# Praise for Courting

'From the first page-turning story of jilted Beatrice, a barmaid, and Frederick, a "spinner of yarns smelling of horses and flashing his winnings", readers are in for a glorious romp. Engaging stories of dashing romance, poetic love and tragic heartbreak, brilliantly sliced through by class, race and gender, swirl across the pages. Love on trial. A reader's delight.' —Constance Backhouse, University of Ottawa, author of *Petticoats and Prejudice*

'This beautifully written book explores the complexity of individual lives with skill, sensitivity and integrity, crafting a new story about love in the past and raising important questions about love in the present. It is also a real page-turner, transporting the reader to diverse emotional and physical spaces through a series of captivating and often deeply moving cases. *Courting* is as important as it is delightful.' —Claire Langhamer, University of London, author of *The English in Love*

'Between 1806 and the 1970s, nearly a thousand jilted lovers in Australia sued for the breach of promise of marriage. They sought damages for money wasted on trousseaux, for the cost of raising children, and for heartache. In telling these stories, this brilliant book shows how the rules of love interacted with the law ... History is rarely written so engagingly.' —Bruce Kercher, Macquarie University, author of *Unruly Child: A History of Law in Australia*

'Delightful and engrossing, *Courting* is filled with stories of infatuation, deception and heartbreak. A beautifully written account of the trials and tribulations of romantic love across the centuries, this is history richly told.' —Anna Clark, University of Technology Sydney, author of *Making Australian History*

'What we find in this deeply researched and elegantly written work is a familiar emotion made oddly strange ... Original and compelling, *Courting* suggests that romantic love, no matter how private and individualized it may feel today, is always shaped by historical and legal contexts. A delight to read, this is an exemplary work that demonstrates the value of law in studying the history of emotions.' —Kathryn Temple, Georgetown University, author of *Loving Justice*

# Courting

## an intimate history of
## love and the law

## Alecia Simmonds

LA TROBE
UNIVERSITY PRESS

IN CONJUNCTION WITH BLACK INC.

Published by La Trobe University Press in conjunction with Black Inc.
Wurundjeri Country
22–24 Northumberland Street
Collingwood VIC 3066, Australia
enquiries@blackincbooks.com
www.blackincbooks.com
www.latrobeuniversitypress.com.au

La Trobe University plays an integral role in Australia's public intellectual life, and is
recognised globally for its research excellence and commitment to ideas and debate.
La Trobe University Press publishes books of high intellectual quality, aimed at general
readers. Titles range across the humanities and sciences, and are written by distinguished
and innovative scholars. La Trobe University Press books are produced in conjunction
with Black Inc., an independent Australian publishing house. The members of the LTUP
Editorial Board are Vice-Chancellor's Fellows Emeritus Professor Robert Manne and
Dr Elizabeth Finkel, and Morry Schwartz and Chris Feik of Black Inc.

9781760642143 (paperback)
9781743823378 (ebook)

A catalogue record for this
book is available from the
National Library of Australia

Cover design by Tristan Main
Text design and typesetting by Beau Lowenstern
Cover image via Getty/Culture Club
Author photograph by Rose Tracey

*To my Nana, Anne Simmonds,*
*who this year celebrates*
*her ninety-third summer.*

*This book has been written on the Gadigal Lands of the
Eora People and I pay my respects to their elders past and present.
The Australia that I have written about always was and always
will be Aboriginal land. Sovereignty was never ceded.*

# Contents

Introduction

# Stories of Love
# from the Archives of Law

*Just a few lines to my ever dear Beattie.*
*My dear love. I am nearly mad.*
*Dear love, I love the ground you walk upon.*
*My dear love. I pity you from the bottom of my heart.*
*You are my love for life.*
*I think it is a yarn about my wife being alive …*
*I think it is spite …*
*Dear, I would like to see you …*[1]

On a squally autumn day in Sydney in March 1914, Beatrice Storey, a barmaid, sued Frederick Chapman, a farmer, for abandoning her on the day of their wedding. To be precise, she claimed £1000 damages in the New South Wales Supreme Court for breach of promise of marriage, a suit that could be used to claim compensation for injuries arising from a broken engagement.

Beatrice had first glimpsed Frederick one year earlier from behind the bar at the Captain Cook Hotel. Cavalier, stocky and a 'spinner of yarns', he breezed into the pub 'smelling of horses and flashing his winnings'.[2] He told her that he had been at the Moore Park races down the road. He also said that he was forty, wealthy and a widower. After a month of giddy infatuation, he presented her with a wedding ring and vowed that he would marry her.

Almost none of what he told her was true.

Beatrice explained from the witness box to the judge and a jury of four that she was thirty years old when she had quit her employment on Frederick's insistence and moved back home with her mother a few doors down on Flinders Street. Yes, she and Frederick had made wedding arrangements at St Barnabas' church on George Street: forty invitations were sent out; the wedding cake and carriage were ordered. She had selected furniture for their new home in Kensington, and he had promised to settle the property upon her as well as gifting her £2000 to furnish the house. 'He said he had plenty of money,' she informed the court; 'in fact, "money to burn."' The day before the wedding, Frederick kissed Beatrice goodbye on the porch of her brother's house and told her not to be late for church.

Frederick never showed up for his wedding. He phoned Beatrice and apologised, asking her to cancel the ceremony as he had just received news that his wife was alive. The marriage would make him a bigamist. Beatrice was livid. Frederick rushed to her house and tried to console her, begging her to take the wedding ring, fumbling his way into an embrace, chaotically trying to kiss her. She pushed him away. In the following weeks Frederick turned to ink and paper, bewailing the maddening effects of passion, confessing that the reports of his wife were 'a yarn' and exhorting that it was his 'greatest wish to marry'. Beatrice converted Frederick's love letters into legal evidence and his passion into proof, in one of the most lucrative breach of promise actions of her decade: £350 compensation for her 'lacerated feelings'.[3]

The next time Beatrice and Frederick appear on the historical record is 23 January 1915 at St Martin's Anglican Church in Kensington. This time Frederick showed up for his wedding.[4]

A little under sixty years later, in the early 1970s, a grandson of Beatrice and Frederick was also sued for breach of promise of marriage, just before the action was abolished. No newspaper bothered to report it, and we only know of the action because in 1986 a Liberal politician, Wilson Tuckey, raised it in federal parliament. 'Paul had a girl called Christine,' he hissed, directing his comments at a Labor MP named Paul, also implying (incorrectly) that an illegitimate child had been born. 'Madame Speaker', the Labor MP interjected. He demanded that Tuckey be censured. He railed against him, calling him a criminal. Later that day, the Labor MP held a press conference outside Parliament House to address the remarks and asked that they be erased from the Hansard minutes. This Labor MP, the grandson of Beatrice and Frederick, was the future Australian prime minister Paul Keating.[5]

*　　*　　*

This book takes as its basis the papery remains of blighted affections found in the records of breach of promise actions to tell a history of love, law and 'lacerated feelings' over the course of two centuries. I settle into the courtrooms of the past, lodged between the scribbling men of the press and the tittering, jeering crowd, and report on a select series of cases plucked from the records of almost 1000 women and men who appeared before judges and juries, carrying proof of their endearment: love letters, lost wages, gifts, jewellery, gossiping neighbours, expert witnesses, trousseaux and tales of misplaced trust.

When we go looking for love in the canons of law, we encounter a different kind of protagonist to those we are accustomed to meeting in histories of romantic love.[6] Here there are no lofty philosophers, sensitive poets or delicate letter-writers penning epistles in the hush of a lady's drawing room. Instead, our feckless Lotharios are shearers, train-drivers, bankrupt shop-keepers, farmers and commercial travellers. Their scorned brides are people like Beatrice Storey: barmaids, domestic servants, seamstresses, nurses, piano teachers and, later in the century, chorus girls and migrants. They are mostly ordinary people of the lower-middle orders who could not afford the luxury of privacy, nor the indulgence of marrying for love alone. Some went to court seeking compensation for lost wages or diminished social and economic status, others for wounded affections or missed romantic opportunities, and many more, like Beatrice, were using the action to pressure their partners to marry them. Women who had been 'seduced' litigated to defend their sexual reputations. Most plaintiffs were refreshingly oblivious or indifferent to the social scorn that the legal action cast upon them: the indignity of having your most private feelings filleted before a public audience; the perceived vulgarity of seeking financial recompense for the unquantifiable pain of a broken heart.

I use litigants' life stories to unpick the entangled histories of love and law, tracking how they became separated over the long arc of the nineteenth and twentieth centuries, and to explore what breach of promise actions tell us about the history of love. If Beatrice Storey had been left at the altar today, for instance, Frederick Chapman would not have been forced by the state to compensate her for her hurt feelings, nor for any financial losses she incurred. The fact that Fred was an intimate, rather than, say, a commercial partner, would likely have denied her a legal remedy.[7] The breach of promise of marriage action is now abolished, seen as a quirky relic of the Victorian era, and the law tends to assume that intimates don't intend to create legal relations.[8] Women are not economically and socially dependent on marriage as they once were, and a failed relationship does not relegate women to the status of damaged goods. Courtship is now defined by love, choice, physical desire and mutual negotiation, rather than by contractual legal obligation.

Fuelled by dating apps that promise a new partner by simply swiping right on your phone, fantasies of romantic plenitude have replaced legal regimes of punishment.

Yet people continue to experience injury, be it financial, emotional or bodily, when intimate promises are broken, and the discovery of deceit in relationships can be life-altering. Rather than seeing the unmooring of love from law as a tale of liberation, by which love was set free from the paternalistic bonds of the state, I question what we have lost in this process, and how we might imagine, legally and socially, an ethics of intimacy.

Instead of turning to law, the Beatrice Storey of today would likely try to overcome her pain by reading self-help books or talking to friends, family and experts, all educated to varying degrees in psychology. The advice she would receive would no doubt revolve around the virtues of resilience, the balm of commodity culture (go out and buy yourself a new dress!) and interrogation of her own psyche (why had she been attracted to such a duplicitous cad in the first place?). Where law would have ascribed fault and demanded a tallying-up of emotional, bodily and financial harm that could be compensated, however awkwardly, by money, therapeutic discourse is uninterested in material loss or ethical responsibility. What was once a public debate about the rules of romance, including its gendered financial costs and the seriousness of its injuries, is now sequestered away in the therapist's clinic. The stories in this book, when viewed as a whole, track why and how this change occurred. Like scholars before me, I argue that the 'coming of the counsellors' by the mid-twentieth century was not a victory but a loss, particularly for women, as responsibility for romantic injury was individualised and feminised, and its pain trivialised drained of economic meaning.[9]

This story of change over time – the shift we can observe in the governance of love from law to psychology – sits alongside my other interest in how courtship shaped and was shaped by changing material circumstances. We might imagine the breach of promise action as a jewel that with each chapter is held up to the light and spun around to illuminate a different aspect of the shared histories of love, loss and law. An absconding domestic servant in the 1800s reveals love's early enmeshment with state power; a propertied gentleman in the 1830s underlines the links between love, lucre and the theft of Aboriginal land; a scheming governess in the 1850s makes us question the gendered dimensions of imperial mobility; an impoverished amateur artist in the 1890s showcases women's struggles against sexual violence; a Parsi trader and a Syrian hawker at the dawn of the twentieth century reveal the racial and religious politics of romance in a globalised world; a flapper shows the commodification of desire; a vaudeville star in the 1920s highlights the history of heartbreak; and a hairdresser poet in the 1930s articulates a feminist ethics of desire. Each biography grounds the nuances of relationships and the idiosyncrasies of character in the broader social and economic context of individual lives.

*   *   *

When I tell my students that they could once have sued a lover for breaking an engagement, they are always astonished and a bit indignant: romance is not a fit subject for law, they say. Their response exposes a cultural assumption that love and law are opposites, conceptual antipodes, each untranslatable and hostile to the other.[10] We think of romance as frolicsome, rebellious, impetuous and wilful, impervious to the monolithic sobriety of law. From the ancients to the romantic poets, love has been a breaker of rules, which is why social contract theorists such as Jean-Jacques Rousseau viewed it with suspicion. 'Lovers never see anyone but themselves, they incessantly attend only to themselves and the only thing they are able to do is love each other,' he complained.[11] While law is rational and generalisable, love is a divine delirium that makes little sense to anyone but the couple afflicted. Ethical or not, today's courting couples can 'ghost' away without consequence; they can break promises or refrain from making them at all. Being true to your own feelings and following your own desires now trumps any notion of duty or honour. Ineffable, exquisitely personal, secretive and mysterious, romantic love, as we imagine it, has nothing to do with the coercive, transparent machinations of our public legal system.

But if we think more deeply, this easy dichotomy between love and law begins to break down. Love has its own laws and exercises its own jurisdiction; like law, it demands, either pleasurably or punitively, that we relinquish our will to a higher order.[12] Love may elevate us – magically transfiguring the world into something as beautiful as our imagined love object – but like law it can also deprive us of autonomy, bestow obligations, punish transgressions and issue commands. And because the stakes in love and law are high, as both change lives, they have a similar interest in evidence: 'How do I know that you are who you say you are?' and 'can I place trust in your words?' are questions asked as anxiously in court as in courtship. Love and law propel us on a quest for proof: we hunt for clues in small gestures, we read signs into bodily disturbances, we discern meaning in happenstance and we detect broad patterns of significance in the minutiae of everyday life.

Many also think of romantic love as the only proper foundation of marriage, and marriage, of course, is an entirely legal creation, 'an artefact of government'.[13] Marriage today is where rules and romance unite – and as breach of promise of *marriage* is the subject of this book, it also determines what kinds of love I can explore. In excluding all love outside heterosexual relationships from its orbit, marriage was a means of institutionalising heterosexuality. Although moments of queer rupture abound in these cases – from cross-dressing in the early colonial period to jealous partners prohibiting romantic same-sex friendships – homosexual relationships did not enter the legal record under the breach of promise action. My study is a history of the regulation of heterosexual courtship. As such, it is also a study of how gender norms were naturalised by languages of love and enshrined in law through marriage.

In the nineteenth century, European people in Australia would have had no difficulty thinking of intimacy as a proper subject of legal regulation. Whether it be a convict being required to apply to the governor to marry, a woman's knowledge that almost everything she owned, including her body, would become the legal property of her husband on her wedding day, a female worker being denied a living wage because the law assumed her primary occupation would be as a wife, or an illegitimate child being unable to inherit, private decisions about marriage had public consequences. They also would have distinguished between the kind of love that led to marriage – chaste, restrained and sanctioned by law, church and the family – and love that was disruptive of the social order – passionate, libidinous, clandestine, illicit and rebellious. Almost every time they opened a newspaper, they would have found reports of cases concerned with the law's efforts to channel love into socially appropriate forms. Whether it be breach of promise of marriage, seduction, criminal conversation (or adultery) or, later in the century, divorce and child custody hearings, courts performed a pedagogical function. Having imbibed the lessons of Augustinian Christian theology, the common law rewarded conjugality and punished concupiscence. Every case of failed intimacy that ended up in the courtroom – romances that never quite reached the altar, babies born out of wedlock, marriages that faltered and fell apart – highlighted the rules dictating what romance ought to look like and the gendered norms that prescribed how women and men should behave.

The Europeans in Australia would also have had an expansive sense of the laws of love. They would have seen the regulation of intimacy as existing on a continuum, beginning with the moral codes internalised by individuals and dispensed by family, kin and church and ending with legislation or a court verdict. A court hearing was usually the final stage after more informal regulatory procedures had failed to produce results: interrogations by a vexed mother in the kitchen; slurs hurled at a suitor by a meddling neighbour; an inquisition by a church; stern words from an employer; or furious letters exchanged by lovers and their relatives, explaining which amorous laws the other party had breached. People accepted the adjudicatory powers of family and kin because love was a collective emotion in which the entire community had a stake, and through which reputations and claims to respectability – whether of an individual, a family, or of a former convict colony – could be won or lost.

Finally, nineteenth-century notions of selfhood made people more amenable to having private romantic decisions publicly arbitrated. Europeans largely defined the self through obedience or sacrifice to social and moral norms, encapsulated in the notion of 'character'. When a man broke his promise to marry because he was in love with someone else, he was not applauded for following his feelings but rather judged for breaching the laws of promise-keeping. He would have been labelled disreputable – the breach altered who he was seen to be as a person – because personhood could not be separated from communal norms.[14] Rather than love being an expression of one's innermost self, unencumbered by social roles, courtship was governed by a series of external norms and rituals, all of which had legal meaning. Were the parents consulted? Did the man visit the woman in her house? Did they go on walks together? Did they discuss the house they would live in? Did they exchange love letters or, later in the century, rings and gifts? If the answer was yes, then a promise of marriage was proved, regardless of whether there had been an explicit proposal. The clear moral content of the rules of courtship, the public nature of its rituals and the economic significance of marriage made romantic love in the nineteenth century easily intelligible to law.

Our journey following the breach of promise action over the course of two centuries terminates with the abolition of the action in 1976, when the state ceded its authority over courtship to couples and their counsellors.[15] There were many obvious reasons why breach of promise finally came to an end. By the 1970s, dating had replaced courtship and legitimated serial monogamy; de-facto arrangements were increasingly popular, which meant marriage was not the only end point for a romance; autonomy in love was privileged over external regulation, whether by the state, church or families; and expectations of marriage had changed with economic affluence after the Second World War: emotional and sexual satisfaction now played a greater role than pragmatic concerns. If marriage was now about finding individual happiness with another person, then no penalty should apply to someone who ended a bad relationship in search of someone more suitable. Romantic love – increasingly unmoored from morality and no longer as dependent as it once was upon financial considerations – was now the only socially legitimate foundation for marriage.[16]

But we also see a more profound change over this time that helps to explain the disentanglement of love and law, a shift in our vision of the self, in the role we give to the law and in how we imagine love. The early decades of the twentieth century are a significant moment of rupture, a period in which both love and law began to declare incompetency in, or a lack of knowledge of, the other's realm. With industrialisation, urbanisation and the shift to consumer society, traditional authority structures anchored in the church, family and community broke down, and a culture of individualism triumphed. A new 'self' emerged, defined by the pursuit of self-fulfillment, authenticity, autonomy and pleasure.[17] Falling in love was increasingly depicted as a rhapsodic encounter with the mysteries of the psyche, a journey into inner worlds, a joyful celebration of sexual passion, although pragmatic considerations still played a part in selecting a spouse. Because evidence of love was now vested in intensely personal bodily desires, and romance was performed far from the invigilating gaze of family, church and community, courtship became increasingly difficult to plead and prove in court.

As people became less inclined to accept the strictures of religion, family or law when it came to romance, they turned more to psychological literature, which by the mid-twentieth century could be found everywhere: in agony-aunt columns, self-help books, psychology clinics, workplaces and cinemas. Like law, psychology channelled individual stories of suffering into a universalist language – but unlike law, as Eva Illouz has argued, psychology relegated 'the romantic and the erotic to the individual's private responsibility'.[18] We see therapeutic discourse washing up in breach of promise as part of the flotsam and jetsam of romances that had run aground – the sex manuals admitted as legal evidence, the love letters brimming with stories of dreams, and the descriptions of heartbreak in terms of nervous shock. Courts, as profoundly polyglot institutions, absorbed the new psychological language used by litigants, lawyers and expert witnesses, and ordered them into juridical logic. From the early twentieth century, we see therapeutic discourse coexisting with law and, over the decades, encroaching upon its domain: like a wartime map, its colours blot and bleed, expanding into more territory, quietly colonising inner worlds, until actions all but cease in the 1950s: people now preferred psychological advice to the judgment of the court.

These changes intersected with shifts in the operation of civil law. If court for people in the nineteenth century was part of the warp and weft of everyday life, a public forum for entertainment or edification, by the mid-twentieth century civil law had become professionalised and rarefied, elevated above the messy emotions of the poor. Early-twentieth-century judges, credentialled with degrees newly offered at Australian universities, grumbled when breach of promise actions were brought in the superior civil courts. The rules of evidence also became more complicated and onerous. Over the course of the twentieth century, the law narrowed its interest in people's amorous lives from the vast terrain of courtship, with its rituals, gifts, letters and romantic wounds, to the contract of marriage and its aftermath: property, taxation, migration, custody and wills. By 1976, civil law had disavowed its authority over romance and declared courtship beyond its jurisdiction. Individual couples, rather than the state, now defined the terms of courtship, aided by a government-funded army of psychologists.

Admittedly, the nation's lawmakers never stopped caring about who and how we love. The same-sex marriage debate in Australia in 2017 highlighted politicians' investment in perpetuating a model of marriage based on life-long, monogamous, heterosexual partnerships. The success of the 'yes' vote also revealed the political power of love as a protest against law's exclusions. The primary argument offered in favour of same-sex marriage was an appeal to love's timelessness and universality: 'Love is love', proclaimed rainbow-coloured banners across Australia. What campaigners meant was that love is a self-evident good, common to all humans across time, regardless of social encumbrances such as race, gender, class or sexuality.

This book is both an affirmation and a refutation of this catchcry. For there is something fundamentally human about falling in love that allows us to feel the amorous tremors of love poetry although centuries may yawn between us and the poet. But love, as I show, is also not just love. When we see doctors giving testimony about the medical effects of heartbreak, or hear a jilted woman's father claiming that in fact it was his feelings that were injured, or read of Beatrice Storey turning around after her court case and marrying Frederick Chapman, or applaud women at the start of the twentieth century for claiming damages for the dinners they had cooked their lovers, we know that we are dealing with an emotion that is profoundly shaped by culture. Love is a creature of its time. And it is in the space between strangeness and familiarity that the history of love can be found.

*     *     *

A hidden museum of love can be found in the archives of law: inside the records from breach of promise cases, which lie bundled in dust-choked boxes in repositories across the country. Often the files appear corpulent, the ribbon straining like a belt. They're filled with all the documents you'd expect to see in a legal case – pleadings, summonses, affidavits, interrogatories and bills of costs – but sometimes unusual things fall out: love letters, train tickets, photographs, receipts for negligees or engagement rings. In Syrian hawker Cissie Zathar's file from 1907, I found a yellowing strip of antique-white lace affixed with a pin to one of her letters to Moses Hanna, her lover in Redfern.

The viscerality of these documents still cuts through me. How could these most intimate, secretive, howling letters end up bundled inside a writ? For the most part, the inner lives of the lower orders do not make their way into archives; posterity was a prerogative of the rich, and states rarely thought to preserve the private lives of ordinary people. Breach of promise cases, I discovered, were an exception. The court transcripts give us the life stories of people who would never have thought to write an autobiography. For the female plaintiffs, these accounts are not coerced, as they would have been in criminal cases, but nor are they written in circumstances of their subjects' choosing. They are partially crafted by lawyers, and they seem to capture people mid-fall, vulnerable, suspended in webs of legality.[19] In this book, I build on what is found in the legal archives by turning to newspaper reports, which published court transcripts, love letters and poems and sometimes offered editorial commentary. For some litigants, I was able to connect with their descendants or rifle through photographs, family papers, asylum records or medical records, or inspect the objects they left behind.

I hope that my archival methodology proves to historians that we might exercise a little less caution than we are accustomed to when dealing with legal records. The idea that the narratives offered by litigants are 'polluted with authority', or a kind of fiction, carefully crafted by lawyers, has become almost a historiographical cliche.[20] It's one that makes perfect sense for medieval historians, who may have only a court transcript and affidavit to rely upon. But historians of the modern period, like myself, have if anything an embarrassment of archival riches. Being able to compare a love letter with an affidavit allows us to understand what people thought the court wanted to hear, as well as what they might have felt in quiet, tender moments. We can contrast private romantic sentiment with public legal norms.

My focus on the life stories of litigants told through the archival remains of their breach of promise actions distinguishes this book from previous studies. In Britain, New Zealand, Australia, the United States and Canada, historians have written superb social and legal histories of the action that illuminate the norms of courtship for working-class people and the influence of the cult of femininity as well as highlighting the paradoxical nature of the suit.[21] It regarded women as dependent on men and destined for marriage, and they were rewarded if they played this part well. It enshrined moral norms around sexual chastity into law, making it a defence for a man to break his promise if a woman was of 'bad character'. Yet as much as the legal framework was steeped in patriarchy, it favoured women in practice, with a vast majority of female litigants winning their actions across the two centuries. As such, it provided financial support for poor women, it offered a lump-sum payment for single mothers, it gave women a means to hold deceitful men to account, and it compelled men like Frederick Chapman to marry. And although legal counsel applauded chaste and modest women, the suit demanded that litigants step into the public sphere to aggressively pursue a man for money – hardly model feminine behaviour. While existing studies tell us much about how the action operated in the nineteenth century, the twentieth century is either ignored or dealt with cursorily.[22] My book is the first comprehensive history of the action across two centuries and as such is able to provide thematic, chronological and biographical analysis.

I have catalogued every Australian action for breach of promise that appeared in newspapers, and before that in the records of the court of civil jurisdiction from 1788. Through this I can say with some certainty whether a litigant was typical or not. I can identify what the average damages were, the class background of litigants, and more idiosyncratic details such as when people began to claim medical injuries for heartbreak, when they began to sue for the cost of their glory boxes, or when and why engagement rings first started appearing in evidence. But in order to produce a peopled history, one in which the reader gets an insight into the inner lives of women and men in the past, a feel for the textures, sounds and smells of the world in which they inhabited, I frame each chapter around a life story and oscillate between the drama of a court case and the wider social and legal context. I selected litigants based on how well they and their cases encapsulated the themes I wanted to examine and did not rule out litigants who left scant remains, as the people most likely to use the suit were underprivileged and ill-educated. Given the success rate of female plaintiffs, concluding each chapter with the verdict of the court would present an overly rosy view of gender relations in the past. By focusing on life stories, rather than just legal stories, we can see what happened after the verdict and quickly learn that the exercise of one's legal rights did not guarantee the enjoyment of one's social rights: moral norms and economic structures generally punished women and forgave men.

*   *   *

This book is divided into four parts, each focused on a period of change in the history of love. Spanning the late 1780s until the 1830s, the cases in the first part reveal love to be tightly entangled with law in the early colony, as the state sought to channel illicit cohabitation into state-sanctioned marriage. The second part comprises a series of chapters set in the mid-Victorian era and examines through the lens of geography the places where courting couples met, visited each other, went on romantic strolls, had sex and proposed. It explores the gendered rules that restricted women's mobility and investigates how romantic love was implicated in colonial civilising missions. The third part, from the 1880s until the First World War, is set against a backdrop of social upheaval and globalisation, which are explored in chapters focusing on sexual violence, social constructions of race and ethnicity, and religion. Finally, the case studies in the fourth section, covering the interwar years, chart the modernisation of love: its entanglement in commodity culture, the restructuring of heartbreak through medical and psychiatric norms and growing feminist consciousness of intimate injustice.

The conclusion and epilogue explore the decline of the action and its aftermath. I query whether we should engage in modern love's exaltation of free will unencumbered by notions of duty, sympathy or honesty. Is there such a thing as an ethics of love? What did we lose in the shift from the legal condemnation of deceit in relationships to psychological exhortations to resilience? Should we take romantic injuries more seriously? How should we economically value intimate labour? History is not simply about avoiding the mistakes of the past – for we never do this anyway. It is at best an exercise in humility: learning that humans are malleable creatures and that the various incarnations of humanity we meet when we travel back in time may sometimes be wiser creatures than ourselves. For Australians, a history of love told from the papery relics of one of our most treasured national icons – the working-class battler – is a corrective to traditional histories of love that tend to favour the bourgeoisie and an antidote to our anaemic national mythologising of stoic, independent blokes and robust women. Frederick Chapman may have been a stockman, larrikin and 'spinner of yarns', but he was also nervous, sentimental and smitten by Beatrice Storey. And far from being a long-suffering heroine of Australian legend, Beatrice took her squandered affections to court and won. Writing a history of courtship from the archival remains of broken hearts allows us to tell national and transnational stories of vulnerability and resistance, of fierce and fragile inner worlds.

# The Rules of Engagement:
# Background to the Action for Breach of
# Promise of Marriage

W hen litigants in breach of promise of marriage actions spoke in court, they shaped their stories to fit the legal elements of the suit, much like litigants today. The success or failure of their cases largely depended on them doing so. So, before we settle into the courtroom, let's acquaint ourselves with what these elements were, and with a brief history of the action.

Between about the fifth and the fifteenth centuries, the breach of promise action resided in the ecclesiastical courts – a special system of courts that administered canon law and resolved spiritual matters such as wills, religious behaviour, courtship, marriage and legitimacy. Ecclesiastical courts had jurisdiction over the soul, so it is natural that love might find its home there.[1] Those who had suffered a broken engagement could sue as a *causa matrimoniales*, and the remedy was not money but marriage: the courts would force a person's partner to marry them under an order for 'specific performance'. During the interregnum in the mid-1600s, the ecclesiastical courts were closed, and people started suing in the common law courts under contract law. The remedy changed from specific performance to financial damages, which made sense in a world where engagements among the wealthy were essentially commercial or property transactions. Men and women, across classes, sued in more or less equal numbers up until the late eighteenth century, which is when the action became feminised and, correspondingly, more about emotional injury. It also became increasingly the preserve of the lower-middle classes. By the Victorian era it was almost exclusively working women who sued in common-law countries around the world, and the damages for the action shifted from contract law, which would aim to put the plaintiff in the same financial position as they had been before the breach, to tort law, or civil wrongs, which recognised compensation for 'lacerated feelings'.[2]

There were four elements that plaintiffs needed to satisfy. There must have been a promise to marry; it must have been unjustifiably broken; the broken promise must have caused emotional, bodily or financial injury; giving rise to financial damages.

Let's begin with the promise to marry. The most obvious people to ask for proof of this would be the lovers themselves, but until the 1870s they were prohibited from giving evidence, because it was thought that the risk of perjury was too great.[3] When lovers were finally permitted to give evidence, the law stipulated that the (usually female) plaintiff's evidence must be corroborated by another witness (either male or female), which made breach of promise the only civil action requiring material corroboration.[4] The justification for this echoed the eye-wateringly sexist law of rape, as the judge in *Howell v Neeld* (1900) opined: 'many men had been subject to extreme danger in consequence of accusations of this kind made by women, which were so easily made and so very hard to disprove'. In 'nine cases out of ten', he declared, 'the women are lying'.[5]

In place of the lovers, the court summoned a range of other people and physical evidence: gossiping neighbours, fretful parents, wedding invitations, dresses and gifts. Love letters provided particularly convincing proof, and they were scrutinised and read aloud in court to the delight of the gallery. They did not need to contain an explicit promise: terms of endearment, amorous language and romantic projections would suffice as proof of a promise of marriage.

While love letters were good evidence, they were not essential. Legal treatises affirmed that romantic gestures without any proof of amorous correspondence could also make a person legally bound to marry. For instance, if a man visited a woman frequently, declared his love for her to her parents or kin, made oaths, published wedding banns (that is, announced the intention to marry in church), took out a wedding licence, promised her a ring, bought furniture, promised to settle money on her, or if they went for romantic walks together, these actions could all be read as proof of a contract of marriage.[6]

Unlike the contract of marriage, it was uncertain whether a woman needed to have offered her consent, and legal opinions on this question changed over time. Writing in 1807, jurist Samuel Comyn asserted that a contract would be formed when 'a man and a woman, being unmarried, mutually promise to marry each other'.[7] In 1826, Joseph Chitty, a leading treatise writer, changed things: the promise of the man, he said, needed to be proved, but all that was required of the woman was that she had 'demeaned herself as if she concurred'.[8] Of greater importance than the woman's consent, for Chitty, was that the couple's parents and friends knew of the engagement.

By 1872, Chitty's guidance had become more performative. A contract could be read into 'a man's visits to a woman and his declaration that he had promised to marry her'. A woman needed to concur, but ideally this would not be too explicit. Quoting from an earlier case, Chitty wrote that being demonstrative would destroy 'that chaste and modest intercourse, which is the pride of the country, and a boldness of manners would probably succeed, by no means friendly to the character of the sex, or the interests of society'.[9] There is a palpable anxiety evident in Chitty's discussion of the consequences of a clod-footed law trampling on the delicate shadowlands of desire, importing a masculine language of contract into the feminine realm of love. Like most concerns about the breach of promise action, it came from a belief that social order rested upon a separation between the public (law) and the private (love). But it also shows a shift from a model of mutual promises between men and women to one based on an active man who offers and a passive woman who demurely accepts. Australian courts agreed. In a case heard in 1850, the defence based its entire argument on the fact that the woman had never consented. 'What was the girl to do or say under the circumstances?' asked the judge, horrified. 'Would you have her cry: "Oh yes! I'll marry you" and go kissing and hugging in the public streets? What a ludicrous idea!' The courtroom filled with laughter.[10]

If explicitly accepting a proposal could be considered bad manners, how did you know when a contract had been formed? The short answer is that you didn't, and that attitudes changed over time. In the nineteenth century, women argued that engagements were forged much earlier than men did. This was partly because women could not be seen to be courting multiple partners without damaging their reputations, and also because, in the absence of other employment opportunities, courtship had a greater significance for women – they were often more keen to formalise arrangements and to lock down a future marriage. Perhaps Lord Byron said it best: 'Man's love is of man's life a thing apart; 'tis woman's whole existence.'[11]

By the twentieth century, changes in romantic culture – including the shift from courtship to serial dating and, corresponding to this, the movement of couples from the home to anonymous commercial leisure arenas – meant the courts began to demand explicit proof of contract. By the 1920s, a promise of marriage articulated publicly or in a love letter, or an engagement ring, or evidence of financial reliance, such as quitting work or collecting items for a trousseau, were generally required by judges and juries to win an action.

The second element – was there a justification for breaking the promise? – was the focus of the defence. In the nineteenth century, the main justification given by men was that the woman was of bad or immoral character, while in the twentieth century it was that they had mutually agreed to end the engagement – a change that reflects a growing acceptance of women's independence and sexuality. Other less common justifications included an incapacity to contract because of being underage, ill or insane; or that the couple had mismatched tempers. Aside from age, the bad character defence was in practice the only one that had any guarantee of success for most of the nineteenth century, and, like the definition of a promise, it changed dramatically over time.

Turning again to our treatise writers, we find Chitty in 1826 giving the following example of bad character drawn from case law. A man sues a woman for breach of promise of marriage. She admits to the breach but says she was justified, as the man was 'destitute of feeling' and had 'gross manners and sentiment'. The court awards in her favour on the grounds that the man had suffered no injury, as he was boorish and therefore 'seemed little calculated to taste [the] pleasures of her society'.[12] By 1834 this man with gross manners had been joined in Chitty's treatise by a 'loose and immodest woman', and by the 1863 edition the man had completely disappeared. A 'loose and immodest woman' was now the exemplar of what it meant to have bad character.[13] It says a lot about the moral burdens placed on women in the Victorian era, as well as about the importance of promise-keeping to definitions of masculine honour, that Chitty now declared that a man was only free to break an engagement if there were 'a want of chastity on the part of the woman or incapacity [illness or being underage] on the part of the man'.[14] Being unchaste or of bad character also had a wider scope than we would imagine today; in the nineteenth century, unchaste behaviour could include laughing 'immoderately', appearing in male spaces such as pubs or workshops, making the first move romantically, or saying the word 'dammit' in public.[15] As the parameters of acceptable behaviour for women expanded in the late nineteenth and twentieth centuries, the defence of bad character fell largely into desuetude, yet women's sexuality continued to be policed. Moral judgment was imported into discussions over whether the plaintiff was the kind of woman to whom a promise of marriage could believably have been made: did she behave more like a mistress than a future wife? Was she dating numerous people?[16]

The final part of the hearing concerned the assessment of damages, and this was where the court addressed the third and fourth elements: was there emotional, material or bodily harm that gave rise to financial damages? Damages were usually determined by a jury, unless the action was brought in a lower court, where the magistrate would decide, or if the breach was admitted, in which case the prothonotary of the Supreme Court exercised judicial power. The main categories of damages were 'loss of settlement' – meaning the value of the marriage – and emotional injury. Damages were partly calculated based on how much the defendant was worth financially, and to this end evidence would be given of the defendant's property portfolios, salaries, land and investments. While this gave plaintiffs a financial incentive to sue wealthy men, money was not the only reason for bringing an action. In many instances, women sued poor men who would never have been able to afford the damages simply as a way of forcing them into marriage, particularly if the woman was pregnant.

Emotional injury – variously called lacerated feelings, wounded affections or loss of honour – comprised the larger portion of damages. As a newspaper commentator in 1891 complained: 'a young and pretty plaintiff will always be able to secure larger damages than a middle-aged and homely woman, although it is obviously the latter who suffers most by the breach of engagement since she may never have another chance of marriage.'[17] Emotional injury – variously called lacerated feelings, wounded affections or loss of honour – comprised the larger portion of the damages, and juries were renowned for giving out very generous awards. A plaintiff could claim exemplary damages aimed at punishing the defendant if it were shown that he had seduced her (that is, had sexual intercourse with her) or if he had falsely accused her of unchastity; she could claim special damages if she had given up her employment, suffered a bodily injury as a result of being jilted or spent money on her trousseau.[18] Although not stated in law, damages would be increased if the woman was considered attractive, educated and accomplished.

While seduction could enflame damages in breach of promise cases, there was also a separate civil action for seduction. Seduction actions often followed, or were brought alongside, breach of promise actions, so we should understand this suit too. Seduction was a civil and criminal action that provided a remedy for loss of services that could be brought by a father on behalf of his daughter or a master on behalf of his servant against the person who had 'seduced' them away. It has its roots in Roman law notions that certain people were property and that other people, specifically their masters, had a property interest in their bodies. This idea worked its way into the British common law of 'master and servant', which allowed a master to sue someone who injured, beat or enticed away his servant for loss of services. In the mid-seventeenth century, this law evolved into the tort (or civil wrong) of seduction, which gave a father, as the master of his household, a common-law right to sue the man who had had sexual intercourse with his daughter if the father could show he had suffered 'loss of services' as a result. Pregnancy was the most common way in which the father could prove loss of service.[19] By the mid-nineteenth century, the action was almost exclusively litigated by fathers defending the sexual honour of their daughters, rather than suing for loss of service. As Constance Backhouse argues, it was a way for the law to redress the sexual double standard that pardoned male sexual licentiousness and demanded female chastity.[20]

Seduction also provided compensation for the very real economic loss that working-class families faced when an unmarried daughter became pregnant. Not only could the daughter no longer work; the disgrace visited upon an unwed mother meant that neither she nor any of her siblings would likely marry thereafter, which was disastrous given that women could not earn a liveable wage.[21] Think of the panic that sets in for the Bennets in *Pride and Prejudice* when Lydia elopes with Wickham, and of Lydia's callow selfishness in privileging a frisson over her sisters' prospects of marriage. For middle-class families like the Bennets, keeping the affair private was crucial to the reputation of the family. A flurry of letters or threats of disinheritance might go some way to pressuring the man to marry. Working-class people, having lost status in the community, wages from their daughter's work and now with a new mouth in the family to feed, had no such luxury.

These were the people who went to court.

# Part 1

## Love in a Penal Colony: 1788–1830

When Mr Sutour fell in love with Miss Cox in the early 1820s, he sent her two parrots, one of which could sing 'My Heart with Love Is Beating', a popular ballad at the time. In the 1830s, Mr Hick pledged his love to Miss Rule with some linen on which he carefully embroidered, with his own hand, his and her initials. And when Miss Stone suspected another woman in Hobart of stealing her lover, she walked to the woman's house, knocked on her door and offered her a box of treats. The woman later told the court that when she opened it, she found pastries crawling with mice, 'sent to vex her'.[1]

No matter how often historians write about the vibrancy of early colonial Australia, a place marked by pleasures 'lively, rough, exciting and cruel', the popular imagination still drifts towards caricature.[2] In television and films, white convict society is presented as a world of stocks, whipping and red-jacketed officers, awash with liquor, prostitution and blasphemy.

Yet the first sixty years of settlement saw people blush, woo, seduce, kiss, gasp, reject and swear vengeance on one another in ways that today seem both odd and familiar. This was a period when the meaning society gave to courtship changed significantly. Heterosexual love arrived with convict colonists in a state of cheerful cohabitation, only to become increasingly beholden, from the 1820s onwards, to bourgeois morality. By the time Australia was granted self-government in the middle of the century, the culture of respectability had triumphed. Expressions of love – once happily erotic, transient and illicit – were placed in the straitjacket of bourgeois, lawful marriage: monogamous, dutiful, patriarchal and restrained. Love and law were now braided together.

Where previous historians have seen breach of promise hearings as public battles over status, involving women who went to court in defence of their honour, I want to see what they have to say about emotions: about the texture, language and politics of romance.[3] After all, when domestic servants and seamstresses took their faithless farmers, sailors and clerks to court, they didn't just claim damages for injured reputations; they also sought compensation for wounded hearts.

# 1.

# 'Swearing by heaven and the moon that he loved her': Honour, Love and Law in the Early Colony

## (*Sutton v Humphrey*, 1806)

*Whereas notwithstanding a General Order ... made public, forbidding any person secreting or harbouring Harriet Sutton from the authority of her parents, she is still unlawfully detained ... it is necessary that the said Harriet Sutton should be delivered into my custody Tomorrow, Monday morning at ten o'clock; Any person or persons whatever who receives, secrets or harbours her after this Notice will suffer such fine and imprisonment for Contempt of the Orders of this Court as the Law directs, in which the necessary Example to the growing Females of this Territory, and good order require to be duly endorsed.*

*By Command of His Excellency ...*
*Sydney*
*June 7 1806*[1]

He slipped away at dawn, leaving behind his mistress, Mrs Palmer, and her endless chores and chastisements, the piled-up dishes in the basin and the unswept floors. Silently closing the door behind him, he padded out onto the dew-spangled lawn, past the creaking windmill on the hill and the screeching pigs in the Domain. Following rocky paths through small, twisted Rows, he turned right at the hanging yards, continued to the swamp around the brickfields, until he was finally on the road to Parramatta. There's no doubt he cut an unusual figure, scrawny inside his ill-fitting coat, head bent, eyes down. For over five hours he walked alongside the clusters of farms that had been carved haphazardly out of the bush, their white wattle-and-daub houses standing guard over swaying throngs of wheat. The dirt scuffed up from his footsteps and a green tunnel of trees arched over him. He needed to move quickly. The outskirts of town were dangerous. The *Gazette* swarmed with stories of natives and bushrangers lurking beyond Sydney Cove.[2]

What happened next depends on whose story you believe. We are certain that on 4 March 1806, a servant of Adolarius Humphrey, the government minerologist, approached this man just outside Parramatta, and that none other than Harriet Sutton stared back at him, 'disguised in man's apparel'. The servant affirmed that Harriet 'was not in woman's cloathes' in the evidence he gave in court after Harriet's father, William Sutton, brought an action against Adolarius for seduction and breach of promise of marriage. The question was whether the encounter was genuinely serendipitous or if the servant had been instructed by Adolarius to meet Harriet on the road. Had Adolarius, as William claimed, 'seduced' Harriet away from her 'comfortable employment' on the promise of marriage? Did he use 'unmeaning words' on Harriet, 'swearing by Heaven and the Moon that he loved her'? Adolarius did not dispute that he had been amorous with Harriet, but he maintained in his defence that he had no idea of Harriet's plans to elope until she and his servant knocked on the door of his barracks.[3]

Today the court transcript of this intimate drama can be found in the *Rough Minutes of the Court of Civil Jurisdiction* – a gargantuan red leather-bound book kept in the papery catacombs of the NSW state archives. It's heavy, requiring two hands to lift, and like a convalescing monarch it asks for delicacy: white gloves, a cushion for its spine and a trolley to transport it from the basement to the reading room. In the *Minutes* you can read the statements put forward by each side. If you're curious to know more, you'll need to consult Governor King's *Letter Book*, kept in the Mitchell Library in Sydney, which contains the proceedings of the Court of Appeal.[4] Here we see William Sutton not so much disputing points of law (as we would expect in an appeal case today) but rather offering an alternative narrative of the case, engaging in creative acts of interpretation to convince Governor King, who was the only judge of the Court of Appeal, why the verdict was unlawful.

Like all the cases in this book, the trials of Harriet, her father William and her suitor Adolarius will appear to have fictive qualities, not just because the conflicting evidence suggests that one side must be lying, but because love is never particularly coherent or ordered. Without any personal diaries or letters describing the affair, the anarchy of infatuation comes to us heavily edited by the pen of law. Yet few in the colony in 1806 were sure what the law was.

*Sutton v Humphrey* took place in the early years of the settlement, when governors issued orders concerning botched romances, litigants represented themselves and, in 1806 at least, no judge or magistrate in the colony had formal legal qualifications.[5] In this chaotic and energetically litigious world, it was not just the facts of a lawsuit that shaped a story, but what litigants, judges and jurors *believed* to be law.[6] Civil law was not yet an elite technical language imposed from above; it was part of the theatre of everyday life. This did not make it democratic – it disproportionately punished the poor, non-Europeans, the ill and women, and it excluded Indigenous people from its protection. Compared to today, however, its tongue was popular, its argumentation was imaginative, and its legal categories were conceptually capacious; it was violent but also violable, and its justice depended upon storytelling.

If the civil law was rogue in this period, then so too was romantic love. Early colonial romance often looked more like that of the late twentieth century than in any other period of history: formal marriage was shunned in favour of de facto relationships or 'common law' marriage; women and men often kept their own personal property; and people would leave each other as they pleased, indifferent to the virtual impossibility, legally, of divorce. Although there was no notion of gender equality in amorous relationships, as we might aim for today, love was yet to be marshalled into the patriarchal confines of state-sanctioned marriage.[7]

This is not to suggest that love romped free from the state. In 1806, the colony's 7000 residents lived cheek by jowl, and people encountered the governor's almost unlimited power at short range. The law's intrusion into their private lives was more severe if they were convicts, who comprised 85 per cent of the population.[8] And if they were women, convict or free, their carnal desires were seen to be of vexing political concern, a problem to be solved by administrators, magistrates, employers and clergy.

In a penal society characterised by discipline, love could inspire a delicious autonomy. It could ignite small insurrections of the heart against the rules of state authorities, fathers and masters.[9] As social stability and public order were believed to emanate from the bonds of obedience that characterised the 'little commonwealth' of the family, it is little wonder that Harriet and Adolarius' clandestine passions would provoke the ire of the governor.[10]

\* \* \*

*Sutton v Humphrey* – the original hearing and the appeal – took place in
June 1806, a rather eventful time in the life of the early colony. As floods,
'squalls and heavy gusts of wind' caused the riverbanks to rise and the only
town clock to fall to the ground, Governor King struggled to keep the crops
alive, while entertaining Māori chief Te Pahi and two natives from Tongat-
apu. For settlers, life looked fretful – a curfew in May promised to imprison
'all Idlers loitering about the Town or Environs after sunset' – and hopeful –
a stray pumpkin seed accidentally dropped in a field of wheat had yielded
thirty-two large, juicy pumpkins.[11] Amid court hearings over trespassing
pigs, unpaid debts, bushranging and burglaries – the latter often involving
Aboriginal people simply resisting the invasion of their country – William
Sutton's case was called in the civil court presided over by Judge Advocate
Richard Atkins. William demanded compensation from Adolarius Humphrey for the seduction and breach of promise of marriage of his daughter,
Harriet Sutton.

It is not certain where the hearing took place. No descriptions survive of
the early colonial court, and historians conjecture that it was either held in
a room next door to the gaol or in an office attached to the judge's house.[12]
Either way, we can imagine large leather-bound registers, treatises and case
books strewn across desks and tumbling onto the floor. Richard Atkins would
have been perched atop a bench presiding over the proceedings. Two assessors – 'fit and proper persons' appointed by Governor King as jurors – were
seated beside Atkins, and below them were Adolarius and William, representing themselves.[13] The low-key courtroom suited the general tenor of civil
legal proceedings: informal, participatory and ribald. Bruce Kercher has written superbly of the Court of Civil Jurisdiction, describing it as a space of lively
conversation between people contesting debts, dignity, wounded bodies and
hurt feelings. In a time before banks, the early colonial world ran on promises, which meant that contract law, still committed at this time to protecting
the virtue of promise-keeping, was regularly engaged.[14]

Judge Atkins was a divisive figure. Those who liked him said he was 'very
prepossessing in appearance, engaging and easy in his manners', and those
who didn't said he was 'a disgrace to human jurisprudence' or, worse, 'a public cheater living in the most boundless dissipation'.[15] Born into the lower
rungs of the baronetcy in England, he behaved accordingly: dissolute, insol-
vent and marinated in liquor. Atkins fled to New South Wales in his forties,
when his inheritance failed to materialise, and creditors were nipping at his
heels. His aristocratic connections won him a position as judge advocate in

1796, a position originally created for military court-martials but with both civil and military dimensions in the colony.[16]

The judiciary was not yet independent of government: Governor King was the only judge on the Court of Appeal, and Atkins was to 'observe and follow such Orders and Directions' as he might receive from the governor 'or another ... Superior Officer'.[17] Atkins was expected to apply the law when presiding over court matters, which sometimes proved difficult on account of his lack of legal training. He confessed to Governor King that his 'Education has not been what is called a Legal one, but a Classical one, with some reading of law.'[18] The reviews of his work were mixed. He discharged his duties to Governor Hunter's 'most perfect satisfaction', and Governor King praised his 'strict justice and impartiality', but Atkins himself would blithely admit that he couldn't advise on certain actions, such as libel or assault, because he didn't know the law.[19] Governor Bligh claimed that under Atkins, 'sentences of death have been pronounced in moments of intoxication'. Yet he had charm. Never did he 'oppress the poor and needy for sordid Lucre', Atkins once pleaded, although he confessed to being an 'Epicurean' who 'prolonged the Convivial hour too far'.[20]

Atkins no doubt felt some sympathy for Adolarius. Not only were both men convinced of their superiority to the convict population; they also both lived their lives on credit.[21] Dark-eyed, thick-browed, louche, large and swarthy, Adolarius looked like an aristocrat gone to seed – well cast for the role he was to play in court that day. Unlike William Sutton, who had come to Australia as a convict and worked hard to re-enter the 'respectable' world, Adolarius was a Regency gentleman. His scientific education elevated him above the grubby world of commerce, and he had been appointed government mineralogist in 1803, thanks to his patron, Charles Greville, a British member of parliament and mineral enthusiast.[22] The position wasn't well paid – Adolarius was on the same wage as William, £91 per year – but the post allowed him adventure, travel and intellectual stimulation.[23] He spent two years dusting rocks and sniffing minerals on exploratory missions in Van Diemen's Land (later Tasmania) with the colony's first judge advocate, David Collins, before deciding in 1805 to return to Sydney Cove. Still in his early twenties, he went to Sydney with the aim, in his words, 'to go wife-hunting' – a sport that seems to have gone awry.[24]

If Atkins was an Epicurean, William Sutton occupied the opposite end of the culinary spectrum. At the time of the breach of promise hearing he was the storekeeper in Newcastle, a settlement two days' ride north of Sydney, where he was responsible for dispensing rations of salt pork, peas, flour and rice to the convicts. He had been sentenced to transportation to New South Wales in 1789, after appearing in the Old Bailey in London on a charge of forgery. He was in his late twenties at the time and had lost his job as an excise officer the year before, when his supervisor discovered that his request for sick leave was a cover for an ignominious sojourn in debtor's prison. Upon his release from debtor's prison, William donned his old work clothes, mocked up a fake excise licence and trundled down to the Bunch of Grapes public house in Cripplegate, Middlesex, where he collected eighteen shillings in arrears owing to the Excise Office. Whether we ascribe his behaviour to hunger or chutzpah, William soon found himself sentenced to death, but he was given 'his majesty's pardon, on condition of being transported for [his] natural life' to Sydney. He petitioned the Home Office to bring his wife and four children with him but was refused.[25]

William arrived in the colony in 1790 and immediately distinguished himself.[26] Having been granted an absolute pardon in 1794, he returned to England and in 1800 boarded *The Porpoise* with his new wife, Ann, and their children, Edward, Sarah and Harriet, bound – this time voluntarily – for Sydney. On the voyage, he met the new commissary, John Palmer, and Palmer's American wife, Susannah, a meeting which yielded work for William, who was granted the post of acting deputy commissary at Parramatta and storekeeper upon his arrival.[27]

As with many members of the respectable working classes, it is hard to get a sense of who William was from archival records: there are no gossipy letters or diaries from which to decipher his character. Governor King was said to have considered him one of two emancipated convicts 'who conducted themselves with the greatest propriety since their conviction'[28] – but we also know that he was dismissed from his post in 1807 for behaving in a 'disorderly and improper manner' towards a superior. A few years later, he was again charged with 'refusing to perform his government labour and acting in opposition to [his] master's order'.[29] I think we can surmise that William was someone who chafed against the yoke of authority, or perhaps what he saw as power without authority. Being literate and numerate, he would have considered himself superior to the average run of convicts, and he would have expected to be treated as such.[30] In a society where the distinction between the bound and the free was clear and determinative for elites but blurred and inconsequential for a rising generation of emancipists, William occupied a slippery social status. With his hard-won dignity and public standing imperilled by his convict past, he summoned every resource in his power to protect himself from social scorn. To this end, William Sutton placed great faith in the common law, that formidable collection of paper and words that had flung him from Middlesex to the other side of the world.

*　　*　　*

These three men – Adolarius Humphrey, William Sutton and Richard Atkins – are our narrators in this chapter. The central protagonist, Harriet Sutton, soon to turn sixteen, is a silent, spectral presence, and I doubt she was even at court. There were no reporters from *The Sydney Gazette* to cover the case, and the archival evidence doesn't mention Harriet being there. Instead, we encounter her as the heroine of a thwarted romance whose plot is told and retold by others. Harriet's story begins not far from the courtroom – a little to the east, up over the hill of Government House, down to Woolloomooloo Bay, twinkling at night with the small bobbing fires of Eora women fishing in bark nowees, and across to the neat rows of fruit trees and tobacco plantations of Woolloomooloo Farm – the residence of commissary John Palmer, his wife Susannah and their four children.

On the day of the hearing, in early June 1806, a procession of witnesses called by William Sutton made their way to the box. The central question for each was whether Harriet left of her own accord on account of a disagreement with Mrs Palmer, or if she was 'seduced' by Adolarius' promise of marriage. Yes, they said, Harriet resented Mrs Palmer 'upbraiding' her about an illicit liaison 'with a gent in her family' and several other suitors. She was probably looking for a way out of service when the handsome Adolarius appeared in the house, the wilds of his untamed beard cascading down into the folds of his cravat. According to a fellow servant, Harriet and Adolarius had two or three romantic encounters in the month before Harriet absconded, including an after-dinner tryst in the orchard. The three of them – Harriet, Adolairus and the servant – 'snuck out to the grove and stayed there till midnight', the servant said. Adolarius swore, with the 'heaven and the moon' as his witnesses, to 'keep and protect' Harriet. When Harriet anxiously asked if he would marry her and what they would do about her father, Adolarius spoke 'in reassuring words'. 'Did not Mr Humphrey use every persuasion to cause Harriet Sutton to leave Mr Palmer's house and go and live with him?' William asked in cross-examination. 'He did,' the servant replied. Another servant spoke of having to walk past Adolarius and Harriet embracing in the hall 'sometimes for ten minutes or more'. He also saw them giddily 'tossing Adolarius' hat' back and forth.[31]

It's a lovely vision, brought to an abrupt halt by Adolarius. 'Did I make her any presents?' he asked one of the servants in cross-examination. She responded in the negative. 'Do you recollect Harriet telling me that she had fixed her affection on Lieutenant Simmons?' he asked another, who conceded that Harriet had indeed written Simmons several letters in the time between her jaunt with Adolarius in the grove and her escape. This servant also recollected Adolarius saying that he had no knowledge of Harriet coming to see him.

So why did Harriet Sutton leave Mrs Palmer's house? Was it because, as Adolarius suggested, Mrs Palmer 'reproved her for some improprieties'? Or did the honeyed words of a hirsute minerologist seduce her away? Either way, both sides agreed that, dressed in men's clothing, she absconded from domestic service on 4 March 1806 and found her way to Adolarius' barracks.[32]

John Palmer took the stand next, looking expensive: silk cravat, aquiline nose, a puff of silvery hair, and a long face resting in a state of imperious regard. Yes, he said, had Harriet still been in service at Woolloomooloo Farm she would have received a provision (or dowry) from him and his wife at the time of her marriage. And no, he did not 'consider her wholly as a servant'. How did he come to know of her escape? He told the court that the morning after Harriet arrived at the barracks, Adolarius set out to find him and clear his name. The two men met on the Parade in Parramatta, and Adolarius asked Palmer if he was missing a servant. When Palmer replied in the affirmative, Adolarius told him he knew exactly where she was.[33]

Palmer said that as the two men were walking back to the barracks, Adolarius claimed he had known nothing of Harriet's plan to come to his house. 'I pledge my honour I have not seduced Harriet Sutton,' Adolarius swore. When he suggested that 'as a young man', Mr Palmer would surely have 'acted as he had done' in the same situation, Mr Palmer told the court that he was adamant: 'I certainly should not.'

No evidence was given as to what happened when Mr Palmer arrived at Adolarius' barracks, but we can assume that Harriet refused to budge. She was still there a few days later when her father William galloped in from Newcastle and banged on Adolarius' front door. John Lewin, the first professional European artist in the colony, had been at Adolarius' barracks when William arrived, and he told the court what he had overheard.

Adolarius said: 'Your daughter, Sir, is in that room and she has locked it and I cannot get in. If she will open it I will put no impediment in the girl's going.'

William ordered Adolarius to open it himself, but Adolarius refused.

'As master of the house,' William urged, Adolarius should 'exercise your authority' and open the door.

Adolarius retorted that he did not consider himself justified in breaking the door.

'Then you should apply for legal authority to break the door.'

Adolarius refused.

In the meantime, Harriet stayed safely in the room with the door locked, listening to her father battling her lover for control over her, insistent, as ever, upon doing as she wished.[34]

*    *    *

This concluded the opening sequence of the hearing of *Sutton v Humphrey*, which was the first joint seduction and breach of promise of marriage action heard in the Australian colonies. Already it gives us a wonderful feeling for the texture of romance in a penal colony. Lovers' oaths and declarations were performed to an audience of many: kin, friends, employers, employees and authorities. Love's arrows might initially be flung at individuals, but they ricocheted around the family – heartbreak and humiliation could be felt by a father as much as a daughter. After all, the breach of promise suit is brought by William Sutton, not by his daughter, and seemingly not even on behalf of his daughter. Sutton told Governor King that he thought Adolarius should be punished for 'trifling and sporting with the wounded feelings of a father'.

Even when love was illicit and clandestine, it demanded an audience. Today, we would probably not invite a friend to accompany us on a midnight tryst with a lover, or we might tell them to leave once we were safely there. Harriet and Adolarius had no such qualms. How do we make sense of the fact that romantic love, an emotion we now associate with the most private and delicate of feelings, could once have been so public?

To begin, we need to imagine our way into a culture that was still largely oral rather than written, and where life was governed by codes of honour that determined personal and family reputations. All the litigants in this story could read and write, but many of the colony's residents could not, and even those who could preferred the evidence of a sworn oath to a written document.[35] Governor Bligh, for instance, in 1806, declared that his 'verbal permission to occupy land was better than a lease, for [a lease] he could take away'.[36] Governor King spent considerable time trying to create a written register of the overlapping land claims in the colony, which until then had been a cacophony of competing oral pledges.[37]

A land grant required a spoken pledge because a lot was at stake, and the same was true of love. When channelled into marriage, love altered the status of each party, turning men into husbands and women into wives, and moving women from the authority and protection of their family or employer to that of their husband. Although women had more civil rights in the colony than in Britain, they were still often dependent on their partners for survival, so it was important to choose well.

For Harriet, as for all domestic servants, even more was at risk. Although her service would have been seen by her family and employer as an interval before marriage, her romantic activity was strictly policed. It's likely that her contract forbade her from engaging in sexual activity, and any courtship should have been subject to the consent of Mr and Mrs Palmer. Failing this, Harriet could be taken to court.[38] Historian Paula Jane Byrne notes that one-fifth of depositions by employers to the Magistrates Bench before 1824 involved 'direct complaints which related to the servants' sexuality.[39] The employment relationship between servants and masters was unlike a usual labour contract: servants were 'bodily owned'; their time and their sexuality were subject, at every hour of the day, to their employer's control.[40] Because women's domestic service, as Adam Smith famously declared, was not 'real work', but rather was seen to be part of the unproductive economy of the household, their leisure time could not be measured and protected as it was for male servants (who for instance refused to start work before 6 a.m.); surveillance was therefore ever-present and intimate.[41] Mr and Mrs Palmer did not consider Harriet as 'just a servant'. They saw themselves as acting *in loco parentis*, providing her with a dowry, ideally teaching her habits of gentility, and permitting or prohibiting her intimacies. The laws of coverture reduced wives, daughters and servants to the property of the men who 'owned' them, so it is also possible that Mr Palmer thought of Harriet as his chattel.[42] Transforming herself from an object owned by others into a wilful romantic subject, acting in defiance of her parents and her employer as well as of the laws that kept women's bodies confined within the home – Harriet's elopement had high stakes. She needed to be able to put faith in Adolarius' words.

With such extraordinary social and legal consequences, love was taken very seriously, and lovers in the colony made their pledges under the eyes of God and the community. This is why Adolarius and Harriet asked a fellow servant to accompany them on their midnight outing, and why Adolarius 'swore by the heavens' in front of this witness. In an oral culture, pledges and oaths were thought to guarantee honesty. We see similar examples in other early breach of promise cases. In one case in the 1830s, a suitor organised a team of witnesses to accompany him on a romantic dinner because, in his words, 'he was about marrying' the woman.[43] Breaking a vow would invite divine retribution, and breaking a pledge would see you subject to community reprisals. Adolarius made himself open to both.

Of course, pledges, vows and oaths were still fallible, and were vulnerable to manipulation by those who might change their minds or take advantage of others' trust. This is where the culture of honour became important. By the early nineteenth century, honour had evolved from a medieval term signifying 'manly courage or noblesse oblige' to mean 'trustworthiness'; an honourable person was someone who had a reputation for fulfilling their moral and social obligations. Honour, writes historian Gregory Laing, was how an oral culture that ran on spoken promises protected itself: if your words did not match your actions, or if you swore a false oath, you sacrificed both your own and your family's honour; you became disreputable.[44] A good name was crucial in commerce, and it was especially important in a penal colony comprised of people with dubious or unknown backgrounds, where traditional kinship networks and guild structures were absent.[45] An honourable reputation could win you and your family social and financial opportunities, while a dishonourable reputation could take everything away. This is what was at stake when Adolarius told Mr Palmer, 'I pledge my honour that I did not seduce Harriet Sutton.'

To grasp the meaning of love in the early 1800s, we need to familiarise ourselves with this vibrant world of gesture, pledges and spoken words, inherited from the oral culture of pre-industrial England. We need to rid ourselves of the modern notion that love is a private and individual emotion. The proofs of love in *Sutton v Humphrey* could have been a bundle of love letters – we know from the hearing that Harriet wrote them. Instead, amorous gestures, oaths and spoken words were considered the best evidence: the toss of a hat, the bond of a kiss, and a vow before God and the community to 'love and take care' of Harriet.[46]

\*     \*     \*

If the early colony was yet to be colonised by the grey ink of the bourgeoisie, it was also yet to have its days parcelled up by calendars and clocks. People rose with the sun and slept with the stars and were only beginning to acquaint themselves with modern time-keeping. With the town clock in a state of disrepair in 1806, a resident helpfully informed his neighbours that he would place his timepiece in the window of his workshop so that people might walk by and know the hour.[47] Judging by the testimony from the next part of the court case, nobody had a watch and few cared much for dates. We know that William left Adolarius with Harriet still locked in the room of the barracks and didn't return until 25 April, at least a month and a half later. A lot happened in between these visits, but the precise dates and times of events are uncertain. This is the story I have managed to piece together.

First, Harriet penned a letter to her father, begging for forgiveness. She had never wanted to go to Mrs and Mr Palmer's house, she said. Her position as a domestic servant had 'always been disagreeable to [her]', and she had been sent there 'contrary to [her] inclinations'. Mrs Palmer made her perform tasks that she thought to be 'impossible'. She also addressed the accusation that she had been 'reproved' by Mrs Palmer for some improprieties. Yes, she wrote, something had happened between her and 'a gent of that family' [the Palmer family] which made her 'situation very uncomfortable'. She didn't mention the hat-tossing and kissing, or the romantic oaths taken under the moon, but simply said that she had seen 'Mr Humphrey two or three times, took a liking to him and threw [herself] under his protection, and found [herself] comfortable'. These are the only direct words we have from Harriet, and they are striking for their discretion. She seems to be trying to reassure her worried father that what would appear to be amorous recklessness was in fact a safe, rational decision.

As Harriet was committing this evidence of their love affair to paper, Adolarius was busy denying the relationship. He met with Governor King, swore an oath that he was not harbouring Harriet, and organised for Harriet to swear an oath to the governor's agent, Mr Grant, affirming that she was acting of her own will. Mr Grant wrote out the oath and 'used all the persuasive means' to make Harriet stay with him. She responded, dramatically, that 'she would make away with herself first' (or commit suicide).[48] Harriet's mother visited her in Adolarius' barracks to try to persuade her, and eventually Harriet left to stay with Mr Grant.

*Adolarius Humphrey, drawn by George Harris in 1803.*

Meanwhile, by mid-April it had become clear to William that the relationship between Harriet and Adolarius was not advancing as he would have liked. He wrote to Adolarius, warning that if he did not return Harriet then he must marry her; failing that, William would apply for 'redress by law'. Before Adolarius could reply, William was once again at his front door, demanding to see Harriet. This time she wasn't there. William took the opportunity to raise the issue of marriage with Adolarius, speaking glowingly not of Harriet's virtues but of his own. He was 'an upright man'; 'his Character was unblemished.' Adolarius was unmoved but assured William he would offer compensation 'in consideration of [William's] great trouble and charges'. In the face of this firm 'no', William called upon Governor King and asked him to intervene. On 27 April, *The Sydney Gazette* published the first of King's general orders concerning Harriet. Her love was now a matter of law.[49]

Reverend Samuel Marsden, infamous moralist and colonial busybody, residing at the time in Parramatta, decided to get involved. He told the court that when he heard that Harriet had absconded, he promptly went to Adolarius' barracks to 'save her' and send her back to the Palmer residence. Either terrified by Governor King's order or cowed into submission by the force of

Marsden's personality, Adolarius offered to marry Harriet and 'hoped that he would be satisfied with that'. Marsden was 'surprized by the offer' and told Adolarius that while marriage 'was a matter for his conscience ... the Government permission must be attained'. He was referring to the licence that all residents, whether convict or free, were required to obtain in order to marry.

Governor King rejected Marsden's application, insisting that William apply on Harriet's behalf. Any minor under sixteen required parental permission. A few days later, following William's application, King granted Harriet and Adolarius a marriage licence, subject to their consent.

William must have felt relieved. It would have seemed that all his cajoling had finally worked. Marriage licence in hand, he, Adolarius and Harriet marched along Parramatta Road towards Marsden's chapel, an impromptu bridal party of three. But just before they reached the chapel, Adolarius 'of a sudden declined it'. Perhaps it was a brave moment of self-assertion against a barrage of government orders, unwanted visits and litigious letters. Or perhaps it was a cowardly refusal to go through with what he had carelessly promised Harriet that night in the orchard, under the fruit trees and the bats at Woolloomooloo farm.

We might have expected Harriet to return despondently to her father, and her lover to go back to his barracks. But the records suggest otherwise. Harriet went into hiding. Around the middle of May, William offered a reward of five guineas for anyone who had information about her whereabouts. 'It is known', ran the newspaper advertisement, 'that several persons must be accessory to her concealment'. When nobody came forward, William changed his strategy. Governor King, at William's behest, delivered another order, threatening a fine or imprisonment for anyone involved in her concealment. 'Good order', King wrote, required that Harriet be returned as a 'necessary Example to the growing Females of this Territory'.[50] If we put these dates together, we have a picture of Harriet dashing from Adolarius' barracks to shelter in friends' houses between 27 April and 8 June. She was 'at large', playing with a furtive autonomy. She was also most likely absent from the hearings that William brought against Adolarius in June 1806.[51]

\*    \*    \*

William Sutton was the first person since the colony's inception to use the breach of promise of marriage suit. The next case was in 1825, and it was not until the 1830s and 1840s that people began to sue with some regularity. We therefore begin our history with a curious silence: why did more people not use the suit? And why did William choose to?

The lack of breach of promise cases was certainly not because the residents of the early colony felt cowed by the courts. They were some of the most litigious people Australia has ever seen. Between 1788 and 1810, over 3000 civil cases were heard in the Court of Civil Jurisdiction.[52] People sued each other over mislaid cabbages and brought defamation actions when someone called them 'a worthless character' or 'a rogue' in the street.[53] Ordinary people, many of them convicts or emancipated convicts, represented themselves in court. They treated the common law as a set of ancient rights and inherited privileges that they could mould to assert their personal and political interests, and to a surprising degree the civil courts accommodated them. Women welcomed the civil law into their cottages, invoking its power against troublesome or abusive partners. When their partners disappeared or returned to England, women appeared before judges demanding maintenance payments for their children; mistresses claimed inheritance rights to the land of their paramour soldiers; and mothers claimed custody rights over children. None of these actions was formally legally permissible, none of these rights existed in law at the time, and many of the women, being either convicts, former convicts or wives, did not strictly have legal standing.[54] Yet the early colonial court interpreted widely its right to adapt the common law to the conditions of the new colony, and the residents of the colony were not shy about bringing their claims to court.[55] If women had wanted to sue their partners for jilting them, they would have.

And yet, until *Sutton v Humphrey*, nobody did.

Barristers in the 1830s often mused upon the reason for the paucity of prior cases. Some thought people in the early colony had tried to avoid the mistakes of England, shunning an action that caused such embarrassment to families. Others decided it was because of the demographic imbalance between women and men.[56] As one barrister in the 1830s explained: in Sydney 'there were twenty-five young men to one young woman, therefore [the woman] could have sustained no loss'.[57] It's true that the ratio of men to women (around seven to one in 1806) played a part.[58] If a woman wanted to find another partner, she could do so with ease; Harriet Sutton had quite a few suitors before her affections settled upon Adolarius. But if the only reason for the lack of cases was demographic, we would still have to explain why cases started to appear in the 1830s and 1840s, when men still outnumbered women by more than two to one in every Australian colony.

To my mind, the rise in breach of promise cases was a legal symptom of a social shift: people in the 1830s began to care about marriage in a way that the people of the early colony, particularly free citizens, did not. As much as authorities sought to regulate love and monitor the affairs of the populace, people resisted by opting for a range of romantic forms forged far from the province of law.

To better understand how love could be at once subject to the power of the governor and largely free of the law of marriage, it's important to disentangle elite discourses from popular practice. For imperial authorities and administrators, marriage had a range of virtues: it would direct women's 'disorderly' sexuality towards reproduction; it would subject convict women, seen as innately wild and treacherous, to the authority of their husbands; it would preoccupy women with the labour of care; and it would ensure that they and their children were provided for by their husbands rather than by the government stores.[59] By the time Governor Macquarie arrived in 1810, the rationale for sending women to the colony had shifted from balancing the sex ratio, and ideally stopping the men from having sex with each other, to bringing wives for the settlers.[60] Evangelicalism, embodied in the meddlesome Samuel Marsden, was on the rise, as were the middle classes, whose claims to political power were based on their perceived moral superiority to the dissolute aristocracy and the working classes. In this evolving culture of respectability, marriage was imagined to provide the moral and economic foundation for a disciplined society. And in a settler colony, dutiful English families would eventually supplant Indigenous families from their land. This was why every governor who travelled to Australia carried instructions to encourage marriage.[61]

The problem was that very few people were interested in lawful monogamous marriage, and colonial authorities were at best desultory in following their instructions to enforce it. While Richard Atkins presided over the dispute between William and Adolarius, his four illegitimate children were probably running around his house.[62] While Governor King considered questions of morals in the Court of Appeal, his wife was raising his two illegitimate children, whom his convict mistress, Ann Innet, had given birth to on Norfolk Island.[63] King and Atkins were not unusual. King reported in 1806 that there were 395 legal wives and 1035 concubines (or de-facto wives) in the colony, and that of the 1832 children born that year, 1025 were illegitimate.[64] Samuel Marsden presented to Governor King a register he had drawn up, which concluded that about two-thirds of the women living in the colony were 'unmarried and concubine'.[65] King was unperturbed. He retorted that the women were simply cohabiting in stable relationships with their partners. He also rejected any proposal to 'lock up the females until they are so fortunate as to obtain husbands'.[66] As much as people like Marsden railed against the vice of the colony, most residents, rich and poor, were blasé about bourgeois Christian morality.

For elite colonists stationed in far-flung regions of the empire, non-normative sexual arrangements were common. The small numbers of white women, the influence of 'savage' customs and the climate were some of the excuses given for white men's moral transgressions or sexual entitlement. 'I was far from good influences – far even from England,' explains Henry Wilcox, weakly, in *Howard's End*, when questioned about his mistress in the Caribbean. 'I was very, very lonely, and longed for a woman's voice.'[67] As for the poor, 'living tally'[68], or common law marriage, was favoured in Britain, Australia and America in the eighteenth and early nineteenth centuries because it allowed women to keep their own property and it meant people could move freely in and out of relationships.[69] Self-divorce among the poor was also common, effected by placing an advertisement in the paper stating that the couple had parted by 'mutual consent' and were not responsible for each other's debts. The colonial courts gave rights to cohabiting couples that they would never have had in England, granting unwed women rights to their partners' property and wages in cases of death or desertion.[70] In the early colonial period, desire for a partner might propel you into many different romantic arrangements, of which lawful marriage was only one.

Seen in this light, William Sutton's efforts to force Adolarius to marry his daughter were unusual, and he was very much an exception in going to court about it. Perhaps he was worried about Harriet's survival. After all, her rebellion was now public knowledge, and she would have been unlikely to find other employment as a domestic servant or even as a seamstress, which would have left her with the options of sex work or bar work, both of which would have made her family disreputable and made her vulnerable to violence. This is why Harriet, in her letter to her father, refers to exchanging one form of 'protection' for another. A young woman alone would find it difficult to protect herself. But this doesn't explain why William Sutton wanted *legal* marriage, or why he wouldn't have been satisfied with Adolarius and Harriet cohabiting. To make sense of William's investment in marriage, we need to delve deeper into what we know of him personally, his desire for status, and his efforts to scrub his family clean of the stain of his convict past.

Prior to William's felony, he occupied one of the rungs of the respectable working classes. His employment as an excise officer was sufficient for him to support a family of four; although troubled by his foray into debtors' prison, he was nonetheless capable of suggesting, when convicted, that he pay for his and his family's passage to Port Jackson. If William rebelled against authority, it was probably because he thought himself to be not really a convict but an exile, which made him superior to those convicts whose abject poverty had led them to crime.[71] Imbibing the growing discourse on respectability in Europe, which celebrated marriage as one of the defining features of the middle classes, William married twice – demonstrating that, unlike most people in the early colony, he believed in the institution of marriage.[72]

He would also have been aware of debates fermenting in the colony between the exclusives and the emancipists. The former believed that convicts and ex-convicts should be kept as a class of people in a state of perpetual subordination, while the latter believed emancipated convicts should be granted all the rights and liberties of free settlers. In 1806, with a majority convict population who were treated more as colonists than as criminals, these discussions were not yet the polarising roar that they would become under Governor Macquarie. Nor did they feature the hereditarianism that would be expressed by the anti-transportation movement of the 1830s, encapsulated best in the words of clergyman Dr Thomas Arnold: 'If they will colonise with convicts,' he opined to John Franklin, 'I am satisfied that the stain should last not only for one whole life, but for more than one generation; that no convict or convict's child should ever be a free citizen, and that even in the third generation, the offspring should be excluded from all offices of honour or authority in the colony.'[73] There was a virulence to anti-convict sentiment in the 1830s that was not yet present in the early 1800s, but discrimination against convicts and their children still existed. In affairs of the heart, it seems that native-born men cared more about their partner's lineage than women did.[74] By 1828, only 8 per cent of native-born men who had married in the colony had married ex-convict women, although 40 per cent of native-born women had married convict or ex-convict men.[75]

William would have known that his re-entry into respectable society might be jeopardised by his convict past, and that his children might be seen to have inherited his previous moral failings. He would also have thought, however, that this exclusion was unjust. Having been expelled from respectable society, William now spent much of his life knocking at its door, arguing his way back in. His daughter's marriage to Adolarius would have consolidated his family's climb up the social ladder, and her rejection would have been a wounding reminder of his past. This is why William tried to convince Adolarius to marry Harriet not by singing her praises, but by pronouncing upon his own 'uprightness' and 'unblemished character'.[76]

If William worried that Adolarius had jilted Harriet because Adolarius thought himself superior, he was correct. In court, Adolarius pleaded in his defence 'how inferior in life Harriet Sutton was to him' and that he had discovered quite 'by chance that her father had once been a prisoner'. Adolarius also claimed that his promise of marriage was not valid because it was not in writing, and he spent much of his defence calling Harriet promiscuous. He asserted that she had at least three suitors on the go as well as a liaison with a 'gent' in the Palmer residence. Adolarius' main defence, however, was William. If there had been a breach of promise of marriage, he argued, there could be no more compelling justification for it than William's convict taint.

There is no record in the trial transcript of Richard Atkins' instructions to the assessors (or jurors), nor do we have access to their deliberations. All we know is that Adolarius' defence was short – probably no more than a few minutes – and convincing. A verdict was declared in favour of William Sutton, but he won damages of just one shilling. Damages like these were called 'contemptuous'; he had won in point of law, but no real injury deserving of proper compensation was conceded.[77]

\*　　\*　　\*

William was furious. He launched an appeal, which was heard by Governor King. As in the original proceedings, he claimed £280 for his financial loss and hurt feelings.[78]

A few weeks later, King – squat, spherical and pouchy – listened attentively from the bench as William explained why Atkins' judgment was 'illegal and improper'. Atkins had not distinguished between the two separate actions William had brought – seduction and breach of promise of marriage – so William now sought to prise them apart. On the charge of seduction, he asked King to recall the testimony of the servants who had seen Harriet and Adolarius 'at the Grove on a Night'. Adolarius used 'every Persuasive Language', he said, 'to induce Harriet to leave Mr Palmer's house'. 'Your Excellency ... will readily see how the Respondent held forth Temptations and Inducements to Harriet Sutton to seduce her from her Situation by unmeaning Language, he said. 'Swearing by Heaven and the Moon that he loved her and would never forsake her. If such Language cannot be called Seduction to an unthinking Female none can.' When Harriet asked him to 'protect her in his House', he answered 'with a soothing Tongue that he would conceal her, and which no doubt he has done'. William directed King's attention to a statement by Mr and Mrs Palmer that 'if [Harriet] behaved herself', it was their intention to 'make a Provisions for her … as she was not considered altogether a Servant'. Finally, he asked King to recall that Adolarius 'refused to exercise his Authority' and open the door Harriet had locked. This concluded William's case for seduction.[79]

As William spoke, Governor King probably leafed through the papers before him, assessing the case. King was a careful thinker and his judgments, writes Bruce Kercher, showed a genuine effort to come to grips with the law. With no formal legal training, King wrote that he found legal decision-making perplexing; he would 'tumble over volume after volume' of English law trying to find the correct answer.[80]

Turning his attention to the breach of promise action, William told King that a 'treaty of marriage' had been forged between himself and Adolarius and reminded him of the marriage licence King had granted, and how Adolarius had 'of a sudden declined it'. This conduct, William railed, 'was not only inconsistent with the British Constitution, but trifling and wantonly sporting with the wounded feelings of a Parent'. According to the 'Laws of England', Adolarius was now obligated to pay William 'half of his or her Fortune'. Adolarius' argument that William's convict past justified the breach of promise should be dismissed, William said: 'If her Father had been a Scavenger, it would be immaterial.' In fact, Adolarius should be fined 'for so unfeelingly reproach[ing] a fellow Creature with past Misfortunes', which was a legal remedy one could, according to William, pursue in England.

King would have retired for a few moments to deliberate, after which he returned to give his verdict. On the question of the breach of promise, King declared that 'no such Obligation took place by the joint application of both Parties', and therefore the appeal must fail. Adolarius needed to consent to the marriage licence. As for the seduction, he thought that 'Harriet Sutton was equally debased in Body and Mind before she eloped from Mr Palmer's protection and Service'. William must have felt crestfallen.

'Yet', King continued, ''tis no less my Belief that the Respondent [Adolarius] was not averse to Harriet Sutton's leaving the respectable Service she was placed in by her Father otherwise it was the Respondent's duty ... not to have welcomed her in to his house.' King declared that by 'entertaining and harbouring her all night I can have no hesitation in considering that [Adolarius] has either directly or indirectly been advising, aiding or consenting in the seduction of Harriett Sutton from her service and of her causing an Expense to Her Father.' He overturned the paltry damages of one shilling and raised them to ten pounds sterling.[81]

*   *   *

Legal historians have warned that court hearings do not necessarily expose 'the truth'. Instead, they reveal the range of narrative possibilities available in a society, and the outcome confirms which story or interpretation was deemed most plausible. If a young woman were to defy her parents and employer today and run away to her boyfriend's house, her story would fit snugly within the tropes of rebellious romance and our reaction would probably be to smile. But in a penal colony at the dawn of the nineteenth century, these same actions suggested different cultural narratives. For Governor King, it was an example of an unruly colonial woman, 'debased in body and mind', repudiating the master–servant bond and threatening public order. Measured against the model of bourgeois femininity – chaste, pious and submissive – women had further to fall than men and were judged, socially and legally, more harshly. In eloping, Harriet had disrupted the smooth functioning of a respectable household and committed transgressions for which she could have been brought before a court: 'neglect of her duties', vagrancy and unchastity or disorderliness. For Adolarius, Atkins and the assessors, the case was about a former convict wrongfully expecting to be able to marry his daughter to someone above her station. For William, it was about family honour, the right of an emancipist and his daughter to be treated with dignity. Each party's version of the truth depended on where they were located in the social hierarchy.

Harriet's case also reveals the malleability of law. Legal actions were not hard, fire-glazed jugs into which litigants would pour their stories. The civil law was still soft and clay-like; ordinary colonists could roll it around in their hands and shape it to their needs. As successful stories became binding precedent, common people, as much as judges and legislators, made law.

The discrepancies between the arguments made in *Sutton v Humphrey* and the law of seduction and breach of promise of marriage found in treatises from the time illuminates the creative ways in which early colonists like William Sutton used the law. Most obviously, refusing to marry Harriet was not a breach of the constitution, and reproaching William for his past misdemeanours did not make Adolarius liable to damages worth 'half his fortune' in either England or Australia.[82] And while a marriage licence would have helped a breach of promise case, neither a licence nor an explicit promise of marriage was required. It was Adolarius' amorous behaviour – his vows to Harriet under the fruit trees and kissing and caressing – that would have made William's case arguable. Instead, both William and King relegated this behaviour to the seduction action. In the civil suit of seduction, the father or the woman's employer was the plaintiff; in breach of promise it was the woman. Perhaps William was suing on Harriet's behalf as she was a minor – but this does not appear in the court minutes, and if it had been the case Harriet should have been the primary witness in her father's seduction case.[83] Finally, while it was possible for Mr Palmer, as Harriet's employer, to sue for 'seduction from employment', it was not possible for William, at least not without proof that Harriet's earnings went directly to his family (although this was no doubt simply assumed).

What I find fascinating about William's speech on seduction is that he does not try to prove that sex took place. In common law seduction cases brought by a father on behalf of a daughter who was without an obvious pregnancy or child, the daughter was usually forced to undergo a medical examination. In this instance, there were no such efforts. Instead, seduction was referred to according to its original medieval meaning as 'seduction from her service'. We see this language elsewhere in the early colony: in 1806, the captain of a ship took out a public notice cautioning the inhabitants of New South Wales against 'harbouring or seducing [sailors] from their duty', and in 1810 the governor threatened to prosecute anyone who attempted to 'seduce or entice away' the girls from the Orphan School, where the daughters of convicts learnt to be domestic servants.[84] A few months after Harriet's case, an editorial in the *Gazette* said that 'excellent moral instruction' could be found in the governor's orders prohibiting 'the seduction of servants from their employ'. '[B]ut for the temptations bestrewed in her path', the article ran, a 'newly arrived' woman 'might gradually have been led into virtuous habits, and have respected industry as the great and only source of real comfort and contentment'. Alas, 'experienced harpies' devoted to 'infamy, and vissistude [sic]', led such 'unwary' women astray with their 'evil counsel, mal example and ... baneful encouragement to dissipation'.[85]

Because industry was believed to lead to virtue and idleness to vice, it made sense to apply the sexualised language of seduction – with its paths bestrewn with 'temptations' – to absconding workers. The imagined servant was someone susceptible to the extraordinary power of words. If in oral cultures, words are more likely to 'do things', as philosopher J.L. Austin argues, then 'reassuring Language' and 'soothing Tongues' could effect a physical seduction.[86] That William could sue on these grounds speaks to the state's concerns about absconding workers in a context of desperate labour shortages, particularly among domestic servants, the hierarchical structure of master–servant relations in the colony, and beliefs about the morally curative powers of work. It is also a wonderful example of the malleability of law at this time. William, Humphrey, Atkins and King – all without legal training – moulded the story to what they thought the law of seduction and breach of promise to be, not what it actually was.

*　　*　　*

We know Harriet only through the words of others – yet the impression she leaves on us is bold. In a world structured by discipline, she acted on desire. The moral and legal codes told women like her that their bodies did not belong in public, particularly not roaming around unchaperoned, and she responded by dressing as a man and exposing the arbitrariness of restrictions based on sex. If her position as a daughter and a domestic servant made her the property of her father and her employer, she responded by 'making off with herself'. She defied her father and her suitor by locking herself in Adolarius' room, and in so doing destabilised the patriarchal norms that gave men access to women's bodies. The hearing constructed her as passive, chaste and impressionable, 'an unthinking female' led from virtue by a 'vile seducer', but she responded by writing back, rationally explaining her motives in letters to her father, and in so doing claiming autonomy. With each transgression she inspired new stories, new judgments and new efforts to shape the stories already circulating about her in the community. Her trials and the subsequent accounts of them – including my own – reveal multiple narratives unfolding over time.

As a modern reader, you might question whether this *is* a love story at all. A romantic vow is broken almost as soon as it is made, a night spent together is followed by wretched betrayal, neither lover seems to want to marry, and the only wounded heart seems to be that nursed by William Sutton. But we should not therefore assume that *Sutton v Humphrey* is not a love story. I am quite convinced that it is. It is just that we encounter love here in a foreign country, and to understand it we need to learn the local language.

Love looked very different in the early colony, and romance among the poor or even middling orders bore little resemblance to what historians have described of nineteenth-century middle-class marriages. Romance depended not on privacy and secrecy, but on publicly performed intimacies and pledges. There were no doubt variations of love that celebrated complete self-revelation, that asked lovers to value each other outside their public roles, but these were not dominant among the poor, and they held little sway in court. In an oral culture that ran on honour and reputation, where individuals were deeply embedded in networks of kin and family, selfhood was largely defined through the status of one's family and one's obedience to social and moral laws. Love was not the delicious whisperings of one's true self, murmured to another, but a collective emotion, monitored and steered by kin.

As an emotion with public dimensions, love was both an appropriate subject for governance and a potential site of political resistance by women. If, in his efforts to control the family story and safeguard its honour, a father was unable to persuade his daughter and her lover into marriage, he might ask the governor to intervene. We know from an 1804 letter to Lord Hobart in the Colonial Office that Governor King believed 'little public assistance is derived to the settlement from the female part of it' unless they were 'usefully employed in their domestic concerns' or 'providing for their families'.[87] King did not think women needed to be legally married, but they did have to be dutifully tucked away in the private world of family – either their own or as a domestic servant – where they would be of no public expense. Any disruption, such as a woman loping furtively and defiantly away from domesticity, was a threat to the paternalistic social order. Women were more likely than men to be brought before the courts for vagrancy, historian Paula Jane Byrne informs us, and in many cases where domestic servants, either convict or free, were arrested for absconding from work, a love affair was found to be the culprit.[88] Harriet's decision to pursue her amorous desires should be seen as a form of protest: against the spatial boundaries that confined her to the home, against the labour conditions that she and other women found 'impossible', and against the moral and state laws that sought to control her sexuality. Romantic love could smooth women's entry into the conjugal family and the domestic sphere, or it could be rebellious, libidinous and anarchic. As an unstable and morally ambiguous force, love was a site of regulation and revolt.

This did not mean that love was only about duty, honour and social order. Historical periods are always cross-cut with intimations of the future and residues of the past. Dominant ideas make their way into the historical record, while alternative realities often remain hidden. This discrepancy is encapsulated in the difference between Harriet's description of her relationship in the letter she wrote to her father and the evidence her fellow servants offered to the court. Kisses in the hallway, flirtatious games and declarations of love under the fruit trees do not make their way into her missive. And being fleeting gestures, they don't usually enter government records. How Harriet decided to describe her and Adolarius' love affair to her father and what she and Adolarius did or felt were two separate things. This should inspire us to think about what other forms of affection might be omitted from government records. For instance, historian Alan Atkinson has analysed convicts' requests for government permission to marry and found that they mostly listed pragmatic reasons – their income and household skills, for instance; at most there might be a declaration of 'mutual affection'.[89] Like Harriet, however, these convicts were appealing to someone with power over them, and it is possible that behind the steady, sober script of officialdom were mutual quickenings of the breath.

*   *   *

And what of Harriet and Adolarius? What can we deduce from the hearing about the nature of their relationship? The court testimony suggests that while Harriet may have absconded because of her distaste for domestic servitude, she also fancied Adolarius. There is evidence that they continued to try to see each other despite the government orders. One witness said that only a week before the first court action, 'Harriet Sutton intended to come to my house, if I would allow her and ... she would go and cognise Mr H of it.' Another said that he saw Harriet and Adolarius meet late at night in a hotel. This seems to imply that they had organised to stay in contact while she went underground. It is even possible that Adolarius' betrayal the day after Harriet arrived at his barracks was a joint decision to ensure that he was not charged with 'aiding and abetting' her. One week before the hearing, when Harriet and Adolarius would have faced prison if they had been caught together, messengers were still darting across the dusty, crooked Rows of the settlement, delivering their notes, and whispering to Adolarius of Harriet's whereabouts.[90]

One of the last times they appear in the historical record together is six years after the hearing, in a letter authorised by Governor Macquarie to the governor of Van Diemen's Land in 1811. Macquarie referred to Harriet as 'an unfortunate young woman who had for some time past estranged herself from her Parents and natural guardians and thrown herself on the Protection of a Mr Humphrey'. We know from Bligh's correspondence that Adolarius had been in Van Diemen's Land since 1807. 'This deluded Girl,' Macquarie's note continued, 'has got a serious sense of her past Indiscretion and has become anxious to place herself under her Father's Roof and Protection.'[91] Given Adolarius' haughty belief in her inferiority, Harriet might have been leveraging some power over him. By this time, William Sutton was wealthy, residing at fashionable Macquarie Place, and he had a 'handsome house' in Pitt Street that he was offering to rent to a 'genteel family'. Macquarie referred to William as 'a reputable man' who was 'desirous to afford her in those Circumstances every parental Tenderness and Affection'.[92] Evidently, William still had no compunction about getting governors involved in his daughter's romantic life. And like Governor King before him, Macquarie was happy to intervene in a family drama. If Harriet wished to accept the offer of 'affectionate Asylum' from her father, he wrote, 'she was not to be detained by Mr Humphrey'.

Macquarie may also have intervened because of a personal dislike of Adolarius. In a letter to the Colonial Office, he reported the difficulties he had experienced with Adolarius on account of the latter's refusal to provide quarterly mineralogical reports. Adolarius had resigned on 1 June 1812 on account of ill health,[93] although Macquarie claimed that in fact he was 'of an indolent Habit and extremely reluctant to take any Trouble Whatever in the Line of his Profession'.[94]

Following Macquarie's letter, Adolarius would have found himself called to Government House and presented with a choice: either return Harriet to her father or marry her. Harriet and Adolarius next appear in the archives together on 28 August 1812, in a record of their wedding in Hobart.[95]

Upon his resignation from the position of government mineralogist, Adolarius was given 200 acres of land stolen from Aboriginal people along the Derwent River, which we can assume Harriet managed alongside him. The couple never had children. Adolarius became a magistrate in 1814, then a coroner, and eventually a member of the Van Diemen's Land parliament.[96] He died in 1829 at the age of forty-seven. Two years after Adolarius' death, Harriet married settler John Kerr and stayed with him for almost twenty years until she died, aged sixty-four, in 1854.[97]

Given Harriet and Adolarius' eventual rise into the colonial establishment, their marriage in 1812 came at an opportune time. Early colonial elites such as Governor King cared little for official marriage, but this would not remain the case for long. The colony was changing. Governor Macquarie – prim and industrious – had arrived, and he came with the cult of marriage in tow.[98]

# 2

# 'Promises and pie-crusts were made to be broken': The Rules of Courtship and the Rise of Lawful Marriage

## (*Cox v Payne*, 1825)

*My Dear Sarah*

*I beg leave to acquaint you it is my intention to sail on Tuesday next if possible, therefore I think it is my duty to inform you that my Affections for you are founded on the most Honourable and pure motives which is possible for any man to be in possession of, and believe me dear Sarah that I am so much interested with respect to your Conduct and Character it is morally impossible for me to propose or wish you to do a single wrong Act which might tend to injure you in the Affection of your Parents or in the eyes of the Publick – I am extremely sorry your Father and Mother should have any Confidence in such a Report particularly when it came from a very loose Character and a person who has no knowledge of me whatever therefore could be any judge of my intention.*

*Believe me Dear Sarah my Affections for you have not been sudden nor precipitant. I have fostered them some time within my breast although you have not been acquainted with it before and now I think you will never have any cause to repent of the promise you made me, as it is my sincere intention to make you a Companion of my future life, should it meet your approbation write me to that effect and it will be one of the happiest moments of my life and believe Dear Sarah that I shall always have your interest at heart.*

*I remain Dear Girl Your Most Affectionate,*

*Jn Payne*[1]

Sarah Cox, young, feisty, and possessed of 'killing beauties',[2] sat at the table on Sunday morning and wrote a brief missive to her lover, Captain John Payne. In front of her was a small wooden box brimful with letters. Beyond that, through a misshapen window, she could see the wink and shimmer of the harbour in summer. On Sundays, the bells of St Philip's church pealed from the hills above, flying across the shingled roofs of Sydney through serpentine rows and into the stillness of the stately new boulevards. They echoed above the shouted greetings of sailors on the government wharf next to Sarah's house and over the clatter of carts carrying tea, salt-pork, leather and china from the docks through the dusty streets.[3] Having lived next to the wharf all her life, Sarah was probably inured to the noise. And anyway, she would have been too focused on the letter to notice anything else.

This was not the first time Sarah had written to Captain Payne. She had known when he first proposed to her that his business in Port Dalrymple, far away in Van Diemen's Land, would compete with her for his attention. In 1822, the first year of their romance, the couple exchanged tender messages on scraps of paper that finned their way between John's liquor business in the south and Sarah's home in Sydney Cove.[4] The following year, when John settled in Sydney, they continued to write. Well, Sarah didn't always write the letters. Mr Todhunter, her sister's beau, had a more elegant hand, so sometimes he would write them for her.[5] But today's letter was not of the kind that Mr Todhunter could write. So Sarah Cox, who has since been described as 'calm',[6] 'amiable'[7] and 'a lady in manner and appearance',[8] put pen to paper:

> Sir,
> I will thank you to send my letters, and everything else you have belonging to me by the bearer, and not give me the trouble of sending any more to an ungrateful wretch as you are.
> S.C.[9]

She then folded the letter six times into a square the size of a stamp, sealed it with black molten wax and told her servant to deliver it to Captain Payne and await his response.[10]

*   *   *

Reading Sarah Cox's words for the first time inspires the kind of shocked delight we feel when *Vanity Fair*'s Becky Sharp flings the gift of Dr Johnson's dictionary out of her carriage window, leaving it at the feet of her loathed etiquette instructor.[11] This is surely not how nineteenth-century women behaved! I first encountered Sarah's letters when reading the colonial newspapers' coverage of her 1825 breach of promise trial, and then discovered the originals in the archives: seven numbered missives, written between 1823 and 1824. The first volley of letters was prompted by a spontaneous, late-night, drunken visit by Captain Payne, which in turn led to him reprimanding Sarah for her florid displays of anger. 'I suppose I have gone too far to be forgiven,' she conceded; 'if so I hope you will return this Note and all of them you might have, but rather would have you keep them and come and see her who loves you more than all the world.' The relationship never recovered. Payne began courting a certain Miss Redmond, whom he later abandoned for a wealthy widow, Mrs Leverton. The seven letters in the archive trace Sarah's reactions to this perfidy, beginning with 'My Dear', tightening into 'Sir', and ending without any address at all, her handwriting scratched into the paper like tiny knife-marks.[12]

With a mixture of fragility and force, Sarah begged to know how Payne was feeling: 'I should presume you think I have feelings as well as yourself, therefore I am determined to know if your mind is altered from what you once thought.' 'Your own Conscience, if you have any, must tell you have injurd me.' His non-response made her frantic: 'I don't know whether you received my letter yesterday ... if you will send me an Answer I will never trouble you any more.' When news of Payne's marriage to Mrs Leverton arrived, Sarah tapped into a rich vein of anger: 'You will be a wretch ... and perhaps in time I shall get someone who will reward me for all my faith.' She boldly announced her intentions to sue him: 'I am led to understand you say you have been told I intend inforcing you to keep your promise. Indeed Sir I do.' The words she anticipated saying on her wedding day had now become a threat of legal action. She continued to demand the return of her letters: 'I am very angry to think you give me so much trouble in Applying for them so often. I can Assure you if you do not send them by the woman I will write until I get them.' Her final note was one of self-redemption: 'the past I will forget, if possible,' she wrote; 'I will be as happy as I was before you broke my peace.'[13]

We know, because Sarah's correspondence ended up in court, that Payne was keeping it for the impending trial: it was used as evidence that he had been released from the marriage contract and proof of Sarah's bad character.

I find Sarah's fury tantalising, partly because it's relatable – any person who has felt the sting of rejection knows the thrill of amorous insult – but mostly because of what her anger reveals about the rules of courtship in the early colony. Captain Payne was not only in breach of common law. He had also transgressed the laws of love. In the early colonial period, love had its own laws, which sometimes complemented and sometimes conflicted with those of the state. If we are to have a sense of how romantic love and law have parted ways over the long arc of modernity, we must begin by investigating their mutual frisson in the early nineteenth century.

*　　*　　*

Sarah Cox felt dizzy and nauseated. Her mouth was parched, her heart thumped and the scent of the large cedar table, warm and spicy, would have been pungent. Her hearing had started with the opening address of her barrister, William Charles Wentworth, his splendid words booming up to the ceiling of the courtroom and sending a hush over the excited chatter of the gallery. 'This is an action to bring such compensation as the law could afford to the injured feelings of the client,' he said. 'The plaintiff is a seamstress apprenticed to the milliner Mrs Forster. Captain Payne carried on a maritime business at Port Dalrymple but now works mostly as a brewer and soap manufacturer in George Street.'[14]

Wentworth was still young, in his mid-twenties, but already his face was cushioned and jowly, his generous belly pressed tight against his waistcoat, and his ruddy skin bore the lines of too much boozing and womanising.[15] He and the defence counsel, Mr Wardell, were wearing wigs and gowns, which, as the people of Sydney remarked, lent the court gravitas. Nobody else at this point, the judge included, had been bothered with official attire.[16]

Wentworth continued: Payne had first caught sight of the sixteen-year-old Miss Cox, who was 'possessing of some attractions', when he was delivering mail from Port Dalrymple to her employer, Mrs Forster. Payne's visits became more frequent, until one morning he handed her a slip of paper, 'asking her whether she had any objections to changing her name to Sarah Payne?' Sarah immediately informed Mrs Forster of the letter, and Mrs Forster told Sarah's mother and father. The next day Payne visited Sarah's parents, declared his intentions to be 'the most honourable', 'and expressed a hope of being allied to the family'. Sarah's parents consented, and he was accepted as Sarah's suitor. On one occasion, Wentworth explained, 'it appears that some misunderstanding arose between the lovers'. 'The whole of the family had retired to bed except for the plaintiff and a female servant.' Payne arrived at Sarah's house intoxicated and wanting to see her. Sarah 'severely reprobated him', saying that if he couldn't select a decent hour to visit then he had better not visit at all. But this falling-out was eventually reconciled. Letters continued to pass between them, 'couched in terms of the strongest affection', until Sarah learnt of Miss Redmond and later Mrs Leverton. 'That money was his object his previous conduct will clearly shew,' claimed Wentworth; 'his first change was from a poor girl to a rich one; and his subsequent change from a rich girl to a rich widow.' Since Payne's marriage to Mrs Leverton, he had also been spreading rumours around Sydney about Sarah. Here Wentworth's address reached a crescendo: 'A case of greater treachery and duplicity never came before the Court of Justice,' he thundered. This case was 'the first of the kind that had been brought before a jury and from the verdict this day he depended that it would be the last.' And then, to the delight of the gallery, Wentworth read Captain Payne's letter proposing marriage out loud.[17]

Sarah was probably glad of her bonnet that day; its hooded wings would have cupped her face and blocked most of the court from view. Captain Payne didn't show up, which was predictable, but his barrister, Mr Wardell, was seated at the same table as Sarah. Wardell was in his thirties and had an almost feminine profile – high cheekbones, sensual lips and large, intelligent eyes framed by luxuriously long sideburns. In front of Sarah on an elevated dais, the court recorder would have been busy scribbling, and behind him, higher up on the bench, sat the chief justice, Mr Francis Forbes – shiny balding head, sharp brown eyes and gaunt, hollowed cheeks – exhausted from overwork. The four jury members were probably leaning against the cedar-panelled stall to her far right, dressed in their finest clothes: white cravats, waistcoats with gleaming buttons, ruffled collars and boots that made a pleasing clop on wooden floors. The jury would spend the next few hours craning their necks towards the witness box in an effort to hear; even when the gallery stopped jeering, the court was a noisy place. The doors opening onto the major thoroughfares of Castlereagh and Elizabeth Streets were left permanently ajar, so all the creaking of carriages and thudding of hooves and the clamour of passers-by ricocheted into the room. Then there was the hammering, crashing and shouting of men working on the construction of the new courthouse across the road, and across from that the roar of the racetrack at Hyde Park.[18]

The courthouse was makeshift – it was originally the Georgian Public School, a school for orphans. Prior to its conversion into a law court, trials were held in the Sydney Hospital. But in 1823 the hospital was declared to be unsuitable;[19] it reeked and groaned with the ill and was bespoiled by hanging washing – sheets, underwear, shirts and dresses flapped indecorously from its verandas.[20] With convict architect Francis Greenway's courthouse yet to be completed, the two-storied Georgian School – chosen for its stately columns and spacious rooms – served as the colony's courthouse for the next two years.[21]

The first people to give evidence for the plaintiff were Mrs Forster and Sarah's sister, Elizabeth Cox. Mrs Forster's interrogation was brief. She affirmed that she saw Captain Payne's letters and heard him 'make declarations of love' to Sarah. Elizabeth said that she too had seen Captain Payne's letters, which were kept in a 'small box on the table near the window', and that he once 'made a promise' of marriage 'to her on the part of her sister'.

'Do you remember what he said?' Wentworth asked.

'He hoped that his eyes might drop out of his head if he did not perform his promise,' she replied.

Now it was Mr Wardell's turn. He stood up, scooped up some letters from the desk and swooped down on Elizabeth like a raven. Yes, Elizabeth said, as he fired a round of questions at her, she could recognise her sister's handwriting and yes, it's true that the packet of letters Wardell thrust into her hand were written by Sarah. As for Sarah's character and the kind of company that she kept, it was 'very little, but good company. Mrs Cooper, Mrs Forster ...'

Wardell interjected: 'Mrs Frazier? Does she keep company with Mrs Frazier?'

Dark murmurs flew around the gallery.

'She does not associate with Mrs Frazier,' Elizabeth said shakily, and then corrected herself. Sarah had walked with Mrs Frazier, but only because Mrs Frazier had been staying at their house. No, she continued, Sarah had not abused Mrs Payne in the street and nor had she been out during the night last year.

Wardell returned to the desk and the last remaining witnesses for the plaintiff were called.

Mr Todhunter, her sister's suitor with the elegant penmanship, said that he 'saw the progress of the attachment' and assisted by writing a few letters for Sarah. Yes, he said, there was one about Payne's 'improper conduct, it was rather a harsh one', but 'she was very much hurt at Captain Payne's conduct', particularly 'when she realised he was married and that there was no chance for her'.

'And what of her appearance?' asked Wardell with a smile. 'Would you say that she is somewhat altered in the last ten months? Would you say that she is "pale and haggard"?'

Todhunter looked at Sarah's sunken eyes and pallid complexion.

'No,' he lied.

Sarah's mother, Mrs Cox, explained that Payne 'had free access to the house', and that he had promised to marry Sarah as soon as he quit the sea. She had warned him that 'we had no fortune but a little Cottage to give her', but Payne didn't mind; he said he 'required nothing but to make Sarah his wife'. Yes, there was the quarrel when he arrived at the family's house late at night, but this was soon made up with letters and a present of a scarf, which Sarah had since courteously returned.

George Williams, a sailor who had worked at Port Dalrymple, testified that Captain Payne was certainly a man of good circumstances, with farms, mills and houses in a number of locations.

The case for the plaintiff concluded with Mrs Beckwith, a friend of Sarah's mother. She remembered Mrs Cox asking Captain Payne 'why he meant to deceive Sarah'. What had been his response? 'That promises and pie-crusts were made to be broken.'[22]

\*　　\*　　\*

Sarah Cox was a 'currency lass', or native-born Australian, who came into the world on 1 January 1805 to convict parents. Her mother, Fanny Morton, arrived in Sydney in 1796, having been convicted for stealing, and her father, Francis Cox, had been in Sydney since 1791 after his penchant for gambling and house robberies propelled him across the ocean on a seven-year sentence, leaving behind a wife and family in Norwich.[23] Francis and Fanny never married, possibly because bigamy laws prohibited remarriage, but more likely because they, like many people in the early colony, didn't have much time for marriage. As I discussed in Chapter One, cohabitation was the norm in the early colony, which meant that many of the native-born – rich and poor – were the children of parents who felt no need to have the law sanction their intimacies. Many of the governors and judges in the early colony had illegitimate children; Sarah's barrister, William Charles Wentworth, was one of three illegitimate children born to D'arcy Wentworth – one of the wealthiest men in the colony – and his convict mistress, Catherine Crowley.[24]

In the twenty years that yawned between Sarah's birth and her breach of promise of marriage action, the colony had changed; it stumbled out from a long night of frolicsome cohabitation and blinked in the glare of a new moral puritanism. Governor Macquarie – prim, indefatigable, his white ruffled cravat buttoned stiff to his chin – had arrived in Sydney Cove in 1810 with government orders exhorting everyone to marry. In a proclamation entitled 'Illicit Intercourse, evils arising therefrom', read aloud in the streets by a town crier, Macquarie lamented 'the scandalous and promiscuous custom so generally and shamelessly adopted, throughout the Colony of Persons of different sexes cohabiting and living together unsanctioned by the legal ties of matrimony'. Women, he noted, were successfully making claims on wills and inheritances of men they had lived with. This practice, he declared, would end. Cohabiting without marriage was a 'scandal to Religion, to Decency and to all good Government', and marriage was essential to 'Morality and Decorum'. Macquarie was determined to 'Encourage Lawful marriage by every possible Means'.[25] Marriage was to be the new norm, and it would be enforced through a system of legal punishments and privileges.

Macquarie and the governors following him offered a range of incentives for marriage, including property and inheritance rights, and they took these rights away from cohabiting couples.[26] Residents, whether convict or free, already required permission from the governor to marry, and this procedure became stricter for convicts in the 1820s and '30s, eventually requiring the sanction of the clergy and, for convicts, their master or mistress.[27] This shift towards a more rigid moral order was not just caused by individual personalities. It was mirrored in other colonies throughout the empire, a product, historians have surmised, of the growth of evangelicalism, masculine public politics, the increasing numbers of white women voyaging to the colonies and the rise of the middle classes, whose struggle for political power rested upon their claims to moral superiority.[28]

The effects of these new legal and moral codes can be seen if we enquire into Wardell's reference to the elusive 'Mrs Eleanor Frazier'. Mrs Frazier was a convict woman who was married to Mr Frazier, and thus benefited from the government policy of permitting convict women who married free settlers to be assigned to work for them as domestic servants – the idea being that they were now under their husband's authority. According to a piece of gossip in *The Australian*, the couple parted 'by mutual consent' in 1824 on account of Mrs Frazier's profligacy and waning amorous interest, which meant she was now a convict 'at large without legal authority'. Five days before a magistrate condemned her to the Female Factory – a grim, three-storey building in Parramatta opened in 1821 to 'house, control, employ and punish' convict women – she reunited with her husband and was again free.[29] At the time of Sarah's hearing, rumours of Mrs Frazier's promiscuity were circulating around the community: 'He got unrequited love,' *The Australian* said of her husband, 'She got Dumps. His tale and her *tale* had been known to all.'[30]

During Wardell's cross-examination of Elizabeth Cox, Elizabeth explained that Mrs Frazier had stayed at the Cox family's house after she had separated from her husband. Realising the social repercussions of being seen in her company, Sarah's father soon asked Mrs Frazier to leave and forbade her from visiting again. Wardell's claim that Sarah was of 'bad character' was based entirely on the allegation that she 'kept improper company' with Mrs Frazier. By the 1820s, a promiscuous woman was seen as socially and morally contaminated. Merely being in her company risked defilement. Had Mrs Frazier been in the same situation twenty years earlier, she would not have suffered the kind of social ostracism we see here, nor would she have been confined to prison for leaving her husband.[31]

Why would colonial authorities bother punishing the unwed and rewarding those who married? Partly for the same reasons we privilege marriage today – the belief that people will be more settled and industrious if they commit to a partner, rear children and become preoccupied with caring and providing for them. But there were also reasons peculiar to the early nineteenth century. Australia was colonised at a time when marriage was changing, from a union forged primarily out of shared property or commercial interests to a companionate model based on a male breadwinner and a dependent spouse. This version of marriage, which institutionalised the divide between a male public sphere and a feminine private sphere, was the peculiar creation of the emerging middle classes. The bourgeoisie argued that unlike the dissolute working classes or the unfeeling aristocracy, they built their marriages on sincerity of feeling, honour, piety and sexual restraint.[32] This reasoning informed Wentworth's argument against Captain Payne: by marrying for money, Payne corrupted the sanctity of love. The opposition between money and marriage had its roots in the dichotomy of public and private, with commerce and self-interest ideally kept separate from the moral haven of home, love and marriage. In muddling these two spheres, Payne, argued Wentworth, had turned marriage into a mercantile transaction. Of course, defence barristers like Wardell would fling the same accusation at plaintiffs, whom they accused of weighing the cost of a broken heart in pounds and shillings.

Marriage also took on a certain urgency in settler-colonial countries. On a pragmatic level, colonisation required both the appropriation of Indigenous land and European colonists to populate it, effected through policies that rewarded those who married and had families.[33] Once forged, these marriages were seen as a safeguard for Western civilisation – a bulwark against the colonies sliding into the sexual licentiousness seen to characterise both Indigenous people and the poor. Edward Eyre wrote that Aboriginal sexual relations were characterised by 'polygamy, and the illicit and almost unlimited intercourse between the sexes';[34] the same criticisms were levelled against the 'lower orders', who, in Justice Forbes' opinion, were plagued by 'licentiousness and debauchery among the single of both sexes'.[35] Edward Eyre drew the comparison directly, concluding that 'I do not yet think the Australian savage is *more* vicious in his propensities or *more* virulent in his passions than are the larger number of the lower classes of what are called civilised communities'.[36] In a settler colony so distant from England – the home of civilisation – the veneer of civility was thin and inhabitants risked descending at any moment into a state of nature.[37] The law's role was to guide these groups towards appropriate civilised behaviour, which meant state-sanctioned marriage.[38]

By the 1830s and 1840s, reports of homosexuality and the sexual licentiousness of the working classes, particularly convicts, had become shrill, particularly from those involved in the movement for self-government and the campaign to end the transportation of convicts to the colony.[39] As the convict population decreased (from 42.8 per cent of the population in 1821 to 22.3 per cent in 1841) and emigration of free settlers from England increased in the 1830s, demands for self-government by political reformers such as Wentworth became urgent.[40] If the colony was to have all the liberties and rights that accompanied British subjects around the world, it needed to make a case for its respectability.[41] The anti-transportation movement argued that the free immigrants of the 1830s and 1840s were a polite and industrious people whose reputation was being tarnished by the colony's bad name. The Bigge and Molesworth inquiries into transportation voyeuristically reported on the sexual licentiousness of convicts, and anti-transportation activists plucked from the scandalised language of these reports to argue that transportation had a corrupting effect on all settlers.[42] The bad character of convicts stood as a proxy for the bad character of the colony, and moral salvation, they argued, lay in marriage.[43] As J.D. Lang told the House of Lords Select Committee on Transportation in 1837, marriage transformed 'women of the lowest character into very respectable persons'.[44]

As the anti-transportation movement and the campaign for self-government grew and marriage became the primary signifier of respectability, offering couples significant material rewards, people began suing in larger numbers for breach of promise of marriage. Of all the cases listed from 1800 to 1850, the majority were heard in the 1830s and 1840s, and barristers used the hearings to offer a kind of moral tutelage for a debauched population: 'the defendant must be taught a lesson', the jury was counselled in an 1830s case, not just for the sake of the plaintiff but for the sake of 'New South Wales, where adultery, seduction and every species of immorality and depravity with all the evils that follow in their train, stalk impudently'.[45] In another case, also in the 1830s, the counsel for the plaintiff 'felt satisfied that the verdict that day would convince the defendant and others that they could not blast the respect of young women with impunity and that even in New South Wales, honour and honesty was the best policy'.[46] A guilty verdict could help to 'remove the stain under which the Colony of New South Wales notoriously labours'.[47] The pedagogical effects of these court hearings could be imbibed by multiple audiences: the court-room gallery, the readers of the British world (newspaper reports of breach of promise circulated around the empire) and the imperial government, which campaigners were pressuring to end transportation and grant the colony civil and political liberties.

If we understand marriage as the pride of the middle classes and a vehicle of moral reform, we can better make sense of Sarah's hearing and the role breach of promise actions played in a society increasingly embarrassed by its criminal origins. Sydney in the 1820s was on the cusp between two worlds. On one side, we have Captain Payne standing in the twilight of the penal colony, blithely declaring that promises, like pie crusts, might be broken, that a person might engage in serial relationships, and that love affairs could be ended with impunity. On the other side we have the arguments made on behalf of Sarah Cox: that a woman could experience no 'greater injury' than a broken engagement and that breaking a vow was an act of 'treachery'. This was the language of a new colony, one where marriage was the foundation of social order and a woman's respectability, along with the respectability of the colony, depended on men keeping their promises of marriage.

*   *   *

With the case for the plaintiff finished, Wardell stalked over to the jury and began his address.

'Why is this the first action of its kind in the colony?' he asked. Because 'the ladies in this country are like horses, very scarce; and my learned Friend would make them still dearer. A gentleman would be afraid to *speak* to a lady for fear of a promise.'[48]

Wardell and Wentworth were adversaries in court, but they had been friends for six years now; in fact, they were known around Sydney as the 'brothers in law'. They had begun a legal practice together and launched the colony's first independent newspaper, *The Australian*.[49] Literary men who dabbled in poetry, they both knew the power of words. To win, Wardell had to create a more plausible story than the one offered by Wentworth.

Recognising that laughter was his greatest weapon, Wardell read excerpts from Sarah's collection of letters, including one from another suitor, called (aptly) Mr Souter. 'Here are a series of letters offering a release,' Wardell declared. 'It would appear that Captain Payne was the only pain that could give her pleasure; yet he was not the only Souter that would suit her.' Laughter rippled around the gallery. Wardell smiled, then continued more seriously: 'I am at a loss to know how this lady can come into Court to look for damages, as she cannot shew a loss sustained; she considers [marriage as] a mercantile contract … if the plaintiff can get a husband, where is the injury?'

Wardell called his first witness, Mr Francis Mitchell, who said that he didn't really know the defendant, but he did know David Souter. At Souter's request, Mitchell had 'sent two parrots with a note to the plaintiff from Mr Souter'. Sarah's face no doubt crimsoned as jeers burst from the crowd behind her.

'Do you know what happened to them?' laughed Wardell.

'I understand they got away from the plaintiff,' he responded. The judge called the laughing gallery to order.

Was Mr Mitchell aware that Mr Souter was shortly to be married to Miss Cox?

'I have heard so, but I do not know from whom. I never heard it from Mr Souter.'

The next witness, John Armstrong, a servant in Mrs Cox's house, was called to the stand. He said that in the past he 'took a great number of notes from the plaintiff to the defendant but Mrs Cox said that they would punish me if I took any more'. Yes, he had heard Mrs Cox call Captain Payne a vagabond and send him out of the house. But Armstrong's credibility was undermined by the next three witnesses, all of whom confirmed that he was frequently intoxicated. The last, Captain Allpike, added that Payne had promised Armstrong '6 gallons and a bottle of rum' as well as 'a new hat and a suit of cloathes' in exchange for evidence – perhaps explaining how Payne had managed to get his hands on David Souter's letter to Sarah.

Wentworth stood for his closing address. 'The defence set-up is two-fold; first, that there was a release [from the contract]; and second that there was no injury sustained.' Refuting the first argument was simple: Sarah's letters, he said, 'contained no proof' of her releasing Payne from his promise. As for the question of the losses sustained by Sarah, 'my learned friend', he said, 'seems really to suppose that women are like that animal to which he made so coarse an allusion; that they are mere machines, and if they get a husband they sustain no injury'. The evidence showed clearly that Sarah had rejected Souter, but even 'supposing it otherwise, is celibacy to be the natural consequence of a breach of such a contract?' As for Payne, 'he continued to court Sarah to within three weeks of his marriage, no doubt because there was always a possibility that Mrs Leverton may reject him ... And although we could not get to the bottom of who circulated the injurious reports about Sarah's character, it was clearly the defendant, for no other person had an interest in vilifying her character.' Reputation, Wentworth said, was why Sarah went to court: 'These reports have been the cause of the action; and by your verdict, Gentlemen of the Jury, you will send her forth to the world free of taint.' 'If such among you as are fathers,' he concluded, 'consider what your feelings would have been, you will award that degree of compensation as will in some measure recompense her for the injury she has sustained.' The gallery murmured their approval, and Wentworth returned to his desk.[50]

Wardell couldn't deny that there had been a promise, and his argument that Sarah had released Payne from the engagement lacked evidence – he admitted this quite freely. Instead, his closing address focused on the demographic peculiarities of the colony. He countered that in a country where the normal narratives of love had been upended by the disproportionate ratio of men to women, Sarah, far from being injured, had plentiful options for marriage. Stories of distressed maidens ruined for life by broken promises simply made no sense here.

Wardell had a point. In 1833, men made up 73 per cent of the population of New South Wales, and in some remote districts men outnumbered women twenty to one.[51] Wardell turned Wentworth's argument that Payne had treated marriage as a mercantile transaction on its head: in encouraging a second lover and bringing the action to court, Sarah was the avaricious schemer, he said: 'a woman never looks so ill as when she comes into court to look for damages, because she could not hold a lover to his promise'.

The jury retired to deliberate, having been instructed by the judge that a promise had been given: Payne's letter to Sarah was irrefutable evidence. A few minutes later they returned with a verdict for Sarah Cox: £100 damages, with costs. In today's terms, Sarah had won about $180,000 dollars. Her reputation restored, she could walk into the world 'free of taint'.[52]

*　　*　　*

Six months after the hearing, however, Sarah gave birth to a child, which Wentworth recorded in his bank book: 18 December 1825, birth of Thomasine Wentworth.[53] Timmie, as she was called, was the illegitimate daughter of William Charles Wentworth and Sarah Cox.

This explained why Sarah, according to Wardell, had looked 'pale and haggard' in court, and it is why I described her as feeling nauseous. While the jury speculated about her chastity, Wentworth and his good friend Wardell knew that Sarah was anything but chaste. Sarah Wentworth's biographer, Carol Liston, who found Timmie's birth certificate, argues that Sarah most likely had morning sickness during the hearing, when she would have been three months pregnant.[54]

It's a delicious piece of colonial gossip, but it had catastrophic consequences for Sarah. Although she won her case, the illegitimate child she was soon to bear meant she lost all claims to respectability.[55]

*　　*　　*

Vaucluse House sits on the curve of a hill, claiming supremacy over all that surrounds it: a lush tropical garden, a gravelly carriage loop, sandstone stables, convict barracks, a vegetable patch and a beach below. It's a gentle twenty-minute drive from the centre of Sydney. The road coils languidly up the headland, elderly fig trees stretching their august limbs over winding footpaths; grand houses point their imperious faces seawards, and the air is sweet and peppery. At the summit, the city appears on the left horizon, flat and two-dimensional, silhouetted against a late-afternoon sky. I am standing in front of the mansion, but there does not appear to be any entrance. From the garden I can see a two-storey, terracotta-coloured building with fairy-tale ramparts and turrets on the roof. Bulging French windows open onto a veranda, but there is definitely no front door.

I walk around to the side of the house where visitors to Sarah Cox and William Charles Wentworth would have arrived and am guided by a carriage loop, as they would have been, to a white gate. Inside I see a courtyard with blue-and-white tiled fountains, ferns in old wine casks, and a covered archway that connects the kitchen and butler's pantry to the rest of the house. By today's standards, the courtyard has a relaxed Ionian beauty, but by elite nineteenth-century standards it would have seemed odd: where was the grand foyer directing people into the formal areas of the house?[56] Why were visitors given immediate access to the house's most private regions, to the obscenity of a cook bent over a wood-fired stove?

Sarah and William were aware of the eccentricities of their house. Between 1827 and 1853, when they lived there, William became the most prominent politician and the wealthiest pastoralist in the country. In normal circumstances, his wife would have supported him through an endless round of dinners, balls and charity events. Entertaining would have been a crucial part of the work performed by Sarah to maintain the family's status and Wentworth's political power.[57] But traces of an unfinished *porte-cochère* – the covering where carriages would drop off visitors – at the end of an empty corridor that now halts abruptly at a wall just inside the house tell a different story. Sarah, in the words of Lady Jane Franklin, was 'very handsome, lady like and amiable, but of course not visited'.[58] If the jury at Sarah Cox's trial thought they would send her into the world free of taint, then the foetus in her stomach produced a different story. 'When a woman falls she falls forever', declared a newspaper in 1847, commenting on Sarah's unchastity, 'she becomes as it were socially dead. Her punishment is indeed worse than death'.[59] Sarah may have exercised her civil and political rights in the courts and won – but when she became Wentworth's mistress and gave birth to two illegitimate children, she lost all social rights to participate in society. As Sarah and William no doubt already knew, love in the early nineteenth century was regulated by a machinery of social laws often more severe than those of the state.

Analysing the entanglement of love and law means exploring how desires were subject to formal government campaigns around marriage. But it also involves excavating *informal* laws of love and acquainting ourselves with how these were adjudicated by the community. Let's start with

*Sarah Wentworth (née Cox), painted by William Nicholas in 1856.*

the family, whose first task in the regulation of love was to ascertain the character of the lover, usually via an inquisition. This was not an inquiry into the person's inner self, personality, moods or favourite pastimes. It was an interrogation into his public status, his reputation in commerce, his social standing and often whether he was concealing a previous marriage. As Captain Payne acknowledged when he expressed 'a hope to be allied with the family', and as Wentworth exhorted when he asked the jury to imagine the injured feelings of Sarah's father, love was more of a collective than a personal experience, an emotion regulated by family and kin. We know from a letter written by Captain Payne to Sarah – found in the archives but not reported in the press – that Sarah's parents had received an unfavourable account of him, which he needed to disprove before he was accepted as Sarah's suitor. 'I am extremely sorry your Father and Mother should have any Confidence in such a Report', Payne wrote. His strategy was to attack the credibility of the informant: 'it came from a very loose Character and a person who has no knowledge of me whatever therefore could not be any judge of my intention'.[60] We have to assume that this satisfied Sarah's parents, as there is no further mention of this rumour. In the case of *Miller v Brett* (1832), the plaintiff's guardians received an anonymous letter charging Mr Brett with bigamy and tasked their friend Chief Constable Jilks with conducting an interrogation.[61] Jilks went 'round to several people' and interviewed them. Although Mr Brett's name was cleared, he considered this to be a slight against his character and broke off the engagement, regretting that he had to 'forego my intention of uniting myself to your family'.[62]

Suitors like Captain Payne and Mr Brett had to submit to these humiliating investigations for a simple reason: Sydney and Hobart, as historians Penny Russell and Kirsten Mackenzie have argued, were cities of immigrants where personal histories were shallow and family pasts unknown, and where people of dubious repute could invent new identities.[63] In the case of bigamy, the consequences for a woman could be dire. If Mr Brett's wife had reappeared after he and Miss Miller had married and had children, Rebecca's children would have been declared illegitimate and the marriage invalid, which would strip her of all economic protection and social status. Bigamy was relatively common in the early colonial period – a sentence of seven years' transportation without one's family, combined with the privileges given to married convicts, almost sanctioned the practice, and the lack of a proper system of marriage registration until 1838 made it hard to track the status of relationships. By the 1820s and 1830s, however, authorities were clamping down on the practice, and the concern of Miss Miller's guardians is a good example of how ordinary people brought their intimate lives into conformity with law.[64] If we add to this murky colonial backdrop love's capacity for imagination and artifice, or for idealised self-portraiture, then one of the fundamental questions of love – 'who are you?' – becomes rather fraught.

Yet privacy was one of the most cherished virtues of nineteenth-century family life, albeit one enjoyed more by the middle classes than the labouring poor. It was also a right habitually impinged upon by the heightened levels of community surveillance that characterised colonial life.[65] 'This place is not like England,' complained convict entrepreneur Mary Reiby, who was Sarah Cox's neighbour and today appears on Australia's twenty-dollar note; 'you are under the Eye of Everyone and your character scrutinised by both rich and poor.'[66] Sydney at this time was a strange mixture of anonymity and claustrophobia; people watched each other with vigilant eyes, and information about people's backgrounds flew on the breath of gossip. Investigations were mostly done through face-to-face interviews, by 'a greedy band of prying police officers and imaginative constables ... raking up all possible information as to the habits of your life', as Mr Brett's defence argued. Letters also circulated around the community, and often the wider empire, in a quest for personal information. Given ships took six months to deliver mail from England, determining someone's true identity could be a long process. In the end, the court judged that Miss Miller's parents' right to investigate her suitor outweighed the suitor's right to privacy.

Once the family had decided the suitor was acceptable, the next stage of regulation involved promise-making, which suitors and parents performed as grand juridical gestures. In the case of *Sutton v Humphrey* (Chapter One), the verbal agreement to marry was referred to as a 'treaty of marriage', while in *Hawthorn v Steel*, which we will examine in the next chapter, the proposal of marriage was called 'a verbal contract'. They 'shook hands and the witness said that it would be disgraceful on either side to break it off without a just cause'.[67] Oaths uttered in front of a community of witnesses ensured that promises were sincere and lawful. In Sarah's case, Captain Payne followed his marriage proposal with a declaration to her sister that 'he hoped his eyes might drop out of his head if he did not perform his promise'.[68] The ceremony attached to these words distinguished promises from idle talk and converted them into what J.L. Austin would call a 'speech-act', where the act of saying something also involves doing something.[69] Like our forebears, we still promise and swear our way to security because our lives can be changed by romance and we know, just as they did, that we can never know another person any more than we can know ourselves. Love makes us beg for reassurance. The difference here is that vows of love carried legal weight and were made to family members, rather than whispered between lovers. Breaching a vow could alter a man's identity: he would be dishonourable, not a man of his word, not to be trusted in marriage or commerce.[70]

Any whiff of caddish behaviour on the part of the suitor saw the establishment of informal courts of love, presided over by family and friends and held anywhere from street corners to gardens or kitchens. Mrs Beckett and her friend Mrs Cooper bundled Payne into Mrs Cooper's house to enquire 'of him his motives for deceiving the young lady'. After interrogations like these, punishment could take the form of slander – for instance, Sarah's mother is accused of calling Payne a 'vagabond' in the street – or worse.[71] In numerous cases defendants were attacked with fists or sticks by furious brothers of jilted women; in one case, discussed in Chapter Three, a family kidnapped the suitor and imprisoned him in their home with a priest until he signed a letter agreeing to marry.[72]

What role was left for lovers in a world where proposals of marriage were offered to family, where getting to know a suitor was a task assigned to the community, and where any faltering of affections was interrogated by, in Jane Austen's words, 'a neighbourhood of voluntary spies'?[73] The many performances and professions of affection that comprised what was then called 'making love' – holding hands, kisses, love letters, walking out together, visits, exchanges of gifts and lockets of hair – were understood to add up to a binding promise.

Love letters in particular opened up 'a space of justice' for lovers, allowing them to write and contest the rules of love and to present an ideal version of themselves.[74] Historians and philosophers have viewed letters as one of the main ways in which the modern 'self' was created. 'One writes in order to become other than what one is,' mused Michel Foucault, 'so as to go beyond a self, so as to invent a self.'[75] Karen Lystra has gone so far as to say that American individualism is largely indebted to the kinds of self-creation involved in writing love letters. 'The nineteenth-century Victorian experience of love was rooted in the concept of an ideal self,' she argues of the American middle-class. 'Not fully expressed in public roles, this ideal self was meant to be revealed to one person only.' Love letters, which were 'totally private', were not just a medium for this ideal self; they created it.[76]

I find Sarah Cox's letters intriguing because they do not fit historical consensus on love letters. Her parents had probably taught her to read and write, and having leafed through her correspondence in Mitchell Library I can attest that she does not appear to have aspired to letter-writing as literature, but approached it as purely functional.[77] She did not seem to see her letters as either private or sacred – her sister told the court they were kept in a wooden box on the table – and she was not always the writer; Mr Todhunter admitted to being the scribe for some of them, as was customary at the time. While they clearly allowed her a space to experiment with adjudicatory power – to interrogate and issue judgment upon Captain Payne – there is otherwise little evidence in her letters of delicate self-portraiture or of a self that has taken flight through words. Instead, reflective of a pre-industrial oral culture, many of her letters read more like speech than literature: 'I was informed I should not think of marrying these two months, nor must I speak to any young man. What do you think of that?' ran one letter without any concluding address.[78]

It's possible that Sarah's letters show the gulf that yawned between the middle classes, for whom writing love letters was a delightful exercise in self-excavation, and the labouring poor, many of whom simply lacked the luxury of time or education to craft epistolary selves for the other's delectation. More likely, to my mind, is the idea that Sarah's letters are indicative of a 'self' that finds expression in the immediacy of spoken words and gestures. The search for an 'authentic self' that lies hidden in the recesses of inner life strikes me as an anachronistic endeavour for early-nineteenth-century working-class people.

\*    \*    \*

Sarah was punished throughout her lifetime for her sexual transgressions with Wentworth. When her first daughter, Timmie, turned seventeen, an age when she could begin meeting suitors, Wentworth was a commanding political figure and Sarah, despite her marriage to Wentworth in 1829, was a social outcast. Like any bourgeois mother in the nineteenth century, Sarah was responsible for orchestrating the marriages of her children, but unlike her more respectable counterparts she was excluded from the circuit of balls and parties where her children could meet gentlemen of equal wealth. So Timmie met her future husband, the barrister Thomas J. Fisher, through Wentworth's sister-in-law, Eliza Wentworth, and in 1844 they married.[79]

Immediately after the wedding, Thomas Fisher cut ties with the Wentworths and forbade Timmie from seeing her parents again, an alienation that lasted for the next twenty years. There was one exception during this time, when Timmie was having complications with her pregnancy and Sarah was permitted to nurse her. After she gave birth, however, the ban was reintroduced. Sarah's sister-in-law Eliza was horrified by Thomas' treatment of Timmie. 'God knows! No one has a higher idea of the duty a wife owes to her husband,' she wrote:

> when his commands are lawful and just and cheerfully and most willingly should I obey them but when his commands infringe and are in direct opposition to those of my heavenly Father I would then most certainly follow the dictates of my own conscience – I cannot comprehend how a husband – a Christian husband could ask his wife to forsake her parents – parents too who have ever evinced the warmest the most devoted affection for their child.[80]

It's a wonderful passage that shows perfectly the multiple and sometimes conflicting levels of law through which love – parental, romantic, divine and conjugal – was regulated.

We might start with the Victorian idea of the family as a site of governance presided over by the husband, whose 'lawful' 'commands' were cheerfully obeyed by the wife. But obedience was not automatic; it was contingent upon the husband's provision, and also on the conformity of the husband's 'commands' to Christian moral norms. Like many women in the nineteenth century, Eliza invokes divine laws as a greater source of authority than the patriarchal laws of the husband, and in so doing justifies disobedience. But there is another law here that informed John's ban, which Eliza carefully avoids: the communal law that stipulates women be chaste until wedlock. By the middle decades of the nineteenth century, female honour was largely defined by sexual chastity, and any breach rendered a woman an outcast and a pollutant; her moral transgression was transmissible to her children. This explains how John could love his wife most earnestly, as he claimed to do, but also inflict such a cruel separation between Sarah and her daughter.

For Sarah, ostracism within the family was exacerbated by social exclusion among the elites. In 1847, after years of being shut out from elite circles, she was invited by the new governor, Sir Charles FitzRoy, to the Queen's birthday ball at Government House. Polite society revolved around Government House, and when it became known that Sarah and two other women of 'doubtful reputation' were on the guest list, people began to retract their acceptances.[81] The chief justice objected to their presence, respectable women took umbrage, and the newspapers discussed the matter: the women should be excluded 'to preserve our wives and daughters safe from the contagion which they might spread', *The Atlas* opined.[82] The scandal was resolved when Sarah, with supreme dignity, declined her invitation.

In the aftermath of the scandal, Sarah decided to move to England. Like Wentworth, who learnt about his father's conviction for highway robbery from a parliamentary debate, Sarah's children learnt of her mother's reputation through newspaper reports. She left in 1853 and Wentworth followed her the year after. Although Sarah longed to return to the 'rustic little paradise' at Vaucluse House, she did so only briefly. The rest of her life was passed in England, where she died and was buried in 1880, far from her beloved William Charles, who rests to this day at Vaucluse House.[83]

\*    \*    \*

'Why do you think Wentworth and Sarah decided to marry?' I ask Mel, a curator at Vaucluse House. It seems like an obvious question, but I ask it because I had spent the previous day communing with Wentworth at Mitchell Library, smiling at his indignant response to being arrested for public drunkenness and reading of his dynastic aspirations: in 1817, proposing marriage to the daughter of the Macarthurs, he wrote to her parents that the marriage would promote 'the future respectability and grandeur of our families'. They rejected him on account of his father's reputation as a highway robber.[84] 'I like to think it was a love-match,' Mel responds. 'Sarah was a strong woman and maybe she was threatening to leave.' I observe that this is certainly supported by the fact that Wentworth went off the rails in the late 1820s, drinking, cursing and philandering his way around Sydney – which may explain why Sarah registered their second child in her own name. 'Sure,' Mel says 'or maybe at the end of the 1820s, Wentworth said, "Alright. I love this woman; she is strong and capable." It may be a bit romantic, but I like to think it was because they were in love.'

In 1829, one month before his marriage to Sarah, William published a poem about her in *The Australian*:

To Sarah
For I must love thee, love thee on
Till life's remotest latest minute
And when the light of fire is gone –
Thou'll find its lamp had thee within it.[85]

Love as we know it today is often found in the shadows of breach of promise hearings: in the wilful passion that trampled on duty, or the desire that scorned promise-keeping and subverted the rules administered by parents and kin. In Sarah's case, we can more easily identify love in the stolen glances we imagine between her and Wentworth than in her relationship with Captain Payne, begun as it was with the stiff formality of a letter to her parents.

Romantic love today asserts itself through will and proves itself through its indifference to law – both formal and informal. But thinking about love historically asks us to suspend these easy reflexes. Sarah and William were shaped by the culture they lived in, a world increasingly intolerant of cohabitation, where marriage was the only legitimate structure for intimate relations between the sexes. People in the early nineteenth century were also primarily concerned with a person's capacity to fulfil social and moral obligations, and with pragmatic considerations such as their ability to pro-vide for a family or perform housekeeping. Today, we like to think that love is a joyful exercise in discovering the person behind the social identity: we pose questions of each other, study each other's gestures and pore over the meaning of words in an effort to divine the true nature of our lover, to access their inner self unencumbered by public roles or cultural norms. For lovers like Sarah and Captain Payne, the opposite was the case: the questions asked concern only the social carapace, the economic and marital roles, and any sordid secrets would be quickly unearthed by a cabal of informants whis-pering in the streets of Sydney. Love and marriage were yet to become the private bonds between individuals that we like to think them to be today. Duty was expected to trump personal happiness. A promise of marriage was not a private utterance to another individual but a public declaration: it enlivened legal obligations. And as the state sought to bring love within the province of law, to channel it into state-sanctioned conjugal forms, commu-nal forms of policing increasingly buttressed or complemented the policies of the state.

It's important to recognise, however, that government campaigns around marriage were not unilateral. Too often, historians envision a prying oppres-sive state struggling to regulate the treasonous ties of the populous; to manage rebellious colonial hearts. Sarah Cox's trial suggests something different. By the time her story of blasted affection came to court, Payne had already been through a series of informal courts of desire; he had been subject to informal laws of love and communal modes of punishment. Both the courts and the community were involved in a shared project to keep men to their promises, because women's reputation and livelihood were dependent upon masculine honour in love. Women lacked the economic ability to support themselves or their children, and so risked becoming a financial burden upon the com-munity. And as Sarah Cox's later life amply demonstrated, women suffered disproportionately for sexual transgressions. Payne may have been punished for his perfidy by the machinery of communal regulation – promise keeping, after all, lay at the heart of definitions of masculine honour in a commercial society – but its sanctions were fleeting compared with those imposed on Sarah, who paid for unchastity with a lifetime of shame.

By 1861, 77 per cent of women in New South Wales over the age of twenty were married, a shift which historians see as indicative of the triumph of respectable culture.[86] Sarah Wentworth's life in many ways confirms this nar-rative, but I think it is worth ending on a note of caution: Sarah moved in elite circles, and there are flickers in her court case of alternative moralities resistant to bourgeois norms. Indeed, for historians, one of the delightful aspects of using court cases is that they show the extraordinary range of competing norms and narratives within a society; they are a theatre for moral contestation, for argument and counterargument. Breach of promise cases can appear like a tower of Babel, where litigants, barristers, judges, jurors and newspaper reporters speak different moral tongues. For instance, Miss Stone won her action in the 1830s even after a landlord described how 'three or four men were continually coming to the house after her'. A neighbour described knocking at her door and Miss Stone appearing 'with her hair about her shoulders, and her back exposed; a man named Mr Kelsey was lying on the bed.'[87] This is most likely the same Mr Kelsey who ten years later successfully defended himself against a breach of promise action. In Kelsey's action a friend, James Loder, confessed to sleeping with the plaintiff and was asked during cross-examination if he was married at the time, to which he responded: 'I was married at the time I speak of knowing the plaintiff. I'm not married now, living with another man's wife is not being married; I can't say that I am not.'[88] Extending our gaze beyond the penal colonies of Tasmania and New South Wales, we see that in the earliest case in Melbourne (1841), brought successfully by Miss Gorman against her partner Mr O'Neil, the backgrounds of the Gormans, notorious brothel owners from Tipperary, was never questioned. A man gave evidence that he had seen Miss Gorman and Mr O'Neil 'lying on the bed' together in her boarding house. He said that he had kissed Miss Gorman 'and had seen Evans playing with her also, and she with him', yet concluded that 'she was a well-conducted person.'[89]

That marriage colonised the romantic imaginaries of most white Australians is borne out in the figures, but we should not assume that this conquest was complete. In witnesses' more candid moments we see the flicker of countervailing forms of heterosexuality – looser, livelier and joyfully indifferent to middle-class marriage, morals and manners.

\* \* \*

The period from the early colony to self-government witnessed a shift in the expression of state power over intimacy: from the almost unbounded commands of early colonial governors seen in the previous chapter to a kind of disciplinary power codified in the common law of marriage and internalised by an increasingly (although never entirely) law-abiding people who had imbibed the norms of Christian morality. By the middle of the century more people were marrying than in the early penal colony, they were marrying in church, and there was an efficient system of registration to codify these relationships. As marriage became the only socially acceptable endpoint for love, courtship too was drawn into the thrall of state power, a fact evidenced by the growing number of breach of promise actions in the 1830s and 1840s. Love and law became deeply and pervasively enmeshed. As suggested in Wentworth's poem to Sarah, love spoke a language of obligation and duty; 'for I must love thee' he wrote, 'love thee on'.

Perhaps it is some compensation for her suffering that Sarah did appear to have a loving marriage. When Wentworth died in Dorset in 1872, Sarah turned to her letter book to grieve: 'it is still like a dream to me,' she wrote to Timmie, 'I can not realise it though I see the empty chair. The light of our dwelling has left us so desolate for he was the one that made our house so very cheerful.'[90]

# Part 2

## Geographies of Desire: 1830–1880

Romance has a geography. Our quest for love makes cartographers of us all. A conventional romantic itinerary – moving from a bar or café to a restaurant, a cinema or a club, and then to the front door, the lounge room, the bedroom, the bed – progresses from public, to semi-public, to private, from light to penumbra to darkness. It's a scenography designed for the delicate performance of self-disclosure; to make desire comply with decorum. Scene changes force galloping passions to pause, and new sets are rolled in to heighten or restrain our feelings. Any disruption to the script can be disastrous.[1] 'I blame the beach,' a friend who lived by the seaside once explained to me when diagnosing the reasons for a break-up. 'Too much, too soon. From day one we were taking romantic strolls at sunset.' Landscapes, cityscapes, and domestic interiors are not just passive backdrops to romance; they actively meddle in our relationships.

Middle-class women and men in the mid-nineteenth century also drew romantic maps and itineraries, although they may now seem charmingly prim: tea in parlour rooms and soft chatter on porches, strolls through gardens or along seaside promenades, pensive walks to and from church, edifying excursions and all-night balls.[2] Couples were introduced via a third party and then, if granted permission by the woman and her family, the man would call at the woman's house, where tea would be sipped, hands squeezed and glances exchanged under the watchful eyes of family. With companionate marriage as the aim, the couple needed to know each other as intimately as possible first, so privacy was essential. Having ushered the couple into a parlour and arranged them on a lounge, the chorus of family well-wishers would silently retreat to the wings to form a coterie of eavesdroppers and tale-tellers. The main setting for courtship was the home, which may have shackled women to domesticity, but also meant that romance was conducted on women's territory, performed at their tempo and presided over by their families.[3]

The few histories written using working-class sources tell us that the poor had a wider terrain within which to fall in love. For women compelled to engage in paid work, there was not such a division between public and private spheres. Women met men while working or through family, neighbourhood or church networks, rather than at balls or through formal introductions. They also had more sex than their middle-class counterparts. This was partly because their parents worked long hours and were less available to supervise, but also because sex, so long as it was to be followed by marriage, was widely acceptable in working-class courtships and, surprisingly, legally sanctioned.[4]

If, as I argue, love and law were linked in the colonial period, then love required solemnised sites where it could be legally enacted: a proposal in a socially approved setting proved an intention to create lawful relations; conversely, certain places would cast doubt on the validity of a romantic contract or compromise the woman's sexual reputation. Whether couples met in gardens or buggies, factories or parlour rooms, romantic geographies – the spaces, places and movements of courting women and men – are ever present in the legal annals of nineteenth-century love.

## 3.

# 'The course of true love': Sex, Space and Gender in Victorian-era Romance

T he Saint James Courthouse in Sydney was damp and smelly and ached with cold. It was June, winter, and currents of icy air whooshed in from the street, sweeping under the broken chairs in the public gallery, whistling through cracks in the partition walls, skimming the putrid water in the privies and blowing miasma from the courtroom floor to the judges' chambers above. When viewed from outside, the building was all classical grandeur: a voluptuous half-dome swelling at its centre, colonnades at the entrance and a high vaulted roof that made it look like the curvy sister to the steepled boxy-ness of Saint James' Church beside it. But as the judges incessantly complained, the interior, particularly the ceiling, was in a 'deplorably bad state'. The roof threatened to collapse with the next downpour of rain.[1]

Selina Carrick, only seventeen years old, would have surveyed its decrepitude from her seat beside her barrister. We don't know if she felt nervous being up there in front of the crowds (anywhere from between 300 to 700 people would have been in the courthouse that day) but we do know that she felt that she had been wronged.[2] Mr William A'Beckett, her barrister, stood to explain her story to the jury.

Selina, daughter of publican John Carrick, met Robert Russell, an ironmonger and gas fitter, while living next door to him on Bridge Street in Sydney in 1839. Robert was thirteen years her senior. An acquaintance developed that ripened into affection and soon led to a marriage proposal. Robert was 'admitted to the house on the footing of an honourable suitor', although Mr Carrick soon found his 'hospitality abused'. After paying Selina 'great attentions', Robert prevailed upon her to 'give up her character and fully accomplished her seduction'. Selina discovered that she was pregnant while on a visit to Maitland, a country town north of Newcastle, and gave birth to a stillborn child. While recovering in Maitland's lying-in hospital she received a letter from Robert, which Mr A'Beckett read aloud:

> Dearest Selina,
>
> I received yours of the 14th instant, on Tuesday, it certainly struck my inmost soul and roused feelings I cannot express. You have brought me to my sense of duty and honor, and never will I let the world brand you with infamy, of which I alone have been the cause. I have not time to say much just now, but in the course of three weeks you will be mine and I yours – but remember, your former acquaintances, such as Mrs. Jones and the like, drops when you become my wife, I intend you will stop at Maitland until I arrive with a friend and get spliced, or married, at once, and come down to Sydney unknown to anyone, in the mean time you may be preparing what you can. Now for your sake and mine also keep your spirits up, and do not suppose for a moment I am trifling with you …
>
> Dear Selina, your much
>
> Attached and honorable
>
> Sydney, Aug. 21. 1840. ROBERT.

Three weeks after sending this letter, the attached and honourable Robert Russell married another woman.

'Could a man carry desolation into the domestic circle?' Mr A'Beckett asked. 'They had heard of the immoral character given the colony elsewhere, that the women were living amongst us in a state of concubinage.' Let's hope that 'by their verdict [the jury] would vindicate the moral reputation of the colony'.[3]

Selina's story tells of the catastrophe that befell women in the nineteenth century who became pregnant out of wedlock and were abandoned by their partners. By 1841 most women in the colony were not, as A'Beckett claimed, living 'in a state of concubinage'. Marriage rates were on the rise, Queen Victoria was on the throne, convict transportation would end in New South Wales that year, and colonists were settling into a new era of respectability. Ignominy now accompanied single mothers, and their families suffered a loss of social status as a result. Selina Carrick – the penurious daughter of a former convict, brought up around her father's pub on Bridge Street – might have asked of her lover, as Tess of the D'Urbervilles bewailed: 'Why didn't you tell me there was danger? Why didn't you warn me? Ladies know what to guard against, because they read novels that tell them of these tricks; but I never had the chance of discovering in that way …'. Selina, like Tess, was not a 'lady'.[4]

But if we look closely at this case, we can see another story, about the geographies of desire that lovers and lawyers mapped in the nineteenth century. Love occupied territories, and it arranged people in places, both imagined and real. Love stories did not just have a time and a place – 'once upon a time in a land far away' – but multiple times and multiple places, a revolving panorama of theatrical stages that were to be entered at specific times to ensure that the course of true love ran smoothly to the altar. Breach of promise cases are useful because they show what happened when true love ran wildly off-piste.

The arguments that prosecutors such as William A'Beckett constructed for their clients give us access to what a courtship in the nineteenth century *should* have looked like. A love affair might take seed in a small neighbourhood, mature through a series of visits to the family home and bloom under parental eyes. In the defence's cross-examination, we see the discrepancies between the ideal and the real: Selina met Robert in his workshop while her father was in England and had sex with him in a park. As questions of moral character were often at issue, breach of promise cases made explicit the otherwise implicit norms around permissible and prohibited places. How did a woman's sallies into pubs or workshops reflect upon her sexual reputation? Where should a romantic introduction or a proposal occur? How did a woman's movements threaten ideas of civilised order? Were romantic walks in a paddock sufficient to signify an intention on both sides to be legally engaged? For white, middle-class people who thought themselves superior to other civilisations partly because of their supposed ability to regulate sexual passion, courtship rituals mattered. Somewhat vexingly for the bourgeoisie, however, these amorous norms were not universal. Breach of promise cases involved acts of translation between classes; the more expansive romantic geographies mapped out by the poor and lower-middling orders were elucidated by litigants and witnesses to barristers, who then sought to explain them to judges and juries. And no matter how well litigants were coached by lawyers to make their peregrinations conform to bourgeois paths of courtship, frisky deviations were exposed.

This chapter will take us on a stroll through the various places where lovers met, visited, walked, imagined living and proposed. In so doing, it differs from the other chapters in the book. Rather than offering legal biographies of Carrick and Russell, I will use their case to present an overview of the geographies of courtship found in hearings from the 1830s to the 1880s. In so doing, I hope to better gauge how landscapes of love varied depending upon class, whether the setting was rural or urban, and how the meaning ascribed to places, and the movements of women, changed over this period. In scholarly literature, the Victorian era is often seen as a time of cultural stasis in the experience of romantic love, 'a seven-decade period of relative stability,' as one American historian put it.[5] In most histories of love, all the exciting shifts happen in the 1880s and 1890s, as women march en masse into the public sphere and new capitalist markets move courtship from the home to the dance hall, via the backseat of a car.[6] This may be true for the United States and Britain, but Australia tells a different story.

From 1830 to 1880 Australia transitioned from the twilight years of a penal colony to a free immigrant society, and as it did so lovers helped to construct an environment based more on pleasure than prohibition. From the landscaping of beaches and parks for romantic picnics to the paths trampled by lovers' feet going to and from church, love played a role in the design of cities and towns. In a settler-colony, this also meant that romance – seen as a spatial and territorial project – helped to consolidate the dispossession and settling of Aboriginal land.

## Meeting

The question of how a couple met was only ever raised in breach of promise cases in urban environments. Rural towns were face-to-face communities where familiarity was assumed, while cities, by contrast, were places where you could slip away for a few months and return, as Robert Russell wrote to Selina, 'unknown to anyone'.[7] They were worlds of strangers, of 'danger and delight', particularly for women.[8] The anonymity of cities and their perceived breakdown of communal authority structures were seen to both license female autonomy and expose women to male predation; anxieties which were exacerbated in a colonial port-city such as Sydney, comprised of people with shadowy backgrounds.[9] If cities throughout Western history have been coded as masculine – the sites of commerce, industry, politics and power – where women represented the threat of sexual disorder, then Sydney in the 1830s and 1840s was seen as a town of festive and frightful inversion, awash in disorderly feminine passions. In the 1837 *Molesworth Inquiry*, which contributed to the ending of convict transportation, witnesses continually depicted Sydney as 'one vast brothel'; and this is what barrister William A'Beckett was referring to when he described the 'immoral reputation of the colony where women lived in a state of concubinage'.[10] In this context, Selina Carrick's perambulations around the city – into its workshops and around its parks – was proof of moral corruption.

'When, precisely, did you meet Robert Russell?' asked the defence barrister, Richard Windeyer, during Selina's cross-examination.

'It was in November 1839, and Father was then in England,' Selina replied.

'Did you not ask Mr Russell to come into the house?'

'No, Mrs Jerome introduced him to me.'

'Where was the introduction then?'

'At Mr Russell's workshop. It was in the evening before dark.'

'When did you next see him?'

'A few nights afterwards at Father's house. I was standing in the door with my mother who asked him in.'

'At what time?'

'About seven o'clock. He stopped for two or three hours. We had nothing to drink, my mother remained in the room.'

'How many times in total did you go to Mr Russell's workshop?'

'Twice', Selina answered – 'but never alone'.

Selina would have known that this was damning evidence. 'She says herself that there was no fit or proper introduction between herself and the defendant, she herself went first to him,' Windeyer pointed out in his closing address. 'Then there was the fact that the girl and her mother stood at the door a few evenings afterwards when the defendant came past,' he continued. 'They invited him to go into the house!' Selina's 'whole conduct, upon her evidence, shews that she must have been a woman of bad and immoral character who had been badly and loosely trained by her parents,' he concluded. Robert was more victim than villain, 'infatuated by the arts of this abandoned and profligate strumpet'.[11]

The first problem with meeting in Robert's workshop was the fact that Selina was a woman in a male space. As we have seen, the gendered separation between public and private spheres meant that any movement by women from the private to the public was seen as a potential threat to civilised order. Romantic love belonged to the private sphere, where it could be channelled into reproduction and would not threaten the ordered rationality of the public sphere with disorderly passions.[12] As Karen Lystra has explained, streets, workshops, courts and public buildings were sites of strict emotional control; gardens and public parks allowed more freedom; verandas and parlour rooms more still, culminating in the interior of the home as a space of unbounded affections.[13] Seen through this lens, Selina brought unruly feminine desire – expansive in its expression and disruptive in its effects – into a place emotionally structured around the discipline of work. Probably knowing this, in court she attempted to rewrite the meeting according to bourgeois courtship etiquette: she said that she was introduced to Robert by a friend and that she didn't go there alone. But the fundamental problem remained. Selina had transgressed the boundaries of the domestic sphere and was exhibiting a dangerous degree of romantic autonomy.

Selina was also accused of being too wilful, by approaching Robert first in his workshop and then inviting him into her house. A few years earlier, another plaintiff, Clarissa Laurie, had been subjected to a fierce cross-examination over her first encounter with her suitor, Mr Beilby, in the Sydney Botanic Gardens. Clarissa denied having 'beckoned to Mr Beilby as he rode by' on his horse, and her sister affirmed that 'Mr Beilby spoke to [Clarissa] first.' Clarissa did confess to having 'nodded to him from the verandah', but only after 'he nodded to me' first.[14] Such cases show how women in the nineteenth century were allowed to respond to romantic gestures but not to initiate them. The ideal woman was sexually innocent and ignorant; her desire might be prodded gently into life by an honourable man's attentions and would then be quickly ushered into the constraints of marriage and reproduction. Of course, so much focus on the need to contain and regulate female sexuality suggested a concurrent vision of women as sexually wilful and depraved, closer to nature than men and ultimately corrupting. Femininity was dualistic, and its animal side was projected onto working-class and non-white women. Sex workers inverted this binary by soliciting men, by corrupting the sanctity of love with the vulgarities of commerce. A romantic introduction that began with a woman beckoning to a man in public could be confused, in this formulation, with prostitution.

In Selina's case, her presence in male workshops and parks caused others to look upon her 'as a common strumpet'. In another case in the 1870s, Mr Spence attacked Miss De Brough's sexual reputation on the basis that he 'met her on the street, the same as any common woman'.[15] Geography was crucial to female sexual reputation, which we can see in the derisive names flung at sex workers: 'street walkers', 'common women', 'public women' and 'vagabonds' (deriving from the Latin *vagari*, to wander). The *Vagrancy Act* allowed police to arrest 'every common prostitute wandering in any street or public highway or being in any place of public resort'.[16] The crime these women committed was not simply spatial transgression, but spatial contamination, which was why defence lawyers in breach of promise actions focused on women's presence in liminal zones – the places where the border between public and private was weakest, such as the doorway where Selina stood with her mother after nightfall. It was in these in-between zones that sex workers could 'infest' the family home with the corruptions of the street.

There are still cultural prohibitions around women propositioning men in public today, but the suggestion that a flirtatious woman might in fact be a 'strumpet', or that a private house might be a brothel, had a particularly sharp resonance in the 1830s and '40s, when political reformers were representing Sydney as awash with prostitution. According to historian Raelene Frances, not all of this was pearl-clutching rhetoric.[17] Working-class women, lacking other vocational opportunities, often engaged in sex work, and they did so almost anywhere they could – pubs, houses, streets, hotels, theatres and brothels. The imbalance between men and women (two men to every one woman by the 1840s) meant demand was high, and many residents came from working-class cultures in England that saw sex work as simply another form of work– one with better pay and conditions than other forms of employment, particularly as the 1840s depression reduced the wages of domestic servants.[18]

The first case in which we see a relaxation of moral strictures on women meeting suitors in the street was in 1881 in Brisbane. Here Mr Bromberg's claim against Miss Ohlrich included the fact that they first 'met on the street near the post office, then again at the Botanical gardens'. He also said that she was constantly seen in the street with other men. Miss Ohrlich was awarded the substantial damages of £250 after the judge directed the jury to ignore this evidence. 'Nothing had been said that was derogatory on her character,' he opined, adding that 'the statement about her walking with other men was no reflection upon her ... she appeared to be a young woman of good character which stood unimpeached.'[19] In 1898, another plaintiff, Miss Higgins, was standing on her balcony in Newtown, Sydney, when Mr Nicholls walked by. They struck up a flirtation and went out for a romantic stroll. The nature of their introduction was never raised by the defence, providing a nice counterpoint to the questions posed to Selina and Clarissa about their encounters sixty years earlier.[20]

These changes can be explained by women's expanding public freedoms in the later decades of the nineteenth century. Industrialisation occurred at a rapid pace in Australia in the 1870s, and as a result breach of promise litigants by the 1880s were more likely to be working in shops or factories, living in boarding houses, travelling to and from work in trains or trams, and spending their leisure time in parks and dance halls or at the beach.[21] Meeting a partner in a park, in the street or on a veranda no longer connoted bad character. As women's sphere of activity widened, so did the parameters of acceptable places to meet a lover.

The sexual geography of cities also changed radically from the 1840s to the 1880s. In the 1840s, people from different socio-economic classes lived cheek-by-jowl in a small inner-city area; the bourgeoisie were yet to radiate out to the wealthier suburbs. A judge could live on the same street as a 'strumpet' (the judge presiding over *Carrick v Russell* stated that he used to live between Selina's and Robert's houses), and sex work could be practised almost anywhere. By the 1880s, in contrast, sex work was confined to specific areas of the city, which liberated most streets from imputation and condemned others, such as Lonsdale Street in Melbourne and George Street in Sydney. It also meant that a woman running a boarding house was no longer necessarily assumed to be a brothel madam, as she might have been in the convict era, unless her boarding house was near a wharf.[22] By the late nineteenth century, it became possible to meet in a boarding house without any imputations, as accommodation for transient workers proliferated and being a landlady came to be seen as a respectable way for women, especially widows, to make money.

While many members of the lower-middling orders might have shared in the moral condemnations of sexually wilful women, breach of promise cases make clear that the triumph of respectable culture was only ever partial. We see this most clearly when the moral universes of barristers, judges and witnesses collide. Mrs Jerome, for instance, who introduced Selina to Robert in his workshop, knew of Selina's frolics with various men in the neighbourhood but said she 'had never seen her doing anything wrong'.[23] The judge in *De Brough v Spence* thought that the case was of a 'disgusting character' after evidence was admitted of Miss De Brough meeting her lover in the street, giving him a famous work of pornography, *Aristotle's Masterpiece*, with all the juicy pages 'marked', and then having sex with him in a hotel. And yet she, like so many other 'immoral' women, won, shedding light on both the rollicking amorous practices of the poor – 'those other Victorians' – and the fact that juries were frequently sympathetic to them.[24] Far from being a classic tale of embourgeoisement – of the working classes becoming respectable – what we see by the 1880s is the middle classes gradually taking up more expansive working-class romantic geographies. When judges in the 1880s directed juries to disregard evidence of couples meeting on streets or in public places, they were echoing views that had long been held by the poor.

## Visiting

If Selina's introduction to Robert was unorthodox (meeting at his workshop in the evening), their courtship at least began correctly. 'He came to pay his addresses to me,' she told the court. 'The Defendant spent almost every evening [at our house] and sat in the public parlour, where my father and mother could see us.'[25] As late as 1885, the author of *Australian Etiquette* advised that although '[i]t is impossible to lay down any rule as to the proper mode of courtship', 'in England and Australia the young man asks the consent of the parents to pay addresses to their daughter'.[26] 'Paying addresses', with its etymological origins in the royal court (to beseech a king or queen for a favour), meant making respectful romantic overtures to the woman and, as the word 'address' still suggests today, it had a location in mind: the woman's family home, specifically the parlour room. The parlour, as previously explained, was too communal to allow for unbounded expressions of desire, yet private enough to permit the exchange of kisses, longing glances and soft words. With companionate marriage as the ideal, it was intended to provide a setting for the couple to get to know each other more intimately (but not too intimately) before committing to marriage. In the words of a barrister in one breach of promise case, a suitor who had obtained parental consent to pay his addresses was 'admitted into the family and allowed those privileges which young persons of respectability must necessarily be admitted to receive, to acquire a sufficient knowledge of each other, before they venture upon the married state.'[27]

Robert visiting Selina every day was on the attentive side; it was acceptable for couples to see each other only once or twice per week. In rural areas, where couples were often separated by distance and bad roads, visiting once every few weeks was considered reasonable. 'Two hours is quite long enough for a call,' ruled *Australian Etiquette*, and 'no young man who would shrink from being guilty of a great impropriety should ever prolong his visits beyond ten o'clock.'[28] This is why Selina was careful to say that Robert only stayed at their house between two to three hours. The danger lay in the possibility of night giving licence to passions once parents were in bed.

Although etiquette manuals were loath to call these dictates 'rules', I would suggest that they were not only rules, but laws. Being a suitor meant being granted rights of access and entry to the woman's house, which is why it was important for the visits to be acknowledged by the woman's parents. Their consent, be it express or implied, converted a trespass upon their property into a romantic visit. A courtship also bestowed responsibilities upon parents that came with the backing of law. In 1827, *The Sydney Gazette* explained that a new rule laid down by the House of Lords declared that 'parents cannot substantiate a claim to compensation [in breach of promise of marriage or seduction actions] if they have been so careless as to leave their daughter sitting up with their suitors after themselves and the rest of the family have retired to bed.'[29] Although this rule was never directly applied in Australia, it is an example of how parental oversight was legally cognisable.

For most litigants between the 1840s and the 1880s, an engagement was difficult to prove without a visit to the family residence, which became a problem for those working away from home such as housekeepers, governesses and domestic servants. For instance, in 1875, Annie Galvin was cross-examined over a courtship that partly took place in the Telegraph Hotel in Maryborough, Queensland. 'It was in the private sitting room,' she explained, 'it was the only parlour they had …' Annie Galvin was a poor governess, and there is something quite heartbreaking about the clunky application of the word 'parlour' to a room in a pub. The judge condemned her for it, directing the jury not to award her extra damages for seduction as she could not be considered 'an honourable woman.'[30] Women in these occupations also lacked the ability to control the tempo of the relationship, and in some instances could not even control rights of entry to their bedrooms. In 1876, Frances Titley, a housekeeper, gave evidence of living in a house with no locks; her predatory employer thought himself entitled to access her room and her body, in spite of her protestations.[31] In some cases, domestic servants didn't even have their own bedrooms. One, Miss Slattery, in 1869 told the court how she slept on the couch in the loungeroom, where her employer's son sexually assaulted her.[32] These cases offer an important antidote to historical narratives that emphasise nineteenth-century women's power to control the pace and space of courtship. This may have been true for middle-class women, but it was often not for their poorer sisters.

The insistence on designated places for courtship – a house or a parlour room – also obscured the inequalities that determined which places were available to working-class people compared to the wealthy. For instance, Miss Steers' relationship with Mr Pitches was carried out entirely during walks up and down the fence separating their two properties, which her barrister struggled to translate to judge and jury: 'There was nothing in all this court-ship that in any way differed from the circumstances that marked that of an ordinary courtship,' he argued with false bombast. 'In nineteen cases out of twenty the persons were as much left to themselves.' The defence disagreed: 'Was it not very strange that [her parents] should never ask him into their house? They do not so much as ask the young man into their house to sit down, although they see him in the garden with their daughter at an unrea-sonable hour of the night.' The fact that Mr Pitches was the Steers' family's landlord no doubt played a part in the family's grudging acceptance of their nightly walks along the fence. 'I did once object to his coming so late in the evening,' Miss Steers' mother explained, but 'nothing changed'. It's also likely that the Steers family didn't feel that they could entertain in their house. 'We are not rich people,' her mother pleaded to the jury.[33] Power dynamics between classes are often implicit in these cases, although they were never acknowledged as such by barristers.

In rural areas where suitors had to travel long distances to see their part-ners, the rules of not staying beyond two hours and staying in the parlour room were impossible to obey. People living on farms would ordinarily invite the suitor to stay overnight, which meant long evenings passed tête-à-tête and giddy trysts in bedrooms. Even in cities, litigants would often admit, as Selina did during her cross-examination, that her lover stayed overnight with her father's permission, which again shows a countervailing working-class morality entirely comfortable with premarital sex, so long as the man agreed to marry in the case of pregnancy.

While sex was off-limits in middle-class houses, couples across all classes would nonetheless engage in intimacies that far exceeded what we imagine of straightlaced Victorians. Bourgeois women played the piano for their partners, much as Jane Austen has led us to believe, but there was also a lot of sitting on laps and a rather surprising amount of kissing.[34] 'Come down as soon as possible and how eagerly and tenderly will I throw my longing arms around your neck and bestow as an offering of my love, innumerable and sincere kisses,' wrote Mr Mellersch, the son of a banker and land-steward, to his lover Miss Heals, the impoverished orphan daughter of a naval lieutenant in 1841, anticipating their next rendezvous in Guildford, Western Austra-lia.[35] In *Fowler v Bayliss* in 1871, the defence challenged whether there had in fact been an engagement because of the absence of kissing in public: 'Did you ever see him kiss her?' the defence asked Miss Fowler's brother. 'Well, no, in fact I don't think he would be likely to kiss her in my presence, but

I have seen other familiarities. I have seen him with his arm around my sister's waist.' Based on this evidence the defence argued that there had been 'no evidence of reciprocity', and this argument won.[36] Contrary to stereotype, physical affection mattered to people in the nineteenth century, and they expected amorous gestures to be performed in public. The point of conducting courtship in parlours in the woman's home was not to stifle romantic sentiments and sexual desire, but to stimulate them in a closely regulated environment.

## Walking out, riding out and trips in horse-drawn buggies

If marriage was equated with settling down, then courtship was a time of mobility. 'Before love settles down into his easy chair,' wrote one journalist in 1869, 'let him have plenty of free and happy exercise – "breathe 'ere" across the open downs, and stolen walks in shady lanes. Then he gets to know thoroughly the disposition and character of his companion.'[37] 'Walking out together' as a synonym for courtship was used across classes, and, as Selina Carrick knew when she told the court that Robert Russell 'used to walk out with me very frequently', it was important legal evidence of an engagement. As a ritualised public performance of heterosexuality, walking out appeared in literature and art as a civilised practice, a way in which couples whose marriages were a communion of soul and minds could get to know each other better. But romantic strolls in Australia never quite resembled pointillist paintings. In place of couples walking arm in arm along rain-slick paths beneath arched canopies of trees were cities blotted with dark corners and country roads that prickled with danger. These geographies also changed over time, as white settler society consolidated its territorial power, the economy flourished on the back of gold and wool, and a free citizenry carved out spaces for pleasure from a society founded on punishment.

Couples were implicitly guided by moral geographies of where one should and should not walk, and at what times, which became explicit when cases came to court.[38] As ever, it was the woman's sexual reputation that was at stake. If walking out sanctioned women's movement into public spaces, it was nonetheless a limited form of autonomy: women would be punished more than men if the couple stumbled into an unsavoury place, the wealthy were expected to be chaperoned, and the use of horse-drawn buggies made women dependent upon men for mobility and more vulnerable to their will.

Walking out together was legally uncontroversial in instances where it began at the woman's house, at her place of work or at church. Walking to and from places coded as masculine, however (such as a workshop), or immoral (such as a pub) was not acceptable. A witness in Selina's case gave damaging evidence that he had seen Selina and Robert together in his workshop and, worse, that Selina had been seen waiting for Robert 'in the passage at Queen's Place in the evening'.[39] Standing alone in a dark passageway waiting for a lover showed an unacceptable degree of autonomy and might be confused with soliciting. Streets and passageways were places that women might pass through alone on their way from one place to another, but loitering or waiting was a masculine privilege.

Yet these norms were subject to debate, as seen in the case of *Rule v Hick* in the 1840s. When Mr Hick claimed that Miss Rule was of bad moral character because she frequented a public house with her sister, the progressive Sydney newspaper *The Monitor* did a wonderful job exposing his hypocrisy. Mr Hick used to walk Miss Rule and her sister home from the pub because her sister worked as a seamstress for the owner of the pub, they explained. 'If . . . the females of a reduced family are not to make dresses, and do needlework for wealthy publicans pray how are they to subsist?' Although the journalist accepted that pubs corrupted feminine virtue, poverty, and not the women, was to blame: 'No wonder poor girls who are dressmakers are so often seduced from the paths of industry,' the writer lamented.[40] Walking to and from pubs may not have been socially acceptable for women, but a colony of largely working-class people who valued commerce and saw moral virtue in work were happy to bend principle to pragmatism.

Selina's mother was accused of 'impropriety' in allowing her daughter to walk out after dark, and indeed even women's letters – which flew with messengers around the streets at night in place of women's bodies – were subject to the rules of propriety: Selina, for instance, was condemned for sending a letter at 11 p.m. In her testimony, Selina countered these accusations by insisting that she met Robert 'in the evening, before dark'. It's a distinction largely lost to us today, but that Europeans in the colony would have understood.[41] In the mid-nineteenth century, a romantic stroll might take place at dusk but not after nightfall without threatening the moral character of the woman and the honour of the man. In drawing a distinction between 'evening' and 'dark', Selina echoed many other plaintiffs at this time who told the court that they went out 'at dusk' or 'before 9 p.m'. These distinctions were inherited from a European intellectual and cultural tradition that was suspicious of the dark. In literature, religious thought and art, night-time inverted social hierarchies and provided a cover for evil deeds. Law ceded power to gangs after sunset, and prostitutes haunted alleyways, melting into doorways at dawn. In the countryside, humans relinquished authority to nature; owls screeched, dogs howled and wolves attacked lonely travellers. And in imaginings of the divine, God was lightness while hell was a dim and fiery place. Evil was equated with blackness.[42] The cultural meaning of darkness helps to explain the colonists' fears of the nocturnal and their campaigns for gas lighting in the streets, which arrived in the year of Selina's trial. For women, any night-time perambulation provoked alarm.

These temporal distinctions were raised more frequently by plaintiffs in the 1830s and 1840s than at any other time, suggesting that they were also a legacy of convict-era curfews. Under Governor Macquarie, town-criers bellowed the time and rang their bells each half-hour, and curfew set in for convicts at 9 p.m.[43] Vagrancy laws affected everyone – convict and free – and were more readily accepted in a penal colony than they would have been elsewhere. The fact that many breach of promise litigants, including Selina, saw 9 p.m. as a cut-off point between the acceptable 'evening' and an unacceptable 'dark' was no doubt indebted to government curfews, and in Selina's case was probably conditioned by the behaviour of her ex-convict father. It also demonstrates that the surveillance of the population did not end with the convict era but continued as society became dominated by free citizens.

Running alongside this suspicion of the night was a competing tradition, seen in literature and art, that imagined night skies as swirling, wonderous and divine, existing for the delectation of lovers: 'If love be blind, it best agrees with night,' whispered Shakespeare's Juliet.[44] Indeed, we know from the 1806 case of *Sutton v Humphrey* that lovers imagined the night sky as an earthly incarnation of heaven, and summoned the moon and stars as witnesses to their pledges. It was not until the 1860s and '70s, however, that litigants spoke freely about meeting after dark. No litigant was challenged over nocturnal walks from the 1880s onwards; instead, night became an acceptable backdrop for romantic rambles. 'They ... had many delightful walks in the moonlight and starlight and talks of love and bliss and the happiness of matrimonial life,' explained a journalist writing about the case of *Wiltshire v Hart* in 1871.[45] 'It is now moonlight enough to make one romantic,' wrote Mr Proctor (artist Thea Proctor's father) to Miss Maunsell in 1878; 'Heavens above – vault studded with stars unutterably bright, through which the moon's unclouded grandeur rolls. It seems like a canopy which love has spread to curtain her sleeping world.'[46] For lovers separated by distance, the night sky collapsed

*The road between Sydney's Botanic Gardens in about 1856,*
*as drawn by Samuel Thomas Gill.*

space and fostered intimacy; Mr Proctor and Miss Maunsell could be miles apart but ensconced under the same moon.

In following lovers on their walks from the 1830s to the 1880s, we witness the proliferation of romantic settings, as the free settler population increased and the colony transformed from a place of penal servitude to an affluent society with dedicated places for business and pleasure. Before the 1850s, lovers in cities strolled in parks, gardens, down to wharves and along riverbanks. In cities and country towns, they might walk to and from church, the theatre or the horse races. In Tasmania, they promenaded around the government paddock and the Domain, and went horse-riding in the countryside, although references to men sleeping with revolvers by their beds suggest that many country people had an uneasy relationship with the bush.[47] Indigenous people were never mentioned in these cases, but Indigenous resistance campaigns against colonisation continued during this time.

By the 1860s, white settlement had expanded, and new leisure spaces opened up in areas once inhabited by Indigenous people. During the convict era in Sydney, Eora fisherwomen would row their nowies out into the harbour, men would go spearfishing along the shore, and they rarely competed with white lovers for Sydney's beaches. By the 1860s this had changed, and couples began to speak in court of their beach frolics. Mr Cunningham was said to have taken Miss Mahoney 'out several times to Coogee and Watson's Bay, Randwick races and other places.'[48] In 1862, Miss Thomas of Adelaide in South Australia was accused by her landlady of spending 'all night on the beach' with Mr Size, and in an 1871 case a couple spoke of going together to Brighton beach, near Melbourne.[49] By the 1870s, barristers spoke of pictur-esque waterside settings as part of the romantic landscape: 'A picnic was got up for these young people on the shores of our beautiful harbour.'[50] The har-bour was the subject of pride, and now imagined to be collectively owned by whites. Breach of promise cases may not tell us exactly when these changes occurred – but when these places are mentioned in court, we know that they have become part of the collective romantic repertoire.

How did our lovers 'walk out' over this forty-year period? From the 1860s onwards, as roads improved and prosperity increased, horse-drawn buggies, carriages and spring-carts made more of an appearance alongside the tra-ditional 'lover's walk'. Like most sanctioned sites of romance, carriages and buggies were perched between public and private. People could be seen in carriages, which is why publican Mr Cunningham, when trying to hide his romance with his domestic servant, asked a barmaid to accompany them so that it looked like a work trip.[51] But they also allowed for intimate tête-à-têtes and physical intimacy, as couples bouncing over potholes were happily jolted together. Miss Walsh and Mr Steane's 'tender attachment', wrote a journalist in Adelaide in 1869, was 'strengthened by the close companionship in a spring cart to and from chapel.'[52] The wealthy Mr Gooch conducted a large part of his courtship with Miss Barron in his horse-drawn buggy in 1869, and in so doing 'acted in every way in the character of a lover'.[53] While Miss Barron no doubt thrilled to her horse-drawn buggy, being driven in either cars or car-riages made women dependent upon men and vulnerable to their caprice, in a way that walking and riding did not. Miss Humphrey, for instance, was promised a Sunday drive to a place outside Adelaide by Mr Kelly, but once they got there he refused to leave. 'You'll not go home tonight, you'll stay with me tonight,' he said, to which she replied: 'I must go, or I would get a scolding.' He would not let her go, and that night he sexually assaulted her.[54] Women were attacked while walking or riding as well, but horses equalised any physical disparities between men and women and, like walking, gave women a way of getting home alone.

Luxury steam ships, with their sweeping decks, also became a place for lovers' strolls, signalling a shift from convict-era associations of ships with sexual debauchery.[55] There were no cases featuring shipboard romances in the 1830s or 1840s, although these have certainly been noted in historical literature among the bourgeoisie. For the working classes, it was with the introduction of steam travel in 1850 and the end of transportation that ships became a site for courtship. When Miss Cameron sued Mr Muir for a broken engagement forged onboard a ship from Scotland to Melbourne in 1857, one journalist was sympathetic:

> Flirtations on board ship, we all know, are very common occurrences. Books, chess, cards, scandal, even eating five times a day, like swine in training for a first-class prize at Baker Street, are excitements that soon cease to stimulate; and then the only resources left the unfortunate water-walled prisoners are to get drunk, to coo, or to quarrel.

The environment of the ship, he continued, stimulated amorous sentiments: 'Who doesn't remember those delightful walks upon the deck, stars burning bright above and eyes glowing almost as bright below...'[56] The writer's vision is indebted to a romantic tradition that saw nature as a site of moral relaxation, where feelings were heightened and true selves revealed. The ship's deck, ideally located between nature and culture, offered all the protections of civilisation and all the abandon of a starry sky unbounded by social rules.

Whether lovers were walking to beaches, church, parks, rivers, picnics, balls or on deck, their romantic strolls included one key feature: they cost little or nothing. Consumer culture had not yet planted its flag in the heart of white Australians, and most leisure arenas had not yet been commodified. Economically, romance was much more democratic than it is today; while other power imbalances existed between men and women, the sexual contract dictating that men pay for dinners and women give cheerfulness or sex in return was yet to be formed.

## Housing

Housing was never discussed in Selina Carrick's case because her pregnancy meant that the couple never had time to plan it, but had Robert Russell committed to the marriage, he would have been expected to find or build a home for them. Indeed, showing a woman the projected marital home, or discussing it with her, was crucial to proving an engagement. Across all classes, marriage without a home was impossible. The home demonstrated the man's capacity to provide for a woman, and it gave physical form to the shift in status that marriage effected for each party. A woman became mistress of her own household and was given more autonomy than she would have had in the parental home, although a bourgeois woman was still expected to retreat within its four walls and would be legally under the 'cover' of her husband. For men, marriage and property were how they achieved full citizenship. Having a home conferred masculine legal rights, such as the right to vote and sit on juries, it increased a man's social status and it was imagined as a refuge from an unfeeling commercial world. The man did not need to own the home – many couples rented – but the couple should not live in a boarding house or have a landlady. Control, as historian Jenni Calder has argued, was crucial.[57] The home was also where the couple's sex life became legitimate and directed towards filling any empty bedrooms with children. Property and housing, therefore, were at the heart of romance, just as its acquisition and imagined white heirs were at the heart of settler colonialism.

In most cases, across class, dreaming about a home was incorporated into courtship. Mr Thomas Mellersch, for instance, gushed to Miss Jane Heals in 1841 that he had 'succeeded in obtaining a place I think you will be pleased with; the view is so picturesque and beautiful and the garden now so cheery, that it only wants your presence to make it complete.' Housing was a shared imaginative project in which the woman – decorative and resourceful – was placed centre-stage. If Mr Mellersch demonstrated his commitment through property, Miss Heals showed her love by discussing it with him. 'Nothing could have more strongly evinced the deep and heartfelt interest you take in my welfare than your anxiety to know the rent I pay,' he wrote in the following missive.[58] The house he was referring to was in the Whadjuk region on Noongar country, near present day Guildford in Western Australia, close to a site where meetings would have been performed and tortoise hunted.[59] Of course, there is no reference to this in their letters: the house was imagined as both exclusive and virgin, a new beginning.

Suitors would pledge houses or property to women and their families as part of marital negotiations: 'He told me he had a great deal of property' was a common claim by jilted women.[60] And courtship would often involve visiting future houses or promised properties. When one South Australian plaintiff told the court that 'On the Sunday he proposed he asked her to go and see his house on Emu Creek,' she was echoing many other women who were whisked away by their suitors in horse-drawn buggies or carts to inspect houses in anticipation of marriage.[61] In 1856, Miss Hood based her claim that there was an engagement partly on the fact that Mr Shorney had discussed with her mother his anxiety about the fireplace: it 'should be nice, should not smoke, and [must be] suitable to Margaret's notions of comfort'.[62] The house was the space into which couples projected their future marital roles, sentimentalising gendered divisions of labour as well as the expectation that women would simply uproot themselves for their husbands: 'I sincerely wish I had the means to make a comfortable home for you and with your consent for you to come and look after me,' Mr Lambswood wrote to Miss Wood in evidence presented in an 1866 case. 'How would you like to live in Kapunda?'[63]

For couples living on the poverty line, who saw marriage as more pragmatic than romantic, the house was all that needed to be discussed. In 1879 Miss Ogden, of Bundaberg in Queensland, described her speedy courtship with Mr Davenport: 'He came down on Sunday and asked me if I would like to get married; and I said, "Yes, if I could get a comfortable home," he asked to take me up to his home and he would pay all expenses. On Boxing Day, we went to the house and he asked me how I would like to stay there; I said very well; he gave me three pounds to buy some things which were needed and we arranged to get married on New Year's Day.'[64] In many ways this is simply an unsentimental version of the weight that all courting couples placed on housing and property. Just as Lizzie Bennet quipped that she loved Darcy when she saw Pemberley, Miss Ogden agreed to marry Mr Davenport when she saw his house in the dusty heat of the Bundaberg hills.

## Seducing

Unlike romantic introductions, visits and walking out, there were no rules devised by the bourgeoisie about where one should and should not have sex with your partner. A woman's claim to respectability and her and her family's honour were premised on sexual chastity. Apart from the aristocratic concern with the transmission of blood and property through family lines, an unplanned pregnancy was a catastrophe for women. In a world without legal abortion, with a gendered labour market that did not pay women adequate wages to survive, without welfare and with a puritanical Christian moral code, an unplanned pregnancy could mean financial and social ruin. The spatial regulation of courtship – ensuring that romance was conducted at home, on chaperoned walks before nightfall, at a picnic or ball – was largely designed to prevent premarital couplings (and pregnancy). It also protected women from unwanted sexual advances.

Histories of love have shown how nineteenth-century systems of courtship, unlike twentieth-century dating, allowed women to control the tempo of the relationship.[65] The problem with these histories, however, is that they're based on middle-class experiences. They assume couples had a parlour room or garden and parents with the time to watch them. They also assume that when sex did happen, it was in a bedroom on the wedding night.

Breach of promise litigants did not always wait for their wedding night to have sex. Engagements were long – on average three years – as men worked to be able to afford a house. In the meantime, couples had sex in parks, on beaches, at friends' houses, in paddocks, under drays and on roads. Selina chose to have sex in the Domain and, if we are to believe the defence, in a neighbour's house and in a passageway in the centre of the city. The tendency to use public spaces for sex can partly be explained by working people's lack of access to private spaces; where else but public parks and beaches could domestic servants who shared rooms be expected to go? Privacy was a luxury. The houses of working people were small, parents shared bedrooms with children, and rooms were often in plain sight of passers-by. But we also shouldn't ignore the balmy climate – a late-night romp on an Australian beach or in a garden was more inviting than a shivering park in England.

Although authorities envisioned parks as places where a healthy populace would play cricket, enjoy nature or promenade with their lovers, they were invariably used by gays, lesbians and the working-classes as settings for giddy 'gambols' and intimate pleasures.[66] Commenting on Sydney's Botanic Gardens, a barrister in an 1837 breach of promise action noted that 'it is notorious that the eyes of our wives and daughters are polluted, and the virtuous portion of the sex driven from those places of public amusement which we loved to witness in the mother country by profligates, adulterers and vagabonds'.[67] Whether it was Fitzroy Gardens in Melbourne, Sydney's Hyde Park and Domain or Hobart's Domain and Paddock, parks were sites of a grand battle between decorum and desire. Landscaping may have subjected the terrain to middle-class rationality and order, but in the English romantic tradition these spaces were wild and relatively free of moral restraint: the voluptuous flowers, earthy scents and exotic trees were suggestive of deep, organic impulses, perfect for intimacy.[68] In 1861, a police inspector reported that 'one Sunday night' he saw 'scenes of immorality' in the Sydney Domain 'that were beyond comprehension'. A number of people 'were in a state of coition at the time, old and young'.[69]

Private houses and rooms were also not particularly private during this time. In Selina's trial, one witness gave evidence that while he was walking along the street one evening he had seen Selina have sex with a man called

Mr Cox. He peered through the (presumably uncurtained) window and had a gawp. Reports like this were quite common in the 1840s.[70]

Many working-class children would have obtained their sexual education from sharing a bedroom with their parents, as a defendant in an 1869 action explained: he 'slept in the same room as his mother and father and a man called Hackett who worked on the farm'.[71] In all these cases involving sex, there is a tension between working-class practice and bourgeois norms of privacy and prudery. By the 1880s, as prosperity increased, voyeuristic accounts of the sex lives of neighbours became less frequent. This is not to suggest that all working people stopped sharing bedrooms – poverty often required it. But couples sought greater privacy, which, counterintuitively, meant public parks remained popular.

These diverse sexual practices were bundled into the legal category of 'seduction': a term that required proof of the woman's sexual passivity and innocence in order to be satisfied. As we have seen, seduction could be brought as a separate legal action alongside the breach of promise action, or it could be pleaded as an exacerbation of the breach of promise, and thereby inflame damages. 'Had she shown that she was a virtuous woman, led astray by the villainy of an artful seducer?' asked the defence in Selina's trial. 'Had she been the seducer or the seduced?'[72] If the latter, law could restore a woman's reputation and compensate her in the form of a lump-sum payment, which would have done more to help single mothers than unreliable weekly maintenance payments. While men may have invoked a woman's 'unchastity' in their defence, treatises and case law affirmed that a woman was chaste and deserving of legal protection so long as sex occurred under a promise of marriage. Of the 211 breach of promise cases in the nineteenth century, 47 per cent were brought by single mothers, who proved their sexual virtue while nursing a child on their hip.[73] All bar two of these litigants were successful.

Finally, geographies of seduction usually included a period of expulsion from the town or city when the woman gave birth. This involved being banished from the family home or the boarding house. Shame was contagious; everyone who shared a space with the woman was tarnished. The wealthy Miss Fletcher contemplated going to New Zealand to save her reputation, while Robert advised Selina to stay in Maitland until the child was born.[74] In most cases involving seduction, the man would book the tickets for a steamer or a train and the woman would travel under his surname, as his wife. There was no socially acceptable place for an unwed mother travelling alone in public. Once the woman had given birth, she would ideally return to the city, married. As Robert Russell's panicked note suggests, a woman's 'fall' also affected men's reputations. Victorians had a much richer vocabulary for shaming duplicitous men than we have today – blackguards, hoary seducers and gay lotharios were just some examples. Interestingly, it was not the sex per se that was deemed unacceptable, but rather the refusal to marry afterwards. This was even more so in Australia, where the absence of a parish structure and poor laws left single mothers dependent on charitable institutions.[75]

## Proposing

There was nothing romantic about Robert Russell's proposal to Selina Carrick: 'I intend you to stop in Maitland until I arrive with a friend and then we get spliced or married at once,' he wrote with indecorous haste.[76] Men tended to behave like this when women fell pregnant. There was no time for ritualised performance; the woman was often already in hospital, so marriage proposals – panicked and perfunctory – were scribbled and delivered by post. 'I now propose to you this,' wrote Mr Nelson to Miss Field in 1850: '[I will send] twenty or thirty pounds to bring you up to Sydney, I will go straight from the steamer to the chapel and marry you ... let me know by return of post that you will marry me then.'[77] A pregnancy forced the couple to take a socially perilous detour from the approved path of love, and private missives replaced public theatrics.

For those couples who stepped merrily and chastely along the socially sanctioned path, a marriage proposal was both a stop on the way to the altar and the resolution to a love plot: the visits, walks, intimate tête-à-têtes and discussion of houses had all been leading to the moment when the man 'popped the question'. We cannot underestimate how vexed this performance was for men personally and for society in general. 'Of all things unpleasant, I think there are few more unpleasant than ... popping the question, when popping time comes,' wrote Australian musical theatre singer and songwriter J. Caulfield in 1879.[78] Novelists, columnists, public speakers, and writers of etiquette and legal treatises spilled much ink scripting the ideal proposal, replete with advice about props and settings. 'The occasion for making a declaration should be well chosen,' advised a journalist in 1879, citing with approval Elizabeth Barrett Browning's suggestion of a night in the country: 'Lead her from the festive boards / Point her to the starry skies'.[79] Sydney Smith, in his 1826 novel *Granby*, counselled against proposing on a gondola, lest the woman say no and the suitor 'be subject to the humiliation of rowing the lady back to shore a sulky, cowed, rejected man.'[80] Places perched between public and private, such as verandas or lounge rooms, were considered ideal, giving spatial expression to the liminal status of the couple (courting but not yet engaged) and offering an easy escape for the man in case of rejection. A journalist in the 1880s thought it obvious that a dinner party, being too public, 'would hardly seem the most suitable occasion for overtures of this description.'[81] The privacy of a lounge room was preferred by one writer in 1876, who gave very specific advice: 'Take a dark night for it. Have the blinds closed, the curtains down and the lamp turned almost out. Sit near enough to her so that you can hook your little finger into hers. Wait until the conversation begins to flag and then quietly remark: "Emma, I want to tell you something ..."'[82]

The advice of etiquette manuals was less nuanced: 'the best way is to apply to the lady in person and receive the answer from her own lips'. The proposal, said *Australian Etiquette*, should be 'bold, manly and earnest.'[83] It was advice which one journalist mocked: 'society tells men "everywhere be bold" but still with the countering whisper in his ear, not too bold.'[84] Being too bold might suggest that the man was well practised in proposals, implying multiple past rejections. Performative awkwardness – with plenty of pauses, half-sentences and embarrassed coughs, offset by gentle squeezes of the hand or looped little fingers – was ideal. One journalist provided a script: '" ... my acts must have shown – that is, you must have seen – I mean, you must be aware that – that—" Pause here but keep your finger firmly locked.'[85] This kind of theatre reflected Victorian-era beliefs in the inexpressibility of love, it dramatised masculine humility and it gave the woman opportunities to encourage or discourage the man. Beliefs in innate differences between the sexes were built into the script: men were the active party and women were responsive. As one writer, paraphrasing the arguments of his more conservative peers, explained, 'A woman ought to wait until she is asked, and she ought not to love until she is loved.' Yet women always held the eviscerating power to decline an offer. A refusal would teach a suitor, 'in a very emphatic way, that there is at least one person in the world who thinks less highly of him than he does of himself'.[86]

In all these incarnations, the proposal was an act of scripted spontaneity. It might assume various forms, but they were all *forms*, replicable, standardised and troublingly inauthentic. No other aspect of courtship was so highly choreographed. The reason for this was primarily legal: the proposal was a speech act. When the words of a proposal were uttered and accepted, they changed the couple's social and legal status: men and women became fiancé(e)s, legally bound to become husbands and wives. To this end, the words spoken needed to be socially believable and legally legible for the community and the state to recognise the engagement and later the marriage. As with all legal utterances, the proposal required solemnity. A proposal could not, as *Australian Etiquette* advised, 'be spoken in a jesting manner', which was also to ensure that men did not propose as a way of obtaining sex (which occurred in a number of breach of promise cases, where proposals were uttered with the urgency of lust).[87] As the law was concerned with evidence, treatises also preferred the proposal to receive public officiation, and family members were ideally given front-row seats.

How obedient were lovers in colonial Australia to this panoply of scripts? The lower and middling orders often had a more pragmatic view of marriage, which meant proposals could be bereft of both sentiment and ceremony. Mr Tuxford's 1856 proposal to Miss Evans, for example, looked more like a family lark than a sublime moment of masculine torment. Mr Tuxford, a volunteer soldier, one evening asked Miss Evans to sit on his knee; when she declined, he hollered to her sister in the kitchen, 'Your sister says she will not be a soldier's wife.' To which the sister responded, 'Does she?' Mr Tuxford then turned to Miss Evans, seated beside him, and said, 'Give me your hand and your word that you will be mine.' Miss Evans replied, 'I will.'[88]

Most marriage proposals over the course of this period took place in the woman's family home; for wealthier couples, they might take place in semi-private places away from home, such as a veranda during a ball, or a garden during a picnic. As the century progressed, however, and factories, cities and boarding houses drew working women into the public sphere, more proposals were made in public. Miss Le Vondare was proposed to in a hotel in the 1870s, and from 1869 there was an increasing number of proposals in buggies, which raised some concern about their sincerity and legality.[89] 'Did you not think it rather tame to be proposed to in a buggy?' jeered the defence barrister to Miss Byrne when she described Mr Malcolm's proposal on the way home from the Mittagong races in 1889.[90] While these settings were certainly unconventional, literature on proposals allowed for them, insofar as men were warned against waiting too long, lest another suitor get in first.

The physical and natural world was ever-present in proposals during this period. 'Now, as we have got to the garden gates, I wish you to make up your mind [about the engagement],' Miss Ohlrich's lover instructed. She hesitated, and at first refused to walk through the gates, until her eventual crossing of Edward Street in Adelaide signified her consent.[91] For some couples, love kept pace with natural time rather than industrial time; it was measured not with clocks and calendars, but through the eternal rhythms of the cosmos. 'It is a beautiful moon,' remarked Miss Wentworth on her way home with her lover Mr Thurgood. 'Yes,' he responded, 'the next moon will see you my wife.' One month later, when the moon rose in the night sky above the town of Emerald Hill and Miss Wentworth found herself abandoned, she turned bitterly to pen and paper: 'I looked upon you as my husband,' she wrote, since that 'memorable night on which I pledged my word to you ... under the beams of the rising moon it was registered in heaven. And now I have only one thing to say, as you gaze on the moon, the full moon of September, in what lanwige [sic] will it speak to you not only this month but for years, nay for your life time, the moon will speak planer [sic] than I do.'[92]

People in the country also marked the tempo of their proposals through the natural world, although in these cases the earth was envisaged in language that was more pragmatic than passionate. Mr Grossert's proposal to Miss Biggin in 1861 was conditional upon his completion of a dam on a neighbour's property and then upon a successful harvest. After this he said he could afford his own farm to settle. Miss Biggin in turn demonstrated her commitment to the relationship by buying him five pounds of seed wheat and one of her father's horses.[93] The natural world was embroiled in these relationships, although, like the relationships themselves, ultimately subordinate to the economic demands of landed capitalism. Like suitors in the city, Mr Grossert could not simply marry Miss Biggin when he wanted, but needed to plan his marital life around the contingencies of an exploitative labour market that paid itinerant manual labourers low wages. However, unlike his peers in the city, his labour was vulnerable to the elements. Flood could destroy a dam, fire could ruin a harvest and seed wheat might spoil in a drought. Unlike Miss Wentworth, Miss Biggin and Mr Thurgood would have thought of nature as more capricious than constant.

Like the marriage proposal, the consent of the woman's parents to the engagement had a geography. Legal treatises imagined the proposal to take place at the woman's home, with the active participation of the woman's family. In *Daniel v Bowes*, which is cited approvingly in contract treatises from the 1830s to the 1880s, the judge thought it was sufficient for the defendant to have 'asked for the lady's hand in the presence of herself and her mother' if the mother 'assented' and the 'lady said nothing' but 'did not dissent'.[94] The fiancée was property to be exchanged between her family and her suitor, and the focus on her parents' consent kept the spectre of feminine desire in check.

In practice, there were no cases where women proposed to men and many where women were chastened for pursuing men, yet women had far more independence from their family than treatises imagined, and this grew alongside their social and legal rights over the century. In a minority of cases, the man sought consent from the woman's parents first, but in most cases the proposal was initially made to the woman. One father in the 1840s responded to a man's proposal by deferring to his daughter, saying 'the girl was of age and capable of judging for herself in such a matter.'[95] From the days of the early colony, women exercised their power to say 'no' to a proposal independent of their parents. Miss Laurie, for example, told the court that when she first received a written marriage proposal from Mr Beilby, she decided not to show it to her father because, in her words, 'I had not made up my mind to have him.'[96] This power of rejection must have been thrilling in a society where women's decision-making ability was almost always subject to male authority.

The fact that proposals generally took place in the woman's home further reinforced the suitor's subservient status as a petitioner. For instance, after Miss Laurie had decided that she would 'have' Mr Beilby, she instructed him to 'come forward and make proposals to my father or I must quit [your] company'; she stayed outside on the veranda while negotiations took place inside.[97] Where it was impossible for a suitor to meet the woman's parents, a letter would suffice, although it needed to state a preference for meeting in person. 'My dear Sir,' wrote Mr Muir to Flora Cameron's father in the 1850s, 'I take the liberty of writing you on a subject regarding which you will justly think I ought to have spoken verbally, ere was my wish, but circumstances prevented.'[98] When viewed in the context of the couple's future relationship, this deference to a woman's family during courtship was an anomaly. Once the couple were wed, the woman was expected to uproot herself and 'cleave' to her husband and his family; it was entirely possible after marriage for neither the woman nor her husband to see her family again.

For couples over the age of twenty-one, the requirement of parental consent was a social norm rather than a legal requirement during this period, and even the social expectation became more flexible between 1840 and 1880. Cases appeared in the late 1870s where there was no evidence of parental involvement, and the court was unfazed by its absence. Miss Le Vondare, for instance, worked in a series of boarding houses and pubs in Rockhampton and Brisbane in Queensland, during which time she met her lover, Mr Simpson. He proposed to her in one of the boarding houses, she accepted without any concern for her parents' opinion, and the jury were not perturbed by this, finding in her favour.[99] The more respectable Miss Belton, a governess in a school in Echuca in Victoria, met her partner, the grazier Mr Macdonald, at her brother's house in 1879. He proposed to her while sitting on a sofa in company with others, she accepted, and again there was no question in court about parental consent.[100] There were still cases where parents refused to give consent based on the girl's age or status, but the evidence suggests that by the late 1870s parental consent was no longer a social necessity. These cases are part of a larger history of intimacy, where a patriarchal family model based on male headship was gradually eroded throughout the nineteenth century by women's increasing public freedoms and by the granting of individual property rights and legal status to children and wives. The court's privileging of women's consent, which in law was only possible if you had 'property in your person' (slaves could not consent because they were seen as property owned by others), was a sign of women's autonomy both from their family and from their future husbands.

## Retreating

Once a proposal had been made and accepted, it was expected that the couple would retreat from society in the lead-up to the wedding. Etiquette manuals advised both men and women to 'schew all flirtations' but not to shut themselves 'away from the rest of the world'; in practice, couples often imposed more serious restraints upon themselves.[101] From the final years of the penal colony until the 1880s, lovers exchanged letters in which they professed not to enjoy socialising, although these statements had an obvious class dimension: there were fewer declarations about relinquishing social pleasures from those whose lives revolved largely around work. Private balls, dinners and parties required leisure time and cultural capital. For Mr Mellersch, there was an inverse relationship between his love of Miss Heals and his loathing of society: 'how dreary and cheerless everything appears now you are away', he wrote; 'the gaiety and dissipation of Perth affords me no satisfaction'. In his next letter he claimed that he had not 'been out much, and probably shall still less. I find I am much altered: I am not so gay and merry as I was before I saw you – not that you have imparted a gloomy tinge to my character, but you have thrown a sort of halo around me which constantly and incessantly follows me.'[102] These descriptions of self-abnegation continued throughout the century. In 1879, Mr Proctor catalogued for Miss Maunsell his virtuous retreat from social amusements: 'I did not go to the ball, and I missed two parties (private) for which invitations were sent me, and a third ball lost my presence, all these in the same week. I have not visited much since my return, and flirting has gone from my gaze like a withering dream: conscience (if lawyers have any) makes cowards of us all ...'[103] Retreating from social engagements was proof of the moral foundations of love, a guarantee of fidelity and a good way to save money in anticipation of marriage. 'To places of amusement I will never go,' wrote Mr Nelson to Miss Field. 'The shilling I might spend there I will save up, and put all in the bank to your credit.'[104] If a woman found that her partner had been socialising, she might use this financial angle to chastise him.

Women's retreat from society following a proposal went beyond declining social outings. Teachers, domestic servants, shopkeepers, governesses and seamstresses all promised to give up work and to move out of their parents' home in anticipation of marriage, a custom which left them socially and economically vulnerable. For instance, Mr Barron refused to allow Miss Gooch to continue her business as a piano instructor and forced her to leave her family home before marriage, which meant she was distanced from her primary support network, without a means of independent support, and burdened with having to re-establish the business after he jilted her.[105] There was also Miss Kelly, who, after running a successful grocery store in a small town in South Australia, sold all the items in her store and the store itself on the promise of a marriage proposal.[106] The withdrawal of engaged women from paid labour and their departure from the family home were symbolic and practical affirmations of feminine submission to men. By the 1880s, however, women had begun to chafe, publicly and privately, against the yoke of subordination. 'If I were like many other poor girls, without means to convey them to another part of the globe, I would be in a fine fix,' wrote Miss Belton to Mr Macdonald in 1879. She was a teacher who had given up work in Australia and stalled her acceptance of a job in New Zealand on account of a marriage proposal. 'I have my own livelihood to get,' she fumed, and 'it's as precious as yours.'[107] These words, written in a private letter, could be read as a feminist rallying-cry for generations of women to come.

## Happily ever after?

Had Selina Carrick and Robert Russell stepped slowly and virtuously along the path of true love, their final destination should have been the altar of their local church. But law and literature recognised that hearts may change and promises may break and so, for women at least, mapped out a geography of heartbreak. Defence counsels in the Victorian era, drawing on a long literary tradition, argued that the ideal woman should respond to jilting by shrinking into psychological and spatial oblivion: 'A pure-minded woman' should 'undergo the heaviest calamity which women sustain – let the clouds of night – of night without a star – obscure that light in which she one moved,' exhorted one barrister in the 1830s. In 'this place', which he described as the 'blackness of darkness', women should martyr themselves to love.[108] Yet the very fact that the action for breach of promise existed suggested another, entirely opposing, possibility: that women dry their eyes, walk out of their bedrooms and into a solicitor's office. Playing the part of the reluctant plaintiff, often dressed in black mourning clothes, blinking in the glare of publicity, was an effort to reconcile the paradox that lay at the heart of the action.

Litigants' responses to the end of their relationships provide a dramatic example of the gendering of spaces. Women, grief-stricken, tended to retreat into the innermost chambers of the home, while men, mobile and independent, threatened to flee to other colonies or countries. 'I cannot describe what agony of mind I suffer,' wrote Miss Maunsell to Mr Cassius when he broke his engagement to her and announced his return to New Zealand in the 1870s. 'As I lie here in bed I hear the people in the street laughing; they seem to be mocking me in my misery.'[109] The family home, envisaged as a refuge from the street, was suddenly exposed to the imagined cackle of public scorn. Where women often suffered a kind of agoraphobia, cowed into their bedrooms by fears of neighbourhood whispers, men looked outwards into colonial space, grateful for the opportunities of escape.

Many men expressed a kind of bravado at the threat of legal action. Mr Wiltshire said that he 'did not care for the exposure as he could clear away to Tasmania or anywhere else'; Mr Hick tried to flee to Launceston; Mr Duggan said he would go to America.[110] Many men tried to take advantage of the fact that there was no inter-colonial legislation allowing for extradition in breach of promise matters, so all they had to do was get across the colony's border. However, they could be thwarted by the law's power to fix people in place: a man trying to leave could be issued with a 'writ of capias' (or a writ upon one's head), which placed him under arrest until the hearing, unless he were wealthy enough to provide sureties or a bond for his release. Not all men threatened to flee – some hid under beds on the day of their marriage, and others brazenly married someone else in the same town. But men were aware of the masculine privileges of mobility, and letters show them wielding it over women.

Selina, however, was not cowed. After her 'confinement' in Maitland, she boarded a train to Sydney, returned to her parents' home and promptly began legal proceedings. Her gruelling cross-examination turned on questions of moral geography: her sexual reputation was tied to her transgressive use of space. Yet Selina's case is also evidence of a countervailing working-class romantic culture that was delightfully resistant to respectable mores. By the 1880s, women en masse had begun to behave more like Selina; meeting their lovers on verandas or at work and strolling with them under swirling night skies. We can attribute this change to women's expanding public freedoms, to the growing affluence and expansion of Australian settler society, and to the middle-class adoption of working-class norms. Selina's case also reminds us that in the colonies, moral principle often bent to economic pragmatism: the costs of raising a child for her, for her family and for the community were tremendous and courts sought to shift this financial burden on to the men responsible.[111] 'The poor are under the protection of the law equally to the rich,' her barrister proclaimed, and the jury agreed, awarding her £300 damages plus costs: triple the average award for the century.[112]

# 4

# 'To have and to hold':
# The Place of Love in a Settler Colony
## (*Hawthorn v Steel*, 1833)

On 3 January 1833, Michael Steel, a 39-year-old man of 'very considerable property', slipped a note into the hand of his lodger, the seventeen-year-old Sarah Hawthorn.[1]

My dear Sarah – I hope I will have the great gratification of meeting you in the garden to-night – I do long so much for a little of your sweet company, and my foot is so bad, I am not able to walk in the paddock.
I am quite devoted to your kind affections.
Your devoted lover,
MICHAEL STEEL[2]

Sarah received the note while lodging in Michael's splendid two-storey terrace in Hobart, a town described as having a 'home-like English aspect'.[3] The public buildings, hewn from white granite, stood along stone footpaths, and snug cottages festooned with geraniums were scribbled across the countryside. Compacted dirt roads curled around the hilly terrain, dipping their toes into the harbour at one end of town and looking up to an amphitheatre of mountains at the other.

Hobart should have been a perfect setting for Michael and Sarah's romance. The 'Paddock' (a public park) was located at the end of their street, and the stroll there in early January, high summer, would have been pleasant. In summer Hobart lost its pale, bleached quality and softened into warm pastels: cornflower skies, green meadows and a bubbling rivulet that ran from the base of Mount Wellington through people's laundries, under the creaking corn mills, alongside the tanneries and into gardens that bloomed with assortments of natives – casuarinas, austrostipa, callistemon – as well as mulberries, cherries, raspberries, strawberries, gooseberries, apples and peas.[4]

For three months, Sarah lived upstairs at Michael's house with her widowed mother, Jane, and her brother, John, while Michael and his sister, Jane, lived downstairs. This set-up could have been very convenient, except that Michael insisted on secrecy; theirs was a clandestine courtship of night strolls, surreptitious missives and words weighted with excess meaning.

'My dear Sir', Sarah had written to Michael on an earlier occasion:

> Your note to me was very flattering. I think you may come upstairs and pay me a visit, as I pay you so many. I have something of importance to communicate to you in the presence of my mother. Come up and pretend to ask for George, and I will ask you in.
> Yours, for ever,
> SARAH HAWTHORN.[5]

They used public settings to communicate private passions. Sarah's brother first noticed their affections when the two families took a Sunday walk to the government garden. Their behaviour, he said, 'could not be mistaken; she leant on Mr Steel's arm ... and after they returned, they went to Mr Steel's parlour for some wine.' As a lodger, Sarah had the perfect excuse to see Michael whenever she wished, although her giddiness could betray her. Recalling the night spent drinking in the parlour, one family friend said: 'I heard Miss Hawthorn laugh immoderately', such that her mother, 'ashamed of her conduct, requested her to come and sit beside her.' In the last letter Michael sent Sarah he declined her invitation to go on an excursion, but promised something more serious: 'My dear Sarah – I am sorry I cannot accompany you to Sandy Bay today; but you have all my affections, and I do intend to make you my lawful wife. – I am, your affectionate lover, Michael Steel.'[6]

If Sarah had read any romance literature, she would have known to beware a lover who demands secrecy: male tyranny and sexual entitlement flourish in dark places. This is why courtship conventions stipulated that Michael ask Sarah's family for permission to begin courting her. But Sarah was young, and she probably delighted in the attention of a wealthy man. If we trust the poet Henry Savery, who met Michael in 1830, she would not have been attracted to his looks. 'His face is not the finest, I'll agree', Savery wrote, channelling a mother counselling her daughter to marry him for his wealth, 'And seldom, a more bashful man you'll see / His shoulders certainly are rather high / But then he has a most expressive eye!'[7] By Michael's own account, he was tall, 'with grey hairs' and a face lined by care and climate.[8] A few days after receiving the promise of marriage, Sarah confessed the details of the courtship to her brother John and handed over Michael's notes. Offended that Michael had not approached him first, John told Sarah to tell Michael to come and speak to him. A fortnight passed and Michael did not appear, so John issued a demand that they meet in the garden. On the morning of 19 January, the two men faced each other.

'What did you mean by this?' John asked, clutching Michael's marriage proposal in his hand.

Michael hesitated, looked askance and then, in a thick Somersetshire accent, responded: 'The fact is, I am not a marrying man.'

'Then how could you think of writing to my sister in the manner in which you have done …?' The garden, once a site of moonlit strolls and interlaced fingers, had become an interrogation chamber.

'I never had any intentions of marrying your sister,' Michael explained sheepishly, 'what I did was merely out of a lark, if I have done anything wrong I am extremely sorry, and will make apology for my conduct.'

'You have behaved in a most dishonourable manner,' John chided. 'I am going to keep the notes.'

Michael, accustomed to being in a position of superiority, tried to gather his dignity. 'But what have you to do with it?' he asked.

'The girl is my sister – she has no father. I am her only protector,' replied John, inflating with self-importance. 'And so it is my duty to question you on the subject.'

'You may do as you please with my notes,' Michael announced, turning to go. 'I am not to be frightened or bounced out of anything.'[9]

The next day John consulted a lawyer, whose first strategy was to dictate a letter to Michael, signed by Mrs Hawthorn, outlining the facts of Michael's breach of promise. The letter expressed Mrs Hawthorn's hopes 'that Mr Steel would feel the necessity of carrying his professions towards her daughter into effect'. Michael understood the meaning of the letter and asked for another meeting with John in the garden: 'If that document compels me to marry your sister, I will make over all my property – and she will not be the gainer of a shilling by me,' he warned. Rumours about Sarah began to spirit out of the

Steel residence: she spent all her time in the kitchen flirting with the servant men; she laughed immoderately during drinks in the parlour; she stormed off after a fight with her brother to go and live at her friend Mrs Donoghue's house. Three months later, the gossip wound its way into a breach of promise of marriage action brought by Sarah Hawthorn and her family against Michael Steel.

*　　*　　*

*Hawthorn v Steel* was the first breach of promise case brought in Tasmania, and its timing, in the early 1830s, is significant. This was a period that witnessed a concerted effort by colonial authorities and new emigrants to convert the gloomy prison of Van Diemen's Land into the respectable home of Tasmania, and marriage was crucial to this mission.[10] From the 1820s through to the 1840s, free emigrants from the respectable lower and middling orders, many funded by government assistance schemes, flooded into Hobart, transforming it from an authoritarian penal colony to a cosmopolitan port city.[11] The moral legitimacy of free settlers' claims to civil rights, as well as their dignity, depended on shaking off the colony's reputation as a place of convict vice and sexual disorder, which in part meant curtailing male sexual entitlement and channelling love and desire into the legal bonds of matrimony.

If we accept that the Steel case, like many of the cases in the 1830s and '40s, was about colonists' claims to respectability, we might also note that this story is told through commentary on gardens, kitchens, parlours, paddocks and vast property empires. This is a story about the geography of intimacy at every level. Its lodging house setting tipped bourgeois courtship conventions on their head: as Michael's lodger, Sarah could not consent to his visits, and nor did Michael have to ask Sarah's brother or mother for permission to see her. They were already in the one house. Impoverished women like Sarah did not have the same power to control male access to intimate places or the tempo of the courtship as bourgeois women. Living in the same dwelling also meant that boarders, live-in domestic servants, governesses or carers could take more initiative in seeing their lovers, by inviting them on excursions or slipping downstairs to visit them, which in turn could threaten their sexual reputation, particularly if the case went to court.

Panning out from the home, we also see in this case the legal significance of land. Property was at the core of romance: the most eligible bachelors, like Michael Steel, owned land, and women like Sarah sued for loss of 'settlement' – the worth of Michael's home, investments and landed interests. I find the word 'settlement' interesting here. In a strictly legal sense, settlement in breach of promise meant the economic and social status that came with being mistress of a home. But it also carried connotations of putting down your roots, and of the emotional connection to place that comes with homemaking. For those whose land was being 'settled', however, it meant the opposite: invasion of the home, loss of livelihood, disruption of social order, fragmentation of family, and perpetual movement to avoid being killed or captured. For all these reasons, 'settlement' is an example of what Freud described as the 'antithetical meaning of primal words'.[12] These are words which, as Jacqueline Rose has put it, 'simultaneously denote one thing and its opposite, and which also possess a kind of magic, since they release you into a world of contradiction.'[13]

If Sarah could sue for loss of settlement, what of the original inhabitants? What violent reality lay behind the romantic appeal of the propertied gentleman? If Sarah fancied Michael Steel because of his properties, much as Lizzie Bennet loved Darcy partly for Pemberley, what if Pemberley was stolen? Keeping our focus on the geography of desire, I want to follow the propertied gentleman in this story from England to Tasmania, from vast estates and parlour rooms to his kitchens and gardens, to explore the links between property and propriety, and to reveal how, in settler colonies, love, land and lucre were entangled.

\*     \*     \*

Michael Steel was in high spirits. It was 1830 and he had just proposed marriage to Betsy Colgrave, or 'Miss C' as he preferred to call her, and was now 'all anxiety respecting her answer.'[14] Betsy lived in Swinbrook in Oxfordshire, near where Michael was born, and there had been a courtship between them seven years earlier before he left for Van Diemen's Land. Now, with a few houses, several farms and a comfortable lifestyle to offer her, he was ready to settle down, and to this end he appointed his brother Joseph, back in Oxfordshire, to be his man on the ground. Michael wrote to Joseph that despite his success in the colonies, he still 'stood in such great need of what I call the one thing needfull', that 'great object, a wife'.[15]

Michael's letters, which were usually tedious accounts of sheep prices and other mundane matters, suddenly became effusive and vulnerable. Announcing his intention to woo Betsy in 1829, he wrote:

> There is nothing I can do that I will not do to obtain her hand and heart ... the joy to me would be beyond expression ... I am too well acquainted with her amiable temper and engaging accomplishments, and as to my appearance, I am told I appear just the same as when I left old England and just as cheerful as ever ...

His homesickness vanished as he rhapsodised about Hobart through the sunny filter of romance.

> [It] is a very pretty town as ever I saw in any part of the world, here are no tythes and taxes to annoy people, here is good wine at 3 shillings per gallon as fine meat, bread and vegetables as ever ... Pray use your utmost persuasion to urge her to come and tell her this is the land of independence, health and real happiness, that we have abundance to spare.[16]

Michael realised that it would not be easy to convince Betsy to sail to the other end of the world for someone whom she had not seen in several years. The colonial papers often featured breach of promise cases involving women who voyaged from Britain on the promise of a love letter only to find themselves friendless and penniless at a colonial port. If Betsy left, she would be vulnerable to Michael's whims. Knowing this, he offered her a formal promise of marriage. I 'consider myself as being her husband until her answer is received by me ... and I also bind myself under the penalty of One Thousand Pounds to make good the contract.'[17]

Joseph's correspondence with Betsy has not survived, but we can assume that he eventually suggested Michael write to her directly. In 1830 Michael wrote:

> I hope she has received my Letter in which I have given her a promise of marriage, a copy of which I also sent to you ... I shall now expect to see her here in a few months ... as you seem to give me such hopes respecting her acceptance of my offer, all I can say more is that if she does come I will do all that is in my power to make her happy and shall from then hope to begin making another odd Steel or Two.[18]

With an eye to posterity and the status of the Steel family name, Michael concluded by congratulating Joseph on the birth of his son: 'at all events I am delighted to think that you have been able to save our family from reproach by wanting a ram, or in other words a son, to wear the names ...'[19] Although Michael Steel later described himself as being 'not a marrying man', we know from his letters that this was not always the case.[20]

\*　　\*　　\*

How did Michael come to live in Van Diemen's Land, on the other side of the world from most of his family and his beloved Betsy Colgrave? As his biographers Gwyneth and Hume Dow note, we can only speculate, as no diaries or letters offer direct reasons.[21] For his 33-year-old sister Jane, who travelled and lived with Michael, romance may have been part of the impetus for the move. A colony with twenty-five men to every one woman held out the promise of a match for a woman hurtling towards spinsterhood. Michael's romantic aspirations, however, never seem to have migrated beyond Oxfordshire, although Van Diemen's Land figured as a place where he would build the fortune needed to secure a respectable wife – a fortune that looked evermore precarious in England.

As the youngest son of a yeoman, or gentleman farmer, the law of primogeniture meant that Michael had no chance of benefiting from his father's patrimony. And by 1823, the year Michael and Jane sailed to Van Diemen's Land, the agricultural boom that had increased his father's wealth had turned to bust in the aftermath of the Napoleonic wars.[22] As industrialisation stripped ordinary textile workers of their livelihoods and drained the financial coffers of minor gentry families like the Steels, the ordered, genteel world of Michael's father exploded into seething revolt. Luddite agitators smashed up machinery, and protestors carrying lanterns swarmed across fields in the textile regions. In the midst of economic depression, rising unemployment, and the mass demobilisation of soldiers, rumours of insurrectionary plots circulated, and the government responded with violent repression. Michael could have remained in England, clinging anxiously to the fringes of the gentry, but he was driven by fantasies of pluck, plenty and family prestige. Like many small capitalists with enough money to escape, his eyes strained towards the antipodes.[23]

Unlike in England, where he was oppressed by feudal 'tythes and taxes', from the 1820s the Australian colonies offered free land grants to settlers based on how much capital they brought. Michael is an exemplary beneficiary of this shift in imperial policy towards capitalist emigration: land previously offered to former convicts would instead be given to free settlers with capital. The Bigge Commission of Inquiry, tabled in parliament in the same year that Michael set sail for Australia, mapped out how the new colonial structure was to work. The imperial government would cut the costs of the previous system of convict transportation – now seen as expensive and ineffective as a crime deterrent – by giving each free settler a grant of land in proportion to his wealth, in return for employing convicts. Convicts would make that land productive, the master would administer punishments, and since he needed to feed and clothe the convicts assigned to him, the master's capital would help to defray the costs of administering the whole system.[24] In Kirsten Mackenzie's words, the gentry's 'want supplied an imperial need ... Unto those who had, more would be given'.[25]

Michael arrived in Hobart with £30,000[26] and £300 of goods and equipment, as well as a letter of recommendation from Lord Bathurst in the Colonial Office saying that he was 'a man of very excellent character and a good practical farmer'.[27] This secured him a land grant of 2000 acres – the most that the government was willing to give at the time – and twenty convict labourers.[28] Within three years, he was able to boast that he had 'already 3000 sheep' on his property in the north-east of Tasmania, near the river Clyde, and he told the surveyor general in the same year that he had 'completed a good and substantial farm house', fenced about 100 acres, planned a barn and 'sown English grasses'.[29] Michael did not just move from place to place; he altered places in the interests of profit. Devoutly religious, he also believed that his work came with the stamp of divine approval. In 1830, he happily mused that 'providence' had been 'bountiful'.[30] The colonial structure was one of Christ, convicts and capitalists, all implicated in the theft of Aboriginal land.

Michael never questioned the morality of his wealth, nor whether the original owners might have a better claim on the land. Imbibing the racism of his time, he saw the Indigenous people as 'filthy', 'ugly' and 'subtle in their attacks' on whites. In February 1827, he described being on his property when a servant returned from an errand to say that four white men had been attacked by natives. 'I instantly armed all my men, some on horseback and some on foot', and they set out to find the attackers. The next day, 'we fell in with them on top of a mountain and poured a strong fire into them and killed their leader and one more.' The rest of the Aboriginal party fled. '[H]ad the country been even and clear,' Michael boasted, 'we should have killed or taken the whole of them, so cowardly are those vagabonds when attacked by bold Englishmen.' From here he drifts nonchalantly into sheep farming, noting that he had 'thought of making money rather fast now [with] 2000 ewes of all ages on the farm this season, having 40 rams amongst them.'[31]

If, as Stuart Macintyre has argued, 'sheep were the shock troops of land seizure', it seems only fitting that Michael concluded a story of murder with rams, a term he also used for sons or heirs.[32] It's a slippage that I find evocative when thinking through the intimacy and the violence of settler rule; when trying to understand how he could write so blithely of killing. To colonise you needed to dispossess the original inhabitants of the land and repopulate it with Europeans.[33] You needed property and progeny, and Michael was committed to securing both.

The shift towards capitalist emigration in the 1820s meant a rapid increase in frontier violence, as new kinds of Britons disembarked in Hobart: free settlers like Michael, interested in building their wealth and status through sheep and soil, through sprawling intergenerational property empires.[34] Prior to the 1820s, as James Boyce has explained, most Europeans in Tasmania were convicts from the industrial and rural poor, and they carried with them the tradition of the commons; a cultural relic from feudal times that gave serfs the right to cultivate or graze animals on common land. Our public parks today can be traced back to this tradition. Unlike the free settlers who came after them, convicts did not claim exclusive possession of the land and they did not trample it with intensive sheep farming. There was conflict with Indigenous people, but on the whole, writes Boyce, it was a system of shared land use.[35] Free settlers, however, arrived with guns, small armies of assigned convicts, sheep and cattle, and a belief in the inviolability of private property, which resulted in an escalation of violence: the roving parties in the 1820s and '30s like the one Michael described; the declaration of martial law in 1828; the Black War from 1829 to 1831; and the 'Black Line' in 1830, when armed white men, including Michael and his younger brother William, formed a line and walked across Tasmania with the aim of killing every Aboriginal person in sight.[36] As William put it, settling was 'bloody work'.[37] It was the work of propertied gentlemen.

The land grants that sanctioned this violence did so through the language of love as much as law. Written in loopy Victorian-era cursive, Michael's grant awarded him 2000 acres 'to HAVE and to HOLD'. If Michael were to marry, he would be rewarded with 'twenty acres more' and another ten for each child.[38] The grant is a legal document whose dynastic vision is flung far into the future, imagining a new white society comprised of married couples and families, and blind to the past, incapable of seeing the people who were already there. As in a marriage, 'to have and to hold' land meant to exercise exclusive possession; it was a sacred and inviolable bond. The law – patriarchal and capitalist – guaranteed a man's right to his property, be it his wife or his land. And like a bride to be, the land was imagined as virgin, awaiting cultivation and existing to bear fruit. 'To essay our fortunes in a wilderness which our labour and enterprise alone could render habitable,' was how Michael and other free settlers described their vision for Tasmania.[39]

The law shared their fantasy of 'wilderness', of virgin land. With its presumption of exclusive property rights, the land grant could not countenance prior occupation. It both sanctioned and denied violence: sanctioned, because it conceived of Aboriginal people as trespassers on the new owner's property; and denied, because in the Victorian imaginary, familial love was incompatible with violence. When violence enters a family estate, wrote nineteenth-century critic John Ruskin, it is no longer home. For Ruskin, home was 'the place of Peace, the shelter not only from all injury but from all terror, doubt and division'.[40] That we are twenty-first-century heirs of this nineteenth-century vision may be part of the reason why we find it difficult to hear massacres and marriage spoken of in one breath.

The grant, like Michael, was also utterly uninterested in the land itself, except in how it might be exploited. I pored over Michael's letters hoping to find some descriptions of his land in Tasmania, but he had decided early on to employ overseers to manage his farms, and his letters are bereft of any feeling for the countryside. To this end, his sensibilities aligned perfectly with those of British property law, which had (and still has) surprisingly little to say about the physical characteristics of the land. For property law to be a useful instrument of empire, it needed to be nomadic, vacant of physical details and applicable to any land, capable of travelling with Englishmen as they prowled the earth in search of a bargain. In Michael's land grant, the textures of the earth are reduced to co-ordinates on a compass – the peppery aromas of a forest after rain, shadows spiriting across rocks, rolling vistas seen from the brow of a hill, the rush of rivers and grasses, are all obliterated, replaced by the chill certainty of numbers – north twenty-five degrees, northeast twenty-five degrees, west forty-four. Rather than the earth, writes legal theorist Nicole Graham, property law concerns itself with people and the relationships between them: who owns it, who can sell it, who can inherit it, et cetera.[41]

Aboriginal property laws, on the other hand, established a system of responsibility for the land, based on knowledge of its physical attributes and farming practices, all of which created the grassy plains abundant with game that lured free settlers like Michael Steel and his flocks of sheep in the first place.[42] In Michael's case, he had convict labour to exploit, and his grant gave him five years to prove that he had 'cultivated or put stock on the land', which is why he boasts to the surveyor of his fences, houses and many ewes: all symbols of permanence.

Michael's approach to the land was ultimately instrumentalist: it was to be exploited for commercial gain so that the Steel family could achieve a position in the gentry. Property was also crucial to Michael's wooing of Betsy. He could have proposed to Betsy earlier than 1829, but he needed to be able to offer her an establishment first. There was a geography to his romantic imagination: he dangled before her 'a good house' or 'a farm' if she preferred, and also Hobart, 'a very pretty town' and a fertile country with abundant produce, 'fine meat, bread and vegetables'.[43]

In 1830, Michael received Betsy's response. 'Now about my intended wife,' he wrote to Joseph after pages of wool reports, 'it seems I have lost her, heaven knows it may be all for the best, but from what has passed, I had great reason to expect her and I have acted accordingly in my plans, yet it is another disappointment, added to the numbers, I must try to return my warmest thanks for the kindness you showed me in the business.'[44]

Conceiving of marriage as business may have been part of the problem. It would have been unlikely for a woman not driven by poverty to uproot her life and move to the largest gaol in the empire unless she was also compelled by love. As Penny Russell puts it, British women 'tended to become colonists because they had chosen to marry a particular man, rather than because they embraced emigration for its own sake'.[45] Michael oscillated between self-pity and bravado. 'I can assure you that I can have plenty of wives,' he wrote, 'but I would have preferred one who was an old acquaintance.'[46] His sister Jane had also suffered disappointment from her Irish lover, who had since married another: 'I said something about Sister getting spliced, but it is all up and Paddy has married another ... I am afraid she takes it to heart, but he was a false, lying scoundrel.'[47]

In less than two years, the same words would be thrown at Michael in every newspaper in the colony.

\*   \*   \*

We now have some background to help explain why Michael behaved as obnoxiously as he did with Sarah. It seems to have been a paltry effort at self-aggrandisement, an amorous trifle intended to soothe his wounded pride – he could have had 'plenty of wives', he had boasted, and Sarah was proof. We also have some idea of how his fortune was made: the 'bloody work' behind the propertied gentleman.[48]

But it would be wrong to think of settler colonialism only happening 'out there' in the wilds of the frontier. Michael's home in Hobart, or Nipaluna, was built on the land of the Muwinina people, who had been dispossessed since settlers began arriving in 1804.[49] Settlers involved in frontier wars may be the most obvious villains of colonisation, but all emigrants who came after them partook of their spoils and continue to do so today. To this end, when thinking through the geography of courtship in settler colonial nations, we need to keep frontier and town in the one frame. Exposing the violent reality behind a 'propertied gentleman' sued for breach of promise shows how Tasmania's gothic, gore-soaked forests are connected to its 'home-like, English' towns. But they are intertwined in another, deeper way as well: it was not just the land that Europeans needed, but the moral legitimacy to take it – the idea that they were spreading the virtues and not just the vices of European civilisation. Here the rituals of courtship and marriage, as symbols of respectability, were crucial. Civilisation could hardly be spread by people lacking in civility. Propriety in love was the velvet glove on the iron fist of property.

This was made clear in the newspaper commentary surrounding the case. If breach of promise today seems like a quirky historical relic, at the time it was treated with utmost gravity. *Hawthorn v Steel* happened at the same time as a trial for false imprisonment; some regular civilians were mistaken for runaway convicts and confined to gaol. It was a common problem in Tasmania, because assigned convicts dressed in normal clothes. Both cases, *The Hobart Town Chronicle* declared, 'demand the most serious attention from every inhabitant in the colony', but the breach of promise action was 'far more to be lamented as a public – or colonial calamity'.[50] The false imprisonment hearing concerned the liberty of the individual and the right to be free from arbitrary state violence. It concerned, in short, the rule of law. The breach of promise hearing revolved around a libertine toying with the affections of a lodger. Yet by colonial standards, the foiled romance was more serious: 'What forms the colony?' the editor asked: 'what renders it worthy of the name, but its respectability – the virtuous and honourable character of the families of which it is composed?' Compared to false imprisonment, the editor continued, the breach of promise action entered:

> more deeply into our domestic life, it pierces the very bosom of our families, it exposes to the open gaze of the multitude the unpremeditated, private conversations and arrangements of individuals on the most delicate of all subjects ... In a word, it ... is calculated ... to break down the barrier, to make fearful inroads on the grand fortress of principle and propriety that forms the chief safeguard of civilisation, of all that renders our existence here desirable.[51]

These were not just the scribblings of one hyperbolic writer. Other newspapers agreed. *The Colonist* considered it to 'be one of those cases where the *private* conduct of an individual affects the *public* interests of the community'.[52] Men who broke their promises, who forced women into the public sphere, threw into chaos the sense of moral order that came with keeping public and private separate.

Who were the 'multitudes' threatening the home, or the citadel? On one level, they could be simply the public – the 'neighbourhood of voluntary spies' peering in through the windows of the bourgeois home, or a court gallery of voyeurs.[53] There was, as scholars have noted, a physical reality to this: the expansion of roads, post offices and newspapers in the early nineteenth century allowed people to observe one another and to disseminate private information in a way unthinkable a generation before.[54] The multitudes could also mean the proletarian masses, particularly in a colony comprised largely of convicts notorious for their loose sexual mores. But if we go back to the editor's words, we can see that it is not just the bourgeoisie, but 'the colony' and then 'civilisation' itself imagined quaking behind a 'fortress of principle and propriety', which makes me think that both class and racial anxieties are lurking here.

The case came to court only two years after the end of the Black Wars, which were conducted on behalf of an empire that couched its genocidal and acquisitive motives in the language of moral uplift. In the tattered twilight of war, it's little wonder that the editor resorted to images of fortresses under siege. The metaphors were born of historical fact, and the breach of promise case exposed how tenuous claims to civility, and thus civilisation, really were.

Let's go back to Sarah and Michael's romance to map out their rogue path through the geography of civilised love.

\*    \*    \*

Michael Steel – prim, rich, devout, ageing, ambitious and amorously wounded – sits on a chair in his house in Hobart nursing his injured foot while Sarah Hawthorne coquettes around him. Who is she? Sarah didn't leave behind an abundance of letters like Michael, but we're fortunate that family historians Judith Carter and Don Bradmore have given us a brief sketch of her family's outline.[55]

Sarah was born in 1817 in Dublin to Jane Hawthorn (née Cramer), a woman of noble blood who had been disinherited by her family at the age of twenty-two after rebelliously marrying George Hawthorn. When Sarah's mother said 'I do' in 1811, she went from being a Cramer – a Protestant family originally from Germany that had owned splendid estates and taken parliamentary offices in Ireland for over 200 years – to a Hawthorn, the lowly wife of a penurious Catholic clerk bereft of bloodline, money and prospects.[56] Livid, her father, Marmaduke Cramer, bequeathed her a shilling before cutting her out of the family.[57]

Between 1811 and 1824, Jane gave birth to seven children, four of whom survived. Sarah was the second youngest. Only a year after the birth of the youngest son, tragedy struck when George died, leaving the family destitute. With no inheritance and four hungry children to feed, Jane was desperate, and with desperation came resourcefulness. She had heard that Jocelyn Thomas, her relative by marriage, had just been appointed acting treasurer of Van Diemen's Land, and she petitioned him on behalf of her family.[58] In 1827, with financial assistance from her brother, she packed off Sarah's two eldest siblings, John, then sixteen, and Frances, fourteen, to be placed under Jocelyn's care.

John gained employment as a clerk in Hobart, where he rented the upstairs rooms in Michael Steel's house, while Frances became a governess on a property not far from Hobart, where she met and later married a free settler, Henry Torlesse.[59] With John and Frances now happily established, Jane boarded the brig *Yare* in 1831 with Sarah, fifteen, and George junior, seven, and sailed for Van Diemen's Land.[60] Upon arrival, the family went straight to Frances and Henry's sprawling stone mansion, 'Rathdowne', built on the

Torlesses' 2500-acre property in the lush Central Highlands. Henry Torlesse had arrived in Van Diemen's Land with a substantial amount of money, accrued from his family's investments in the East India Company, which won him the largest land grant possible.[61] And like Michael, his settlement meant unsettling the original owners, driving the Big River People – a group of between 400 and 500 Indigenous people – from their fertile, watery planes.[62] The story of the Torlesse family's wealth shows how two forms of British imperialism, one based on remote economic and political domination and the other on domination through settlement, could connive to reproduce European power and privilege.

Perhaps Sarah inherited her mother's appetite for doomed romances. While the rest of the family busied themselves assisting Frances with her new baby, Sarah exchanged meaningful glances with the next-door neighbour, Samuel Wells, son of former colonial secretary Thomas Wells. Sarah and Samuel were too young to marry, and both families objected to the match. But the couple was insistent. A bargain between the families was struck, one that we see in numerous Victorian-era novels: the couple had to wait three years before marrying, in which time they were not to see each other. If they were still in love after that, consent would be given to their marriage. The families shook hands and declared it a 'contract'.[63] Anguished by the separation, Sarah mooned around the house until her mother decided that the family would move in with John in Hobart.

The intention was probably to distract Sarah from the pursuit of love, but her amorous imagination had been awakened, and she searched for the next hero. She arrived in Hobart in October 1832 and by December she was having romantic rendezvous and swapping love letters with Michael Steel. Six months later, on 11 May 1833, the meaning of these exchanges was debated in Tasmania's Supreme Court.[64]

\*　　\*　　\*

The hearing took place in autumn, in a courthouse no more than ten years old. It was a severe, rectangular building with four columns guarding its entranceway, an ornate pediment, arched, cathedral-like windows, a circular turret and no heating, all of which gave it the feel of a medieval castle. At night, a lonely lamp post flickered in the street outside, casting a pool of yellow light on the rubbly road. During the day you could see down the slope of Macquarie Street to the tall ships floating in the harbour and across to the paddocks that wound around the lobes of Salamanca Bay.[65]

This being the first breach of promise case heard in the colony, a crowd of people turned up to watch, staying from ten in the morning, when the hearing began, until nine at night, when the assessors announced their verdict.[66] It was one of the most talked-about events in Hobart that year; *The Hobart Town Chronicle* described it as a 'sensation'.[67]

Michael was present at the hearing, but it's uncertain whether Sarah was there. The press would usually have commented on the demeanour of the plaintiff, but there is no reference to her. Sarah's case was put by Mr Gellibrand, a man of about thirty with a soft, hairless face that was still boyish: round cheeks, heavy-lidded eyes and an alabaster complexion irradiated by golden curls. Gellibrand had arrived in the colony in 1823 – clever, young, and fearless – and after trumpeting the democratic rights of man, including the right to trial by jury, came into conflict with the authoritarian Governor Arthur. He had been removed from his position as attorney-general in 1827 and was now practising exclusively as a barrister.[68]

Gellibrand began the hearing by assuring the gallery of the respectability of the characters: Michael was a man of great wealth and Sarah was the niece of Jocelyn Thomas. This allowed him to pre-empt the defence, which he knew would try to cast aspersions on Sarah's character. From here, he told the story of their courtship: Sarah had been lodging at Mr Steel's house, 'an intimacy commenced, Mr Steel took a fancy to Miss Hawthorn, and proposed marriage'. It would have been 'the fair and open way to consult the wishes of her family', he noted, but Steel had 'peculiar notions'. Even after John requested that Michael speak to him, he still didn't come forward. When the two men finally met, Michael 'declared that he never had any serious intentions; that he was not a marrying man; and that it was all a lark'.

Next came Mrs Hawthorn's 'very feeling letter', inquiring as to what his objection to marriage may be. Of course, 'there was none'. Instead, Michael 'spread a report industriously and invidiously against her reputation and compels this young lady to come into court'. The gallery was sombre as Gellibrand spoke, pervaded by an atmosphere of 'gravity' which lasted until he read aloud their correspondence. The letters' descriptions of trysts in the garden and strolls in the paddock were too much, the *Chronicle* reported, and 'produced an abundance of mirth' from those present.

Gellibrand ended his address with high drama. He turned directly to Michael Steel, who would have been sitting with his counsel, and thundered:

*The Hobart Court House.*

'I say it to his face, in preference of saying it behind his back. That if possessed of one spark of honour or humanity, he would not have treated the widow and this poor girl who has no one but her brother to protect her, in so base and unworthy a manner.' With that, all the elements of the case for the plaintiff were established: the written proof, the virtuous plaintiff, the rakish libertine and the justification for the action: the Hawthorns had come to court not for money but for honour, to clean a tarnished reputation.[69]

The plaintiff's case rested on reputation and letters, while the defence focused on geography and gesture. Mr Horne, the defence solicitor, pounced upon John Hawthorn: 'During the time that you resided at Mr Steel's, did their family ever visit you?' he asked. John had previously described the family's living arrangements. 'Mr Steel and his sister lived in the lower part, [John] with his mother and sister in the upper,' and 'they visited Mr and Miss Steel but the latter were not in the habit of visiting them.' Now, Horne wanted specifics. 'Never' did Michael visit his family, John conceded, although he 'did come upstairs once ... for the purpose of asking him and his sister for a walk.'

Next, Horne read aloud from Sarah's letter: '"I think you may come upstairs to pay me a visit, as I pay you so many,"' he said, mockingly. 'Here was a young lady paying a great many visits to a man and requesting that he would pay her one in return. A novel kind of courtship indeed.' Where Gellibrand had suggested that Michael was at fault for not obtaining consent from the Hawthorns, Horne flipped this argument on its head. Why didn't John seek out Mr Steel? John had received Michael's note about making Sarah his 'lawful wife' on 7 January, but he had 'taken no steps' to speak to Mr Steel until 19 January. John replied meekly that he had 'waited for Mr Steel to make some communication to him on the subject'. Horne turned to the assessors: 'A gentleman who talks as you have heard him today, of his duty in protecting his sister, and suffers a match to be hatched up in the same house, clandestinely, and who then comes before you to ask damages at your hands; such conduct is anything but what it ought to be.'

Horne now focused on his main defence: that Sarah Hawthorne was a woman of 'levity', meaning carefree or 'improper'; it was a subcategory of the defence of 'bad character' and could be used to justify breaking a promise of marriage. 'Was it not in consequence of a quarrel between you and your sister that she left Mr Steel's?' asked Horne. John was offended: 'I will not answer that question.'

Horne apologised: 'I exceedingly regret, for the sake of human nature, that I am compelled to put this question, but if I can shew that by her levity of conduct then Gentlemen (turning to the jury), you will form your opinion.' John was 'quite affected', according to the *Colonial Times*, and admitted that they had indeed quarrelled, and Sarah had left.[70] There was more damning evidence to come.

Michael's sister Jane testified that she and Sarah used to be friends, that Sarah would visit her while Jane was making puddings in the kitchen, but that they were not friendly anymore as Sarah 'did not conduct herself [to Jane's] wishes'. Jane's testimony alluded to Sarah's behaviour in the parlour room, which a Steel family friend, Richard Cook, relayed to the court. They were playing backgammon, there had been some wine, and then 'Miss Hawthorne laughed immoderately'. Newspapers reported that something else was imputed here, but the evidence was dismissed. It was too lewd to be repeated in print, *The Colonist* explained, and unfortunately the archival record of the case has been destroyed, so we have no way of knowing precisely what was said.[71] On top of the parlour-room incident, Cook added that Sarah had 'taken every opportunity of being in the kitchen with the servant-men', although he conceded on cross-examination that this might be because she prepared the family meals in the kitchen and she needed to pass through the kitchen to get to her apartment.

Mr Goordhand, an assigned convict, said that he had given Sarah some earrings as a romantic gift, and that she had remarked that 'she would sooner marry a prisoner than marry Mr Steel'. The final witness was poor Samuel Wells, who only months before had professed his undying love for Sarah. He gave proof of their contract of marriage. With Horne's command of narrative, Steel went from libertine to victim, caught in as 'complete [a] trap' as Horne had 'ever heard of'.

Later, newspapers would applaud Horne's defence, but on the day the audience sided with Mr Gellibrand. Gellibrand finished his closing speech, appealing 'powerfully' to the assessors as fathers and brothers, and the 'thronged courtroom' rewarded him with a 'burst of applause'. After only two hours, the assessors returned with a verdict for Sarah of £200, double the average damages awarded during the nineteenth century, based on Michael's investments, his houses and his many splendid acres.[72]

\*     \*     \*

At the beginning of this chapter, I suggested that this case was about the geography of intimacy. It shows how gendered moral norms were incorporated into law and how British ideals of civility in love played out in the colonies. Let's look more closely at precisely what these norms were, and how each side attempted to use space, place and movement to discredit the characters of their opponents.

We can start with Horne's first argument: that Sarah visited Michael more than he visited her. This wasn't just a matter of sexual precocity; it went to the question of whether a promise had been made. In sarcastically referring to it as 'a novel mode of courtship indeed', Horne was referring to the conventions, found in literature and law, which set out what a promise of marriage should look like – where it should happen, who should be there and how they should behave.

The nineteenth-century legal writer C.G. Addison explained that a promise existed 'when the defendant, having called upon the plaintiff, to whom he paid his addresses, at her father's house, said to the father, "I have pledged my honor to marry her in six months."'[73] The precedent for this was the case of *Cork v Baker*, in which it was ruled that such a declaration was 'sufficient evidence of a promise of marriage'.[74] The law assumed, at a minimum, a family home where a woman could be visited, and parents who could watch over the courtship and who could be petitioned for consent. Men did the visiting; women granted or denied them entry.

Nothing about Sarah's living arrangements had been imagined in law. She had no family home, no father to be petitioned for consent, and the relationship with her suitor was secretive. Even if Michael had petitioned Sarah's brother or mother, he could hardly have been admitted to his own house as a suitor. The Hawthorns attempted to approximate respectability and formality by referring to 'visits to their apartment', but serendipitous meetings in shared spaces such as the garden or the kitchen were inevitable. In Sarah's case, she liked Michael, but many poor women had no choice but to board in houses with transient male workers, and they were often more vulnerable to sexual assault. Sarah might have enjoyed flirting with the servant men in the kitchen, but it is also possible that she was simply cooking, or that it was easier to flirt with them but she would have preferred to be left alone as she made the family meals. Either way, the gendered division of labour, her family's poverty and the sexual double standard conspired to make her subject to the charge of 'levity' or bad character.

The ideal woman imagined by legal treatises was a dutiful daughter who sat passively in the family parlour, waiting to be romantically awakened. Sarah's courtship was 'novel' because she was active; she pursued her own desires while Michael, sitting supine nursing his foot, responded. Sarah did the visiting, Sarah invited Michael to roam around Hobart, and Sarah did all this without her family's knowledge. This left her in direct contravention of British marriage law, which demanded transparency and which, in Addison's words, regarded 'with jealousy and dislike all clandestine contracts for the celebration of marriage'.[75] The rationale for this was partly about protecting heiresses from abduction,[76] and partly about guaranteeing that property stayed in possession of the gentry. The law's 'jealousy' of clandestine courtships was also a recognition of the dangerous autonomy that romance inspired in women, who enflamed with desire, might flout parental advice and tumble headlong into disastrous unions.

Sarah was a wilful romantic subject *par excellence*. Not only was she the pursuer rather than the pursued, but she also fought back against her brother's censure and promptly left to go and live with Mrs Donoghue. Running away from the family home was transgressive behaviour of the highest order: Sarah's brother refused to talk about it in court, and Mr Horne apologised for having to ask about it. Yet he must, he said, because if proved, Sarah's relocation to the house of a family friend raised questions about her reputation.[77] Autonomous movement made her suspect.

Sarah's rebellious stomps around the city were one problem. The other was that she refused to conform to the emotional rules that governed certain places. If this mattered generally to the evolving culture of middle-class manners, it was even more so in the most far-flung British colony, where gendered performances of propriety guaranteed the moral legitimacy of colonial property, stolen from the original inhabitants. A woman's respectability was measured by her capacity to understand the rules of comportment and to exhibit appropriate levels of self-restraint. Historian Mary Poovey puts it perfectly: 'the ideal woman of the nineteenth century was a being whose natural modesty and emotional self-control prevented her sexuality from obtruding.'[78] This explains why Sarah's 'immoderate laughter' in the parlour room became linked to her sexual reputation, and why it was considered evidence of her bad character. Sarah throwing her head back and chortling was a vision of the female body in the throes of pleasure. Behaving like this was bad enough, wrote *The Colonist*, but to bring evidence of that night into a public courtroom threatened to corrupt the general public. Laughter, spreading from the body to the body politic, was contagious.[79]

This is not to suggest that Michael escaped scot-free. The imputations against his character were also based on an understanding of moral geography and of his deviation from appropriate behaviour as a 'gentleman'. At issue was the tension between his two roles of landlord and suitor. Even if Michael had behaved more decently, his status as a landlord would still have made him an awkward suitor. As a landlord, he had a duty to protect women residing 'under his roof', which implied a responsibility to shield them from predatorial sexuality, to vet potential suitors and to intervene if a romance went awry. As Gellibrand argued, the idea of a proprietor acting as a predator was a confusion of categories, 'deeply distressing' to colonial society.[80]

This wasn't the first time Michael had been accused of being dishonourable. When confronted by John in the garden, Michael had tried to de-escalate the situation by suggesting that he apologise for any offence he had caused. John shot back that this would not be sufficient: 'you have behaved dishonourably,' he chided, and spoke of Michael's 'duty' to protect Sarah.[81] The language of honour was intelligible to both law and morality and escalated the issue from a breach of social etiquette to a breach of law.[82]

Possibly because we are used to thinking of dating as a time of freedom, it has tended to go unnoticed by historians that in the nineteenth century courtship enlivened legal obligations, including rights and responsibilities in relation to space. For instance, case law and legal treatises from the period refer to men visiting 'on the terms' of a suitor once they had received permission from the woman's parents.[83] What they mean is that a suitor was given visitation rights to enter the private domain of the home and to converse with the woman, and with this came the responsibility to fulfil the promise of marriage. It was a legal status that could be compared today with that of an owner or lessee who is given rights of access and entry to land and obligations to maintain it. Similar rights and obligations attached to the families of courting couples. In the case of *Cork v Baker*, the judge wrote that the father had 'a right to make the inquiry' of the suitor and to receive a correct answer; that is, he had a right to information for the purpose of governance and surveillance.[84] The dispute between Michael and John was therefore what lawyers would call a jurisdictional question: who had authority over Sarah, and who had a responsibility to protect her?

*The Hobart Town Chronicle* declared that Michael was to blame: 'What! A person in the character of the defendant, a gentleman of mature years, with the plaintiff and her mother as lodgers in his own house, whom he was in a manner bound as a citizen and a landlord to protect, at least from external harm, to play thus with the feelings of a young female ...'[85] Mr Horne, on the other hand, picked up on John's statement in the garden that he had a 'duty' to interrogate Michael because 'he was her brother and only protector'. Why, then, Horne asked, had it taken John so long to perform the investigation? Both men were accused of failing to appropriately protect a woman 'in his own house'. The problem was that in a boarding house, the question of whose house it was was never settled.

The assessors decided that the responsibility ultimately lay with Michael, which may also have been an acknowledgment of the power imbalance between the two men. As well as being wealthy and well connected, Michael had the power to throw John's family out of his house whenever he wished. And it is not too long a bow to draw to say that these power differences between the two men were reliant upon one larger act of colonial violence.

\*     \*     \*

On 9 February 1833, Michael Steel sat at his desk in Hobart and penned a gloomy letter to his brother Joseph in England. It was only a few weeks after his confrontation in the garden with John, and legal proceedings would have commenced. 'Wool is at a loss,' he began, and he longed 'to be able to come home upon a cruise of pleasure and stop for a year in my native land to see and be seen by old acquaintances once more.' He was lonely. Mr Cooke, the family friend who would later give evidence at the hearing, 'was a nice young man and his company seems very agreeable to us,' but otherwise 'we have little society here.' The problem, Michael wrote, was that 'all were looking for gain'.

A few years earlier, he had told Betsy Colgrave that he was 'just as healthy and happy [in Hobart] as at home', but now his self-portrait had darkened: he described his grey hairs and worried that Joseph 'would not know me I am so altered since you saw me [by] care and climate'. He concluded: may 'God grant that we may yet live to see each other once again before we enter into the land where all things are forgotten.'[86] Unsurprisingly, there is no mention of the breach of promise action, although Michael's anxiety about it simmers beneath the surface.

There are no other surviving letters from 1833, so we have no way of judging how Michael felt about the hearing, although given his almost priggish sense of moral rectitude, I imagine he would have felt it to be personally and socially catastrophic. He was also beginning to move into finance, making money by issuing loans for mortgages, and so his entire business depended upon his reputation, upon being seen to be a man of his word. The action was no doubt a setback.

Michael usually wrote two or three letters to his brother per year, so 1833 is unusual for only having the one letter, written in February. The next is not until January 1834, by which time he had recovered his good humour, abandoned his plans of going to England, and was now trying to encourage his brother to emigrate. 'It will be the happiest day I ever spent in my life to see you once more,' he wrote, 'and remember you will have a good house and ale to come to and the most hearty welcome that was shown or offered to a brother.' From the intimate geographies of home, Michael panned out to the charm of Van Diemen's Land: 'indeed this country is now getting very much improved as we have no blacks or bushrangers to fear, with a soil most beautiful and climate the finest in the world.'[87] His invitation is breathtaking for its honesty – the reality of massacre is openly acknowledged. His fantasy of a family reunion in a land of abundance was always dependent upon Aboriginal erasure.

Michael returned to England in 1840, and within five months married Martha Moore, the daughter of a respectable farmer from Warwickshire. His vision was always to have returned triumphantly as a member of the gentry, and this was recorded in his wedding certificate. Name: Michael Steel. Occupation: 'gentleman'.[88] He and Martha never had the 'rams' so longed for by Michael, but he wrote warmly of his two daughters, born in 1842 and 1843, as his 'dear little girls'. The family returned to Hobart in 1845 and continued to amass wealth through mortgage lending, gold speculation and property acquisition in Tasmania and Port Phillip, although both Michael and Martha always wrote of returning to England. In 1854 they set sail from Hobart and spent the rest of their lives in 'Begbroke House', an impressive country mansion with a swooping circular drive near Blenheim Palace in Oxfordshire. After many years of bad health, Michael died at the age of seventy-one on 27 August 1865.[89]

Like Michael, Sarah Hawthorn also recovered from the scandal of the breach of promise action. Questions of honour in colonial society were often a balance of principle and pragmatism, writes Penny Russell.[90] For all the moral condemnation litigants might receive in court, a colony of convicts had an interest in cultivating a certain amnesia about the past. In 1835, two years after the action, Sarah married Dr George Francis Huston in New Norfolk, in the south-east of Van Diemen's Land, and went on to have six children.[91] There is a reason why Victorian-era romances end at the marriage: on a practical level, marriage meant entering into a cycle of childbearing, lactation, child-rearing and domestic labour. Although none of Sarah's letters survive, George Huston's résumé – justice of the peace, member of the municipal council of New Norfolk, superintendent surgeon of the Hospital for the Insane, and member of the Tasmanian House of Assembly – suggests that at the very least she married an interesting man, perhaps even a man of honour. Sarah died at the age of eighty-nine in 1898.[92]

\*     \*     \*

I confess that when thinking about love, law and geography, I chose the case of *Hawthorn v Steel* because I found the politics of the boarding house fascinating. From wild laughter in a parlour room, to love letters passed from a landlord to a lodger, to a delayed confrontation between a brother and his sister's deceiver, both sides based their arguments on the appropriate behaviour of men and women in specific spaces. Women bore the burden of these expectations much more than men; their bodies were more constricted and more scrutinised, and they were punished more harshly if they transgressed. Even when a jury found in favour of a woman, as in this case, the law was premised upon an ideal of male honour, which had as its counterpart feminine fragility.

Curiously, although Michael Steel has featured in histories of Tasmania, the breach of promise action against him has not.[93] He was unusual, historians have noted, for his willingness to write openly about the murder of Aboriginal people before the commencement of martial law. There is little doubt that other propertied gentlemen in colonial Australia had similar stories to tell, but Steel was one of the few who wrote so candidly. His violence has received scholarly attention, but I suspect his breach of promise action has been deliberately kept out of the historical record.[94] Gwyneth and Hume Dow were scrupulous biographers who gathered an impressive archive of letters, newspaper reports and legal documents pertaining to the Steel family to tell a history of class formation in rural areas in the colonies, yet strangely there is no mention of the hearing. It is possible that they somehow missed it – but unlikely, given it was written about in every newspaper in the country. It would not surprise me if the breach of promise action was omitted from their history because courtship was considered irrelevant to the serious business of capitalism and colonialism.

By attending to the geography of desire, my goal in this chapter has been to argue the contrary – to show how land, love and the law were intimately entangled in settler societies. Land grants were written as a family romance – parcels of countryside were allotted 'to have and to hold' – and the colonial theft of Aboriginal land depended for its moral justification on the rituals of courtship. This is why *Hawthorn v Steel* was considered such a dangerous case in 1833, in the aftermath of the Black Wars, when European settlement was still seen to be precarious, and when the colony was struggling to shake off its reputation for vice. 'Who would be safe,' the Colonist asked, if men like Michael Steel trifled with the sanctity of a marriage proposal? Love, assisted by law, was a means of regulating space, and conforming to its rules was a guarantee that white settlement in Tasmania, still no more than thirty years old, looked civilised.

5.

# 'A system of deception': Sexual Reputation and Global Mobility

## (*Stewart v Byrnes*, 1857)

On 21 March 1857, Henry Byrnes – young, smitten, and wretched with worry – burst into Mrs Leed's Hotel. 'I have received two letters,' he announced. 'Which am I to believe?'[1]

It was late, 11.30 p.m., and he had ridden almost forty miles from the town of Orange to Bathurst, having been summoned by a letter from his betrothed, Ellen Stewart. 'Mrs Wise has aspersed my character,' it ran; 'if you do not believe such lies you must come immediately to Bathurst to defend me.'[2]

Ellen, a governess, was now standing before him in the parlour with her mother, Mrs Stewart, the police officer Captain Battye, and her barrister, Mr Dalley. 'Prepossessing' was how Mr Dalley would later describe her,[3] although tonight she was vexed and hard.[4] The other letter Henry had received was from Ellen's friend Mrs Wise. He retrieved the letters from his satchel and Ellen walked over, snatched the one from Mrs Wise, and began reading it aloud:

Strictly Private and Confidential, and keep this.

'My dear Mr Byrnes, – It grieves me very much to be obliged to write to you as I must do ...

Before your engagement I had doubts – this from the best of motives. I struggled against them, confessing them only to yourself and I may say, to herself ... In spite of this plain-speaking I saw her permit the same intimacy and the same familiarity which I had so much blamed before with Charles ... All of Sunday afternoon was passed together, in the manner of

132

Saturday evening; the evening on which you left could not be mistaken by anyone who witnessed it …[5]

Here Ellen's voice lowered to a murmur, and she read the next few paragraphs to herself. Her eyes skimmed over something about a fight between her mother, Mrs Stewart and Mrs Wise. Mrs Wise had warned her mother that Henry's father would not consent to Ellen and Henry's marriage when the engagement had been for less than six months, to which Ellen's mother had retorted that she too would not have consented had she known that Henry was dependent upon his father. Anyway, her mother had sniffed, she had been cautioned against her daughter marrying a tradesman. Ellen hummed her way through the letter until, in a high, shocked voice, she began reading to the room again:

We have had parties each evening since, and I too found that ill was only before me; that there was intimacy and romping, dancing with Charles Wise enough for the whole room to remark, and other conduct convinced me at once that she was deceiving both you and me … she, I must say as well as her mother, so completely threw off the mask they have been wearing, that I saw at once all deception was at an end – that the daughter had been playing a part and she will continue to play her part, and miserable as it is for you to be awakened to these facts, it is better that you should be awakened now than find yourself married to one who had deceived you … I must urge you to weigh my words well, and bear in mind I have never deceived you, and I have your interest in heart as if you were my own brother. Any letter you may receive from Miss Stewart must be a deception … I have completely found her out.[6]

Ellen gripped the letter in her hands and levelled her gaze at Henry: 'if you dare to believe such lies you are released from our engagement,' she said, 'and I will sue you.'[7]

Henry looked back at her, stunned. Wouldn't tears be more fitting than the threat of legal action? Ellen's mother – a lady of grace and gravitas – intervened.

'How can you speak so to Mr Byrnes?' she chided. 'Is he not honourable? Is he not here?'

'Yes,' Henry reassured her, referring to Mrs Wise's letter, 'I do not believe a word of it.' He promised to go to Mrs Wise's house the next morning and seek an explanation.

Ellen softened, and she and Henry sank down onto the couch, Henry's arm gently wrapped around her waist. He was exhausted but stayed and talked with Ellen and her mother for the next few hours. Mrs Stewart showed him the French wedding veil she had bought for Ellen, and Ellen even tried it on in front of him. At two-thirty in the morning, Henry bid the Stewarts farewell. He shook hands with Mrs Stewart, embraced Ellen, kissed her, and promised to call on them the next day, once he had spoken to Mrs Wise.[8]

Henry next saw his betrothed and her mother a few months later – from the witness box. He had not called on her the next morning, and after visiting Mrs Wise, who was an old family friend and confidante of Henry's, he had never spoken to Ellen again. As a consequence, Ellen had launched two actions: one against Mr and Mrs Wise for defamation, and the other against Henry for breach of promise of marriage. Heard on two consecutive days, the newspapers reported both cases under a single headline: 'Scandal.'[9]

\*　　\*　　\*

Mrs Wise's letter raised a question that continues to lie at the heart of romantic love today: who are you really? Our tendency to paint flattering self-portraits when we fall in love, and to relish those of our lovers makes this a worthwhile inquiry, as does the fact that intimacy makes us vulnerable to suffering: a bad match can mean financial or emotional abuse, violence, or being burdened with the expense and labour of rearing a child. We want to know our partner thoroughly to make sure that they are someone we can depend on. Whether we are prompted by passion or a fear of perfidy, love turns us into obsessive investigators, scrutinising our lovers for clues that might reveal their true selves.

We may share the same language as Mrs Wise, but this should not lull us into thinking that our investigations are the same. In trying to 'find out' or expose Ellen Stewart, Mrs Wise was not only speculating about her innermost desires; she was also commenting on Ellen's deviation from moral and social norms. Ellen's character was under scrutiny, revealed by her breach of courtship etiquette, which in turn cast doubt on her affection for Henry. Engagements demanded that each party retreat from social activities before marriage, not 'romp and dance' all night with other people.

But Mrs Wise's doubts went further. Cavorting at a ball led her to conclude, as Ellen later recalled, that both Ellen and her mother were engaged in a 'system of deception'.[10] To understand this rather dramatic language and Mrs Wise's fretfulness, we need to imagine our way back into the British Empire in the 1850s.

What was it about Ellen Stewart that aroused Mrs Wise's suspicion? As she says, the ball was only the last straw – she had long had her doubts. This was an odd thing to write, given Ellen had been staying with Mrs Wise as a friend for five months prior to the ball. Then only a small provincial town, Bathurst was no doubt a lonely place for Mrs Wise, and she had invited Ellen to stay to keep her company and help with social engagements. According to Mr Dalley, Ellen had been considered 'an ornament to the house', 'just the sort of person to make a party go off well'.[11] Ellen had happily agreed to the arrangement and had given up her paid employment as a governess.

Herein lay the problem. Ellen may have had impeccable manners, her piano-playing may have been peerless, but she had no money. Ellen and her mother, otherwise ladies, both stooped to work as governesses; not the vulgar, upstart variety seen in tradesmen's daughters, but the more noble variation that fell under the label of 'distressed gentility'.[12] Mrs Stewart's unhappy marriage may have robbed them of their wealth, but nobody could deny their aristocratic accomplishments. This did not, however, place them above suspicion. As novelists of the day warned, governesses could be either Jane Eyres – hardworking, downtrodden and virtuous – or Becky Sharpes – scheming, libidinous and instrumentalist.[13] Either way, Ellen Stewart was already inside the walls of the bourgeois family home, moving unchaperoned around ballrooms, bedrooms and parlours. With marriage, she would change legally and irrevocably from masked interloper to insider. Mrs Wise needed to move quickly.

The moral suspicion generated by Ellen's movements within the home were related to her movements outside the home. If mobility for men was a sign of autonomy and citizenship, for women it came with a whiff of danger and sexual depravity. Governesses needed to be mobile to support themselves. Their contracts were short – usually between six months and three years – and they would travel alone around the country, with only letters of recommendation to vouch for them.[14] Like the flood of emigrants who arrived in Australia chasing gold in the 1850s, they could slough off their past and walk into each new posting a new person. As scholars tracking the careers of fraudsters, imposters, black sheep and interlopers throughout the British Empire have revealed, imperialism provided many opportunities for self-reinvention.[15] The proponents of British imperialism may have thought of the empire as a moral venture, spreading the softer virtues of trade and civility around the world, but it tended to attract some of Britain's least moral members. In the Australian colonies – filled as they were with former convicts, nouveau riche gold-diggers and emigrants of dubious repute – Mrs Wise's question 'who are you *really?*' took on a certain urgency.[16]

One of the issues for the court in the defamation action, however, was whether Mrs Wise had the authority to ask these questions. As a friend, she was not in a privileged relationship to Henry (as she would have been if she were his parent) so what legal right did she have to cast imputations on Ellen's character? Even if interrogations into a person's background and moral conduct were sometimes warranted, how was this to be balanced against the middle-class right to privacy or the duty to not besmirch the reputations of your neighbours in a world that ran on credit, both socially and commercially? Such questions arose from deeper tensions: how was companionate marriage, imagined as domestic stasis, to be reconciled with a population more mobile than at any other time in history?[17] Who had the authority to regulate love and to conduct inquiries into the truth of someone's character? How was romantic love, which demanded intimate knowledge of one's partner, to be found in a world of fraudsters and schemers? Having travelled from Jamaica to France to England to Australia, Jane and Julia Stewart embodied all the possibilities and perils of global mobility in an age of empire.

## Jane Stewart

One of Ellen's proudest memories, she would later tell her granddaughter, Mrs Gertrude Marion Cardew, was being collected in an ambassadorial carriage out the front of Madame Baseus' school in Paris. It was February 1848, and she was eleven years old. Back then, she was not called Ellen, but Jane Stewart. 'Grannie always had a vivid recollection of the carriage from the British Embassy calling for her', wrote Mrs Cardew, 'and feeling very important as she drove through the streets, escorted by French soldiers with tricolours cockades in their hats, and of her safe arrival at the embassy.'[18] With her little head bumping against the window of the carriage, Jane would have looked out to see a city in revolt. Thronging crowds had sheltered behind barricades, omnibuses were overturned and used as protection from the guns of municipal guards, trees were felled, and pamphlets hastily pasted on walls proclaimed the right to work, the right to vote and the rights of man: 'Liberté, egalité, fraternité.' Alexis de Tocqueville had known the 1848 uprising was coming. 'We are sleeping together in a volcano,' he

*Julia Gertrude Stewart.*

had brooded, eyeing the rising unemployment, failed harvests, economic depression and lack of enfranchisement (only one per cent of the population were entitled to vote). 'A wind of revolution blows, the storm is on the horizon.'[19] By the time Jane's carriage bumped down the cobblestones, the city of light had darkened.

The passport Jane was given by the French revolutionary guards to pass through the streets of Paris was little bigger than a postage stamp, and it can be found today in the Stewart family papers in the Mitchell Library in Sydney. In the 1940s, Mrs Cardew pasted it into a leatherbound book containing the letters, poems, songs, autobiographies and official documents of her grandmother, Jane, and great-grandmother, Julia Gertrude Stewart. The words 'Dans La Révolution de 1848 – Liberté, Egalité et Fraternité' are handwritten in black calligraphy around the edges, and at its centre fly four French flags embossed in gold. Eleven-year-old Jane carried her passport to the British embassy and to the 'belle maison' of the British ambassador's wife, Lady Normandy, where she stayed until her mother made arrangements. Eventually Lord Musgrave, Lady Normandy's son, escorted her to England.[20]

That Jane remembered a moment of historical terror as an affirmation of her personal status could have been a product of her age – adventure being a genre favoured by children for scripting their lives – but I think it may say more about her desire to obliterate the shame of poverty she felt in early life, or the discrepancy between her family's aristocratic connections and their penurious finances. By the time she was retelling the story to her grand-daughter, it had become a kind of origin myth, a beginning point from which she could trace a seamless line between a noble, cosmopolitan past and her genteel present. Her mother, Julia Gertrude (Mrs Stewart earlier in this chapter), probably remembered the revolution differently.

Jane was not actually enrolled in Madame Baseus' school but rather at an English school for girls in Paris run by two sisters, 'The Misses Martines'. When revolution broke out, Julia was working as a governess in Galway, Ireland, teaching the Lawrence daughters the finer points of embroidery, singing, painting, piano-playing and European languages, and it was here that she received an alarming letter from the Misses Martines:

> Dear Miss Stewart
>
> I am sure you will sympathise with us in the misfortune which has just befallen us – both my Sister and myself are still so stunned – with the sud-denness of the trouble that it appears like a dream. But so it is that late disturbances in Paris have so alarmed the Parents of our own pupils that they have all been removed from us within the space of three days in con-sequence of which we have been compelled to close our establishment and return to England without a farthing in the wide world – we were not able to bring your dear child with us not having the means so to do but have left her with the care of Madame Baseus who keeps a school at no 70 Rue de Chaillot. She will keep her for a week or two ...[21]

Her daughter had been abandoned, left in a strange school as the city around her blazed, and Julia had one or two weeks to organise her res-cue. Thankfully, Julia was a savvy woman, and her connections were her currency. In a matter of days, she had contacted Lady Normandy in the British embassy (she was the sister of Jane's paternal grandmother), who organised for her son to escort Jane across the British Channel to Grove Mill House in Hertfordshire, the home of Lady Normandy's sister. Lady Normandy also organised for Julia to sail from Ireland to Hertfordshire,[22] and within a few weeks, mother and daughter were reunited in one of the most fashionable houses in England. It was a journey that would set a pat-tern for the Stewarts, whose migrations were both compelled by historical circumstance and enabled by elite contacts. Theirs was a privileged yet precarious cosmopolitanism.

*   *   *

How did Jane, raised in Paris among Ladies and Lords, come to be Ellen, a governess in Australia? According to a birth certificate found in the Stewart family papers, Jane was born to John Oliphant Murray, the British attaché in Paris, and Julia Gertrude Stewart in 1837. More precisely, she was born on the Rue Saint Honoré in Paris, an elegant, serpentine street that winds through the centre of the city, taking in tall frothy apartments, the Tuileries gardens, and the turquoise dome of the Opéra Garnier. Although there are no official documents verifying it, Mrs Cardew writes that John and Julia's marriage was an unhappy one and Julia eventually decided to leave him and strike out on her own as a governess.[23]

While Julia taught among her friends in the French and German nobility, Jane was placed with the Misses Martines, paid for by a bequest from the British government, called Queen Anne's Bounty, which was established to assist in the education of the children of families who had served their country. Julia wrote of the agony of leaving her daughter, 'I could not bear quitting the one object of affection which still bound me to life, however wretched that life might be', but financially she was left with no other option. When Julia worked with families in Paris, she was able to see Jane each Sunday. When she worked overseas, their intimacy subsisted in letters.

Jane would write to her mother in a mixture of French and English, rhapsodising about presents she had received – 'a little red shawl to put under my manteau' – and of the games she played at school – 'When we go out we take our hoops and run with them and we have great fun.' When the 1848 revolution arrived, she wrote a heartbreaking letter to her mother in French from Lady Normandy's house:

Ma très chère maman,
    … Lady Normandy ne sais pas comment m'envoyer en Ireland … et bien que toi tu le saviet … moi je suis trop jeune pour voyager toute seule.
    Adieu chère Maman, je t'embrasse comme je t'aime.
    J. Stewart'[24]

('Lady Normandy doesn't know how I am to be sent to Ireland, and as you well know, I am too young to voyage alone. Goodbye my dear mother, I kiss you, and how I love you.')

After reuniting at Grove Mill House, mother and daughter spent two years living together in England before they left for Australia. Julia opened her own school, charging £100 per pupil. If we are to believe her own story, she only came to Australia because friends encouraged her to do so. 'I was induced,' she explained in her unfinished memoir, 'through the brilliant prospects held out to me by those high in office and Court favour at the time to leave England for Australia.'[25] A more likely explanation is that her pupils in England may have been dwindling because she was unable to provide a piano (piano-playing was a necessary accomplishment for any lady), and finding work elsewhere was difficult.[26] Governesses were ideally younger than Julia (she was then fifty years old), and the 1840s witnessed economic depression, bank failures and high unemployment in England.[27] Many genteel families lost their fortunes, and their unwed daughters were forced into the only occupation besides marriage acceptable for middle-class women: governessing.

The *Amity Hall* sailed from Southampton around midday on 4 December 1849 with Julia and Jane on board, bound for the Australian colonies. Julia was carrying 'not merely private letters of introduction, but one from her Majesty's Prime Minister (Earl Grey) to the Governor, Sir Charles Fitz-Roy.'[28] What Julia does not mention in her memoir is that the Stewarts' voyage had been paid for by a priest, the Reverend Olger, and that they sailed with the second-class passengers. On Monday 13 May 1850, the *Argus* reported the arrival of a 'Mrs and Miss Stewart' in Melbourne.[29] A few days later they sailed to Sydney. Julia wrote that she arrived 'with my little girl, then scarce 13 years of age! With no friend or relative to meet me, no income to secure the means of existence in a land so totally different to those I had been accustomed to all my life.'[30] In place of family or friends to meet her, she carried a bundle of letters written by some of the richest and most powerful people in England.

\* \* \*

Jane loathed Sydney at first, and Julia's memoir is punctuated with her daughter's plaintive cries at night. The letter of recommendation from Earl Grey to Governor FitzRoy came to nothing, and Julia instead found work at Miss

Moore's Seminary for Young Ladies,[31] a prestigious finishing school in Sydney. With characteristic chutzpah, Julia organised for the governor to pay her rent at the place she'd been staying as she had run out of money. She and Jane then settled into a bedroom at the seminary.

Jane was an awkward fit among her peers: younger and poorer but more polished and worldly. Her status was also ambiguous. Was she a pupil? Or the daughter of a governess? The other girls had all come from elite colonial families, and as Julia chortled to herself, 'no Ladies Verey, Gower or Howard of the Old British Peerage could have been prouder of their noble ancestry than these young "parvenues" of N South Wales (I had nearly said Botany Bay).'[32] This was not merely affectation on the girls' part. As gentry men engaged in the socially fluid worlds of commerce, property, or politics, gentry women assumed the labour of asserting class distinction, a task that required the conjuring of ancient lineages and the sniffing out of interlopers.[33] It was a skill they learnt early in life.

'Many were the petty annoyances [Jane] had to endure,' wrote Julia, the 'covert whispers' or 'glance of the eye'. The cruelties – barely perceptible and therefore unpunishable – infuriated Jane. Her 'temper, under perpetual trial' meant that she became irritable' even towards Julia, whom she accused of being 'wilfully blind' to the insults she suffered. The situation came to a head one day in the music room when Jane sat down for the half-hour allotted to her and practised some polkas and waltzes. A certain Miss Riley stalked into the room, peered over her shoulder at the sheet music and declared that it was not in fact Jane's but Miss Lamb's. 'How could you think of touching music belonging to any of the young ladies?' she asked, indignant. 'You are not to consider yourself among them.' 'Oh Reader, think of the pollution!' Julia laughed in a telling aside. Jane could bear no more and rushed out of the room. Always the heroine of her own story, Julia went straight to Miss Moore to insist on a public apology, warning that 'if it was not forthcoming' she would withdraw from the school 'as the insult offered, if passed over, would in the eyes of all preclude my being of any use to her Pupils for the future'. Miss More agreed and organised the reconciliation. Miss Riley 'said she was very sorry' to Julia and offered her hand to Jane.[34]

Two years after this incident, Jane was working as a governess in the homes of Australia's elite families with daughters much like the girls she had met at Miss Moore's finishing school. She travelled with her mother, first to a wealthy solicitor's family in the northern suburbs of Sydney, then to Adelaide, and by 1855, at the age of eighteen, she was working for the Docker family in Victoria. Families raved about her. Sarah Docker received a gushing letter from her sister in England, who had met her daughter Josephine, saying how delighted she was that Sarah had found such a good governess. If all her children turned out like Josephine, she wrote, 'who was a credit to her training', she had no cause for anxiety.[35] Julia, however, found the situation more worrisome.

Folded within the Stewart family papers are a series of draft moral advice letters from Julia to Jane, to which Julia gave the rather long and alarming title: 'Letters to my daughter, aged fifteen, on all the subjects calculated to influence the character and fate of a young women, from circumstances obliged early in life to quit the maternal guidance and protection and, in the "Halls of the Stranger" gain a scanty pittance as "The Governess!!" The well-read Julia drew upon a cornucopia of British fiction and commentary that identified the character of 'the governess' as an infinitely interesting and troubling persona. Numerous inquiries in the 1840s and '50s were conducted into the low pay and poor working conditions of governesses in Britain, which feminist social reformers used to argue for the improvement of women's employment opportunities as a whole and for equality of education between women and men. These inquiries informed Charlotte Brontë's picture of Jane Eyre's treatment by the Reed family at Gateshead – the brutal assaults and humiliations she was subject to – as well as her grim descriptions of Lowood School for Girls, where governesses in training were all but starved.[36] It also gives some context to Julia's concern about the 'trials' Jane would be sure to experience in the 'halls of the stranger'. Julia wrote of the 'trembling anxiety' she felt as a mother when reflecting on the 'dependent position' of her daughter, which 'would lay her open to censure far more than a girl of the same age in affluent circumstances with a Father or Brother to resent remarks'.[37]

The literary context also helps to explain why Julia, when reflecting upon all the moments in Jane's life after she came to Australia, settled upon the music room scene to elucidate her character. I suspect it is no coincidence that *Jane Eyre* begins with an analogous scene: Jane perched on a window seat, hiding behind the curtains in the Reeds' library, daring to read a book owned by the family. 'You have no business to take our books,' taunts John Reed; 'you are a dependant, mamma says; you have no money; your father left you none; you ought to beg, and not to live here with gentleman's children like us.'[38] In both scenes there is the problem of what Julia calls 'pollution', the supposed contamination of a bourgeois body politic by a working-class pollutant, touching and infecting the property of the privileged.

It was not just the governess's humiliating work conditions that worried reformers, but also the sexual and class disorder she came to represent. On the one hand, the idea of a genteel woman of reduced circumstances educating other people's children made sense to Victorians. Confined to the domestic sphere and devoted to inculcating morality, manners and knowledge of Western civilisation in children, she was doing the same work as any middle-class mother. Her bourgeois status guaranteed her moral rectitude and her chastity. On the other hand, the governess was paid, like any working-class man or woman. She usurped the natural role of the biological mother. And she was asked to restrain her own sexual desires while in the bloom of youth.[39] In order to govern her charges, she needed to be able to govern herself. To this end, her sexuality was seen as both 'necessary and unreliable', particularly at a time of economic disruption, when Victorian gender ideology emphasised the role of chaste, middle-class women in guaranteeing social order. According to historian Mary Poovey, contemporaries worried that the governess was 'the conduit through which working-class habits would infiltrate the middle-class home'.[40]

Julia would never have conceived of either herself or Jane as a working-class threat to the middle-class home. Rather, in another half-written memoir, 'Passages in the Life of a Finishing Governess', she recalls her first charge, Mathilde, saying to her: 'Mamma has told me Madame that you never were a governess before, that you are a lady like herself, and have lived in Society, so I hope to like you.'[41] Yet Julia's concerns about the dangers of sexuality simmer beneath her advice. 'The little girl,' she wrote of Jane, 'just emerging from childhood to Youth, who a few short weeks since stood by her Mother's side ... has now entered a world where disappointments, trials and temptations are thick around.' She cautioned her to beware of 'temptations, amusing deceptions, and fleeting enjoyments'. In an ordinary middle-class family, Julia would have been able to watch over Jane's courtships, to help her to distinguish an amusing deception from an amorous delight, or to steer her away from the fleeting and ephemeral towards the certain and the dependable. For Julia, the threat lay not in Jane but in her host families; she went 'young and unprotected in the house of another'.[42]

## Ellen Jane Marion Murray-Stewart

The defamation and breach of promise actions were held consecutively over two days in October 1857 at the Bathurst Courthouse, which delighted the town gossips. There had been 'so much excitement', one journal commented.

'A considerable crowd [had] assembled to listen.'[43] As Justice Therry later remembered, the cases were 'the leading topic of conversation ... there was scarcely a person at Bathurst who did not express some opinion, *pro or con ...*'[44]

The breach of promise action was straightforwardly resolved: the promise of marriage was easily proved in love letters, where the engagement was discussed, and the defence cast no imputations on Ellen's moral character. The defamation action, which included both slander (spoken words that cast doubt on Ellen's chastity) and libel (Mrs Wise's letter), was more complicated. Ten years earlier the law around defamation had changed in Australia, and it would continue to do so around the common law world. There was still the requirement that defamatory words be both damaging to the reputation of the plaintiff and public, however the usual requirement that women alleging sexual slander prove 'special damage', meaning 'the loss of an upcoming marriage with a specific person' was abolished, making it easier for women to sue for defamatory allegations of sexual immorality.[45]

As the witnesses to the alleged slander against Ellen Stewart disobeyed their summons, Ellen's case rested entirely on Mrs Wise's letter to Henry Byrnes. The letter had damaged Miss Stewart's reputation, Chief Justice Alfred Stephen, who was presiding over both matters, explained to the jury, resulting in her loss of 'home, loss of character, and an establishment'.[46] Had Mrs Wise not written the letter, Ellen would have been the respectable wife of a business-owner and the mistress of her own household. This meant the central legal question for the court was whether Mrs Wise had legal authority to send the letter. Was she in a privileged relationship to Henry Byrnes (like a doctor to a patient, a teacher to a student, or a lawyer to his client)? To prove this, she would have to show that she had been delegated parental authority by Henry's parents and was thereby duty-bound to tell him what she believed to be true. Further, she needed to show that she had not acted out of malice.[47]

Although separate actions, journalists struggled to distinguish between the breach of promise action and the defamation action, and for good reason. Each hearing repeated the same stories and cast of witnesses: mother and daughter on the Stewarts' side, and father and son on the Byrnes' side. Only one gossipy needlewoman who had been stationed with the Wises offered an outsider's perspective. Mr and Mrs Wise would never have stooped so low as to give evidence in a public hearing, and the other members of the gentry, the Suttors and Mrs Marsh who had been summoned to give evidence on slander, had disappeared. Equally confusing for journalists was that Miss Stewart had changed her name. No longer the dowdy Jane Stewart, she had refashioned herself as the mellifluous Ellen Jane Marion Murray-Stewart. More like a lilting sentence than a name, her mother had insisted on the change. It gave Ellen gravitas, dignity and, significantly, a father.[48]

That a person could reinvent themselves through a simple change of name spoke to a recurring motif of both hearings: deception. Mr Dalley, barrister for the plaintiff, claimed that Mrs Wise had deceived Miss Stewart, who had placed 'perfect confidence in her' as a friend only to find that she had manufactured a malice against her.[49] Mrs Wise said that Miss Stewart had deceived both her and Mr Byrnes, feigning affection while romping with Charley Wise. Mr Holroyd, barrister for the defence, argued that Mrs Wise had a duty to reveal this deception, and that she had done so with motherly tenderness rather than malice. Mrs Stewart said that she had been deceived by Mr Byrnes, who had not told her of his financial dependence and that she now realised that Mr and Mrs Wise were in fact foes masquerading as friends.[50] In short, nobody knew who anybody really was, and none of them could be trusted.

Over the two days of hearings, Mr Dalley thrilled to his role as master storyteller and advocate for the impecunious and 'unprotected' Miss Stewart. Short, jovial and nuggety, with a thick, bullish neck and square jaw, Dalley was the son of convict parents and spent his life championing the rights of the native-born. He had always imagined himself working in Hordern's drapery store in Sydney, but an archbishop encouraged him to continue his studies, and having been articled to a clerk in 1846 he was finally admitted to the bar in 1856, a year before the Stewart hearings. Chief Justice Stephen would later describe him as 'loveable, himself a lover of romance, and in whose company no man could feel dull'.[51] Much the same could be said of Chief Justice Stephen – the handsome, worldly, theatre-loving flautist – who also served on the legislative council.[52] On the other side, for the Wise and Byrnes families were Mr Wise's brother, Edward Wise, scrupulous, morally upright and a lover of poetry,[53] and Mr Holroyd, a short-tempered polyglot who had learnt Arabic during his jaunts around the Middle East.[54]

Mr Dalley began each hearing with the backdrop to the dispute. In October 1856, nineteen-year-old Miss Stewart had endured the arduous, boggy, four-day journey over the Blue Mountains from Sydney to Bathurst to pay a visit to Mrs Wise. Mrs Wise lived in what Bathurst locals referred to as 'the big house'.[55] She was the niece of New South Wales first chief justice, Sir Frances Forbes, and she had married George Foster Wise, magistrate, businessman and later immigration agent, in 1842. An obituary would later describe her as 'possessed of unusual social qualities and powers of conversation' and 'ever the centre of a circle of friends'.[56]

Mrs Wise warmed to Miss Stewart immediately and insisted that she stay on in her house as a friend. Although not mentioned by Mr Dalley, it's likely that Mrs Wise was lonely.[57] She had no children of her own and would have considered herself above friendship with the servants. Like other gen-teel women who advertised for a lady's companion, the invitation to Ellen contained a blend of intimacy and instrumentalism and, quite possibly, char-ity. Mrs Wise was committed to philanthropic causes, and Ellen might have appealed to her for this reason. Not only was Ellen well educated, religious and refined, she was also penniless and in need of saving. Mrs Wise later described her as an 'ungrateful girl' given all the kindness she had received.[58]

As for Ellen, who had been a peripatetic governess for four years on short-term, unreliable contracts, earning around £60 per year, the offer had obvious attractions.[59] No longer a governess, Ellen could style herself as a friend of Mrs Wise, Bathurst's 'leader of fashion'.[60] At twenty years of age, with raven locks and creamy skin, she was ripe for romance with a man of superior class status. Governesses, at least in England, were off limits for both middle-class men, who saw them as too lowly, and working-class men, who saw them as middle-class women.[61] In Australia, given the demographic discrepancy between men and women (still 138 white men for every 100 women in 1861, with more of a gap in regional areas[62]), governesses had a better chance of marrying, but the demands of their work, specifically the expectation that they neutralise their sexuality, would have stifled romantic opportunities. In accepting Mrs Wise's post, Ellen moved from being the chaperone to the ball to being the 'ornament' of the ball. She was cosmopolitan, clever and had grown, Dalley said, to be 'a great beauty'.

Dalley explained that Henry Byrnes met Miss Stewart while visiting the Wises, with whom he was both friends and business partners.[63] There are no surviving portraits of Henry, but we know he was young, ambitious, well con-nected and romantic.[64] He and Miss Stewart would go for horse rides, gossip about the various legal celebrities who stayed with the Wise family during Assize week (when the Supreme Court was on circuit in the country), or sit tête-à-tête in the drawing room upstairs.[65] Just before leaving Bathurst to establish an outlet for the Wise and Byrnes Co. store in Orange, Henry pro-posed, and Ellen's mother Julia happily gave her consent. Henry gave Ellen a watch and an engagement ring, and Ellen stitched lockets of her hair into love letters for him. In March 1857, with Assize week approaching, Henry left

Bathurst for Orange and their relationship continued in letters.[66]

There were no torrid passions in Ellen's letters to Henry. She reported on the weather ('one constant pour of rain'), Mrs Wise's anxiety when some 'evil persons' threw rocks at her window, and their visitors, many of whom would later be involved in her case: 'Mr Dalley has come up from Sydney, but Justice Therry is stuck at Blackheath. Mr Dowling paid us a farewell visit on Friday.' She wrote of Mr Fox's sermon and finally, at the end of the letter, asked after Henry's health. 'Did you get wet, and are you quite well?' She concluded 'with best love and many kisses. Ever yours affectionately, E.J.M. Murray-Stewart.' During Assize week, she missed the post one day and wrote a short letter at three in the morning the next, 'knocked up' after a night of dancing. There was some warmth – 'Suffice it to say that I wish you were with me, for I have so much to tell you about everything' – and some self-absorption: 'but more about myself, which I have not time to write now.' Promising to write more next time, she signed off 'with many many loves and kisses'.[67]

Henry had reason to worry. People in love will always find the time to write – the desire for an imagined communion with a new partner has, across the centuries, felt compulsive. Where Ellen's letters were breezy and newsy, Henry's were anguished and love-struck. 'I feel very lonely without you,' he wrote in reply, 'and shall be truly happy when the time arrives for our marriage, until then days will seem as weeks and weeks as years, for my affections are so completely wrapped up in you that I do not like to be *separated* from you a moment, and if it is at all possible, I would like to be married before June.' These effusions later became evidence of a promise of marriage, as did his report that he had just written to his father to 'tell him of the happiest act of my life, namely, my engagement with you'.[68]

There was nothing in the letters about Charley Wise, the dashing young cousin of Mrs Wise, although he was most likely the cause of Henry's nervousness and of Ellen's tardiness. Yes, said Henry when giving evidence in the defamation action, he had spoken on 'several occasions' to Miss Stewart about Charley Wise, and 'on one or two occasions he had found Charley Wise and Miss Stewart in a room together, and much too friendly for his liking.'[69] There was one instance where he had found Charley in a room alone with Ellen, crying because he had learnt something about Ellen's past.[70] Worried about their intimacy flourishing while he was away in Orange, Henry asked Mrs Wise to 'acquaint him if Miss Stewart manifested the slightest friendship for Charles', and told Ellen that he would not carry out his engagement if she didn't 'cut [Charley] altogether'.[71]

Ellen denied everything. Yes, she said, she had once walked in company with Charley, but that was before she was engaged. She also recalled a time when 'Mrs Marsh refused to go out with her if Charles accompanied them, as she said the great object was to "do propriety."' As for her changing her name, she had never wished to be married in the name of Murray-Stewart, but Henry had insisted.[72] When Julia entered the witness box, she laid any questions over Ellen's name to rest: 'Her daughter had at her request taken the name of Murray about two years ago,' she explained. Julia's 'maiden name was Stewart, she had borne that name for many years, but if she had her right name it would be Murray, as that was her husband's name.'[73]

There was an oddity in the defamation hearing that preoccupied the press: Ellen had found out about Mrs Wise's 'slander' a few days before the final ball, and yet she didn't leave. Mrs Wise said that it would be better for Ellen's reputation around Bathurst to stay, and Ellen, intriguingly, agreed. Newspapers ruminated on how awkward those last few days must have been for Ellen, although Mr Dalley gave them a simple explanation: 'She was compelled to remain,' he explained, 'because she had no home to go to.'[74] Having grown up in poverty, Dalley knew that exercising the most basic right to move depended on having money or connections.

Dalley took the material of the Stewart case – a dispute over marriage between three rather snobby families – and turned it into an anti-aristocratic allegory. His reconstruction of events took an imaginative detour via the British Empire, travelling back and forth between old-world British corruption and nascent Australian republicanism. The 'lady patroness', Mrs Wise, he said, was living in 'a kind of provincial government house', part of 'a small exclusive party' that had 'banded to together to crush and ruin an unprotected girl'. Mrs Wise had ridden roughshod over the Stewarts' right to privacy and good reputation and used 'the vast machinery of England in collecting from all sorts of people the materials of her family history'.

He depicted Henry as a milquetoast, effeminised by his financial reliance upon his father and the dictates of his elite friends. 'He was reduced to the position of utter helplessness,' Dalley lamented, 'one of those young men who could do nothing for themselves'. Dalley's speech was sprinkled with the masculinist rhetoric of democracy and self-government, which had been granted (partially) to New South Wales two years prior to the case, and with the chatter of the goldfields located a few miles from Bathurst, where inherited power was being challenged by the egalitarianism of luck and toil.[75]

Chief Justice Stephen also had a transnational approach to the defamation case. He had socialised with Mrs Stewart in the past at Government
House and knew of her French background.[76] On the question of 'the sin of
flirtation', he advised the jury that 'what would be perfectly correct and in
keeping with a Frenchwoman would in an Englishwoman be ridiculous or
grossly improper.' Of course, designating a 'young girl a flirt and unfit for a
wife' was libellous, he argued; 'it would be monstrous' to say otherwise. But
what evidence had been offered of Miss Stewart's 'immorality or inconti-
nence'?[77] Stephen was himself a colonial offshoot of a cosmopolitan imperial
family and was also on the organising committee for the Paris Exhibition
at the time, which may have inspired his outlook. But his argument – that
the law needed to cultivate a transnational perspective when adjudicating
intimate transgressions – had wider implications.[78] It was a plea for moral
pluralism in a world of mobile emigrants.

In making this argument, Stephen identified one of the causes of the dispute. A defamation and a breach of promise of marriage case, both of which
turned on accusations of deceit on all sides, were at heart about the scope
for imposture facilitated by manners and the possibility for self-reinvention
enabled by mobility. Over a period of five months, the affluent Wise family
had invited Ellen, a near-stranger, to move in with them, to share confidences
and intimacies, because she had 'considerable personal accomplishments'.
She had similar manners to theirs, and these manners suggested similar
morals. This was also no doubt why the Wises' good friend, Henry Byrnes,
thought she would make an excellent wife. Yet Ellen was also culturally suspect. Her movements around the country as a governess in search of work
meant that each new town had offered opportunities for reinvention (she
had even changed her name), and her unchaperoned movements around the
home facilitated illicit sexual liaisons. This was more so at Mrs Wise's house,
where her status as a 'friend', rather than a governess, gave her an ambiguous
autonomy: she was free to spend her time as she wished but was financially
dependent on the Wise family.

When Ellen took advantage of her freedom of movement, meeting Charley Wise for walks or spending evenings in his company, she was lectured
about 'doing propriety'. Her mobility – the walks, dances and intimate conversations in private rooms – were breaches of etiquette and raised suspicions
about her moral character. Who was she *really*? This was already a question
asked of any governess, on account of the discrepancy between their class
and their cultural capital. They were poor, working women with elegant,

genteel manners, a combination that had troubled the British since at least Lord Chesterfield's *Advice to His Illegitimate Son* in the late eighteenth century: could manners be unmoored from morals?[79]

During this period, sensational novels about the governesses' 'masks' and secrets proliferated.[80] Although finishing governesses like the Stewarts were hired for their knowledge of etiquette, their lack of financial status highlighted the possibility that their manners were a disguise, simply a series of scripted behaviours that could gain them entry into the halls of the most illustrious homes in order to sap a family's fortunes from within. It was a concern exacerbated by the vast numbers of etiquette manuals in the eighteenth and nineteenth centuries aimed at the working classes, which also implied that innate aristocratic grace may be a learnt choreography of class. Mrs Wise identified two moments as crucial to the Stewarts' unmasking. The first was when Miss Stewart danced with Charley, and the second was when Mrs Stewart yelled at Mrs Wise for interfering in the engagement. The former was a breach of courtship etiquette, suggesting Ellen's lack of affection for Henry and a lack of sexual restraint. The latter was a breach of Victorian gendered codes of decorum which prohibited female anger, particularly in a context where Mrs Wise was simply asking for a longer engagement so that the couple might get to know each other better. Both incidents suggested that the Stewarts were incapable of governing their emotions – a crucial marker of bourgeois identity – and that they were grasping and scheming, hatching a hasty loveless marriage to replenish their own coffers.

That these vexed questions about deception and character were raised in the context of romance is understandable. As Mr Holroyd argued, modern companionate marriage was distinguished from the property transactions of the premodern world by love, by each partner having 'perfect confidence' in the other.[81] It was cupid and not cupidity that escorted couples to the altar. Further, the distinction between love and commerce, indebted to the public/private distinction, was weighted with moral judgment: prostitutes, in bringing the market into the bedroom, were an example of moral corruption *par excellence*. Yet in a labour market that failed to pay women liveable wages, marriage was necessarily driven by economics, which meant that the question of whether someone was marrying for love or money was ever-present and ever-perplexing. In this formulation, lovers did not battle against social and moral encumbrances to reveal their true selves but rather saw the self as inseparable from moral rules. The term they gave to this self was 'character' and, being comprised of outward expression, it was capable of being monitored and judged by others.

The question in the Stewart defamation hearing was who besides lovers had the authority to inquire into and judge someone's character, and how was this duty to be balanced against 'the duty not to slander our neighbour'? When Mr Holroyd argued that Henry had 'constituted Mrs Wise his agent' and delegated her 'parental authority', he argued that parent and child were in a legally privileged relationship in romance, much like doctor and patient in medicine. He later claimed that Mrs Wise was expressing 'fraternal affection' in looking out for Henry.[82] Culturally, romantic love was an emotion with communal dimensions that required familial regulation. It was accepted that the law supported the family's duty to regulate courtship, but how wide was the 'family circle'? Could any friend of the family be designated a legal agent?

The answer, Dalley argued, depended upon whether the duty fell upon a woman or a man. He could not see how 'any lady' could be so 'indelicate' as to pursue the path taken by Mrs Wise, laughingly referring to her as Henry's 'solicitor'. The joke lay in the incongruity between the erasure of a wife's legal agency under the laws of marriage, and the notion that she would then be given the authority to be a 'legal agent'. 'If the duty' to tell Henry Byrnes about Miss Stewart's conduct 'devolved upon the Wise family it was surely the husband's place to perform it,' he argued. Chief Justice Stephen agreed, and went further, suggesting that women may also not have the same right to free speech: 'The duties of man to man required free expression of opinion. A father for instance must not be restrained in speech to his children. But what duty did Mrs Wise owe Mr Byrnes or society?'[83] In so arguing, Dalley and Stephen took a legalistic, not to mention misogynistic, approach to the issue, ignoring the plethora of literature at the time that gave women responsibility to preside over love.[84]

As love and emotions were increasingly relegated to the private sphere in the late-eighteenth and nineteenth centuries, women became their chief custodians.[85] Young girls were educated in matters of the heart by romantic novels, and wives were preoccupied with matchmaking as much in real life as in books. For wealthy women, authority in matters of romance meant the power to determine the transmission of property between families, and the management of social hierarchy. It gave them the power to exclude certain families from marrying into elite circles and to prop up those of declining fortunes. This private regulation of social hierarchy and class status was no small power to wield.

Letters like the one written by Mrs Wise made clear that married women were operating their own courts of romance as self-appointed judges, advocates and juries. But as seen in the words used to describe such women – 'interfering', 'meddlesome' or, courtesy of Dickens, 'pecksniffian' – people in the nineteenth century were uneasy about feminine authority in romance.[86] A father's patriarchal right to intervene in a courtship was never questioned in breach of promise cases. Women needed to be more careful, lest their expression of judgment appear too masculine or malicious. This is why Mrs Wise wrote that she 'would not interfere any more' in a letter to Henry that can only be described as blatant interference; and that she had acted with the 'best, kindest, most charitable feelings'. Ultimately, gendered prohibitions against women exercising authority meant that a woman's judgment might be dismissed as malice, where a man's would be applauded as sound reasoning. Chief Justice Stephen advised the jury that the Wise family's defence rested entirely upon whether the jury could find that Mrs Wise was obligated by a higher duty.[87]

It is a testament to how socially vexed the questions of gender, deception and romantic authority were in the Victorian era that the jury could not come to an agreement. The breach of promise case was easily and swiftly proved, with Ellen Stewart, at least on paper, walking out of the court £500 richer. The defamation action, however, resulted in a hung jury. After being locked up all night in the Bathurst Courthouse, the jurors had failed to come to agreement: eight thought that Mrs Wise had a privileged relationship with Henry, which negatived her libellous letter, and four didn't. On a practical level, this meant that Ellen's £500 should have gone straight to Mr Dalley for legal fees, but Henry refused to pay.

Henry appealed the breach of promise decision, arguing, in the main, that one of the jurors was biased against him. The juror had been heard in a pub before the trial boasting that he would 'sheet it home' to Henry. Curiously, this wasn't the only grounds for a retrial. Henry argued that Ellen's flirtation with Charley had not been the primary reason he had decided the marriage with Ellen was 'impossible'; rather, the reason was to be found in two other letters he had written to Mrs Stewart seeking information about her and her family history. Mr Holroyd had asked for those two letters to be produced, but Mrs Stewart had refused, and the judge had not compelled them. As *The Sydney Morning Herald* later reported, the letters contained 'certain matters [not named] which had come to his knowledge in reference to Mrs Stewart's family', matters so unseemly that they could not be mentioned in court.[88]

## Julia Gertrude Stewart

According to the Stewart family papers in the Mitchell Library archives, Julia Gertrude Stewart, mother of Ellen Jane, grew up in a castle in Jamaica: Stewart Castle, to be precise, in the parish of Trelawny.[89] Her family's three-storey mansion, built with cut-limestone and surrounded by forests of fruit trees – mango, guinep, ackee and coolie plum – was as august and imposing as it was vulnerable. The compound walls were pockmarked with almost 100 gun ports, and inside there was a fortified privy, two detached towers, a 2.5-metre-deep well, and an armoured courtyard large enough to secure people and animals, guaranteeing survival in case of a siege. Like other planter houses in the area, it stood high and imperious on a hill, allowing Julia's father, James Stewart II, and before that her grandfather, James Stewart I, to keep watch over the 300-odd enslaved Africans working on his sugar plantations. It also gave him a good vantage point from which to spy any renegade Maroons (former slaves) who might slip down from their mountain hideouts to foment rebellion among his workers.[90]

James Stewart's letters patent predicted insurrections. A noble Scottish family that traced its lineage to the House of Stewart in 1298, the Stewarts had been awarded land in Jamaica through a Royal Proclamation by Charles II in the 1600s, which James Stewart I turned to his advantage. Still in his early twenties, he sailed from Galloway in Scotland to Jamaica in 1754, stopping in America en route to collect enslaved Africans. The patent granted him land contingent upon him 'opening up ten acres every year', 'keeping four negroes for every one hundred acres of land', and serving in case of 'Insurrection, Mutiny, Rebellion or Invasion which may happen in our said Island'. Uprisings by enslaved Africans had been a feature of Jamaican life since at least the 1650s.[91] In the almost eighty years that the Stewarts lived there, they would have witnessed a war with the Maroons at the turn of the eighteenth century, revolts in 1816 and 1820, and over 2500 people fleeing plantations in the 1820s.[92]

By the time of abolition in the 1830s, Stewart Castle had transitioned from sugar production to cattle, and when James Stewart died in 1828, the family were subsisting on a charitable bequest from the Jamaican parliament.[93] From an early age, Julia knew what it meant to live with high rank and low credit.

Julia arrived in the world in ominous circumstances. While her other five siblings have birth certificates from Jamaica, Julia's is English and dated 1798, the year after the Deed of Mortgage for the Stewart Castle Plantation.[94] Her pregnant mother, Elizabeth Christiana (née Dallas) had travelled to London with James Stewart II, who by then was a prominent public figure, to meet with two merchants. Feeling the pinch of poverty, the Stewarts agreed to mortgage their castle as well as '240-odd slaves' months before Julia was born.[95] However, there is no mention of living with financial distress or the fear of slave insurrections in Julia's memoirs; instead, she writes about 'Old Jamaica' in nostalgic, eulogistic tones. They were 'palmy days'; her father was 'wealthy and influential', and her mother was of noble stock (Julia's maternal aunt was the mother of the poet Lord Byron).[96]

Life in Jamaica for Julia would have revolved around the bustle of activity at the castle, which in 1799 stretched to 1200 acres. An 1835 watercolour of the property painted from one of the bordering hills shows dusty roads that wind through sugar works belching forth black smoke from tall stone chimneys and around Spanish-looking houses that served as slave quarters. There is a palm tree in the foreground and the Caribbean Sea twinkles on the horizon, with high puffs of cloud in the sky. The painting was commissioned by a merchant, Richard Shelden, who bought the estate in 1830, two years after Julia's father died.[97]

James Stewart's obituary in *The Royal Gazette* in 1828 mourned the death of one of the country's 'most distinguished legislators' who was 'born to the inheritance of an ample fortune' but whose 'zealous commitment to the public service saw him neglect his private affairs'. He had been 'cool and determined' as a major in the Maroon war, 'plain and perspicuous' as a representative in the House of Assembly, 'uniformly impartial' as a judge of the Supreme Court and the Slave Courts, but his patrimony was 'irretrievably ruined' in the later years of his life. Julia later attributed the family's loss of fortune to his bad investment in Spanish stocks and, implicitly, to the end of slavery. The obituary concluded that James Stewart's 'grateful country' nonetheless 'cheered his declining years with a liberal grant' of £700 per annum for the next thirty years of his life.[98] Julia used some of this money to leave Jamaica in her thirties and voyage to Paris.

As she would later explain, it was there that she met and fell in love with her cousin John Oliphant Murray, the British attaché in Paris and ten years her junior.[99] Auburn-haired, rosy-cheeked and with a mischievous cherubic mouth, John Oliphant was a man of fashion and charm whose family occupied pages of *Burke's Peerage*.[100] Julia claimed that the couple were married in a church in Paris in 1836, although she said the church had since burned down. 'About five months afterwards,' she discovered that she had been 'deceived that no marriage in France was legal or binding save the civil contract before "Le Maire de l'Arrondisement" in which the parties are at the time residing'. She was already pregnant with Ellen Jane and presumably pressured John Oliphant Murray to make the union official according to French law, but he refused. 'We had a severe altercation on the subject and parted never to meet again six months before my Daughter's birth.'[101]

From this point onwards, Julia's family name was the cornerstone of her identity and the foundation of her business. With her family's fortune gone and no husband to support either her or her child, she depended entirely upon her noble blood, her elegance and her genteel accomplishments. Mrs Cardew, her descendant, wrote that Julia gave up her husband's name of Murray, although 'this was her name by right', preferring Stewart, of which she was immensely proud.[102] 'Now for my debut as "The Governess!"', Julia wrote in her memoir, describing how she drew work from her friends in the French and English nobility.[103] Her mark of distinction was that she was born to the aristocracy and styled herself as French. By the time she arrived in Australia, Julia was a snob by trade.

Julia did not expect to find people in Australia who knew her illustrious family history, and she recalled her 'unqualified happiness' at meeting a community of former West Indian families in Sydney who 'knew I was a gentlewoman and treated me as such'. There was Lady Forbes, cousin of Mrs Wise and wife of Chief Justice Forbes; the Pinnock family, whose property bordered that of her mother's family in Jamaica; and Colonel and Mrs Barnley – all of whom had lived in 'Old Jamaica'. The 'West Indian Families of former days', wrote Julia, were distinguished by their 'warm-hearted feelings' at least 'before the ruin of their fortunes and … of that once splendid land.'[104] At the time that Julia was writing, Jamaica had become a country of free citizens. Families like the Pinnocks did not in fact go to ruin but rather received compensation from the British government in 1835 for the loss of their slaves, which they then channelled into accumulating capital in colonies such as Australia. For historians investigating the legacies of British slave-ownership these transnational ties show the interconnections between slave histories and settler colonial histories.[105] For Julia, in the 1850s, these people were a reassuring reminder of her true nobility.

What went wrong? What did Henry Byrnes hear about Julia's family that meant he was unable to marry the person from whom he 'could not be separated'?[106] While all of Henry's love letters survive in the state records office, the two letters he wrote to Mrs Stewart have vanished. The information was so defamatory that no newspaper could report it, and they were not produced in court. The diarists we might turn to, such as the gossipy John Milbank Marsh, brother of Mrs Wise, are missing the years of the litigation, and Julia did not keep them in her memoirs.[107] Either that, or her descendant, Gertrude Cardew, did not include them.

### Gertrude Marion Cardew

I had suspicions about Julia's story when reading through the Stewart family archive. The person who had collated the papers in the 1940s and 1950s, Mrs Gertrude Marion Augusta Cardew, bore the names of her grandmother and her great-grandmother, and her correspondence was sent from a rather prestigious address in Sydney.[108] Here was a woman with an eye to posterity and a keen interest in her noble bloodline.

I began to notice that most of the official correspondence sent from the Public Records of Jamaica did not include Julia Gertrude. There was a typed letter sent to Mrs Cardew in 1946 containing 'the data which we have been able to gather on your ancestor, the Honourable James Stewart of Trelawny'. Under the title 'FAMILY OF JAMES STEWART' are listed seven children born between 1763 and 1809, but no mention of Julia. Instead, we have Mrs Cardew's insistent annotation in pen at the bottom: 'Julia Gertrude Stewart was born in England ... Date of her birth was 1798.'[109] It is possible that the fact that Julia was born in England explains why there is no record of her in Jamaica – but for such a public figure as James Stewart, one would expect at least some record of her existence. Mrs Cardew scribbled family trees onto sheets of paper inserting Julia into the bloodline: 'Julia Gertrude born in England 1798 married John Oliphant Murray, son of 8th Baron Elibank. There was one child of the marriage, a daughter Ellen Jane Marion.'

There is a photograph of Julia as an elderly woman taken in the 1870s. She gazes pensively into the middle distance, her lips pressed together in a secretive half-smile. Her hair falls loosely just beneath her ears and her starched black dress is draped in white lace. Around the photograph, Gertrude Cardew has confused their first names: 'Gertrude Julia Stewart, daughter of Hon James Stewart of Stewart Castle Trelawney, Jamaica and mother of Ellen Jane,' she wrote. Julia 'married her cousin in Paris 1836, the Honourable John Oliphant Murray and the name of Murray Stewart was assumed, but the marriage being unhappy she assumed for herself and her daughter her maiden name of "Stewart".'[110] And yet I could find no proof. Julia herself said in court that she had only asked Jane to assume the name of Murray at the age of eighteen.[111] Given that the marriage laws of the Australian colonies in the 1850s

*Ellen Jane Stewart.*

did not demand official ceremony, why did Julia not try to obtain some documentation of her marriage? The church may have burned down, but surely a priest or clerical official could have verified the union.[112]

There were other questions, too: why was there no mention of Julia Gertrude or Ellen Jane in any public record of John Oliphant Murray? Julia had said that he had been punished for his treatment of her, and yet the public records show that he ended up in the esteemed position of concierge to the King of Bavaria.[113] Why did Julia never turn to any of her siblings for support? Why would she sail to Australia if, as she claimed in her memoirs, any member of the British or French aristocracy might have employed her? It also seems strange that Mrs Cardew, so punctilious in her research, included birth certificates for some members of the family but not for Ellen. All births of British nationals overseas were officially recorded at the time, and the certificate would not have been difficult to obtain.

Today, digitised records make birth certificates easy to find. Perplexed by Henry's claim in the appeal, I scrolled through the names on the UK, Foreign and Overseas Registers of British Subjects, 1627–1965. In handwritten print at the bottom of the register for the year 1837 I found Ellen, once again with a different name. Here she was 'Ellen Janet Mary'. The category for parents' names is divided in two: Christian and surname. Under Christian name there is Julia

Gertrude Stewart and under surname there is a blank space. There is no father recorded; instead there is the abbreviation: Illeg. Meaning: illegitimate.[114]

This does not mean that John Oliphant Murray was not Ellen's father. History, as this book shows, is overpopulated with caddish men abandoning women after a night of passion. But it does raise doubts about his and Julia's marriage. It might also explain why the Jamaican archives contain no reference to Julia in any of their information on the Stewart family. She and her illegitimate daughter Ellen Jane were very likely retrospectively wiped from the family tree as illegitimacy became less acceptable in the Victorian era. This is surely also why the Jamaican records of 1843 don't mention James Stewart's three other illegitimate children, born to a woman, Elizabeth Steele, who was classified as a 'free quadroon'.[115] Late-eighteenth- and early-nineteenth-century Jamaica, much like Australia, turned a blind eye to extramarital liaisons, and in the Stewarts' case all the children were given the Stewart name.

James Stewart received the highest honours upon his death, and Julia was raised to believe that she could trade on his good name. But James Stewart lived the life of a Regency imperial aristocrat. Julia, on the other hand, gave birth to her illegitimate child in the year Queen Victoria ascended the throne. By the time Ellen received her first marriage proposal in 1856, having her mother's maiden name as a surname spoke not of an ancient bloodline but of a history of moral disgrace. In the words that the law gave children like Ellen, she was an 'outcast' – she 'hath no father'.[116].

Like dominoes clattering one against the other, the oblique facts of *Stewart v Byrnes* suddenly became clear and interconnected. Everything led back to the scandal of Ellen's birth: the strange scene in the Wises' house when Charley wept to Ellen that he had discovered something unutterable about her past; Julia's insistence that Ellen change her name to Stewart-Murray; and Henry asking that she marry in the name of Murray.

That Mrs Wise found out about Ellen's illegitimacy in the first place is characteristic of imperial mobilities. As much as Julia Gertrude might travel around the globe to escape a shameful past, she had to anticipate other people from her past being equally mobile – people far more judgmental than their forbears and who, in the wake of abolition, felt an extra need for respectability. James Stewart's extramarital liaisons would have been viewed very differently by the next generation of white Jamaican families, such as the Forbes, the Barnsleys and the Pinnocks, all of whom had known him in Jamaica. I suspect that this group of people who had travelled from Jamaica to Australia knew about Julia's past from the outset and simply thought it unseemly to discuss it publicly or to inquire too deeply into it – until her daughter looked as though she might marry into their ranks, at which point they wrote letters, spoked in hushed tones, and finally closed the door against her.

## Ellen Jane Marion Steel and Julia Gertrude Stewart

If you drive east from Bathurst, past sandstone pubs, through cool, shadowy tunnels of poplar trees and then up into bleached scrubby mountain planes that roll on and on until the horizon, you'll find a picturesque village called Rockley. It's small – the population is less than 200 – and perfectly silent, except for the whistles and warbles of Australian birds. At its base, weeping willows turn the riverbank into an impressionist painting, and at its height, even above the steepled churches, sits a 'gracious' colonial home with a cream-coloured picket fence, 'Chislehurst'. It was built by the well-pedigreed Watson Augustus Steel II in 1871 for his three children, Watson Augustus Steel III, Gertrude and Isabella, and for their mother, Ellen Jane Marion Steel.[117]

Watson Augustus Steele II was the son of the original grantee of Rockley and one of the wealthiest landowners in the area. In 1860, he received a pledge from Julia Stewart, outlining the circumstances of her marriage to John Murray. The pledge was written two years after Henry had unsuccessfully appealed the breach of promise action and one year after Ellen had once again appeared in the newspapers, this time for insolvency.[118] The £500 Henry owed her was listed as a 'bad debt', and she had creditors in Sydney chasing her for millinery and a writing desk.[119]

There may have been love between Watson and Ellen but, like many Victorian marriages, there was also convenience and financial need. The scandal surrounding the litigation would have damaged Ellen's chances of marriage and her employment options. Although litigants often went to court to save their reputations, the details that might emerge during the hearing, and the very fact of publicly appearing in court, had the potential to do more harm than good. When Julia pledged that she had married John Murray in a church in Paris in 1836 and that Ellen Jane was therefore not technically illegitimate, she was writing for their lives.

On Valentine's Day in 1860 at All Saints' Church in Bathurst, the Reverend Fox pronounced Ellen and Watson husband and wife. There are no surviving love letters between them, and the only commentary from Julia is a boast to descendants of Lord Byron in England (who seemed barely to know her) that Ellen had married well. The couple featured in *Empire*'s list of marriages as the union of 'MURRAY-STEEL'. Ellen was referred to as 'Ellen Jane Marion, only daughter of the Honourable John Oliphant Murray, Scotland.'[120] Julia had been erased and Ellen was once again traced to a father who was as good as fictitious.

Ellen never possessed her mother's love of writing, and nor did Watson Augustus Steel II. In the absence of family papers, it is difficult to imagine what their marriage was like. We do have, however, bundles of letters sent between 'Grandma Julia' and Ellen's children, counselling them on feminine comportment and chastening them for bad grammar.[121] We also have a stunning collection of children's clothes, sewed by Julia and now in a national museum.[122] What troubles me most about these letters are the various street names, all without numbers, from which Julia wrote. Ellen would not have wanted for anything financially after her marriage, but this was no guarantee that her mother received a share of the spoils. An archivist at Bathurst Archives kindly stood with me over a colonial-era map of the city, trying to trace the precise areas where Julia lived. We find her, from 1860 until her death in 1876, in at least four different addresses, all located, the archivist tells me, in the industrial ends of town.[123] The last years of Julia's life were passed much as she had lived: with a constant and restless mobility, less an expression of freedom than a mark of the fugitive.

*   *   *

The Stewart trials remind us of the urgency of the question *who are you really?* in colonial-era love affairs. The cases revolved around two problems heightened by the accelerated movement of people in the nineteenth century: how do we know what we think we know about a lover? and who has the authority to interrogate and judge lovers? These questions would rarely have troubled the small communities of the early modern world, where a person's continuous connection to a place and the community's knowledge of that person's family over generations provided a trustworthy means to evaluate character.

Nineteenth-century Australia, however, was no such place. Among the gold miners and former convicts parading their finery were governesses, women who were in the business of spreading civilisation yet who had some of the most obvious features of the uncivilised: vagrant in their search for work, unfeminine in their need to work, and sexually ungoverned at their places of work. The suspicions that attached to governesses were exacerbated in a world of strangers, and even more so in the realm of love, where 'perfect confidence' was demanded of potential partners.

Ellen's and Julia's life stories also show the benefits of a peopled history – looking beyond court cases to excavate personal stories that bring the local and the global into dialogue. Discarding the usual imperial routes from Britain to Australia, we travel instead from a plantation society in Jamaica to the metropoles of France and England to the settler colony of New South Wales, and in so doing we illuminate the entangled histories of slave societies and settler colonialism. We see how disparate places and histories were bound together by the families, personal information and capital that shifted between them and how the opportunities for self-reinvention afforded by empire were cruelled by the simultaneous movement of people from home.

Most importantly, Julia and Ellen's story provides a corrective to celebratory histories of mobility – the histories of uninterrupted 'flows' of people, of frictionless cosmopolitanism, rebellious moving subjects who slip across national borders evading the eyes and laws of the state, of escaped convicts, rebels and sailors, mostly men, many of whom left destitute women at home.[124] Julia's movements around the globe appear more like a series of personal emergencies, motivated by declining family fortunes, poverty, perfidious men, and a moral code that punished women more than men for sexual transgressions. For historians, mobility may be best understood by examining its constraints – the imperial structures and class privileges that made it possible for some people to move and not for others, and the cultural suspicion that greeted mobile women while celebrating the autonomy and adventure of men.

*   *   *

I pull into the Bathurst cemetery at dusk, wanting to find a public monument to Julia and Ellen. After all, Watson Augustus Steel I has a plaque on the pioneers' wall in Bathurst, and Watson Augustus III devoted much of his life to triumphantly writing his grandfather into the nation's history.[125] A local historian of Bathurst's historical houses admits that the genre tends to favour the men who built the houses rather than the women who lived in them, and Chislehurst, in local histories, appears as the home of the family of Watson Augustus Steel II.

Bathurst cemetery is denominationally divided, and the Church of England section is vast, over a kilometre long and wide, although conveniently there is a part reserved for 'old' graves. As clouds blush, shadows grow long, and the sun becomes a jewel in the sky, I bend down to inspect gravestones that are now little more than lichen-freckled concrete, the names long since smoothed away by wind and rain. I start to doubt the possibility of ever finding them. And then, at the very bottom of the cemetery I spot three marble crosses. The first one I see is for Ellen and Watson's son, Watson Augustus Steel III, and the second for their youngest daughter, Isabella Blanche Steel. The third is not, as I would have imagined, for Ellen and Watson, but for Ellen and her mother Julia. When Ellen died in 1928, twenty years after Watson, the newspaper reported that she had 'always expressed a strong desire to be buried in Bathurst'. Their tombstone is a magnificent structure, with four white marble steps leading up to the cross. Julia would have been pleased. There is no mention of John Oliphant Murray. The inscription, etched in black, finally tells the truth: 'Julia Gertrude, Daughter of the Honorable James Stewart of Stewart Castle, Parish of Trelawney, Jamaica; Also, Ellen Jane Marion Steel, Daughter of the Above ...'

# Part 3

## Intimate
## Encounters:
## 1880–1914

The years 1880–1914 have been cordoned off from the flow of time and garlanded with a mellifluous epithet: 'la belle époque'. Though not all was voluptuous splendour. This was a period of rupture, when old certainties were thrown into doubt and habits of thought questioned. Writers scribbled visions of imagined futures – some apocalyptic, some utopian – as institutions disintegrated around them. Dreamers experimented with communal living, women adopted radical fashions, artists painted in shockingly new ways, and simmering conflicts – between bosses and workers, women and men, or colonies and empires – bubbled to the surface[1]. Gazing back on the shifting relations between 'masters and servants, husbands and wives, parents and children', Virginia Woolf insouciantly declared in 1925 that 'on or about December 1910 human character changed'.[2]

In Australia, the long economic boom of the Victorian era came to a spectacular end in the late 1880s and 1890s, and the police, military and special agents flooded city streets to quell mass strikes by hungry workers. Feminists demanded the right to vote and called upon the state to protect them from male violence. Print journalism flourished, its stories pulsing around the globe in new underwater telegraph cables. And as unprecedented numbers of people moved around the world, the Australian colonies erected racially exclusive borders in response to frightful visions of 'Asian hordes'.[3] By the early twentieth century, British imperial fantasies of cosmopolitanism had ceded to the exclusionary demands of a sovereign white nation, embodied in the White Australia Policy and legislatively enshrined in the *Immigration Restriction Act* of 1901.[4]

And in the midst of this social upheaval, people courted, and spoke about courting, in hitherto unimaginable ways. Intimate life broke free of medical and scientific textbooks or religious doctrine, and found its way into newspapers, social-scientific studies, sexological research, literature and art. There were panicked public discussions about sex trafficking, venereal disease, the declining birth rate, homosexuality, marriage and divorce. Intimacy was the stuff of everyday conversations, and the factory girl, the shop girl and the 'new woman' were held responsible for moral, racial and national decline.[5]

Scandalous divorce hearings and criminal sex trials were one way that private life became a subject of public debate, and the sheer number of cases during this period has led historians to declare it 'the age of the trial'.[6] Yet breach of promise has not been part of this history, because scholars have tended to see the suit as Victorian; they have assumed that the turn of the century witnessed the action's decline.[7] In Australia, however (and I suspect in other Western countries that saw social disruption during this period) there were in fact more cases reported in the press between 1880 and 1914 than in the entire nineteenth century. Women used breach of promise hearings to protest male violence, while non-European migrants went to court to sooth wounded feelings and to assert their right to dignity. The gradual unravelling of love from law that we witness later in this book began in this period of fierce contestation, as traditional authority structures broke down and people looked for new models to make sense of intimate relationships.

6.

# 'The Jezebel of Sydney': Courtship, Coercion and Intimate Violence

## (*Vaughan v McRae*, 1891)

yles McRae MLA was a monster of male entitlement. Almost any person who read the Australian newspapers in the year 1891 would have thought so. Six feet tall, forty-nine years old, jowly, moustachioed and in the habit of smoking three to four pipes per day,[1] Myles consolidated his commercial success with a parliamentary position. And as his wife Clara McRae's petition for judicial separation revealed, he matched public power with private tyranny. Clara was forty-two years old when she stood in front of the Divorce Court in Sydney and recounted his abuse. He 'dragged her about by the hair of her head',[2] she said, and 'called her vile and filthy names'. When she tried to stop him hitting one of their five children, he 'struck her on the back and ordered that she leave the house'. He beat her on the corners of King and George Streets in Sydney, blackening her eyes. Her staff suffered his violence too. Clara once arrived home from church with her children to find the servants complaining 'that the respondent had been walking about the house in almost a state of nudity, attempting to take indecent liberties with them.' Myles' feelings of sexual dominance thrived on the discomfort of others. 'The respondent would leave the house in his nightshirt and proceed to the river, about forty yards distant, and there bathe in a state of nudity before his daughters and the servants.'[3] Myles' abuse of Clara was such a 'common occurrence' that she couldn't provide all dates or accounts of it in her affidavit.[4]

And then there was his adultery. Clara listed numerous affairs and, most damningly, a bottle that she found in a drawer in his office labelled 'for outward application only.' She presented it to a doctor (Dr Reid), along with a sample of Myles' underwear, who confirmed her suspicions of venereal disease. When she confronted Myles about it, he beat her, pushing her against an open window in his office and accusing her of 'infecting him with the disease'.[5] She fled to her father's house in Paddington.

Among the governesses, servants and doctors Clara summonsed to court to support her case was the 'young and prepossessing Ilma Vaughan', whom Myles had allegedly 'violently seduced' under a promise of marriage.[6] Clara's divorce petition was the first time Ilma brought to public light her stories of Myles' brutality. The next time she did so would be in her breach of promise of marriage claim, and by then Myles' reputation would be in tatters: 'We are not so short of men or manhood in this colony as to be forced to seek lawmakers in the ranks of brutal seducers, hypocritical adulterers or men who for their own purposes would wink at the ravishing of a helpless girl,' thundered *The Daily Telegraph*.[7]

Myles McRae resigned from his parliamentary position in December 1891.

*   *   *

I was surprised to see the likes of Myles McRae in my breach of promise cases. This book is meant to be a history of romantic love and law, based on a suit that awarded damages for wounded hearts, not intimate abuse. But cases where love and violence intermingled popped up continuously throughout the nineteenth and twentieth centuries, with the peak number recorded in the 1880s and 1890s. This may in part be attributed to changes in the laws of evidence in the 1870s that allowed plaintiffs to give testimony in their own suits (rather than relying on their fathers to bring a seduction action), but that doesn't explain the decline in actions involving intimate violence in the early decades of the twentieth century. A more likely explanation is that in the 1880s and 1890s, much like in the #MeToo era, men's entitlement to women's bodies was being challenged. Historian Marilyn Lake has described the gender wars in the late-nineteenth century as 'one of the greatest political struggles in Australian history'.[8] Women, in the words of historian Susan Magarey, went on a marriage 'strike', with 51 per cent of women aged between twenty-five and twenty-nine in 1901 recorded as unmarried,[9] and feminist publications such as *The Dawn* and *Women's Voice* setting out to reform masculinity and the politics of love. In 1886, four white men were hanged for their part in the gang rape of a white sixteen-year-old girl from Sydney's slums and in 1891, the year Myles found himself in court, the Victorian parliament debated the castration of rapists.[10]

Litigants like Clara and Ilma were the historical antecedents for contemporary feminism; they were part of a movement comprised of both activist and non-activist women that provided some of the first public discussion of intimate violence in a legal setting. In having the courage to appear in court and tell their stories to an all-male courtroom, these women helped to lift the veil of privacy that had shrouded sex, marriage and male violence in the nineteenth century. They were not prosecuting the stereotypical villain of criminal law – the stranger rapist in a park– they were suing their lovers, their fiancées and their husbands, self-purported exemplars of masculinity.

In Australia, there is still only a burgeoning literature on the history of intimate violence; a topic so shrouded in secrecy is difficult to trace and scholars have largely turned to criminal and divorce records for illumination.[11] But it is not just in suits for marital cruelty or child custody that we find our evidence. There is an extraordinary archive of pain, lust, violence and resilience found in the civil court transcripts for seduction, breach of promise, and maintenance as well. Somewhat serendipitously, we have found in the figure of Myles McRae someone who was sued no fewer than three times in one year under all of these actions.

Myles might have been a monster of male entitlement, but he was also a well-loved and respected man who was certainly not alone in thinking that coercion was an acceptable element of love and lust. In the stories of Myles, Clara and Ilma, we can see that the law sanctioned violence not only within marriage but also between courting couples; a fact that scholars have to date ignored.[12] Courtship appears less as a time of independence for women, as academics have optimistically argued, than as the first chafing of a marital yoke.[13] The women who challenged these conventions brought about nothing less than the birth of a new intimate order: to protest the abuse of one's body or psyche is to make a radical claim to autonomy.[14] While Elizabeth Cady Stanton stood before the US Congress in 1892 and demanded a right to 'self-sovereignty', ordinary women like Ilma and Clara invited law into their bedchambers to restructure the rules of romance and to claim the right to an intimate life free from violence.[15]

## Myles McRae

Myles McRae was born on New Year's Day 1845 into a family of boys, the seventh of eight sons. His parents were Alexander and Mary McRae, two Scottish

Presbyterians hailing from the fighting clan of the McKenzies,[16] who had set sail for Australia in 1837 on clergyman Reverend John Dunmore Lang's promises of antipodean bounty.[17] The McRaes were people of the land. Alexander worked as a stockman in the Hunter Valley and then purchased his own property in the area, while Mary cared for the family and worked on the farm.[18]

Myles, while proud of his humble origins, spent his life seeking opulence. Ambition propelled him to the goldfields in the 1860s, fossicking first at Lambing Flat, or present-day Young, and then in the Widden Mountains near Grenfell.[19] When the mud in the bottom of his pan failed to glitter, he became a merchant and land speculator around the Illawarra and southern Sydney in the 1870s and 1880s.

At the end of summer in 1871, Myles married Clara Charlotte Taylor, the daughter of a wealthy timber merchant family who lived between Paddington in Sydney and the Hunter Valley. Clara was twenty-two, and Catholic, and Myles was twenty-seven, and Presbyterian, when he slipped a gold band on her finger, engraved with her name on the inside. Reverend Lang pronounced them husband and wife at Scot's Presbyterian Church in central Sydney.[20] We don't know how they met, or whether the decision to have a Presbyterian wedding ceremony was a source of conflict. Until at least the 1960s, people would furrow their brows at relationships between Catholics and Protestants, and families would skip the wedding ceremony rather than enter the church of a different denomination. Mixed marriages, it was thought, could result in marital strife: religion determined the choice of education for children, job opportunities and friendship circles, while a child from a previous marriage would be declared illegitimate if baptised in a different faith. I would speculate that the Presbyterian ceremony was one of Clara's first submissions of will, an act that signified the effacement of her prior identity as a Catholic and her incorporation into the tight-knit McRae clan.

In the 1880s Clara and Myles moved to Morpeth, the main commercial hub of the Hunter Valley until the completion of the rail link between Sydney and Newcastle in 1890 doomed it to economic irrelevance.[21] Morpeth was, and is, a picturesque town. Willows drooped on the banks of the Hunter River, rickety wooden piers poked into rivers and paddle-steamers churned their oversized wheels, puffing black smoke into the air. Pelicans, plovers and curlews keeled over lagoons.[22] Myles stood amid the bustle of the wharves, watching his lucerne make its way to Newcastle and Sydney, and walked through streets that had been dignified during the 1860s and '70s with monumental civic architecture: an austere grey-stone church, a courthouse of terracotta red and cream, and a regal School of Arts with Corinthian columns and a classical pediment.

It was at the School of Arts that Myles was first elected as an alderman to the borough of Morpeth in 1885. Following this success, he was elected alderman of Kogarah and Hurstville in southern Sydney in 1886 and 1887, and in 1889 he ran successfully as a member of the Legislative Assembly for Morpeth.[23]

If Myles' public speeches and letters from this time might give us a sense of who he was as a person, then we could begin by saying that there is something of the careerist in someone so hungry for titles and volatile in his sympathies. His position on the question of protectionism versus free trade oscillated from being in favour of both in 1874[24] to being staunchly in favour of free trade in 1887 when he ran unsuccessfully for the Legislative Council,[25] to an avowed protectionist when he ran successfully for the Legislative Assembly in 1889.[26] By then, it appears, he had anticipated that an electorate of farmers would want their produce protected by government tariffs. Myles railed against 'improvident', 'careless' and 'extravagant expenditure' and boasted of having 'pressed hundreds of tons of hay, mown, reaped, dug, fenced split and could take his stand against any man he came across',[27] yet he moved through the world girt by luxury: adorned in gold watches, chains and sleeve links, twinkling with diamond pins and rings, shaded by a silk umbrella.[28] He celebrated democracy and full manhood suffrage but argued for the restriction of public office to the wealthy: 'they should place themselves in a substantial position before they ask people to give them suffrages (applause)'.[29] He also showed little respect for the popular vote. When his election campaign failed in 1887 he penned a fiery letter to the people of Morpeth: 'Unfortunately for the best interests of this country, constituencies return men ... who prostitute the representative function and make it subservient to meet their own base vile ends.' Myles saw himself as standing above personal interest, uniting a people polarised along class lines: 'I believe thoroughly in the recognition of the rights and privileges of all classes of the community to do as their conscience dictates, I have always stood aloof, my platform being a purely Australian one.' His mission, it seems, was divine: 'I would like to see my countrymen united in brotherly love, which to my mind is the very essence of Christianity.'[30]

A man of such rhapsodic egotism was contemptuous of social graces. He would interrupt his rivals at public debates and bluster over the top of them such that they would threaten to leave if he didn't stop.[31] He usurped the role of the mayor in greeting a public dignitary at Morpeth train station, offering him, according to the mayor, 'the freedom of the town, without authority', causing a public skirmish.[32] Myles crashed through the delicate, ritualised world of nineteenth-century government like a drunken giant. 'I would like to know who constituted him as an authority on receptions,' he railed in *The Maitland Mercury* against the mayor, 'did he get his diploma from the gods?'[33] For Myles, money, liberally distributed, gave a better claim to authority than mere diplomas or institutional hierarchy. As he reminded electors, he 'was not born with a silver spoon in his mouth' yet was generous with his largesse, and one can detect in his behaviour a susceptibility to humiliation that comes from economic power without cultural authority.[34] Wealth bought him access to the halls of government, but the rules remained illegible and he banged against them with clumsy rage.

Finally, Myles cared about his family and he cared about women, or so he told his electors. 'The first duty of men is to their families,' he said in 1887 to rapturous applause. When he ran for election in 1889 he promised to give the whole of his salary to a widows and orphans fund, although once elected he reduced that promise to fifty pounds.[35] If Clara had never petitioned Myles for a divorce, we might have believed his public persona. It is through an item in the newspaper that appeared on 4 July 1890 entitled 'An MP in the divorce court'[36] that we begin to get a different perspective on Myles' life as seen through the eyes of his wife, Clara Charlotte McRae.

## Clara Charlotte McRae (née Taylor)

Within the colossal folder marked *McRae v McRae* at the State Records Office is an affidavit written by Clara McRae which could also be read, in part, as her autobiography and as a biography of Myles.[37] Affidavits are stories of the self, written in moments of vulnerability and desperation, according to the conventions of law. Historian Arlette Farge says it best: 'usually the archive does not describe people in full. It cuts them out of their daily lives, cements them in some complaint or pitiful denial and even when they are consenting, pins them down like trembling butterflies.'[38] Myles' public life can be easily traced in newspapers, whereas women like Clara are best exhumed in legal records, because women were excluded from almost all forms of civic life in nineteenth-century Australia. The bundle of papers before me, tied with pink string, is a 'tear in time'; a crevice which we can slip down to listen to eavesdrop on the conversations of the marginalised and the silenced.[39]

I turn to Clara's affidavit and begin reading. 'I was married to Myles McRae hereinafter called the Respondent on the fourth day of March in the year of Our Lord one thousand eight hundred and seventy-one by the Reverend Doctor Lang'. The handwriting is not hers but belongs to a clerk of the court – neat, loopy italics. 'Myles is forty ~~seven~~ nine years of age' and their children include 'William aged ~~sixteen~~ eighteen years, Percival aged ~~fourteen~~ sixteen years, Reginald aged twelve fourteen years, Kathleen aged ten eleven years and Josephine aged seven nine years'.[40] Each correction tells a story of struggle, of Clara's failed efforts to leave Myles. The affidavit is dated 1890 but she must have first petitioned for judicial separation in 1888.

I read on. She was born in Sydney and Myles was born in Dunmore. 'That before marriage, I was a Spinster living with and supported by my father and mother'. Myles was a 'Batchelor', then a 'commissioning agent', and 'since marriage has made large sums of money by speculating in land'. These bare descriptions are rich in detail about the different universes inhabited by men and women. Clara had no existence outside her relationship to others. She moved from dependency (her parents) to dependency (Myles). There was no life beyond marriage. Myles on the other hand experiences marriage as a launching pad from which to sally forth into the world, occupying a range of different titles: bachelor, husband, commissioning agent, land speculator. The only path for Clara was from daughter to spinster to wife to mother.

Clara lists the places where she and Myles lived together: Goulburn Terrace, Surry Hills, York Terrace, Pyrmont Bridge Road, Paddington and Petersham. In 1883 they moved to an estate called Bonnie Doon on the Cook's River, about ten miles from Sydney, and lived between there and Morpeth until their separation. After this come pages and pages of sorrow narrated in the strangely self-confident language of law. 'I charge', she declares 'that he was guilty of great cruelty to me, that on several occasions he has struck me with great violence'. Myles hit her with hair-brushes,[41] knocked her down in streets, humiliated her in front of servants and children, left her without money and 'struck her about her body with his clenched fist and ... said in effect that all women were alike to him, and he cared no more for her children than the dust beneath his feet'.[42] She writes of a body in pain, now anaesthetised by the language of law. The evidence of Clara's suffering strikes me most acutely when at the end of the statement I see her signature: tremulous, blotted, almost illegible. She is shaking so much that she can't hold the pen still. It looks like the scribblings of a frightened child.[43]

What can explain Myles' violence? To my mind, there seems to be a link between his confession that he could not have fellow alderman question him without 'giving expression to his indignation' and his domestic violence. Myles could not countenance any challenge to his authority in public or in private. His grandiosity, desire for public power and seemingly unassailable self-esteem were possibly built on a foundation of self-doubt; a feeling that unlike Clara he was not born into a world of privilege and power. I would speculate that his attraction to Clara was no doubt partly a product of her family's wealth and connections, but that this would have also given rise to humiliating feelings of dependence. Violence was a means to turn 'impotence into omnipotence'.[44] When I read back over the affidavit, I see that Myles' violence did not seem to be a product of jealousy or fear that Clara might leave him, but rather a sense of entitlement to dominate the family. He hit Clara when she challenged his authority to discipline his children; when she accused him of carrying venereal disease; when she chastised him for being unduly familiar with the governesses or servants; when she queried him about his adulterous affairs; and, finally, when she sat on the veranda reading over a statement that I now have in front of me from 1888 first petitioning for a judicial separation. Myles responded with force to any limit placed upon his perceived right to control women's and children's bodies. We can also read a certain misogyny into Myles' alleged comment that 'all women are the same to me' that might possibly be traced back to growing up in a family of eight boys, and in a culture where public life was entirely dominated by men.[45]

I think it's important to speculate on these personal impulses because not all men in the nineteenth century beat their wives, although they could have done so. But Myles' violence is not just the product of family history or a bullish personality. His cruelty to Clara and her decision to separate from him are born of larger historical forces. Myles and Clara lived through a period when the meaning of marriage changed, when the balance of the law's scales on the question of marital violence began to tilt more towards prohibition than permission, and when wives, in their journey from being the property of their husbands to separate legal persons, packed their bags, closed the front door and walked into the divorce courts.

\*    \*    \*

When Clara said 'I do' at the altar of Scots Church in Sydney in 1871, her legal identity vanished; she transformed from a woman to a wife, and effectively, to the property of Myles McRae. Indebted to the Christian idea still celebrated by some today that marriage makes a husband and wife 'one flesh', the doctrine of coverture made Clara and Myles 'one person and that person [was] the husband', in the words of one famous legal commentator.[46] Coverture was a formidable apparatus of female oppression that sanctioned and enforced domestic violence. It was a regime of coercive control allowing men to direct and control the household income, to beat or rape their wife, and to isolate their partner from family or friends. Fortunately for Clara, coverture began to crumble in her lifetime thanks to two major legal innovations: the first was the right to divorce enacted in all Australian colonies by 1873,[47] and the second was married women's right to keep their own earnings and to own property, granted in 1879.[48] Both of these laws fractured the Christian ideal of marital unity with a simple and radical idea: husbands and wives do not necessarily always share a common interest. And it was in the stories of private torment that women brought to the public theatre of the divorce courts that bourgeois beliefs in companionate marriage came undone.

Clara argued for a judicial separation based on two grounds: marital cruelty and adultery. Extraordinarily, Myles did not contest any of Clara's testimony. He instructed his solicitors to challenge the alimony and custody claims, but he would let the argument in her divorce application stand. Justice Foster awarded Clara the judicial separation and then three months later found in her favour for the alimony proceedings. She would lose her three sons but be granted custody of her two daughters. Clara could see her sons and Myles could see his daughters for two hours twice a year: 11–1 p.m. on the first days of April and October. In a society where she had no presumed rights to her own children, this was considered a win.

The star witness for Clara's claim that Myles had committed adultery was Ilma Vaughan. Six months later, Ilma appeared in court again, this time as a plaintiff in her own action against Myles for breach of promise of marriage.

## Ilma Vaughan

The *Vaughan v McRae* case file in the state records office is disappointingly thin – no letters and no affidavits – and like most poor women Ilma and her mother Petronella left scant other remains.[49] To understand how their life paths crossed over with the McRaes' we'd best be going to court. In 1891 this means entering the Dickensian labyrinth of St James' courthouse, with its

*Ilma Vaughan.*

overflowing barristers' chambers and leaky roof, walking past the anterooms where genteel ladies who want to see but not be seen are taking turns to peek into the little glass peep-holes in the doors that look directly onto the witness box, and descending into the armpit of the public gallery where crowds are rushing for the seats reserved for the press and the clerk of the court has to raise his voice and tell them that it's standing room only.[50] It means witnessing, as one of the tabloids reported, 'the sensation of the week'.[51]

*   *   *

Gamine, with dark curly hair, olive skin and some residual baby-fat softening her jawline,[52] Ilma Vaughan stood in the witness box and swore that she was born in the British Honduras (or Belize) in 1872. Her father was 'a mahogany merchant and European gentleman' hailing from Surrey in England who died when she was young, leaving her Spanish mother, Petronella, and her two siblings in penury. After passing some years in New Zealand the family moved to Australia twice: once in 1884 and the second time in 1888. Petronella sought accommodation at Myles' real estate agency and Myles found them a house in Granville, one of the new suburbs that had sprung up around Sydney in the past decade. As Ilma recounted, he visited them there soon after: 'I don't suppose you know me now,' he said when Ilma opened the door. 'I am Myles McRae, the first time I saw you, you were quite little, but you have grown a big girl now.' We can imagine the carnivorous glint in his eyes. 'You must feel very dull here, you ought to get married, it would be much better for you.'

Ilma told the court that she said she had no desire to get married, to which Myles responded: 'then you are very silly, as you would make a good match.'[53]

Ilma's delivery was calm, almost nonchalant, until the cedar doors creaked open at the far end of the court room. Myles McRae blithely sauntered inside, and whispers flew through the gallery as he took his seat at the solicitor's table. He leant into the heaviness of his lower back and folded his arms across his light summer suit. Ilma had been reciting the same narrative she had given at the McRae divorce hearing and now stopped and shot Myles 'a glance of withering scorn.'[54] Justice Innes – a staunch churchman with wavy grey hair and bristly mutton chops – remained sombre. He was a conservative with a genius for sympathy, people said. He told her to continue.[55]

On a second visit, Myles asked Ilma to join him for a walk. While strolling out on Granville Road he proposed marriage, assuring her that his wife had divorced him four years earlier. Her reply was blunt. Ilma 'did not care for him sufficiently well to marry him', but given that her mother was in 'reduced circumstances' she 'was willing to make some sacrifice for her'. Ilma says that when they returned to the house Petronella expressed some surprise, but 'was willing to consent if her daughter was not opposed to the match'. A few days later, Myles organised a house in Mount Victoria for Petronella to take charge of as a housekeeper, and on Saturday evening Ilma and her mother boarded a train and travelled two-and-a-half hours west of Sydney. Before leaving, Myles said that he 'would visit them occasionally, but those visits would be brief as he had so much business to do at the Legislative Assembly.'[56]

From this point onwards, Ilma's testimony assumes the form of a dream sequence, or a nightmare. She awakes later that night to the sound of Myles being reprimanded by her mother for arriving late, at 11 p.m. She remembers Myles rushing into her bedroom and kissing her roughly. 'How dare you enter my room,' she exclaimed. 'I'm sorry,' he replied, flustered, 'I was so anxious to see you that I just couldn't wait.' She has tea with Myles and her mother, and he gives her a gentleman's diamond ring, saying that it belonged to his brother Donald but should do for the time being. It's too big. She places another ring alongside it to stop it sliding off. While Ilma is preparing some candles in Myles' room, he walks in and locks the door behind him. Ilma screams. Her mother rushes to the room, rattles the doorknob and hammers against the door, demanding to be let in. Despite Ilma's struggles, he is 'intimate' with her. Ilma finally manages to escape, bursting out of the room in tears with her night-dress torn from her back. Petronella yells at Myles that she would 'instantly take proceedings against him' and orders him to leave the house. Myles defies her to take him to court, adding 'besides, I am married to your daughter ... what is the use of your proceeding against me?' He points to the engagement ring and says: 'you cannot say or do anything now because I have put a ring on her finger.'[57] The next morning, they all breakfast together and Myles and Ilma go for a walk to collect ferns at a 'fairy glen' in the bush. Over the next few weeks, the couple move around hotels and boarding houses, with Ilma dependent upon Myles for money. He beats her and rapes her numerous times, she claims. On one occasion during a walk through the Domain, he knocks her down and rapes her while she is unconscious. Ilma finally settles in Manly, where she confronts Myles about his marriage. When he admits that he was not in fact divorced she threatens to sue him for breach of promise of marriage. He responds with insouciance: 'I am accustomed to courts, and as I am a member of the Legislative Assembly everyone would take my side.'[58]

\*   \*   \*

Assuming that Ilma was telling the truth, her story begs the question, which continues to be asked today: how to explain men's sexual violence? Was this the sordid exploitation of an impoverished girl by an unscrupulous man? Did his libido just see an easy opportunity in Ilma? Or did Myles care for Ilma, and if so, how did he reconcile this with sexual coercion?

Let's begin at the level of the personal. In 1888, when Myles knocked on Ilma's front door, Clara was in the process of leaving him. In her petition for judicial separation, she said that it became clear in 1888 and 1889 that Myles 'had some other lady in view'. During one of their fights he tore up Clara's 'private papers, including her marriage-lines [or marriage certificate] and took the photos of himself, which he gave to a girl named Ilma Vaughan.'[59] Clara hired a private detective and clairvoyant called Madame Laetitia, who lived in Short Street in Redfern, to confirm her suspicions. Pen and notebook in hand, Madame Laetitia fluttered across streets, melted into crowds and lurked in shadows in pursuit of Ilma and Myles. She followed them through the gleaming glass doors of the brand-new Hotel Metropole and interviewed cleaners after they had left, who testified to seeing Myles leave Ilma's room at 5 a.m.[60] Madame Laetitia silently slipped on board a ferry that carried Myles and Ilma from Circular Quay to Mosman and then followed them to the shore, where she busily recorded their frolic in her notebook. There were no letters written by Myles submitted into evidence, but Clara's evidence, combined with that of Ilma's, suggests that while Ilma may have had very few feelings for Myles, Myles was seemingly enamoured of her. Why would he then abuse someone he professed to want to marry?

It's possible that sexual violence was the dark side of Myles' benevolence: having bought Ilma with hotels, gifts and living expenses he now owned her and could dispose of her as he wished. And being young, poor and friend-less, Ilma made an easy target. The disparity between their class positions was also undoubtedly a factor. Myles had employed Ilma's sister as a governess and her family was financially indebted to him, possibly creating paternal-istic relations of beneficence and authority on one side and obeisance on the other. Ilma was not a domestic servant, but she might have had a lot in common with the centuries of servant women before her whose bodies were regarded as the property of their masters or who had fallen for their whis-pered promises of marriage.

But reading through other breach of promise cases from this period, and turning our mind to literature, we see that coercion was not the sole preserve of gentlemanly seducers and penurious girls. Sexual violence against women transcended class and was built into cultural scripts of seduction. In Casanova, for instance, sex was likened to conquest: 'you have to rush modesty by example, leading over the barrier of shame and victory is certain'.[61] And as historian Joanna Bourke has argued in her his-tory of rape: 'nineteenth century Penny Dreadfuls recounted stories of lust and violation in gruesome detail. Romances lovingly depict their heroines being "ravished" against their will'.[62] Turning to breach of promise cases from the period we see how these tropes worked their way into the court-ships of the respectable poor, justifying sexual violence. 'I asked him what he meant treating me in the way he did at Pinda,' testified Ms Pascoe in an 1882 suit after telling the court that the defendant had held her hands down and violently raped her during a walk through the country.[63] The defend-ant, a clerk, allegedly replied that 'this was his idea of real love'.[64] The 1903 case Yeo v Fox involved Mr Fox, a grazier, coming into Ms Yeo's room, plac-ing his hand over her mouth and raping her, followed by a flurry of love letters ending with 'a thousand kisses and tons of love from your darling boy, George'.[65] Tropes of coercive seduction made sense in a culture that equated femininity with sexual modesty and eroticised male dominance; there was little scope for female initiatory desire. They worked to convert non-consent into consent and gave rapists a narrative to offer to the courts.

The normalisation of coercion as a part of romance also helps us to explain how Ilma, Petronella and Myles could have happily breakfasted together the very day after he had allegedly raped Ilma. This is not to suggest that there was social consensus on the matter. Violence chafed against middle-class beliefs in companionate marriage as well as models of masculinity based on affective restraint, and by the 1890s social reformers were recasting non-consensual seduction as violence, not romance. Sexual violence was subject to contestation and breach of promise plaintiffs, like Ilma, who told their stories of abuse in court were part of a growing chorus of protest against male sexual entitlement.

It wasn't just cultural narratives that legitimised Myles' violence. Law also played a part. Let's return to Myles holding up Ilma's hand, pointing to the engagement ring and claiming that he couldn't be charged because he had made a promise of marriage. It's a scenario that is almost illegible to us today; promising to marry someone doesn't mean that you can rape them. Even legal historians would have difficulty understanding it, given we tend to begin our analysis of marital violence at the altar, not at courtship. Historians who have sought to understand how rape in marriage was legally justified usually start with Lord Hale's dictum in 1736: 'the husband cannot be guilty of a rape committed by himself upon his lawful wife, for by their mutual consent and contract, the wife hath given up herself in this kind unto her husband, which she cannot retract.'[66] The husband and wife entered into a contract whose terms were written by the state, and which neither party could alter or leave.[67] A husband could not rape his wife because rape was an act of trespass and he couldn't trespass upon property he already owned.

What fascinates me about Myles' justification for raping Ilma is that it suggests that the rules of coverture that allowed men to rape their wives began not with marriage but with courtship. And we find, looking at other breach of promise cases, that Myles was not unusual in thinking that the promise of marriage retrospectively legitimised his violence. In *Bawden v Pascoe* (1882) the plaintiff reported that the defendant said to her before raping her: 'I promised you I would marry you and once I make a promise I keep it.' She resisted and told him she would scream, to which he responded, 'people would not think anything the worse of him.'[68] Legal commentary in newspapers echoed these views. Relatedly, betrothed women in the nineteenth century could not dispose of their own property without their fiancés' consent.[69] Not just marriage, but a *promise* of marriage, made women's bodies and their possessions the property of their suitors.

How did a promise of marriage come to have this significance? We need to go back to ecclesiastical law to understand it. Prior to the Interregnum (which is when the ecclesiastic courts were first closed down in England), promises to marry were separated into two kinds: promises made in the present tense, which were regarded as a valid and indissoluble marriage[70]; and promises to marry made in the future tense, which would not be enforced unless they had been followed by sexual intercourse, after which the promise constituted an indissoluble marriage.[71] That is, a promise of marriage could mean marriage, and marriage, according to the sacramental view, gave the husband dominion over the wife's body.

The legal construction of promises to marry as creating a 'valid marriage' persisted after the ecclesiastic courts closed and the action moved to contract under the common law. Nineteenth-century legal treatises noted that sex performed under a promise of marriage was to be treated the same as sex in marriage: 'if the suitor renewed his promise of marriage after the illicit intercourse had taken place, the subsequent promise would be binding.'[72] The darker side of this logic is that it gave men sexual rights to women's bodies.[73] A promise of marriage could retrospectively erase the fact of sexual violence.

This also helps us to explain why Ilma Vaughan's lawyers categorised the Mount Victoria rape as part of the breach of promise action and the rape in the park as an assault. At first this was troubling to me – why would they only be holding McRae responsible for the assault in the Domain, particularly given the assault in the Mount Victoria house had the corroborating evidence of Ilma's mother? The answer seems to be that they accepted Myles' reasoning: a ring and a promise of marriage legitimised what would otherwise have been rape. Justice Innes, when later commenting on the case, also affirmed this reasoning: 'One would suppose that a mother who valued the character and happiness of her daughter would have insisted upon something very definite being done in the way of reparation. She would tell him: "You are going to marry my daughter and that is the best reparation you can make for the outrage."'[74] Nobody considers the possibility of criminal prosecution for rape. Myles' violence may have been a product of individual impulse, but it was buttressed by law and culture.

The defence, of course, arrived at very different conclusions. They denied the violence, calling into question Ilma's credibility and suggesting that if the violence did happen, it was legitimate because Ilma was the 'jezebel of Sydney'.[75]

*   *   *

Preparing to cross-examine Ilma, Myles' barrister, Mr Want, paced around the court like a lion tamer: twirled black moustache, theatrical eyebrows and a shiny bald head popping out of his flapping black cape.[76] He had a thick pile of Ilma's letters in his hand.

'Did you have anything more to do with Myles after he told you in Manly that he was just fooling with you and was not in fact divorced?'

'No, nothing,' she replied.

To establish her case, Ilma needed to show that she always believed that Myles was capable of marriage and that, upon being disabused of this idea, she broke contact with him.

Mr Want opened the first letter and began to read:

5th June 1890.
Clifton House, Manly
My dear Myles,
I received your letters alright, but as I told you before, I cannot pay my debts unless you send me five pounds more, because I cannot go without decent clothes. I never dress gaudily, because I am too much of a lady for that, but if you have any sense you will agree with me that I can't do without clothes. You know very well that if I could get the money anywhere else I would. I suppose you think I delight in asking you for it. I cannot tell you what I feel when I have to ask you for it, but I must remember I am writing to a door or some other dumb article. [77]

'It is no handwriting of mine,' Ilma insisted, as soon as Mr Want finished reading. She needed to deny it because the date was incriminating: it was written weeks after Myles had told her he was not divorced. Mr Want moved on to the next letter, written by Ilma to her mother a day after the previous letter, and which she admitted to writing:

Dear Mother,
I had just finished writing the few lines that I sent you when Mr George Tindall, the one who wants to marry me, came in. He was delighted to see me, he said, looking so well. He wishes me to marry him. But I for my part, prefer a very handsome young man who is after me, a Mr Ted Baker, and I think more of Mr Baker's little finger than Mr Tyndall's whole body ...

Mr Baker took me to a grand concert last night and saw me home, which we did not reach until 12 o'clock. I was very prettily dressed in a cream dress with pink camellias in my hair ... Mr McRae is very anxious for me to marry one or the other, but you know, mamma, flirting is delightful and more so when one is young ...[78]

This letter went to the question of Ilma's character and credibility, which meant her chastity, in the most expansive sense of the word, including her friendships, her flirtations, what she wore and what time she arrived home. Yes, Ilma said, she had always led a pure life up to the time the defendant violated her. Yes, Mr Curwin did ask her to marry him, but she refused. And yes, he did want to put his arm around her waist, but she would not let him.

Mr Want opened another letter: 'I wish I had never come to see my relations as I most foolishly did,' he read. 'I am worried out of my mind and nobody to care for me. If I had never seen Thomas Bray I would have been very different; but I suppose I shall always be the jezebel of Sydney.'[79]

'Objection!' Ilma's solicitor, Mr Gannon, leapt to his feet. 'If these letters were said to be in the Plaintiff's handwriting, she ought to be allowed to see the contents of them.'

Justice Innes agreed: 'They may or may not turn out to be absolute forgeries concocted for the purposes of this case. It is grossly unfair. Why not show the letters to her first and give her an opportunity of seeing whether it is in her writing or not? Assuming that it is true what she says, that she, a mere child, outraged as she has been, basely corrupted ...'

'I am taking a course which is always taken,' Mr Want replied as Ilma inspected the letters.

'I never wrote that,' Ilma said decisively.

Mr Want continued. 'Did you ever write this to Mr McRae: "I know that I am not a good woman. I have been spoilt from my childhood. My grandmother's words come back to me now. She said, 'before you saw your brothers you were innocent as an angel.' I am very miserable. I wish I was dead, only when I think of you, who have been so kind to me I want to live."'[80]

'I did not write that,' Ilma retorted. Mr Want handed her the letter for closer inspection. Yes, she admitted, the handwriting was hers, but she 'must not have been in her proper senses ... I have no past life to be ashamed of at all ... No man touched me till Myles McRae did.' The reference to her brother, she said, was in relation to him swearing. And no, she did not write to Myles after the assault in the domain, she 'merely wrote for money.'[81]

Mr Want continued to read Ilma's letters to Myles: 'Think of me if you can as a girl who was innocence. Such a lot of badness always seems to cross my path. Henceforth I will try to turn over a new leaf and try to think of religion. I am always thinking of Thomas Bray.' Ilma chuckled: 'It's true, I am always thinking of Thomas Bray.' A final letter written in magniloquent prose ended abruptly with the words: 'For God's sake come and bring me five pounds' and sent howls of mirth through the courtroom.[82]

Justice Innes banged his gavel.

'If that improper conduct is repeated here, I shall have the court cleared,' he warned. 'Here is one of the saddest tales from whatever aspect it is looked at, that was ever revealed in a court of justice, yet there are people calling themselves men who laugh, gazing here with prurient eyes on this poor girl under this terrible ordeal. It is a scandal to manhood. It is no laughing matter that this poor girl should have been ruined and left in distress and despair.'[83]

Justice Innes was exhausted. There was still half an hour remaining, but he had had enough. 'The air in this court is stifling,' he declared, and then, looking at the rows of barristers in the gallery, he winked; 'and this court is crowded with a lot of people who seem to rank among the unemployed.' Laughter broke out and they adjourned until Monday, 10.30 a.m.[84]

\*   \*   \*

The newspapers loved Ilma Vaughan. One referred to her as 'the gentle Ilma', another printed her portrait, and many more applauded her composure.[85] Where the testimony delivered on the first day sounded rehearsed, her letters and response to cross-examination sparkled with spontaneity and dramatic richness. To my mind, Ilma saw herself as a romantic heroine, bejewelled and beloved by all, swanning from grand concert to romantic promenade, followed by a train of male votaries. She did not regard her acceptance of Myles' offer of marriage as prohibiting her from frolicking in love's pastures; she obsesses over Thomas Bray and, in her own words 'is always full of suitors for my hand.'[86] She understands that her sexuality gives her power over men, and she wields it quite magnificently. 'Flirting is delightful', as she says, particularly when it pays for expenses and elevates her from suburban Granville into a lofty world of hotels and balls. But it would be a mistake to celebrate this as an unbounded expression of agency. It's obvious from her letters that Ilma has no way of valuing herself outside of male attention. Dependent upon men for survival, she plays the part which they expect of her. Ilma, in Roland Barthes' words, 'loves in order to receive recognition'. 'She knows herself to be an object but cannot think of any destination for herself other than that of an ornament in the museum of the masters.'[87] And it is Ilma's status as an object that explains why she so often conceives of herself in a passive register, photographed, acted upon rather than acting, seen by others rather than seeing.

Lamenting how 'such a lot of badness always seems to come my way'[88] was also a way for Ilma to navigate the sexual double standard, which we see in panicked real-life form when she writes of being 'worried out of my mind' about her sexual reputation.[89] Her flirtations may have given her power, but they also skated perilously close to promiscuity and its attendant social ostracism. Ilma needed to disavow her sexual volition to maintain claims to chastity, which is also what Innes does when he garners the sympathy of the court for her by suggesting that she was a 'mere child' subject to 'outrages'.[90] By the late nineteenth century, sexology acknowledged that women like Ilma experience sexual pleasure and shifts in courtship allowed her to have serial romances, but marriage remained her primary purpose in life and chastity was crucial to securing a partner.[91] As a poor migrant woman, Ilma's entire economic and social future and that of her family depended on her making a good match. The pressure would have been enormous.

By invoking Ilma's prior sexual history and her multiple flirtations, the defence was implying that she must have yielded voluntarily. If rape was a crime understood as a trespass upon another man's property, a promiscuous woman could not be raped, as nobody in particular owned her; she was collectively owned. Women continue to suffer this kind of public humiliation when they attempt to hold perpetrators of sexual violence to account, and society continues to circulate narratives that work to stop us from believing them. Unjust as it is, the idea that a promiscuous woman is somehow complicit in her rape is comprehensible to contemporary readers. The truly shocking part of Ilma's cross-examination is the idea that being a victim of child sexual assault also destroyed her chastity. The references to Ilma's brothers 'spoiling' her continued throughout the hearing, with Ilma insisting that she meant that they swore in front of her. She denied the abuse, confirming that 'no man touched me till Myles McRae'.[92] But a range of witnesses, including Myles, testified that she had told them she had been 'violated by her brother'.[93] Both sides agreed that this evidence destroyed Ilma's character. The defence introduced it as a justification for the breach of promise, while the case for the plaintiff queried why Myles had continued to be engaged to

Ilma after being made aware of her assault: 'As soon as you heard a suggestion about her moral character you left?' the counsel for the plaintiff asked. Myles assented, only to be ambushed later when it was proved that he continued to have a relationship with her after she had told him of her brother's assault.[94] Curiously, the most humane response to Ilma's abuse came from Myles: 'I took compassion on the girl and felt a loathsomeness for her brother. The story she told me was enough to make a stone weep.'[95] But in law, where questions of female character still rested on chastity, there was no scope for compassion or for a recognition of the subjective impact of Ilma's injury; even Ilma frames the attack from an outsider's perspective: her body has been 'spoiled' for the use of others. Victorian-era constructions of femininity as chaste, pious, submissive and fragile meant rape constituted a form of contamination, in which the sin of the perpetrator was shared by his victim.[96] Rape was not so much a form of violence as a moral scandal, one which harmed the victim's reputation.

The defence also used Ilma's poverty and her economic dependence upon Myles as proof of her unchastity. Witnesses in the hearing later reported that Ilma had told them her family was so penurious her mother wanted her to work as a prostitute. There was an implied double meaning in Ilma's letter stating that she 'never dresses gaudily', which at the time meant engaging in sex work.[97] With this evidence, the defence hoped to reduce the jury's sympathy for Ilma. Prostitutes could not be raped as they were already considered common property, and an impoverished woman, even if she were not a sex worker, might be considered habituated to violence. As Georges Vigarello has argued in relation to rape in early-modern France, 'poverty never encouraged vigilance of judges whereas wealth predisposed them to indulgence'.[98] This is why the defence introduced evidence of Ilma begging Myles for money, writing letter after letter asking him to take care of her debts.

The curious part in Ilma's trial is that the strategy didn't work – her letters asking for money were interpreted instead as a sign of Myles' neglect. As the gossipy tabloid the Sydney *Truth* commented: Myles had '"engaged" himself to marry her ... The mother and daughter seem to have accepted the situation after a while, and the girl lived under his protection for a time. Even in this Myles McRae proved true to his nature, for he actually left her to run up a bill for a boarding house, and when she visited him at the Parliament House he abused and threatened her, and refused to pay her debt – a debt really incurred by him.'[99] Once again, coverture seems to have extended to courtship, meaning a betrothed woman's debts were considered her suitor's responsibility. Legal texts were explicit about the extension of this principle to cohabiting couples, as treatise writer Josiah William Smith explained: the 'law allowed for coverture for debts' he wrote 'in instances where the couple lived together as if man and wife'.[100] Blackstone also stated that husbands were responsible for all debts incurred by the woman before marriage.[101] This principle made sense in a context where women were denied access to a liveable wage, but it was also a source of humiliation. We feel the pangs of women's abjection in Ilma's letters: 'You know very well that if I could get the money anywhere else I would. I suppose you think I delight in asking you for it. I cannot tell you what I feel when I have to ask you for it ...'[102]

\*   \*   \*

By day four of the hearing, whatever confidence Myles once felt had vanished. He complained of being tormented by insomnia, waking in a twist of sweaty sheets over the last few nights, wishing for death.[103] His prediction that everyone would take his side could not have been more wrong. Outside the courthouse Australia was in the grip of a moral panic over the vulnerability of factory girls to male predation, as urbanisation and industrialisation sent women into streets, factories, offices and parks, beyond the 'protection' of respectable men. Social Purity societies such as the Society for the Promotion of Morality were preaching 'manly self-restraint' in order to 'protect both women and men from vice and disease', while feminists were seeking legal protections for women.[104] Prompted by British legal reform, legislation had been introduced into the NSW parliament to increase the age of consent from thirteen to sixteen,[105] and in 1887 the Seduction Punishment Bill was tabled, providing for criminal penalties for seduction, or sex induced by a man under a promise of marriage,[106] possibly inspired by similar legislation in some American states.[107] What's more, the eastern colonies had just plummeted into an economic depression caused by the avarice of land speculators like Myles. In 1892, at this particular moment in history, he looked like an archetypal villain.

Justice Innes called Myles McRae to the stand.[108]

Dressed in a well-cut suit, occasionally dabbing his face with a handkerchief,[109] Myles told a story of personal benevolence and generous displays of friendship towards the Vaughan family. He said that when they first arrived on the doorstep of the real estate agency he owned in 1884, he found them a house, employed Ilma's sister Nina as a governess and lent them money.

They disappeared for five years, but when he next received a letter from Petronella in 1889 he rushed to her aid and, upon finding her 'ill and in reduced circumstances', lent her money. Petronella, he said, 'expressed sympathy with him in his trouble with his wife.' She said she could 'get good evidence for him' because Nina had kept a diary during her time as governess and 'knew that his wife had split his head open with an ornament'. Having failed to defend himself at his divorce hearing, Myles was using the breach of promise action to set the record straight.

As for the story told by Ilma Vaughan and her mother, there was 'not a word of truth in it'. In fact, 'it was pure friendship that urged him in his acts of kindness' towards Ilma. He had never given her a ring and 'the statement about his locking her in his room, tearing her clothes and assaulting her was absolutely false. He had nothing to do with the girl the whole time he was at Mount Victoria.' The time they spent together 'was innocent', although marred somewhat by Ilma's tendency towards fabulation, demonstrated most spectacularly by the picnic invitation she extended to him at Mossman's Bay on behalf of 'the son of a Lord'. When he got there, he said, 'there was no picnic, no host and no son of a Lord'.

'Once and for all,' Justice Innes asked with gravity, 'I understand you to say that you never on any occasion took any liberties with her, either with or without her consent – never assaulted her or touched her in any way?'

'Never.'

Mr Gannon rose to commence his cross-examination.

'Did you defend the divorce action?'

'No.'

'Was adultery one of the charges?'

'Yes.'

'With whom?'

'Ilma Vaughan.'

Justice Innes butted in: 'And yet with your knowledge that the present case was pending, you allowed the suit to go undefended?'

'I took the advice of my solicitor.'

Gannon continued: 'Did you see Madame Laetitia at the Metropole?'

'No, I did not know her by sight.'

'Did you know that she swore in the Divorce Court that she saw you misconducting yourself with the plaintiff at Mossman's?'

'It's false, I don't believe she was at Mossman's.'

'Did you escort about a young woman from the Fresh Food and Ice Co.?'

'No.'

'Why did the servant Catherine Smith leave? Was it not because of your indecent behaviour?'

'No.'

'Did you not often pass through the house in a state of nudity?'

Myles' face flushed red and his voice rose.

'NEVER.'

'And what about the evidence given in the Divorce Court about your … health?'

'I appeal to Your Honor for protection!' Myles howled. 'Dr Reid swore falsely! It is absolutely not true.' And from here nobody could catch what Myles said. As one newspaper reported, 'he went off into a wild declamation of the circumstances attending his domestic affairs and worked himself up into a state of frenzy.' Justice Innes banged his gavel and called him to order, but Myles bellowed over the top of him. Mr Want admonished him, but Myles could hear nobody other than himself. 'If the witness is not in a fit state to be examined the case will have to be adjourned,' Justice Innes declared. 'I wish I was dead,' Myles yelped. 'I haven't slept a wink all night.' He violently rubbed his face with his handkerchief and then collapsed in sobs.

'You were not so tender hearted when you saw your wife carried out of the Divorce Court,' Gannon lectured.

'That is false,' Myles replied balefully.

Justice Innes stood and walked away from the bench.

'You must restrain yourself or leave the court,' warned Mr Want.

Myles took a sip of water and wiped his brow.

'There are no further questions.'[110]

\* \* \*

The rest of the day was taken up with evidence given by the lodging-house owners with whom Ilma had lived – all of them testifying to her bad character. Mr Twomer said that she would 'spread tales that she was going to marry several influential persons, including Lord Bertie, Hon. R. Carrington and other such personages.' 'Her language was not altogether choice' and 'she used to read to him letters written by herself, which she said were offers of marriage she had received.' 'On one occasion he saw Miss Vaughan standing in the backyard with a young man, who had his arms around her,' and after this he asked her to leave. 'And that so shocked you that you gave them notice to clear out?' asked Innes. 'No wonder you're not a married man when you are so easily shocked!' The gallery laughed at his prudishness.

Annie Raynor, a lodging-house owner and wife of the district registrar at Granville, said that Ilma claimed her brother had 'taken a knife and threatened her life and ... that her mother and brother ill-treated her because she could not make money by getting married.' Annie said Ilma had admitted to lying to her family about her romantic life, saying 'she was going to marry wealthy people', which was untrue; she wrote a confession to her family, which she read aloud to Annie. Finally, another lodging-house operator, Kate Mary Hartley, said that 'when she came home she saw Ilma going in to lunch with her hair dressed all in flowers'. Mrs Hartley spoke to her and told her that she could not go to dinner that way. Ilma remained for four or five days and was asked to leave after Clara McRae informed her of Ilma's affair with Myles. Ilma begged to be allowed to remain for the night as she had no money, which Mrs Hartley permitted. 'Except her peculiar way of dressing,' Mrs Hartley admitted, 'she saw nothing wrong about her.'[111]

\* \* \*

Myles' and Ilma's talent for fiction made it challenging to determine the truth. 'There were great improbabilities on both sides,' declared Justice Innes, which meant character was crucial to assessments of each side's credibility. If we were to interpret the fact that Myles did not seek to defend the adultery charge as an admission that he and Ilma were in an adulterous relationship, then the question a contemporary lawyer would pose would be whether Ilma consented to have sex, which would require a forensic examination of her mental state. Breach of promise of marriage actions, however, downplayed questions of consent and emphasised questions of character. As we can see in the cross-examination of Myles, Justice Innes didn't care whether Ilma had consented: 'Did you behave improperly towards her with or without her consent?' he asked. His concern was with Myles' behaviour and Myles' sexual history. Some feminist academics have suggested that breach of promise cases put men in the spotlight, making them bear the burden of proof. Scholar Estelle Freedman argues that breach of promise defined 'the problem in terms of male words and actions rather than female chasteness or virginity, effectively putting the onus on men to explain why marriage had not occurred after sexual relations ...' Breach of promise, she argues, was a kind of salvation for women, a historical example of how the law developed an alternative framework to punish sexual violence.[112]

While it's certainly refreshing to see Myles subject to the kind of examination about his sexual history that women have always had to endure, the testimony from the boarding-house owners shows that the law, at least in Australia, was just as concerned with female chastity. Ilma was said to be 'unchaste and of bad character' because she wore flowers in her hair when leaving the house, because a man had put his arm around her waist, because she fought with her mother, because she was the victim of child sexual assault, because she swore and because she invented aristocratic romantic suitors. Judging by previous breach of promise cases, this expansive definition of bad character is not surprising. In the mid-nineteenth century a woman who laughed too loudly in public, wore men's trousers or swore could be found to be unchaste.[113]

Nonetheless, Justice Innes defended Ilma's character. In his instructions to the jury, given on day five of the hearing, Innes noted that while the defence had introduced evidence of Ilma's ostentatious dress and coquetry in an effort to 'condemn' her, 'it actually said nothing against the girl's character'.[114] Yes, Ilma was 'flighty and engaged in flirtation, but did not the diary entries and letters show that she had regard to her character?'[115] Given judges are weighted with the responsibility of expressing community values, Innes' defence of Ilma suggests that definitions of character were in the process of change. He was on the side of those seeking to narrow the definition of female good character from a wide range of supposedly 'unfeminine' behaviour to the narrower question of chastity, which Ilma frets over in her letters.

Myles' reputation, on the other hand, had been buried in the divorce court. The 'Defendant ... came into court convicted on his own admission of adultery with this young woman and cruelty towards his wife, and yet he wept here about his wounded character', he fulminated. This was not to suggest that they should believe Ilma. Her story 'was highly improbable', Innes said, 'and under ordinary circumstances it was extremely unlikely that the assault was committed. The jury must ask themselves whether it was likely or probable that if this girl was subjected to the outrage which she and her mother declared she was, the defendant would have been allowed to remain an inmate of the house for the rest of the evening and the whole of next day, and that the mother would have allowed her daughter to go wandering about the bush with the defendant on Sunday ... It was for the jury to say whether they were satisfied with their explanation.'[116]

In the end, the jury believed Ilma, which suggests that for certain segments of the population coercion was still a normal part of courtship. Ilma was awarded £500 damages for breach of promise of marriage, although the jury found for Myles on the assault in the Domain.[117]

*     *     *

Court verdicts can leave us with a false sense of triumph. The result is declared, the victorious party grins and hugs their supporters, the loser slumps in his chair, the judge sweeps away in his folds of black cloth and the newspapers report on the proceedings as though they were sport: someone won and someone lost. In this case, we could leave Ilma, Clara and Myles, satisfied that justice was served. Ilma blinks in the midday sun on King Street with £500 in her pocket, Clara has ample money to survive with her two daughters, all of them safe from Myles' tyranny, and Myles is sent out to pasture in some small country town, where he dies impoverished by court costs.

When we look beyond the immediate verdict, however, we find a more complicated picture. Like many abusive men, Myles' desire for dominance and control could not countenance the higher authority of the law. He launched an appeal against the breach of promise damages award, which resulted in Ilma's £500 being reduced to £179 when the Prothonotary awarded Myles costs for the assault charge. After this, the only further trace I could find of Ilma was in the Gosford New South Wales Pioneer Register, where she is recorded as having married Davide Talarico in 1899. She spent the rest of her short life in the labour of care, raising six children until her death in 1918.[118]

Myles, predictably, also did not respect the court's verdict in the alimony case. The McRae file contains a packet of letters sent between solicitors that show how pyrrhic court victories can be. Clara began court proceedings against Myles for unpaid alimony in October 1892 and he paid the full amount after being threatened with contempt of court. But this was still not the end. A statement in the file written by Clara, dated one year later, October 1893, shows that £114 were still owing. 'That I verily believe therefore the said respondent is well able to pay the said alimony but that he desires to put me to as much trouble and inconvenience as he can by reason of his non-payment thereof,' she wrote. Myles must have paid the money, as the letters then stop. There are no further records of Myles and Clara's intimate life together except for Myles' will, in which he left everything to Clara, and his tombstone, where she is referred to as his 'dearly loved wife'.[119]

Clara and Myles reconciled, but we can only speculate as to how and why. It's possible that he reformed his behaviour and they ended up in a harmonious marriage. It's also possible, and in fact more likely, that Clara could not economically survive without him and she found life without her three sons unbearable. Myles may also have missed his daughters, although his working hours probably meant he spent little time with his family. Even if Clara did not return to Myles entirely of her own choosing, I like to think she would have returned a stronger woman than before. This may be wildly hopeful, but I couldn't help but smile to see that when Clara signed her last alimony claim she did so with a confident, steady hand.

As for Myles, public memory is short when it comes to gender violence by bourgeois men. Myles was mayor of Kogarah in Sydney's south from 1895–96 and again in 1901–04. His business prospered and his wealth continued to grow until he died, now nicknamed 'Myles the Millionaire', at the age of eighty-one in 1926.[120] His fortunes were celebrated in the major national newspapers and his annus horribilis vanished from the public record. Clara died six months after Myles, and you can see their graves in the Wonona cemetery today. Myles is buried in the Presbyterian section and Clara is buried a safe distance away in the Catholic section.

*   *   *

I came to the story of Myles, Clara and Ilma through Ilma's breach of promise case, and found myself captivated by its historical peculiarities: the strangely nonchalant way in which Ilma described sexual violence; the court's acceptance that a promise of marriage permitted rape. And then there was the paradox that runs through all stories of intimate violence, of how our most elevated ideas of love, sex, marriage or courtship could be coupled with coercion and cruelty. Unlike the question so often asked of victims of rape and domestic violence today – why didn't you fight back or leave? – the question I wanted to ask was: how can we explain men's violence towards those they profess, or once professed, to love? And at a time when marriage law sanctioned intimate violence, why did some men choose to inflict pain upon their intimates while others did not?

Myles' personal susceptibility to humiliation and his tendency to respond to any challenge to his authority with violence are threads that runs through this chapter. Yet Myles also felt entitled to dominate because for a large part of his life, law and society expected this of men. Law sanctioned behaviour that we recognise today as domestic abuse. As Ilma's case shows, coverture extended beyond the marital bed and into the realm of courtship. The fiction of marital unity that allowed husbands to rape their wives and to control the family income did not disappear with reforms to divorce law or the *Married Women's Property Act*. Its shadow is long – extending well into the twentieth century – and cast a chill over courting couples.

The story of Myles McRae is worth remembering as male violence is once again a topic of popular and parliamentary debate and women are demanding a right to sexual self-sovereignty. His story reveals the public and personal conditions that made male violence possible in the late-nineteenth century and humbles us in our assertions that the #MeToo moment is 'unprecedented'. Women much less privileged than us have long called upon the state to restructure the rules of intimacy and curtail male entitlement, yet Myles' rise back to the ranks of respectability warns us against any premature celebrations. Patriarchy has a remarkable capacity to dust itself off and get back up again. If historical amnesia is part of the masculinist armoury against women, then stories like this are part of our arsenal against forgetting.

7.

# 'A Hong Kong romance':
# Race, Religion and the Politics of Desire

## (*Lucas v Palmer*, 1892)

There was boisterous weather across Australia on the day of James Lucas hearing. It was 28 June 1892, and the newspapers howled with stories of inclemency: boorish winds had knocked a chimney stack over in Ballarat and killed two men; sheeting rain had blinded drivers in Melbourne, causing buggies to collide; snow had been dumped on inland towns, and the climate in Sydney was 'rough'.[1]

Having spent the last fifteen years in the tropics, James Lucas, formerly James Sorab Lucas and before that Jamsetjee Sorabjee, probably felt it. The NSW District Court was not built with a view to comfort. Its sandstone façade, high shingled roof and cavernous rooms were originally intended as convict barracks, and later as an asylum for female immigrants. Now part of a complex of government buildings, including a vaccination centre for smallpox, the court was impressive, gothic and cold. Like the building's former residents, James was in transit. Right now, he probably longed to go home to Hong Kong.[2]

James would have been seated behind his barrister, Richard Colonna-Close, a plump, genteel chap known for his long brown whiskers, eccentric clothes and 'flowery oratory'. Colonna-Close was pitched against defence solicitor Harold Morgan, a man with a thin moustache and a face that settled naturally into an ironic smile. Perched above them on a wooden dais was Justice Gibson – thick black eyebrows offset by a cloud of silvery hair. Clara Palmer, twenty-two years old, 'prepossessing' and 'becomingly dressed', would have been seated to his left.[3]

Colonna-Close stood to give his opening address. Like every barrister hired to represent a male plaintiff in a breach of promise action before him – and there had been only five in the last century – he began with the obvious. No, he said, it was not usual for a man to sue a woman for breach of promise of marriage. But James Lucas did not want a 'large sum of money', just enough to justify bringing the action and to show 'that men were naturally as liable to attachment to women as women were to men'.[4] It was, after all, the 1890s, and conceptions of essential differences between men and women were being challenged. To be wounded in love, Colonna-Close implied, was human, and James had suffered emotionally and financially when he pursued Clara to Australia. He then narrated James and Clara's story to the jury.

In 1887, 28-year-old James Lucas was running a successful business as a merchant in Hong Kong when Clara Palmer, an Englishwoman, moved into a lodging house next door. With his high cheekbones and glimmering brown eyes, James was regarded by some as 'comely', and Clara no doubt agreed. Seventeen years old, she was living in Hong Kong with her sister and brother-in-law, Mr and Mrs Curiambux. Her family had been in the food shipping and import business and were now trying their luck in Hong Kong as restaurateurs. Both single and eminently eligible, Clara and James fell in love.

Over the next year and a half, James consulted letter-writing manuals to give English form to his feelings, and Clara responded with torrid epistles of her own. She adorned herself in the silver bangles he gave her, and friends saw them driving together through the twinkling streets of Wan-Chai. A friendship developed between James and Mr and Mrs Curiambux, and it was eventually decided that they would board in James' house at a rate of £5 per week. After only two months, Clara and James became engaged at Clara's urging, and James showered her with presents. Convinced that marriage was a certainty, James tolerated the non-payment of board by Clara's family for some time, but after sixteen months and not a penny passing hands, he took action.

In 1889, James burst into the quarters of his house occupied by the Curiambux, accompanied by a bailiff. He had taken the matter to court and secured a verdict in his favour. Mr Curiambux, having received the summons weeks earlier, had fled to Macao – geographically close to Hong Kong but jurisdictionally far from the reach of English law – leaving his wife and Clara alone in the apartment. Before leaving, Clara chastised James for resorting to such 'ungentlemanly' behaviour as litigation and warned that suing her family had caused her 'feelings to cool'.[5]

For two years, James heard nothing from Clara, until in 1891 she returned to Hong Kong in search of him. She was now twenty-one and no longer under the control of her family: marriage, she told James, was something she would decide for herself. She said that she and the Curiambux were moving to Australia, and she discussed the possibility of James following so that they could begin a new life together. She sat on his knee, kissed him and told him that if he behaved himself like a gentleman and settled the case against her brother-in-law, ensuring the warrant for his arrest was withdrawn, they would marry. James, elated yet cautious, agreed but asked for a letter affirming her promise of marriage. He even gave Clara an example of the kind of letter he wanted: 'I should have married you in Hong Kong,' he suggested she write. 'If you do love me come over to Australia and I give you my sincere word and promise I must marry you there in any part of Australia.' It was a contract disguised as a love letter.[6]

Clara responded with a more candid missive of her own:

My own darling James,
I would prefer, my darling, to express my feelings in the way I think best. I really do not think a love letter composed by a third party should be made use of by anyone who wished to convey their truthful sentiments. You will, I am sure, appreciate this letter much more than the one you asked me to copy and address to you. You have shown yourself sufficient now, my dearest, to be deserving of all my attention and respect, and if you will only continue to conduct yourself on similar lines in the future how happy you will make me …

Hardly effusive, Clara at least sounded sincere, and James, upon reading her words, felt satisfied. He discharged Curiambux's debts, withdrew the warrant, sold his businesses, packed up his house and bought tickets for a steamer to Australia. Clara continued to write to him from Sydney, then Melbourne, although her ardour soon subsided. She warned that business was not good, and eventually she advised that he should not come to Australia at all. But it was too late. With Clara's letters in his suitcase, James sailed from Hong Kong for Melbourne in the summer of 1892.

As Colonna-Close explained to the jury: 'On arrival [James] discovered to his great sorrow that her affection for him had turned to coldness', so he came to court in search of 'something in the shape of cash as a balm to his wounded heart and as compensation for the loss he had sustained by giving up his Hong Kong business'.[7]

\*     \*     \*

*Lucas v Palmer* was the first interracial breach of promise case to be heard in an Australian court, and as journalists noted at the time, it 'reversed the usual order of things'.[8] Here was a love affair that crossed oceans and ethnicities, and where a man, rather than a woman, claimed hurt feelings. The newspapers, judging by their headlines, were uncertain how to describe it. Some resorted to racial binary: 'A Colored Lover and a White Girl'. Another focused on gender inversion: 'A Man Sues for Breach of Promise'. One invoked Orientalist titillation: 'A Hong-Kong Romance'. And another drew on the trope of universal, colour-blind love: 'Blighted Affections. He Wants Damages from His Sweet-Heart.'[9]

Australian reporters also weren't sure how to racially classify James. Some described him as 'coloured', others highlighted his religion ('he is a Hindoo'), and another speculated on his class ('a coloured gentleman').[10] Other papers, such as the *Newcastle Morning Herald* and the tabloid *Evening News*, did not mention race at all, captivated instead by the spectacle of a female defendant.[11] If there is one thing that the reporting of the case suggests, it is that the language of race in the 1890s was messy, plural and contested.[12] And this was even more so in the realm of love, where Orientalist cultural traditions sanctioning inter-racial desire rubbed against an evolving discourse of whiteness and blood purity. There is brow-furrowing in the reporting, but also winks and smiles. In the early 1890s, a romance between a European woman and a South Asian man might provoke amusement, anxiety or both.

If we examine legislation and political speeches, however, the view is quite different. *Lucas v Palmer* came at a time when white settler colonies such as Australia, America, Canada and New Zealand were erecting racially exclusive borders in defiance of the purported cosmopolitanism of empire. Four years after James' case, New South Wales would pass the *Coloured Races Restriction and Regulation Act*, extending immigration restrictions that had previously been applied to people from China to 'all persons belonging to any coloured race inhabiting the Continent of Asia or the Continent of Africa or any island adjacent thereto, or any island in the Pacific or Indian oceans'.[13] After this came the *Immigration Restriction Act* of 1901, shutting the nation's borders to 'Asiatics'.[14] The quest for racial homogeneity, write Marilyn Lake and Henry Reynolds, had the effect of categorising non-Europeans – previously recognised in their multiple identities as, for instance, Chinese, Hindu, Muslim, Malay, Thai, Congolese or Syrian – into one monolithic category: not-white.

A global colour line was being drawn: 'literacy tests, passports, surveillance, the census and the passport were all beginning to divide the world between white and not white.'[15] By the turn of the century, the formal equality of status once promised to all subjects of the British Empire had been challenged by the sovereign rights of nation states to racially exclude, discriminate and incarcerate. The freedom to travel and the right to high wages, good labour conditions and self-government were defined as the rights of white men. Racial plurality, of course, still existed; the White Australia Policy was an attempt to impose upon it a punitive and hierarchical racial binary.[16]

There was fear underpinning these laws – the military might of Japan, the unprecedented movement of non-Europeans around the world in search of better living conditions, and the economic threat this was seen to pose to white labour – and there was hubris. White people had begun to think of themselves as rather miraculous specimens, unique in their capacity for reason and self-government, elevated in their civilisation and, as racial scientists were beginning to argue, 'pure' of blood. Notions of white supremacy reinforced the idea that European love affairs were the pinnacle of tenderness, emotional refinement and economic security, contrasted with the masculine tyranny or libidinous excesses of non-Europeans. To this end, it was argued, whites should only marry among themselves. Any woman who envisaged herself as a 'worthy, prospective wife and mother' should not 'mate herself with a member of the lower race', declared an Australian book of marital advice in 1900: 'A Negro, A Hindoo and a Chinaman, although all civilised after a fashion, would no more be her husband than would an Australian black.'[17] Henry Parkes had anticipated anti-miscegenation laws in Australia in 1888 when he argued against the admission of any class of persons 'whom we are not prepared to advance to all our franchises, to all our privileges as citizens and to all our social rights, including the right of marriage'.[18] He would have been inspired by many southern states in America, which in the wake of emancipation had made it illegal for white men and women to marry African Americans, Native Americans, Asian people or people of mixed-descent, among others.[19] Interracial desire was seen as unnatural and as a source of racial degeneracy. The boundaries of legitimate sex, like the boundaries of the state, solidified around colour; whiteness became the natural homeland of romantic love.

In plotting out this wider context, I am drawing upon a vast body of work that has examined the rise of 'whiteness' as a privileged racial category at the dawn of the twentieth century.[20] But where does the story of James and Clara fit in? No newspaper expressed concern about racial degeneration, and there was no discussion of interracial romance as 'unnatural'. James' racial identity seemed unstable, defined by the malleable bonds of culture, language, religion or British imperial citizenship. As he would argue in a later court hearing, he was not 'black', but rather 'an Indian-born British subject'.[21] When considered in the context of other interracial breach of promise cases from the nineteenth and early twentieth centuries, *Lucas v Palmer* appears poised at a moment of transition: in the 1890s, racial identity was more flexible than it would be only a few decades later. The case also allows us insight into how race was articulated, enforced and contested, not simply through legislation, courts and conduct books, but through the private and personal languages of love.

## James and Clara in the witness box

*Lucas v Palmer* began with Colonna-Close's opening address, and James seated behind him, listening closely. This was not James' first time in court, so he felt confident taking part in proceedings, even interjecting when he thought Colonna-Close needed assistance.

Having given the jury a precis of the love affair, Colonna-Close opened one of the love letters in the bundle he held in his hands.

'You will see from the letters I will read to you,' he said, 'how the course of true love progresses and how the terms of endearment increase. This letter concludes with the words "Chin Chin,"' he remarked, smiling. 'I do not know what that means, but perhaps you do. I am not up with these little love passages and endearing expressions.' It was an effort to normalise, or more accurately whiten, James and Clara's relationship – to absorb evidence of cultural difference into the European diction of youthful love.

Unaware of this strategy, James sang out from his seat: 'Oh, that's Chinese for what you would call *ta ta*.' The courtroom burst into laughter.

Colonna-Close continued: 'The letters became more endearing,' especially when Clara pleaded with James to forgive her family's debt. And although she didn't write for the two years that she was in Macao, the engagement was immediately renewed when James and Clara met again in Hong Kong.[22] Colonna-Close then called James as the first witness to the stand.

James began his testimony by describinig how well the Curiambux family had first treated him, even saying that he was 'the only gentleman in Hong Kong'.

'Was that the defendant?' the judge asked, trying to pinpoint who had said what.

Yes, James replied, Clara had said it. She was 'always very pleased'. She was 'chatty' and wanted 'to marry me, my Lord'.

'Oh, I see,' the judge mused: 'she proposed to you.' The courtroom broke out in cackles. 'And what did you say?'

'I say yes. I will marry you.' One of the most significant moments of his life was reduced to a joke as the courtroom heaved with laughter. It was a response that would come to characterise the hearing, no matter how plainly factual the details of his love affair. James continued over the top of it, explaining how he had paid for Clara's passage to Australia and given her 'many presents' before she left. It was difficult to find her once he arrived in Australia, he said, but when they made contact he discovered that 'she was quite a different woman'.

'How do you mean?' asked the judge.

'Before she always run and kiss me,' James recalled. 'But this time she ask me to sit down, my lordship.' He tried to 'make love to her ... the same as I do before'. But Clara would not allow it. He reminded her of her promise, 'but she only laughed' at him and said nothing.

With James' examination over, Close ambled back to his chair and Mr Morgan took the floor for his cross-examination.

'Have you ever threatened Curiambux?' he asked.

'No,' James replied.

'How long did you know the defendant before you proposed to her?'

'She proposed to marry me,' James said; 'that was about two months after.'

'You wrote a number of letters to the defendant. Have you a large experience in writing love letters?'

'I take it from a book. A book I use ... I use this book in my business.' Laughter once again ricocheted around the gallery. Mr Morgan changed tack.

'Do you know about the Wanchai arson case?' he asked. Until this point, James had been unruffled by the questions and the humiliating laughter from the crowd. But this accusation was too much. His voice became loud and tense.

'I explain myself. It was a fire.'

'There was a charge of arson, and you were arrested, were you not?'

'It was a fire, yes, and the jury said: "not guilty." It was about a year ago.'

'Did you take any steps against Curiambux here? A summons in the Water Police Court?'

'Yes, and the magistrate non-suited [or dismissed the action] until the finish of this case.'

The cross-examination over, James walked back to his seat.[23]

\*   \*   \*

James' ethnicity was not an explicit focal point of the hearing. Neither Close nor Morgan noted that an interracial romance was an anomaly in an Australian court, and nothing was said directly about James' South Asian origins or his skin colour. But if we look closely at the language used in the hearing and the reaction of the gallery, it becomes apparent that both were saturated in presumptions of white superiority. Let's take a moment to examine how race and romance interacted in the hearing and how ideas of racial difference were affirmed or challenged by the language of love.

We can begin, perhaps counterintuitively, with laughter. What was so funny about James' translation of the Chinese phrase 'chin chin'? Why did the gallery laugh every time he opened his mouth? Henri Bergson's notion of laughter erupting from a 'collision between two discursive universes', or two antithetical ways of seeing the world, helps to explain the racial dynamics behind the laughter in James' case.[24] If a white male plaintiff would usually be laughed out of court, as the judge would later claim, it was because there was a disjuncture between what a man was supposed to be – emotionally restrained, powerful, stoic – and the amorously wounded, somewhat pathetic role that a breach of promise plaintiff was asked to play. For James, this was exacerbated by his supposed lack of linguistic competency. *The Daily Telegraph* published James' entire testimony, complete with his accent and creolised English, as well as the reaction of the court, while *The Leader* reported that he spoke English 'very lamely'.[25] This was the first time a person's accent was reported on in a breach of promise case in Australia, although the court would have heard a range of accents – English, Scottish, Irish and continental European – throughout the nineteenth century.[26]

It could be argued that this focus on English literacy as a signifier of whiteness was a uniquely late-nineteenth and early-twentieth century form of racism that found its most extreme manifestations in Australia's *Naturalisation Act* and the dictation test. Under the *Immigration Act*, migrants entering Australia were required to write fifty words in any European language, as chosen and dictated by an immigration officer. Between 1910 and 1949, nobody passed the test.[27] But an American case involving two African Americans reported in the Australian press in 1828 used precisely the same form of discrimination. The defendant 'knew all the "Massas" of the jury', wrote the reporter, adopting a Southern creole patois, which disappeared abruptly when the journalist realised that the two lovers 'probably spoke in

Dutch'. The lovers' first encounter, usually a moment of high romance, was reduced to slapstick: "How, gawd it mit you?" "Hail goot," said I.' The reader's sympathy was dashed with a bucket of mockery.[28]

Farce was a crucial weapon in assertions of white superiority, arising from what Homi Bhabha has described as colonial notions of the 'doubleness' of the native; that they were 'almost but not quite, almost but not white'.[29] People like James, with their wealth, English manners and pretensions to English romance were seen as poor imitations of whites, comical in their efforts and their failures. In the American case, the defendant was reported to be in 'tolerably smartish dress and appeared as if he had been in the metropolis taking lessons off perfidious lovers'. The judge ruled that he 'could see no reason why these humble Africans should not, in imitation of their betters, appeal to a jury for damages,' and said that the damages should be steep enough to 'act as a lesson to those coloured gentry, in their attempts to imitate fashionable infidelity'.[30] Similarly, the *Australian Star* noted that James Lucas' letters 'were not the product of his fervor and originality but had been copied from a book,' which highlighted his racial difference and reduced his status; after all, letter-writing manuals were intended to teach polite conduct to the working classes.[31]

There were other ways in which racial discourse seeped into James' hearing, without needing to be explicitly mentioned. When Clara gave her testimony, the defence played on tropes of the scheming Oriental despot extorting marriage under threat: 'When she wanted to go to Australia he told her that she would have to marry him, or if she didn't he would stop her.'[32] This was James, in the words of her barrister Harold Morgan, as 'the designing Lucas' who had Clara's family in his 'clutches'. Clara admitted that she would have married him, but only if he had reached an appropriate standard of manhood and 'behaved like a gentleman'. Here we have Clara acting as both prize and pedagogue, the pure white woman teaching her Oriental lover how to improve his status. The fact that James sued Clara, Morgan argued, was a sign of lack of cultural competency and buffoonery in the practices of romantic love: 'The thing was absurd'.[33]

Like many relationships between white women and non-white men, James and Clara inverted the usual power dynamics between men and women. In a white supremacist society, white women would often have more social and cultural capital than their non-white partners, and with both parties discriminated against in the labour market, their economic status was more equal, albeit equally difficult. When white men had relationships with non-white women, they may have been socially ostracised, but their economic standing was not directly affected. The opposite was true for white women, who would rise or fall in accordance with the economic and social status of their husbands.[34] The idea, then, that a white woman would choose to reduce her status through marriage with a non-white man was almost unfathomable.

At stake was the status of non-white masculinity and the capacity for non-white men to conform to the gender norms of love and marriage. Marriage and courtship prescribed male dominance: men, as active agents, proposed to women once they were capable of providing for a family, and while marriage enhanced men's social and political status, they were not financially reliant upon it. By these standards, James appeared hopelessly effeminate: Clara proposed to him, she had cultural and linguistic mastery over him, and he occupied a feminine position in a legal action that existed to redress women's emotional and social reliance on marriage. This perception of James as effeminate may explain why some newspapers referred to him incorrectly as a merchant from 'East India'.[35] In European hierarchies of South Asian men, Bengalis (from East India) were seen as foppish by contrast to the more masculine Sikhs.[36]

James' chances of salvaging his case, as Close realised, depended on his wealth. To be socially acceptable, a cross-cultural romance depended upon a fantasy of riches; non-white men needed to be 'dark-skinned princelings'.[37] A man needed an independent fortune to thrive in a society that excluded both him and his partner from the labour market. To this end, Close insisted, James was not, as he had described himself, 'a shop-keeper' but 'a successful merchant'. This was the guarantee of James' manhood and a prerequisite for his role as lover in an Orientalist romance.[38]

Ultimately, however, Close's strategy appears to have been to efface James' ethnicity by framing the relationship in the universalist language of European love. 'There was no difference between the feelings of a man or a woman when such feelings were violated and subject to the pangs of disappointment', said Close, assimilating James into a vision of a common humanity defined by emotional susceptibility. Everyone knew the sting of unrequited love. [39]

In so arguing, Close invoked a long tradition in romantic literature that celebrated love's egalitarian potential: colour-bind and indifferent to gender and class. 'What then is colour in estimating the griefs of a forsaken and ill-treated female?' asked the barrister in the 1828 American case. 'She was poor, it was true; and in a humble sphere of life but love levels all distinctions …

The blind god was no judge, and no respecter of colours; his darts penetrated deep, not skin deep; his client though black, was flesh and blood, and possessed affections, passions, resentments and sensibilities.' Racial difference was acknowledged in order to be disavowed, dissolved within an essentialised language of love.[40]

In all these ways, race was constructed through romance: through the homogenising language of whiteness that sought to incorporate cultural difference into a script of European love; through the notion of doubleness – the idea that non-Europeans were similar enough to Europeans to appear reformed and recognisable, but different enough to be inherently deficient of feeling; through humour that depended upon a collision between European authenticity and Oriental mimicry; and through Orientalist stereotypes of the scheming Asian male who could oscillate between tyranny and effeminacy.

\*   \*   \*

Described by the press as 'becomingly dressed', Clara, if she followed the fashions of the 1890s, would have swished to the witness box in a bell-shaped skirt nipped at the waist and a shirt with a high, graceful neckline. As manners and morals loosened, so did the stiff attire of the Victorian era, and Clara, with her global travel and her insouciant flirtations, was a woman of her time.

She began her testimony by denying almost everything James had said. No, she told her barrister, Mr Morgan, she had never proposed to James, nor had she received any jewellery, at least no watch or engagement ring. Although, yes, she might have been given a pair of silver bracelets and a chain. She had never been riding, walking or driving out with James in Hong Kong, and as for the letters, she had returned most of them. When her family wanted to come to Australia, she and her sister had simply gone to James to ask him to withdraw the verdict against her brother-in-law. James had said that he would only do so if she wrote a letter promising to marry him, and he gave her an example of the kind of letter he wanted. Morgan read to the court James' model letter:

My Darling James,
I have received your loving letter, and I am grieved to find you still express

doubts as to my promises and appear to fear I am deceiving you. My dearest, the time you allude to was quite different from now. I was then a minor. I am now over 21 years, and I can make my own selection, and marry whom I please. I assure you, my darling, you have no cause to doubt me. I love you, my sweet dear, truly and sincerely.

... I accept the ring you gave me with the pledge it accompanies. From this day, I am yours and yours only and will remain so till death parts us ...
Believe me, I am your ever-loving,
CLARA PALMER.

After this came Clara's reply to James' request, in which she gently chastised him, saying she preferred 'to express her feelings' how she thought best, before reassuring him:

Believe me, my dearest James, I desire to have you respected by everyone, and when circumstances bring us together shortly – I hope soon – we shall appreciate each other's company the more. I greatly deplore my approaching departure from Hong Kong, but I shall look forward with great joy to your visit to Australia, and I shall then show you by thought, word and deed how much I admire your dearest person, and shall do everything to make you feel happy in your new home ...
Believe me to be, my dearest James, yours very sincerely,
Clara.

Morgan returned to the lawyer's table while Colonna-Close stood, gathered up a bundle of letters, and began his cross-examination.

'Do you admit to having written, in a letter dated June 30, 1891, that you would marry James "if he behaved himself like a gentleman"?' Colonna-Close asked, waving the letter at Clara.

'Yes,' Clara replied.

'Is it not a fact that Lucas paid your passage money to Australia?'

'I swear he did not.'

'Who has the receipt?'

'My sister has.'

Colonna-Close returned to the letter. 'Why did you write this to him when you were leaving Hong Kong?'

'I disliked the man so much that I would have done anything to get away from him.'

'But you could get away from him without writing the letter. You were on board the steamer.'

'He would have stopped us from going if I had not written the letter.' And anyway, Clara continued, at the time of writing the letter she had 'heard that he was married'. Yes, she conceded, she 'should have written him from Port Darling in Victoria, telling him she disliked him, instead of penning him a deceptive letter. But after she left Hong Kong, she thought no more about him.'

Pulling another letter from his bundle, Colonna-Close asked: 'How is it that you wrote him a letter from Port Darling beginning "Dear James" if you did not think about him?'

'I intended to write to him from Melbourne to prevent him coming.'

'You knew he was going to Australia for something more than to make money?'

Clara Palmer smiled coyly: 'Certainly.'

'Then how is it that you did not write to him of the double purpose of his visit to Australia instead of referring only to business, and telling him that business was bad here?'

'I knew he was fond of making money and I thought that would stop him.'

Colonna-Close returned to his seat and Mr Morgan declared that he would call Clara's sister, but the judge objected.

What was the point, when there was a letter written by the girl in which she stated that she was willing to marry Lucas and Lucas was willing to marry her, Justice Gibson asked. 'Leave the case to the jury. Had the action been brought by a white man he would in all probability have been laughed at.' Gibson was not referring to the reaction of the public gallery but to the reaction of the jury, which in previous breach of promise cases brought by men had laughed the matters out of court.

Mr Morgan nodded and began his closing address. The jury had, he said, 'a degrading spectacle before them in a man suing for breach of promise. What were they to think of a man who sent a letter to a girl to be re-addressed to him, setting forth a number of false statements about her affection for him?' And Clara, when she received that letter, 'did not despatch it to him, but ... sent one less ardent in its tone. There was no love in the subsequent few letters. Would any man receiving such letters from a girl on the strength of them give up his business and go to a strange country to her?'

James, Morgan insisted, 'must have known that the girl did not like him. She had simply acted toward him as she did to free her brother-in-law ... from the clutches of the designing Lucas.'

Colonna-Close did not address Morgan's arguments. He simply said that his client wanted nominal damages, which was reasonable given that he had allowed the defendant and her sister and brother-in-law to stay in his house without charge for over a year. James, he said, was still willing to marry Clara despite what she had done, but failing that, he wanted to return to Hong Kong 'vindicated from the stigma of having been made a fool of'.[41] As James may have realised, every word of the trial would later be reprinted in the Hong Kong press.[42]

\*    \*    \*

If the barristers and judges only mentioned James' ethnicity obliquely, some newspapers, as previously mentioned, were more explicit, while others didn't mention it at all.[43] To understand this diversity of reactions, we need to place *Lucas v Palmer* within the context of other breach of promise cases involving non-white litigants across the nineteenth and early-twentieth centuries. Although the sample size is small, the judgments, newspaper commentary and testimony of litigants reveal clear shifts in white perceptions of interracial romance.

In the earliest reported case, from 1856, an unnamed Chinese man in Drayton, Queensland took out – and then dropped – a writ for breach of promise against a European woman. This provoked a kind of chuckling curiosity on the part of the press. *The Perth Gazette* commented: 'We live in strange times do we not?'[44] Another journalist reported:

It appears that the loving and fascinating Celestial had been paying his addresses to the lady in question for some time, and at length gave vent to his passion by making a virtuous declaration of his love. In an unguarded moment he 'popped the question' of questions to the fair one and oh happiness supreme he found himself the bridegroom elect of his dazzling mistress ...

But fancy the horror, grief and dismay which was depicted upon the countenance of the faithful lover, when, in a few weeks afterwards, he found 'the fickle fair one' had allied herself in matrimonial bonds to another, and he, horror of horrors, a European.

Immediately love gives place to intense hate in the bosom of the unhappy celestial, and as he conceived he had not been treated in accordance with the strict principles of English law and justice, he issued a summons to the fair one ...

A little reflection, however, led him to conclude that his case was a hopeless one, and so he goes and tries his fascinating smiles with another, obtains her consent and proclaims to the world that at length has succeeded in obtaining a European lady for a bride.[45]

There is an obvious racism behind the journalist's humour. The idea of a lowly 'Celestial' – a racial slur used to describe citizens of the 'Celestial Empire', or China – experiencing the heights of romantic love was seen as comical. There is the hubristic notion that 'pure' white women are the ultimate romantic prize, and that Chinese men would inevitably suffer humiliation when competing with European men.

Yet the journalist does not condemn the affair. Instead, he appears tickled by it. He notes with little concern that the Chinese man went on to marry a different European woman. Chinese people are othered in such reports, but romance draws them into a common humanity. Meanwhile, the Chinese man does not seem to have felt that he was prohibited from falling in love with European women, and he believed he had a legal right to compensation when they broke their promises.

The timing of this case is crucial to understanding the reaction of the press. Chinese migrants began arriving in significant numbers in Australia with the gold rush in the early 1850s, and the response by white Australians was at first one of cross-cultural inquisitiveness. The fact that almost all Chinese migrants were men provoked some alarm, and there was discussion of the possibility of encouraging Malay women to come to Australia to marry them. White women, it was presumed, would only want to marry white men. But unlike the United States and Canada, where legislation prohibited sex or marriage between Chinese men and white women, no laws were passed in Australia regulating such intimacies. When the first scattered reports appeared of interracial marriages, the coverage, writes historian Kate Bagnall, initially expressed 'curiosity', but this did not last long.[46] From the 1860s until the turn of the century, the dominant response from white commentators in the press and parliament was one of abhorrence at the 'ruination' of white girls and women, the pollution of the British race and the 'creation of a piebald breed'.[47] This became part of a wider debate about Chinese immigration that focused on the spectres of cheap labour, opium dens, the seduction of women and the squalor of Chinese camps.

Yet these were elite discourses, and what happened on the ground tells a very different story. Chinese men and European women, of course, continued to fall in love and to marry. Understanding the discrepancy between the views expressed by politicians and the press and the experiences of ordinary people may help us to make sense of the range of reactions to James Lucas and Clara Palmer in the 1890s. Historian Alexander Yarwood argues that the racially discriminatory legislation introduced during this period didn't reflect popular sentiment against Asian migrants but pre-empted it; or, as Lake and Reynolds argue, it imposed a binary on what had previously been racial plurality.[48] There was no 'groundswell of excited popular feeling' demanding immigration restrictions in the 1890s, Yarwood points out, and there had been no major influx of migrants in that decade.[49] The number of Chinese migrants living in Australia had decreased to 30,342 in 1901 from about 38,000 during the gold rushes; there were 4681 South Asian people in Australia in 1901 and even fewer Syrians, Afghans and Japanese.[50] Even parliamentarians' vehement racism around the time of federation, Yarwood argues, should be distinguished from 'the thorough-going racialism of the post-1930s'.[51] This context helps to make sense of the rather blasé reaction by the press to James and Clara's affair.

In the newspaper reports of the two interracial breach of promise cases in the 1890s (including James and Clara's), there was no suggestion that interracial romance was unnatural, nor was there mention of purity of Anglo-Saxon blood or racial degeneration, although these ideas appeared in legal proceedings involving interracial affairs in America at the time.[52] Racial ideology spoke many tongues – from indifference to Orientalism; from insistence on a racial binary to assertions of a common humanity – and none of these discourses entirely disappeared in the early-twentieth century. They were, however, increasingly muffled by the booming voice of 'race science', which lectured the new white nation about immutable racial traits based in blood and biology. By the 1920s, the vocabulary for describing non-Europeans would narrow, and this was evident in reports of breach of promise cases. Gan Dah, an Indian plaintiff in a 1920 case, was simply referred to as 'black', 'a colored man' or 'a Hindoo' – the latter was a catch-all term for South Asians regardless of their actual religion. Tatanoa Kooiso, a Japanese defendant in a 1923 case, was called a 'Jap'.

Unlike James Lucas or the Chinese man from Drayton, both of whom felt confident pursuing European women, Gan Dah expressed internalised racism.[53] He had met Lizzie Lenton in a store in Redfern, Sydney, in 1919, and after some time he asked her if she was married. When she replied in the negative and expressed romantic interest in Gan Dah, he gloomily responded, 'You are white and I am black.' Marriage would be impossible. Lizzie disagreed: 'there were plenty of white girls married to black men', she chirped, and they began courting. He showered her with jewellery and money and eventually asked her to write out an agreement stating that she promised to marry him. She refused and broke off the engagement. Where James Lucas' case was largely argued on the grounds that he, like any man, suffered emotionally from amorous betrayal, Gan Dah's case was purely about monetary compensation. James Lucas' barrister had sought to draw him into a common humanity defined by shared emotional sensibilities, but this was no longer considered a viable strategy by the time Gan Dah brought a surprisingly similar case to court. With no evidence presented of Gan Dah's emotional suffering, the judge said he couldn't 'estimate the blight on his affections' but awarded him £8 compensation as a precise return of monies spent.[54]

The case brought by Tatanoa Kooiso, a Japanese importer and manufacturing agent, also reveals the growing taboo against interracial relationships. Kooiso had met a shop assistant named Rowan in 1921 in Sydney. They courted, and eventually Rowan 'succumbed to his blandishments' and became pregnant. Kooiso promised her marriage and they moved into an apartment together, but trouble erupted when she began to suspect that he was a spy and a philanderer. Recalling his frustrations during this period, Kooiso told the court how 'annoyed' this made him. 'I am not a spy,' he declared. Rowan eventually moved out after 'a violent quarrel over another girl', and Kooiso married another European woman.[55]

An article in *The Bulletin* railing against the fact that Kooiso had 'transferred his affections to another white girl' was reprinted in a number of newspapers. The source of the problem, the author claimed, was 'American cinema':

There is no getting away from the unpleasant fact that Australian girls have become familiar in the picture theatre with the spectacle of at least one Japanese screen-actor resident in America, and of mimes got up as Africans, making love to white women and being glorified in the process. There is no weightier count in the indictment against American screen 'art' than that it has clothed miscegenation with a false glamour of romance – and this is a country where preservation of race-purity is the all-in-all.

The author concluded with a call for less 'Hollywood offal' and more 'healthy Australian sentiment'.[56]

This was the first time the words race-purity and 'miscegenation' were used in commentary on an Australian breach of promise hearing (the latter term had been invented in America in 1864), and it shows a shift in racial thinking.[57] Where the Chinese man from Drayton was described as a 'fascinating and loving Celestial', breach of promise defendant Abu Bakar in 1893 as a 'dusky Princeling', and James and Clara's relationship as a 'Hong Kong romance', Kooiso and Rowan had engaged in 'miscegenation'; their romance threatened the purity of white bloodlines.

The 1920s cases show a hardening of racial ideologies, whereby interracial marriage came to be seen as biologically hazardous. But the commentary also alludes to a counter-discourse, in which 'the false glamour of romance' continued to sanction love across colour-lines. While America was enforcing anti-miscegenation laws and Australia was ensuring white blood purity through the *Immigration Restriction Act*, disobedient fantasies of the exotic, of difference and quite possibly of the prohibited pulsed through a burgeoning film, music and radio industry and into the desires of ordinary people.

\* \* \*

With Clara's cross-examination over, there was nothing left but for the judge to sum up. 'Although actions of this character were very uncommon,' he began, 'the plaintiff had a perfect right to claim damages if he considered he had suffered through the defendant breaking her promise.' He noted that if James was awarded high damages, it was likely that Clara would go to gaol, as she had no means of paying them – but this caution aside, it was clear that he thought James should win. The jury retired and within an hour returned a three-quarters majority verdict in favour of James, which the parties accepted.[58]

I concede that I did not expect James to win his case. He was not white, for one thing. And he was a man. In the first Australian breach of promise action brought by a man against a woman in 1849, the defence lawyer argued successfully that he 'could readily understand how a woman felt after such a disappointment', as it might blight her prospects for life, for love "tis woman's whole existence"'. But 'being jilted made a man wiser.' He also argued that 'every woman had a perfect right, even at the altar, to break her vow of marriage, without rendering herself amenable to the law.'[59] The jury agreed,

as they did again in another case by a man, in 1871, when the defence barrister argued that a woman abandoned by her partner had had her 'worldly
prospects blasted, but a man suffered not one jot'.[60]

By the 1880s, however, as women's public status began to rise and as law
professionalised, pushing the contractual elements of the action to the fore,
men began winning their actions. The sums claimed were usually nominal:
£30 in an 1880 case and one shilling plus costs in an 1889 case – but in 1902,
a man won £150.[61] The same trends were happening in England, with one
journalist commenting in 1893 that the actions were 'the inevitable consequence of the aggression of the women's rights movements'.[62]

When a judge, in 1903, quoted Shakespeare at the jury and told them
that a man, like Macduff, must 'feel it as a man', a commentator in the South
Australian press took him to task:

> Some years ago, before the political equality of woman with man was estab-
> lished, there was an unwritten code which looked askance at actions for
> breach of promise brought by men. But things are changed now. Either
> men should have the same sympathy when they are jilted as is accorded
> to women, or woman, the equal of man, should scorn to look to a jury to
> repair her lacerated heart.[63]

Of course, women had not obtained anything near equality with men:
there were no women in Australian federal parliament until the 1940s, no
women on the judiciary until 1965, and women had to wait until the 1990s
before they had equal jury franchise to men. Equality in work opportunities
and wages was (and remains) an ideal, which meant women were still more
dependent upon marriage than men were. While acknowledging that men
also suffered from heartbreak no doubt helped to break down stereotypes
of stolid, laconic masculinity, the debate revealed the limitations of formal
political equality, blind as it is to the structural inequality that kept women
reliant upon legal actions such as breach of promise.

James Lucas brought his action at just the right time, as the law was beginning to be more sympathetic to male plaintiffs. With the verdict and costs in
his favour, he walked out of the court with £40 and his honour vindicated.[64]

## James Lucas

If we were to end the story here, we would have learnt a lot about how settler societies assimilated, excluded or 'othered' non-European migrants, but

very little about the migrants themselves. Absorbing James' case into a larger national narrative, means obliterating his life beyond the courtroom and beyond state borders. When we say that James' decision to sue Clara was unusual, we can only mean that it was atypical from an Anglo-European perspective. But if, instead of confining his story to that icy day in June when he appeared in the District Court, we try to uncover who he was before and after it, the action appears utterly predictable.

James was not of Hindu faith, as newspapers assumed, but Parsi. He was raised among people who delighted in going to court.[65]

Reconstructing James' story is no easy task. He left behind no letters or diaries and there are no judgment papers surviving from his breach of promise case. I have tracked down newspaper commentary, his Australian immigration papers, a later court case, and two palm cards from the Hong Kong archives.[66] Opportunities for archival snooping are sadly limited. Clara Palmer also disappears from the historical record following the case. Nonetheless, I hope to use these archival fragments to give James' case a wider, more global context, and to contribute to a historical understanding of how legal cultures have travelled with people. Scholars have written fascinating studies that look at law's mobility: how captains of ships extended sovereignty into 'undiscovered' lands, or how sovereign rulers declared themselves immune to foreign laws.[67] But to date, few studies exist of how ordinary people, such as James Lucas, carried legal cultures with them. Beginning with James' immigration papers, we can begin reconstructing his life by sailing back home with him to India. Not to east India, or to Hong Kong or Bengal, as the Australian press assumed, but to a town called Broach (or Bharuch today) in west India, where James began his life among weavers, cotton-farmers, merchants and sailors.[68]

## JAMSETJEE SORABJEE

Broach was the oldest city in Gujarat, a place long fabled as a market for India and the world. Over 8000 years ago, the *Periplus Maris Erythraei* (CE 80) recorded ships from Arabia and Persia drifting into the harbour with Italian wines, white dates and sweet lotus, as well as gold, silver, topaz, coral and velvet, and sailing out again laden with rice, sugar, salt, ebony, horn, cinnamon, sandalwood and gossamer-light sashes and muslin. Broach was a watery world: canals spread like capillaries from the rivers that wound through the city – the Narmada and the Dhadhar – and during the rainy months, from July to September, flat-bottomed canoes, ferries and dinghies carrying food, cloth and spices wended their way into the inland towns of the region.[69]

In 1848, James was born blinking into the last glints of the city's former splendour. Since the seventeenth century, Broach had been in decline, usurped by the ports of Surat and Bombay that had been favoured by the Portuguese and the British. Weavers who had once shuffled out of their huts at sunrise to set up looms in the shade of the mango and guava trees could no longer compete with the steam-powered cotton manufactures in the larger cities. The commercial dealers left in search of more prosperous markets, and the ship builders sailed to busier harbours. In 1851, the census registered the population at 290,984, the majority of whom were Hindu or Muslim. The group that had decreased most from the 1820s to the 1850s were the Parsis, or Persians. This is significant, because although every newspaper in Australia called James Lucas a Hindu, in fact he identified as Parsi.[70]

We don't know much about James' family, but we do know that he travelled on British and Indian passports and registered himself as 'Persian'. This would have made him racially ambiguous in both Australia and colonial India, where Parsis were ranked higher than Hindus or Muslims and a rigorous practice of exogamy led to Parsis being paler-skinned than other Indians.[71] James would have been brought up in the Zoroastrian religion and would have imbibed Parsi tales of their (self-declared) miraculous history. For James, growing up in the 1850s, when Muslim and Parsi riots broke out in Broach, the origin story that he was taught would most likely have emphasised the Parsi flight from Muslim persecution. In this version, Parsis fled from Persia in the fourteenth century as the region around present-day Iran converted from Zoroastrianism to Islam, although a competing account argues that the original Parsis were part of an oceanic trading diaspora, sea-merchants who were already familiar with Gujarat.[72]

According to oral tradition, when the Parsis arrived in India, the local ruler sent them a bowl brimful with milk, signifying that there was no room for more people in the state. The Parsi leader placed a teaspoon of sugar into the milk and returned it: your bowl will not overflow, but simply be sweetened by our presence. Who could refuse such poetry? The Parsis were permitted to stay, subject to five rules, including that they cease being warriors and become merchants, that they not try to convert people, and that the women adopt the local dress. Under the Mughal empire, Parsis were agriculturalists, weavers and merchants, but as the East India Company gained influence in the eighteenth century, Parsis, already outsiders within the community, carved out a role for themselves as mercantile middlemen between Europeans and Indians. By the time James entered the world, their star was rising: the British spoke of them as wealthy, well-mannered, well-spoken and loyal to the ruling elite.[73]

Learning about his faith growing up, James would have received a course in socially responsible capitalism. Unlike Catholicism, which cautions against the corruption of riches, or Islam, which stipulates fasting, Zoroastrianism is comfortable with pleasure and prosperity so long as they are tempered by munificence. According to the 3000-year-old teachings of Zarathustra Spitama, Zoroastrians should reject asceticism, live well, be dutiful and truthful, honour promises and give to the community. 'Good thoughts, good words and good deeds' were, and still are, the guiding precepts for Parsis. The *Avesta* (or Parsi scriptures) would have taught James that the universe was the site of a cosmic struggle: the forces of order, goodness, truth and light versus the dark forces of evil, deception and disorder. Parsis emphasised moral responsibility. What role James played in this spiritual drama was up to him.[74]

Being a good Zoroastrian meant James should marry within the Parsi community – monogamously, although divorce became available in 1865. As leaders worried about the fading of Parsi identity with Parsi mobility around the globe, opposition to interfaith marriages grew in the 1890s, but such marriages had not been uncommon in the nineteenth century; many wealthy Parsis who socialised and traded with Europeans married European women. A young man's parents or friends could help to arrange a marriage, or he might simply fall in love, in which case the *Parsi Marriage and Divorce Act* (1865) required parental consent if the couple were aged under twenty-one. Marriage was a foundational institution in Parsi culture. The *Avesta* described it as favoured by God: a man with a 'fire, cattle, wife [and] children' was more likely to be able to withstand 'physical and mental afflictions and to lead a religious and virtuous life'. Marriage was also a source of happiness: 'What a delicious breath marriage sends forth,' sang Zarathustra Spitama, 'the violet's bed not sweeter.' Betrothal was a 'promise of truthful adherence to a marriage contract', and to break it was 'considered to be a great sin'. While Parsi culture clearly favoured marriage, the injunction to marry within the community meant James would not have been looked down upon for remaining single if he could not find a Parsi spouse. Being single was, and continues to be, a valid social identity for Parsis.[75]

James came into adulthood during the period of British Crown rule over the subcontinent (1858–1947), when Parsis were governed by English law. Unlike Muslims and Hindus, whose civil disputes were settled through the colonial court's application of Anglo-Hindu and Islamic family law, Parsis became deeply invested in British common law. Being merchants, they took to commercial law with gusto, while in the areas of marriage, inheritance, trusts and defamation, 'Parsi values made their imprint on British law'.[76] Historian Mitra Sharafi explains that what may have appeared to be a process of assimilation was in fact a successful bid for autonomy: jurists established their own tradition of Parsi law from within British law. Parsi students sailed to England to study law and the community became famous for producing lawyers, judges and litigants. In the early twentieth century Parsis represented only 0.6 per cent of the population in Bombay, yet, extraordinarily, they made up almost one-fifth of the parties in the reported case law. Suits between Parsis constituted 5 per cent of all reported cases.[77] As Parsis turned to the state to resolve disputes rather than to their own religious or community authorities, 'the litigious Parsi' became a familiar trope in nineteenth-century Indian newspapers.[78] As someone who prosecuted no fewer than eleven civil actions in the Australian courts during his two decades in Australia, James Lucas was an example of the litigious Parsi *par excellence*.

We have only a few dates and a scattering of sources from which to plot James' story, but the archive gives us some idea of his movements.

In Broach during his childhood in the 1850s, James and his family would most likely have lived in Parsivad, a quarter that had belonged to the Parsis for over six centuries. Parsivad was a well-to-do area of town, a place where rambling mansions with ochre-coloured porticos and classical archways lurched higgledy-piggledy over rutted stone cart tracks, and where the scent of ginger biscuits wafted from the doors of Parsi bakeries. James would have gone to a Parsi school that offered a Westernised education, and his ability to read and write English would have placed him at an advantage in dealing with the British.[79]

If James was later accused by Clara of 'loving money', we can hardly blame him. James grew up in a world of mercantile promise sanctioned by religion. He said he was not 'a good scholar', which barred him from the professions but left open the possibility of making his fortune in commerce and trade.[80] We can imagine the young James in Broach, dreaming of adventure as he watched the boats serpent their way through the city's waterways, out past the brackish tidal lagoons to the fog and salt-clouds of the port. We can also imagine stories of Parsi fortunes made from shipbuilding, the opium trade between China and Bombay or the cotton trade between Bombay, China, and Britain fuelling his decision to leave his hometown. I also wonder how the lack of a homeland for Parsi people – historically defined by commercial restlessness and flight – might have played into his decision.

This was (at least) James' second relocation. Although he was born in Broach, one of his solicitors described him as a 'native of Bombay', which suggests he and his family were probably part of the great migration of Parsis from the Guajarati hinterland to the commercial metropolis sometime in the 1850s or 1860s.[81] We know from the archival records that James' first job in Hong Kong was as a police officer, which suggests two possibilities: either he paid his own way there (with savings or as an indentured labourer on a boat) or he was recruited from the Bombay Native Infantry in the late 1860s or 1870s. In Hong Kong, he would have been promised a higher salary and lower cost of living than in India and a favourable exchange rate set by the police force to remit money back home. He might also have heard about the commercial possibilities on offer in Hong Kong from the Parsi merchants who had long operated out of Canton.[82]

In the early to mid-1870s, a steamship carrying James – then still using the name Jamsetjee Sorabjee – drifted into Hong Kong's Victoria Harbour. If it was morning, the bay would likely have been wreathed in mist, and the captain would have navigated with the aid of fog horns, bells and the booming signal guns discharged by the lighthouse. When the fog cleared, James would have found himself surrounded by tall ships fluttering with the flags of many nations, a flotilla of sampans, 'great, clumsy-looking' junks and ferries taking people and their luggage to the pier. He would have seen the city rising, almost mythically, from the water's edge. Beyond the tallest buildings, his gaze would have been drawn skywards up a steep green hill that ascended terrace by jagged terrace into the towering granite ridges of Victoria Peak.[83]

Bananas, poinsettias, tree ferns, scarlet passion flowers, banyans, dates and sago grew wildly from Hong Kong's great rocky core. Around the precipitous escarpment at its centre, secret stairwells took the place of roads and rickshaws and palanquins replaced horse-drawn carriages. Once James was ashore, he would have turned east, past the harbourside grog shops, gambling dens, opium parlours and brothels into the wide, foliage-lined streets that led to the police headquarters on Hollywood Road.

James arrived in Hong Kong during a period of relative quiet. The Qing Dynasty had ceded Hong Kong to the British in 1842, ending the first Opium

War and converting a community of around 6000 fishers into a busy entrepot between East and West. At first Hong Kong had the feel of a frontier town: streets were perilous at night, home burglaries were rife, murders were common, the bay was a nest of pirates, and the police force was corrupt. James was recruited as part of efforts to reform the police force and increase its numbers, which by the 1870s had started to pay off. In 1866, for example, 384 people were convicted of highway robbery; a decade later, in 1876, this had dwindled to twenty-four, in a population of 139,144.[84]

The British had divided the Hong Kong police force into three sections. 'Group A' comprised eighty-five European constables, 'Group B' 165 Indian constables, and 'Group C' 187 Chinese constables. The groups rarely spoke to one another, and so James would have passed his days with his Indian compatriots. He would have patrolled the streets in uniform, arresting people for opium possession, unregistered gambling, pickpocketing, or the dumping of rubbish in the watercourse.[85] By 1877, however, James had tired of the force. That year, he signed a promissory note to a fellow Indian, Allanjee Devojee, probably to pay for his trip back to India. He did not return to Hong Kong until 1884.[86]

## James Sorab Lucas

In 1880, while back in India, James signalled his allegiance to the British by Anglicising his names and giving himself a new surname, which was a common strategy used by Parsis. Lenders took on names such as 'Readymoney', and professionals signalled their specialisation by assuming names such as 'Engineer'.[87] Jamsetjee Sorabjee became James Sorab (or Sorabjee) Lucas.[88] We don't know what vocation James pursued in India, but his name change probably coincided with his entry into the world of commerce. In 1884 he appears again in the Hong Kong archive, this time suing a man called Gomes for £500 over the proprietorship of two public houses.[89] The British had a monopoly over land ownership in Hong Kong, so it's likely the court case (from which no judgment papers have survived) was over a lease agreement. In the same year, James became landlord of the Rose, Shamrock and Thistle hotel, and in 1887 he extended his commercial portfolio when he became the proprietor of a boutique shop, the Victoria Emporium on the busy Queen's Road East in Wan Chai.[90] By 1890 he was a wealthy man and the proprietor of two more general stores, one in Yee Wo Street and the other on Hollywood Road, near where he had first begun his working life in the police force around twenty years earlier.[91]

On the day James met Clara Palmer in 1887, he was a well-established businessman of almost forty years of age (not thirty, as he would later tell the court).[92] He was impressively multilingual, having learnt English at school and in business, Cantonese in the police force, Gujarati from his family and Marathi and/or Hindi in Bombay. James first saw Clara when he walked into his neighbour's house one day, looking for an Indian man he knew.[93] James' house, like all the houses on his street, was a Chinese-style *tong lau* or tenement, that comprised a ground-floor shop with three or four storeys of accommodation above it.[94] It was a housing style designed for blended families and itinerant workers, suited to a city where hundreds of thousands of people were crammed onto a rock that was only eighteen kilometres long and no more than eight kilometres wide.[95]

As the court would later hear, Clara and her family had moved into James' house as tenants and James and Clara's courtship had ripened. He wrote Clara 'many many letters', showered her with gifts and, typical of Parsi romance, adorned her with jewellery.[96] Within months of first exchanging glances, the pair were engaged to be married. No one seems to have expressed concern about Clara and James being of different ethnicities.[97]

Why did James wait so long before trying to recover the rental arrears owed to him by the Curiambux? He probably thought he and Clara were getting married and was simply playing the part of the dutiful husband, providing for Clara and her family, and at having to push an intimate affair into public light. James may also have felt a sense of shame at having been duped. Parsis sued happily and frequently over domestic matters, but usually only once the transgression had already become public knowledge. Before that point, a good reputation depended upon keeping the matter within the community.[98] As for the Curiambux, I can only assume that they were in straitened circumstances and probably swindlers. They have since disappeared from the historical record. James boarded the steamer in pursuit of Clara in the summer of 1891, carrying her letters in his suitcase: 'if you behave yourself as a gentleman should shore [sic] is nothing to prevent us being married' she had written. He also had another motivation for leaving Hong Kong.

In 1890, a shop James owned caught fire and he was accused of arson, which no doubt horrified him, as a former police officer. Fires were common during this period, and insurance companies had become suspicious. The jury acquitted James, but the fire raises the possibility that his decision to move was more self-interested than he acknowledged. By the time he departed for Australia, settling comfortably into the grand saloon with other first-class passengers, he had a handsome insurance pay-out in his pockets and nothing in Hong Kong to keep him there.[99]

On 21 January 1891, the shipping news in *The Age* reported the arrival of James S. Lucas in Melbourne.[100] Clara's letters had been sealed with her address on the back, and he set out to find her. Like most visitors to Melbourne, James was no doubt dazzled by the city's size (almost half a million people, double the population of Hong Kong at the time) and its opulence. Wide, stately streets were lined with banks and train stations that looked like chateaux, and the skyline undulated with domed rooftops, occasionally pierced with spires or turrets. Trams rattled across the city, passing terraces with ornate cast-iron balconies. Conductors bellowing 'Tickets, please' ferried around a suave population that had grown rich on gold and property speculation, and who were about to lose it all in the depression later that year.[101]

Having found Clara in the house where she was living with her sister and brother-in-law, James declared his love for her. He asked to stay with the family but was told they had no spare rooms. Eventually, Clara's sister took him aside and stated firmly that Clara would not be marrying him. James was wasting his time.[102]

At some point between James' arrival in Melbourne in January and his court case in June, he and the Curiambux family both moved to Sydney. James didn't simply give up on Clara; he demanded justice. First, he filed a claim for outstanding debt against Mr Curiambux in the Magistrates Court. Then he filed for breach of promise of marriage in the District Court.[103] As much as James may have identified with Europeans – enough to change his name and seek out a European wife – he also knew not to trust them. For all Clara's exhortations for James to be more gentlemanly, he had no access to the white European social world of dinner parties, picnics and balls, where the codes of gentlemanly conduct could be monitored and enforced, and where a man like Curiambux might be shamed into honouring his debt, or a woman like Clara chastised for taking a flirtation too far.

Instead, James behaved like any rational Parsi would in his situation: he sought protection in the law. Although breach of promise actions were not used by Parsis in India at this time, Parsis were adept at manipulating British legal actions for their own ends.[104] Raised in a culture that valorised marriage and saw a broken engagement as a sin, James went to court. His perceived right to legal redress was distinctively Parsi, but it also reminds me of the writing of critical race theorists almost a century later, responding to Marxist cries to replace the alienated language of contract with 'community' and 'trust'. White people can afford to be blasé about legal rights, critical race theorists have argued, because their rights are usually protected. But racism has taught other communities to prefer the formal protection of a legal relationship over pledges of white goodwill.[105]

## James Lucas

We know from James' immigration certificate that he didn't return to Hong Kong after his breach of promise case, but stayed in Australia and opened a confectionary store in Katoomba, in the Blue Mountains west of Sydney.[106] From 1893 until 1901, James lived a quiet life. In winter, icy winds would sprint up over the escarpment, blowing sleet onto the bleak deserted streets of the town, making the hairs on his legs stand on end, and rattling the windows of his store. In summer, the heat was scorching. Grubby-faced children would count out their pennies on the counter, slavering over the sugar sticks, brandy balls and peppermint drops. He also sold postage stamps and Indian specialities to locals and tourists.

James' world – small, stationary and financially comfortable – was unusual among South Asian migrants at the time, most of whom were hawkers. As the century came to a close, James would have seen his countrymen referred to as part of an 'Asiatic problem' in the newspapers and as a 'nuisance' in the licensing courts. Unlike James, these men were poor, highly visible with their turbans, less likely to speak English and, for authorities, vexingly mobile. He might also have noticed a certain anxiety on the part of the Crown in discussing the problem. In 1893, the solicitor-general advised magistrates that they could use their discretion to deny South Asians hawker's licences, but that they must be careful 'not to discriminate against British subjects'.[107] The solution was simply to deny licences to anyone who didn't 'understand the English language sufficiently'. It was the same solution that would be used in the *Immigration Restriction Act*.

The problem of Indian migrants for white politicians and administrators lay in the tension between their status as British subjects – members of an imagined imperial citizenry that, as Queen Victoria had promised, did not discriminate on the grounds of 'race or creed' – and the sovereign right of emerging nations to exclude people on racial grounds. Of course, the British promise of equality was only ever a fantasy – as residents of a 'dependent colony', Indians were never considered capable of governing

themselves, unlike the white self-governing colonies, and a century of imperial bloodshed and plunder had disabused most Indians of any belief in
British justice. Subjecthood did not translate into citizenship rights. But
the promise of formal equality still provided a powerful argument in Indian
demands for increased civic status. For Indian migrants abroad, belonging
to an imagined imperial citizenry offered a riposte to the everyday humiliations of white nationalism.

While James went about making his life in Katoomba small and sed-
entary, the government busily legislated walls around him. In 1893, James
had sailed into Australia without a passport. At immigration checkpoints he
needed only to prove that he was not a coolie labourer. During his breach of
promise action, he described his plans to return to Hong Kong. By 1901, he
no longer had a right to return to Australia if he left, and he could not move
interstate in search of work. By 1905, he was disqualified from citizenship.
James and other Asian people who had been living in Australia prior to the
*Immigration Restriction Act* were now relegated to a subordinate civil, political and social status: they could not vote, receive a pension, hold public office,
bring their families out or sit on juries.[108]

In 1901, James moved two hours west of Katoomba to the small town of
Mudgee. Here, in the soft green valley belonging to the Wiradjuri people,
James pursed the typically Parsi vocation of produce merchant.[109] Mudgee
was the hometown of one of Australia's best-known poets, Henry Law-
son (1867–1922), whose verses about tin-shed schools, wallaby tracks and
mateship provided the thread from which myths of egalitarian Australian
identity were woven. James' experiences in Mudgee add a darker pattern to
the national cloth.

In 1903, two years after moving to Mudgee, he launched an action in the
local court against Robert Large, a miner, bartender and general ne'er-do-
well, seeking an order to restrain Large from using malicious language against
him. We don't know what Large had said to him, but it would be surprising
if it did not contain a racial inflection. James lost the case but secured from
Large a 'promise not to use malicious language'.[110]

Six years later, on 12 June 1909, James was milling around with other
traders and farmers at the Mudgee auction house when George Roth – son
of a famed viticulturalist, Adam Roth – murmured something insulting to
him. Half an hour later, Roth followed James outside and continued his attack
more publicly, telling one of James' customers, 'Don't talk to that black bug-
ger. Talk to a white man.' James responded by suing Roth for defamation,

*James Sorab Lucas in 1921,*
*photographed for a certificate exempting him from the dictation test.*

seeking £500 damages in the NSW Supreme Court. Defamation had long been used by men in commerce to protect their reputations, but James was also demanding dignity and respect. He claimed he had been 'injured in his credit, reputation and circumstances', and that Roth had spoken 'falsely and maliciously'. James was not black, his barrister argued, but 'an Indian-born British Subject'. The judge made no effort to hide his hostility towards James, stating that 'it was questionable whether the language was defamatory at all'. The jury nevertheless found in James' favour, but awarded him trifling damages of £5. The formal equality of law was preserved, but a discriminatory effect was still achieved. The court not only reflected the community's racial prejudice; it enforced it.[111]

James' litigiousness (I have found no fewer than eleven court actions involving him) was part of the Parsi cultural heritage he had brought with him to Australia twenty years earlier. He had internalised the law's promise of formal equality, and without access to the commercial and social networks of white society, he sought protection in the formalities of the court. He may not have turned to law primarily for financial compensation – scholarship on the Parsis in India suggests that many wanted nothing more than public recognition of harms suffered.[112] By this standard, James often won.

\*   \*   \*

When James sat to have his photo taken for a certificate exempting him from the dictation test in 1921, he was seventy-three years old and his face had crinkled with age. The skin around his cheeks looked as thin as a butterfly's wing, cross-hatched with tiny lines. His dark eyes drooped under rumpled lids and his beard was a fleecy white. Both his hands were crippled. In one photograph, James faces the camera directly; the other is in profile. The photographs, along with thumb prints and hand prints mandated by the immigration department, replicated those taken by police – the non-European migrant had been criminalised. From side-on, you can still see glimpses of the handsome young man: the aquiline nose, the high, haughty cheekbones and the head tossed cockily to one side. His eyes which at first glance appear fatigued or resigned, upon closer inspection have the steadiness of defiance.

Accompanying his application were three letters of support. He was of 'splendid character', a journalist friend in Mudgee had initially written, before, perhaps embarrassed by such effusiveness, crossing out 'splendid' and replacing it with 'good'. Another referee described James as 'quiet', and another said he was of 'industrious habits'.[113] These are the last words I found written about James Lucas. Characteristically mobile, he had recently arrived back in Australia from Hannover in Germany via London, and was now en route to India.

\*   \*   \*

There are multiple backdrops against which we could cast the life of James Lucas. We could view him in light of his court action and examine how his story of dashed romance reflected the mixed reactions to interracial romance at the turn of the century. Although legislators may have been separating the world into white and black, at the level of popular discourse, race was still a debatable and flexible idea in the 1890s, complicated by culture, class, linguistic ability and imperial identity.

If we were to end our analysis here, however, we would only be contributing to knowledge of how white courts and white people have regarded the interaction between race and romance. To dignify people like James with historical nuance, we need to acknowledge them as subjects in their own right. We need to take the few scraps they left in the archive and engage, as readers and writers, in a shared act of historical imagination. We need to ask what may have led James to sue Clara Palmer, and what happened next?

It is only by telling the story of James' life in its entirety, beginning in a Parsi community in the far west of India, that we can understand his case against Clara. An action that appeared anomalous to a white Australian population made perfect sense to a Parsi merchant who belonged to a litigious culture, creative in its uses of British law. It made sense to someone schooled in the Zoroastrian tradition, raised to honour his promises and to feel acutely the sting of deceit. As the years pass and we see James in his sixties still suing to secure his reputation, we see how law operated as a resource for Parsi migrants as they faced the cruelties of discrimination. If we think of civil law not as a monolithic, top-down institution but as culturally hybrid, made up of the legal cultures that litigants bring with them, we can see how that legal baggage could alter the scope of the law itself.

In some respects, James Lucas cuts a strange figure in a book about intimacy. His relationship with Clara Palmer appears like an aberration in an otherwise solitary life. The references James provided for his immigration certificate were mostly officials, although the effusiveness of the journalist perhaps suggests a genuine friendship. It is also possible that James, for all his supposed cantankerousness, was a sensitive man, a romantic who packed up a successful life in Hong Kong to pursue his lover. Jilted, he turned to litigation and, against all odds, won.

Where James went after he boarded the steamer out of Melbourne in 1923 is uncertain. I could find no grave for him. If he did make it back to Bombay or Baruch to die, his body would have been carried up to a Parsi temple of silence eventually to disappear with the birds into the sky.

# 8

# 'I'm not dying for a man': Modernity, Migration and the Colour of Love

## (*Zathar v Hanna*, 1907)

T he file labelled 'Moses Hanna: no. 17464' arrives at my desk looking pleasingly fat. Yellowing papers curl around a tattered grey belt; their messy bulk almost bursts the latch. I have been at the NSW State Archives all morning, white gloves on, tracking down the court documents for a 1907 case involving two Syrians, Cissie Zathar and Moses Hanna. The archives are an arcadia of silence, occasionally broken by an excited murmur as researchers – heads bent over powdery bundles of paper – commune with the dead.

I take out the file and observe the documents before me: typed script, purple ink, black and red government stamps. Unlike case files I have inspected from the nineteenth century, which are sepia-coloured, bound with rusted pins and hand-written in the loopy decadence of Victorian-era cursive, these documents are formalised. They are the products of what philosopher Max Weber called 'good record-keeping': the bloodless ledgers that the modern bureaucracies of capitalism required. They are the fruits of law's disenchantment.[1]

Which is why, as I make my way through Moses Hanna's pleadings, I gasp when my gloved hand brushes against something unusual: two pieces of antique-white lace, brittle with age, pinned to a collection of letters in the middle of the file. Cissie, a hawker in the Tamworth region, had sent the lace to Moses requesting more from his warehouse in Redfern, and Moses had later admitted it into court as proof that their relationship was purely professional. But as anyone who has been in love will know, people contrive all sorts of reasons to contact each other.

Cissie and Moses had agreed not to write of 'love or marriage', lest Moses' father discover their clandestine relationship. For four years, Moses wrote over seventy-four letters to Cissie, and Cissie responded with coded references – she was his 'friend' – and less coded eruptions of distress at Moses' neglect: 'every train I went and looked on the platform [for you]', she wrote in one letter. 'Please let me know if you want to come. I am full up of waiting.' The lace, I think, was simply an excuse to write to him.[2]

Now here it is before me, more than a century since Cissie attached it to her letter while living in Mrs Varney's boarding house on Peel Street, Tamworth, in the years when she clattered down sun-baked dirt tracks with her horse and cart, selling cashmere men's socks, tablecloths, silk handkerchiefs, tape measures and drapery to people on bush properties. When Cissie posted the lace in 1904, she surely had not the least thought of it being converted into legal evidence against her or, nearly 120 years later, into an archival relic for us.[3]

\*   \*   \*

If the language of state administration was to be, as Weber argued, drained of emotion – *sine ira et studio*, 'without hatred and passion' – how do we explain the bundle of letters and lace hidden inside Moses' case file?[4] How can we incorporate love into our narratives of modernity when the modern world, according to theorists, is characterised by disenchantment, scientism, rationality and secularism? What would modern love look like if we envisaged it beyond the norms of white culture; if, when discussing the shift from Victorian-era courtship to twentieth-century romance, we went beyond the dance halls and picture palaces inhabited by amorous white couples to imagine the lives and loves of people like Cissie and Moses?

When Cissie and Moses appeared in court in the first decade of the twentieth century, newspaper columnists turned themselves into amateur anthropologists, scribbling observations about Syrian romantic practices. 'Florrie Frivolous', writing in *Truth*, thought that the case was 'funny because of the nationality of the pair, and the mixture of Syrian and English betrothal customs', while 'A Lady's Letter' in *The Bulletin* explained what these customs comprised. Referring to Cissie as 'goods and chattel', she declared that 'apparently in Syria an appointment is made with the goods; the prospective buyer calls and looks at the countenance of the property; and if he is not satisfied, he just goes away.'[5] *The Bulletin* thought Cissie was 'like the heroine of Song of Solomon ... dark but comely, of pronounced Semitic type.'[6] A few years earlier, Syria had been described in newspapers as a place where 'life is more natural and less restrained than in the western world.'[7] Through Cissie's case, such coverage suggested, readers could travel back in time, acquaint themselves with this exotic people and observe their antiquated romantic customs.

But unlike the ventriloquised participants in ethnological surveys, or the mute skulls under the phrenologist's gaze, Cissie had a chance to speak back. As a plaintiff telling her own story, she transformed from object to subject, and a particularly defiant one at that. Columnists may have depicted her as languishing in tradition, but Cissie appeared as a quintessentially modern woman: economically independent, mobile, autonomous and peddling the shiny objects and fickle fashions of an industrialised, globalised world.[8] She was at ease in public spaces such as courts, roads and marketplaces, happily making a spectacle of herself at a time when visibility was usually a privilege granted by the media to white, bourgeois women. And she was brazen in her pursuit of romance. Law courts may have provided a forum in which race was defined and enforced – but as the case of *Zathar v Hanna* suggests, court was also a volatile, multi-vocal place where racial and gender stereotypes were contested and sometimes shattered.[9]

If people's identities appeared more global and more complex than newspapers liked to imagine, then so too did their love affairs. Efforts to caricature Syrian romance as mired in the past stalled against the evidence of Cissie and Moses' improvised, culturally hybrid relationship. The couple spoke self-consciously about drawing upon practices from Australia as much as from Syria, and in so doing they allow us to bring the history of emotions into dialogue with histories of migration and modernity. Where global history has long spoken about 'multiple modernities' as a challenge to Eurocentric definitions of modernity – which see modernity as secular, capitalist and individualist – histories of love generally continue to imagine a white mono-culture of diners, motorcars, commodity consumption and sexual desire.[10] Travelling with Cissie and Moses on steamships, trains and in Cissie's horse and cart, and following them as they call upon kin, priests and finally the state to resolve their amorous grievances, allows us insight into a romance which, I argue, was peculiarly modern by virtue of its cultural and legal plurality, its imaginative blending of new and old worlds, and the lovers' mobility. It also helps us to understand processes of migrant acculturation, specifically how their cultural understandings of love and law interacted with romantic laws and norms in Australia. It begins the work of uncoupling modern love from a European context and casting it upon a world stage.

## Cissie Zathar

Cissie Zathar hailed from Zahle, a 'city of wine and poetry' nestled in the picturesque Beqaa Valley in what is now Lebanon. Zahle was famed for the crystalline Berdawni River that ran through it, beginning in the snow-capped mountains above the town, meandering desultorily along the vineyards that raked down the surrounding hills and coursing through a limestone ravine that still cleaves the town in two. Lebanon was yet to achieve independence, so Cissie would have identified as Zahlawi, from Mount Lebanon in Syria, within the Ottoman Empire.[11]

Cissie's daughter, Queenie Sada, recalled her mother coming from a prosperous family. In a three-page biography of Cissie, passed on to me by her descendants, Queenie says that her mother was born in 1883, the daughter of George and Sada Zathar (née Bakhash), who owned 'a large two-storey home, valuable vineyards, sheep, a horse or two and a donkey or two'. Cissie had one sister, Fa'hmie. Each morning, the stock would be taken up into the hilly country above their home for grazing, and in summer Cissie and her family would likely have dined in one of Zahle's riverside restaurants, her parents sipping wine or arak and Cissie and Fa'hmie nibbling on mezze as warm winds spiced with the scents of charred meat wafted past.[12]

Although newspapers loved to imagine people like Cissie voyaging from a pre-modern Orient to the modern West, Cissie's ability to leave Zahle was entirely a product of modernisation. A new political regime established in Mount Lebanon in the mid-nineteenth century encouraged free trade, resulting in an acceleration of the area's integration into the world economy. Beirut developed into a cosmopolitan port city with at least ten steam navigation lines operating from its shores, and European goods flooded the market. Cash replaced barter, literacy levels and average life expectancy rose, and the population expanded. These shifts, historians say, triggered a shift in people's *mentalité*, seen in the rise of autonomous economic motivation and a desire for material wealth. It also resulted in an export-driven economy focused on silk production and a shift towards monoculture farming (almost half of all cultivated land was allocated to mulberry trees), leading to a need to import basic commodities such as wheat. In the 1880s and 1890s, the Mount Lebanon region plummeted into depression when Chinese and Japanese silk flooded the European market.[13] Cissie's uncle Abdullah Backash, a merchant, migrated to Australia, along with the first wave of Syrian/Lebanese migrants during this period.[14] In 1901, after a disagreement with her father, Cissie also travelled the fifty-five kilometres from Zahle to Beirut, where she boarded a steamer bound for Sydney.[15]

Who was Cissie Zathar besides a 'comely' woman? She was wilful, impetuous, clever, adventurous and brave. She was also partially blind in one eye. Having been raised in a female-dominated household, I suspect that she chafed against the authority of her father and yearned for autonomy. By the time the time she sailed alone from Beirut at the age of eighteen, her uncle Abdullah had been living in Sydney since 1888. Perhaps it was her uncle who had nourished her imagination with the fantasy of a world beyond Zahle, where she might put her hands in her pockets and feel the cool clink of coins, and where she might be mistress of her own fortune.[16] It is also possible that Cissie's voyage was unplanned, and that Abdullah received a shock when he opened the door of his drapery shop in 1901 to find Cissie standing there.[17]

The timing of Cissie's arrival in Australia was fortuitous. She walked off the gang plank and into the clamour of Port Botany just months before the iron gate of the *Immigration Restriction Act* slammed the nation's border shut to 'Asiatics'. Had she arrived after December 1901, she would have been made to sit the discriminatory dictation test, or to apply for an exemption, before being allowed entry.[18] Instead, she sauntered past the immigration officials and went in search of Abdullah.

Over the next few weeks, Cissie stayed with her uncle and his wife above their shop on Elizabeth Street in Redfern, a busy, arterial road that teemed with humanity: the screech of trams, the clop of horses, the rustle of turbaned South Asians and Syrians carrying heavily laden baskets, and the laughter and chatter of female hawkers and their children socialising in Redfern Park. Abdulla's shop signage, like that of other stores on the street – Anad Bossara, Stanton Melick, Callie Hanush and J.T. Malouf – was hand-painted in a serpentine script with letters that dipped and curled. Had Cissie peered into these shops, she would have glimpsed a small theatre of Syrian proprietors, squat on their haunches, haggling with travelling hawkers – mostly Syrian men and women or South Asian men – over bolts of fabric, ribbons, thimbles, razors, handkerchiefs, underwear and other 'fancy goods'.[19]

Referred to by whites as 'Darkest Redfern' or 'the Syrian Colony', the few blocks around Elizabeth Street and Phillip Street were the economic centre of Syrian and South Asian life in Sydney. There were small cottages surrounded by white picket fences, grand five-storey warehouses with factories out the back, and draperies like the one owned by Abdullah. The warehouses were generally owned by Syrian men and were filled with goods bought locally or imported from France, England, Germany and Syria.[20]

Queenie writes that Cissie, while in Redfern, decided to 'commence her own soft goods business', backed by her uncle and his friend Mr Coorey, who owned one of the warehouses on Elizabeth Street. The early Lebanese migrants to Australia were careful not to compete with one another when setting up businesses, which may explain how Cissie ended up in the inland town of Tamworth, some 400 kilometres north-west of Sydney, residing with family friends. Mr Coorey sent her a first load of goods, and Cissie began her trade as a travelling saleswoman: 'from a pram, she graduated to a horse and small cart, called a "Dog Cart"', Queenie explained. She may have applied for a hawker's licence in Tamworth (there are no court records of her application), or she may have bought one on the black market. There was a push to stop the granting of hawker's licences, and the Redfern Local Court had stopped giving out licences to 'Asiatics' in 1895, but some licences continued to be granted.[21] Cissie would grow to love 'dear old Tamworth', as she called it; perhaps it reminded her of Zahle, surrounded as it is by undulating hills and parsed in two by the Peel River. But culturally, she could not have been further from home. She had gone from being part of a majority Melkite Christian community in the cosmopolitan Ottoman Empire to part of a spurned minority in a largely white town where few spoke her language or understood her past. The loneliness, which Moses and Cissie later wrote about to each other, must have been deep.[22]

\* \* \*

In 1902, Cissie returned to Redfern to restock. While there she met Joseph Hanna, owner of one of the largest warehouses, who suggested she should buy from his store instead. She went inside and there, among the twenty-five machinists busily sewing out the back, was Joseph's handsome, moustachioed son, Moses. Moses introduced himself and whispered for Cissie to come back later to speak with him privately. Thus began a clandestine love affair that would last until 1906.

In Cissie's statement of claim, she described Moses escorting her to the theatre and the circus, visiting her in Tamworth – unbeknown to his father – and showering her with presents: a silk handkerchief embroidered with his initial 'M', sweets, a black silk dress and an engagement ring. He promised her a wedding on Ascension Thursday in 1904.

The day arrived, but no wedding. Moses apologised, vowing that they would marry once his finances improved, but Cissie soon lost patience. She said that for all his oaths, gifts and sweet words, Moses had still not told Father Yasbeck, the local Maronite priest, of their engagement, and his affections seemed to be 'fading'. In June 1906, having received a letter from Moses telling her 'not to be foolish as there were plenty of single men to marry', she boarded a train from Tamworth to Sydney. Upon meeting Moses at his father's warehouse, she bellowed a long incantation in Arabic and put a curse on him.[23]

Not content with conjuring divine forces, Cissie also turned to the secular courts of law. There is no discussion in the hearing of why she took legal action. She could read and write English, so it is possible that she knew about breach of promise cases from newspapers. She was also part of a community that had been in Australia for over twenty years, so perhaps a friend encouraged her. Either way, on 6 June 1907, all major newspapers in the country reported on one of the most intriguing breach of promise cases heard that century. As the tabloid *Evening News* headline explained it:

SYRIAN ROMANCE. HAWKER AND MERCHANT. ALLEGED BREACH OF PROMISE. KISSED HER AND GAVE HER SWEETS. HE SWORE BY SAINT MAROON.[24]

\*   \*   \*

Cissie and Moses' case was one of only ten breach of promise cases involving non-European litigants heard between 1807 and 1910, and the only one that was not interracial. The couple were seen through many of the same Orientalist tropes as other litigants classified as 'Asiatic', but the fact that they were Syrian gave them a different status to other migrants. As we saw in the last chapter, in the 1890s and 1900s, settler colonies such as Australia, America, Canada and New Zealand were erecting racially exclusive borders, drawing a 'global colour line' and attempting to reduce the previous multiplicity of racial identities into one simple binary: white and not-white.[25] With only 1800 Syrians living in Australia (at least according to official publications), the Syrian community was small relative to the larger South Asian and Chinese communities, and might have slipped under the radar were it not for the conundrum Syrians posed to the administrators of the White Australia Policy: how were a Christian people who looked white 'and who had migrated in family groups' as permanent settlers to be racially classified?[26]

Geographically, Syrians were seen as Asian, and so fell under the category of prohibited migrants for the purposes of the *Immigration Restriction Act (1901)*, and they were classified as 'Aboriginal natives of Asia' under the *Naturalisation Act (1903)*.[27] Yet what precisely constituted an 'Aboriginal native of Asia', 'European blood' or a 'British subject' were contentious questions when it came to people from the eastern Mediterranean. A South Australian senator in 1903 claimed that Syrians should be given naturalisation rights (such as voting and owning property) because they were 'good citizens' and 'of the same race as the great founder of Christianity'.[28] Further, unlike South Asian and Chinese migrants, who were overwhelmingly men, Syrians tended to move as families. This, it was argued, meant that they would not undercut wages, as they had families to support, and that they posed no threat of miscegenation. Mr Azbourik, the interpreter in Cissie's trial, wrote in a letter to prime minister Alfred Deakin in 1910 that Syrians were physically and culturally akin to Europeans: they 'are Caucasians', he argued, 'and they are a white race as much as the English. Their looks, habits, cultures, religions and blood are those of Europeans, but they are more intelligent'.[29] By 1914, immigration minister Atlee Hunt had come around. The question of how to classify Syrians had 'caused the department considerable difficulty', he wrote in a 1914 memorandum. Although they had 'dark hair and sallow appearance', they nonetheless approximated 'far more closely European types than to those of India or part of Asia'. In fact, 'they cannot be distinguished from people of Southern Italy, Spain [or] Greece.' Being a British subject, it appeared, was largely about convincingly performing whiteness. Were they Christian? Were they good citizens? Did they want to own property (usually the reason for applying for naturalisation)? Did they speak English? Did they have families? Was their skin pigment light? In short, were they assimilable?

Of course, not everybody was so sympathetic. Commentators and government ministers opposed to Syrian migrants caricatured them according to the usual panoply of racist stereotypes used to justify discrimination. Blocked by social and legislative discrimination from other employment opportunities, they became shopkeepers and hawkers, and were generally loathed for their itinerancy.[30] As one commentator wrote in 1896:

> The Syrian is often little better than an offensive nuisance – unscrupulous in his dealings, unclean in his habits, cunning and treacherous, able to live, as the saying goes, on the smell of an oily rag ... He is commonly never his own master, but merely the hireling, if not the actual slave, of thriving Oriental importers of gimmicks ... It is in the country districts, rather than in the cities and towns, that their worst qualities are displayed and their influence most felt. There the [hawkers] come into sharp competition with the country storekeeper, who pays rents and taxes from which the itinerant vendor is exempt. But the most objectionable feature about them is their tendency to terrorise women and children in the bush ...[31]

Here Syrian men appear as both emasculated and hyper-masculine, a roving, uncontained and threatening sexual presence. The purportedly putrid, low-rent houses occupied by Syrians led to a belief that they would undercut white men's wages, because they did not require the same standard of living; and as mobile traders, they were seen as shadowy, slippery and evasive, shirking the financial obligations of citizenship and difficult to control. Being female did not let Cissie off the hook. In 1906, *The Bulletin* declared that 'some of the women, usually the aged and the ugly, do a little hawking with baskets of cheap rubbish. They will never take no for an answer and when they can't make a sale, they become abusive.'[32]

For twenty years, Syrians – their vices and their virtues – were the subject of an extended public debate over how to classify them: were they white or coloured? By the 1920s, the negative voices had been effectively drowned out by a concerted campaign by 'respectable' Syrians, and Syrians won the formal right to be naturalised and to immigrate, although in practice only very small numbers were allowed to enter the country.[33]

These arguments were circulating in newspapers and in parliament when Cissie and Moses were exchanging silk handkerchiefs and enjoying romantic soirées, and they should alert us to how extraordinary a case like this would have appeared at the time. Syrians had no public forums in which to tell their stories in Australia, even less so if they were women. When Cissie walked purposefully to the witness box on 6 June 1907, she rejected the disenfranchisement of her people and turned herself into a powerful, rights-bearing subject, demanding redress from a lover who had deceived her and claiming a public platform in a civic sphere that systematically excluded and silenced her.

## Cissie in the witness box

The hearing of *Zathar v Hanna* began in the NSW Supreme Court on a Thursday and took seven days, making it one of Australia's longest breach of promise hearings. The twelve white male jurors had their wages increased on account of its length.

Presiding over the case as acting justice of the Supreme Court was Richard Sly – thick black beard, charcoal eyebrows and long, pronounced nose. Highly strung, he was renowned for his habit of nervously twirling a piece of pink tape while addressing the court.[34] This was only the third time Sly had acted in a judicial capacity (he was otherwise still a barrister) and, judging by the copious notes he scribbled during the hearing, he took his role very seriously.

Appearing for Cissie was barrister Richard Windeyer and for Moses there was James Gannon. Seated at two tables at the front of the court, facing the bench, the two barristers could not have come from more distant worlds. As the son of Sir William Charles Windeyer, Richard was born into legal aristocracy. He was educated at the exclusive Sydney Grammar School, then at the University of Sydney, after which he went, ineluctably, to the bar.[35] James, meanwhile, was the son of a coach proprietor and educated in public schools. He studied law while working in the public service and with his warmth, wit and carelessness of speech was beloved by all who met him: an 'Irish gentleman from his heels to his hat', people said.[36]

After declaring the proceedings open, Justice Sly nodded to Windeyer, who stood to give his opening address.

'The parties are both Syrians,' Windeyer began, noting that they were 'not Mahommedans, but Roman Catholics,' a crucial detail in whitening Cissie and Moses and getting the jury onside. He then summarised their love affair. The couple became engaged in 1905, Moses 'gave her an engagement ring, according to the European custom', and they exchanged multitudinous letters, one of which contained a request to meet 'as early as 3.00 in the morning when [Moses] was passing through Tamworth'. As the jury would see, however, the letters were 'cunningly couched so as to be impersonal communications'. In a surprise manoeuvre, Windeyer then requested to tender further evidence of seduction, or 'intercourse under a promise of marriage', in aggravation of damages. Gannon objected, as he had been given no notice, but was overruled by Sly. Whispers flew through the public gallery. Windeyer called Cissie Zathar to the stand.[37]

Cissie walked to the witness box wearing her evidence: a black silk dress, a silk handkerchief in her hand and an engagement ring on her finger, all given to her by Moses. She said that she was twenty-four years old and had arrived in Australia six years ago. She had met Moses in 1902 in his father's store in Redfern. Moses had asked her to come back and speak to him privately; when she did, he asked her if she had a boy and if she thought she would get married in Australia. 'It's hard to tell,' she replied, to which he responded: 'I might be your boy for all you know.' Embarrassed, Cissie tried to change the subject: 'I am talking business now,' she said, but Moses persisted. 'We can do business and talk too.'

Once Cissie had switched her business to the Hannas' warehouse, she began to stay at the Hannas' home during her visits to Sydney, as was customary among Syrian migrants. This allowed her romance with Moses to blossom under the cover of commerce. In 1903, Moses proposed marriage: 'If you think you like me, and I will suit you for a husband, say "Yes"; if not there is not harm done.' Cissie told Moses that they had not known each other for long and that it sounded like he was 'making fun' of her. 'I never joke,' Moses replied; 'Cissie, by Saint Maroon I mean to marry you.' The courtroom filled with laughter, but Cissie continued over the top of it: 'Saint Maroon was Moses's saint,' she explained patiently.

Mr Gannon leapt upon the gallery's mirth. 'Which Moses? Moses the defendant?' he joked.

'Yes,' Cissie replied flatly. 'When we say a thing like that by a saint, we intend to do it. He also gave me a handkerchief with M for Moses on it.' She handed the silk handkerchief to Mr Gannon, who examined it with theatrical inquisitiveness.

'That's not M at all. It's W upside down.' More laughter filled the gallery.

'He told me it was M for Moses,' Cissie said, 'to remind me of my "husband left behind in Sydney".'

She recounted how on one occasion, Moses tried to stop her from speaking to another man. 'I said, "Moses, I think you are getting very strict on me. You have given me a handkerchief as a token of marriage. When do you think we get married?"' Moses assured her that in in a year and a half he would receive his half-share of the family business. 'At that time,' said Cissie, 'the words Hanna and Son were on the signboard of the shop, but since then the words "and Son" [have] been painted out.'

Justice Sly wrote down her words and later underlined this part in his notebook. It was proof of the Hanna family's efforts to avoid the company being liable for damages arising from the action.

After a month, before leaving Redfern, Moses said, 'Cissie, when you write to me, don't write a love letter or a married letter. Just write a business letter and say: "Dear Friend" until I see you myself.'

Cissie next saw Moses in September 1904, when he alighted from a train in Tamworth. 'I have come to see you,' he effused; 'when you were in Sydney I fell in love with you. I always keep thinking of you, and you are always on my mind. I told my father I was going to Queensland.'

It was during Moses' stay in Tamworth, she said, that he 'gained his object' and had sex with her under a promise of marriage. Cissie had recently moved into Mrs Varney's boarding house in west Tamworth, close to the Peel River. 'Come down to Sydney and get married at Easter – on Ascension Thursday,' Moses told her, adding 'my home is yours, or will be shortly.' Cissie needed more reassurance: 'No one hears what you say to me but God,' she said. 'I call Him to witness between you and me'.

'All right,' Moses replied, 'I give you my promise and my honour. You take it from me. I won't deceive you.' He kissed her and gave her sweets, and when they parted, they once again exchanged handkerchiefs. Later, he sent her a silk dress, the same one she was wearing in court.

Things went sour, she said, in Easter 1905. She was once again in Sydney, and Moses told her they may not be able to be married for some time. 'We owe a lot of money, and if we married now our business would be upset. When our debt of nearly £300 is paid there is nothing to stop us.' But Cissie, in her words, was 'full up of waiting'. She asked Hanna senior if he thought his son would make a good husband. Hanna avoided the question. In April 1906, she again pressed the issue: 'Moses, the best thing we do is get married if you like,' to which he replied: 'It is Lent time now, and we can't get married, but we will the first week after Easter.'

Cissie continued: 'A week later I asked him if he had told Father Yasbeck, the priest, of our approaching marriage. He said, "No, I don't think I am fit to marry you now. I think you will be very sorry if you get married."'

'I am very sorry if you think you are a man, Moses,' she spat back.

'Cissie, don't be angry,' he pleaded. 'I'll keep my word yet. I went to confession the other day and the priest would not give me absolution until I promised to marry you. Anyway, in this country people are engaged six or seven years and then get married.'

'Are you engaged to me in this country's fashion?' she asked. If so, he should get her an engagement ring. When Moses later presented her with a ring and asked her not to say anything of it to his father, she retorted: 'No fear. If he asks me I will tell him no lies. I'll say you bought it and paid for it and that you are going to marry me.' Whether consciously or not, Cissie had begun collecting legal evidence.

On the eve of her departure for Tamworth in 1905, Cissie said that her uncle Abdullah asked Moses about his promise of marriage. 'I like the girl,' Moses admitted, 'but I want to ask my father. If my father says no, I can't.' In June 1906, she received a letter from Moses telling her 'not to be foolish as there were lots of single men to marry'.

'I came to Sydney at once and saw him,' she recalled. 'He said, "I tell you fair and square, I've changed my mind." I said: "Moses, for two and a half years, I've waited for you. You've done me harm, and after all you've changed your mind." I put the curse on him.'

'It is rather long, isn't it?' inquired Windeyer.

'Yes.'

'Oh well, we won't bother about it,' he said, ending Cissie's examination in chief.[38]

*   *   *

Commentators described *Zathar v Hanna* as a 'yellowish case' involving 'curious' Syrian customs. Cissie was an 'elderly brownish siren who had beguiled little kid Moses', a 'lady who hawked things with a horse and cart – a hawkeress or hawkerine', and an 'illiterate woman with a glass eye' who 'could not read or write even in her own language' (this was untrue).[39] One writer thought she was a 'highly intelligent young woman' whose unadorned speech and quick responses made her 'probably the best witness that number two jury court has seen for many a day'.[40] Overall, however, the tone was one of amusement at Cissie's ethnic difference and at the exotic Syrian rituals being played out in modern, white Australia.[41]

Applying traditional theories of modernity would lead us towards much the same analysis. If the modern world is defined by the shrinking influence of religion, a rupture with tradition, the liberation of the individual from the authority of the family, and by literacy, rationality and urbanity, the romance of Cissie and Moses looks distinctly premodern.[42] Cissie's evidence told of curses and Levantine oaths. Maronite priests were summoned to adjudicate disputes, the patriarch of the family decided upon love matches, and commercial relationships were built on patronage and gift-giving. The line between public and private was blurred. But this analysis defines modernity in European terms and measures non-Europeans against it. Instead, I want to examine Cissie's evidence using a notion of modernity that sees it as plural and locally specific, starting with a vision of Cissie as a quintessential modern woman.

## The new woman

First seen shopping, cycling, protesting, dating or working her way into the public sphere in the 1880s and 1890s, the 'new woman' was a symbol of a peculiarly modern feminine identity, dramatising a break from the Victorian era.[43] Unlike the modesty, piety and thrift that defined the femininity of her forebears, the new woman was political, fashionable and comfortable in public. Her modernity was defined against the perceived servitude of Victorian-era women and against colonialist imaginings of her opposite: the oppression and poverty of women in the East, consigned to invisibility by the tyranny of custom.[44]

Historians have long recognised the imagined whiteness of the 'new woman', both in terms of the wealth that her consumption presumed and the colonial discourses that proclaimed her superiority.[45] There is now a flourishing literature on feminine colonial modernities: Chinese businesswomen who travelled, romanced or created families around the Pacific; Bangladeshi women sailing the Indian Ocean, made mobile by distant marriages.[46] Yet when we think about a 'modern' woman in the early twentieth century, the popular imaginary still conjures a white suffragette in a jaunty hat, whooshing around on her bicycle, or a waifish flapper coquettishly dangling a cigarette from tapered fingers. To this end, it's worth not simply proclaiming Cissie to be modern, but explaining precisely what modernity looked like from the perspective of an early twentieth-century Syrian woman.

Cissie's occupation as a hawker was crucial to her modernity, although hawking is yet to be included among the new feminine identities historians have catalogued at the turn of the twentieth century: the typist, the factory girl, the secretary, the screen star or the beauty contestant. If the department store is seen as the archetypal site of modernity, hawking might seem like a relic from an archaic Eastern past.[47] Yet hawking was a new occupation for Syrian women, a result of the modern processes of globalisation that brought migrant labour populations into the lower-class sectors of wealthy nations. While no doubt the result of a discriminatory labour force, hawking gave women economic independence and turned them into agents of the modern world in the bush.[48]

A letter Cissie sent to Moses in 1905 gives us a glimpse of what was inside her 'buster'. She was writing to Moses for more stock: half a dozen cashmere men's socks, Valenciennes lace, pearl buttons, silk handkerchiefs, aprons, a set of cards, half a dozen tape measures, garters and two yards of tablecloth.[49] Newspaper articles from the time also mention Syrian women selling aromatic soaps, cosmetics and small domestic wares.[50] Like the women themselves, these commodities were the fruits of globalisation, made possible by the late nineteenth-century transport revolution, the intensification of capitalism, and the development of steam manufacture and an industrial labour force. Although anti-immigration commentators denigrated these wares as 'gimmicks', people in the bush experienced them as wonders.

Literature from the period gives us a rich sense of what hawkers meant to people in regional areas. 'Underneath the honey gums', wrote Myra Morris in 1925, a hawker 'takes out all his homely wares / Bringing a touch, provoking, gay / of streets and cities far away / what goods are there from Ali's pack?'[51] Through the senses – touch, sight and smell –hawkers introduced people in the bush to the commodified enjoyments of the metropolis. The exchange of goods prompted a rare form of sociability that crossed the racial divides of white Australia. Patrick White's depiction of the Syrian hawker in *The Aunt's Story* (1948) is one of the most vivid descriptions of how a day on the farm was transformed by a visit:

> From a good distance you could see the dirty canvas swaying and topping above the cart, and there was time to shout a warning, to call, 'The Syrian! Here comes the Syr-i-urn!'
>
> Everyone ran out. It made quite a scattering of fowls.
>
> Gertie said the Syrian sold trash, but everybody liked to buy, and Gertie even, to touch and choose, it was exciting as the cart grated through the yard. Turkeys gobbled. Dogs barked. The day was changed, which once had been flat as a pastry board. Now it was full of talk and laughing and the whining of the Syrian's mangy dog, and the jingled harness of his old blue horse. Now there was no question of work, now that the Syrian had come.[52]

It is a symptom of the masculine gendering of the bush that female hawkers have been erased in Australian literature on hawking, yet newspaper commentary at the time noted that Syrian hawkers were almost all women, which in turn led to stereotypes of Syrian men's 'laziness'.[53] While it is important not to paint too celebratory an account of female hawkers – they hawked because they had few other options; the work was arduous and not always profitable; and they were vulnerable to violence – it cannot be underestimated how radically modern the occupation was for women. The division of labour – whereby most men worked in warehouses in the city and women (as well as some men) worked as hawkers in the bush – inverted the traditional dichotomy between women, invisible in the home, and men, mobile and engaged in public pursuits. Hawking gave Syrian women a very public occupation and, significantly, economic autonomy.

In the same year as Cissie's trial, the Harvester judgment determined the meaning of a liveable wage for white men and women, holding that a man should be paid sufficiently to keep a wife and three children in frugal comfort.[54] Men were breadwinners, women were dependants. As a hawker, Cissie fell outside this legal scheme. She could, and did, charge whatever prices she liked, and, as her barrister noted, she was a successful businesswoman. Her letters show her assertively listing items that she needed to sell, determining her own work schedule, tallying costs, demanding fulfilment of promissory notes and even, at one point, lending the Hannas £40. She tells Moses not to write the prices on garments in English, so that she can charge whatever she likes.[55] Although women worked in silk production in Syria, hawking was not a female occupation there. In fact, Syrian men complained about women working as hawkers in Australia, and one even called for magistrates to ban them.[56] Like the anxieties provoked by the autonomy of the factory girl or the office girl, female hawkers were a challenge to patriarchal power.

Hawking also gave rise to new ways of conducting romance. Although Moses ended up submitting to the will of his father, it is significant that the couple were able to escape the invigilating gaze of their families for four years. Cissie's mobility around the countryside allowed for Moses' clandestine visits, and they converted the commodities they sold into expressions of love. Silk, for Cissie and Moses, was not just a pleasurable fabric; it was also a language that they understood and that connected them to their past in Syria. That their engagement was signified by an exchange of silk handkerchiefs was peculiarly Syrian; by the early twentieth century, the European language

'A typical Syrian hawker', as depicted in
The Sydney Illustrated News *in 1892.*

of handkerchiefs, dramatised in Desdemona's dropping of the 'spotted hand-kerchief' in Othello's library, had all but vanished, as cheap cottons turned handkerchiefs into utilitarian items. While lovers giving each other presents or rings may be seen across the centuries, the culturally hybrid meanings given to Cissie and Moses' gifts were unique, an example of how they were adapting as migrants to a new environment. Gifts gave their private feelings public form, and they also became, in the words of Othello, 'ocular proof' used by Cissie in both legal and quasi-legal settings. It was a distinctively modern solution to a modern problem: living in a world without witnesses and conducting a love affair 'at large'.

Finally, Cissie's economic self-sufficiency and her habituation to being visible and mobile meant she responded to being jilted not with passive resig-nation but with a spectacular series of confrontations. She responded to a letter breaking off the affair by jumping on a train, travelling over ten hours alone to the city, expressing her rage at Moses, putting a curse on him, and then taking him to court: all wilful activities, made possible by the ease with which she traversed the public sphere.

These factors may partly explain the spiritedness Cissie demonstrated in court. She converted an action that asked women to play the part of fragile, wounded maidens into a theatre for women's empowerment. She was matter-of-fact about her sexuality and blunt in her declarations of independence from men. When asked whether Moses kissed her after meeting her on the train platform, Cissie responded, insouciantly: 'Doesn't a man, when he is engaged to a girl, kiss her?' One commentator remarked that 'when Cissie was asked why she didn't alarm the household when, as she alleged, [Moses] attempted to anticipate the marriage ceremony, she caused a laugh in court by inquiring: 'Why should I scream when he was going to marry me?'[57] On another occasion, when asked by Gannon whether she had proposed marriage to Moses, a certain Mr Malanck and a litany of other men, she replied: 'No, I'm not dying for a man.'[58]

Of course, Cissie did not need a man because she was earning enough money to support herself. How much that was, however, she refused to tell the court. Yes, she told Mr Gannon in another sparky exchange, she had received a letter from Syria saying that her sister's husband was dead and that he had left her a lot of money.

'Who is going to pay your expenses in this case?'

'That is my business.'

'It is a bit of my business too … Who paid your witnesses to come down and give evidence?'

'I won't tell you anything.'[59]

Cissie's refusal to submit to the authority of the court and to men in general may be partly ascribed to her personality. A woman who travelled the world alone, worked by herself and chose to live by herself had a feisty independence of spirit. But I also suspect that these experiences helped to forge her identity. To paraphrase Simone de Beauvoir, Cissie was not born, but made; she was made by a life of mobility and the quest for economic autonomy.

## Moses Hanna in the witness box

Moses Hanna, possibly aged twenty-one but most likely a few years older, walked to the witness box on 8 June 1907. 'Boy Moses' was how *The Bulletin* referred to him, mocking his claim to have been 'sixteen when Cissie blandished him her best eye – or he mashed her.'[60] ('Mashing' was a new term for flirting that appeared in the 1890s.) The defence launched by Gannon was firstly that there had been no promise of marriage and secondly that Moses had been underage, and therefore incompetent to contract marriage. 'He denied having seduced the lady; he denied having kissed her; he denied knowing her age; in fact, he repudiated Cissie wholesale and retail except as a customer at the shop of his Syrian parent,' *The Bulletin* reporter quipped.[61] Moses stood in front of the jury – plump and moustachioed – knowing that his task was not just to say that there had been no romance, or that he was too young to marry, but that the woman he once loved was comically old and monstrously wilful.

Moses' testimony began with his origins: he said he was born at Kfarsghab in Syria, came to New South Wales in 1901, and was a Maronite Christian, while Cissie was a Malakite. He said he first saw Cissie in 1902, when she came to his father's shop. She chose some goods and returned thirteen months later, requesting more goods on credit.

'In May 1904 when she came to Sydney,' Gannon prompted, 'did you meet her?'

'Yes, after she had been in the city two or three days, she said to me: "Moses, since I have seen you, I confess I have fallen in love with you. I love you too much and would like to marry you."'

'What did you say to that?'

'I said, "Cissie, you know I am too young to marry", and she answered, "Moses if you are frightened to marry young and that your father would not leave you any property when he dies, I promise you that I will make your life more comfortable and better than your father would."'

'What was your answer then?'

'I told her that when I was bigger, if I could find a nice girl with plenty of money, I would marry her.'

'You're quite a Britisher,' Gannon laughed. 'What did she say?'

'She said: "Moses, you don't know what women are, especially young ones. If you marry a nice young girl she might love other men, or other men might love her and she might leave you, but if you marry me, I promise you I will be true to you."'

'Yes, what then?'

'I said, "You are only joking, you are older than me. If you want to get married, you can go and marry a man the same age as yourself."'

In Moses' version of events, the situation came to a head when Cissie's uncle confronted him: 'My niece says she likes you and would like to marry you,' Moses recalled Abdullah saying. 'I said: "You know very well I will never marry her." Then I left his shop and went to my father's shop. Cissie followed me and I said to my father: "One or the other, me or her," and my father then turned to her and said, "Cissie, clear out."'

When asked about the ring, Moses replied: 'My father went to the jeweller's and obtained the ring. It was a present from the firm and was paid for by the firm of J. Hanna and Son.'

Mr Windeyer now stood to cross-examine Moses. Like a shark circling its prey, he narrowed in slowly.

'Except that she "rushed" you with a proposal in 1905, there was nothing between you but business matters?'

'No, nothing but business.'

'Do you put photographs of your customers in your room?'

'Our practice is to put photos of relatives and customers in the room and hers might have been among them.'

'Did you put her photo in a frame?'

'I might have, but I do not remember.'

'Did you write this? "We received your photo you sent to us. Thank you very much. We put it in a large frame and hung it in your room."'

'My father dictates and I only write what my father says.'

'When Cissie wrote to you, "I do not believe you care for me," and you replied: "When I see you I will show you whether I care for you," did that "I" mean you yourself or Hanna and Son?'

'I was very weak in English at the time.'

'Have you ever seen these words: "Moses says you look after your health and business. No harm about the other thing. There is plenty of time. No joke."'

'I saw those words.'

'Will you swear you never wrote them?'

'I can't remember.'

'Did you tell the priest you never used those words?'

'I told the priest I did write some of those words. I don't think I wrote "No joke."'

Windeyer returned to his seat and Moses left the stand.[62]

*   *   *

The newspapers had a field day with Moses' evidence: 'Syrian Romance / Maronites and Malakites / It was all business,' proclaimed the *Evening News*. 'Moses, I Love You / What Moses Wanted' ran the *Australian Star*, followed by the question: 'Were They Lovers?'[63]

Behind the inquiry into whether there was a romantic relationship lay another question: was Cissie Zathar loveable? Was it plausible to imagine a relationship with this person? Who was permitted into the realm of love?

And what was it about Cissie specifically that made it possible to paint her as unattractive or unmarriageable?

Age was the determining factor here. It was not sufficient for the defence to argue that Moses was underage. For the relationship to be implausible, Cissie needed to be an 'old woman', at least forty, creating a 'farcical' age gap between them.[64] Like romance fiction, which was and still is filled with fatherly heroes and girlish heroines, breach of promise cases usually involved men who were older than their lovers, and rarely the other way around. Economically, this had its foundation in the fact that women were valued for reproduction, and men were expected to financially provide for a family, which meant working for many years before they could afford to marry. But it was also because Victorian and early-twentieth-century culture valorised female chastity and eroticised inequality between men and women. It was a model of romance that gave a legitimating gloss to the power imbalance between women and men but was increasingly out of step with women's growing political and economic freedoms.

The idea that love was the exclusive domain of the young can be seen in cases throughout the nineteenth and twentieth centuries.[65] In 1849, a case involving a man in his sixties was laughed out of court: 'What love, what affection could an old man like that have?' the defence asked.[66] Barristers in such cases generally argued that damages were sought for a breach of contract, where marriage was a 'straightforward business arrangement', which seemed to reflect how older lovers saw themselves.[67]

Understanding this context helps to explain the defence's line of argument against Cissie – and it was one that had to battle against Cissie's actual appearance. As one commentator put it, 'Cissie was so good to look at, it seemed a shame to call her forty.'[68] Cissie claimed to be twenty-four, but without a parish or state registry to verify her birth, the defence was free to try to paint her as old and unattractive. The sexuality of the modern woman came with a use-by date, after which she was expected to bow out from the theatre of romance.

\*   \*   \*

Three more witnesses were called over the next few days of the hearing. First came Moses' father, Joseph Hanna, who told the court that he had come to Australia eleven years ago, residing first in Melbourne, then Adelaide and then Broken Hill. He said that he knew his son was underage at the time of the alleged engagement because he had recorded the date of Moses' birth in the Book of Baptism, located in Syria, and had copied the details into a notebook before leaving. Opening to the relevant page of the notebook, Joseph read it aloud.

Windeyer approached the witness box, asked to see the notebook, and after inspecting the ink closely, made a challenge: 'Will you swear that the entry in the book was not made since you were in Sydney?'

'I will swear they were not made in Sydney,' Joseph replied. Windeyer informed Justice Sly that he thought the ink was new and asked for a government analyst to examine it. Sly assented, and the notebook was given to a clerk of the court.

Windeyer continued: 'Do you remember a conversation with Father Yasbeck with regard to your son promising to marry Cissie?'

'I had no such conversation.'

'Was not Moses' name omitted [from the company register and the store] after receiving of the writ?'

'His name was not omitted owing to the writ, but because I wanted to make provision in the event of my death, because the business might be swallowed up by Moses.' Laughter spilled out of the courtroom.

Joseph Hanna left the witness box and Father Dadah – flowing white beard and flapping black robes – next took the oath. He said that he remembered in 1906 having a conversation with Moses about his relationship with Cissie, during which Moses denied having promised her marriage. He said he reported the conversation to Cissie, and she later sent him one of Moses' letters as proof.

With Justice Sly's permission, Gannon gave the original letter to the jury, advising them to take note: the copied version contained the words 'I will marry you, no joke', at the top of the letter while the original didn't. The jury were left to come to their own conclusion about why the letter was missing a piece at the top and whether it did, in fact, contain a promise of marriage.

The last person to be interviewed was Mr Hamnet, the government analyst. He told the court that he could identify approximately, by aid of microscopic examination, the age of inks.

'Do you see that little black book?' asked Windeyer, gesturing towards Joseph Hanna's notebook.

'Yes.'

'Have you examined the ink?'

'Yes, I think it to be from ten to twelve months old,' Mr Hammet said.

It was modern ink, he explained, and was universally used.

As Windeyer continued his examination, the jury passed the notebook from one to another, peering at the entries with a pocket microscope.[69]

## Love and religion in the modern world

'A Comedy in Inks. Entries from the Book of Baptisms. Eleven Months or Eleven Years Old', ran the headline in *The Evening News* that night. *The Australian Star* seemed to enjoy exaggerating the modern skills of the government analyst being applied to such an archaic document: 'after microscopical and chemical analysis', the ink was found to be no more than a year old, it reported.[70]

It could be argued that the press was simply picking up on the significance ascribed to religion by the parties themselves. Progression towards marriage was marked at specific points on the Christian calendar (they could not marry during Lent, although Ascension Thursday or Easter Sunday were appropriate); God was summoned as witness to Moses' pledges; Saint Maroon authorised his promises; and Maronite priests such as Father Dadah acted as judges. Here was a love affair structured by sacral authority at every level. As a mobile, global and increasingly bureaucratic form of authority with jurisdiction over love and its discontents, Levantine religion was a source and an agent of modernisation. To understand the sacred rules of romance that Cissie and Moses were adhering to, we need to return to their homeland in the Ottoman Empire.

From the fifteenth century onwards, Turkish rulers divided residents of the Ottoman Empire into 'millets', semi-autonomous legal-administrative groupings based on religion rather than geography. For instance, Melkites (like Cissie) formed one millet, and Maronites (like Moses) formed another. No matter where somebody was in the empire, they were subject to the laws of their millet. These millets were the main reference for personal law (marriage, divorce and custody), social control and education. Religious leaders were vested with responsibility to maintain order for the Ottoman rulers, including keeping birth, marriage and death registers for their communities.[71]

In the nineteenth century, particularly under sultan Abdülhamid II, who ruled from 1876 to 1909, governance was modernised. Each millet came to be administered under the rules of its own constitution, and information contained in documents such as the Book of Baptism was sent to local registry offices. The development of a modern bureaucratic imperial state under the Ottomans depended upon the traditional record-keeping systems of religion.[72] As civil society was predicated on religious sect, the millet system 'organised a church into a nationality', writes Anne Monsour, which proved useful in a world of global mobility.[73] If priests accompanied migrants, Syrians could carry their laws with them around the world, allowing them to carve out small spaces of legal and cultural autonomy. We see this in the role played by Maronite priests in Cissie and Moses' dispute and in each party's lack of respect for state law. The Hannas were at ease submitting doctored evidence (a torn letter) to the court, but Moses found it impossible to lie when asked to swear under oath that he hadn't torn it.[74] Religious authority, not state authority, compelled him to tell the truth. Law, so often seen as halting at national borders, in fact moved with migrants around the globe, colliding with or supplementing the laws of their host nations.[75]

Priests also played a crucial pedagogical role, both at home in Syria and abroad, offering English classes to migrants and establishing Christian schools. Literacy was not only necessary for reading the Bible, but also for commercial negotiations, and as Mount Lebanon opened to global trade, the millet system provided a structure for commerce that continued in Australia. As Jim McKay notes, Syrians established commercial networks based on religious sect: hawkers who were 'Orthodox migrants from Kousba went to Naswer Abdullah's warehouse ... Melkites from Zahle found J.G. Malouf ... and Maronites from Kfarsghab turned to the Lahoods, the Hannas or the Cooreys.'[76]

Children were encouraged to marry their co-religionists; in the case of mixed marriages, the woman was expected to adopt the man's religion. For those living abroad, if a suitable spouse could not be found, they were expected to return to Syria, find a partner in their village, and return to their new country with their bride or husband.[77] While religious networks converted easily into commercial networks, the prohibition against mixed marriages, as Cissie and Moses' case suggests, was at odds with the intimacies that could spring up in new worlds. Migration threw people who would once have been separated together, and unconventional romances blossomed.[78]

Cissie's testimony also shows us how Syrian migrants used religion to navigate peculiarly modern problems that arose from mobility. Having crossed oceans and vast tracts of land, and now isolated in Tamworth without family or kin structures, Cissie invoked the power of divine sanction to keep Moses to his word: 'Nobody can hear you but me, so I will summon God and you can pledge before him.' She also invoked the power of priests in unconventional ways. In cross-examination, she admitted that while married couples went to priests to resolve their problems, courting couples did this less so. Her decision to appeal to Father Yazbeck was a cultural innovation borne of a new environment and the absence of traditional support networks. Eventually, having exhausted the influence of the established church, Cissie invested herself with otherworldly powers and put a curse on Moses. Appealing to secular Australian law was the final step in what had been a journey through sacral authority structures.[79]

Tradition and modernity jostle against each other in Cissie's evidence. Like all migrants, Cissie and Moses were great improvisers, loyal to a recollected past and alert to the customs of their new nation. They submitted their love affair to the jurisdiction of the church, much as Syrians had done for centuries, but they also drew upon the conventions they observed in Australia. This is surely romance at its most creolised and cosmopolitan, adapting and responding to new and old customs and in the process inventing new ones.

Religious traditions are not usually seen as central to how people fell in love in a rapidly modernising world. This is a product of a Eurocentric bias in the scholarship and of the overblown claims to secularism made by traditional theorists of modernity. Distinguishing a secular, modern West from a religious, premodern East makes little sense when examining courtship and marriage. Although the absence of an official state religion in Australia made the legal institution of marriage a matter for the state rather than the church, at the level of popular discourse marriage was still considered a holy sacrament for much of the twentieth century. Like Syrians, white Australians were ferociously sectarian and frowned upon marriages between people of different faiths until well into the 1960s. Only six years before Cissie's hearing, the judge in *Stores v Cottarn* (1901) stated that he had no hesitation in saying that '"mixed" marriages between Roman Catholics and Protestants were a huge mistake, and productive of a great amount of misery and evil.'[80] Although love was beginning to wriggle free from the institutional and imaginative grip that religion had for centuries held over it, we should not overstate the gulf between an imagined religious premodernity and a secular modernity, or the difference between Levantine religions and Western Christianity.

## The verdict

In his instructions to the jury, Justice Sly made clear that he did not trust the Hannas. The first question to consider, he said, was whether Moses had been underage in 1906; if the jury found that he was, that would be the end of the matter. Sly reminded the jury that the government analyst believed the ink in Joseph Hanna's notebook was less than a year old. He also encouraged the jury to think about the sign on the family store and about Moses' inclusion as partner in the company register in 1904: if Moses was as young as Joseph claimed he was, he had been listed as a partner in the business at the age of fourteen. 'If the jury could not trust the defendant's evidence' on these matters, Sly said, 'they might be influenced by that fact throughout the whole case.'

The second question was whether there had been a promise of marriage. Sly drew the jury's attention to the handkerchief, the ring and Cissie's detailed account of the couple's conversations. Could she really have invented all those details? Would a girl, 'unless stung by wrong, come into court and tell of her own dishonour'?

Two and a half hours later, the foreman of the jury returned to announce the verdict: Cissie Zathar won on all counts, leaving court £250 richer.[81]

*      *      *

Whatever feelings of triumph Cissie may have felt must soon have been dashed when Moses declared himself bankrupt days later, as 'quidless as his famous namesake was when he was slumbering among the bulrushes.'[82] In the State Records Office, I examine a navy leatherbound volume titled *Register of Firms: 25195* – about as wide as my fully extended arms – and see the legal trace of this cunning. In January 1907, a red pen is struck through the name Moses Hanna, and Joseph Hanna is declared 'sole owner' of the family business.[83]

Somewhat pitifully, Cissie continued to write to Moses during the bankruptcy matter, and there are a series of pleading letters threaded into Moses' bankruptcy file. 'I thought you held no more spite,' she wrote in 1908, complaining that her earlier letters had gone unanswered. 'Don't let your temper get the better of you and don't take advice from other people, as I did.' We might speculate from this that Cissie brought the action to pressure Moses into marriage, or that she didn't anticipate that it would lead to a complete rupture in their relationship. She continued to write to Moses asking for goods, which, like the lace, seem like an excuse to make contact. 'If you don't mind write me and let me know how you are,' she pleaded in 1907. Moses collected her letters and submitted them into court, possibly still prosecuting his innocence in the breach of promise action. I suspect that Cissie simply missed Moses. She probably longed for him and for the person she had been in the relationship – now extinguished – a version of herself crafted partly out of his words and partly out of hers.[84]

In 1909, Moses sought a discharge from his bankruptcy. Cissie did not contest it, meaning she never received her £250 pounds.[85] Moses left the next year for Kfarsghab and returned in 1912 with a wife. Perhaps he went home because the Hannas felt they had been disgraced and thought that finding a local bride would be difficult; perhaps his father had always intended him to marry someone from his village. Upon Moses' return, 'and Sons' was once again painted onto the sign outside the Redfern store, and soon the business was thriving. In 1918, Moses opened a store in Armidale, in the New England region of New South Wales and, in 1951, a newspaper article commemorated his fifty years in the country: he was a 'splendid citizen' whose 'generous support to all worthy causes and his backing of improvements for civic progress never falters.' In the division that white Australia drew (and draws) between 'model migrants' and 'undesirables', Moses fell firmly into the former camp. 'He is a Britisher to the backbone,' the writer concluded, echoing Windeyer's remarks from almost half a century before.[86] Moses died a wealthy man in 1962.

Moses' life is easy to trace through the archives. Cissie's, like most migrant women's, is more oblique, preserved in the recollections of her daughter rather than in public documents. Judging by the many properties she owned, Cissie's action against Moses was not driven by financial need. In 1908, she opened a soft goods and drapery business in Tamworth, and when flood damage ruined that business in 1910 she promptly rented another property. By 1915, she had her own store in the centre of town.[87]

Cissie eventually stopped mourning her relationship with Moses. She married Henry Beresford in 1911 and, following his death, George Davis in 1915, and in 1926 a widower, James Murphy. Her first two marriages were tragically cut short by illness – diphtheria and typhoid – leaving Cissie at one stage with three children and a business to run. She was 'coping with children's ailments galore,' wrote Queenie, 'coughs, colds, teething, convulsions, typhoid fever – with both sons in hospital at the same time.'[88]

There is a photograph of Cissie and George Davis out the front of their shop in Marius Street, Tamworth, in 1916 – unpainted wooden panels, dirt footpath, corrugated iron roof and a sign saying G. Davis, although Cissie was in fact the proprietor. There is Cissie, dressed in a long black skirt, cinched and gathered at the waist, and a white blouse buttoned high at the neck. She is nursing a bundle of white cotton cloth – her first son, George – and at her side is five-year-old Queenie. Cissie looks sturdy, her feet rooted to the earth, hip-width apart, her gaze levelled at the camera and a small smile resting on her lips. Her husband looks like a Hollywood cowboy, his hat dipped over his eyes, a smirk on his face, tight pants, shirt and boots. Dashing and wilful, George Davis was born to an Aboriginal mother and European father near Coonamble and worked as a contractor, shearing, fencing and ringbarking. When I asked Cissie's descendants how they think Cissie and George met, they responded, laconically, that it was probably because they both had dark skin. Historical research has reached similar conclusions about other migrants: Cissie seemingly lacked the prejudices of most white women at the time, and, having passed almost a decade travelling around the outskirts of towns, she, like many hawkers, would have encountered and perhaps stayed with Aboriginal people. There is a significant archive of cross-cultural interactions between South Asian, Syrian and Aboriginal people, which is only beginning to receive historical attention.[89]

Cissie spent the rest of her life either in country towns or on farming and grazing properties. Ever resourceful, she returned to Lebanon briefly in 1926 when she received news that a cousin was trying to swindle her out of her share of her late father's estate. For nine months, she battled him in court until she won her portion. Following her third husband's death in 1949, Cissie lived on the significant rents from her many properties and spent a few years in Sydney living with her sons, before returning to Tamworth to live with Queenie. 'How lovely to be back in dear old Tamworth,' she said as they drove into town from the airport in the early 1960s. Religious like her mother, Queenie wrote that Cissie 'passed into her maker's loving arms on 7 January 1962'.[90]

\*     \*     \*

With its archival relics, curses, strident heroine, Maronite priests and trips around the world, *Zathar v Hanna* immediately sparked my curiosity. But there's a more personal reason why I found this case resonant. When Cissie described meeting Moses at the Tamworth train station, and when I saw where Hanna and Sons was once located in Elizabeth Street, I knew intimately what these places looked like. My high-school years were spent in Tamworth, and most of my adult life has been spent in Redfern, a few blocks away from the old 'Little Syria'. While I have long known of Redfern's

Lebanese history, I was fascinated to find that my hometown, which I had long thought of as overwhelmingly white, rural and conservative, was once home to an eighteen-year-old Syrian woman who clopped about with her horse and cart, selling 'fancy goods'. My school uniforms, always bought from Hanna's Clothing Store in Armidale, suddenly took on new meaning. And then, serendipitously, while attending a lecture on researching Lebanese history, I found myself sitting next to an old university friend, who told me that she was tracking down her husband's Lebanese ancestry. 'It's the Hanna family,' she explained, and I smiled. We eventually worked out that her husband was a descendant of Moses' brother, Mansour.

Cissie and Moses' romance is an important corrective to dominant histories of modern love, which have tended to focus on white men and women. Here instead we have a vision of love 'at large' in the world – peripatetic, culturally hybrid and sustained across vast distances. Cissie was in every respect a modern woman, living off her own earnings, voyaging across oceans and peddling the shiny trinkets of the modern world to people in the bush, all while in hot pursuit of Moses Hanna.

Like other migrants, Cissie and Moses did not arrive in Australia as blank slates but rather travelled with laws of love from their home country. These laws met and mingled with the laws of love in Australia, creating, in the words of one commentator, 'a curious mixture of Syrian and British customs'.[91] Historians have since termed this process 'acculturation': the means by which migrants adapt to a new environment. It is also an example of the legally pluralistic nature of modern love – the laws, customs and rituals migrants invoked from a remembered past interlaced with the novelties of the present.

# Part 4

## Modern Love: 1914–1939

The years from 1914 to 1939, bookended by the two great wars, have been somewhat maligned in popular consciousness. We speak about first-wave and second-wave feminism, as though nothing happened in between women's struggle for the vote and the sexual revolution of the 1960s and 1970s. And while today's bookstores are packed with popular tomes on the world wars, there is much less on what happened between them. In fact, the interwar years witnessed massive transformations triggered by the growth of social movements. Vigorous feminist activism focused on women's right to assume public roles and to be financially compensated for the domestic labour they performed in private, while around the world communist movements and anti-colonial independence campaigns jostled alongside the rise of fascism. In Western cities, the glittering indulgences of the roaring twenties were followed by the great depression of the 1930s.

The vast social shifts that began in the 1880s and 1890s – urbanisation, secularisation, the transition from a society of producers to a society of consumers, women's expanding public freedoms, and the rise of sexology and psychology – were accelerated by the First World War, and these shifts in turn stimulated dramatic changes in how people conducted their intimate lives. As American historian Beth Bailey has noted, courtship became serial dating, 'a private act conducted in a public world'.[1] Couples wooed each other at dance halls, amusement parks, vaudeville theatres, on public transport, at work, or at any number of new leisure arenas, and power relations shifted accordingly: parents could no longer control relationships as they had done in the nineteenth century, and the market, as both a metaphor and as a site of romance, restructured intimacy. Now, archetypal romantic partnerships involved an active man who paid for dinners, gifts and amusements, and a passive woman who offered him her cheerfulness or sexual favours in return. If sex was now central to married life, as Marie Stopes counselled in her book *Married Love* in 1918, then it was also important to courtship, although no woman could 'go all the way' without sacrificing her reputation.

The well-defined course of true love seen in the nineteenth century was over, and with it a moral edifice that translated easily into law. In its place was a focus on subjective sexual and romantic feelings, informed by media and expertly interpreted by psychologists. In breach of promise cases from this period, litigants, barristers, judges and juries confessed to being uncertain of the etiquette of this new style of courtship, how it might be proved and whether it was legally enforceable. As romance became unmoored from its traditional anchor points and drifted further into the opaque waters now charted by experts, love and law became increasing disentangled. Historians have documented the radical shifts in romance during this period, but nothing has yet been written on the role of law in seeking to govern amorous emotions: on the problems of evidence, love and loss so peculiar to the people of the jazz age.

# 9

# 'And you call this a lady's trousseau!': Courtship, Candour and Commodity Culture

## (*Rodriguez v O'Mara*, 1916)

Verona Rodriguez was a member of the 'Silly Swift Set', a group composed of 'flighty flappers, frisky matrons and brainless slackers of the idle rich class'. At least this is what the gossip columnists said in 1916. Scribblers cast a stony gaze over Verona and her friends, indignantly documenting their rendezvous at a notorious Hay Street café in Perth, where they were seen 'smoking, tangoing, joy-riding and behaving generally as if life were a long round of flighty pleasures and there was no such thing as a war on'. The newspapers wrote of a certain 'Have-A-Banana Club' that the Swift Set frequented, a place that 'reminds one of the night clubs of London – beautiful fairies with their nymphlike forms and clinging dresses puffing the fragrant Russian cigarettes'.[2]

Verona's first brush with the law came when the Have-A-Banana Club was raided by police: the tango dancers reportedly 'gathered up their tight skirts, threw away their half-smoked cigarettes, left their half-drunk wine in the teacups ... and fluttered out into the night'.[3] The second was when Verona, who by day was a school teacher – twenty years old, beautiful, vivacious and clever – brought a breach of promise action against another member of the Silly Swift Set, 27-year-old Adelaide resident John O'Mara, a 'good-looking ... young man of idle habits, sporting proclivities and independent means'.[4] As another newspaper reported at the time, 'few civil cases which have been dealt with in the Supreme Court have aroused more attention'.[5]

Over the course of a three-day hearing, Verona's and John's letters and telegrams were read out in court, and the couple divulged stories of their intimacies which readers would have found either dangerously or delightfully modern. They had met when Verona was staying at a mutual friend's house and John suggested that she join a motoring party to a hotel for a late supper. John claimed Verona had sat on his knee in the back seat of the car, and Verona said he told her she was 'the nicest little girl he had ever met'. Over the next seven days, they motored around the countryside and lunched at exclusive hotels. They smoked cigarettes, went to the theatre, kissed, made plans for their honeymoon in either Honolulu or the Orient, and murmured softly to each other on a friend's balcony into the small hours.

John, who liked to call himself 'Mr Rothschild', paid for everything. When he announced his return to Adelaide, Verona suggested they become engaged. He didn't get down on one knee, she later laughed. 'It was 1916,' after all. John agreed to the 'understanding' and promised to send her an engagement ring, so long as they each had the right to rescind the engagement when he returned.[6]

A flurry of letters followed John home to Adelaide: 'already crowds of people know of our engagement', Verona gushed, but she was reluctant to 'make our thing public until you send me the ring'. In the meantime, she resigned from her position as a teacher and began 'updating' her trousseau, purchasing sixteen hats, blouses, night-gowns, pyjamas, boots and shoes, oils, face creams, polish, perfume and lotions from Brennan's department store. When Verona's epistles were met with silence, her marriage preparations stalled, and her ebullience turned to rebuke. She sent a telegram demanding that John write to her mother asking for permission to marry and, after that, chastised John for not being 'manly' enough to write and tell her that his affections had waned. Verona thought marriage should be about happiness and that 'there was not much happiness without love'.[7]

Nonetheless, when John returned to Perth in January for three weeks, passions were rekindled. The couple spent all their time together and Verona later claimed the engagement was renewed, although John denied it.

John's second departure for Adelaide witnessed a repeat of the first: Verona's letters were met with silence, he refused to write to her parents for permission, and the ring never arrived.[8]

Eventually, Verona consulted her solicitors. She claimed £5000 for breach of promise of marriage, including £180 for her trousseau. The gossip columnists declared the case to be 'the first lesson in the history of the Silly Swift Set',[9] and the judge thought Verona's trousseau was 'the most extraordinary thing he had ever seen'.[10] The case represented a dramatic encounter between consumer culture, new masculine and feminine identities, romance and the law. It was a case that put modern love on trial.

*   *   *

For long-time readers of newspaper accounts of salacious legal cases, *Rodriguez v O'Mara* would have appeared markedly different from those of thirty years earlier. Victorian-era cases had been rather ascetic affairs. While property and furniture featured as pledges of love, women rarely claimed their trousseaux as damages, engagement rings were seldom produced, and store-bought gifts, particularly jewellery, were scant.[11] While Verona and John were more affluent than most early twentieth-century litigants, their wealth alone does not explain the cluttering of their romance with commodities. Rather, their case exemplifies, extravagantly, a larger cross-class trend that began in the 1890s and would continue well into the next century: consumer culture's colonisation of romantic love.

Verona and John's affair conforms with much of what we already know about early-twentieth-century romance. Verona was romantically assertive, and she imagined romance, marriage and femininity as things that needed to be bought. John qualified Victorian-era ideas of manliness with the very twentieth-century confession that such ideals crumbled in the face of sexual desire, which – as Freud had by then explained – was not something over which people had complete control. John also thought that romance could be purchased, and he knew that his financial capital translated into sexual capital. John and Verona were exemplars of the new gender identities to which early-twentieth-century consumer culture, helped along by cinema, radio, advertising, popular magazines and sexology, gave rise.[12]

The couple also embraced a modern idea of marriage based on love and desire rather than duty, which explains why they agreed to a trial engagement. If love was to be the foundation of marriage, romantic exploration needed to be liberated from contract, so that full self-disclosure and intimacy were possible. Parents were only consulted after the engagement had been agreed on, and the courtship mostly took place far from their gaze: in hotels, theatres and new modes of transport such as steamers and motorcars.

The gossip columnists' fixation on the women of the Swift Set and the court's shock at Verona's trousseau show the blatant gendering of this new world of sexualised consumerism. Women, seen throughout the nineteenth century as biologically predestined for the private sphere, were delegated the labour of shopping for the family, yet they were derided as extravagant or selfish for performing this role. That the flourishing of twentieth-century industrial economies and the smooth running of households depended on their purchases passed unnoticed.[13] Ultimately, the city's hotels, theatres and dance halls beckoned young lovers such as John and Verona to their brightly lit rooms – but inside, a balcony of tight-lipped moralists peered down at the lovers and frowned, fretting about declining birth rates, work habits, thrift and propriety.

These aspects of Verona and John's affair will be familiar to anyone who has read F. Scott Fitzgerald or Evelyn Waugh. What is surprising about their romance, and what contradicts current scholarship, are its legal nuances, from their very appearance in court to the legal meanings they assigned to romantic objects. Scholars in Britain and America have assumed that the breach of promise action all but died with Queen Victoria. The action's presumption of female dependence on marriage and its privileging of con- tractual duty over desire meant that by the early twentieth century, breach of promise 'was seen as a legal action out of step with modern intimacies'.[14] In England, there were 'fewer and fewer' cases, while in America the action's focus on emotional wounds 'doomed it', as 'courts and legislatures became uncomfortable with awarding money for emotional harms.'[15]

Yet in Australia, the early twentieth century is when the action springs to life. From 1900 to 1930 there were 523 cases reported in the newspapers, compared with 211 in the entire nineteenth century. Not only were there more cases being reported, they played out in a radically altered way. The typi- cal nineteenth-century hearing, with its love letters, gossiping neighbours and invigilating families, suddenly became strewn with *things*. From ostrich feathers, books and rings to nighties, knickers, smelling salts and lotions, romantic objects took centre stage. Amorous gifts were given an economic and epistemic value, as both the price and the proof of love.

Verona, who upon her death in 1976 was described as personifying the 'gay 1920s in Perth', and whose case turned entirely on the relationship between morals, material proof and materialism, embodied these historical shifts in love and law.[16] Her love letters, the items she selected for her trousseau and her cosmopolitan, luxurious and ultimately tragic life give us intimate knowledge of the possibilities and pleasures that twentieth-century romance opened to certain women, as well as its social costs and cruelties. Her story also suggests a link between the proliferation of cases in the early twentieth century and the sudden appearance of romantic commodities in court. Verona went to court seeking compensation for the money and job opportunities she had lost in anticipation of marriage. Like other women of her generation, she applied an economic valuation to all aspects of love. The court, in turn, functioned as a spectacular moral theatre where consumer desires could be disciplined, new romantic identities could be performed, new courtship practices could be debated, and new laws of love defined.

The abundance of commodities in early-twentieth-century cases was a reflection not only of sexualised consumerism, but also of the popular and legal desire for evidence in a rapidly changing romantic terrain. As courtship ceased to be policed by family and as Victorian formalities loosened, the rules of romance became open to debate. While the engagement ring became solid, almost incontrovertible legal proof of an engagement, the trousseau became a suspect item, emblematic (if it was too copious) of the woman's uncontained consumer passions: sensationalist, sensual and obscene, offensive to the rationalist, forensic visual cultures of law. In the economics of romance, commodities bought by men had probative and monetary value; those bought by women were suspicious.

In Verona's life story, we can observe how the uncoupling of law from love gave rise in the early twentieth century to an explosion of law, reflecting a quest for candour as much as for costs, as amorous words were uncoupled from their conventional legal meanings and consumer culture put a new price on love.

\*    \*    \*

Verona Rodriguez knew from a young age that she was special. Her birthday, she informed the editor of the Children's Pages of Perth's *Daily News* in 1907, was on 'December 25 ... a day known to everybody; don't you think?'[17] Considered 'a Christmas box' for her family, Verona was born on the schooner *Sree Pas-Sair* in the milky-blue waters off the far northwest coast of Australia in 1895.[18] She would later swear that she was born to a Spanish father – pearl-diver and hotelier Filomeno Rodriguez – and a Cornish mother – businesswoman Maud Miller. When writing to John O'Mara, she jokingly referred to herself as 'the Dago in the West', and Filomeno's naturalisation papers describe him as Spanish. The truth was more interesting, and more obvious for anyone familiar with the cosmopolitanism of the pearling frontier.[19]

Filomeno was in fact only part-Spanish. He was born in 1864 on the island of Bantayan, in the province of Cebu in the Philippines, to a Spanish planter and serial philanderer, José Rodriguez, and an unnamed, unmarried Filipina woman. Verona's descendants speculate that she may have been a domestic servant.[20] Filomeno would have learnt to dive beneath soaring black volcanic cliffs in the cerulean waters of Cebu, ducking into coral reefs that had been harvested for pearls since the mid-nineteenth century. He likely acquired his Catholicism and his ability to read from the Spanish missionaries who fluttered like moths garbed in dusty brown robes around Bantayan, busily building schools, erecting churches and claiming souls. By the age of twenty-two, Filomeno had earned enough money as a pearl-diver to strike out with his own lugger. In the 1880s he recruited a group of ten divers, mostly Englishmen, on Thursday Island, and together they scoured the ocean bed for pearls, sailing down through the exhausted reefs of the Torres Strait, North West Cape and New Guinea until they arrived at the abundant and unexplored reefs around Cossack in the northwest of Australia.[21]

The pearling industry ran on muscle, breath and racialised cruelty, but its quick fortunes depended on luck – and Filomeno was a lucky man. En route to Cossack he moored at Turtle Island, off the west coast of Australia, and found himself in a thicket of reef encrusted in pearl shells: *Pinctada maxim*, to be precise, the mother- of-pearl variety whose shells had curled, crinoline lips rimmed in gold and silver. A few days later, he arrived at Cossack bearing seventeen tons of pearl shell, worth about £3000, which gave him enough capital to purchase a boat and several luggers. He now also had the money to marry.

In 1890, Filomeno exchanged marriage vows with Maud Guinevere Miller in the school at Cossack. It was a grimly appropriate location for the marriage, given Maud should still have been in class. She was only twelve-and-a-half years old, six months over the legal age of marriage for women in Western Australia at the time. Perhaps Maud's parents, Cornish miners driven by poverty to Adelaide and then to Cossack, thought that the devoutly religious, hard-working and fabulously wealthy Filomeno was a good match for their daughter. For his part, Filomeno probably thought it wise to marry into a local white family. The air in the late nineteenth century was pungent

with talk of racial exclusion, and the marriage would have ensured his integration into the white community. Soon after their marriage, the couple
moved to Broome, around 800 kilometres north of Cossack. By the time
Verona, their fourth child, was born in 1895, Maud was only eighteen years
old.[22]

There are two black-and-white photographs of Verona that her son,
88-year-old Michael Prevost, sent to me. The first is a generic colonial-era
photograph: moustachioed men with lined faces dressed in pressed white
linens stare unsmilingly from beneath their hats – some pith helmets, some
straw boaters – into the camera. They're assembled in front of a wooden balcony enclosed with rattan blinds and wear the same garbs of imperial rule
you might see anywhere from Africa to India to Australia. To their right is
a man in a diving suit; his helmet rests on a wooden plinth in the centre of
the frame. The diver, Michael informs me, is Filomino. He is likely model-
ling a new type of diving suit, a costume that would not look out of place
at a steam-punk convention, complete with calf-high boots weighted with
metal. His youngest daughter, Carolina, is by his side, and on the other side
of the diving helmet stands Verona, about five or six years old, a tiny waif
peeping over her brother Joe's shoulder, tucked in next to her father. Here
we catch a glimpse of the world in which she rollicked around for the first
ten years of her life.

Verona was raised in an idyllic corner of the world, a place closer to Asia
than to the capital cities of Australia. The ocean in Broome shimmers a pale,
opalescent blue, hot winds blow red dust into flurries, frog-song fills the air
at night, and during the day the heat has the effect of an acoustic dampener –
all is mute and still. When Verona went to the pier with her father during the
laying-in season in Broome (that is, when pearl shells were harvested, from
April until August) she would see the polyethnic melee of the pearling industry in full swing – Indonesian, Timorese, Malaysian, Filipino, Melanesian and
Japanese divers; American, English, Dutch, Japanese and Australian owners –
alongside Afghan and Bangladeshi camel traders and the local Yawuru and
Goolarabooloo people. As historian Henry Reynolds has written, the Australia that lies north of the Tropic of Capricorn 'was never and could never
have been white'.[23]

Cosmopolitan, however, is too romantic a term for early-twentieth-century Broome. Growing up among people of different ethnicities also meant
that Verona witnessed first-hand an industry divided by race. The pearling
industry was exempt from the White Australia Policy, not for progressive

reasons but because pearling was too lucrative to lose to Dutch Indonesia, and the labour was seen as too dangerous for white men to perform. By the time Verona was born, strategies were in place to prevent Aboriginal people being sold into slavery on pearl luggers, as had been the practice from the 1860s. Instead, she would have seen a labour force of primarily Asian divers and white owners. As parliamentary inquiries into conditions in the industry confirmed during this period, brown foreign bodies were seen as cheaper and more expendable.[24] Brown people could endure the illnesses, the shark attacks, the indentureship, the ten-hour days, the mean provisions, the tyrannical captains and the 10 per cent death rate because they were more 'fatalistic', it was argued. This was no work for the 'coming man' of white Australia.[25]

Young Verona was no doubt keenly aware of racism. But in her father's standing in the community, she also registered how money could insulate non–Anglo Saxons from racism's humiliations, albeit never entirely. Filomeno, a self-identified Manilaman (or Filipino), owned a fleet of fourteen luggers, a number of houses and blocks of land in desirable locations, and Broome's first hotel. This no doubt aided his election to Broome Municipal Council in 1900. Verona saw her father being treated differently to other non-whites because of his wealth, his marriage to a white woman and his Christianity. Yet she would also have known that no matter how impressive her father's financial success and no matter how esteemed his public positions, he still felt the barbs of prejudice. When Filomeno won shipping races, he was accused of cheating; when he generously sailed writer Daisy Bates around Aboriginal missions, she publicly described his boat as filthy. Filomeno's wealth, people murmured, was ill-gained, a product of illegal Kanaka labour. Verona would have seen that money gave her family a passport to whiteness and social mobility, but that the passport could be confiscated at any time. She learnt early in life that in white Australia, it was easier to deny her Filipino heritage and simply replace it with Spanish.[26]

The second photograph is labelled 'Rodriguez Family Photo' and was taken around 1912, by which time all ten children had been born. Verona is seventeen years old; her hair is long, wavy and pulled up at the sides, and she looks like she's laughing – her eyes are crinkled with joy. Filomeno and his mother-in-law Caroline Miller are seated, with the children gathered around them. Standing to Verona's right is her mother, Maud Miller, whose large, impressive, lace-bound bosom dominates the space between Filomeno's and Caroline's heads. At the time the family posed for this photograph, they were commuting between Broome and Perth. Filomeno had built Gantheaume House in the wealthy Perth suburb of Claremont in the early 1900s, so that the children could live there under the guardianship of Caroline while attending the city's best Catholic schools. When Verona arrived in Perth in 1905, she walked into a city awash in new money from the Kalgoorlie goldfields. Today Perth appears to many visitors as relaxed to the point of being sleepy, but in the early twentieth century, it was fast and rich, more like an antipodean San Francisco.[27]

In her school years, Verona was brilliant and precocious, in the last throes of childish unselfconsciousness. We know from newspaper articles that she was busy doing good deeds – performing in plays to fundraise for the local orphanage – and writing to the editor about her labours. In a series of letters from 1907 to 1909 she wrote of bringing the orphans 'flowers … and a few sweets' and taking them down to have 'tea on the beach'. While some of the children preferred to walk, she 'thought it was glorious running down the hills'. Verona's body thrummed with vitality and pleasure; her senses were alive to the world. Verona at eleven was still subject, not object; her body was for doing things, not for looking at. With comic imitative maturity, she provided readers with an official report on the state of the orphanage, which she measured, characteristically, through commodities: 'They have a great deal of toys there, nearly everything imaginable.' And she apologised to the editor for her tardiness in writing – 'you must think that I have forgotten you'. She was certain of her place at the centre of everyone's universe.[28]

Verona's writing vibrates with cleverness, and *The Daily News* was filled with formal proof of her academic prowess. She took out prizes in arithmetic, algebra, religious studies and music. She decided in her final year of schooling that she would like to study medicine, and the school organised a mathematics teacher of the highest calibre to teach her. In her matriculating exam she won a place at Melbourne University and in 1915 she began her medical studies. But in the same year there was a crash in the pearling industry, and her father decided that he would only pay for the two sons' university fees. In the hierarchy of family priorities, sisters came second. Verona was sacrificed and sent back to the west. She became a teacher at a girl's convent school, and soon she started mingling with the Swift Set.[29]

There is another photograph of Verona, which first inspired me to write on her case. It is a staged photograph that accompanied an article on her breach of promise action in the gossip pages. Her signature is in the bottom corner, and I would guess that she had offered it to the newspaper in a happier moment. I have not seen a photograph of any earlier litigant given so much space in a newspaper, and it distinguishes Verona from her nineteenth-century counterparts. Like other women in the twentieth century, her femininity was asserted not through modesty and self-effacement but through spectacular public display.[30]

In this photograph, Verona is in profile, perched on a rock with her dainty features and thick black hair silhouetted against a white backdrop. She is in her late teens and dressed like a Grecian deity – festooned in white robes that fall in loose folds around her small frame, her hair wound up into a loose bun and encircled in a crown of silver; she is a figure of insouciant grace. Unlike the eleven-year-old Verona – the active, laughing girl who thought it glorious to run down hills – this Verona is stationary, a statue existing for the gaze of others. Yet in posing for the photograph and sending it to the paper, she is also mistress of her own self-creation. Verona has matured from the children's pages to the gossip pages. They report on the clothes she wore to a friend's engagement party, and she intends to use them to announce her engagement to John O'Mara. Verona is no passive doll – she knows that modern femininity needs to be seen, and she has created a product for popular consumption. What this Verona, sitting resplendent on a rock, is yet to learn, however, is that control over her creation – its reception and circulation – is not entirely in her hands. She could not have imagined the humiliating text that would soon wrap around her image.[31]

*   *   *

On 11 December 1916, Verona Rodriguez and her grandmother Caroline walked through the whitewashed foyer and along the scarlet-red carpets of Western Australia's new Supreme Court, until they reached courtroom number two. Verona had convinced Caroline to pay the £215 legal fees for one of Perth's best barristers, the rotund, convivial former politician Sir Walter James, and to register the action in Caroline's name. At the age of twenty, Verona was not legally competent, so Caroline was her 'next friend'.[32] Outside the court, however, Verona was friendless. 'Everyone had dropped the girl because of her breach of promise action', a Perth resident later gossiped.[33] It would have been considered unseemly among members of Perth's high society to air one's dirty laundry in public, particularly using an action that was associated with shop girls and seamstresses.

According to *The Sun*, once the courtroom doors opened 'there was a rush for seats, and during the remainder of the day it was "standing room only" for curious pressmen and members of the Devil's Brigade [lawyers]. For those not in the swim there wasn't even standing room.'[34] Verona and Caroline walked past the thronging crowds and took their seats behind their legal team. At 10.30 a.m., the judge's associate rose to his feet and proclaimed: 'All stand.' He then knocked three times on a door behind the bench, and Chief Justice Robert McMillan swished through it: handsome, clean-shaven, head held aloofly high. McMillan was almost sixty years old. A self-identified man of the Victorian era, his diligence had just earned him a knighthood – 'Sir' was added before his name in the court documents.[35]

McMillan lowered himself into his chair, prepared his notebook, and then inclined his head towards Sir Walter, who rose to address the six members of the jury. It was not a bombastic opening, more a factual precis of the claims: Verona said that the promise of marriage was made in August 1915 and repeated in 1916, while John said that there was no promise, or if there was it was tentative and he had only agreed to it because Verona had pressed him. 'If this is true,' opined Sir Walter, 'the defendant was a weak man, a mere puppet in the hands of a woman'. Sir Walter said that he would show that in August 1915 John proposed marriage to Verona and promised on several occasions 'to give her a ring'. Verona had purchased her trousseau with John's encouragement; he had 'suggested that she bring it up to date'. Sir Walter concluded by saying that he was confident the breach of promise would be established by the couple's correspondence.[36]

Verona then took the stand. She told the court that she had been acquainted with John for three or four weeks before he proposed to her. 'We were alone together in the evening,' she said, on the side veranda of their friends' house. 'It was very late. He said I was the nicest little girl he had ever met, and that he would very much like to make me his wife ... and he said he would come next morning and give me a ring.'[37]

'And what reply did you make?' asked Sir Walter.

'I think I said I would because I liked him,' Verona answered, before continuing: 'The next morning he came with Mr Moss Maloney and we went to the Savoy to lunch. John had several calls to make and said he had not time to get the ring but would send me one and a gold wristlet watch from Adelaide ...' Reflecting on the relationship, she said: 'We behaved more like an engaged couple than as mere friends.'

Sir Walter then stood and read aloud from Verona's love letters:

Dearest Jack – This is my first love letter, so you will please have to pardon it if it is only just so-so … Well dear, I do miss you and very much wish you were here again. After leaving Fremantle yesterday we motored home, called in to see mother on our way and broke the news of our engagement to her very quietly. I told her you were writing. Of course, and naturally, she was surprised at its suddenness but I explained that we were very fond of one another and that I really think an engagement makes one fully realise the serious side of the matter …

I expect the news was well round the convent today. I don't want to make the thing public until you send me the ring and then I shall only be too delighted to proclaim it to the outside world. Trust children for advertising anything – I used to do it myself once …

After we had finished lunch (and of course a smoke) we wandered round town for the rest of the afternoon. Went to a fortune-tellers, who told me the maddest things out. Mum's the word. Moss says he intends driving us around in his car for our honeymoon. He is a bit premature … I think if we ever do go on a honeymoon trip we can dispense with his or anybody else's services (N'est-ce pas?) Mother thinks I have known you for nearly all the time you were in Perth. You must not say otherwise for she may think we are rushing things. But Jack what does it matter; you seem to be very fond of me and I know that I'm very fond of you and have not felt that I could marry any other person before I met you … I think I will say 'au revoir' for the present. Bye-bye dear, this time. Ever so much love from yours. Ron xx

After this, said Sir Walter, came a telegram from Jack in Adelaide: 'arrived safely; pleasant trip. Writing later. Best love, Jack'.

Sir Walter didn't comment on the brevity of Jack's message, but picked up the next of Verona's letters and began reading:

Dearest Jack – it seems just ages since you left here, yet it is only one short week today. I wish you were coming back … It is marvellous how stories leak out, but already crowds of people know of our engagement. It is most annoying as I didn't want it announced before you had written to mother. Still that part, writing to mother, is merely a matter of form. For if I liked anything or anybody no parent could stop me from having that. I'm a little bit determined, I think. However, there's no need to worry about the parents' consent part for I have had a chat with mother and I think all is serene. They like you very much. Hurrah!

It's a silly idea but I guess the announcement of the engagement had better take place soon. Silly idea, I mean, as far as a newspaper is concerned. The two lady writers from the *Cygnet* (our society paper) and the *Daily News* have written for permission to announce it. I'm waiting to hear from you, though. Send your father's Christian name too, will you. Silly idea, but I suppose we must adhere to convention ...

When do you expect to be over here again ... I'm really very lonely without you and I cannot tell you how much I miss you. Certainly I have been enjoying myself since you departed, but it isn't the real enjoyment and pleasure ... au revoir, with all my love, Ron.[38]

## Love letters

Jaunty, gossipy, warm and a little pretentious, Verona was judged by newspaper columnists to be an excellent correspondent. 'She is a school-teacher by profession, but she could earn a good living as a lady writer', opined the writer for *Truth*.[39] But would her letters be sufficient, as Sir Walter had confidently declared, to establish a promise of marriage? I have little doubt that a few decades earlier she would have easily won the case. The letters' explicit mention of community and family recognition of the engagement, the terms of endearment and the discussion of honeymoons would have been seen to reflect a prior contract to marry. But the nineteenth century was a different world from the one Verona moved in.

I find Verona's letters fascinating because they appear perched between two eras: steeped in the twentieth century but shot through with the past. We see two competing models of feminine identity: a Victorian woman concerned with formality and morality, and a twentieth-century woman who performs for an imagined crowd of thousands yet is answerable only to her own feelings and conscience.

When Verona asks John to write to her mother for formal approval of their engagement, we meet the Victorian-era Verona. We encounter her again when she calls John 'unmanly', 'cowardly' and 'ungentlemanly' for breaking his promise of marriage. It is in moments of crisis, when Verona is trying to compel John to keep his word, that she has recourse to the social and moral norms of the nineteenth century, invoking a traditional model of masculine honour based on promise-keeping in commerce and love. When it becomes clear that John has been 'playing' with her, she mentions her family's displeasure – 'mother thinks it strange you not writing' – and the censure of friends: 'I don't want to think what Glennie says of you: "would not trust Jack O'Mara walking from one door to another."'[40] Victorian-era courtship norms imposed a higher moral standard on men to fulfil their promises, they cocooned women in bonds of community and family, and they gave extra-judicial powers to family and kin to shame wayward lovers into honouring their word. They were also legible to the dictates of law.

Existing alongside this prim and censorious Verona is another, more dominant, person: a quintessential modern woman. If one Verona needs parental consent before she can tell people of her engagement, the other is a woman of galloping passions and independent desires who professes she does 'not care' what her parents' think, and who regards family approval as 'merely a matter of form'. For this Verona, there is no higher moral law than her own feelings and desires. She is 'determined'. She has 'grit'. This Verona privileges mutual love over bourgeois Victorian-era values: 'I shouldn't care to marry a person who didn't love me, even if I loved him ever so much,' she writes. 'Such things as money and position don't appeal to me in the least, for the man I marry I'll marry for himself even if he were the poorest of the poor.'[41] In reality, her family had just lost substantial capital in the pearling crash, and if anyone was using marriage for social mobility, it was probably Verona. But the idea that love was indifferent to class gained legitimacy in the twentieth century, particularly for women, as sexual desire became increasingly important and courtship came to be structured around an exchange between masculine financial stability and feminine beauty.[42]

For women, including Verona, the flipside of the elevation of romantic love was that men were now increasingly compelled by their fluctuating desires. The Victorian Verona called John 'unmanly' for jilting her, but the twentieth-century Verona asked for honesty: 'Don't think that you must bind yourself to me. Only write and let me know your wishes.' She invited him to prove his masculinity not by keeping his promise, but by having the courage to tell her that he had changed his mind: 'If you have any reasons for not writing, wouldn't it be more manly to tell them and not keep silent – well, it does seem cowardly.' Where a Victorian-era woman might have appealed first to male chivalry and then to the law, the Edwardian-era Verona recognised the vulnerable position she was in and chafed against it: 'Don't think this letter is a please-take-me-back-in-your-affection kind [of] pleading one', she wrote; 'I don't want to make a pathetic appeal, but for the past weeks you have spoilt my happiness and made me a butt for ridicule …' And in contrast to the Victorian era, when the community would have rallied around a jilted woman and shamed the man into keeping his promise, by the early twentieth century the community, while still keen to exercise judgment, cared less about male honour. Verona's letters reveal that she was in fact more concerned about community perceptions than about her own feelings: 'Your silence doesn't make things altogether pleasant for me. That I don't mind very much for myself because it is always the girl who suffers. But still, from other people's point of view, it is queer.'[43]

In the twentieth century, the small, moral community of the Victorian period had been replaced by an anonymous, amoral crowd that had no personal stake in men keeping their promises but were ferocious in their judgment of women. Yet the new century also held out the promise of a meaningful life for women through work rather than marriage. Verona's final letter to John sees her reaching for this: 'I've grown very tired of a butterfly existence and want to do something worthwhile for myself, without being entirely dependent on others', she declares, outlining her scheme to establish a 'decent girls' school'. 'I want something to live for, something to do, and not to be wasting precious time, as I have this last year', she continues. 'I'm going to be a keen business woman – money and the education of young minds.' This final letter brims with pathos: she can only establish the school, she explains, if John will lend her the money, and she is still 'aching' for him to write back. Having given up on romantic transfiguration, Verona seeks emancipation in work. She wants to use her 'brains', but her dreams are thwarted by structural forces: a sexed labour market that pays women half the wages of men and a society that still sees marriage as women's ultimate destiny.[44]

I feel sympathy for Verona, but there is also something rather alarming about her letters. Sir Walter described them as 'typical', but to my mind they lacked a crucial ingredient: curiosity about her lover. This is particularly striking because the couple had only known each other for a week when they got engaged, and the engagement was contingent upon them developing a deeper intimacy. One would expect their correspondence to be a space for mutual self-revelation, with each side begging the other for more biographical details, but Verona asks John no questions about his past or who he is outside his social roles. Far from creating a space of intimacy, Verona's letters read like updates on preparations for a show.

During the engagement, Verona calls the gossip of schoolchildren 'advertising'; she thrills to being contacted by the newspapers; every social interaction, whether with family, close friends or acquaintances on the street, is an opportunity to bask in the fame that romance has given her.

The engagement is less about her relationship with John than about a rhapsodic encounter with herself. Verona imagines performing for multitudes, moving giddily through a world of public pleasures, existing entirely through the gaze of others. She thrills to the idea of being watched.

It would be wrong to think that such vanity was simply a personality defect. I think Verona embodies a larger historical process; in broad terms, she reflects a new psychological type that emerged with a new social order. As American historian Warren Susman argues, the shift from a nineteenth-century producer society to a twentieth-century consumer society triggered a change in how people presented themselves, from 'character' to 'personality'. Where people in the nineteenth century 'built' their characters through self-abnegation and self-control, ensuring that their individual conduct conformed with the moral and social order, people in the twentieth century 'developed' their personalities through self-gratification and self-expression, 'striving to become one with a higher self', rather than with a higher moral order. Personality, writes Susman, 'is the quality of being someone', of distinguishing oneself from the crowd and at the same time appealing to the crowd, of being well liked, influencing others and impressing people. Where character was built through the sublimation of desire into work and duty, personality was developed through leisure and consumption, particularly if you were a woman.[45]

Twentieth-century women were applauded not so much for being virtuous and chaste as for being fashionable or having good complexions. They also had more opportunities to perform to a crowd, as new developments such as the cinema, the department store and urbanisation created spheres in which women were put on display. 'The spectacular modern woman', writes historian Liz Conor, triumphed over her modest, thrifty, nineteenth-century predecessor. Visual culture and its attendant regimes of self-discipline were now essential to definitions of femininity. With her fantasies of crowds, her abundant trousseau and her love of publicity, Verona Rodriguez lived the new cult and culture of personality.[46]

These vast social and psychological changes created new romantic practices, which in turn required a redrafting of the rules of love. Revisiting Verona and John's courtship helps us to map out these changes. Their first meeting (at a family friend's house) and the circumstance of their engagement (on the veranda) would not have been surprising for middle-class people in the nineteenth century. What makes their courtship peculiarly modern is that little of the intervening time was spent with Verona's family. They went to the theatre, lunched and took supper at hotels; they motored to a weir outside Perth; and they spoke until the small hours of the evening – all without the knowledge of their families. So little did Verona's family know of John that she could tell them she had known him for three weeks rather than one, and they were none the wiser. Her request to know John's father's name to pass it on to the gossip pages is telling in its awkwardness: a vast readership would soon learn of Verona's engagement to someone whom she herself barely knew. John later told the court that he boasted of his engagement to Verona to his sister and his mother, but they both thought it was a joke because he could not remember her name. (She had written it down for him in his little brown book, but he didn't want to consult it in front of his family.) Courtship for Verona and John had moved beyond the jurisdiction of family to become 'a private act conducted in a public world'.[47]

A romance that took place in hotels, restaurants, theatres and motorcars was also more expensive than a visit to the family home and a walk around a park. When love affairs played out in a commodified public sphere, the language of love became tainted with market: romance was now an 'investment'. Verona later asked John to come to Perth 'for a fair settling up' of their affair. Beth Bailey argues that this shift altered the power dynamics of courtship. When courtship moved from the feminine sphere of the home to the masculine market, women relinquished control over the tempo and space of romance, and dating assumed the form of a financial transaction: men paid for outings and women offered their cheerfulness, beauty and, increasingly, sex in return. The norms of masculinity also altered according to a new commercial logic. Young men, as Eva Illouz has argued, no longer needed to prove their manhood by being the head of a household. They now had the option of becoming 'sexual capitalists': the more women they accumulated, the more manly they were.[48]

It's not just that men like John O'Mara acquired less social and economic status through marriage than they would have in the nineteenth century; their promises of marriage also became increasingly difficult to prove. Although on one level heterosexuality was now a visible performance, 'conducted at eye-level on the street', it also became invisible to interested witnesses.[49] Amorous words uttered in private were ephemeral, romantic gestures were ambiguous, and promises could dissipate into air. 'It's wonderful how news carries,' Verona wrote bitterly to John, 'and when it was rumoured that I was engaged to you, I felt so silly, people coming up and saying, "Is it true; where's your ring?"'[50] It is in this context that lovers turned to romantic commodities for proof.

Looking back at Sir Walter's opening address, his confidence that Verona and John's correspondence would establish the promise appears to have been mere bluster. Rather than parsing Verona's letters to prove a promise of marriage, he instead devoted his time to explaining the absence of an engagement ring. Sir Walter would have been aware of the shifting rules of evidence in breach of promise cases, and he would have known that the vast gestural vocabulary of nineteenth-century romance – its visits, walking out, kisses and love letters – had, over the past twenty years, narrowed to the width of a finger.

### The engagement ring

Verona spent her courtship with John vexed by the absence of an engagement ring. John first promised to buy her one on the veranda. Then he promised to send one over from Adelaide. Later he boasted that he would get her 'a nicer ring' than that of her friend. The court was also perturbed by the absence of a ring, and Sir Walter blamed John's inconstancy – 'he was a man of many promises'. In his defence cross-examination, Mr Villeneuve Smith – a tall, devastatingly clever barrister who sported a large pince-nez hanging from a black silk ribbon pinned to his suit – also focused on the ring.

'Why did you not mention the ring before he left?'

'Because I thought he would be man enough to send it.'

'Did he take the measurement of your finger? I thought that was one of the greatest pleasures – measuring the lady's finger with a little extra squeeze or two.'[51]

It was a clever strategy by the defence. In slipping from the visual to the tactile, Villeneuve Smith attempted to shift questions of character from masculine promise-keeping to Verona's sexuality, uncontained by marriage and its visual cues of exclusive possession.

Why did people care so much about the engagement ring? The ring's origins in Biblical and Roman law as a pledge to marry and as a symbol of possession explain in the broadest terms why the ring mattered. To be converted into law, the rites and rituals of marriage required public witnessing, as they continue to do today. Had Verona received the ring, it would have enacted a change in her status, propelling her upon a journey from single woman to wife.

Examining breach of promise cases in the nineteenth century, however, we find that the engagement ring has not always held such social and legal significance. There are no engagement rings mentioned in cases from the first half of the nineteenth century, very few (only twenty-two) in the second half, and in actions where rings are mentioned they have little weight as legal evidence. Legal treatises and etiquette books are also surprisingly silent on the subject. The 1888 edition of *Manners and Rules of Good Society* stipulates the 'return of letters and presents' in the case of a broken engagement, but nowhere considers what to do with a ring. *Chitty on Contract* – the pre-eminent contract treatise – has no reference to rings as proof of contract to marry throughout the nineteenth century. The rituals of courtship, such as visiting, walking out, obtaining parental consent, kissing and writing, were seen to convert romance into contract in a court of law.[52] Chitty's first mention of a ring is in 1912, in a section on the return of presents in the case of a broken engagement, and it is not until the 1921 edition that a ring appears under proof of contract. The historical shift that the engagement ring registers is evident in the American case of *Horan v Earle*, cited with approval by Chitty in 1921: 'Whatever the expression of earlier cases, then, a promise to marry cannot be inferred alone at this day from one's devoted attention, frequent visits and apparently exclusive attachment. Nor from mere presents or letters, not to the point ... But the giving and acceptance of an engagement ring, if properly shown, becomes a most important circumstance.'[53] This is not to suggest that engagement rings were unknown in the nineteenth century, but simply that their ubiquity in the twentieth century also saw their increased importance as legal objects.

Engagement rings appeared en masse in Australian courts in the first decade of the twentieth century, and barristers began to demand them as proof. This resulted in confusion, as working-class litigants who couldn't afford rings struggled to explain their naked fingers. When Miss Brown was asked by a barrister in 1909 if she had 'ever heard of a girl being engaged without a ring', she responded, blithely: 'plenty of them'.[54] In 1915, Miss Bell told the court that 'she had never received any ring from him nor any presents as he always pleaded poverty'.[55] Judicial clarity on the probative weight of the ring first appears in the 1929 case of *Manterfield v Bloomfield*. The defence argued that 'there had never been any definite engagement, as disclosed by the binding symbol of a ring, and it was not enough for the jury to be of the sentimental opinion that having proceeded so far with his friendship for the plaintiff, the defendant ought to have gone further and married her.' The jury found for the defence.[56] Tracing how the engagement ring became elevated to the status of legal evidence provides us with a wonderful example of the vernacular life of civil law: a system of rules developed over time from the stories and material culture of everyday people, rather than necessarily being imposed by legislators, judges or lawyers.

The reasons Verona gave for wanting a ring were typical of other cases from the early twentieth century. She said that she didn't 'want to make the thing public until you send me the ring', and allegedly claimed that a ring would make things 'more serious'.[57] In the context of twentieth-century dating, unlike nineteenth-century courtship, Verona and other women needed a ring to make their affairs 'serious' because the opposite had become socially accept-able: women and men might go out motoring or dining without any suggestion that this behaviour implied a promise to marry, and many twentieth-century defendants admitted to 'a flirtation' but denied an engagement. A culture of dating based on short-term serial monogamy, in which couples were phys-ically intimate before committing to marriage, had sprung up in place of courtship. A ring and the circumstances of its gifting now mattered.

As women based their cases around rings, men in turn claimed that the rings were merely 'friendship rings' or 'given in jest'. Etiquette manuals were indignant about these matters. 'I might add', advised Eleanor Aimes in 1935, 'that there is no "friendship" ring. Either it is a ring of betrothal, in which case the girl accepts it, or it is purely a gift of jewellery, and must be declined.'[58] Mr Walker claimed that when Miss Robottom asked him for a ring in 1914, he 'brought up the top of a whiskey bottle cork carved in the shape of a ring, and told her as a joke she ought to be married in ten or twenty years.'[59] To ascertain intention to create legal relations, the court was now tasked with distinguishing solemnity from jest for both women and men. If judges in the nineteenth century thought it sufficient for a girl's parents to consent, judges in the twentieth century directed juries to decide cases based on whether the woman had accepted the ring or not. For their part, women relished the power consent gave them. In the 1910 case of *Ezzy v Blondsmith*, the plaintiff greeted Blondsmith's marriage proposal with the words: 'What rot! I have not known you long enough', and returned the ring three days later.[60]

As much as women enjoyed their freedom to be discerning in their choice of a partner, however, they were also cautious about accepting rings, because they knew that a ring signalled a loss of freedom. In the 1904 case of *Horton v Keenan*, the woman was not allowed by her suitor to board a ship alone until he had given her an engagement ring.[61] In the 1900 case of *Wildie v Constable*, the plaintiff assured the jury that she never went 'walking with anyone else while she had the ring'.[62] At the very moment that women were becoming more financially independent, socially mobile and sexually liberated, the practice of ring-giving emerged to hobble women's autonomy and to mark them as the exclusive possessions of men.


\*     \*     \*


Verona would have awoken on the second day of her trial to find her love letters and her testimony splashed across most of the nation's newspapers. The trial transcript took up almost an entire page of *The Daily News*, fanning out around advertisements for Dr Lyon's Tooth Powder that – improbably – guaranteed women 'a good complexion' and for Lockyer's Hair Restorer, which exhorted: 'Don't Look Old!' When the journalists filed their stories on day two after lunch, they reported that the crowds had swelled with the arrival of 'a large number of office girls during the luncheon hour'. By this stage, Verona had endured cross-examination for at least three hours and was reportedly looking exhausted.[63]

She had told the court that Jack 'called himself Mr Rothschild', and that he had 'paid for a lot of cigarettes'. Why did she sign her love letter 'Bow-Wow'? Because it was John's pet-name for her. Yes, they passed time alone together – at Cottesloe beach, on a trip to Armadale, at the Perth Cup races and on the veranda of her grandmother's house. And no, it was not true that she had resigned from being a teacher because of poor health, rather than because of her engagement. There were doctors' certificates testifying to her illness, but that was simply because she was 'foxing the government', trying to get money for sick leave.[64]

Villeneuve Smith moved on to Verona's claim for her trousseau, beginning with the sixteen hats.

'I suppose you wore a different hat each day while he was here. Hats are fetching, are they not?'

'I don't know.'

'Sixteen hats! That's a bit tall?'

'Yes, but there are a lot of things to come off [the list of items].'

'Yes, but it's a pity they didn't come off before. You are charging us with them?'

Sir Walter James interjected: 'No we are not. We are not charging you for sixteen hats. There are items we say are trousseau items.'

But Villeneuve Smith had tapped into a rich vein of comedic potential, and with the gallery roaring with laughter, he bowled along.

'Did you wear them all?'

'I have some of them now.'

'Did you produce them? Have you brought them?'

'No.'

'On January 24 you bought pyjamas?'

'Ladies' pyjamas.'

'You also bought three night dresses. Do you wear both?'

'Yes.'

'On February 4 you bought more pyjamas and on the same date another lot. Have you produced these pyjamas? I only want to know if they are ladies' pyjamas or not?'

'They are ladies' pyjamas.'

'Well, I want you to produce them. I want someone to feel them.' The court erupted again in hoots of laughter. 'How about night dresses ... What do you want with pyjamas if you wear night-gowns? Perhaps you bought them for your trip to Honolulu.'

'I wanted them for my trousseau!'

Inspecting the itemised list of Verona's trousseau, Villeneuve Smith turned to the dresses and skirts. 'That's pretty expensive, is it not? ... 45 pounds 2 shillings and 6 pence for a lady earning 2 pounds and 10 shillings per week!'

'No, Mr Smith.'

'I don't wonder at people not getting married. Who was to buy this trousseau?'

'I was to buy it and my father was to pay for it.'

'Your father authorised you to buy it?'

'It is a father's duty to pay for it.'

'Don't you know he has not paid for a single penny?'

'Yes.'

'Then on February 9 you buy a manicure set. Is that an adjunct of a trousseau?'

'Yes.'

'Cream and paste! That's for pasting the face, isn't it?'

'That's for sunburn.'

'Vaseline! Is that for a lady's trousseau?'

'No.'

'Soap?'

'No.'

'Polish! Lotion and perfume! Oil and rum! I suppose that's bay rum?'

Laughter roiled around the gallery.

'Yes.'

'Salts! I suppose that's merely smelling salts?'

'Yes.'

'And you call this a lady's trousseau.'[65]

*   *   *

Mr Villeneuve Smith was not the only person shocked at Verona's trousseau. It made newspaper headlines the next day: 'THE TROUSSEAU / Some remarkable Evidence / Hats and Pyjamas / Oil, Rum and Salts', declared *The Daily News*.[66] Justice McMillan, later writing about the case in his notebook, wrote that 'the trousseau was the source of the estrangement', although John O'Mara said nothing about the trousseau being the cause of his loss of interest.[67] Here, we might assume, was a collective masculine disciplining of feminine consumer excess. Social panics over the relationship between modern women and the market, their susceptibility to superficial attractions, their extravagance, frivolity and ruinous love of finery, their slide from luxury to lechery, all leapt out of Verona's trousseau. Social condemnation was also more ferocious because of wartime austerity measures. Emphasising the extravagant cost of the trousseau and O'Mara's reputed wealth spoke to a shadow world of opulence inhabited by the rich while the rest of the world, at war, suffered material privations. As one commentator remarked: 'while 25,000 West Australians are suffering all the horrors of war, gilded young slackers (and slackeresses) are at perfect liberty to indulge in idle, vulgar and vicious enjoyment.' At a time when other men and women were answering the 'call to duty', John and Verona appeared to be 'shirkers' in all spheres of life.[68]

But I think that this only partly explains the court's reaction. Two years later, a series of government inquiries into the basic wage and the cost of living for adult women workers found most of Verona's items essentials rather than luxuries. Soap, Vaseline, powder, corsets, camisoles, knickers and even a kimono were among the items listed as crucial by the NSW Board of Trade to a single, working woman's wardrobe on top of domestic items such as aprons, work clothes such as blouses, jackets and skirts, and leisurewear such as bathing costumes, sportscoats and sandshoes. As an expanding services sector drew more women into the workforce and consumer culture reconfigured feminine identity, how much it cost to be a modern woman became a topic of public and legal debate – discussed, as ever, by old white men. So why did it cause such an uproar?[69]

Part of the problem lay in its copiousness – one hat was acceptable; sixteen were excessive. Justice McMillan later complained that Verona might have bought 'most of the items' for herself 'for everyday use', but it could be argued, and indeed was argued, that most of the items of any woman's trousseau could be repurposed by single women. This also doesn't explain the court's laughter at Verona's cosmetics and powders. To understand these reactions, we need to track the changing cultural meaning and legal status of the trousseau from the nineteenth to the twentieth century, to see how it became brimful with anxieties about young women's imagined preference for sensual pleasures over marriage and motherhood.

There were no trousseaux claimed as part of damages in the first half of the nineteenth century and very few in the second half. It's possible that this was because women felt that they could not claim damages for home-made products, but if this were the case one would expect it in descriptions of marriage preparations (such as getting a wedding dress). The trousseau, it seems, was simply a luxury beyond the reach of most working people. The women who claimed damages for their trousseaux were wealthier than the average litigant, and the court welcomed their claims for the same reason as judges and juries welcomed engagement rings: they were material proof, evidence of quantifiable loss in an action that, troublingly, awarded monetary compensation for unquantifiable emotional harm. There was also no doubt a bias by upper-middle-class judges towards middle-class women. When debates raged in Britain and America in the late nineteenth century over whether the action should be abolished, the trousseau was singled out as a cost that deserved compensation. In Britain, Mr Herschell's unsuccessful Bill to Abolish Breach of Promise of Marriage in 1879 left open the possibility of claiming pecuniary loss, 'such as that incurred by purchasing a trousseau or giving up a situation', but abolished 'attempts to appraise in cash the value of outraged feelings and blighted expectations'. In jurisprudential terms, it was an effort to strip the action of its tortious elements, which allowed compensation for emotional loss, and reduce it to contract.[70]

In Australia the trousseau was uncontentious throughout the long nineteenth century. In most cases, the woman was referred to as 'preparing' her trousseau by hand, implying its non-economic value, and the few who brought evidence of it to court did so as both proof of a promise and proof of loss. Lawyers always claimed it under the category of 'general damages', rather than as 'special damages' – the latter required material proof of damage – and it was usually referred to as something that the woman's parents had paid for. In 1901, when a barrister tried to humiliate a woman for her trousseau, he was chastened by the woman and by the court. 'What was the trousseau made of? What did you get?' the lawyer asked. 'What do you think I got?' she snapped back. When her mother gave evidence that she had bought half a dozen night dresses, the barrister cried out 'Good Lord!' and the judge was not impressed: 'I must ask you not to express yourself so,' he said, awarding the woman damages for 'the home she has lost, the expense she has incurred and the possible loss of reputation.'[71]

In the first decade of the twentieth century more women brought their trousseaux to court, reflecting the rise in working people's disposable income, women's increased participation in the workforce and the birth of consumer culture. As the farmer Mr Dickenson explained in 1907, when asked whether he had bought his first wife a trousseau: 'She did not have one. There were none in those days, only a dress.'[72] The contents of the trousseau also changed from mostly handmade items to a mixture of handmade and store-bought. A new world of store-based credit made shopping more accessible to working-class people, much to the shock of wealthy judges: 'are there really places where you can get a trousseau on time payment?' asked a judge in 1910. 'Many such places,' counsel responded soberly.[73]

Judges were sympathetic to women's claims for compensation in this decade. One judge asked a woman whether the clothing in her trousseau was 'old fashioned by this time', and another accepted a woman's argument that money should be awarded both for the cost of the items in her trousseau and for her 'fancy work' – the embroidery she had done on them.[74] As I discuss in Chapter Ten (*Allan v Growden*) this litigant, like other women who demanded compensation for cooked meals and housework performed while courting, foreshadowed later feminist arguments by applying an economic valuation to unpaid domestic labour.

The first sign that the trousseau was becoming suspect can be seen in its migration from the body of newspaper articles to their headlines in the 1910s: '100 Pound Trousseau' was splashed across the page in an account of one 1911 case, and in 1913 another headline screamed: 'Girl Buys Trousseau.'[75] Both female litigants won their cases, but a sensationalist press appears to have thought that hinting at a woman's underwear and nightgowns might appeal to readers' voyeurism. In 1915, one year before Verona's case, Miss

McQuilkin became the first woman to lose her case because of her extravagant trousseau, which she valued at £233. 'If Your Honour looks at the list, you would think she was starting an underclothing shop.' The judge agreed. 'Preposterous!' he bellowed when Miss McQuilkin informed him that the four night-dresses bought for her sister were for their trips together.[76] In some cases, male defendants used the trousseau to invoke stereotypes of gold-digging women. 'When a girl rings in a glory box ... you want to be very careful,' said Mr Cunningham-Armstrong in 1914, provoking waves of laughter. 'I felt like I was a lamb about to be fleeced.' The fact that this woman paid for her trousseau from her own wages as a music teacher was not going to ruin a good joke.[77] In 1921, Miss Sharpies lost her case after the judge declared the prices affixed to the items of her trousseau to be 'monstrous', and the defence barrister, much like Villeneuve Smith, played to its salaciousness: 'I would like to have a look at the dozen nightgowns at 30 pounds,' he leered. 'They must have butterflies all over them. I know something about nighties.'[78]

On the other side were the 'sensible young ladies' with modest trousseaux comprised of a mixture of 'hand-worked' and purchased items, all of which would be used in their imagined future home or in their role as wives. These women generally valued their trousseaux at around £30 pounds, and when asked about its contents never mentioned anything beyond house linen, cutlery, night-dresses and undergarments. By the 1930s, the courts had established a series of precedents for determining the legitimacy of a woman's trousseau. She must have purchased the items with her own money, and anything that suggested pleasure for the woman outside her role as mother or wife would be ridiculed, resulting in the woman losing her case. The court turned what could have been an act of self-fashioning for women into a performance of self-abnegation. Women worked in the public sphere to buy their way back into the private.[79]

To my mind, the trousseau's inextricable links to domesticity – to the 'sacred' institution of marriage and to an idealised version of wifehood based on self-renunciation – explains the alarm provoked by Verona's lavish purchases. Legally, the trousseau was haunted by the ghost of coverture, which in the nineteenth century had restricted a wife's right to 'contract in the marketplace' to 'necessities'. Once engaged to be married, a woman had no need for luxury, and she certainly had no need to attract men; her engagement signalled her retreat from public life. Like the items in a trousseau, an engaged woman occupied a liminal space, not yet settled into the marital home but

*Verona Rodriguez.*

no longer belonging to her family home. The trousseau marked its owner's entry into a new phase of life as wife and mother. Preparing it should train the woman in the art of thrift and household management, and show that she was preparing to subsume her sense of self into that of her husband and children. This explains why the Board of Trade could condone single working women spending money on clothes, cosmetics and leisurewear, while the courts berated engaged women for doing the same thing.

In this context, we can see that Verona's trousseau was part of a wider judicial trend that sought to punish the perceived excesses of modern femininity and reaffirm marriage as an institution elevated from the market, bound by duty rather than desire. The more consumer culture beckoned women to its seductive commodity displays, offering to fill their trousseaux with pleasurable new objects, the more the court affirmed the trousseau as a symbol of resistant Victorian morality, emblematic of a future wife's frugality. The objects in a woman's trousseau revealed her feminine identity, and in the court's eyes there were now two options: she was either a sensible housewife or a hedonistic flapper.

Although courts were comfortable policing women's consumer pleasures, the procedural question of how to do this, in the case of the trousseau, was a source of vexation. How could the court reconcile the requirement for litigants to produce evidence with the illicit sensory pleasure that a box of silk negligees might arouse? Early twentieth-century law increasingly saw itself as a science whose rules of evidence were underpinned by the positivist link between sight, object and truth. This epistemological connection (the word 'evidence' comes from the Latin *videre*, meaning 'to see'), combined with legal mistrust of women's testimony, lay behind Villeneuve Smith's request that the silk pyjamas be brought to court. But this created a conundrum. 'Just imagine,' Sir Walter protested, 'three suits of ladies' pyjamas, being produced in court – the height of indecency!' It not only 'embarrassed' the woman but also risked turning the court into a site of erotic titillation rather than rational inquiry. At issue was a confrontation between three visual registers: Victorian decorum, modern spectacle and legal forensics.

Sir Walter voiced his objections early, but as Verona's cross-examination proceeded it became clear that the objects in her trousseau didn't need to be produced in order to titillate. The court's tradition of physically producing objects so as to 'activate a fully rational, disembodied objectivism' was inverted, and the court descended into an imagined emporium of erotica.[80] In the absence of visual proof, Villeneuve Smith piqued the audience's imagination by highlighting items that engaged the 'lowest' senses: smell (the perfumes and oils) and touch (the pyjamas, which he wanted 'someone to feel'). These senses implicated the body and turned court participants into voyeurs. This is why Verona's trousseau, in the end, was never produced, and nor was any woman's in the history of the action. In sacrificing legal forensics to Victorian decorum, the court sought to establish its reputation as an institution of scientific rationality, distant from modern feminine and consumerist spectacles.

And what of Verona h rself? What meaning did all those extravagant dresses, powders and lotions have for her? None of her letters or legal testimony give us an answer, but I would speculate that Verona was seeking to insulate herself from prejudice and poverty. The references to her ethnicity in reports of the case – a 'dusky butterfly' or 'Portuguese' – hint at how she was racially othered in the very white world of Perth. Her son Michael remembers his mother rolling her eyes at the petty discriminations she experienced. 'They can say what they want,' she'd laugh; 'we're richer than them all.' To this end, Verona's trousseau was both aspirational and protective. She moved in elite circles thanks to high-school ties, but she still needed to work as a teacher because her father could not support her medical studies. Returning to Perth after her triumphal departure must have been disquieting. Perhaps her grandmother Caroline, the woman to whom Verona was closer 'than anyone else in the world', told Verona about the abject poverty in which she (Caroline) had been raised. Unlike her grandmother, however, Verona knew, through cinema, magazines and books, that glamour could be purchased, and that beauty gave her capital on the marriage market.[81]

Verona's imaginings of her future married life were rebellious and romantic. She claimed no costs for household items because she never imagined herself being trapped in a house with children. The toiletries and clothes in her trousseau were indeed for everyday use, as Justice McMillan alleged, because she imagined no sharp division between her married life and her single one. Her trousseau did not symbolise a deferral of pleasure but a continuation of it, but with a more secure financial basis through John O'Mara. Marriage, as she said in her letters to John, would increase her fame, and Verona wanted to look the part.

*  *  *

On the trial's final day, *Rodriguez v O'Mara* looked more like a sporting event than a court hearing. 'The spectators blocked the entrances to the court, and the passages to the rear of the press boxes', one journalist complained. 'Standing room was at a premium' and 'the atmosphere [was] stifling.' John was scheduled to give testimony, and then a verdict would be released.[82]

Press reports of John were flattering. He was a 'spruce-looking young man', twenty-seven years old, and certainly not the 'idle-rich, time-wasting' gent that some reports 'would lead the public to believe'. John was 'alert, intelligent though quiet', and one paper joked that he was a member of the IWW, or the 'I Won't Wed' Club.[83]

John took the stand. No, he said, he and Verona had not met at the Haynes' house, but rather at the Ozone Club, where he had gone with a friend to see Miss Haynes. They had decided to go for a motor, and Verona was invited to come along. 'Miss Haynes sat between me and [my friend] and Verona sat on my knee. This was the first time I had met the plaintiff.' After this came outings to Kalamunda, the theatre, a pantomime, and nightly visits to the Haynes' house. Yes, they discussed an engagement on the veranda, but it was only a tentative agreement, and nothing was said about a ring. 'I was willing provided I had the right to withdraw when I returned at Christmas.' Yes, he introduced Verona to his mother, but it was clumsy, as he 'could not think of her name so left it at "Miss"', after which Verona wrote her name in his pocketbook. When the ring was raised, he told her that 'there is plenty of time … when I come back at Christmas'. Later, in Adelaide, he received a number of letters and telegrams from Verona, to which he did not reply. When she finally asked him to release her from the engagement, he agreed and said he would come to Perth 'to silence the ridicule which she said had been heaped upon her'. When he arrived in January, they 'just shook hands' on the pier, but afterwards, as he drove her home, she said, 'Couldn't you love me again?' He replied: 'No, Ron, I couldn't.' During the three weeks he was in Perth they went with friends to the races and motoring around the countryside. No, they had not planned a honeymoon in Honolulu, he had no idea she had resigned from her job, and he 'did not hear a word of the trousseau and had never suggested its purchase'. Yes, he had paid for all their outings and came to resent it, he said, recalling an occasion when he was asked to foot the bill for a dinner he hadn't attended; he said he had remarked at the time that he would 'have to become a Rothschild to keep the kite flying'. After leaving Perth, he didn't hear from Verona again until he received her letters in May, which he did not answer.

If the strategy of the defence during cross-examination was to depict Verona as frivolous, promiscuous and deceitful, the strategy of the counsel for the plaintiff was to paint John as caddish, indolent and offensively rich. Given so many men were at war, this should have been an easy task.

'I submit that you are an idle young man with money to burn,' began Sir Walter.

'You are wrong,' John replied, adding that he was manager of his family's estate, which had lost significant revenue recently because of a change in liquor laws. The sum worth of their estate was only £37,000. He was no Rothschild. Sir Walter changed tack.

'You're a very cautious man in love affairs?'

'It is wise to be so.'

'What experience have you had?'

'This experience.'

'But did you not behave as if you were engaged?'

'How would you say an engaged couple behave?'

Sir Walter shuffled his notes and left the question unanswered. 'When you went away, were your feelings towards her like those you had to any other girl?'

'I had a little more for her, I think ... I was going to give it deep consideration ...'

'You said you were going to save her from being the butt of ridicule? How could you do that except by putting a ring on her finger?'

'Could I not come over and take the responsibility of having released her?'

'What steps did you take to show the world you had released her?'

'I met her and took her out.'

'Would not that tend to confirm the idea that you were engaged?'

'I don't think so.'

'Did you never put your arm round her waist?'

'No, I might have put my arm near her waist.'

'Didn't you kiss her at all?'

'Yes, on the first night.'

'More than once?'

'Yes.'

'After that night did you kiss her?'

'No.'

'Well, what on earth were you wasting time ... for? Were her verbal expressions of love pleasant to you?'

'They were like water off a duck's back.' Laughter again filled the courtroom.[84] Sir Walter declared his cross-examination over, and John stepped out of the witness box.

Justice McMillan needed little time before beginning his directions to the jury. He began by drily remarking that 'the jury would derive much assistance from counsels' remarks. It had been a real education to listen to two such experts in the art of love.' Muffled laughter could be heard in the gallery. Sir Walter, the judge said, had depicted Verona as a child, but McMillan thought 'she was a child who knew a good deal'. His only surprise was 'to find that she had been for a considerable time a state school teacher, a position which one would hardly have expected to find her.' Turning to John, McMillan said that although he had been portrayed as 'a kind of South Australian Rothschild', in fact 'his wealth had been considerably exaggerated'. Widening his perspective to the action itself, he said that despite arguments that breach of promise 'should be done away with', he was of the opinion that there were some instances where it was justified, but 'was not quite sure that the case before them was one of them'.

And what of the conflicting facts put before the jury? McMillan, like so many judges in breach of promise cases before him, turned to literature for authority. 'George Bernard Shaw', he said, was a 'philosopher ... one of whose theories was that it was always the woman who ran after the man. That was the motive of his play *Man and Superman*. Shaw thought that although the man proposed, it was the woman who took very good care that he did so'. McMillan said that he agreed with the defence that Verona had initiated the engagement, and that 'there was a good deal to show that the plaintiff had made up her mind at a very early stage that the defendant was worth getting'. The only question was whether their relationship had been anything more than 'what one would call a gorgeous flirtation'.

Could Verona's version of events be believed? No, he thought. She had admitted to lying to the Education Department about her sick leave, and she had made numerous false statements. Could a promise of marriage be inferred from the couple's behaviour? 'Sometimes people drifted into engagements, but there was no drifting in the case under review, because there was no time for it ... With some girls kissing and going to theatres with a man, and like acts, would go a long way, but with others more giddy and flighty such instances would certainly not serve to prove an engagement, because otherwise the same girl would be engaged to a great number of men'. McMillan observed that juries needed to infer a promise from the 'usual' behaviour of courting couples, but conceded that he may not know what this was anymore. Like Verona's grandmother, he was 'of that antiquated type' that some referred to as 'Victorian', and that Grandma Caroline 'probably thought that if the plaintiff and defendant were not engaged, they should have been'. He noted that no love letters were exchanged by the couple after the defendant's return to Perth, and that the jury must ask themselves whether 'the absence of a ring fitted in better with the plaintiff's or the defendant's' story'.

Regarding the trousseau, Justice McMillan said that 'he hoped the jury knew more about [it] than he did. All he could say from his limited knowledge was that the account presented by the plaintiff for her trousseau was the most extraordinary document he had ever seen in his life', and that the articles listed were 'largely in everyday use' by Verona. Concluding, he opined that Verona was not any worse off after her acquaintance with John. He was, 'after all, one of many men who were in the habit of giving her a good time'.[85]

*   *   *

If the task of law is to provide clarity, to neutrally demarcate the permissible from the impermissible, McMillan's judgment shows law struggling to perform this task. The moral anchor points of Victorian-era courtship were no longer available. It was difficult for the courts in the early twentieth century to reflect social norms and morals when these were radically in flux and generational divisions in romantic practices seemed wider than ever.

When Sir Walter had asked John O'Mara, 'Did you not behave as an engaged couple?', John's answer – 'How would you say an engaged couple behave?' – was left hanging in the courtroom. When John mused on the ethics of love, elements of nineteenth- and twentieth-century norms mingled haphazardly in his reflections. 'If a lady appealed to me, I would not allow myself to be drawn so near as to make a life promise,' he later explained to the court. 'I would take time to think. That is if I had time to think ... Of course, if I was drawn straight in ...' Laughter drowned out the rest of his musings on the ethics of love. His description of falling in love as an instantaneous reaction to the 'appeal' of a girl was typically modern; his caution and his understanding of a promise of marriage as a serious life-long commitment were typically Victorian; but then his confession that these principles would fall away if he was quickly 'drawn in' was a twentieth-century endorsement of the power of unconscious sexual attraction. In laughing at this confession, the people in the gallery were very different from observers of a few decades earlier, who would have been horrified by such flippancy.

The language of the market had not only entered courtship; it had also infiltrated law. The jury were referred to by McMillan as 'business men', rather than 'fathers and brothers' as they were in the nineteenth century, and the promise of marriage was 'a business proposal', the existence of which they should assess 'without feeling'.[86] Legal decision-making was dispassionate, as cold and rational as commerce. The defence did not argue that Verona was 'unchaste' but used the more popular twentieth-century defence: that she had rescinded the contract. Yet gender norms found a way into Justice McMillan's directions to the jury and, to my mind, ultimately decided the case. The twentieth century had given birth to a new type of woman: 'giddy and flighty', someone who was 'given a good time' by many men and for whom 'kissing and going to theatres' meant little. The law draws distinctions to determine who can be compensated and who cannot; who has suffered and who has not, and sexual reputation still mattered in this assessment. Like sexually autonomous women before her, Verona was deemed incapable of suffering. She was cast out from law's protection.

The jury took only thirty minutes to return a verdict in favour of the defendant.[87]

## Ronnie

Verona's life after the hearing comes to me in archival fragments – photographs, court records, newspaper articles – and in the wistful, witty musings of her son, Michael Prevost.

A search for Verona in Perth's State Records Office brings up another court hearing: *Grave v Grave*. Here we find Verona on a ship bound for Sydney only two months after her trial. She passes her days writing letters to her lover. 'My Darling – the boat will be in Albany in a couple of hours ... in saying "au revoir" yesterday to the two people I love best in this world, I thought my heart would break.' She delights in the receipt of his lettergrams – 'I have read and re-read them again and again and in fact know them off by heart now' – and boasts that she has been 'most industrious the whole way across, and [has] quite finished embroidering one of my "nighties" and I am on a second one now.' She reads four books and all her magazines and finds the crowd on the boat generally 'nice', except for 'some vaudeville artists from Melrose, who were the last thing in vulgarity'.[88]

She has plenty of time to sew and read because she has promised her lover to stay in her cabin and not to disembark at Adelaide. Dinner, however, proves difficult. She 'needs to make an appearance'. She dines in the first sitting, 'of course', but finds Mr Lavan sitting at the far end of her table. He had been the instructing solicitor for the defence in her case. 'The old beast had the impertinence to bid me good-day,' she huffs, although she appreciates his discretion: 'he has not pointed me out nor has he, I think, been speaking of me.' Verona is a consummate artist. Her lover is mistrustful, and she provides him with a reassuring self-portrait, painted in subdued tones. She goes to bed early and upon waking walks thirteen-and-a-half laps of the deck with the bishop of Goulburn, 'a dry old wit'. She reports on the young men on their way to military college. 'They're boys, the eldest of whom is 18, who love to do a great deal of "swank". Their only regret is that there are not any presentable flappers on board to whom their "swank" might appeal.' The implication, of course, is that Verona is no longer a flapper. Her letters alternate between gush – she is 'always your sweetheart' – and panic – 'Destroy this and all other letters I write. It is best. Likewise destroy the enclosed telegram. I'm afraid of letters going astray.' Verona is now pregnant, and she is writing to the father of her child, Mr Fred Grave.[89]

Fred kept Verona's letters in his desk drawer 'for sentimental reasons', as well as a photograph of her. They were the proof that his wife, Chris Grave, used to petition for divorce on the grounds of adultery in 1917. Chris and Fred had befriended Verona in the lead-up to her breach of promise of marriage case out of pity. They saw how she had been socially ostracised and reached out to her. It all seemed very benevolent, until an anonymous letter addressed to Chris appeared in their mailbox:

> Madam, it behoves you to keep an eye on your husband and that notorious breach of promise creature. He meets her every Monday, Wednesday and Friday Night at Claremont Railway Station.
> Yours, A Claremont well-wisher.

Chris Grave went immediately to see Verona, but Verona wasn't home; when Chris raised the letter with Fred, he berated her for not trusting him. In any case, he said, Verona would be leaving for Sydney in a few weeks. Chris apologised and sent a telegram to Verona wishing her safe travels, but she was now on the alert. In February 1917, she went into her husband's study to call him for dinner and found him hurriedly stuffing a letter into his coat pocket. When he left to run an errand after supper, she found his coat, extracted the letter, and read about Verona's time on board the *Zealandia*. Verona's letters were unsigned, but Chris knew the handwriting. And who else would describe sea-sickness as *mal-de-mer* or prefer *au revoir* to goodbye? When confronted with the proof, Fred 'unblushingly confessed'. 'As you know so much, you might as well know all,' he said. 'She is going to give me a little son. I love her more than I do you. I'm going to stick to her.' The affair had been going on for nine months, he said. In May 1917, Chris filed for divorce in front of Chief Justice McMillan.[90]

Comparing the dates in Chris Graves' petition to those of Verona's breach of promise action, McMillan now declared Verona's action to have been 'the most impudent claim he had heard in any court of law'. While demanding damages for wounded feelings from John O'Mara, she had been in love with Fred Grave and possibly already pregnant. It doesn't seem to have occurred to McMillan that Verona's pregnancy may have been the reason she decided to pursue the action against John – had her action been successful, it would have provided her and her child with independent financial security. Following the Graves' divorce hearing, Verona's letters landed on the gossip pages of the sensationalist press across the nation: 'a most remarkable story of a fast, furious, guileful and clever young lady has been received from our Perth Correspondent', gushed Melbourne's *Truth*. Verona had longed for fame; she now had its poor cousin, notoriety.[91]

The son Fred dreamt of never arrived. He and Verona married in 1917, and Verona gave birth to two girls, Shirley and Joan. Their births were registered in 1918 and 1919, but I suspect Shirley was born earlier, and that they waited to register her until after their wedding to ensure her legitimacy. Verona Grave was now the wife of a wealthy engineer and distributor of motor cars, living in a splendid harbourside property, bowling around town in the latest-model Ford. Money no doubt cushioned her somewhat against the raised eyebrows of Perth society, but it provided no protection against Fred's violence. 'He was a monster of a man,' Michael tells me. Looking back at her letters from the ship to Sydney, we can see all the signs of coercive control. He demands that she not leave her cabin and makes her vow not to go ashore in Adelaide; she begs him for permission to see her friend Ida in Melbourne. When Fred died suddenly of cerebral syphilis in 1924, Verona felt relief. She was now a merry widow.[92]

The next glimpse I get of Verona is in a book about the famous pilot Charles Kingsford Smith. Following Fred's death, she spent time in Broome with her family. She was now twenty-nine – 'beautiful, capricious, intelligent and volatile'. She met 'Smithy' when her car broke down while driving south from Broome. The author of the book interviewed Michael for the details: 'A search party, led by Smithy, went out and found them. The affair – and there certainly was an affair – started soon after. It was conducted … in Broome and Perth, far from discreetly.' According to local legend, Smithy would land in Broome with a motorbike lashed to the undercarriage of his plane, and 'within minutes of parking he would be off to see Ronnie'. Michael says that there was 'considerable correspondence between them which, unfortunately, was all destroyed in the 1950s'. He is not sure how long the affair lasted, but it 'eventually just fizzled out. The reasons for this, I understand, were Ron's unwillingness to settle down after her very unhappy marriage'. Another problem, he says, was that 'Ron was extremely rich whereas Smithy was far from so'.[93]

The next image I find of Verona is a photograph from 1927. She is sitting atop an elephant in India, dressed in full flapper regalia. A lady traveller, she has joined a climbing expedition in the Himalayas, having placed her two daughters in an exclusive boarding school. Her smile beams out from beneath her stylish toque hat. *The Sunday Times* in Perth carries reports of her travels 'through most of Europe and America' and her triumphant return to Perth in a sports car – 'an Imperial Chrysler, as pretty a car as human ingenuity can fashion'.[94]

A film written, but never made, about Verona, overseen by one of her grandsons, depicts her cavorting around the world in the 1920s: she dances the Charleston under crystal chandeliers in London; her portrait is painted in Paris and in New York; and she is introduced to a wealthy Australian wool-buyer, Benjamin Prevost, whom she marries in 1928. For the next decade they live between England and Australia. Verona gives birth in 1938 to their only child, Michael Prevost.[95]

On 3 August 1940, the sky darkens. Verona appears in the Family Notices section of *The West Australian* as the mother of Joan Grave, a brilliant medical student at Melbourne University who has died in a car accident. Joan was driving with friends to Canberra when the car skidded off the road and struck a tree. She is remembered as someone 'around whom was an atmosphere of radiant happiness'. Verona never recovers from the shock.[96]

The film script depicts Verona in an asylum in 1941, vacant-eyed, nursing dolls in bed, being visited by young Michael. Meanwhile, her husband consults psychiatrists. In reality, Verona's mental illness was more protracted. Throughout the 1940s and 1950s, she was placed by her well-meaning husband in the best institutions around the world, just as mental illness was being reconceived as a problem of brain chemistry and drugs were replacing talk therapy. She received shock therapy in New York and was placed on a diet of pills. Finally, her husband consulted a doctor who recommended a full-frontal lobotomy, and he agreed.[97]

When I ask Michael to reflect upon his relationship with his mother, who fell into depression only three years after he was born, he writes: 'I loved mother without ever liking her. By the time I came along there wasn't much left to like.' The lobotomy did not make her into a vegetable, as Hollywood films would tell us, but it did alter her personality irrevocably. The warmth, the vivacity and the brilliance were gone, but the hardness and self-absorption remained. Verona was a woman who had learnt from a young age the peculiarly feminine power of exclusion, who monitored her invitation lists closely, who could forgive herself but not others. She loved Michael but had no way to express it. In the last years of her life, Verona moved to England to be close to him. She died there in 1976, and her ashes were returned to Australia 'to be buried beside her beloved daughter Joan'.[98]

\*     \*     \*

The Covid-19 pandemic prevents me from travelling to Perth, so I search for material traces of Verona near where I live. I ask the Sydney Powerhouse Museum if I can view their collection of trousseaux from the early twentieth century, to see what kind of nighties Verona might have been embroidering onboard the *Zealandia*. Like the barrister in her case, I want to feel the clothes that caused the court such offence.

I am taken into the museum's warehouse, where I walk past a selection of Australian cultural relics: shiny green-and-gold 1980s Olympics swimming costumes ; sequins and feather boas from *The Adventures of Priscilla, Queen of the Desert*; a wooden sleigh used in early Antarctic expeditions. When we arrive in the section that houses the trousseaux, a hush comes over us and everything shimmers. I am handed a delicate, peach-coloured *crêpe-de-Chine* night-singlet, embroidered with cherubs playing horns and violins while swinging prettily on garlands of white flowers. It comes from the trousseau of Miss Schofield. Miss Steeper's trousseau, meanwhile, included a pewter-coloured silk night-dress and bed jacket, while Miss Rose, probably of more humble origins, knitted her own pink pyjamas. Time collapses when I touch the buttery softness of the silk night-dresses. These clothes have defied the secrecy of romance and the ineluctable slide of fashion towards oblivion.

My quest for deeper knowledge of the world inhabited by early-twentieth-century litigants is not entirely rational. It is a search for knowledge through the senses and the emotions. On top of all the research I have done in the archives, I want to imagine their world through my fingers – to feel the tactile pleasures that tantalised women like Verona and made the court blush.

It was a similar desire to know, through sight and touch, that brought romantic objects into the courtroom. Historians have never asked why ordinary people in the modern world began bringing their love tokens to court, presumably because no historian has engaged seriously with breach of promise cases after the nineteenth century. If they had, the sudden cluttering of the courtroom with rings, gifts and trousseaux would surely have begged an explanation. We could list the obvious reasons – the industrial revolution, the birth of commodity culture, globalisation, modern media – but this only tells us why people bought the objects, not the specific meanings they ascribed to them, either personally or in court. Examining Verona's case alongside other early-twentieth-century cases offers us a more nuanced understanding of how and why love tokens were elevated to the status of legal proof. Material evidence replaced traditional ways of proving romance because the rules of romance were in flux and ordinary people – who now conducted their courtships far from the invigilating gaze of family – looked for incontrovertible, visual evidence of commitment. Rings and trousseaux were easily intelligible to a legal culture that was in the process of professionalising, of becoming increasingly scientific and positivist in outlook, and that preferred the calculability of contract to the vagaries of tortious emotional damages. Finally, claiming compensation for a trousseau also tells a story of modern women's growing financial autonomy. As the intimate items of the trousseau washed up in court like emotional debris, judges became disciplinarians of women's participation in consumer culture – and female plaintiffs, almost all of whom had won their cases in the nineteenth century, began to lose.

When Verona died in 1976, her obituarist omitted any reference to her scandalous legal cases, her unhappy marriage to Mr Grave or her full-frontal lobotomy (as one might expect). Instead, he wrote: 'with her died an inkling of the gay 1920s in Perth and more than a hint of the exotic in her early life in Broome'.[99] Verona had a heightened sensitivity to the promises of the twentieth century, but also suffered its gendered cruelties. When I think of her, I imagine the clever eleven-year-old girl penning letters to newspapers about how glorious it is to run down hills, her head tossed back, her body galloping, her eyes crinkling with laughter.

## 10.

# 'A very finely acted part':
# Proof, Performance and the Legal
# History of Heartbreak

## (*Daniels v Culverhouse*, 1920)

Whenvaudeville dancer Sydney Culverhouse arrived in the hotel room of his former lover and dancing partner Daisy Yates, he found her lying supine on a bed, 'crying, and very white'; she said she 'could not realise that this was goodbye'. As the men downstairs in the Marble Bar sipped martinis under brilliant chandeliers, relieved that the war was over, Daisy languished upstairs in heartbreak. She was 'refusing to eat or take anything at all', Sydney recalled, except for the sedative veronal. She warned him that he might 'find her dead some day'. Daisy, whose career in Australia had started to lag, had previously agreed to travel to America to find work and now begged Sydney to come with her. 'It is absolutely impossible,' Sydney replied firmly. 'I have my contract here and besides, think of my engagement to Maggie.' Upon hearing this, he said, Daisy became 'hysterical'.[1]

Daisy herself admitted she had been 'crazy with grief' ever since Maggie Dickinson had 'danced off with Sydney's heart' during a pantomime in 1917.[2] For the three years previous, Daisy and Sydney had appeared as a dancing duo, posing as brother and sister. Both originally from Britain, their careers had whisked them around the world: from the Moulin Rouge in Paris to the London Coliseum, to Johannesburg and Vienna. Daisy Yates was an 'incomparable artiste Anglaise', the Parisian gazette *Le Radical* declared in 1914.[3] 'The dancing of the clever pair is unusually attractive', gushed Melbourne's *Table Talk* in 1915, 'causing something of a furore every night'.[4] In 1917, Sydney left Daisy in Sydney to tour around Australia and New Zealand, playing the part of 'Civilisation' in a celebrated 'war ballet' alongside Maggie Dickinson, who played 'Peace' and Ruby Grainger who played 'War'. As Maggie and Sydney fell in love on stage, Daisy, who was said to be 'resting', awaited his return.[5] In August 1918, she received a letter from Sydney:

> I feel I must make my confession to you at last. I have bottled it up for a long time. The fact is, I am madly and hopelessly in love with Maggie. Don't think I am trying to hurt you by confessing this; but I should feel such a cad when we meet if you did not know … I shall still be the same thoughtful boy to you, and have your interest at heart both financially and otherwise; but I cannot be the same old Syd … It had to come, Daisy, sooner or later, and here it is … Please take this letter in the spirit it is written, and at least give me credit for being honourable.[6]

This was not the first time Sydney had become infatuated with another woman. Daisy said he had first promised her marriage after she had complained about him 'flying around with other women' on money he had borrowed from her. 'We were very happy before all this rot with Miss Dickinson started,' she told the court, hoping that this affair, like all the others, would pass. 'Think things over quietly and see if you cannot come to my way of thinking, dear.' But when they met in person in October 1918, Sydney's feelings were unchanged. 'There was a storm', he later recalled, but Daisy eventually 'cooled down and agreed to go to America' to find work. Any repose that Daisy felt, however, was temporary.[7]

She later secretly followed Maggie and Sydney back to Maggie's room in a boarding house and burst in upon them. 'Are you going to give him up?' she asked Maggie in a quavering voice. 'No,' Maggie replied calmly. 'I was crying,' Daisy said later, 'I did not know what I was doing … I was not in good health and had been fretting.' Eventually Daisy stopped wailing and Sydney even claimed that she offered to go to the marriage registry to take out a marriage certificate for them, no doubt bitterly. But when Maggie accompanied Daisy to her taxi, Daisy 'became angry' again. 'Go back to your lover,' she shouted from the taxi window.[8]

During her breach of promise of marriage hearing in 1920, Daisy denied having been in a 'tearing rage', although admitted that she had been 'crazy with grief'. With no witnesses, and no explicit proof of a marital promise, her case depended upon a convincing display of romantic anguish. While Sydney argued that 'she was shamming' and that 'it was a very finely acted part',

Daisy performed sincerity for the court and denied that she was performing at all. Having been trained in pantomime and vaudeville – among the most lavish and overwrought of theatrical arts – Daisy now needed to perfect the performance of authentic suffering for a courtroom suspicious of her every gesture and every word.[9]

*　　*　　*

Daisy and Sydney's hearing turned on a series of questions that arose in the early twentieth century and which continue to trouble cases concerning emotional damage today. How can tears, shock, torment, sorrow, despair or fury be translated into the anaesthetised language of law? What kinds of evidence make private suffering intelligible to a public court? How do gender norms define what displays of emotion are appropriate or inappropriate for men and women? And how can the law reconcile its demand that plaintiffs perform their suffering, both in and outside of court, with an insistence upon the relationship between truth and sincerity? In short, how is the private drama of heartbreak to be staged in a law court anxious to distance itself from theatre, particularly the counterfeit emotions and 'vulgarity' of vaudeville?[10]

At the time that Daisy brought her action against Sydney, these questions were still new. In nineteenth-century breach of promise cases, damages were rarely pleaded because romantic suffering was presumed to be a natural consequence of women's dependence upon marriage and their innate susceptibility to emotion. By the early decades of the twentieth century, however, heartbreak had become a subject of interrogation and a prompt for theatrics. As women like Daisy suffered less in a material sense than their Victorian counterparts – they could now find another partner and pursue work instead of marriage (albeit constrained by low wages) – the court demanded that they show their suffering more. Cast adrift from its economic moorings, breach of promise drifted deeper into the opaque waters of injured feelings. In the United States, this shift towards emotional injury has been seen by historians as signalling the death knell of the action as 'courts became uncomfortable with awarding money for emotional harms'.[11] In England it has been argued that 'purely emotional suffering became a suspect head of damage' in the early twentieth century, heralding the action's demise, although contrary to this, a foundational study of breach of promise argued that the cases continued apace until the 1940s.[12] In Australia, actions for breach of promise continued well into the twentieth century, and judges and jurors, suspicious of the evidence of women, became expert in interpreting their gestures, voice and appearance in court. As we saw in Chapter Six (*Vaughan v McRae*), in civil law, breach of promise of marriage was the only action which demanded the plaintiff's testimony be corroborated, because women were thought to be untrustworthy. Meanwhile, romances performed at picture palaces, theatres and on radio were introducing audiences to a coterie of manipulative, avaricious women for whom there had been no counterpart in the nineteenth century: the vamp, the gold-digger and the flapper.[13] For litigants like Daisy, mastering the performance of pain became crucial to legal success.

Describing or showing one's despair was one method of expressing heartbreak. Another was to medicalise it, which we see in Daisy's descriptions of herself being not in 'good health' or 'hysterical'. The interwar years were remarkable for ushering in a new medical language of heartbreak, as women like Daisy borrowed psychological categories of trauma from victims of war and industry. As the First World War legitimised public outpourings of grief and upended traditional forms of authority, medical and psychological experts stepped in to provide people with a new language of suffering. Following the advice of doctors who increasingly appeared as expert witnesses, courts came to recognise emotional harm that had been validated by expert knowledge. This convergence of law, medicine and psychology, combined with women's audacity to demand that their feelings be taken seriously, led to heartbreak being categorised as a form of suffering warranting medical and legal intervention.

These novel expressions of heartbreak signalled a new chapter in the history of love: psychology, united with medicine, had encroached upon law's governance of romance, and in the process amorous anguish came to be understood in emotional rather than material terms. The emphasis shifted from loss of economic security, social status or settlement (a house) towards a greater focus on women's bodily and psychic pain. Romantic love, once understood as a profoundly collective and social emotion, with fault that could be ascribed and financial harms that could be calculated by law – was increasingly individualised and psychologised. Few cases exemplify these changes more clearly than that of Daisy Yates, a woman who performed – on stage and in the court –all the pleasures and pain of the modern body.

## Daisy Yates

On 31 December 1918, 'charming' Daisy Yates was featured in the newspaper *Graphic of Australia*. Aside from court records, this is the only interview with Daisy that remains. The text is wrapped around a stage photograph of her. With her sleek flapper's bob – wavy and blonde – pencilled eyebrows, blooming cheeks and coquettish grin, Daisy looks like a modern woman. Her large brown eyes blink out at the camera over a plush white fur coat, and her teeth, endearingly crooked, give her a cheeky, gamine quality. She's probably in her late twenties. 'Yes! I am an English girl, but as my mother was half French, half Italian, I cannot claim to be of purely British blood. My father is a church of England clergyman,' she explained, while changing into a costume in her dressing room at the King's Theatre in Adelaide. 'Of course, it is looked on as a joke in our profession to call oneself the daughter of a clergyman, but in my case, at least it is the truth.'[14]

Daisy tells the interviewer that she ran away from home to become a dancer. After meeting an agent in London, she landed a job in a musical production as the understudy for the female lead, after which her career flourished. She 'donned the trunks and hose' and cross-dressed as the principal boy in pantomimes such as *Dick Whittington* and later 'returned to skirts as principal girl' in *The House That Jack Built* and as a dancer in *What ho! Ragtime.*

In her late twenties, Daisy sailed across the channel to work on a revue at the Moulin Rouge in Paris. Sadly, she sighed, Paris was 'no longer the unlimitedly gay city it was reputed to be, and even shows symptoms of becoming slightly puritanical.' While in Paris, she sent for Sydney to join her: 'We were so well suited to each other,' she added wistfully, probably aware that he was at that moment dancing with Maggie Dickinson to rapturous reviews. 'We played in the musical pantomime *The Girl on the Film* and danced together at the London Coliseum.' With a degree of false modesty, Daisy told the interviewer that one of her 'little hobbies' was to 'write my own song and dance items'. 'I never have had a dancing lesson in my life,' she marvelled, 'but have just trained myself. Dancing is to me the greatest joy!'[15]

*    *    *

Magazines like *Graphic of Australia* were part of the burgeoning print culture in the late nineteenth and early twentieth centuries that helped to elevate dancers such as Daisy to stardom and to commercialise vaudeville, musical theatre and pantomime. They have also bequeathed to the historian a rich archive through which we can trace the careers of performers and test their own accounts of their lives against the record.

Searching through the archives, I discover that Daisy Yates' father was not in fact a clergyman, and nor (predictably) was her name Daisy Yates. Ellen Maingay Ellis was born in Jersey in the Channel Islands in 1884, one of seven children of George Frederick Wilfred Ellis and Ellen Mary Robins. As a younger man, her Cambridge-educated father had worked as a Roman Catholic school teacher. In 1879, tired of teaching, he approached the Bishop of Truro and the Archbishop of Canterbury, claiming to be an ordained Roman Catholic deacon who had suffered a crisis of faith and wanted to join the Church of England. They believed him – he presented them with a forged ordination certificate – and awarded him clergy posts in Cornwall, Middlesex and the Channel Islands. In 1880, he married Daisy's mother, Ellen Robins, daughter of a wealthy banker and patron of the parish of Wetheringsett in Suffolk. When the position of Rector became vacant at Wetheringsett in 1883, George Ellis successfully applied on the recommendation of his father-in-law and was granted a handsome stipend of £980 per year as well as a stately rectory.[16]

Daisy was born one year later, in 1884.[17] The first four years of her life would have been spent in opulence, as *The Ipswich Journal* reported: 'Mr Ellis ... made the acquaintance of nearly every person in the parish by handsomely entertaining them at his place.' He 'furnished his home in a superb fashion and spent a large sum in laying out his grounds and in purchasing land to let out as allotments, and for a time he had a very favourable reputation in the parish.'[18] He married twelve couples, although his tendency to shirk marriage ceremonies and to request 'neighbouring clergymen to perform these duties for him' piqued suspicion. In early 1888, an investigator from Scotland Yard began inquiries, after which Mr Ellis hastily sold the household possessions, vacated his post and moved his family to his father-in-law's house in Essex, where he bided his time until a police officer knocked on his door. Daisy was four years old when her father was given the remarkably severe sentence of seven years' hard labour in Ipswich Prison, and she was eleven when he was discharged. (An act of parliament was later passed to validate the marriages he had officiated.)[19] Upon release, Daisy's father altered his name and became a theatre manager until his death in 1904. In short, Daisy grew up knowing the value of a good performance and the price of a poor imitation.[20]

It's likely that Daisy learnt to dance and sing by watching performers on the stage of her father's theatre in the 1890s and 1900s, a period when the theatrical arts, and society in general, were in the throes of radical change.

This was a time when urban metropolises grew wide and tall; when streets were made sleepless by electric lamp posts, sensuous with the displays of department stores, tense with the shriek of trams, and frenetic with the rush of people moving from home to footpath to office to venue. Philosopher Georg Simmel wrote about the 'intensification of nervous life', as people in the metropolis confronted 'a dizzying variety of sensations with every walk across the street'. Cities in the West throbbed with people keen to spend their disposable income on new forms of entertainment. Theatre managers sniffed a new clientele, and vaudeville was born.[21]

During the 1880s and 1890s, across Europe, the United States, Australasia and Canada, the masculine, working-class culture of nineteenth-century music halls and minstrel shows was converted into family-oriented variety or cabaret entertainment called vaudeville (etymologically *voix de ville*, songs or voices of the village). However, during its period of cultural dominance from 1890 to 1930, vaudeville never entirely shook off its morally suspect origins. A vaudeville show might feature comic sketches, female wrestlers, animal trainers, acrobats, magic tricks, chorus girls, minstrel shows and burlesque, as well as opera singers and classically trained dancers, all for the price of a few shillings. In offering something for everyone, it was the first form of global mass entertainment, and people at the time recognised it as profoundly modern.[22] '[It is] a sign of our nervous, precipitate age, which finds no repose for long and prolix entertainment,' mused the founder of the first cabaret in Berlin.[23]

Daisy described her early career as a 'variety artist'. She supported herself as an actress until 1906, when she married fellow music-hall artist Thomas Daniels in a shotgun wedding, having met him working on the vaudeville circuits in England. We know little about these years and nothing about Daisy's daughter, except that her mother helped with child-minding when Daisy went back to work three years later. It was then that her career blossomed.[24]

The advertisements and reviews for Daisy Yates are voluminous. In Britain she first appears as a star performer in newspapers in 1909, when she would have been twenty-five years old, in advertisements for the pantomime *Dick Whittington* and the musical *Clare Duval*. In 1910, she developed her own comic sketch called 'Impressions', offering 'impersonations of various people', which she performed in a vaudeville show at the Hull Hippodrome in 1910. For a woman to appear on a vaudeville stage and be funny, mocking, talented and clever, in a context where women were usually confined to the role of comic feeds, the butts of jokes or sexual objects, was an act of defiance. Her chutzpah cannot be understated. Yet Daisy also probably knew that as an

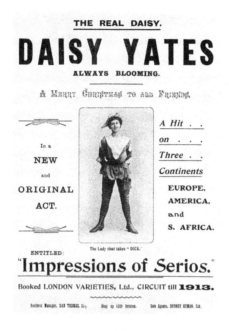

*A poster advertising Daisy Yates' 1913 tour,* Always Blooming.

entertainer her sexual reputation was always in doubt, and that her life – the international travel, the mixed-gender workforce, the absence of domestic or caring responsibilities while on tour, the high wages, the salacious costumes and routines – transgressed the norms of femininity for her time.[25]

In offering a model of liberated femininity for public consumption – international, mobile, erotic and economically independent – and introducing audiences to shocking new music and dance, Daisy helped to bring the modern world to ordinary people. Although we often think of 'modernity' as a vast amorphous process, it could not have happened without the gramophone recordings, the musicians and dancers like Daisy. She was one of the many vaudeville stars who transported the American jazz age to Europe, England and Australasia.

By April 1914, on the eve of the First World War, we see Daisy's name in the pages of the entertainment sections in the major French presses. As dark clouds rolled in over the rooftops of Paris, Daisy and other music-hall performers kept the lights twinkling – pirouetting, tightrope walking, tangoing, singing, joking and fire-breathing the audience into mass distraction. Parisians adored Daisy: '*L'étoile Anglaise achève de donner un esprit vraiment Parisien*', rhapsodised *L'Aurore* in 1914, while others commented on her '*grâce*'.[26]

It was during her time in Paris that Daisy noticed a young, blond English-man in the dining room at her hotel and asked to be seated next to him. By this stage she was separated from Thomas Daniels following a disastrous trip to South Africa in 1911, during which he had accused her of having an affair with a music conductor. Thomas had stopped sending her child-support money and had begun his own affair with actress Hilda Attenborough in 1912. So when the dashing dancer and theatre manager Sydney Culverhouse intro-duced himself, Daisy let herself be charmed. What happened next depends upon whose story you believe. Sydney claimed that Daisy left letters for him each day after work, inviting him up to her room, and that inevitably they became lovers. Daisy maintained – quite improbably – that there was no sex-ual intimacy until she had divorced her husband, which she did in 1916.[27]

As Daisy was the star, Sydney changed his stage surname to Yates, and they began their career as a sister and brother dancing duo until the outbreak of the First World War. In an interview in Australia, Sydney described the drama of their last moments in Paris: 'The newspaper offices were bringing out special editions almost every hour, and when their paper stock became depleted they published extraordinary editions on plain paper bags.' In the whirl of panic, Sydney and Daisy continued their final rehearsals for a show until 'a uniformed official' appeared one day and 'read out a declaration ordering all men to immediately join their regiments. All our musicians, stage-hands, and artists simply had to lay down their tools'. For the next ten days, Sydney and Daisy tried to get train tickets out of Paris, a near-impossible task as martial law had been declared and trains were being used to take troops to the front. When their tickets finally came through, they journeyed from Paris to Dieppe, a seven-hour trip that took them over two days because of delays. They slept on the sand in Dieppe, as all accommo-dation was full, and boarded a boat the next day to Newhaven, England.[28]

Relying on transnational music networks, Daisy and Sydney travelled from England to South Africa for work, although they were also in pursuit of Thomas Daniels, whom Daisy now wanted to divorce.[29] Once there, they discovered that Thomas had moved to Australia, so when a talent scout from an Australian firm, J.C. Williamson Company, offered them a contract, they accepted immediately. In April 1915 they disembarked in Melbourne, having signed a joint contract that included travel and a £20-per-week salary and stipulated that they were to only dance with each other.[30]

At a time when international performers were scant because of the war, Daisy and Sydney were an instant hit, performing in every major city in

Australia and New Zealand. They tangoed in the musical *The Girl in the Taxi* in Adelaide, did a 'whirlwind dance to irresistibly gay music' in Brisbane, performed the 'Apache dance' at the Tivoli theatre in Sydney and performed alongside Dame Nellie Melba in Melbourne. Until 1918, Daisy was the more successful of the pair, and Sydney was often referred to as her partner rather than by name. 'Miss Yates goes into her numbers heart and soul,' *The Sunday Times* sang in 1916. 'She is spun round by her partner so that she seems gossamer light.'[31] When their contract was up in 1916, they secured another with the Tivoli Follies. Immediately, their twirls, acrobatic leaps and experimental waltzes were declared to be 'perhaps the most enjoyable part of the entertainment', drawing 'hearty and well-deserved applause'.[32]

Daisy was said to be 'resting' throughout 1918, but the truth was exposed when a newspaper article in November 1918 reported that she had taken out a writ for breach of contract against J.C. Williamson. Mr Welton, the manager of J.C. Williamson, had put forward his sister-in-law Maggie Dickinson to perform the lead role in the 1918 musical season, dancing with Sydney. As Sydney and Daisy could only be contracted together, Daisy was part of the agreement. She was not required to perform, but nor was she permitted to dance with any other company, and nor could she return to England. Daisy was not thrilled, and she said so both to Sydney and to the company, but at Sydney's urging she eventually contented herself with receiving his photographs and letters while he toured and she stayed in Melbourne.[33]

Daisy's first inkling that all was not well came when Sydney revealed in 1918 that he had been offered a separate contract, although he reassured her that they would split the income. Daisy felt betrayed and sent Sydney what he later described as an 'All is lost' letter. 'I'd be a damned fool if I said No,' he responded. Soon after, he confessed by letter that he was 'madly and hopelessly in love with Maggie'. When he suggested Daisy travel to America for work, she agreed, but on condition that she receive an assurance from him, the meaning of which became a subject of legal dispute.

'Dear Daisy,' it ran, 'I swear that if anything happens to my present affairs I will come back to you and marry you if you are willing on those conditions. This I swear to you on my most solemn vow of Masonry. The 11 day of October 1918. Love Syd.'

For the next month, Daisy wrote letters begging Sydney to come back. She pleaded with him on the telephone, she ambushed Sydney and Maggie in the boarding house and she wept, raged, bargained and threatened 'self-destruction'. It must have been an excruciating time for her – she had lost a confidante, a lover, a creative partner and, significantly, a work contract. 'I never want anyone to dance with me but you,' she wrote in 1918, 'I know all your funny little ways, and you know mine.' In November 1918, she wrote warning that if Sydney did not come back, she would 'go and fight for my rights'. By 1919, she had brought the action against J.C. Williamson for breach of contract, which was settled in her favour for £150, and when she saw an advertisement for Maggie and Sydney's engagement, she took out a writ for breach of promise.[34] By 1920, her career was back on track and she was performing to rave reviews in the Tait's Australian production of *Mother Hubbard*. Financially sound, she arrived at the Melbourne Supreme Court on 20 May 1920, demanding compensation from Sydney Culverhouse for her hurt and humiliation.[35]

### Daisy Yates in the witness box

Daisy and Sydney's case was heard on a typical autumn day in Melbourne: the sky was bloated with rain and flurries of amber leaves tumbled down wide, windblown streets. With their Renaissance revivalist arches, severe blinded windows and Italianate circular courtyard, the law courts occupy a grand and solemn space in Melbourne's business district. Yet according to the newspapers, Daisy and Sydney's hearing looked more like entertainment than law: 'The court was crowded each day, people waited around the doors for admission like the "early door" crowd at the theatres', Brisbane's *Truth* reported. 'The entrances were guarded by policemen who prevented overcrowding but as soon as an individual, having just popped in for an hour or so, made his or her exit, another rushed to fill the vacant seat.' The clerk impotently informed the gallery that applause and laughter were banned. Daisy and Sydney sat behind their barristers across the courtroom from each other; their every gesture commented on by the press.[36]

Justice Mann, whose unfailing decorum and short stature had earned him the nickname 'the little gentleman', was presiding over the hearing with a jury of four. He called the court to order, then nodded to Mr Hogan – a distinguished barrister and fierce Roman Catholic representing Daisy – who stood to give his opening address.

'The parties first met in Paris in 1914,' Mr Hogan began, and proceeded to describe their life together. Their relationship had been 'very loving', but their main 'controversy' had been Sydney's tendency to spend the larger portion of their joint income entertaining other women. 'Fed up,' Daisy insisted that 'they should have a definite understanding about their future marriage, to which Sydney replied: "Well Daisy, I am quite ready and willing to marry you if you will marry me." The wedding was delayed, however, by Sydney's later confession that he was 'not in a fit state of health'. He suggested that they marry in America once their contracts had expired, and Daisy agreed.[37]

Hogan described Sydney's departure on tour at the end of 1917, and Sydney's eventual admissions that he had signed a separate contract and fallen in love with Maggie. Yet when they discussed the matter in person, Hogan said, Sydney assured Daisy that Maggie 'was only one of his passing infatuations'.[38] In a letter later that month, however, which Hogan read aloud to the court, Sydney described himself as 'a very desperate and worried man', reporting that the firm was considering cancelling his and Maggie's performance.[39] 'And now you turn up,' he had chided Daisy, 'with no thoughts but of self-destruction', saying that 'you are prepared to die', 'little thinking of your worried boy, who would have the finger of scorn pointed at him, and might be hounded out of the country, branded as a rotter.'[40] In the same letter, Sydney said that he was 'bound tightly by a cord of honour to two women' and asked Daisy 'to hear the appeal of his sorrow and "get work"'.[41] The gallery jeered at Sydney's expense.[42]

Mr Hogan then called Daisy Yates to the witness box.

'Now, please remember, Miss Yates, that this is a speaking part and not a dancing part,' he joked, 'so kindly speak up so that the judge and jury can hear you.' Daisy smiled and commenced her testimony, recapitulating his story. They had been 'sweethearts' since their meeting in Paris, she explained. 'At that time I had a flat in London. Sydney said that I had better send my furniture to his mother's house. I did so, and I also went there to live ...'

'And when he said to you: "We are going to be married", did you believe him?'

'Yes. Around June 1917 he borrowed some money from me – a mere matter of five pounds,' she replied.[43] 'He wanted it, he said, to pay back to a lady.' Daisy agreed to lend him the money but also expressed her irritation: '"You are always flirting with other women, and you are doing it under the cloak of being my brother."'[44] Turning to the jury, she explained: 'All this time, you see, he was really engaged to me. So I asked him what he intended to do in regard to the matter. He replied: "Oh, we will get married."'

'And what did you say to that?'

'I agreed ...'

'But you did not [marry]?'

'No, a week or so afterward he came to me and told me that he was in bad health, and that it was quite impossible for him to marry me at that time.'[45]

'For what specific reason?'[46]

Daisy hesitated. 'Must I tell the court?'

'Yes, now that you have gone that far.'

'He said to me, "I have been going with another woman and I have contracted a disease." He added, "It will be better to let things stand over until we have finished our contract in Australia, and then we can go to another country." To that proposition I agreed.'

'How was it you came to separate?'

Daisy described being usurped by Maggie and a rumour she had seen in a magazine that Sydney and Maggie were engaged. During this part of the testimony, the press reported, Daisy 'appeared to be much affected, and frequently applied her handkerchief to her eyes. She answered questions in a very low voice and had to be asked to speak up.' She said that on her request, Sydney had contradicted the engagement rumour in the magazine's next issue.[47] When she brought an action against J.C. Williamson a month later, she had 'very little money', was 'crazy with grief' and 'not in good health ... I had been fretting'.

'I have some photographs here that [Sydney] gave you,' Hogan said. 'There are some inscriptions on the back of them.'[48] Turning one over, he read aloud:

To the biggest dam'd nuisance extant, with a heart of gold and with all your faults possible, and come what may, I shall never forget.

From the rotter,

Syd.

Passing one of the photographs to the jury, Hogan explained with a smile, 'And this one, as you can see, is a very good [photo] of the rotter.' Laughter roiled around the courtroom.

'You saw an announcement in the *Herald* of December 1919 that the defendant intended to marry Maggie Dickinson?'

'Yes, there were photographs of the pair of them in the newspaper ... Subsequently I placed the matter in the hands of my solicitor and a writ was issued.'[49]

*  *  *

Mr Macfarlane – a former classics professor and newly appointed King's Counsel – rose in his chair to begin his cross-examination. McFarlane had a reputation for his 'rough' handling of witnesses, and Daisy probably braced herself. He began by suggesting that Daisy had lied about her age on her marriage certificate, which she admitted to doing because she did not have her parents' consent. Had she also, Macfarlane asked, lied to the Divorce Court about living with Sydney without being married. Daisy tried to wriggle out of this accusation:

'I was not living with him,' she replied.

'Really and truly were you not?'

'Do you wish me to state whether I was living with him as his mistress?' she shot back, pre-empting his line of attack.

'Yes.'

'Well, I was not doing anything of the kind. What privileges I allowed him were because I loved him.'

'... When you first met him in Paris you were staying at the same hotel?'

'Yes.'

'And you used to receive him as a visitor in your bedroom?'

'It is a common rule amongst members of the theatrical profession to receive visitors in a bedroom.'

'But he would be there at nighttime, would he not?'

'I cannot remember that in Paris he was in my room late at night.'

'Well, I will put the matter plain to you. Did intimate relations take place between you and Sydney before you left Paris?'

'Certainly not.'

The cross-examination continued in this vein, with Mr Macfarlane asking about their sleeping arrangements in London, Johannesburg, Melbourne and Adelaide.

'And you say that sexual intercourse never occurred between you until when?'

'Until I obtained a decree from the court for a divorce.'

'From that time onwards, I suggest that you were his mistress.'

'No, intimacy between us only occurred now and then.'

'You were lovers?'

'We may have been lovers.'

'You looked upon the man as belonging to you?'

'Well, yes.'

'And you granted him indulgences now and then because you loved him?'

'Yes.'

'And you are bringing this action against him because you love him?'

'Perhaps so.'

'And in the hope that you may force him to marry you?'

'Again, perhaps so.'

'Money never entered into it?'

'No.'

'But perhaps you have another motive?'

'What do you mean?'

'What about the motive of revenge?'

Here Daisy burst into tears. 'Revenge!' she cried, 'That is untrue! I am not actuated by such motive.'

'Jealousy of course would have nothing to do with your actions?'

'No, I have never been jealous of anybody.'

'Did you ever tell anyone that you intended to make Sydney suffer?'

'No,' Daisy responded decidedly.

'What?'

'Well not as far as I know. At times, of course, when I was distracted I may have said things that I hardly knew what I did say. I hoped almost right up to the end that he would come back to me.'

Next came Mr Macfarlane's questions about Sydney's alleged venereal disease, which he declared to be a 'diabolical lie'. Daisy insisted she had not made it up and nor had she spread rumours about Sydney suffering from syphilis to thwart his engagement to Maggie. Unable to gain any ground on this front, with Daisy even naming the doctors that Sydney had consulted, McFarlane moved to an easier target: the promise to marry in the written assurance.

'You say that he agreed [to marry you], if you did not succeed in getting your passport?'

'Yes, and he gave me a memo so that I should have it in black and white.'

'But in the memo he says: "If anything happens to my present affairs". It says nothing about "if you do not get your passport". So the most important thing is left out of this memo?'

'I can't help that …'

'You also wrote: "If you will come back to me at the end of your contract I will drop everything", and you added, "I want you now, but at the end of two or three months, I may not."'

'I meant that I wanted him then, but that if we continued to be parted for two or three months, he might kill all the love I had for him ... When one is silly with grief one does not stop to think of every word one writes ...'

'You suggest that you are heartbroken over this business?'

'I am.'

'But on the stage, you have made a game of it all? ... You have been acting with [comedian] Jack Cannot recently? And in that act you two made a travesty of this very case? ... He kisses you, doesn't he, and he says – what? – he says, "You won't tell the missus."'

'On one occasion only that I know of, he added "or sue me for breach of promise."'[50]

*   *   *

Was Daisy Yates truly 'heartbroken over this business', or was she merely acting, concealing her true motivations of revenge, greed or jealousy? Who has the right to feel disappointed in love? Could a mistress be promised marriage and feel despair at being jilted? And is ill-health a recognised symptom of 'fretting' over a lover, or a reason for postponing a wedding? These were new questions for juries to consider in the early twentieth century, and they were the questions around which Daisy's examination turned. They continued the next day, when Sydney was placed in the witness box. He described her being 'hysterical', and he read out letters in which he had urged her to 'not cry and make yourself ill'. He also argued that her sobs had been mere performance. Yes, he said, as an actor he should have been able to detect her 'shamming', but Daisy's was a 'finely acted part'.[51]

Legally, questions about Daisy's broken heart would inform the determination of damages (the largest 'head' of damages was for injured feelings), but they also shed light on her motivation for bringing the action and whether there had been a promise to marry. On this last point, Mr Hogan had said that there had been two promises: the first had been verbal, given after Daisy complained about Sydney 'flying around' with other women, and the second written. As Mr Hogan and Daisy no doubt knew, however, the written 'memo' was at best ambiguous and at worst unconvincing. A more plausible reading, as McFarlane argued, was that Sydney had agreed to marry Daisy if his 'present situation' with Maggie changed, and indeed this seems to be what Daisy pleaded with him in her later letters. It was a contingent promise, and in the law of breach of promise, a contingent promise was not enforceable. To this extent, the case rested on the verbal promise, which, given in private with neither witnesses nor material proof, came down to the question of who to believe: Sydney or Daisy?[52]

By the time Daisy stepped out of the witness box, Sydney did not look like a particularly pleasant chap. He was, in his own words, 'a rotter': a philandering, self-absorbed, unempathetic, cravenly instrumentalist rotter. He was now also suspected of carrying a venereal disease. Daisy's credibility, on the other hand, would be determined by a more delicate test. Was she genuinely stricken with grief over the affair? If so, it would seem likely that she had been promised more than a status as mistress. Amorous distress would also give her a culturally acceptable reason for having come to court, demonstrating her feminine vulnerability in matters of the heart. In court, she needed to act out her anguish but not attract suspicion that she was acting (a somewhat difficult expectation for an actress), and she needed to tell the court of her suffering in a language that rendered heartbreak serious. In short, she needed to translate the acute and anarchic wordlessness of pain into legal form.

Had Daisy brought her case to court fifty years earlier, she would never have been challenged on her experience of heartbreak. A woman's suffering only became determinative of damages around the turn of the twentieth century. In the nineteenth century, once a woman had established a promise of marriage, she was not asked to provide proof of lacerated feelings. For 'virtuous' women, anguish was seen as a natural consequence of femininity and of a gendered labour market that made women socially and economically dependent upon marriage. Indeed, women's susceptibility to love and its torments meant that anguish was imputed even in cases where it was clearly absent. 'This was not a case where any great amount of sentimental feeling was involved,' explained a judge in 1869. 'Still, feelings were involved, and no woman could be treated in this way without being injured'[53]

There were exceptions, gradations and hierarchies, even in the nineteenth century, specifically that a woman's susceptibility to heartbreak was indexed to her social status and virginal purity. Being middle-aged or unchaste was generally assumed to diminish a woman's capacity to suffer, while being virginal, 'prepossessing' or wealthy increased it. Throughout the nineteenth century, any action involving a female plaintiff in her late thirties or older was argued strictly on its contractual merits. Women deemed unchaste were also assumed not to suffer: 'She could not be so affected by the disappointment, and no such violence would be done to her feelings as there would be if she were a good and virtuous young woman whose character was unblemished,' argued the attorney-general in *Field v Nelson* (1850).[54] However, if the plaintiff's counsel could show that she had been brutishly seduced, the woman was redeemed and the weight of her suffering intensified.

In the nineteenth century, sexual reputation was dealt with through the defence of unchastity, which, if proven, completely justified a man breaking his promise of marriage. By the time Daisy brought her action, however, the defence of unchastity had all but disappeared, as sexual norms began to wriggle free from Christian morality. Twentieth-century sexology, popular Freudianism and emerging consumer culture considered women's sexual expression as natural, while the emergence of a dating culture saw women and men become intimate more quickly. Sexual reputation was still discussed, but moral boundaries were no longer so clearly delineated. Barristers argued over whether a promise of marriage could be made between people of loose morals and whether an unchaste woman could suffer heartbreak.

Macfarlane's interrogation of Daisy about her and Sydney's sleeping arrangements was part of this wider shift. He resumed the theme the next day, turning to the sexual reputation of people in the theatre. 'The parties belonged to the stage, and there was a certain degree and deal of freedom in their relations.' They were not like 'respectable people', he said. They might pass letters in endearing terms to each other, but this was not to imply a marital promise. Classification became significant: were Daisy and Sydney 'sweethearts' and 'lovers', as Daisy maintained, or was she a 'mistress', as Macfarlane argued, a term weighted with moral condemnation. These arguments would have been perfectly acceptable in the nineteenth century. By 1920, however, definitions of 'respectability' were changing, and the term 'mistress' had started to sound anachronistic. As reflected in other cases from this period, the relationship between a woman's sexuality and her suffering had become unsettled. While evidence of sexual licentiousness could still condemn a woman, it might just as likely be ignored. More definitive was whether or not the woman could show how much she had suffered.

Where nineteenth-century women were applauded for their self-composure, twentieth-century women were condemned if they failed to dramatise their grief – but Daisy's performance was flawless. She was a picture of femininity in distress. Importantly, she laid claim to emotions – love and grief – that were considered evidence of genuine heartbreak, unlike more suspect emotions such as jealousy, greed and vengeance, which might cause a woman to lose her suit. An excess of rationality could also provoke suspicion: a Ms Field lost her case after giving 'her evidence coolly and intelligently' and 'only on one occasion display[ing] any warmth of feeling',[55] while a Ms Jaeger lost her action because of her 'cheerful[ness]': the judge mused that she 'did not impress him in the box as having suffered much in her feelings'.[56] In contrast, a plaintiff who emoted in court was almost always guaranteed of success, as the defence counsel in *Cooper v Barnett* (1905) grumbled: 'give me a pretty woman, well dressed, who will cry at the right time and I'll get her a verdict from any jury'.[57]

Performing her grief both in and out of court was one way Daisy could convince the court of her suffering. The other was to package her pain in a language that was legible to early-twentieth-century courts: that of psychosomatic injury. Daisy, like other women, turned to medicine and psychology to legitimate her anguish; she discussed heartbreak as a psychic harm with bodily effects. In drawing upon new scientific expertise to authenticate her pain, Daisy was very much a creature of the modern world.

When heartbreak was raised in the early-to-mid nineteenth century (always a rare occurrence), the language used was usually Biblical in provenance – the woman was 'afflicted' – and the most common effects were somnambulism and agoraphobia: a woman might confine herself to her bedroom or sleepwalk down a corridor, shrieking. From the 1880s to the First World War, descriptions of heartbreak changed. A language of health crept into women's testimony, although nothing more precise than that of 'falling ill' or 'being under medical attendance'.[58] The period after the First World War, however, marked a shift towards a psychological language of shock, nervous breakdowns and neurasthenia and physical symptoms attributed to them. The language used to describe Daisy – 'hysterical' or 'crazy with grief' – was already being usurped by this more technical, expert terminology.

In 1918, Ms Broadhurst gave evidence that Mr Archer's letter had given her a 'terrible shock' resulting in neurasthenia. The following year, Ms Chadwick told the court that being jilted came as 'a terrible shock to her; her nerves and eyes were affected, she could not sleep and had to take to wearing glasses'.[59] This language continued into the 1930s, when Miss Allan described how her nervous breakdown caused her legs to become paralysed, and into the 1950s, when (a different) Ms Chadwick reported that she had 'lost two and a half stone and couldn't work for months because I had a nervous breakdown'.[60] Women reported seeing doctors or entering hospitals much more frequently in this period.[61] In 1931, Miss Lory summoned her doctor as a medical witness and he gave a precise diagnosis of the effects of heartbreak on the body:

she had a very worried appearance, face drawn, eyes looked red, skin dark under lids, muscles of face twitching, melancholy tone of voice. Her hand grip was listless, pulse – 95, soft and slightly irregular. There was a tremor noticeable in the hand. She complained of loss of appetite and almost complete loss of sleep, restlessness and inability to concentrate.

It would be 'three to six months before she could start the business again', he said, as 'she felt strongly the injury to her affections'.[62] Women drew upon this new medical language of suffering to prove their pain to courts that had never completely trusted their testimony and which now demanded proof of their distress.

Although the language of health may appear to have arrived suddenly in the court records, we can trace this shift to the nineteenth century and vast processes of secularisation, whereby science challenged the explanatory power of religion. By the late-nineteenth and early-twentieth centuries doctors had consolidated their authority through professionalisation (the NSW branch of the British Medical Association was established in 1880) and they had a new role to play in public debate.[63] Science was placed in the service of social reform movements aimed at 'curing' high crime, unemployment and a steadily declining birth rate.[64] Evolution, race and heredity became features of national debate, and supposedly 'scientific' solutions were proposed to counter the perceived threats of racial decay and the rise of Asian powers: pronatalism at the turn of the century and eugenics in the interwar years.

As doctors with an interest in the emerging field of psychology turned their minds to the problems of the time, a more refined language of psychosomatic harm developed, which we see in the testimony of breach of promise claimants. The constant use of the word 'shock' by plaintiffs, beginning in the 1880s, was indebted to the literature produced by surgeons examining the effects of railway accidents (a frequent cause of injury in the nineteenth century). Surgeons John Erichsen in 1866 and Herbert Page in 1883 argued that victims of railway accidents suffered emotional harm, which Page termed 'nervous shock'. Page went so far as to suggest that people could experience shock without having any physical injuries, an alarming notion for a legal system that preferred visible, verifiable proof. As large numbers of victims litigated their complaints, a body of precedent developed which stipulated that emotional injury needed to be accompanied by some kind of physical injury, proven by doctors. Lawyers in breach of promise cases would have been aware of these cases, as negligence and breach of promise both fell within the domain of torts. Although it is possible that plaintiffs genuinely experienced a feeling of 'shock' upon being jilted, it would also make sense if lawyers had encouraged the use of this language to make their clients' grief more credible.

The psychosomatic symptoms described by plaintiffs were indebted to new psychological categories that emerged after the First World War. Psychology obtained greater legitimacy during this period, when psychologists claimed authority in a crowded market of unregistered physicians and doctors specialising in 'nerve and brain complaints'.[65] Their success, according to Stephen Garton, could be ascribed to a combination of their effectiveness in treating shellshock and their more conciliatory approach to the medical establishment. In the 1920s, most metropolitan hospitals were operating psychological clinics,[66] and the rates of voluntary admissions rose dramatically as the categories of mental illness expanded to include more 'stress-related' illness such as financial anxiety, worry and grief, and as psychological discourse spread through the popular press.[67]

Significantly, psychology had delved into the question of heartbreak and concluded that its symptoms were psychosomatic. Freud and Breuer's *Studies on Hysteria* included the case history of Fraulein Elisabeth Von R., whose secret and unreciprocated feelings for the son of a family friend manifested in fatigue and in 'great pains' in her legs while walking.[68] In 1926, Ernest Snowden, an English clinical psychologist, published an article on 'The Conversion Neurosis', in which he described a condition whereby the 'psychological disturbance is converted into a bodily symptom which is usually a disturbance of function in some part of the body'. He noted that this could be seen in shellshocked soldiers and in women who had fallen victim to a breach of promise of marriage. He cited the case study of a 23-year-old woman who was jilted after announcing her pregnancy and as a result lost the use of her left arm.[69] The popularisation of such theories explains why breach of promise plaintiffs around this time found themselves going blind upon being jilted, being rendered speechless, or, in Daisy Yates' case, losing her pallor and her appetite.

Psychological discourse appeared in breach of promise cases almost immediately after the First World War, as returned soldiers and jilted plaintiffs began to report remarkably similar symptoms. In 1916, Mr Finch, like other defendants who claimed that they were 'medically unfit'[70] for marriage, told the court that he suffered from shellshock, the symptoms of which included insomnia and neurasthenia. The next year, Ms Broadhurst claimed that the 'shock' of a letter breaking off the engagement had caused her to suffer from neurasthenia.[71] In 1918, Ms Chadwick reported that the 'shock' of jilting had caused her insomnia and partial blindness.[72] Emotional injury gained legitimacy by being attached to male trauma. Heartbroken women elevated blasted love to the status of a military wound and found medical proof of their anguish in their wakeful bodies and jangling nerves.

The pathologisation of romantic suffering also had roots in the pronatalist and eugenicist beliefs circulating at the time. Psychology, medicine and popular periodicals all stressed that women's purpose was to be wives and 'mothers of the new race'. This imbued spinsterdom with an aura of illness. Ms White reportedly told Mr Proude that they should marry because if she had 'no children, it may affect my health'.[73] These ideas coincided with a narrowing of the colonial family: spinsters, who had previously held defined roles in large extended families, were increasingly cast as economic burdens. If a woman's ultimate goal in life was motherhood, then being jilted meant a pathological deviation from a biologically predestined path. Love could make you go mad.

Of course, there was nothing new about linking love to madness. From Dido and Aeneas to Shakespeare's *Midsummer Night's Dream*, love has often been depicted as a divine delirium, condemning its unhappy protagonists to an exquisite torture. Yet the reshaping of the family unit, combined with the new medical and psychological analysis of love, undoubtedly changed how people experienced heartbreak.

In the Public Records Office in Victoria, I ask for nineteenth- and twentieth-century asylum records. These large books – as wide as the table – contain photographs of patients and handwritten case studies. They are vast compendiums of suffering, the papery traces of troubled minds. Opening the files for Yarra Bend Asylum, I find that Janet Wilkinson, in 1883, was the first woman diagnosed with a love-related psychological illness – in her case, dementia caused by 'disappointment in love'. There were no such cases before her, but after her, cases appear quite frequently. In 1906, Alice Graham's delusions were attributed to 'disappointment in love affairs' and 'heredity'. In 1903, Sarah Pins suffered a three-day case of 'shock' that was 'caused by reflecting on the character of her lover'.[74] The most common symptom caused by 'love affairs' was 'acute melancholia'; 'delusions' and 'dementia' were also common. The Inspector General for the Insane's report for 1912 listed 'love affairs' as a distinct category under causes of illness.[75]

When Daisy described herself as having been in 'ill-health' as a result of the broken relationship, her words carried a distinct medical, psychological and legal meaning that has been lost in our more cavalier (or callous) times.

## Sydney Culverhouse in the witness box

On the day Sydney gave his testimony, hordes of people flocked to the court, spilling out into the cloisters. 'Hardly adapted to the requirements of a place of public entertainment, the First Civil Court was uncomfortably crowded this morning,' grumbled *The Argus*. As Macfarlane would later explain, Sydney and Daisy had decided against 'dragging their friends into the witness-box', so Sydney would be the last witness. 'It was a fight to the finish between themselves.'

Sydney, even by his own barrister's admission, made a terrible witness. Yes, he said during cross-examination by Mr Hogan, he had heard his counsel describe Daisy as his 'rejected mistress', but he 'would not use' that term: 'I hate the word mistress.' But had he not, 'on oath, applied it to her in documents filed in court'? 'I have, but that was in writing, not in speech.' The gallery laughed, but Sydney continued, clumsily, 'Yes, she was my mistress.'

Having established Sydney's flexible approach to words uttered under oath, Mr Hogan moved on to his failure to honour contracts. Yes, Sydney agreed, they did have a verbal agreement that they would always dance together, and yes, he had broken that agreement because he fell in love with Maggie Dickinson.

'Is it not the fact that you saw which side your bread was buttered on when you wrote to the plaintiff in this connection: "I have made up my mind to stay in Australia until I do get some money"?'

'Partly, but it was partly sentiment.'

'Two days later you wrote to the plaintiff: "That silly idea of refusing work with anyone but me must come out of your head; that is, if you want to work again out here. It would be a different thing if we were home. But we are not, and I don't mind what I do so long as the money is forthcoming." Does that mean that if the two of you had been among your own people, you would have done the decent thing by the plaintiff?'

'What do you mean by "the decent thing"?'

'The decent thing is to keep your word, sir, if you ask me. Did you mean that in Australia you did not care a Continental damn for any consideration but money?'

'Certainly not. I meant that the plaintiff could have other partners at home, because there is bigger scope there.'

' … You wrote to Miss Yates after [confessing you had signed a separate contract]?'

'Yes.'

'You addressed her as "My Love" and concluded with kisses?'

'Yes.'

'Then you were writing a letter full of love talk to one girl while in love with another?' Hogan continued. 'You say in this letter: "Think of me in my position, caught and bound tightly, by the cord of honour, to two women." Whom were these two women?'

'Miss Yates and Miss Dickinson.'

'What was the cord of honour binding you to Miss Yates?'

'To look after her financially, to see she did not want.'

'How would that cause you to write that you were "broken up in spirit as well as in honour", unless you were bound in honour by a promise to marry in regard to both girls?'

'I was financially embarrassed. I had four pound per week to live on. Instead of going back to America, Miss Yates came back here, planted herself down in the hotel and said: "Here I am, and here I am going to stay."'

'I see! She would not get out of your way.' Hogan opened one of Sydney's letters to Daisy and began reading from it. 'Then you say: "Would it not be wonderful to look into the mirror and see a contented healthy face reflected, and to think that though you paid the price, you made someone happy."' Looking up from the letter, he asked, 'What price was she to pay?'

'The price of separation.'

'Then it wasn't really your financial position that had broken your spirit, but the refusal of Miss Yates to go away. You would have been happy had she gone. She was to pay the price. The woman pays. Is that the position? Then you say: "Don't cry. Do not make yourself ill about this heart appeal of mine, but try to win out for the sake of poor old Syd." Does that mean, "I promised to marry you, but efface yourself for the sake of making me happy"?'

'She was lying in the hotel room, refusing to eat or take anything at all. She was in the habit of taking Veronal, and she threatened to take an overdose and said I would find her dead some day … It was a very finely acted part, she was shamming, and it did not take her long to get over it.'[76]

*   *   *

Sydney's testimony reveals another possible way of reading the history of heartbreak in the early twentieth century: women came to court with stories of heartbreak because in fact they suffered more than they had in the nineteenth century. Sydney represented a new type of twentieth-century manhood, one that achieved masculinity not through marriage but through promiscuity, and women bore the brunt of his sexual entitlement. In the Victorian era, masculinity had been defined through promise-keeping, both romantic and commercial, and achieved through marriage and fatherhood as men assumed governance of the home. Men's behaviour during courtship was monitored by the family and community, and perfidy was severely punished. Indeed, in Victorian literature, men who break their promises to marry are often cast out of the community or even killed. A person's selection of a partner was also informed by moral standards exterior to the self. Couples fell in love because they came from similar moral, social and economic worlds, not because their partner was 'sexy' or because they craved self-validation.[77]

With its catchcries of freedom and choice, the modern world, after the First World War, replaced this ritualised romance with an unregulated and competitive sexual marketplace. As male power within the family was eroded by legal reforms granting women property and personal rights, men asserted their dominance in the sexual arena, proving their masculinity by accumulating sexual conquests. A new dating culture developed, unmoored from morality and community regulation, and with very different gender expectations for men and women. Sex-advice literature and popular culture encouraged women to seek love to ground their identity, given they still did not have equal opportunities for self-actualisation in the public sphere. Men, meanwhile, became sexual capitalists, competing against one another, and marriage was no longer assumed to be the endpoint of romance. In this new world, women not only suffered more from love, but therapeutic culture individualised and interiorised fault. A man was attracted to a woman not because of external standards such as her morality or economic standing, but because of attractions deeply intimate to the self: personality and sexual charm. If the relationship failed, male sexual entitlement was not to blame so much as the woman's appearance or psychological makeup. Experts told women so.[78]

This provocative thesis has been argued by sociologist Eva Illouz, and there is much in her explanation of modern love that helps to explain why Sydney caused Daisy such pain.[79] Sydney could be seen as a sexual capitalist *par excellence*, 'flying around' with other women, reluctant to marry and even incapable of marrying because of a disease he had contracted from a lover. As Daisy had a more successful career, he was unlikely to prove his masculine dominance at work or at home. And having chosen a potentially effeminising career in dance and entertainment, at a time when other men were testing their masculinity in battle, Sydney proved his manhood instead by collecting women. He expected Daisy to accept this, which she did until she demanded marriage.

Later, when Sydney met Maggie, he behaved like the ideal consumer: a rational, self-maximising individual who was happy to discard Daisy for a woman who offered more economic, social and sexual value. The affair was both highly emotional – he was 'madly and truly in love with Maggie' – and highly rational – he 'knew what side his bread was buttered on'. And as Daisy and Sydney were far from their families and communities of birth, living in a peripatetic world of performers, his actions had little immediate social consequence. In the vaudeville community, their dispute was seen as a private matter to be fought out between the two of them: this explains why nobody else gave evidence. Finally, Sydney maintained his sovereignty during the affair, while Daisy dissolved: her sense of self, her identity as a dancer and her future had all been bound up in her relationship. Sydney demanded to exercise his freedom of choice without Daisy 'standing in his way', and he even asked for her emotional support in this endeavour, imploring her to sacrifice herself for 'poor old Syd'.

Yet Sydney's insistence that he was 'not a cad' and that he was 'bound by a cord of honour between two women' suggests that the luxurious brushstrokes of Illouz's sociological thesis could benefit from a historian's careful gradations and detail. Why would a philandering louse in the twentieth century care about honour? Why would he be fearful of being 'hounded out of the country' if men now enjoyed unfettered access to a vast sexual marketplace of desire? Most obviously, because the romantic arena he inhabited was not in fact detached from morality but rather saturated in it, and Sydney feared social reprisal.

Sydney's terror of being 'branded as a rotter' and having 'the finger of scorn pointed at him' suggest that male sexual licentiousness was still subject to community policing. A new dating market may have opened, but it was not unregulated. As numerous historians have pointed out, male sexuality was considered a major problem in the late nineteenth and early twentieth centuries, with concerns about venereal disease, violent 'sex maniacs' and adulterers the subject of public debate and targeted by the social purity movement. Male sexual appetite, it was thought, would corrupt the nation's young women, and indeed nothing was so damning in Daisy and Sydney's trial as the evidence that he had contracted gonorrhoea. In the

years following the First World War, a renewed emphasis on domestic masculinity replaced the prewar idealisation of heroic, militaristic masculinity.
If there had been a 'flight from domesticity' in the late nineteenth century,
as historian John Tosh has argued, then it has since been shown that that
flight had been 'impaled on the barbed wire of the Somme', and men
returned happily to home and hearth following the ravages of mechanised
warfare.[80] This is not to suggest that Illouz's thesis has no merit, simply that
the sexually licentious forms of masculinity that she sees emerging in the
twentieth century sometimes competed, merged or mingled with older
models of manhood, in which sexual transgressions were policed by the
community, sexual reputation mattered, and the natural teleology of romantic desire was marriage.

Rather than exemplifying the liberated, commodified sexuality of the
jazz age, Sydney and Daisy's trial illuminates a period of contestation over
the ethics of love. Behaving honourably mattered to Sydney; we know this
from his letters. This was partly because his career depended on his public
reputation, but also because he clearly cared about his personal integrity. Yet
never was a man more conflicted! Sydney argued that 'at least [he] behaved
honourably' in one breath, and signed his letters 'Syd, the rotter' the next. He
wrote about the 'cord of honour' that bound him to 'two women' but knew
that monogamy necessitated a choice, and if he chose Maggie this would
mean breaking his word to Daisy. Sydney hollowed the term honour of its
substantive meaning; what remained was a dry husk of proceduralism. Like
other men involved in twentieth century breach of promise suits, he defined
being 'honourable' and 'decent' not as *keeping* his word, but as being open
about *breaking* it. The key value to protect was autonomy, and self-revelation
ensured that both sides could make informed decisions. Confession had
become an act of chivalry.

Of course, one of the strongest arguments against this thin conception of
romantic ethics came in the form of women's tears, lamentations and threats
of self-destruction. A performance of suffering was an appeal, a reminder of
a legal and moral obligation. Heartbreak challenged a man's 'right' to choose
with a personal plea based on inter-dependency. For Sydney's self-conception
as an honourable man to be plausible, he needed Daisy's cheerful consent to
their break-up. When she wept and refused to release him, he claimed that
her suffering was 'a finely acted part' and that she was motivated by revenge.
The alternative explanation – that his broken promise had caused her real
agony – would have left him open to ethical interrogation, and a lawsuit.

\*  \*  \*

Daisy should not have won her breach of promise action – at least the judge didn't think so. Both parties, he said, 'had done a certain amount of acting' in the witness box, and neither had called corroborative evidence. In these circumstances, the jury should pay 'particular attention to the documents'. The judge 'thought it strange' that Sydney and Daisy had not married immediately after she had complained about him borrowing money. The reason suggested (that Sydney had a venereal disease) seemed unbelievable. He 'did not think that any man anxious to delay his marriage would give the reasons alleged, even if those reasons existed'. The second promise – the written memo – was a conditional promise that 'seemed to bear the defendant out'. That said, if the jury found for the plaintiff, they should 'take into account her humiliation and her lessened value and chance in the marriage market'. Nothing was said about her loss of future 'settlement' or her economic security. Extraordinarily, after the jury had retired for five minutes, the judge called them back with another pointer: 'if they considered that the defence was correct in saying that his promise to marry was conditional on his not marrying Miss Dickinson, it was their duty to find for the defendant.' Of course, he had just told them that this was the correct interpretation.[81]

After two hours of deliberation, the jury returned. On the first element of the offence – had a promise of marriage been breached? – they answered yes. On the calculation of damages – how much hurt and humiliation had Daisy suffered? – they gave an exemplary award. Daisy Yates was to be compensated £500. It was a significant win: more than double the average damages for the twentieth century.[82]

\*  \*  \*

Daisy's exit from the crowded doors of Melbourne's first civil court might appear like the final performance in one of her shows. We have sat through a whirl of disconnected acts featuring a charlatan priest, a cross-dressing dancer, a romance at the Moulin Rouge, the outbreak of war, success on the stage, heartbreak in hotels, and a courtroom drama. But these scenes are all woven from the thread of modernity. They emerged from a 'nervous and precipitous age' that invented frenetic theatrical pleasures, turned courtship into the accumulation of sexual capital, diagnosed bodily and psychic pain in terms borrowed from medicine and psychology, and demanded that proof of suffering be performed to a courtroom audience of sceptics. This was not simply an age of skittish minds, but of minds that sought out novel ways of knowing and new, bodily forms of evidence.[83] Yet as much as Daisy and Sydney twirled their way into the modern world, they kept step to an older rhythm and, like others, were judged harshly if they moved out of time. As much as Justice Mann insisted that his court was 'not a court of morals but a court of law', the jury was unable to disentangle morals from love, because morality – whether thought of as honour, decency or manliness – still mattered to romance.[84]

Too often when we think about the jazz age, we imagine a world of unbounded pleasures: waifish flappers with thin cigarettes spinning with abandon past a line of dandies; the joyful anarchy of vaudeville and early cinema; the thrill of motoring or steaming around the world. If we think about pain during this period, it is usually of masculine suffering, on the fields of the Somme or in the minds of shellshocked veterans who stalked the light-striped corridors of the modern asylum. I have set out to show in this chapter that heartbreak belongs to this history, and that in the early twentieth century it assumed a distinctly modern form. Women like Daisy understood and expressed their hurt feelings as an issue of bodily and psychological health, and in court this language earned them significant damages.

\*     \*     \*

I am sitting in the National Library of Australia listening to 'By Heck' from the American musical *So Long Letty*, which the sheet music tells me was 'sung with charming success by Daisy Yates and Sydney Yates'. There is a photograph of Daisy and Sydney on the cover, with Sydney centre stage – dinner suit, bow tie and a delicate, androgynous face – and Daisy hovering behind him, staring fixedly into the camera. They performed it in 1915 and it must have been one of the first times Australian audiences saw the foxtrot, with its strict four-four time disrupted by whimsical ragtime syncopation. I can imagine the musical – described as one that 'bubbles over with laughable pretty tunes, youth and beauty' – distracting an anxious nation that had recently lurched into war. I can also imagine Daisy dancing to it, unaware that only two years later she would waltz with Sydney for the last time.[85] I'm not sure how much we can read into a photo, but I like to think there is something in those narrowed, purposeful eyes of Daisy's that suggests defiance – that no matter what the blond-haired man taking up all the space on the cover may do, she would, in her own words, 'fight for her rights'.[86]

Daisy's breach of promise action was not the last time she was in court. In 1923 she slipped and fell, twisting her ankle while performing in *The Peep Show* for J.C. Williamson.[87] She demanded, and won, £150 compensation for her injury and claimed that the company had agreed verbally to re-employ her once she had recovered.[88] Her written agreement with the company, however, suggested otherwise, and when they refused to offer her work she sued, unsuccessfully, for breach of contract.[89] Yet this setback did not dim her career, and she continued to sing and twirl into the dying years of vaudeville. In the National Library, I flip through the rectangular vaudeville flyers and see her headlining throughout the 1920s, alongside female crack-shooters, singers of sentimental ballads and stand-up comics. In 1927 she appears as part of a comedy duo with Yorke Gray, a talented female impersonator, revue writer, dancer, singer and comedian. In 1930 the newspapers announce their marriage and in 1935, Daisy and Yorke moved to New Zealand, where they continued to perform together. Yorke died in 1943, when Daisy was one year shy of her sixtieth birthday. According to a vaudeville and pantomime website, Daisy 'was still to be seen in Parnell Road, Remuera in 1981'. She died, aged 100, in 1984.[90]

With no diaries, no surviving relatives and only short excerpts from her letters, it's difficult to get a sense of who Daisy was when she wasn't flitting across a public stage. Interviews like that in *The Graphic of Australia* need to be read judiciously, as they primarily served as advertising for shows. But this interview, recorded after 'a strenuous rehearsal, with dress rehearsal to follow', seems to have caught her in a vulnerable moment, and she appears disarmingly honest. 'I am a very quiet person,' she begins, '... and I love motoring, not to sit at the wheel, but to cuddle under a rug whilst someone else does the work.' Having spent much of her life crossdressing, she thought that there was 'a lot of the boy in me'. 'I am well used to looking after myself,' she says. 'I like to sew and to make all my own undies and do the mending.' Her 'great particular pal is a canary which is so clever it understands all I can say,' and she once had 'a black Persian cat. It was a most brainy animal.' Her parting words are heavy with faux humility: 'Hope I have not been too dull,' she smiles. And then she gathers up her furs, her sequins, her silk and sash-ays out of the room, ready for the next performance.[91]

11.

# 'It must be her baking, that's always to blame': Love, Law and Feminist Consciousness

*(Allan v Growden, 1938)*

The file marked *Allan v Growden* (1938) is delivered to my desk in the Western Australian state archives: black-and-white photographs, poems typed in faint purple ink, letters so long they have chapter headings, and a patent for herbal remedies spill out from a large plastic sheath. I eye the documents with anticipation, like delicacies in a voluptuous banquet. I also feel vindicated. Yesterday, the archivist had told me that I should return to Sydney and consult newspaper accounts of the case online. 'Very few of our papers survived,' she sniffed, 'and certainly not judgment papers of the kind you're looking for.' With a steely smile, I asked for the guide to the collections and passed a day jotting down names and numbers. Now, dipping my hand into the folder, I retrieve a photograph of the litigants I had been looking for: Robina Marwick Allan – hairdresser, beautician, clairvoyant, poet and amateur psychologist – and Frederick Growden – police constable. They are pictured in a curvaceous black Ford Cabriolet convertible, Robina in furs and Frederick in a dinner suit. Heads turned towards the camera, they gaze out across the decades, like cinema stars from the golden era.[1]

There is no date on the photograph but I assume it was taken in the first years of their romance, sometime in the early 1930s. When Frederick met Robina, she was a local Perth personality. Captured in profile in newspaper advertisements, she looked stylish and distinctively modern: permed chestnut bob, fine features, pale skin and an arch half-smile. She claimed to be a 'widely travelled hostess and specialist in Psycho Beauty Culture', capable of making women 'look ten years younger in thirty minutes'.[2] She offered women-only lectures on 'Supreme Healing Power' in outback towns in Western Australia.[3] Frederick, slick, dark-haired and dapper, was in his fifties but could pass for his early forties. In a time of economic austerity, they rolled around town in Frederick's convertible, making appearances at the theatre, clubs and cinema. When Frederick was posted to Fremantle, Robina gifted him tablecloths, ebony elephants and paintings. Frederick helped Robina financially when her business failed, and they passed moments of quiet intimacy together, making up stories about the bird in the nest outside Robina's flat. 'Two doves were seen to visit her early this morning,' Robina wrote suggestively. 'Birdie is not the saint she has been credited [to be].' The relationship went off-piste in 1934 when Frederick confessed to having 'a flutter' with a barmaid – 'the lowest kind of woman', Robina glowered. When the flutter developed into a relationship, Frederick demoted Robina to friendship, and Robina responded with furious letters and violent confrontations. By 1937, Frederick said that Robina had made his life a 'perfect hell'. Robina wrote that if he didn't return, she would die. Instead, in 1938 she sued him for unlawful detention of goods, assault and breach of promise of marriage.[4]

I skim the court documents and am struck by how familiar they seem; by Robina's sophisticated, proto-feminist critique and her joyful carnality. 'She can't get a husband, dear me / What a shame / It must be her cooking that / is always to blame', runs a poem entitled 'She'. At one o'clock in the morning Robina scribbled to Frederick, 'I am longing for one great night of nights. The night of all nights' and asked what gossipy condemnation would follow a woman who dared to name her desire and pursue a man. She began with her own experiences, then mapped them onto women as a collective, bewailing their impotence in one letter then threatening vengeance in the next. 'Unfortunately women are helpless, and it is all in your power to act as you wish', she wrote, although in another missive she threatened to attack Frederick and his new partner with her walking stick: 'Revenge is sweet. I haven't lost everything not to get back in full.' Love compelled Robina to write, and in her letters she reflected upon her desires, plumbed her and her partner's inner worlds, and fashioned a self and an ideal vision of a relationship.

When Robina's love affair with Frederick failed, it was in the collision between the ideal and the real, and between how Frederick regarded her and how she regarded herself, that a feminist politics was born. Of course, Robina would not have called herself a feminist: in the popular imagination, feminism in the interwar years belonged to elite and bourgeois women, and their self-presentation and demands were rather sexless. But in her poetry, her letters and her court case, Robina foreshadowed later feminist demands and ideas. She expanded from personal experience to collective grievance, she re-examined her experience of desire, romance and heartbreak through a critical lens, and she claimed a right to use coercion, both the state's and her own, to redress her suffering.

Converting love into law meant finding fault, it meant confronting the law's objectivist epistemology with the forms of knowing born of subjective experience, tallying the financial costs of love, protesting intimate violence and taking seriously her emotional injury to make a claim on law to intercede. At a time when law was beginning to retreat from the etiquette of courtship, when the breach of promise action was increasingly referred to as a Victorian relic, Robina used the action to make the very modern argument that the personal was political.[5]

## *Allan v Growden*: Day one

The Western Australian newspapers thrilled to the news that Robina Marwick Allan, who traded and wrote under the name Brendah Barrye, was suing Frederick Growden. It was 1938, and the action would be the first breach of promise case in the state for six years. 'Growden says he was merely a friend of Miss Allan / Letters read' proclaimed *The Daily News*.[6] 'Plaintiff's "poetic" leanings', *The West Australian* rang out.[7] News of the case spread across the nation, and outlets from Melbourne to Townsville in Northern Queensland reported on the 'Case against policeman'.[8]

It was not the first time Robina and Frederick had confronted each other in court; one paper referred to it as a 'sequel'.[9] A year earlier, Frederick, dressed in civilian's clothes, had bundled Robina into his motor car with the aid of Lillian Bodinner (the barmaid) and charged her with 'creating a disturbance'.[10] Robina appeared in the police court, dressed in a 'smart dust coat, small black hat and frock', and claimed that she had been accosted while strolling down Hay Street at seven o'clock at night.[11] The reason, her solicitor argued, was that she had just issued a writ for breach of promise against Growden.[12] The arrest was intimidation and an abuse of power. Growden and Bodinner, on the other hand, said that they had been innocently idling in a motor car outside a café when Robina spotted them, yelled abuse and attempted to hit them with her walking stick. The magistrate believed Growden but let Robina off with a caution and costs.[13]

*Miss Brendah Barrye, Psycho Beauty Specialist*

*Robina Allan, a.k.a. Brendah Barrye, in 1936.*

Now, on 19 October, in the swelter of a heat wave, Robina and Frederick were again facing each other in court. This time they were in the monumental grandeur of the Western Australian Supreme Court, with its Corinthian columns, serpentine stairwells, dark wooden furnishings and baking windowless rooms. Representing Robina was Thomas John Hughes, a fervent unionist, 'larrikin populist' and one-time Labour politician. Growden had hired the more conservative, moustachioed H.P. Downing (King's Counsel). Presiding over the matter was Justice John Dwyer, tall, blue-eyed and fair, who would later be remembered as having 'one of the finest, most incisive minds' in the state. Members of the public packed the seats of the gallery, spilling out of the courtroom and into the corridors.[14]

Robina sat in the witness box – fifty, bespectacled, her bobbed hair dyed platinum blonde, and dressed in a smart suit with polka dots and large red buttons. She began her testimony with evidence of Growden's initial romantic attentions: in 1931 he would ring her up or call upon her at work or at home, she said. When problems with his philandering arose, she would berate him: 'if he wished to keep company with [me] he must cease running around with other women'. Growden was transferred to Fremantle in 1933, and he urged her to leave the hotel where she boarded to live with him.

329

When she asked whether this meant he intended to marry her, he had replied in the affirmative. They inspected a house together in Fremantle, and when Robina objected that it was too near the gaol, Growden agreed to build them a home instead. The relationship bubbled along until Growden received the alarming news from someone in the 'eastern states' that Robina was already married.[15] Extraordinarily, however, there were two Robina Marwick Allans. The Robina he had discovered was her first cousin; they were both named after their grandmother.

Robina told the court that Growden had continued to send her affectionate letters when they were apart. At this point, Mr Hughes interrupted her testimony and read one of the letters aloud to the jury:

> Dear Brendah,
> Sorry to learn that you have been confined to barracks with 'flu. Should like to have been handy in order to look after you, poor woman ...
>
> I will be away this weekend. The sergeant at York is laid up and I have to go over there to take charge during Saturday, Sunday and Monday celebrations. So you may not have the pleasure of hearing my sonorous voice for some time ...
>
> You may be permitted to have a gorge on specially prepared cauliflower and sweet potatoes etc following closely upon my return to Fremantle. You need not worry about the cabbage; I shall attend to that myself ...
>
> You did not say how the organ was going. Are you sure it is giving satisfaction? Heavens, won't I have a feast of music when I return home!...
>
> By Cripes, Dave, it's cold up here these times. A few degrees of frost last night, in my toes, like a refrigerator ...
>
> Well, sweetie, bye bye, Love—
> FREDERICK

Robina explained that after some time, Growden told her that he had been 'keeping company' with a barmaid. 'You can't do a thing like that after all these years,' she said, to which he responded that Robina was 'a married woman' and an 'imposter'. They parted, Robina said, but when he returned to the shop later that day, he took her hand and put it against his face, saying: 'You've been a very loyal woman to me. We'll make it up – don't worry anymore.' When she asked about the barmaid, he replied, 'I'll dump her. You've received me with open arms. Let us be happy and we'll continue with our engagement.'[16]

Robina had not been well, and so Growden sent her away on a holiday, 'for which he kindly paid', but upon her return she found the barmaid still skulking around. 'You can't go on like this – running around with this woman. People are talking about you and it's very bad for my business', she chided. Once again, Growden said that if Robina could forgive him, he would consider getting married. Sometime later, she visited him at his flat in Fremantle, but he wouldn't let her in as there was another woman inside. Robina told the court that he 'ran her downstairs, grasping her arm' until 'she cried out with pain'.[17] The confrontation ended with Frederick again arresting Robina and taking her to the Fremantle police station, where he 'pushed her down and injured her so seriously that she was unable to work for around six weeks'.[18] Her requests for the return of her property went unanswered, and eventually, he told her flatly that he would not marry as he believed she was a bigamist. 'It was not true that she had ever been married', she reportedly reassured the court.[19]

Mr Downing walked to the centre of the room to cross-examine her. Yes, Robina said, she had conducted business under the name of Brendah Barrye in the Bon Marche Arcade but had to give it up in 1936, as she had been 'too ill and too worried to carry it on'. Frederick's behaviour had caused her to have a 'nervous breakdown', and 'both her legs became paralysed'.[20]

'Did you tell him that you did not wish his friendship with you to interfere with his friendship with other women?'

'No.'

Had she 'pursed Growden very vigorously'?

'No.'

'You have what you call other admirers, haven't you?'

'Most women have.'

'So you had a lover?'

'I think I said before that most women have other admirers.'

'I see.'

Mr Downing opened one of Robina's letters and read a snippet to the jury. '"Come back soon, dearest, or I will run amok with somebody." He was objecting to you writing these letters?'

'No, he was delighted and answered them.'

'Here's a long letter', said Downing, counting out fifteen pages.

'It was probably in reply to a twenty-page letter from him', Robina shot back. 'He was always writing loving letters. In fact, it was his long suit.'

'Did you write two poems entitled "He" and "She"?'

'Yes.'

'I suppose "He" means Growden and "She" means you?'

'Not necessarily. I had written hundreds of poems.' They were 'of general application and could be read by anybody … Some men, however much they loved women, do not respect them,' she mused. Frederick 'was incapable of respecting a woman'.

'How old are you, Miss Allan?'

'As old as I feel.'

'Are you a psychologist?'

'No.'

'A clairvoyant?'

'No. I profess to be nothing but a woman.'[21]

## Robina Marwick Allan (or Brendah Barrye)

Who was Robina Allan? She may have professed to be 'nothing but a woman', but a woman who sued a man in the 1930s was never 'nothing'. In the court room, her identity was fiercely contested in a series of conflicting character studies. The self-portrait Robina offered the court – vulnerable, long-suffering, faithful, thoughtful and ready for marriage – was a product of the legal requirements of the action, crafted in dialogue with cultural tropes and gender stereotypes. To prove a promise of marriage, she needed to show that she was marriageable – that she was not simply a 'mistress'. This question turned on similar evidence of her sexual reputation as had the defence of 'unchastity' in the nineteenth century. Robina sought to prove her respectability by counterposing herself to a barmaid – a licentious creature in the popular imagination – and by casting Frederick as an abusive philanderer.[22] Her testimony, like that of all plaintiffs, was not just autobiography but also a critical biography of the defendant.

While Robina framed her story as a narrative of exculpation, the defence told theirs through a series of accusatory rhetorical questions that sought to pass as facts. Robina was depicted as libidinous (had she had many lovers?), sexually aggressive (had she pursued Growden 'vigorously'?), deluded (had she mistaken friendship for love?) and possessed of mysterious or illicit powers (clairvoyancy had been criminally prosecuted in Western Australia, and psychology – still a new field of study – was often mistaken for divination).[23] Yet unlike women accused of unchastity before her, Robina claimed a right to an active sexuality and affirmed, in a delightfully matter-of-fact tone, that she had a plethora of lovers. She challenged law's conservatism and the sexual double standard with a modern constructin of femininity at ease with women's sensuality. Remarkably, she did this as a fifty-year-old woman, at a time when youth and beauty were the markers of womanhood and the prerequisites for feminine sexuality.[24]

Usually, the glimpse of litigants that legal records give us ends here, with their affidavits and testimony in court. Litigants' stories begin the moment they meet their partner and end with the pain of a broken heart. *Allan v Growden*, by contrast, comes with an usually rich archive. In this extensive collection of fifteen-page letters, cantankerous poems and typed memos, we find a form of life writing, which in wrestling with love's small cruelties gives rise to what would later be termed feminist politics.

*　　*　　*

The archives do not have much to say about Robina's early life. She was born in 1887 in Victoria, the youngest daughter of Julia Allan (née Collins) and William Allan. She had two sisters and two brothers, and her father worked as postmaster; she grew up in the rungs of the middling sorts.[25] An advertisement for her hair and beauty business tells us that she spent her youth travelling around Paris and London, and in 1927 she set up business in Perth as a self-described 'specialist in Psycho Beauty Culture', meaning she offered beauty treatments, haircuts, spiritualist readings and sex advice. By then she would have been forty. Four years later, she met Frederick Growden during one of his visits to Perth from the country.[26]

The letters, poems and photographs in the *Allan v Growden* file skip the couple's first year together and begin in 1932, one year after they met. Happy love has no place in legal records; the state took an interest in love letters only when romance went askew. Three of Frederick's letters were submitted as evidence – Robina said she had destroyed the rest. Her letters, however, comprise over fifty typed pages.[27]

In 1932 and 1933, as stock markets crashed, businesses closed and hungry people tramped dusty roads in search of work, Robina sat in her 'boudoir' above a noisy pub in Perth and penned voluminous letters to Frederick, oscillating between delirium and despair, bravado and self-abasement. Still in the flushes of early love, her writing is visceral, vital and pulses with carnality. 'How I miss you,' she wrote in 1933. 'Come back soon dear for I am sure life is of no interest without you. Yes I miss you in the morning, because – well,

I miss you? I miss you in the evening (because I want you) and I miss you in the night, because I love you.' Frederick had gone away for work, and Robina anticipated his return, imagining her sexual pleasure. 'Somehow I expect you back all of a sudden and I'm feeling real fit,' she enthused. 'Oh what a feast I'll have. I'll start at your eyes and finish at your clear beautiful feet. I'll have the night of my life when you return. Oh what is life without love? Nothing!!' When Robina was not writing to Frederick in her 'little room', she was reading novels. 'Fortunately I am kept in books, and sometimes read in bed for an hour or so,' she wrote chattily in 1932. 'These love stories are all right in books. But I know a lassie at present who could play a good part in reality. But as Shakespeare says: All's well that ends well. So we will see.' She went to the cinema and the theatre, which, along with her books, gave her a rich repertoire of love stories, through which she fashioned a sense of herself as a romantic heroine, and against which she judged Frederick's deviations.[28]

In these early letters, Robina's outpourings of desire were followed by consternation. Frederick refused to commit to the relationship. He was a reluctant letter-writer when away, which sent Robina spiralling into introspection and self-doubt. Turning to her typewriter, she chastised Frederick and tried to persuade him to accept love on her terms:

> I can't be like you, love all, and worship none.
> You know me so well that you are afraid of me and rightly so too.
> If you had not returned Sunday it would have been all over. But you came back only to torture me, by saying you have someone else ...
> I can't pretend to be satisfied knowing there is someone else.
> Let it end with a little suffering.
> You will not miss me ... If you do? A man's privilege is always there.
> Now my dear, I am hurting myself and it is only the beginning ...
> Unfortunately women are helpless, and it is in your power to act as you wish. All I can say is while I am with you I am lost in happiness, there is no explanation needed.
> Goodbye darling ...[29]

Here is love as self-sacrifice. A woman might find solace in worldly pursuits, or muster some power by threatening to leave, but ultimately, as Robina wrote in another letter to Frederick, 'life is [of] no interest' without him. The world and the self dissolves around an unstable love object. Romance derails her ambition and makes her vulnerable to Frederick's whims. She relishes self-abasement; comes alive through suffering and is complicit in her own misery. 'It's no use, dear, I surrender. You can have my car, bankbook, everything. If you only come back,' she wrote. 'I'm discontented and miserable. I would go to Sydney or Melbourne in a minute if I thought you were not coming back to me. And there I would live and take all I could get and look for more. Here I am different. I want to give all.' Love for Robina was a divine delirium, which she was powerless to resist: 'Well dearest, I must conclude that a woman is mad to give all and get nothing in return.' She recognised injustice and submitted.

Of course, this performance of suffering was intended to persuade Frederick to return and to commit to her monogamously. Her anguish comprised an ethical claim and an argument for change. She also summoned a community of critics to judge him, reporting that a mutual friend had said, 'My dear, don't have anything to do with him etc etc', and that a man she met at work had 'made violent love' to her and had wept when told of how Frederick had 'cleared out and left me'. When Robina criticised Frederick directly, she acknowledged the norms of feminine passivity that she was breaking, retreated, apologised, and then reared up and crashed through them again:

And now I must draw in my horns again, or else I'll say something, and again offend the tender feelings of my precious lover and be told I am running amok ... wait, just wait, my boy, there will be nothing left of you to run amok with when I have finished with you ... if you are returning in a few weeks then I'll wait and we'll run amok together.[30]

The letters from 1934 to 1936 are of an entirely different character. In these years, Robina learnt of Frederick's relationship with Miss Bodinner, and she became the subject of 'slander' in Perth. Her business suffered and she was forced to close it in 1936, although it seems that her frayed nerves, as much as the gossip about the barmaid, were to blame. In the same year, with financial assistance from Frederick, she went on a lecturing tour in northwestern Australia offering perms (that took six hours) and women-only talks. 'Miss Barrye is a widely travelled woman with a great psychic power', her advertisements ran.[31] I suspect Robina was probably one of many working-class women in this period who supplemented their primary income by giving paid spiritualist talks or readings, which sometimes crossed into counselling about sex and reproduction.[32]

As her relationship with Frederick deteriorated, Robina began to reflect on the gendered norms of love and on Frederick's breaches of romantic ethics. She put a price on what she had lost, and she demanded justice.

In one of the few surviving letters from Frederick to Robina, he calls her insane – 'I have told you on a former occasion that you sometimes give one the impression that you are not quite right mentally. Last night's episode was one of those unfortunate instances.' The Robina of 1932 would have agreed – 'is it any wonder I'm mad', she laughed, reflecting on her ill-treatment. By 1934, however, her self-laceration had turned to critique. Rejecting his 'vile accusations', she instead 'made a study' of Frederick. The problem, she argued, originated in his career as a police officer, or perhaps in 'some personal happening in the past'. Either way, he saw the world too simplistically in terms of 'good and bad' people. In some letters, Robina was simply angry: 'Let me get out for God's sake; I'm fed up and tired', she wrote in 1935. 'You have nothing to offer and nothing to give.' She dissected Frederick's misogyny:

If a woman is a gold-digger she is bad in your estimation. If a woman lives alone and asks for nothing she is bad, also, in your estimation. If she wants a home and gets it for herself she again is bad ... if I go off quietly and buy what I want, for myself, I am bad. If I ask you to get anything for me, I am bad.

In another letter she concluded: 'A man that has so little respect for a woman, and gives so little, deserves only what you must be getting – a life alone.'

That Frederick was indeed a brute – eye-wateringly racist and sexist even for his time – is amply evinced in a letter he wrote chastising Robina in 1934:

Unfortunately you are one of those presumptuous creatures who will insist in everlastingly getting beyond themselves. Give them an inch and they will take a mile, treat them to a little kindness and attention, give them a little ordinary gentlemanly treatment and they immediately kick over the traces after the style of the n___r whom one imprudently well treats and has to be belted back to submission again.[33]

With the scales falling from her eyes, Robina consulted a solicitor in 1935 and again in 1937, when she issued a writ for breach of promise of marriage. Her letters from these years offer a lucid assessment of what she had lost. Frederick's sexual licentiousness meant a loss of social standing, which had damaged her business. 'You must realise that you have ruined my reputation in your last final flutter with the barmaid. We are the talk of Perth. And if I am to face slander, you must help me to pull my business together. I can't starve.' His treatment of her had caused her mental injury, which in turn illuminated the unreciprocated labour of care she had offered throughout the relationship. 'When you were ill my bed was your rest home and I was your nurse. Now that you have caused me such mental agony and sickness you leave me to starve.' How much did he owe her? 'My dear boy you can never repay me for the past twelve months,' she wrote; '100 pounds would not cover the loss of business.' Her wounds were deep and enduring: 'Have you stopped to think for one moment what our parting meant to me, just everything. And now think what it may mean, a life of disgust and distrust towards everybody. Man, woman, yes and even child.' In the mixture of pain and legal remedy, feminist consciousness was born. In her final letters, she contemplated the drudgery of 'settled' life for women and came to relish her singledom: 'I no more want to settle down than you do because I would be a failure from start to finish. I may put too much salt in the fish and make a fearful hash of housekeeping.' She conceded that it was 'nice to have someone to call your own', but concluded: 'We have a lot to be thankful for and that is, our freedom.'[34]

Robina's movement from individual anguish to collective grievance is seen most clearly in her poetry, and in the language she eventually used in court. The poem 'She', written in 1934, critiques a world in which women value themselves according to rigid notions of beauty – 'her legs are too thin / and her head is too small' – and in which sexual attractiveness is reserved for the young – 'she has little to lose and nothing to gain / And is past the age where she might be vain'. It mocks the notion that women would find fulfilment in domesticity and that finding a husband was a woman's ultimate goal: The final lines of the poem run:

The pots and the pans she
Simply adores? (Oh yes)
And is wonderfully happy just
Staying in doors
She is not a bit selfish
As you will see ...
But she can't get a husband
Poor thing. What a shame

It must be her cooking that's always
To blame.

By contrast, the poem 'He' depicts male bombast, privilege and impunity:

There isn't a thing that he cannot do
And there isn't a girl that He will not speak to
... he is always right and never wrong ...'[35]

Obviously, the poems were based on her experience with Frederick, yet in court she stated that they were 'of general application': 'some men are incapable of respecting women', she observed. Implicit in Robina's discontent at the power imbalance between men and women was an argument for an ethics of love based on reciprocity and equality. If she cares for Frederick when he is sick, then why doesn't he care for her? With her breach of promise action, she called upon law to enforce an ethics of intimacy and to provide compensation for her loss. In so doing, she followed in a long line of breach of promise claimants who, from the 1920s onwards, used the action to provide legal redress for their exploitation in romantic relationships.

While Robina wrote letters and poetry about her unpaid domestic labour, other breach of promise litigants claimed compensation through the category of 'special damages', which allowed redress for quantifiable financial loss such as money spent on a trousseau, wages lost from quitting one's employment, or bodily injury caused by heartbreak. With extraordinary chutzpah and innovation, women from the 1920s onwards began claiming damages for their labours of care through this category. When bank manager Alan Lindsay told Pauline Lory in 1931 that he would pay her back 'for what you spent on the box' (meaning her trousseau), Pauline responded with steely confidence: 'No, Alan ... It is not only what I spent you will have to pay me back. It is more than that.' In court she explained: 'I had nursed his mother and done all the housework for him.'[36] In 1933, Kathleen Brown charged Charles Shearston for the 10,000 meals she had cooked for him over a twenty-two-year engagement,[37] and in 1920 Ms Exton claimed an extra £90 for 'services rendered', arguing that she should be paid for the housework she had performed.[38] All these women won their actions. In making these claims, women blurred the liberal distinction between economics and emotion, labour and love. They exposed the economic foundations of romance and demanded financial redress for squandered care. These claims suggest that arguments for the economic valuation of care began not with middle-class feminists such as Linda Littlejohn in the 1930s or the wages for housework campaigns of the 1970s, but with working-class women at the turn of the century – which makes sense, given working women had for centuries been paid for domestic labour.[39]

The law not only accepted women packaging claims for lost wages in a heart-balm suit: judges demanded it. When women attempted to claim for unpaid labour using other actions, they were generally unsuccessful. In 1912, Ms Hine, who had been in a relationship with Mr Schmidt, attempted to recover six years' worth of wages for housekeeping but was awarded the 'trifling damages' of £25. The judge lamented the outcome: 'She could have sued for breach of promise of marriage; but she didn't take that course'. Because her claim was for lost wages, the judge directed the jury that to award damages, they must find a contract. This would have been relatively easy in a breach of promise action but was virtually impossible in the absence of a written contract for domestic service.[40] By contrast, in 1946, Mrs Crowley, a widow, sued Mr Dive for breach of promise to marriage after her position as a housekeeper developed into a romantic relationship. She said she had 'washed and ironed and mended and nursed the family for three years', yet had received 'no wage or any other consideration'. When asked why she had done this, she said simply, 'because I loved him … because I was going to be his wife'. Mrs Crowley won £125 damages, the equivalent of her wages for two years.[41]

## *Allan v Growden*: Day two

On the second day of the hearing, Robina went straight into the witness box for cross-examination, this time over her alleged violence. Of the alleged 'disturbance' at Growden's apartment, she said: 'He threw me on the floor. It was Growden who created a disturbance'. No, she had not tried to assault Miss Bodinner when she saw her in a car in Hay Street. Bodinner and Growden had been waiting to accost her. As for her prosecution for 'creating a disturbance', that was 'unfair' and she could call a witness to prove it.[42]

Her cross-examination over, Robina assumed her seat in the gallery. Growden, described by one journalist as '[y]ounger looking than fifty, dressed in light grey [and] square chinned', took the stand. He reportedly gave his testimony 'with no dearth of vigour', partly to compete with Robina's 'curt interjections' and 'gusts of laughter', which flew at him from the back of the courtroom.[43]

Growden said that he had been in the police force for thirty-seven years and that his relationship with Robina had always been one of friendship. He had lent her money over the years, but he had never proposed marriage, 'at any time, at any place or under any circumstance'.[44]

'"Any time" will do,' remarked Justice Dwyer archly.

Growden described the incident at his apartment, when Robina had entered 'uninvited'. He had been mending a water tap in an adjoining flat and came home to find Robina sitting on the settee. '"Now I don't want to make a scene," she had said, 'and looked to be under the influence of alcohol.' He told her that 'there was nothing to make a scene about' and suggested she should leave. When she didn't, he took her by the right arm and pushed her towards the door, at which point she cried for help 'in a loud voice', attracting the attention of other residents. 'This woman walked into my flat uninvited and refused to go out, so I simply put her out,' Growden explained to the assembled neighbours.[45] Robina had 'looked at the people and said: "It's quite all right. Thank you."' Later that day she went to Beaconsfield police station, where he was working, and 'continued to be abusive'. When she refused to leave, he 'had to put her out'. He concluded his testimony with a description of her violence towards Miss Bodinner in the car. She 'struck her with a heavy walking stick' and tried to strike her again later in the day, which is why Growden took her to the police station. As for the goods she claimed he had detained, he didn't have any of her things, except for some that she had given him. 'And tuppeny-ha'penny things they were.'[46]

Mr Hughes, described by his biographer as 'chunky and energetic', stood to cross-examine Growden.[47] Yes, Growden conceded, he had taken Robina out driving and to the theatres, but he had pointed out early on that their relations must be those of friendship only. The question of marriage was never mentioned. When he became aware that she was becoming attached to him, he repeatedly 'knocked her back'. He had 'a perfectly fair, square and honourable understanding with her and if she did not choose to live up to it, that was her fault alone'. In fact, he 'repeatedly told Robina that she was losing her sense of proportion and was becoming like a noxious weed which had to be continually chopped back'. She wanted 'his friendship at first to save her business, and she got it; she then tried to inveigle him into a love-entanglement and he refused to be drawn into it'. 'Many people had warned him that she was a dangerous woman and that he had to be on his guard against her.'[48]

Yes, he said that he did write a letter in 1935 that ended: 'Kindest regards and love, yours sincerely Growdie. Followed by seven crosses, denoting kisses', but that was because 'she owed me one hundred pounds and I had to do something to keep sweet with her.' As for the letter that ended, 'Well sweetie, bye bye, love Frederick', he could only say that he may have been her 'sweetie', but he was 'certainly not her fiancé'.

'You were her sweetie?' queried Mr Hughes

'She was not the only sweetie I had. I never let her be anything but a friend, despite her efforts.'

'Do you consider that the closing words of that letter are tantamount to "yours faithfully" merely?'[49]

Justice Dwyer interrupted, with a certain sly gaiety: 'Not "faithfully".'

Growden became agitated. 'Have I not told you over and over again, Mr Hughes, it was friendship, pure friendship. I told her I already had a girl-friend, and she said, "Can't you spare me some time? A couple of nights a week?" My reply to that was: "Well, she is not particular whom she goes out with so I expect I can." At this point, the newspapers reported, Growden 'half rose from the chair' in a 'dramatic scene' and declaimed: 'Look here, Mr Hughes. Get this and get it plain. If you can produce one single genu-ine love letter written by me to the plaintiff I will immediately instruct my counsel to abandon the defence and make a settlement. Do you get that, Mr Hughes?'[50]

Hughes now shifted his focus to the apartment Robina said they had furnished together, which Growden flatly denied. No, he had 'furnished the Fremantle flat with "bachelor" furniture. Robina had not assisted him to choose it'. As for his inquiries into Robina's marital status, he began them after the present proceedings had been instituted.[51] When Robina had persisted with her claim that he had promised to marry her, he told her that she was 'the most atrocious liar he had ever met in his life'.[52] He reminded her that he had paid for her to go to Melbourne to see her dying mother; her treatment of him in return, in his opinion, was nothing short of blackmail.[53]

Nellie Fling, a widow and one of Growden's neighbours, was next in the witness box. 'Growden did not appear to be using excessive force when lead-ing Robina out of his flat,' she said, although under cross-examination she conceded that she had intervened at the time and said to Growden, 'Don't do that.' She had later seen Robina in the street; 'she waved her stick, blas-phemed and said that if she could not do the defendant any harm she would throw herself under the wheels of his car.' Taking pity on Robina, Mrs Fling had invited her inside for a cup of tea. Robin declined, 'but said she would like a glass of brandy'. Nellie said she had asked Robina, 'Are you engaged to him?' and Robina had replied: 'Oh no, but he's not going to have five years out of my life and get away with it.'[54]

## Love and violence

From Growden allegedly 'giving Robina a thrashing' and 'throwing [her] on the floor' to Robina allegedly breaking into Growden's house, scratching him on the face and attacking her romantic rival, *Allen v Growden* was a case where desire was spiked with violence.[55]

To my mind, explaining Growden's violence is fairly straightforward. Drawing on decades of feminist theory, we might speculate that he felt entitled to abuse Robina's body, and that the law and social norms sanctioned his right to assault her. Other cases from the twentieth century also suggest that men felt they had a right to give their romantic partners a beating, so long as they didn't cause sustained injury; the same arguments were heard in cases of marital cruelty. As a police officer, Growden was accustomed to wielding authority, and his letter to Robina showed that he expected women to exist in a state of submission. If they got too uppity, they needed to be 'beaten down', a sentiment which expresses with perfect clarity how violence buttresses relationships based on male domination and female submission. That Growden's argument relied so heavily on his financial beneficence to Robina also suggests a sense of ownership, implying that he could do as he liked to his property.

Robina's violence, on the other hand, provokes questions that academics are yet to theorise. When women's violence is addressed, it is usually in the context of self-defence. What I noticed in breach of promise cases, however, is that between the 1890s and the 1920s, women became quite shockingly aggressive – and the courts not only accepted such behaviour but actively condoned it. When Mr Schwabe jilted Ms Henry in 1912, for instance, she stabbed him with a hat pin.[56] Ms Bushby broke her umbrella over the head of Mr Beardsall.[57] Ms Caulfield met Mr Edge at a bench on Flinders Street in Melbourne, pulled a shotgun from her purse and fired four shots. She was acquitted on a charge of manslaughter and, like the other women mentioned, went on to win substantial damages.[58]

Although contract treatises recognised that a plea of mismatched tempers could mitigate damages, judges suggested otherwise.[59] On hearing that Ms Cooper had given Mr Barnett 'a smack in the face such that his hat fell off' when she caught him strolling off the ferry with another woman, the judge blithely observed: 'I have often wished a woman had the physical strength to give the man it back.'[60] When Ms Bentley in 1913 told the court that she had continued to entertain the duplicitous Mr Clews, who had seduced her, the judge asked: 'Why didn't you throw scalding water on him when he came to your house? You would have been entitled to do so.'[61] Why would a bourgeois court condone female violence? One possible explanation is that women's expanding public freedoms at the turn of the century coincided with a campaign to reform male sexuality.[62] As Victorian strictures of feminine comportment were discarded, women experimented with anger in ways that corresponded with their new political rights. And the courts, keen to enforce a model of masculine domestic responsibility were willing to outsource punitive powers to the women who bore the brunt of male entitlement.

The first decades of the twentieth century also witnessed public uncertainty about the rules of romance. As we saw in the previous chapter, a new dating culture had emerged, but it had not yet supplanted Victorian-era courtship conventions, and most women were still economically dependent on marriage. As more working-class women started to live independently in cities, and as the ability of the family and of communities to regulate courtship waned, courts accepted that women were capable of regulating their own courtships, with physical force if necessary.

There were fewer cases involving female violence towards men in the interwar years, and in those cases where extreme violence appeared, women usually lost their case. The forms of women's aggression also became less florid and more standardised, increasingly scripted by American popular culture.[63] Gone were the hat-pin stabbings and brolly-bashings; these were now consistently replaced by a swift hard slap to the face. In a series of letters addressed to her suitor as either 'Gee Boy!' or 'Gosh Boy!', Zelda Ellis in 1931 replied to his letter ending their engagement: 'oh what a fibber! You just did NOT tell me you were finished with me. You story teller! What you want is a darned good slap – a hard one.'[64] A slap to a man's face was the most common form of violence by women from the 1920s until the 1950s, and courts seemed to accept that women had a right to do this. Anything beyond this, however – particularly extreme behaviour such as beating people with a walking stick or breaking into an apartment, as we find in Robina's case – received neither cultural nor judicial sanction.

There are a number of explanations for this change. First, taking violence into one's own hands is usually justified on the grounds that some entitlement or right has been violated. By the 1920s and 1930s, women no longer had a right to expect that a romantic relationship would lead to marriage if there had been no explicit proposal. Frederick blithely told the court that Robina was one of many 'sweeties' at the same time as he swore that their relationship was 'fair, square and honourable', a phrase that it would have been unthinkable to apply to his circumstances only thirty years earlier. With men's right to date multiple women affirmed by law and society, women lost their authority to punish and regulate. We see this in a letter Frederick wrote to Robina after she attacked him and two female friends in a car. He argued that she had a 'false sense of proprietorship'. 'By what right, authority or stretch of imagination do you claim the privilege to admonish lady friends of mine who beset themselves in my car?' he asked.[65]

Frederick's use of the word proprietorship is revealing. In the Western legal tradition, the concept of rights developed alongside notions of private property – only people who had property, in the form of their own person or that of others, were considered to have rights. This is why slaves, children, the mentally ill and women did not have rights: they were owned by others.[66] The norms of feminine propriety prohibited women from violently attacking men for most of the nineteenth century, but so did the notion that they had no personal rights in romance – they were the property of men, not the other way around. As women's rights and freedom of expression expanded and as coverture was slowly dismantled, we see women from the 1890s onwards attacking their suitors and claiming a right of possession. Until the 1920s, the courts affirmed this. (There had never been any doubt that a male partner had rights of possession over a woman; rape in marriage was not abolished in all states in Australia until 1992.)[67] After the 1920s, however, the rules of dating changed to permit casual relationships, and women could no longer assume proprietorial rights to a man who had romanced them.

Some historians have seen the 1920s and 1930s as an era not of liberation for women, but of the beginning of new forms of discipline and self-surveillance. This is the moment when federation-era feminism, with its widespread demands for citizenship status and involvement in public life, was channelled by popular culture and commodity culture into a world of consumption, with its standardised forms of femininity characterised by self-doubt, obsession with the body and self-laceration.[68] Shifts in romantic culture, to my mind, affirm this thesis.

It is perhaps no surprise, then, that threats of suicide also increased in this period. It is uncertain whether nineteenth-century female litigants ever attempted suicide, but I do know from reading over two hundred cases from that era that not one of them ever reported a suicide attempt in court; to have done so would have been to admit a sin against God and to invite a criminal prosecution. By contrast, interwar and mid-twentieth-century women were constantly threatening to kill themselves. The choreography of violence has a history, and its changes here can be ascribed to a number of factors. The increasing secularisation of society removed fears of moral sin, and declining levels of family and community regulation of romance increased the psychic burden placed on jilted women, no doubt conspiring in their desires for self-annihilation. Meanwhile suicide was a favourite end for thwarted love affairs in cinema and literature of the time. As physical violence by women towards men became less acceptable, it was turned inwards, directed towards the self. Twentieth-century courts never questioned or chastised women for attempting suicide; rather, such threats tended to be seen as further proof of the injury to a woman's affections.

## *Allan v Growden*: Day three

The final day of the hearing passed swiftly and predictably. Everybody – the jury, counsel and judge – seemed to know what the verdict would be. Mr Downing for the defence argued that there had been no corroboration, given Robina had called no witnesses and the epistolary evidence of the promise of marriage seemed 'most shadowy'.[69] 'The plaintiff had produced no letter stating, or even implying, any such promise – and if any such letter had been written by the defendant, it was hardly likely that the plaintiff would have destroyed it.' As to the alleged assault, her story was 'to say the least, unconvincing'. 'She had produced no evidence whatever to prove that the defendant merited censure or even complaint from her.'

Hughes, on the other hand, focused on romantic practices and behaviour – an argument that would have had a high chance of success in the nineteenth century, but which was now on shaky ground. Growden 'held himself out to the world' as 'Miss Allan's lover', he began. 'He had behaved in exactly the manner in which a man who was "keeping company" with a lady would behave. He had asserted that he had been at great pains to define his relationship with the plaintiff as one of friendship only, and had continually rejected her overtures. Yet strange to say, he had always called on her immediately when he returned from the country, and thenceforward frequently when he was living in town.' And then there were Growden's letters. 'It could not be denied that "sweetie" was American for "sweetheart",' he argued. '[Growden] said that he had used the term merely because he wished to keep "sweet" with her as she owed him money. If that were a new prescription for keeping "sweet" with debtors, [he] could foresee a striking change occurring in the phraseology of the creditors' reminders which most people received from time to time!' The courtroom filled with laughter. Growden's actions 'had been consistent with those of a man who was wooing a woman.' Finally, Growden's efforts to prove that Robina was married showed 'a guilty conscience'. He only bothered with it because he thought that Robina had a case.[70]

Justice Dwyer, like almost every judge before him, began by outlining the contractual nature of the action: 'in order to succeed in her action the plaintiff must establish that there was a promise of marriage, and that it had been broken.' Yet he thought that 'anybody who read the letters submitted in evidence would be satisfied from them that there had never been a promise of marriage.' He didn't discount the possibility that the duration of a relationship over a significant period of time, as well as the exchange of money, words and endearments, might be circumstances that could help in ascertaining whether the association was intended to 'continue as far as the altar.' Yet in this case, he said, the letters simply did not bear out that construction. 'In the present day one would hesitate to take words like "sweetie" as of any consequence', and the money had been simply for business. As for the action for assault, he thought Growden's ejectment of Robina from his property needed to be taken in light of her 'mental and physical attitude' towards him and his friends, which had become 'violent'. As for the detention of goods, they were gifts always intended to become his property. The question of their return was one of ethics, not law. He 'should return them as a matter of good feeling ... not as a matter of legal remedy.' Dwyer's concluding remarks formed newspaper headlines the next day: 'In these days one must assume the possibility of platonic and other friendships not intended to lead to matrimonial bonds.'[71]

*   *   *

Anybody who read about the case would have learnt a very clear lesson: so long as there was no explicit proposal of marriage, a person had a right, much like a customer, to try as many different partners as they desired. It can't be denied that Robina was not a model witness, and having read her love letters I would agree with the judge that there is no explicit or even implicit promise of marriage. But women with far more compelling evidence in the 1930s,

'40s and '50s also lost their cases, with similar reasoning from the judge in their directions to the jury. Quite simply, it could no longer be assumed that all romantic relationship were intended to end at the altar. There now needed to be mutual contractual intent.

This simple, legalistic reasoning reflects a vast shift in the social construction of gender identities and in the organisation of romance in the twentieth century. A dating culture defined by freedom of choice and sexual desire had emerged, and it brought about a corresponding shift in masculine and feminine identities. In the interwar years, masculinity was seen to be under threat, as women's rights expanded, manual labour was replaced by bureaucratised white-collar jobs that 'sapped' male virility, the depression exposed poor men's inability to provide for their families, and the shellshocked or mutilated victims of war provided living proof of male fragility.[72] In this context, as Eva Illouz and others have argued, modern masculinity was proved through heterosexuality.[73] Men like Frederick asserted their masculine entitlement to 'sexual freedom', and all-male courtrooms affirmed it. At the same time, the contractual elements of the breach of promise action appeared in its modern, proceduralist form: was there contractual intent? If an explicit promise could not be proved, damages could not be awarded.

If Frederick could relish his sexual freedom, then why couldn't Robina? After all, modern women were defined through advertising and popular Freudianism as sensual creatures, and sexually active women no longer faced the same kind of moral censure as they had in the nineteenth century. Illouz argues that the dating arenas of the twentieth century disadvantaged women because their reproductive years were limited and they needed commitment to be able to provide for a child.[74] This may be true in certain cases, but Robina expressed no desire for children and was likely past her reproductive years at the time of their relationship. Alongside the obvious psychological desire for amorous affirmation, there were very real economic reasons why women for most of the twentieth century wanted marriage more than men did. Women in Australia did not get equal pay until 1969, and until then most were paid half the wages of men. While jobs in the services sector and the professions were increasingly open to women, women were still expected or forced to retire after becoming engaged. So long as this was the case, marriage mattered more to women than to men. Further, if a reproductive clock placed pressure on them to marry quickly, then so too did the sexualised dating culture of the twentieth century, which limited feminine beauty to the young and encouraged women to exchange sexual attractiveness for male property and status. Robina, like other women, knew that whatever limited power she might exercise over men through her sexuality, it came with a use-by date.

Robina's case affirms these broad social shifts, but it also suggests something that has passed unnoticed in the scholarship. It was not just organised middle-class feminists who protested the social organisation of intimacy. Ordinary, working-class women like Robina developed what we now see as feminist consciousness through their lived experience of the disadvantages and disappointments they faced in romance. If, as I have argued, an awareness of gender, economics and power could arise from women tallying the costs of failed romance and packaging their pain in legal form, then so too did the failure to be granted legal redress. Robina walked out of court in 1938, no doubt furious at the verdict, but she reappeared in the newspaper a year later – this time in the opinion pages. For the next eleven years, she exchanged the court of law for the court of public opinion, and in the weekly letters section of the paper we see her advocating for improvements in women's status and opining on the ethics of love.

In 1939, Robina's first letter to the editor, under the name of Brendah Barrye, appeared on the question of marriage proposals. 'Girls should propose! Every year of her life, as a mother, is of great value to the country. If a girl does not (or cannot) show her deep affection for a man, he naturally thinks he is not wanted – and very often the home-wrecker takes her place.'[75] On the eve of war, she was brimming with pro-natalist rhetoric about the citizen mothers whose country needed them to breed an army of warriors (and she was also clearly still cranky about the barmaid). Writing on average twice per month, Robina advocated for the rights of 'bachelor women', 'war spinsters' and women who had given birth outside wedlock.[76] She campaigned for the release from prison of a nurse accused of administering abortions and for the release of a woman, Evelyn Newman, gaoled for two years for committing infanticide. Convinced of the systemic male bias of law, she called for 'lady lawyers to act in such cases as Evelyn Newman's, women on the jury, more women in parliament, police women to track scoundrels down who desert fallen women. And a cage in the zoo of two years' imprisonment, when they catch them.'[77] She argued for a pension for spinsters aged fifty and over, the 'most badly treated of all women'. She shared many opinions on love, including that engagements should be limited to three years, and that a man who advertised that he could 'wash and iron' was a 'bargain'. She flipped the gold-digger trope on its head, arguing that many men were not looking for love but for 'a spinster with a comfortable business or a widow with a furnished home'.[78] She also thought that parliament would benefit from having an Aboriginal representative.[79]

This is not to suggest that Robina was a model feminist. She thought that women should not wear slacks to work, she railed against young women 'dancing and howling' down Hay Street at two in the morning, she blamed mothers for the sins of their promiscuous daughters, and she developed a curious moral taxonomy around smokers:

> Women street smokers are disgusting; afternoon tea smokers are worse. Lounge smokers are in their place, but women who smoke without asking permission are common. The man who lights a cigarette in his mouth and offers it to a flapper is a cad. And the man who objects to his wife smoking but who thinks it smart for girls to smoke is a rotter. The proprietress who smokes during business hours loses respect but the tired business woman who retires to her boudoir and smokes after business hours is to be congratulated. She offends nobody.[80]

Who else could this tired businesswoman be but Robina herself? In 1948, the opinion pages ran a feature on Robina as their 'most prolific letter-writer'.[81] When asked what type of person wrote letters to the paper, she responded: 'If you're not afraid to say what you believe to be right, you're probably a sterling character with large quantities of public spirit.' To be able to 'express your opinion in print before thousands of readers is sheer democratic tops.' Her opinions had won her 'several marriage proposals', but by this stage she had decided to live out her days in blessed singledom. The article concluded with her correcting several inaccuracies:

> Brendah Barrye IS a woman, not a man.
> She is not a man-hater
> She does not sit in a hotel lounge all day sneering at people who drink[82]

In 1951, an article appeared in *The Mirror* entitled 'Brendah Barrye as Heart Renovator'. The journalist reported that Robina had finally registered a business which she had been operating successfully for two years, 'Divorce Anonymous'. 'Into her modestly furnished Hay Street Rooms come women – and men – whose homes are in danger of being broken up.'[83] Robina had borrowed the idea from an American company that tried to dissuade couples from divorcing by making them listen to a panel of divorcees detailing the horrors of life post-divorce. Taking a more therapeutic approach, Robina dispensed with the panel and created a space where unhappy couples could talk to her. Her desire for profits as a beautician, however, and the misogynistic underpinnings of 1950s psychological culture, produced a rather toxic combination for the women she counselled:

> The trouble is often with the wives themselves, you know. They've got their man and they let themselves go dowdy. The men see a bright piece of fluff around town, like a blonde barmaid or shopgirl and they chase it, but what they really want is someone to darn their socks ... I've had lots of cases where the wife has come in for a 'fuss up' and when the husband has seen her he falls in love all over again. Then I just leave them together and they usually go away quite happy.[84]

Robina's final career as a 'heart renovator', as the newspaper called her, is a perfect end to the story of how love and law became disentangled in the mid-twentieth century, reflecting a broader shift in the governance of love from law to psychology. People in the 1950s were caught in a bind: on the one hand, marriage continued to be the cornerstone of society, and therefore divorce needed to be discouraged. On the other hand, the post-war boom had freed them somewhat from the need to marry for survival, and couples primarily now expected sexual and emotional fulfilment from their partner. And as Robina's comments demonstrate, women suffered in this shift to psychology. Women were blamed when men cheated on them, and a battery of experts (including Robina) sought to profit from their self-doubt. Married couples who might once have gone straight to court were rerouted through a dense web of counsellors, psychologists and divorce experts. For courting couples, legal options were severely frowned upon by the 1950s. In their place was psychology, which vested responsibility for love in an individual's psyche, in their family background and in the supposed sexual failures of women.

*   *   *

Robina eventually conformed to the gender norms of the 1950s, but her court hearing and the abundant archival evidence paints a picture of a sophisticated, funny, tempestuous and indignant woman who would easily fit our contemporary definition of a feminist. Yet judging by the scholarly literature, the idea that we would find feminist arguments in a breach of promise action is surprising. Although historians have acknowledged the agency of litigants, there has been an assumption, shared by academics and interwar feminists, that the women who used the action had to accept its gendered legal narratives.[85] In the post-federation era, when women were claiming independent citizenship rights, the action forced them back into dependency on men and marriage, argues law academic Margaret Thornton.[86] And feminists in the 1940s, almost all of whom were bourgeois women, agreed.

In an article titled 'Equality of Sexes and Breach of Promise', an unnamed 'feminist' described the action as the 'most humiliating and degrading to which women can avail themselves' and argued that it ought to be 'scrapped'.[87] From the 1920s onwards, it was increasingly argued that the action was a relic of the Victorian era, when women had no vocation other than marriage and needed the law's protection against dishonourable men. Breach of promise was seen as complicit in the tyranny of loveless marriages: inescapable, duty-bound, and oppressive, as revealed in salacious detail each morning in the newspaper reports from the Divorce Courts. Now that women were 'equal', they should marry for love and take being jilted 'like a man', one commentator argued.[88] If there is feminism to be found in breach of promise, we might expect to see it in the action's decline in the 1950s or abolition in 1975, signalling both women's expanding economic freedoms and a growing emphasis on love in marriage that made marrying out of obligation distasteful.[89] That a woman such as Robina might use the action to critique gender norms, or to argue for the economic value of her domestic labour, has escaped feminist writers across the twentieth century.

I have tried to use the life story of Robina Allan to tell a more empirically grounded, more complex and less celebratory story. I suggest that in the frictions, the crises and the failures of romantic love, a distinctly feminist consciousness emerged that would later take collective form in the sexual revolts of the 1960s and 1970s. Crucially, I argue that this consciousness was dependent upon women conceiving of themselves as having a legal right to redress for romantic harm. It was the linking of love and law that illuminated the material foundations of romance, unveiling the myths of love to expose economically quantifiable domestic labour. It demanded women take their suffering seriously as an injury that attracted the attention of law.

By the time of Robina's death in 1960, law had been supplanted by psychology as the primary explanatory structure used for the governance of love. Intimate injustices were privatised, psychologised and individualised. Relationships were now governed by norms negotiated between partners, not by legal rules. There are obvious benefits to these changes: couples now had more autonomy to define their relationships and more freedom to abandon a miserable relationship in pursuit of a better one. Unlike the notions of fault and blame that lie at the heart of juridical discourse, therapeutic discourse encourages mutual reflection and transformation. Yet I am reluctant to see these developments as the triumph of love over sexist tradition. Rather, I would suggest that this is the final chapter in a story of how love, in its lawlessness, lost many of its ethical and material foundations. It explains why people who suffer serious emotional damage from relationships today have no legal avenues for redress.

# 12.

# From Law to Therapy: Abolishing Breach of Promise of Marriage

W inter had just arrived when the Australian parliament met in the early days of June 1976. The first snow of the season had settled on the nearby Snowy Mountains and icy winds blew frosted breath down the valleys, across the lakes and into the silent streets of Canberra, sending flurries of amber leaves into the air, twisting and lifting the hems of women's skirts.[1] Bob Ellicott, the Liberal attorney-general, stood on the carpet of the House of Representatives to give his second reading speech for a bill to amend the *Marriage Act 1961* (Cth).

Marriage, divorce and the politics of sex had been hot topics of debate for a decade, and the previous Labor government, under Prime Minister Gough Whitlam, had packaged the reforms demanded by feminist, queer, Marxist and civil rights protestors into voluminous bundles of legislation. The year before, in 1975, the government had introduced the *Family Law Act*, which aimed to reduce 'the bitterness and humiliation' of separation by establishing no-fault divorce. Under the act, an army of counsellors and psychologists were employed to work alongside Family Court judges to encourage 'parties to be reconciled or to terminate their relationships amicably through the use of marriage counselling.'[2] Never before in Australian history had so many unhappy couples rushed to dissolve their unions. At the time Ellicott was introducing his bill, the Family Court was processing over 1000 applications for divorce each week.[3] The institution of marriage was in crisis, Ellicott warned, and the bill now before the House was intended to 'avert [its] breakdown.'[4] Where the *Family Law Act* had '[upheld] the institution of marriage' by offering a new 'cure', this bill would focus on 'prevention', specifically, therapy. Before couples took 'the decisive step to enter into marriage', they would be educated in 'the nature, dimensions and responsibilities of marriage'.[5] By funding premarital and marriage counselling, Ellicott's bill would further modernise intimacy: private passions would be guided by psychological expertise, and the moral stigma once associated with a broken relationship would be replaced by rational therapeutic judgment. There were two other clauses in the bill bringing marriage into step with modern sensibilities: the distinction between illegitimate and legitimate children was to be further diminished in legislation, and the 'virtually obsolete' action for breach of promise of marriage would be abolished.[6]

Three months later, the bill passed into statute, signalling not simply the retreat of law from the etiquette of romance, but a formal shift in the governance of heterosexual love: from the courts of law to the psychologist's couch; from juridical judgment to therapeutic expertise.

When the Australian government removed the possibility of suing for breach of promise of marriage, it was following the lead of other common law countries and states: South Australia in 1971, Britain in 1971, New Zealand in 1975, and some American states as early as the 1930s.[7] Parliamentarians in all Anglophone countries generally agreed on the causes of the action's demise. Times had changed, they said, and to suggest that women were delicate creatures dependent upon marriage for a vocation, or that their reputations would be ruined by being jilted, was incorrect and patronising. With women's increased social and political status came a more egalitarian vision of marriage, one based on desire, compatibility and negotiation rather than obedience, duty and contractual obligation. Divorce reform had enshrined visions of companionate marriage into law: if a couple found that they were unhappy or incompatible, either party could freely terminate the relationship. It was not the state's role to determine fault, and each couple should negotiate their own relationship norms. Historians have agreed that the abolition of the action signified women's growing independence and the incorporation of feminist emphases on equality over protection into law. Women's entry en masse into the workforce, the post-war welfare state and the triumph of 'companionate marriage' had made the action 'a relic'.[8]

Yet the *Marriage (Amendment) Act 1976* did not just rid the law of what had come to be seen as a sexist historical anachronism. By injecting significant funding into premarital counselling and psychological services, it legally codified a crucial shift in the relationship between law, love and psychology, a shift which has been missing from historical analyses. In abolishing the action, law ceded its authority over heterosexual romantic love to psychology, formalising a process that had begun in the early twentieth century and ended, not in the 1970s with the action's legislative demise, but in the postwar years when people stopped bringing their stories of wounded feelings to court. It was ordinary people, not politicians, who in substance ended the action, much as it had been everyday people who shaped what the court accepted as proof of a relationship or evidence of suffering throughout the action's history.

Over the course of the twentieth century, the declining authority of religion and the decreased role played by families in courtship coincided with the mass dissemination of therapeutic discourse in magazines, cinema and workplaces and the expansion of psychological services. People dating in the mid-twentieth century had a new explanatory framework through which to understand intimacy; one which, like law, ordered individual stories of suffering into a universalist language of norms, but which, unlike law, relegated 'the romantic and erotic to private responsibility' and blamed women for their romantic pain.[9] The abolition of the action certainly signified advancements in women's status and shifts in the meaning of marriage, but I want to offer a less celebratory historical narrative by interrogating what was lost in the gradual movement from law to psychology, from public debate around the ethics of love to private rumination, from definitive legal allocations of fault to endless psychological exploration, from compensation for psychic and economic injury to the individualisation of emotional harm.

Before we knock on the psychologist's door, however, let's take a walk down the corridor and peer into the other rooms to examine more closely the reasons politicians at the time and historians since have given for abolishing the action. To be clear, I am not suggesting that the rise of therapeutic discourse was the sole reason for the action's demise. Rather, it needs to be analysed alongside the two other main reasons for ending the action: the first being shifts in the meaning of courtship and marriage, from duty and obligation to romantic love and desire; and the second being women's increased political and social status. A better analysis is that these three discourses – psychology, feminism and romantic love – conceptually borrowed from one another over the course of the twentieth century and, working in concert, ultimately succeeded in bringing the action to an end.

\*　　\*　　\*

Since the eighteenth and nineteenth centuries, marriage had been imagined by bourgeois writers and nascent feminists as a union based on affection and equality rather than dependence and duty, and those who subscribed to these views were the first to criticise the action in Australia. Breach of promise 'has to answer for many miserable matches', declared an article that did the rounds of colonial papers in 1856. 'Before it is too late, one of the engaged couples makes the discovery of incompatibility of temper or of some other objection, but the fear of law proceedings and damages prevents the timely retreat and the contract is completed which dooms both to unhappiness for life'.[10] In suggesting that marital misery was preferable to a broken engagement, or that marriage was a mere contract like any other, the suit was offensive to visions of companionate marriage. 'Atticus', writing to *The Northern Argus* in 1885, explained that those in favour of abolishing the action regarded marriage not 'as a contract but as a sacrament ... which should be removed from the sordid area of everyday obligations'.[11]

Few in the nineteenth century would have disagreed that love and happiness were ideal foundations for marriage, yet so long as working- and middle-class women's livelihoods depended on a husband, they were luxuries – added extras to economic considerations. As the pragmatic Charlotte Lucas advised Elizabeth Bennet in *Pride and Prejudice*, 'Happiness in marriage is entirely a matter of chance'.[12] While Britain debated bills to abolish breach of promise in the 1870s, Australians had no such legislative prompt, only a notice of a bill abolishing the action in New South Wales in 1889 that soon disappeared without ever being introduced.[13] With concerted government and community efforts at the turn of the century to reform male sexuality, Australians, as one columnist opined, thought the action had a 'restraining influence over some, and those the worst of men'.[14] Whether it be to punish caddish men or to protect vulnerable women, the high rates of success for plaintiffs attest to wide-scale community acceptance of the action throughout the nineteenth century.

By the early twentieth century, in the wake of divorce-law reform, middle-class women's entry into paid work, the emergence of dating culture and the spread of psychological views on the importance of sexual desire in marriage, the idea of marrying for anything other than love became increasingly culturally unacceptable among the middle classes. 'To the woman who simply wants a husband of any kind, make, shape or age, for the purpose of giving her three meals a day and clothes to wear, no redress should be given, as she merely aims at legal concubinage,' wrote a commentator in 1907, arguing for the abolition of the action.[15] It was a common refrain from elite women, and it also speaks to an historical truth: marrying for love alone was a privilege reserved for those whose needs were already met. Working-class women, the women most likely to use the suit, may have chosen their partners based on affection, but economic factors were equally, if not more, important. And if the woman had quit her paid employment upon becoming engaged, moved out of her home, birthed a child or prepared a trousseau, being jilted meant incurring serious financial and reputational loss.

One of the key shifts in commentary on the action from the nineteenth to the twentieth century was that cultural disapproval of marriage as a financial bargain shifted from a critique of economic structures or families to condemnation of 'avaricious' women. A new vocabulary used to shame 'scheming' women wended its way from cinemas and popular magazines into commentary on the action and the courtroom, and working-class plaintiffs trying to marry across class boundaries were monstrously reconfigured as legal concubines, amateurs, racketeers, swindlers and gold-diggers: grasping seductresses who mined the gentle pastures of love for financial gain. In Australia, Britain and America, the misogynistic fantasy of the gold-digger was one of, if not *the*, primary reasons given by politicians for abolishing the suit.

'This field of litigation has always been regarded as the peculiar prerogative, the recognised hunting ground of the "gold-digger"', wrote one commentator in 1930. Yet her 'depredations never really become known', the article ran, because men would rather pay than face the humiliation of a court case'. The proportion of men who preferred to settle for breach of promise was as high as 'five to one', the author claimed.[16] Judges also increasingly asked juries to discern whether the woman was motivated purely by money: 'did she give them the impression that she was just a gold-digger?' asked a judge in a 1937 case.[17]

That these arguments arose in the early and mid-twentieth century – the period when romance became commodified and courtship was restructured as a transaction – is not coincidental. The emergence of a commercial dating arena solidified men's and women's roles in dating: men paid for dinners, dancing, cinema or theatre, and women gave their cheerfulness, love and, increasingly, sex in return.[18] Men had economic power; women offered emotional and sexual sustenance. American GIs stationed in Australia during the Second World War further schooled local women in American models of romance, and by the 1950s dating culture was entrenched.[19] The language of vamps and gold-diggers was used to denigrate women who made explicit the implicit terms of this sexual contract, who supposedly feigned self-sacrificing love to selfishly profit, and who were seen to usurp male financial power. It also worked to police the boundaries of class once sexuality, unmoored from morality, had made marriage markets more democratic. If sex appeal was now a reason to marry in its own right, working women could exchange sexual attractiveness for wealth; they could marry into elite ranks that would have been firmly closed to them only a few decades earlier. Films like *Gentlemen Prefer Blondes* (1953), which included a breach of promise action, reflected cultural anxieties about the capacity for sex to disrupt class hierarchies.[20]

The problem of gold-digging may have been seen to have been caused by duplicitous women, but as commentators pointed out, it went hand in hand with the assumptions that underlay the breach of promise action; the suit saw marriage as no different from 'a promise to buy a radio set or a crate of lobsters'.[21] The law, this argument suggested, should instead reflect modern marriages, where love was quarantined from the market, determined purely by affection and desire, a product of mutual negotiation between two equals parties.

Early-twentieth-century feminists shared these criticisms of the action. They did not challenge constructions of plaintiffs as gold-diggers, but rather viewed them as 'degraded' by profiting from a law that reduced women to 'concubines'. 'Surely if a woman accounted herself as man's equal, she would be humiliated to accept and build her future on that money,' argued one feminist in 1940. 'What modern woman, priding herself on belonging to this splendid new era of femininity, wants to make use of a vindictive law, evolved in days when it was almost a crime to be an old maid?'[22] Her argument, like those of many other early feminists, was more hopeful than empirical. When certain American states abolished the action in the 1930s, Australian women wrote in favour of the changes. 'There has always been an underlying principle [in the action] that the woman is weak and defenceless and is without the means to make her own living or to protect herself from the machinations of man,' a commentator in *The Women's Weekly* observed; 'the adoption of universal suffrage, the entry of women into important places in the professions, in business and industry and more lately into high public office has changed her status from that of the weak dependent into an independent and self-sufficient equal of man.'[23] By the mid-twentieth century, the action was regarded as a symbol of Victorian-era subjugation and one of many laws that needed to be repealed for women's emancipation. The only cases deemed acceptable were those involving direct pecuniary loss, such as the cost of a trousseau, and those involving an illegitimate child, given the stigma and financial hardship faced by single mothers.

Feminists downplayed the significance of economic factors binding women to marriage in a manner that reflected their own privilege, and they assumed that changes in women's legal and civil status would be sufficient to grant them autonomy from marriage. They failed to predict that advancements in women's legal and civil status would do little to alter women's dependence upon marriage so long as a sexed labour market denied women economic autonomy. Like us, they were living in the fog of the present. They could not know that although white women could stand for federal parliament from 1902, none would be elected for another forty years, that equal pay would not be introduced until 1969, or that married women would be barred from the public service until the 1970s. Excited by the new work opportunities they saw opening up around them, none could have guessed that to this day, the legacy of 'men's' and 'women's' work would mean that female-dominated jobs are clustered at the lower end of the pay spectrum.[24]

It is certainly true that changes in women's civil status helped society to reimagine femininity as economically independent, rational and autonomous. But it was the post-war economic boom and the creation of the welfare state by the 1940s Labor governments – specifically child endowment, a widow's pension and unemployment and sickness benefits – that were most significant in releasing women from dependency upon marriage and, in the process, recreating marriage. As marriage became uncoupled from financial necessity in the post-war years, marriage and romantic love became soldered together, argues British historian Clare Langhamer.[25] In 1949, an Australian commentator noted that breach of promise cases had become rare 'since the war', and by the early 1970s the action was referred to as a 'Victorian variety of heartbalm'.[26] By the time it was formally abolished in 1976, social welfare legislation and the extraordinary affluence of the post-war era had long eroded the action's economic foundations.

Finally, historians have also attributed the action's demise to shifts in how it was understood by the courts. In Britain, it has been argued that in the twentieth century the action returned to its contractual roots, and so came to seem out of step with modern ideas of marriage. Alternatively, historians in America have argued that the tortious elements of the action (that is, the elements that focused on emotional damages) doomed it, as courts became uncomfortable with awarding money for psychological harm.[27]

To my mind, there is evidence for each of these interpretations. More important is the fact that law became professionalised at the turn of the twentieth century, and was increasingly subject to an instrumentalist and bureaucratic logic that privileged 'good record keeping', in Weber's words.[28] It demanded visual evidence, be it of suffering, economic loss or an engagement, and it became more focused on formal equality of contract, as seen in the fact that men began to win their cases. Neither of these demands sat easily with an action based on invisible and unquantifiable emotional suffering. Judges also became increasingly disgruntled with the action, particularly in the Supreme Court. Whereas civil law had been part of everyday life in the early nineteenth century, by the early twentieth century it was becoming a rarefied institution, removed from the grubbiness and vagaries of working-class people's disputes over love. Here we see the beginnings of the divided legal system we live with today: the working classes are channelled into the criminal law while the wealthy have the comfort of the civil courts. The rich suffer financial damages; the poor suffer prison.

In short, although commentators at the time often ascribed the death of the action to its misuse by gold-diggers, they mistook a misogynistic caricature for the cause. Professionalisation explains the judiciary's growing distaste for the action, while post-war economic affluence, the creation of the welfare state, women's increased status, and social consensus about the superiority of love-based marriages explain why people stopped bringing actions by the 1950s. The codification of women's formal equality into law explains the abolition of the action in the 1970s. So long as a sexed labour market and absence of welfare provisions denied most of the working poor love-based marriages, the action remained relevant, even if victims of male deceit were now reimagined as aggressors and the working-class plaintiffs as villainesses.

*    *    *

If we were to conclude our analysis here, it would be a story of how love was set free in the twentieth century, liberated from law and the sordidness of commerce, and how women – economically independent, sexually emancipated, confident and resilient – no longer needed legal 'protection' or compensation for their broken hearts. By the 1950s they were just as capable as men of navigating dating culture, and the law had no need to pry into their intimate negotiations. A bad relationship was a misfortune but not seriously damaging – you just picked yourself up, dusted yourself off and got back out there. Romantic love – anarchic, exhilarating, joyful or terrifying – had neither want nor need for governance.

But modern governance, as the philosopher Michel Foucault has taught us, is not confined to politics, the state or law. In fact, it is far more likely to be found in precisely those places that claim to be setting you free: a self-help book, a marriage manual, a classroom or a psychologist's office.[29] While unhappy fiancés by the mid-twentieth century were unlikely to seek legal resolution to their conflict, a battery of experts, counsellors, agony aunts, friends and family extracted their confessions and demanded self-scrutiny. As Foucault claimed, individuals were no longer judged against criteria of guilt or innocence, but of normal or deviant, healthy or unhealthy.[30] As part of this shift, by the 1950s, the heartbroken woman rather than the perfidious man bore the burden of a relationship's failure.

Discussing the bill that abolished breach of promise of marriage, Ellicott explained: 'The most significant part of this measure is that we are giving grants for premarital education' to help inform 'the attitude of those entering marriage'.[31] The bill prescribed a one-month minimum period of notice of intended marriage, during which time all couples would be directed towards voluntary premarital counselling services, while couples under eighteen and without parental consent would be legally obliged to undergo counselling.[32] He noted the introduction of counselling as part of matrimonial reforms in the 1950s and '60s, as well as the psychological services funded under the *Family Law Act* in 1975. Where breach of promise punished people who acted on their doubts after getting engaged, longer engagements and premarital counselling would help couples to explore uncertainty without sanction.

There was certainly benefit in not ascribing punitive sanctions to a broken engagement; however, we also know from breach of promise cases that the decision to break off an engagement often lay not with the couple, but with one party, and was often prompted not merely by second thoughts but by unethical or cruel behaviour. The psychological and economic damage caused was often severe, particularly if a child was involved. Rather than going to court, aggrieved parties now had one avenue open to them: therapy. The courts confined their jurisdiction over relationships to questions of property and custody, while counsellors and psychologists took over the governance of emotions.

The potted history that Ellicott mapped out for his bill, starting with the reforms of the 1950s and '60s, could begin much earlier. The provisions replacing parental consent with that of a psychologist was the culmination of an historical process that began in the early twentieth century with the 'coming of the counsellors', experts who supplanted the waning power that families, churches and communities exercised over private life. With industrialisation, urbanisation and the shift to consumer society, the story goes, traditional authority structures broke down and a culture of individualism triumphed. A new 'self' emerged, defined by the pursuit of self-fulfilment, authenticity, autonomy and pleasure, replacing the internalised moral norms of the Victorian era. The models once used to make sense of intimate relationships, specifically Christian morality, no longer held up, and psychology swept in to offer a new explanatory apparatus at a moment of social upheaval.[33] Psychology, however, was no less a system of governance than law. Indeed, psychological advice was often issued in a juridical register; they shared the same language of objective, universal rules derived from individual cases. For instance, the best-selling 1931 book *How to Be Happy Though Human* promised to explain a lack of romantic feeling through a series of case studies, from which the author would 'deduce certain general laws of conduct which may be of use to those who feel their own love fading.'[34] Twentieth-century psychology sought to identify universal laws that originated within the self and family. This process was at once antinomian – in that it encouraged people to be true to themselves, to follow their own laws – and deeply juridical – therapists, as we will see, clearly ascribed fault, but the sphere of responsibility was narrowed to women.

Breach of promise offers us a partial lens into this process. Women described their romantic anguish through therapeutic categories such as a nervous disorder or nervous breakdown up until people all but stopped bringing cases in the 1950s. The meaning of heartbreak in the psychological literature, however, shifted dramatically. As historians have noted, the heterogeneity of therapeutic advice in the early twentieth century narrowed in the 1930s, '40s and '50s and its message – which could be read everywhere from etiquette manuals to agony aunt columns to the pages of women's magazines and popular newspapers – was increasingly uniform. It focused on self-sufficiency, independence, resilience and keeping people within the bounds of an increasingly tight definition of 'normal'.[35] Where suffering from nervous shock as a result of being jilted suggested an irruption in a person's psyche caused by the behaviour of someone else, being labelling 'neurotic' suggested that the problem lay within; it was a pathological inability to recover. This also implied that the harm of a broken engagement was trivial, something that most 'normal' people could overcome.

In 1951 'researcher' Hilda Holland, for instance, in her book *What Keeps You from the Altar?*, answered the question posed by the title: 'the fault is probably within yourself'. With chapter titles such as 'Love and Neurosis' and 'Are You Emotionally Mature?' Holland concluded that many women were, 'partial deserters' from marriage because of a 'morbid obsession against household duties' and an 'intense dislike of housekeeping'.[36] Mr Gould, a widely publicised New York psychologist, also placed the blame squarely on women's shoulders: 'If a young woman failed in a love affair, the fault was hers, generally,' he proclaimed in a public lecture in 1936. She was to blame for entering into a 'hot love affair' in the first place, which was itself a 'thoroughly abnormal condition', and she was to blame for her suffering.

> Any girl who cannot throw off an unfortunate love affair, buy herself a new dress, apply a brand-new shade of lipstick, and dash out to attract a new home and more suitable beau, is suffering a neurosis. The sign of a healthy emotional life is the ability to outlive the suitable or the un-gettable man and to attract someone else. The girl who can't do that is simply a poor neurotic who has such a fixation that it amounts almost to mania.[37]

Gould's remedies – consumerism, re-entry into a hedonic dating culture, a reaffirmation of gender identity and emotional resilience – were now the tonics prescribed for broken hearts. The responsibility for romantic pain was feminised, and legal redress was shunned. 'Keep your dignity and do not wear your heart on your sleeve and most certainly do not tell the world that your love was something which can now be settled by repayment in cold hard cash,' advised agony aunt Lesley Deane in 1939 when a woman wrote to say that she wanted to launch a suit for breach of promise. 'Revenge is a high-flavoured sweet that leaves a bitter taste in the mouth,' she warned. 'Brooding has inspired you towards more rancour,' but any action that the woman pursued in the courts would bring 'just the opposite to happiness and satisfaction.'[38] Where the dishonourable man loomed large in nineteenth-century commentary, attracting a delightful arsenal of adjectives to shame him – a gay lothario, a black guardian, a vile seducer, a cad, a bounder, a louse – he disappears entirely in twentieth-century psychological discourse.

Dressed in the authoritative language of scientific expertise, mid-century psychology repackaged women's romantic suffering into universal laws of conduct and rearranged the emotions associated with love and heartbreak into the normal and the pathological. Emotions such as anger and rancour, which focused on the partner rather than the self, were prohibited and considered unhealthy. Emotions which implied judgment of men, such as brooding or fixation, were pathologised. Strong feelings, such as the giddiness of passion, were 'abnormal', and a refusal to perform domestic labour was a sign of 'neurosis' and to blame for a lack of romantic 'success'. These prescriptions were aimed at designing a new inner landscape for women, a new feminine subjectivity. The imagined ideal woman of therapeutic discourse was self-sacrificing in her devotion to the domestic, self-regulating in her rational avoidance of all-consuming passions, docile in her refusal to judge and amnesiac in her refusal to brood. She was also infinitely emotionally self-recuperating, thanks to both economic markets and marriage markets; the former allowed her to buy her way to sexiness and the latter to exchange one man for another. It's revealing that an American film advising young people about dating, *Choosing for Happiness*, distributed in 1950 by the NSW education department, is entirely bereft of romantic anguish. Young women are depicted dancing their way through a dizzying line-up of romantic partners, dating for months at a time, developing intimacies, rationally deciding upon their incompatibility, and blithely selecting the next one from an assembly line of masculinity. No tears are shed, no feelings are hurt, no dreams are dashed.[39]

The stories of real women who appeared in court in the 1930s and 1940s tell a very different story. In 1947, 45-year-old divorcee Mrs Linda Crowley described how she 'suffered a nervous breakdown, her hair went grey and she had been under a doctor's care' ever since she was jilted by her lover – and employer – Mr Dive. She described spending three years working as his housekeeper, washing, ironing and mending clothes and nursing the family 'because she loved him and was going to be his wife'. She recuperated her financial losses in the £125 of damages she was able to claim.[40] For 33-year-old Miss Lyons, in 1935, it was the 'uncertainty about whether she was to be married' or not that 'injured' her health and caused her to suffer a 'nervous disorder'.[41] When Miss Carr in 1937 was left to support an illegitimate child, the defence asked: 'what humiliation is there in these days about broken-off engagements?'[42] The emergence of a dating culture and the notion that an engagement might be a trial period rather than a contract had rendered these questions legitimate. Therapeutic discourse had also shifted a broken engagement from a question of morality – with all its emotions of humiliation, shame, and anger – to rationality: it was now simply a matter of incompatibility. Yet in the inter-war years and throughout the 1940s the courts were a bastion of resistance to the therapeutic reordering of intimacy that absolved men of responsibility. Miss Smith was granted £1,500 damages and the judge called Mr Carr a 'wicked' perjurer.[43] Judges advised juries to take into account a woman's feelings, social status and health when awarding damages. Giving evidence of suffering, as I have shown in Chapter Nine (*Daniels v Culverhouse*), also became more important in the twentieth century. If counsellors outside court were telling women to put on a bit of lippy, buy a new dress and get back out there, judges and juries were carefully assessing the costs of love: the domestic labour performed for free under a promise of marriage, the emotional injuries, the financial burden, and reputational damage of an unwanted pregnancy.

Although courts continued to financially reward the women who appeared before them, the social costs of filing a suit became much higher by the 1950s. A breach of promise action did not just mean having your private life filleted before the public, or being called a gold-digger. It also meant potentially being labelled abnormal. There were still doctors willing to treat women, and women's own self-diagnoses continued to place the emphasis on nervous shock or breakdown, but dominant psychological opinions about broken hearts had shifted.

*     *     *

If we were to imagine the three reasons for the action's demise in dialogue – that is, women's increasing social status and independence, shifts in understandings of marriage, and the mass dissemination of psychological discourse – then the conversation would be at times harmonious and at other times prickly. On the one hand, feminism and psychology worked together to reconfigure marriage as a private bond defined by romance, equality and mutual respect; they agreed that the family was the origin of people's suffering, and second-wave feminism's focus on consciousness-raising borrowed from psychological beliefs in the emancipatory potential of talk therapy.[44] When counsellors marched into the Family Court it was seen as a victory for feminism and for romantic love.[45] The state, in receding from the moral regulation of intimate life, would actively protect people's right to privacy, which in turn encouraged a model of love based on emotional authenticity rather than social rules.

On the other hand, by the 1960s feminists such as Betty Friedan and Shulamith Firestone had issued excoriating critiques of the misogynistic elements in psychology, showing that 'diagnoses such as hysteria and depression had been forged by men to delegitimise, exclude and render powerless women who were in fact protesting their social condition' and that any relaxing in sexual mores was exclusively to the benefit of men.[46] So long as women were denied genuine autonomy in a male-dominated society – blocked in pursuing their careers and trapped in domesticity – they would invest romance with greater significance and suffer disproportionately from failed affairs. As we have seen, mid-century psychological discourse burdened women with the responsibility for the emotional maintenance of relationships and blamed them when they went awry. It's little wonder that when Elizabeth Evatt, the first chief justice of the Family Court of Australia, commented in 1973 on the abolition of the action in Britain, she expressed ambivalence: 'it remains to be seen whether this will be for the benefit of women or not.'[47] A sexist historical anachronism had finally been laid to rest, but was it really so anachronistic? Did the state's affirmation of the right to privacy now just leave women without redress and subject to intimate exploitation and harm?

In some ways, the action died much as it had lived: with a question mark over its head, fissured with contradiction. In making unchastity a complete defence, the suit enshrined the sexual double standard into law; in being the only civil suit that demanded that women's evidence be corroborated, the action legally codified a patriarchal mistrust of women's evidence; and although a small number of men used the action, its *raison d'être* was premised upon female dependence: it presumed that a woman was economically reliant upon marriage, her primary social status was as a wife, and her emotional injuries upon being jilted were severe and life-long. By the 1970s, very few people in any Anglophone country would have recognised this version of either femininity or marriage, and when Ellicott stated in 1976 that abolishing the action was 'in line with the equality of the sexes', few would have disagreed.[48]

Yet the elements of the action tell us little about how it was used in practice. As this book has shown, the women who sued their lovers wielded the suit in profoundly feminist ways: refusing their victim-status by aggressively prosecuting for economic and emotional injuries suffered, advancing feminist arguments around the labour of care, protesting sexual violence, and demanding an ethics of relationship. While it is possible that the women who brought actions were more courageous, wilful and empowered than their peers, the legal process itself also produced feminist political subjects. If therapy encouraged women to replace judgment with self-blame and to channel love into a private language devoid of moral norms or economic responsibility, the common law demanded the opposite. The action asked women to appear on a public stage at a time when they had little or no voice in parliament, in courts or in the press; it required them not simply to tell their stories, but to stand in judgment of men. In demandng proof of 'lacerated feelings' or financial loss, it ensured that women take their own feelings seriously and it elevated private pain to a question of public justice. In awarding an economic valuation of housework or child-rearing, the action put a price on unremunerated feminine labours of love. The almost one thousand cases in Australia's history of breach of promise of marriage are not a historical curiosity or an anachronism but fundamental to our feminist past and instructive of a feminist future.

# Epilogue

I t's December 2022 and Sydney is in bloom. Great swags of bougain-
villea – lurid pinks and siren reds – hang languidly down the sides of
terrace houses, streets carpeted in soft purple jacaranda flowers radiate an otherworldly aura, and the summer sun – already high and brilliant
at eight in the morning – illuminates the underside of leaves, setting their
veined patterns aglow like small stained-glass windows. For academics, summer means conference season, and today I am on my way to a symposium
on the theme of love, law and money. Legal theorists, historians, sociolo-
gists and anthropologists from around the world will meet to discuss some
provocative, albeit familiar questions. Why is deception or fraud legally com-
pensable when practised by a stranger in a commercial setting but difficult
to litigate when done by an intimate? Why does the law assume that people in intimate relations do not intend to create legal relationships and what
does it take to rebut this? Why, given all that we know about the suffering
people experience when their romantic partners or family members deceive
them – the depression, anxiety, financial loss, bodily injury and sometimes
suicide – does the law insist that these harms are beyond legal remedies? And
in what ways do women bear the brunt of the law's reluctance to go beyond
the front door of the house?[1]

The conference chair begins by noting that these scholarly questions
bleed into the personal – simply mentioning the symposia to friends works as
a prompt for intimate revelation. Everyone seems to have a story to tell either
about themselves or someone they know having been duped, hurt or deceived
by a loved one. As she speaks, my mind drifts to a coffee chat I had recently
with a friend, Stephanie Wood, a writer and journalist. A few years earlier,
Steph had met a man online – an architect and grazier with two grown children, a rather pleasing yacht, a house in the Southern Highlands and, topping

it all off, a flop of thick curly brown hair and a wry, haughty demeanour. She fell in love. But over the course of a year her excitement turned to confusion, anxiety, self-doubt and debilitating grief as she struggled to make sense of his endless cancellations, his evasions, his rubbery stories, his refusal to introduce her to his family, his obvious lies. I remember her therapist counselling her to challenge her 'trust issues', and I recall her telling me how her life was falling apart, how she would curl up in bed unable to talk to anyone, incapable of work. One day, when he cancelled on a romantic holiday, leaving Steph stranded at the airport, she walked over to the flight assistant and asked if his name was on her list. Nothing, she was told, although he had sat on a couch opposite Steph when supposedly booking the flight. When Steph decided to investigate him more fully, she found that he had been struck off the register of architects for fraud, the yacht was someone else's, the photograph of a ute bogged in a paddock he had sent her was taken from Google Images, there was no country house, and Steph was one of many women he was seeing. Steph told me at the café that she hadn't dated anyone since – she had lost trust in her own capacity to judge character.[2]

I also think about two cases that had been in the news that month. Renae Marsden, a sixteen-year-old girl whose friend Camila Zeidan had created a fictitious young man called Brayden Spiteri to live out a passionate online romantic relationship with her, even discussing wedding plans. When 'Brayden' suddenly ended the relationship without explanation, Marsden was devastated and suicided.[3] There was also Lydia Abdelmalek, a woman who seduced other women online pretending to be an actor, exchanging torrid messages, asking them for nude photographs and then blackmailing them.[4] Even with such serious injuries, the courts have struggled to find legal remedies. In Renae Marsden's case, the Coronial Court concluded that no criminal offence had been committed, although a direct line could be drawn between her friend's deceit and her death. Abdelmalek was found guilty of stalking, but this does not capture the harm experienced by her victims – it offers no remedy for their emotional distress, and only provides a punishment if the deceit escalates to physical or cyber-stalking.

Steph might have sued under the tort of deceit, although I doubt that she would have won. The courts in Australia are unwilling to apply a remedy designed for commercial cases to intimate matters, particularly if there is no direct financial loss. It said as much in a case involving paternity fraud – conduct in an intimate relationship is not to be held to a legal standard.[5] I wonder, as I have often wondered while researching this book, why we didn't just reform the breach of promise action rather than prohibiting it? What fantasy led us to believe that it was out of date? With the expansion of digital technologies and online dating services in the twenty-first century, the need for the law to regulate romance – a realm populated by smiling wolves – has possibly never been more urgent. In any case, as Elaine Hasday has argued, the law's self-declared reluctance to intervene in romantic, sexual or familial contexts is by necessity a form of governance, one that in refusing to punish ends up condoning the behaviour of liars and frauds.[6]

Over the next two days at the conference, I feast upon a smorgasbord of intellectual delicacies. I hear about how au pairs are given no legal protection because they work within the realm of family; their pay is explicitly referred to in European law as 'pocket money' and their employers as 'hosts'. I learn that the formula used to calculate child support in Australia does not include childcare; the social presumption that costs will be borne by the mother is implicitly enshrined in law. I also listen to papers on the law's efforts to regulate romantic injury. A colleague discusses a 2011 case involving Dr Neil Wallman, who gave a dating agency more than two million dollars over the course of three years. The agency promised romantic introductions and concocted fictional lovers for him, all of whom demanded money before disappearing. He won his action against the agency for breach of trust, deceit, misrepresentation and misleading conduct, although the fraudulent lovers were not parties to the litigation. It's similar to the 2018 English case of Tereza Burki, who successfully sued a dating agency for deceit and misrepresentation after she paid £12,600 pounds in membership fees on the promise that they had a substantial number of wealthy men who were open to having children. She later discovered there were only 100 active men on the agency's books.[7] We discuss how important the financial element was in these cases – emotional injury in law needs, in general, to attach to bodily or financial harm – and the fact that they involved a company rather than a person. Dr Orit Gan, a legal theorist, speaks up to say that this is not the case in Israel, where they still have the action for breach of promise of marriage. I'm shocked. I had presumed that only civil law countries still had it in very limited form. That night she emails me about a leading case.

Having spent the last ten years reading over a thousand breach of promise cases, mostly from the Victorian era and early twentieth century, I find it strange, almost uncanny, to read such a familiar story in its twenty-first-century incarnation. The case is from 2004 and the litigants are not the wealthy plaintiffs in present-day deceit cases, but a woman and man who worked in a tobacco company; she was a secretary and he was a manager. They were both married to other people when they commenced a long-term relationship, although she appears never to have lived with her husband. The manager had a key to her apartment and went there every day, showering her and her son with gifts, including a car. He suggested that she 'forego mainte-nance for her son', as he would look after 'all his needs' and promised her that if she divorced her husband, he would divorce his wife and they would start a family together. Buoyed by this prospect, she divorced her husband and soon fell pregnant to the manager. This was not her first pregnancy to him, but it was the first time she had wanted to keep it, with a vision of their family in mind. When he refused to divorce his wife, she decided to carry on with her pregnancy, after which he severed all ties with her. She responded by bringing an action for breach of promise of marriage, loss of marriage expectations, mental anguish and loss of spiritual and emotional support in the Magistrates Court, which she won. She was granted a lump-sum payment of 35,000 new shekels (A$15,045). He appealed to the District Court, arguing that as a mar-ried person, he could not make a promise of marriage and that such a promise would be void for being immoral and contrary to public policy. The District Court upheld his appeal, finding that 'the voidance of marriage agreements by married men allows the married man to try to rehabilitate his marriage', which would not be possible if the court bound him to his promise to divorce his wife. In other words, it would be better for a married man to try to repair his relationship than to be legally forced or encouraged into another mar-riage. She appealed this judgment in the Supreme Court.[8]

It's refreshing, given the limits placed on litigating intimate injuries in Australian, American, Canadian and English courts, to read a judgment that takes seriously and applies feminist thought on the issue. The argument that married men should be immune from litigation was quickly dismissed by Justice Barak; such reasoning was out of date given the legal recognition of cohabitation and the absurdity of creating a special status for married people. Instead, the majority judgment went straight to the crux of the matter: why should injuries in domestic or romantic contexts be beyond legal redress? It might be argued, Justice Barak noted, that 'the agreement to marry falls within the realm of emotion' and is therefore found 'in the sphere where the law rec-ognises the freedom of the individual to honour his promise or not to honour it'. But this argument ignores the damage caused to the other party and sug-gests that the law of contracts 'stops on the threshold of the family home'. This, he stated, would be neither true nor satisfactory. 'The promise of marriage sometimes leads to reliance and various plans for realising it', and this can lead to an adverse change in a person's position, and to substantial financial expenditure. 'Ignoring this reality of life is wrong and unjustifiable,' he stated. 'Freedom of marriage does not give rise to a freedom to cause damage to others.' Given that the law already regulates contracts that are based upon emotional foundations, such as child maintenance or the joint ownership of assets between spouses, there is no reason why it would not also recognise a contract made between romantic partners. 'The expenses and damages should not be borne randomly by one of the parties (usually the weaker party) but this should be determined by the rules of contractual liability.' The original order of the Magistrates Court was reinstated, and the plaintiff was granted a lump-sum payment.[9]

I don't expect any Anglophone country to reintroduce a reformed version of the breach of promise action – one free of gender bias that applies to cohabitation as well as marriage – but the Israeli case, when read in light of the action's history, shows the need for legal reform. Rather than having one specific action, we might insert emotional injury into pre-existing actions such as fraud, or extend torts such as deceit and misrepresentation into the romantic realm; we might begin by asking questions about vulnerability and reliance and by interrogating the harms, whether they be manifest on the body, the mind or the wallet, caused by deceit, misrepresentation or simply changing your mind. We might begin with an ethics of love in which all the frolicsome freedoms and delights of romance exist side by side with a duty to take care of each other. And we might admit, with some humility, that the people in the past who took lacerated feelings seriously may have been wiser creatures than ourselves.

# Acknowledgments

A novelist friend once told me that he couldn't tell me what he was writing about because if he did there would be no point in writing it. Fiction demands secrecy, he said. Non-fiction, I replied, demands the opposite: compulsive chatter, an endless discussion of ideas, and the interminable circulation of papers. As a result, when non-fiction authors like me come to the end of their books, we have many people to thank.

I would like to begin by expressing my profound gratitude to the team at Black Inc./La Trobe University Press and in particular to my editor, Denise O'Dea, who reached into the vast, swirling morass of words I gave her and miraculously pulled out a book. Sage, unflappable, judicious and sparklingly clever, Denise is the best kind of editor – I am so very lucky to have been able to work with her. Before Denise, my editor was the wonderful Julia Carlomagno, and I returned years later to her expert advice and words of encouragement when editing *Courting*. I thank Chris Feik for agreeing to take a punt on a rather niche topic and the publicity team at Black Inc. for all their marketing nous – of which I have none.

This book was made possible by two very generous grants awarded to me as a Merewether Scholar by the State Library of New South Wales and as a Chancellor's Postdoctoral Research Fellow at the University of Technology Sydney. I would particularly like to thank Rachel Franks, Richard Neville and all the archivists and librarians at Mitchell Library for their expertise, excellent conversation, and for allowing me to use the scholars' room at the end of this project. Is there a more beautiful library in the world than Mitchell Library? And can there be any desk more inspirational than that of Donald Horne? At UTS I would like to thank Jenni Millbank, who supervised the very first article I ever wrote on breach of promise of marriage (an embarrassingly long time ago) and Shaunnagh Dorsett, who, in supervising my postdoc, generously shared her insights on legal history and introduced me to the nerdy pleasures of FileMaker Pro. I would also like to thank all my delightful, witty, terrifically smart and politically engaged colleagues at UTS – never has a faculty been so happy as ours! And I couldn't imagine another workplace where colleagues are also your most cherished confidantes, your closest friends, and your best readers. I would particularly like to thank Isabel Karpin, my current supervisor, for her unerring support and friendship and our dean, Anita Stuhmcke, who is kind, sage and fearless.

In the final months of this book, I reached out to all the experts in my field to read and comment on various chapters and I was humbled by their generosity and the depth and breadth of their knowledge. Many people saved me from errors – of fact or interpretation – not to mention my love of rococo sentences. Here I would like to thank Paula Hamilton, Bruce Kercher, Marilyn Lake, Katherine Biber, Sacha Molotoritz, Paula Jane Byrne, Grace Karskens, Jane Lydon, Mel Fyfe, Ann Curthoys, Kirsten McKenzie, Lisa Ford, Isabella Alexander, Eric Reiter, Devleena Ghosh, Zora Simic, Anne Monsour, Sophie Loy-Wilson, Tamson Pietsch, Melissa Bellanta and Renata Grossi. All of these people wrote extensive comments on chapters, pointed out mortifying errors and challenged my interpretations in the most helpful ways possible. I can only pledge to have the same scholarly generosity towards future generations that they have modelled. I would also like to thank the institutions that invited me to present work in progress, in particular the Melbourne and Sydney Feminist History Groups, faculty history seminars at the University of Sydney and the University of New South Wales, the Max Planck Institute in Berlin, Concordia University in Canada and the internal research seminars at UTS.

And where would this book be without all the fascinating and provocative conversations I have had over the years with my colleagues in the field of law, history and emotions? Katie Barclay, Sharon Crozier de Rosa, Penny Edmonds, Eric Reiter and Kate Rossmanith – thank you! I would also like to thank people who read drafts along the way, particularly Nikki Lengkeek, Penny Russell, Aviva Tuffield and the members of my own writing group – Las Campaneras – not mentioned above: Judith Keene, Ruth Balint and Frances Clark. Early drafts of sections of this book were published in the *Australian Feminist Law Journal* 45.1 (2019), pp. 131–57 and 23.1 (2005), pp. 99–120, and in *The Journal of Legal History* 38.2 (2017), pp. 179–202. I would like to thank the editors and reviewers of these journals for their immensely helpful feedback and particularly Joy Damousi and the late Patrick White, who provided feedback on the very first article on breach of promise I published (too long ago).

My heartfelt gratitude goes out to all the archivists and librarians without whom I would never have been able to complete this book, in particular Emily Hanna at the State Records Office NSW, David Whiteford at the State Records Office Western Australia, Christie and other archivists at the Old Court House Law Museum in Perth and all the archivists in the public records office in Victoria, Queensland, South Australia, Tasmania and the University of Melbourne Archives. In Bathurst I was treated to the most delightful hospitality and extraordinary expertise of Kim Bagot-Hiller, Lee Steele and Sarah Swift. For each chapter I attempted to contact the descendants of my protagonists and I am particularly grateful to the charming Michael Prevost, Peggy Aeschlimann and Steven Donnelly (on behalf of the Donnelly and Koscez families) for sharing their stories and family archives.

I am lucky to be surrounded by the cleverest, funniest and warmest of friends who have shown extraordinary forbearance of my tendency to turn all conversations to the history of love. I have been sustained over the years by the chatter of (in no order) David Carter, Siobhan Petri, Anthea Vogl, Penny Crofts, Bec Whish, Hope Earl, Emily McCosker, Catriona Menzies-Pike, Lisa Ford, Michael Dulaney, Tim Brunero, Michael Hugill, Kiera Lindsay, Hannah Forsyth, Sophie Loy-Wilson, Elva Darnell, Dan Stacey, Huon Curtis, Brian Opeskin, Jenni Millbank, Eugene Schofield-Georgeson, Kathryn Greenman, Tamson Pietsch, Ruth Higgins, Miranda Kaye, Trish Luker, Claire McLisky, Daniel Vaughan, Yane Svetiev, Richard White, Cath Bishop, Samia Khatun, Siobhan Moylan, Ivan Ah-Sam, Andrew Wong, Kyle Clasky, Tessa Zettle, Steph Wood, Alex Roginski, James Herrington and Gab Abramowitz. I particularly want to thank my dear friend Rose Tracey for her superb professional photography.

I am extremely grateful to my family for their love. If I have a passion for reading, writing, research and politics, then it is because of my parents, Helen and Greg Simmonds. My siblings Tara and James Simmonds are among my closest friends, and I am always grateful for their humour. Isadora Mae, Zachary and Phil Mathews and Karla Delgado have also brought me such joy.

Finally, this book would never have been written without my two closest readers and companions: Anna Clark and James Jiang. In the many many years that it took to write this book, Anna and James were the first people whom I would call when I had an idea or when I felt compelled to read out a paragraph or a sentence. They were the first to receive a draft of every chapter that I wrote, and their feedback always struck the perfect balance between criticism, encouragement and care. They are both terribly brilliant in starkly different ways and this book is richer because of their words.

# Image Credits

Portrait of A.W.H. Humphrey by George Prideaux Robert Harris, 1803. National Library of Australia, Humphrey Collection.

Portrait of Sarah Wentworth (née Cox) by William Nicholas, 1856. Museums of History NSW, Vaucluse House Collection.

*Road between Botanic Gardens, Sydney*, by Samuel Thomas Gill, c. 1856. Dixson Library, State Library of New South Wales.

*The Court House, Hobart Town*, from *Hobart Town Magazine* Vol. III, No. 13, March 1834. W. L. Crowther Library, State Library of Tasmania.

Portraits of Julia Gertrude Stewart and Ellen Jane Stewart, from the Stewart and Steel Family Papers 1280–1963 MLMSS 1218/1. Author's own photos.

Ilma Vaughan, from *The Bulletin*, 28 March 1891, via Trove.

James Sorab Lucas, Certificate Exempting from Dictation Test No. 2829, 11 October 1921, National Archives of Australia.

'A Typical Syrian Hawker', *The Sydney Illustrated News*, 19 November 1892, via Trove.

Photograph of Verona Rodriguez courtesy of her son, Michael Prevost.

Poster advertising Daisy Yates, *Always Blooming*, c. 1913. Chronicle / Alamy Stock Photo.

Robina Allan, a.k.a. Brenda Barrye, *Sunday Times* (Perth, Western Australia), 29 March 1936, via Trove.

# Notes

## Abbreviations

| | |
|---|---|
| AE | *The Adelaide Express* |
| AENEGA | *Armidale Express and New England General Advertiser* |
| AT | *Adelaide Times* |
| AMI | Australian Marriage Index: 1788–1850 |
| ATCJ | *Australian Town and Country Journal* |
| BFP | *Bathurst Free Press and Mining Journal* |
| Bell's Life | *Bell's Life in Sydney and Sporting Reviewer* |
| BA | *Bendigo Advertiser* |
| CT | *Colonial Times* |
| CCJP | Court of Civil Jurisdiction Proceedings |
| DD | *The Darling Downs and General Advertiser* |
| GA | *Geelong Advertiser* |
| GEPP | *Goulburn Evening Penny Post* |
| GT | *Gympie Times and Mary River Mining Gazette* |
| HRA | Historical Records of Australia |
| HRNSW | Historical Records of NSW |
| HTC | *Hobart Town Chronicle* |
| IM | *Illawarra Mercury* |
| LE | *Launceston Examiner* |
| MM | *Maitland Mercury and Hunter River General Advertiser* |
| NAA | National Archives of Australia |
| NA | *Northern Argus* |
| NBN | *Nambucca and Bellinger News* |
| NMH | *Newcastle Morning Herald and Miners' Advocate* |
| NS | *Northern Star, Lismore NSW* |
| MC | *Maryborough Chronicle, Wide Bay and Burnett Advertiser* |
| ML | Mitchell Library (in the State Library of NSW) |
| NSWCSP | New South Wales Colonial Secretary's Papers, 1788-1856. |
| OMA | *Ovens and Murray Advertiser* |
| PG | *Perth Gazette and Western Australian Journal* |
| PROV | Public Records of Victoria |
| SAWC | *South Australian Weekly Chronicle* |
| SAR | *South Australian Register* |

Notes

SG          *Sydney Gazette*
SLNSW       State Library of New South Wales
SH          *Sydney Herald*
SM          *The Sydney Monitor*
SMH         *Sydney Morning Herald*
SRNSW       State Records of New South Wales
TA          *The Australian*
TDT         *The Daily Telegraph*
TSH         *The Sydney Herald*
TWC         *The Western Champion and General Advertiser for the Central-Western Districts* (Qld)
WT          *Weekly Times*

## Introduction

1   Frederick Chapman, as cited in '"Couldn't Marry Me"', *The Sun*, 24 March 1914; 'An Abandoned Wedding', TDT, 25 March 1914, p. 15. See also *Storey v Chapman*, SRNSW, Judgment Papers, Container 20/11055, no. 143.

2   David Day, *Paul Keating: The Biography* (HarperCollins, 2015), p. 5.

3   '"Couldn't Marry Me"', *The Sun*, 24 March 1914; 'An Abandoned Wedding', TDT, 25 March 1914, 15. See also *Storey v Chapman*, SRNSW, Judgment Papers, Container 20/11055, no. 143.

4   AMI: registration place: Randwick, NSW; registration year: 1915; registration number: 1348.

5   Day, *Paul Keating*, pp. 136, 287.

6   Histories of love generally focus on the bourgeoisie. For Britain and Europe, see Leonore Davidoff and Catherine Hall, *Family Fortunes: Men and Women of the English Middle Class, 1780–1850* (Routledge, 2015); Peter Gay, *The Tender Passion: The Bourgeois Experience, Victoria to Freud, Vol. 2* (W.W. Norton and Co., 1999); Peter Gay, *The Naked Heart: The Bourgeois Experience, Victoria to Freud, Vol. 4* (W.W. Norton and Co., 1996). For exceptions, see: Clare Langhamer, *The English in Love: The Story of an Emotional Revolution* (Oxford University Press, 2013); Ginger Frost, *Promises Broken: Courtship, Class and Gender in Victorian England* (University of Virginia Press, 1995). For America, see: Eva Illouz, *Why Love Hurts: A Sociological Explanation* (Polity, 2013); Karen Lystra, *Searching the Heart: Women, Men and Romantic Love in Nineteenth-Century America* (Oxford University Press, 1992). For Australia, see: Penny Russell, *A Wish of Distinction: Colonial Gentility and Femininity* (Melbourne University Press, 1994); Hsu-Ming Teo, 'Love Writes: Gender and Romantic Love in Australian Love Letters', 1860–1960, *Australian Feminist Studies* 20:48 (2016), pp. 343–61.

7   Jill Elaine Hasday, *Intimate Lies and the Law* (Oxford University Press, 2019), pp. 1–18.

8   This is in spite of recent judicial opinion advising against presumptions. See: *Ashton v Pratt* (NSWCA, 2015).

9   My argument is indebted to Eva Illouz, although differs in that I focus on working-class people and the law. See: Illouz, *Why Love Hurts* and *Cold Intimacies: The Making of Emotional Capitalism* (Polity, 2007). See also Christopher Lasch, *The Culture of Narcissism: American Life in an Age of Diminishing Expectations* (W.W. Norton and Co., 2018).

10    For scholarship on love and law see: Peter Goodrich, *Law in the Courts of Love: Literature and Other Minor Jurisprudences* (Routledge, 1996); Goodrich, 'Epistolary Justice: The Love Letter as Law', *Yale Journal of Law and Humanities* 9 (1997), pp. 245–295; James Martel, *Love Is a Sweet Chain: Desire, Autonomy and Friendship in Liberal Political Theory* (Routledge, 2012); Eric H. Reiter, *Wounded Feelings: Litigating Emotions in Quebec, 1870–90* (University of Toronto Press, 2020); Alecia Simmonds, 'Promises and Pie-Crusts Were Made to Be Broken: Breach of Promise of Marriage and the Regulation of Courtship in Early Colonial Australia', *Australian Feminist Law Journal* 23:1 (2005), pp. 99–120; Renata Grossi, *Looking for Love in the Legal Discourse of Marriage* (ANU Press, 2014); Steedman, *History and the Law: A Love Story* (Cambridge University Press, 2020).

11    Jean-Jacques Rousseau, *Julie ou La Nouvelle Heloise* (Pennsylvania State University Press, 1968), pp. 261–62.

12    Goodrich, *Law in the Courts of Love.*

13    Nan Hunter, 'Marriage, Law and Gender: A Feminist Inquiry', in Lisa Duggan and Nan Hunter (eds), *Sex Wars: Sexual Dissent and Political Culture* (Routledge, 1995), p. 110.

14    Warren Susman, 'Personality and the Making of Twentieth-Century Culture', in Susman, *Culture as History: The Transformation of American Society in the Twentieth Century* (Pantheon, 1984), pp. 271–85; Illouz, *Why Love Hurts*, pp. 1–3, 20–30.

15    Clause 21, *Marriage Amendment Act 1976* (Cth). This inserted s. 111A into the *Marriage Act 1961* (Cth), which abolished the action for breach of promise of marriage.

16    Langhamer made this argument around the significance of the post-war years. See Langhamer, *The English in Love*, pp. 4–8.

17    See Susman, 'Personality', pp. 271–85.

18    Illouz, *Why Love Hurts*, p. 4.

19    Arlette Farge, *Le Gout de l'Archive* (Editions du Seuil, 1989), p. 6; Carolyn Steedman, *Dust: The Archive and Cultural History* (Rutgers University Press, 2002), pp. 45–55.

20    Edward Muir and Guido Ruggiero, 'Introduction: The Crime of History', in Muir and Ruggiero (eds), *History from Crime* (Johns Hopkins University Press, 1994), p. ix; Natalie Zemon Davis, *Fiction in the Archives: Pardon Tales and Their Tellers in Sixteenth-Century France* (Cambridge University Press, 1987), pp. 1–26.

21    In the US, see: Michael Grossberg, *Governing the Hearth: Law and the Family in Nineteenth-Century America* (University of North Carolina Press, 1985). In Britain, see: Saskia Lettmaier, *Broken Engagements: The Action for Breach of Promise of Marriage and the Feminist Ideal, 1800–1940* (Oxford University Press, 2010); Frost, *Promises Broken*. In Canada, see: Rosemary Coombe, 'The Most Disgusting, Disgraceful and Iniquitous Proceeding in Our Law: The Action for Breach of Promise of Marriage in Nineteenth-Century Ontario', *University of Toronto Law Journal* 38:1 (1988), pp. 65-69. In New Zealand, see: Megan Simpson, 'The Action for Breach of Promise of Marriage in Early Colonial New Zealand', *Victoria University of Wellington Law Review* 41 (2010), p. 473.

22    Frost 'arbitrarily' ends her study in 1900. Lettmaier devotes most of her book to the nineteenth century. See: Frost, *Promises Broken*, p. 11; Lettmaier, *Broken Engagements*, p. 12.

# Notes

## The Rules of Engagement

1 Goodrich, *Law in the Courts of Love*, p. 19.
2 Lettmaier, *Broken Engagements*, pp. 19–24.
3 *Evidence (Further Amendment) Act 1869* 32 Vic., c. 68; Assented to in all the Australian colonies except Victoria as *An Act for the Further Amendment of the Law of Evidence*, s. 2 (Western Australia: 1871; New South Wales: 1876; South Australia: 1870; Queensland: 1874; Tasmania: 1870; note that Victoria did pass an *Act for the Further Amendment of the Law of Evidence* in 1876, however it did not require corroboration.).
4 Edmund Powell, William Blake Odgers and Walter Blake Odgers, *Powell's Principles and Practice of the Law of Evidence*, 10th edition (Butterworth, 1921), p. 447.
5 *Howell v Neeld* (1900), NSWSC, *NS*, 17 March 1900, p. 4.
6 Joseph Chitty, *A Practical Treatise on the Law of Contracts Not Under Seal, and Upon the Usual Defences to the Actions Thereon* (G. and C. Merriam, 1872), pp. 585–87.
7 Samuel Comyn, *A Treatise of the Law Relative to Contracts and Agreements Not Under Seal: With Cases and Decisions Thereon in the Action of Assumpsit, Vol. 2* (A. Strahan, 1807), p. 408.
8 Chitty, *A Practical Treatise* (1826), p. 158.
9 Chitty, *A Practical Treatise* (1872), p. 585. Citing: *Wightman v Coates* (1818), 15 Mass. 4, Parker, C.J.
10 *Field v Nelson* (1850), SCNSW, as cited in *Bell's Life*, 6 July 1850, p. 1.
11 Lord George Gordon Byron, 'Donna Julia's Letter, Canto 1', *Don Juan* (1824).
12 Chitty, *A Practical Treatise* (1826), p. 159.
13 Chitty, *A Treatise on the Law of Contracts* (H. Sweet, 1863), p. 491.
14 Chitty, *A Treatise on the Law of Contracts*, p. 491.
15 See for example: *Heals v Mellersch* (1842), WASC, *PG*, 16 April 1842, 2–3; *Hawthorn v Steel* (1833), TASSC, *SG*, 11 June 1833, p. 4.
16 See: *Daniels v Culverhouse* (1920), VICSC, *GA*, 21 May 1920, p. 5.
17 'Breach of Promise Actions', *GA*, 27 March 1891, p. 1.
18 Sedgwick et al., *A Treatise on the Measure of Damages*, 9th edition (Baker Voorhis, 1920), pp. 1272–83; Lettmaier, *Broken Engagements*, p. 47.
19 Jane Larson, 'Women Understand So Little' ... A Feminist Rethinking of the Seduction Action', *Columbia Law Review* 93:2 (1993), pp. 375–93.
20 Constance Backhouse, 'The Tort of Seduction: Fathers and Daughters in Nineteenth-Century Canada', *Dalhousie Law Journal* 10:1 (1986), p. 47.
21 Larson, 'Women Understand So Little', pp. 375–93.

## Part 1 – Love in a Penal Colony

1 *Cox v Payne* (1825), NSWSC (17 May 1825), as cited in *Sydney Gazette*, 19 May 1825; *Rule v Hick* (1836) NSWSC (16 September 1836), as cited in *Sydney Gazette*, 27 September 1836; *Stone v Macarthur* (1833) TASSC (9 October 1833), as cited in *The Tasmanian*, 11 October 1833.
2 Grace Karskens, *The Colony: A History of Early Sydney* (Allen and Unwin, 2010), p. 2.
3 Kirsten McKenzie, *Scandal in the Colonies: Sydney and Cape Town, 1820–1850* (Melbourne University Press, 2004), pp. 90–110; Bruce Kercher, *Debt, Seduction and Other Disasters: The Birth of Civil Law in Convict New South Wales* (The Federation Press, 1996), pp. 97–104.

## 1. Honour, Love and Law in the Early Colony (*Sutton v Humphrey*, 1806)

1  'General Orders', *SG*, 8 June 1806, p. 1.

2  See Karskens, *The Colony*, pp. 98–188; *SG*, 17 February 1805, p. 2; 6 April 1806, p. 2.

3  *Sutton v Humphrey* (1806) *CCJP*, 2/8148; Philip Gidley King, *Letter Books*, vol. 4, 12 June 1806.

4  King, *Letter Books*, vol. 4, 12 June 1806.

5  The first legally qualified judge was Richard Dore, who arrived in 1798 but died in 1800 and was replaced by the legally unqualified Richard Atkins. It was not until barrister Ellis Bent arrived in 1810 that court procedure became professional.

6  For popular conceptions of law, see: Paula J. Byrne, *Criminal Law and Colonial Subject: New South Wales, 1810–1830* (Cambridge University Press, 1993); Alex C. Castles, *An Australian Legal History* (Law Book Co., 1982); Bruce Kercher, *An Unruly Child: A History of Law in Australia* (Routledge, 1995).

7  See: Patricia Grimshaw et al., *Creating a Nation: 1778–1990* (McPhee Gribble, 1994), pp. 49–50; Kercher, *An Unruly Child*, pp. 50–51; Alecia Simmonds, 'The History of Non-Indigenous Marriage', in *The Cambridge Legal History of Australia* (Cambridge University Press, 2022), pp. 456–81.

8  Carol J. Baxter (ed.), *Musters of New South Wales and Norfolk Island, 1805–1806* (Australian Biographical and Genealogical Record, 1989).

9  Joy Damousi, *Depraved and Disorderly: Female Convicts, Sexuality and Gender in Colonial Australia* (Cambridge University Press), p. 62.

10  For the family as the 'little commonwealth', see Jean-Jacques Rousseau, *La Nouvelle Heloise*, pp. 261–67.

11  'General Orders', *SG*, 18 May 1806, p. 1; 'Bench of Magistrates', *SG*, 8 June 1806, p. 3; 'Sydney', 18 May, 1806, p. 2.

12  Kercher, personal correspondence, 21 May 2018; Byrne, personal correspondence, 21 November 2020.

13  Kercher, *Debt, Seduction*, p. 10.

14  Kercher, *An Unruly Child*; Kercher, *Debt, Seduction*.

15  Governor William Bligh and John Macarthur, as cited in J.M. Bennett, 'Richard Atkins', *Australian Dictionary of Biography*, https://adb.anu.edu.au

16  Bennett, 'Richard Atkins'.

17  *HRA*, IV/I, p. 1.

18  Richard Atkins, as cited in Kercher, *Debt, Seduction*, p. 28.

19  Philip Gidley King to Evan Nepean, 10 March 1801; King to John King, 21 August 1801, as cited in Alan Atkinson, 'Richard Atkins: The Women's Judge', *Journal of Australian Colonial History* 1:1 (April 1999), p. 129; and Bennett, 'Richard Atkins'.

20  Richard Atkins, as cited in Kercher, *Debt, Seduction*, p. 28.

21  See Kercher, 'Commerce and the Development of Contract Law in Early New South Wales', *Law and History Review* 9:2 (1991), p. 273.

22  Lord Hobart to P.G. King , 1 March 1804, *HRA* series I, vol. IV, p. 36.

23  L. Macquarie, 'A List of Persons Holding Civil and Military Employments in His Majesty's Colony', 1810, *HRNSW*, series 1, vol. 7, p. 367.

24  G.H. Stancombe, 'Humphrey, Adolarius William Henry', *Australian Dictionary of Biography*, https://adb.anu.edu.au.

25  Trial of William Sutton, July 1789, *Old Bailey Proceedings Online*, www.oldbaileyonline.org, t17890708-7.

26    David Collins, *An Account of the English Colony, Vol. 1* (1798), Chapter XVIII,
       Project Gutenberg, https://www.gutenberg.org.
27    Margaret Steven, 'John Palmer', *Australian Dictionary of Biography*.
28    Collins, *An Account of the English Colony*, Chapter XVIII.
29    See: Collins, *An Account of the English Colony*; and Michael Flynn, *The Second
       Fleet: Britan's Grim Convict Armada of 1790* (Library of Australian History, 1993),
       pp. 559–60.
30    Although over 50 per cent of convicts could read and write, considerably more
       than in England. See Richards, 'An Australian Map of British and Irish Literacy in
       1841', pp. 345–59.
31    *Sutton v Humphrey* (1806) CCJP, 2/8148.
32    *Sutton v Humphrey* (1806) CCJP, 2/8148.
33    *Sutton v Humphrey* (1806) CCJP, 2/8148.
34    *Sutton v Humphrey* (1806) CCJP, 2/8148.
35    See Alan Atkinson, *The Europeans in Australia, Vol. 1: The Beginning* (Oxford
       University Press, 1997), pp. 18, 124.
36    William Bligh, as cited in Atkinson, *The Europeans in Australia*, p. xi.
37    Karskens, *The Colony*, p. 184.
38    Byrne, *Criminal Law and Colonial Subject*, pp. 38–50.
39    Byrne, *Criminal Law and Colonial Subject*, p. 47.
40    Byrne, *Criminal Law and Colonial Subject*, p. 47; see also: Damousi, *Depraved and
       Disorderly*, pp. 65ff.
41    Adam Smith, *Lectures on Jurisprudence*, as cited in Steedman, *Master and Servant*, p. 22.
42    Linad K. Kerber, *No Constitutional Right to be Ladies: Women and the Obligations
       of Citizenship* (Hill and Wang, 1998), p. xxiii.
43    *Miller v Brett* SCNSW (1832), *SG*, 21 June 1832, p. 3.
44    Gregory L. Laing, 'Bound by Words: Oath-taking and Oath-breaking in Medieval
       Iceland and Anglo-Saxon England', PhD thesis, Western Michigan University,
       2014, pp. 1–21.
45    Penny Russell and Nigel Worden, 'Introduction', in Russell and Worden (eds),
       *Honourable Intentions? Violence and Virtue in Australian and Cape Colonies, c.
       1750–1850* (Routledge, 2016), p. 11.
46    *Sutton v Humphrey* (1806) CCJP, 1788–1814, 2/8148.
47    'Sydney', *SG*, 8 June 1806, p. 3.
48    *Sutton v Humphrey* (1806) CCJP, 2/8148.
49    'General Orders', *SG*, 27 April 1806, p. 4.
50    'General Orders', *SG*, 8 June 1806, p. 1.
51    *Sutton v Humphrey* (1806) CCJP, 2/8148.
52    Kercher, *Debt, Seduction*, p. 63.
53    CCJ, Series 2656, container 2/8148, SRNSW, pp. 644, 645.
54    See Kercher, *Debt, Seduction*, pp. 1–76.
55    William Blackstone, *Commentaries on the Laws of England in Four Books, Vol. 1*
       (J.B. Lippincott, 1753), p. 111.
56    *Cox v Payne* NSWSC (1825), *TA*, 19 May 1825; *Miller v Brett* NSWSC (1832), *TSH*,
       21 June 1832.
57    *Miller v Brett* NSWSC (1832), *TSH*, 21 June 1832, p. 2.
58    Baxter, *Musters of New South Wales*, PRO Reel 72.

59 Simmonds, 'The History of Non-Indigenous Marriage', pp 456–81; Hilary Golder and Diane Kirkby, 'Marriage and Divorce Law Before the *Family Law Act 1975*', in Kirkby (ed.), *Sex, Power and Justice: Historical Perspectives of Law in Australia* (Oxford University Press, 1995), pp. 150–67.

60 Catie Gilchrist, 'Male Convict Sexuality in the Penal Colonies of Australia, 1820–1850', PhD thesis, University of Sydney, 2004, p. 21.

61 Grimshaw et al., *Creating a Nation*, pp. 49ff; Grace Karskens, *People of the River: Lost Worlds of Early Australia* (Allen and Unwin, 2020), pp. 325–56.

62 Atkinson, 'Richard Atkins', p. 135.

63 A.G.L. Shaw, 'Philip Gidley King', *Australian Dictionary of Biography*.

64 King to Palmer, 12 August 1806, *HRNSW*, series 1, vol. VI, p. 162.

65 'Marsden's Female Muster, 1806', in Baxter, *Musters of New South Wales and Norfolk Island*.

66 Marsden, 'A Statement of the Married and Unmarried Women' in *Letter Received by Banks from William Bligh*, Banks Papers, SLNSW, 40.71.

67 E.M. Forster, *Howard's End* (Penguin, 2012), p. 246.

68 Kercher, *An Unruly Child*, pp. 50–51.

69 See: Ginger Frost, *Living in Sin: Cohabiting as Husband and Wife in Nineteenth-Century England* (Manchester University Press, 2008); Karskens, *People of the River*, pp. 325–56; Kercher, *An Unruly Child*, pp. 50–51.

70 Kercher, *An Unruly Child*, p. 49ff.

71 Although I could find no official correspondence referring to him as an exile, this categorisation makes sense given it was his decision to exile himself. I thank Grace Karskens for illuminating this.

72 Trial of William Sutton, July 1789, *Old Bailey Proceedings Online*, www. oldbaileyonline.org, t17890708-7; Collins, *An Account of the English Colony, Vol. 1*.

73 Arthur Penrhyn Stanley, *The Life and Correspondence of Thomas Arnold, Vol. II*, 4th edition (B. Fellowes, 1845), p. 48.

74 Karskens, *People of the River*, p. 356. Examining native-born women's marriages to former convicts, Karskens argues that 'their marriage choices and the support of their parents throw a very different light on the ideology of the 'convict stain' imported by English free settlers, the idea that convicts and their progeny were corrupting and untouchable. Such notions were countered by the many women and their families who welcomed convicts and ex-convicts into their intimate lives.' The case of *Sutton v Humphrey* provides a counterpoint.

75 Portia Robinson, *The Hatch and Brood of Time*, as cited in Karskens, *People of the River*, pp. 331, 355–56.

76 *Sutton v Humphrey* (1806) CCJP, 2/8148.

77 *Sutton v Humphrey* (1806) CCJP, 2/8148.

78 *Sutton v Humphrey* (1806); King, *Letter Books, Vol. 4*.

79 *Sutton v Humphrey* (1806); King, *Letter Books, Vol. 4*.

80 King, as cited in Kercher, *Debt, Seduction*, p. 12.

81 *Sutton v Humphrey* (1806); King, *Letter Books, Vol. 4*.

82 Kercher, *Debt, Seduction*, pp. 97–100.

83 Samuel Comyn, *A Treatise of the Law Relative to Contracts and Agreements Not Under Seal ... Vol. 2* (A. Strahan, 1807), p. 408.

84 'Classified Advertising', *SG*, 21 September 1806, p. 2; 'Advertising', *SG*, 28 January 1810, p. 2.

85 'Sydney', *SG*, 19 October 1806, p. 1.

86 J.L. Austin, *How to Do Things with Words* (Oxford University Press, 1962).

87 King to Hobart, 1 March 1804, Letter No.3, *HRA* Series 1, Vol IV, p. 483.

88 Byrne, *Criminal Law and Colonial Subject*, pp. 47ff.

89 Alan Atkinson, 'Convicts and Courtship', in Grimshaw et al. (eds), *Families in Colonial Australia* (Allen and Unwin, 1985), pp 27–29.

90 *Sutton v Humphrey* (1806) CCJP, 1788–1814, 2/8148.

91 Letter to Captain Murray the Commandant at Hobart Town from William Campbell on behalf of Governor Macquarie, *NSWCSP*, 27 June 1811, pp. 25–6.

92 Letter to Captain Murray the Commandant at Hobart Town from William Campbell on behalf of Governor Macquarie, 27 June 1811, *NSWCSP*, p. 25–6.

93 'Government and General Orders', 1 June 1812, *NSWCSP*, p. 298.

94 Macquarie to Bathurst, 28 April 1814, *HRA,* Series 1, Volume 8, p. 158.

95 Registrar General's Department, 36/01 1812/0120.

96 Stancombe, 'Adolarius William Henry Humphrey'.

97 Stancombe, 'Adolarius William Henry Humphrey'.

98 Lachlan Macquarie, 'Illicit Intercourse, Evils Arising Therefrom', NRS 1043, Colonial Secretary: Digest of Proclamations and General Orders, 1791–1821, SZ756, reel 6039 (25 February 1810), p. 579.

## 2. The Rules of Courtship and the Rise of Lawful Marriage (*Cox v Payne*, 1825)

1 *Cox v Payne* (1825) SRNSW, NRS 13471 [9/5198]. See: *Australian*, 19 May 1825, p. 4; *SG*, 19 May 1825, p. 3.

2 Letter from David Souter to Sarah Cox, *Cox v Payne* (1825) SRNSW, NRS 13471 [9/5198].

3 Descriptions of Sydney taken from: Karskens, *The Colony,* pp. 189–233; File 01 Colonial Box, Early Sydney (images) ON 609/Box 11/nos. 495-506; *Paintings from the Collections*, Room 1, Mitchell Library; perusing the *Sydney Gazette* for these years; Sarah Cox's house is from Carol Liston, *Sarah Wentworth: Mistress of Vaucluse* (Historic Houses Trust of NSW, 1988), p. 10.

4 *Cox v Payne* (1825) SRNSW NRS 13471 [9/5198].

5 *Cox v Payne* (1825) SCNSW, *Australian,* 19 May 1825, p. 4; *SG*, 19 May 1825, p. 3.

6 Liston, *Sarah Wentworth*, p. 23.

7 Lady Jane Franklin, cited in Liston, *Sarah Wentworth*, p. 119.

8 James McArthur, as cited in Liston, *Sarah Wentworth*, p. 129.

9 *Cox v Payne* (1825) SRNSW, NRS 13471 [9/5198].

10 *Cox v Payne* (1825) SRNSW NRS 13471 [9/5198].

11 W.M. Thackeray, *Vanity Fair* (Harper and Brothers, 1848).

12 *Cox v Payne* (1825) SRNSW, NRS 13471 [9/5198]. See: *Australian*, 19 May 1825, p. 4; *SG*, 19 May 1825, p. 3.

13 *Cox v Payne* (1825) SRNSW NRS 13471 [9/5198]. See: *Australian*, 19 May 1825, p. 4; *SG*, 19 May 1825, p. 3.

14 *Cox v Payne,* (1825) SCNSW, *Australian,* 19 May 1825, p. 3 *SG,* 19 May 1825, p. 4.

15 See Cochrane, *Colonial Ambition*, pp. 1-25; Michael Persse, 'William Charles Wentworth,' *Australian Dictionary of Biography*.

16 Kercher, *An Unruly Child*, pp. 94, 152.

17    *Cox v Payne* (1825) SRNSW, NRS 13471 [9/5198] See: *Australian*, 19 May 1825, p. 4;
      *SG*, 19 May 1825, p. 3.

18    Descriptions include: John Edwards, 'Robert Wardell', *Dictionary of Sydney*, 2013:
      *https://dictionaryofsydney.org/person/wardell_robert*; Frances Forbes as described
      in Kercher, *An Unruly Child*, p. 83; C.H. Currey, 'Sir Francis Forbes', *Australian
      Dictionary of Biography*; Bennett, *A History of the Supreme Court of New South
      Wales* (Law Book Company, 1974), p. 5.

19    Bennett, *A History of the Supreme Court of New South Wales*, p. 4.

20    Karskens, *The Colony*, p. 190.

21    Bennett, *A History of the Supreme Court of New South Wales*, p. 5.

22    *Cox v Payne,* (1825) SCNSW, *Australian*, 19 May 1825, p. 3; *SG*, 19 May 1825, p. 4.

23    Liston, *Sarah Wentworth*, pp. 7–13; Liston, 'The Damned Whore and the Public
      Man: Sarah and William Wentworth', in Penny Russell (ed.), *For Richer, for Poorer:
      Early Colonial Marriages* (Melbourne University Press, 1994), p. 116.

24    Persse, 'Willian Charles Wentworth'.

25    Macquarie, 'Illicit Intercourse, Evils Arising Therefrom'.

26    Grimshaw et al., *Creating a Nation*, pp. 49–50; Kercher, *An Unruly Child*,
      pp. 50–51; Golder and Kirkby, 'Marriage and Divorce Law', p. 152.

27    See: Frank Bongiorno, *The Sex Lives of Australians* (Black Inc., 2015), p. 10;
      Atkinson, 'Convicts and Courtship', p. 19.

28    Marian Aveling, 'Imagining New South Wales as a Gendered Society, 1783–
      1821', *Australian Historical Studies* 25:98 (1992), pp 10–11; Deborah Cohen,
      *Family Secrets: Shame and Privacy in Modern Britain* (Oxford University Press,
      2017), p. 45; Joan Landes, *Women and the Public Sphere in the Age of the French
      Revolution* (Cornell University Press, 1988), p. 2.

29    Karskens, *People of the River*, p. 325.

30    'Fashionables and Shewings Up', *Australian*, 12 May 1825, p. 3; 'Police Office', 5 May
      1825, p. 3; *Cox v Payne* (1825) SCNSW, *Australian*, 19 May 1825, p. 3; *SG*, 19 May
      1825, p. 4.

31    On the increasing moral rigidity at this time, see Bongiorno, *The Sex Lives of
      Australians*, p. 9.

32    See generally: Norma Basch, 'Marriage and Domestic Relations', in Michael
      Grossberg and Christopher Tomlins (eds), *The Cambridge History of Law in
      America* (Cambridge University Press, 2008), p. 247; Lawrence Stone, *The Family,
      Sex and Marriage in England, 1500–1800* (Penguin, 1979); for Australia, see
      Simmonds, 'The History of Non-Indigenous Marriage'; Grimshaw et al., *Creating
      a Nation*, pp. 49–50.

33    Russell, *For Richer, for Poorer*, pp. 1–10.

34    Edward Eyre, *Journals of Expeditions of Discovery into Central Australia ... Vol. 2*
      (Libraries Board of South Australia, 1962), p. 372.

35    *R v Maloney* (1836) NSWSC , *SH*, 15 February 1836, p. 2.

36    Eyre, *Journals*, p. 321.

37    Penny Russell, 'The Brash Colonial: Class and Comportment in Nineteenth-
      Century Australia', *Transactions of the Royal Historical Society* 12 (2002), pp. 431–53.

38    Penny Russell, *Savage or Civilised? Manners in Colonial Australia* (UNSW Press,
      2010); McKenzie, *Scandal in the Colonies*; Simmonds, 'Promises and Pie-Crusts
      Were Made to Be Broken', pp. 99–120.

39    Bongiorno, *The Sex Lives of Australians*, pp. 14–20.

40    McKenzie, *Scandal in the Colonies*, p. 50.

41    Russell, *Savage or Civilised?*; McKenzie, *Scandal in the Colonies*.

42    John Hirst, *Convict Society and Its Enemies* (Allen and Unwin, 1983), pp. 21–27.

43    Bongiorno, *The Sex Lives of Australians*, pp. 14–20.

44    J.D. Lang, as cited in Hilary Golder, *Divorce in Nineteenth-Century New South Wales* (UNSW Press, 1985), p. 26.

45    *Laurie v Beilby* (1837) NSWSC, *SG*, 21 March 1837, p. 3.

46    *Rule v Hick* (1836) NSWSC, *SH*, 29 September 1836, p. 2.

47    *Laurie v Beilby* (1837) NSWSC, *SG*, 21 March 1837, p. 3.

48    *Cox v Payne* (1825) SCNSW, *Australian*, 19 May 1825, p. 3; *SG*, 19 May 1825, p. 4.

49    Kercher, *An Unruly Child*, pp. 68, 84, 95.

50    *Cox v Payne* (1825) SCNSW, *Australian*, 19 May 1825, p. 3; *SG*, 19 May 1825, p. 4.

51    Liz Rushen, 'Marriage Options for Immigrant Women in Colonial Australia in the 1830s', *Journal of Australian Colonial History* 16 (2014), p. 111.

52    *Cox v Payne* (1825) SCNSW, *Australian*, 19 May 1825, p. 3; *SG*, 19 May 1825, p. 4.

53    Liston, *Sarah Wentworth*, pp. 16–19.

54    Liston, *Sarah Wentworth*, pp. 16–19.

55    Russell, 'The Brash Colonial', pp. 431–53.

56    Liston, 'The Damned Whore and the Public Man', pp. 114–15.

57    Penny Russell, *A Wish of Distinction: Colonial Gentility and Femininity* (Melbourne University Press, 1994).

58    Lady Jane Franklin, as cited in Liston, 'The Damned Whore and the Public Man', p. 121.

59    *SMH*, as cited in Liston, 'The Damned Whore and the Public Man', p. 125.

60    Letter from John Payne to Sarah Cox, February 1822, *Cox v Payne* (1825) SRNSW, NRS 13471 [9/5198].

61    *Miller v Brett* SCNSW (1832), *SG*, 21 June 1832, p. 3.

62    *Miller v Brett* SCNSW (1832) *SG*, 21 June 1832, p. 3.

63    Russell, *A Wish of Distinction*; Russell, *Savage or Civilised? Manners in Colonial Australia*; McKenzie, *Scandal in the Colonies*; McKenzie, *A Swindler's Progress*.

64    See Melanie Methot, *Much Married: Bigamy in Australia, 1816–1950s* (research project, 2023).

65    *Miller v Brett* SCNSW (1832), *SG*, 21 June 1832, p. 3.

66    Mary Reibey, as cited in Karskens, *The Colony*, p. 333.

67    *Hawthorn v Steel* (1833) TASSC, *SG*, 11 June 1833.

68    *Cox v Payne* (1825) SCNSW, *Australian*, 19 May 1825, p. 3; *SG*, 19 May 1825, p. 4.

69    J.L. Austin, *How to Do Things with Words* (J.L. Urstom, 1962).

70    See also McKenzie, 'Of Convicts and Capitalists', pp. 199–222.

71    *Cox v Payne* (1825) NSWSC, *SG*, 19 May 1825, p. 4.

72    *Fletcher v Headlam* (1883) TASSC, *NMH*, 13 April 1883, p. 2.

73    Jane Austen, *Northanger Abbey*.

74    Goodrich, 'Epistolary Justice', p. 252.

75    Ruas, Charles, 'An Interview with Michel Foucault', in *Death and the Labyrinth*, trans. C. Ruas (Althone Press, 1987), p. 182.

76    Lystra, *Searching the Heart*, p. 7.

77    Wentworth Family Letters, CY 702.

78    *Cox v Payne* (1825), NRS 13471 [9/5198].

79  Liston, *Sarah Wentworth*.

80  Eliza Wentworth, as cited in Liston, *Sarah Wentworth*, p. 45.

81  Liston, *Sarah Wentworth*, pp. 46–54.

82  *The Atlas* (14 November 1846) in Liston, *Sarah Wentworth*, p. 49.

83  Liston, *Sarah Wentworth*, p. 111.

84  Wentworth's Legal Letter Book, MLA 1440; Michael Persse, 'William Charles Wentworth'.

85  *The Australian*, September 1829, as cited in Liston, *Sarah Wentworth*, p. 21.

86  Australian Census, 1861, as cited first in Golder, *Divorce in Nineteenth-Century New South Wales*, p. 29.

87  *Stone v Macarthur* (1833) TASSC, *The Tasmanian*, 11 October 1833, p. 5.

88  *Wrathall v Kelsey* (1844) TASSC, *CT*, 17 September 1844, p. 2.

89  *Gorman v O'Neil* (1841) VICSC, *Port Philip Gazette*, 20 November 1841, p. 3.

90  Sarah Wentworth, letter dated 20 March 1872, Liston, *Sarah Wentworth*, p. 90.

## Part 2 – Geographies of Desire

1   I am indebted to the work of Morrison et al., 'Critical Geographies of Love as Spatial, Relational and Political', *Progress in Human Geography* 37:4, pp. 505–21; Yi-Fu Tuan, *Romantic Geography: In Search of the Sublime Landscape* (University of Wisconsin Press, 2014); Pamela Schirmeister, *The Consolations of Space*.

2   See Peter Ward, 'Courtship and Social Space in Nineteenth-Century English Canada', Canadian Historical Review 68:1 (1987), pp. 35–62; Lystra, *Searching the Heart*, p. 18; Russell, *A Wish of Distinction*, p. 133.

3   Beth Bailey, *From Front Porch to Back Seat: Courtship in Twentieth-Century America* (Johns Hopkins University Press, 1989), p. 21.

4   Frost, *Promises Broken*, p. 63.

## 3. Sex, Space and Gender in Victorian-era Romance: 1830–1880

1   Bennett, *A History of the Supreme Court*, p. 9; J.Rae (artist), 'Supreme Court and St James Church from Elizabeth St', 1842 (pictorial collection, Mitchell Library, NSW).

2   Figures estimated from Lord Alfred Stephen. See Bennett, *A History of the Supreme Court*, p. 10.

3   *Carrick v Russell* (1841) NSWSC, *SH*, 3 June 1841, p. 2. See also: *SG*, 3 June 1841, p. 2.

4   Thomas Hardy, *Tess of the D'Urbervilles* (Penguin, 2003), p. 91.

5   Lystra, *Searching the Heart*, p. 8.

6   Bailey, *From Front Porch to Back Seat*; in sociology see: Illouz, *Cold Intimacies* and Illouz, *Consuming the Romantic Utopia: Love and the Cultural Contradictions of Capitalism* (University of California Press, 1997).

7   *Carrick v Russell* (NSWSC) 1841, *SH*, 3 June 1841, p. 2.

8   Judith Walkowitz, *City of Dreadful Delight: Narratives of Sexual Danger in Late-Victorian London* (University of Chicago Press, 1992).

9   Katie Barclay, 'Mapping the Spaces of Seduction: Morality, Gender and the City in Early Nineteenth-Century Britain'; McKenzie, *Scandal in the Colonies*; Russell, *Civilised or Savage?*.

10  Hirst, *Convict Society and Its Enemies*, pp. 21–27; Bongiorno, *The Sex Lives of Australians*, pp. 14–20.

11  *Carrick v Russell* (NSWSC) 1841, *SH*, 3 June 1841, p. 2. See also: *SG*, 3 June 1841, p. 2.

12    Carole Pateman, *The Disorder of Women: Women, Love and the Social Iustice*, pp. 27–29.
13    Lystra, *Searching the Heart*, pp. 17, 126.
14    *Laurie v Beilby* (1837) NSWSC, *SG*, 21 March 1837, p. 3.
15    *De Brough v Spence* (1870) VICSC *Empire*, 19 August 1870, p. 2.
16    *Vagrancy Act NSW* (1835).
17    Raelene Frances, *Selling Sex: A Hidden History of Prostitution* (UNSW Press, 2007), pp. 10ff.
18    Frances, *Selling Sex*, p. 34.
19    *Ohlrich v Bromberg* (1881) QLDSC, *Telegraph*, 24 May 1881, p. 2.
20    *Higgins v Nicholls* (1898) NSWSC, *SMH*, 2 September 1898, p. 3.
21    Jill Julius Matthews, *Dance Hall and Picture Palace: Sydney's Romance with Modernity* (Currency Press, 2005).
22    Frances, *Selling Sex*, pp. 74–95 and 113–68. The *Vagrancy Act NSW* (1835) NSW included 'houses kept or purported to be kept for the reception lodgings or entertainment of travellers'.
23    *Carrick v Russell* (NSWSC) 1841, *SH*, Thursday 3 June 1841, p. 2. See also: *SG*, 3 June 1841, p. 2.
24    *De Brough v Spence* (1870) VICSC, *Empire*, 19 August 1870, p. 2
25    *Carrick v Russell* (1841) NSWSC, SH, 3 June 1841, p. 2. See also: SG, 3 June 1841, p. 2.
26    *Australian Etiquette*, p. 189.
27    *Laurie v Beilby* (1837) SCNSW, *SG*, 21 March 1837, p. 3.
28    *Australian Etiquette*, p. 200.
29    'The Ministry', *SG*, Monday 8 October 1827, p. 3.
30    *Galvin v Simson* (1875) VICSC *The Age*, 18 November 1875, p. 3.
31    *Titley v Moltine* (1875) VICSC, *Leader*, 6 November 1875, p. 21.
32    *Slattery v Maher* (1869) VICSC, *Bendigo Advertiser* 1869, p. 3.
33    *Steers v Pitches* (1857) VICSC, *OMA*, 13 August 1857, p. 3.
34    *Evans v Tuxford* (1855) SASC, *SAR*, 13 September 1855, p. 3.
35    *Heal v Mellersch* (1841) WASC, *Inquirer*, 20 April 1842, p. 3.
36    *Fowler v Bayliss* (1871) NSWSC, *GT*, August 1871, p. 3.
37    'Should Marriage Engagements Be Long', *BA*, 15 June 1869, p. 3.
38    Barclay, 'Mapping the Spaces of Seduction'.
39    *Carrick v Russell* (NSWSC) 1841, *SH*, Thursday 3 June 1841, p. 2. See also: *SG*, 3 June 1841, p. 2.
40    *Rule v Hick* (1836) NSWSC, *SM*, Saturday 1 October 1836, p. 2.
41    *Carrick v Russell* (NSWSC) 1841, *SH*, Thursday 3 June 1841.
42    See Koslofsky, *Evening's Empire*.
43    Karskens, *The Colony*, p. 213.
44    William Shakespeare, *The Tragedy of Romeo and Juliet*, Act III, Scene II.
45    *Wiltshire v Hart* (1871) VICSC, *Weekly Times* 10 June 1871, p. 14.
46    *Maunsell v Proctor* (1878) NSWSC, *ATCJ*, 18 May 1878, p. 14.
47    *Stewart v Byrnes* (1857) *SMH*, 12 October 1857, p. 2.
48    *Mahoney v Cunningham* (1861) *IM*, 15 November 1861, p. 2.
49    *Thomas v Size* (1865) *The Cornwall Chronicle*, 11 October 1865, p. 3; *Wiltshire v Hart* (1871) VICSC, *WT*, 10 June 1871, p. 14.
50    *Maunsell v Proctor* (1878) NSWSC, *ATCJ*, 18 May 1878, p. 14.

51  *Mahoney v Cunningham* (1861), *IM*, 15 November 1861, p. 2.
52  *Walsh v Steane* (1869) *BA*, 1 May 1869, p. 2.
53  *Barron v Gooch* (1869) *NA*, 17 September 1869, p. 3.
54  *Humphrey v Kelly* (1870) *The Herald*, 2 November 1870, p. 3.
55  See: *Stone v Macarthur* (1833) TASSC, *The Tasmanian*, 11 October 1833, p. 5;
    *Rule v Hick* (1836) NSWSC, *SM*, 1 October 1836, p. 2.
56  'Country Comments on Passing Events', *SMH*, 2 September 1857, p. 2.
57  Calder, *The Victorian Home*, pp. 9–11.
58  *Heals v Mellersch* (1841) WASC, *Inquirer*, 20 April 1842, p. 3.
59  See 'About the Whadjuk Region', : https://www.noongarculture.org.au/whadjuk.
60  See for example: *Rule v Hick* (1836) NSWSC, *SM*, Saturday 1 October 1836, p. 2
    and *Humphrey v Kelly* (1870) *The Herald*, 2 November 1870, p. 3.
61  *Walsh v Steane* (1869) *BA*, 1 May 1869, p. 2.
62  *Hood v Shorney* (1856) *AT*, 23 September 1856, p. 2.
63  *Wood v Lambswood* (1866) *AE*, 12 September 1866, p. 3.
64  *Ogden v Davenport* (1879) *MC*, 3 April 1879, p. 2.
65  Bailey, *From Front Porch to Back Seat*; Ward, 'Courtship and Social Space', pp. 35–62;
    (America) Lystra, *Searching the Heart*; (Britain) Leonore Davidoff, *The Best Circles*.
66  Holmes et al., *Reading the Garden*; Holmes, 'Gardens', pp. 152–62.
67  *Laurie v Beilby* SCNSW (1837), *SG*, 21 March 1837, 3.
68  Holmes et al., *Reading the Garden*, pp. 152–62.
69  As cited in Hoskins, 'The Core of the City', 7–24.
70  *Carrick v Russell* (NSWSC) 1841, *SH*, Thursday 3 June 1841, p. 2. See also: *SG*,
    3 June 1841, p. 2.
71  *Slattery v Maher* (1869) VICSC, *BA*, 1869, p. 3.
72  *Carrick v Russell* (NSWSC) 1841, *SH*, Thursday 3 June 1841, p. 2. See also: *SG*,
    3 June 1841, p. 2.
73  Alecia Simmonds, 'Gay Lotharios and Innocent Eves: Child Maintenance,
    Masculinities and the Action for Breach of Promise of Marriage in Colonial
    Australia', *Law in Context* 34:1 (2016), pp. 58–75.
74  *Fletcher v Headlam* (1883) TASSC, *LE*, 4 April 1883, p. 3.
75  Simmonds, 'Gay Lotharios', pp. 58–75.
76  *Carrick v Russell* (NSWSC) 1841, *SH*, Thursday 3 June 1841, p. 2. See also: *SG*,
    3 June 1841, p. 2.
77  *Field v Nelson* (1850) NSWSC, *Bell's Life*, 6 July 1850, p. 1.
78  John Caulfield, Jr and John Caulfield, 'Popping the Question', Enk Davidson, 1879.
79  'Popping the Question', *The Herald*, 30 December 1879, p. 3.
80  Sydney Smith, *Granby*, as cited in 'Popping the Question Properly',
    *The Queenslander*, 21 January 1871, p. 7.
81  'Popping the Question' *The Burrangong Argus*, 5 April 1882, p. 4.
82  'Popping the Question', *Queanbeyan Age*, 12 May 1875, p. 4.
83  *Australian Etiquette: Or the Rules and Usages of Best Society in the Australian
    Colonies* (J.M. Dent, 1886), p. 194.
84  'Popping the Question Properly', *The Queenslander*, 21 January 1871, p. 7.
85  'Popping the Question', *Queanbeyan Age*, 12 May 1875, p. 4.
86  'Popping the Question', *AENEGA*, 7 October 1871, p. 4.
87  *Australian Etiquette*, p. 194.

88  *Evans v Tuxford* (1855) SASC, *SAR,* 13 September 1855, p. 3.

89  *Le Vondare v Simpson* (1879) QLDSC, *DD,* 26 April 1879, p. 3.

90  *Byrne v Malcolm* (1889) NSWSC, *DT,* 15 March 1889, p. 3.

91  *Ohlrich v Bromberg* (1881) QLDSC, as cited in *The Telegraph,* 24 May 1881, p. 2.

92  *Wentworth v Thurgood* (1868) NSWSC, *Empire,* 10 November 1868, p. 3.

93  *Biggin v Grossert* (1863) SASC, *SAWC,* 16 May 1863, p. 2.

94  *Daniel v Bowes,* as cited in Chitty, *A Practical Treatise on the Law of Contracts,* 1872, pp. 158–59.

95  *Rule v Hick* (1836) NSWSC, *SM,* Saturday 1 October 1836, p. 2.

96  *Laurie v Beilby* SCNSW (1837) *SG,* 21 March 1837, 3.

97  *Laurie v Beilby* SCNSW (1837) *SG,* 21 March 1837, 3.

98  *Cameron v Muir* (1857) VICSC, *The Age,* 13 August 1857, p. 6.

99  *Le Vondare v Simpson* (1879) QLDSC, *DD,* 26 April 1879, p. 3.

100  *Belton v Macdonald* (1891) SASC, *Evening Journal,* 17 February 1891, p. 4.

101  *Australian Etiquette,* p. 198.

102  *Heals v Mellersch* (1841) WASC, *Inquirer,* 20 April 1842, p. 3.

103  *Maunsell v Proctor* (1878) NSWSC, *ATCJ,* 18 May 1878, p. 14.

104  *Field v Nelson* (1850) NSWSC, *Bell's Life,* 6 July 1850, p. 1.

105  *Barron v Gooch* (1869), *Northern Argus,* 17 September 1869, p. 3.

106  *Kelly v Butler* (1875), *The South Australian Advertiser,* 23 April 1875, p. 2.

107  *Belton v Macdonald* (1891) SASC, *Evening Journal,* 17 February 1891, p. 4.

108  *Miller v Brett* (1832) as cited in *SG,* 21 June 1832, p. 3.

109  *Maunsell v Cassius* (1872) VICSC, as cited in *The Age,* 19 March 1872, p. 3.

110  *Wiltshire v Hart* (1871) VICSC, as cited in *WT,* 10 June 1871, p. 14; *Rule v Hick* (1836) NSWSC, *SM,* Saturday 1 October 1836, p. 2; *Stewart v Duggan* (1890) NSWSC, *NMH,* 15 April 1890, p. 7.

111  Penny Russell, 'Honour, Morality and Sexuality in Nineteenth-Century Sydney', in P. Russell and N. Worden (eds), *Honourable Intentions,* pp. 202–218.

112  *Carrick v Russell* (NSWSC) 1841, *SH,* Thursday 3 June 1841, p. 2.

## 4. The Place of Love in a Settler Colony (*Hawthorn v Steel,* 1833)

1  *Hawthorn v Steel* (1833) TASSC, *Austral-Asiatic Review,* 14 May 1833, p. 3 (As no Tasmanian judgment papers survive for May 1833, I have used the following newspaper reports. See 'Tasmania Court Records, 1830-1845' Call Number: MLMSS 4476X, ML. For newspapers, see: *HTC,* 14 May 1833, p. 2, *CT,* 14 May 1833, p. 3 and *SG,* Tuesday 11 June 1833, p. 4. There was no relevant discrepancy between the reports).

2  *Hawthorn v Steel* (1833) TASSC, *CT,* 14 May 1833, p. 3.

3  Louisa Anne Meredith, *My Home in Tasmania, During a Residence of Nine Years* (John Murray, 1852), chapter 2. See: Gutenberg.net.au.

4  I have used a number of sources to reconstruct this image including Meredith, *My Home in Tasmania*; J. Feldheim, *Tasmania Old and New, 1804–1914* (J. Feldheim, 1914); David Burn, *A Picture of Van Diemen's Land* (Cat and Fiddle Press, 1973); the paintings of Mary Morton Allport (1806–1895) http://stors.tas.gov.au; James Boyce, *Van Diemen's Land: A History* (Black Inc., 2008), p. 156.

5  *Hawthorn v Steel* (1833) TASSC, *SG,* 11 June 1833, p. 4.

6  *Hawthorn v Steel* (1833) TASSC, *SG,* 11 June 1833, p. 4.

7  Henry Savery, *The Hermit in Van Diemen's Land: From the Colonial Times* (Andrew Bent, 1829), p. 147.

8    Steel Family Papers, 9 February 1833, Item: 1981.0134.00008.

9    *Hawthorn v Steel* (1833) TASSC, *SG*, 11 June 1833, p. 4.

10   Boyce, *Van Diemen's Land*, p. 1.

11   Russell and Worden, 'Introduction', in *Honourable Intentions*, p. 9.

12   Sigmund Freud, *The Antithetical Meaning of Primal Words*, trans. James Strachey (The Hogarth Press, 1957).

13   Jacqueline Rose, 'Pointing the Finger: On Camus' *The Plague*', *London Review of Books* 42:7 (May 2020).

14   Steel Family Papers, 15 January 1830, Item: 1981.0134.00008.

15   Steel Family Papers, 10 May 1829, Item: 1981.0134.00008.

16   Steel Family Papers, 10 May 1829, Item: 1981.0134.00008.

17   Steel Family Papers, 10 May 1829, Item: 1981.0134.00008.

18   Steel Family Papers, 15 May 1830, Item: 1981.0134.00008.

19   Steel Family Papers, 15 May 1830, Item: 1981.0134.00008.

20   *Hawthorn v Steel* (1833) TASSC, *SG*, 11 June 1833, p. 4.

21   Gwyneth and Hume Dow, *Landfall in Van Diemen's Land: The Steels' Quest for Greener Pastures* (Footprint, 1990), p. 6.

22   Dow, *Landfall in Van Diemen's Land*, pp. 1–25.

23   Kirsten Mackenzie, *A Swindler's Progress: Nobles and Convicts in the Age of Liberty* (Harvard University Press, 2010), pp. 181–99.

24   Mackenzie, *A Swindler's Progress*, pp. 194–96.

25   Mackenzie, *A Swindler's Progress*, p. 196.

26   To be precise he arrived with 10,000 dineros, each worth 5 shillings, and he made up the full £30,000 with the help of a loan of £300 from his sister Jane. See: Dow, *Landfall in Van Diemen's Land*, p. 12.

27   Lord Bathurst to Lieutenant-Governor Sorell, 31 March 1823, TAS CSO, 1/114/2839.

28   Deeds of Land Grants, 1804–1935, for Michael Steel, Tasmania, Land and Surveys Department, 354/1/6 – Land and Surveys Department 354/1/8.

29   Michael Steel to surveyor-general, 26 July 1826, TAS Land and Surveys Department, 1/111/131-3 .

30   Steel Family Papers, December 1830, Item: 1981.0134.00008.

31   Steel Family Papers, 21 February 1827, Item: 1981.0134.00008.

32   Stuart Macintyre, *A Concise History of Australia* (Cambridge University Press, 2020), p. 58.

33   Ann McGrath, *Illicit Love: Interracial Sex and Marriage in the United States and Australia* (University of Nebraska Press, 2015), p. 3. This argument was first made by Patrick Wolfe, 'Settler Colonialism and the Elimination of the Native', *Journal of Genocide Research* 8:4 (2006), pp. 387–409.

34   Boyce, *Van Diemen's Land*, pp. 155, 188.

35   Boyce, *Van Diemen's Land*, pp. 6–10.

36   Boyce, *Van Diemen's Land*, pp. 10, 186.

37   *Steel Family Papers*, 20 February 1830, Item: 1981.0134.0000.

38   Deeds of Land Grants, 1804–1935, for Michael Steel, Tasmania, Land and Surveys Department, 354/1/6 – Land and Surveys Department, 354/1/8.

39   This was a petition to the lieutenant-governor of Van Diemen's Land against quit rents (a feudal land tax) that Michael and 31 other landed proprietors signed and published in the *Hobart Town Courier*, 1 June 1832, p. 1.

40   John Ruskin, 'Lecture II: Lilies: Of Queens' Gardens', in *Sesame and Lilies* (George Allen, 1894).

41   Nicole Graham, 'Owning the Earth', in *Exploring Wild Law: The Philosophy of Earth Jurisprudence* (Wakefield Press, 2011), pp. 259–70.

42   Graham, 'Owning the Earth', p. 265.

43   Steel Family Papers, 10 May 1829, Item: 1981.0134.00008.

44   Steel Family Papers, 12 April 1830, Item: 1981.0134.00008.

45   Russell, 'Introduction', in *For Richer, for Poorer*, p. 9.

46   Steel Family Papers, 31 December 1830, Item: 1981.0134.00008.

47   Steel Family Papers, 31 December 1830, Item: 1981.0134.00008.

48   Steel Family Papers, 20 February 1830, Item: 1981.0134.00007.

49   Ryan, *The Aboriginal Tasmanians*.

50   *Hawthorn v Steel* (1833) TASSC, *HTC*, 14 May 1833, p. 2.

51   *Hawthorn v Steel* (1833) TASSC, *HTC*, May 1833, p. 2.

52   *Hawthorn v Steel* (1833) TASSC, *Colonist*, 21 May 1833, p. 3.

53   Jane Austen, *Northanger Abbey* (Little, 2007), p. 203.

54   Atkinson, 'Honour, Information and Religion', in Russell and Worden (eds), *Honourable Intentions*, p. 82.

55   Judith Carter and Don Bradmore, 'The Hawthorn Family', *Ancestry* 36:2 (2015) 99–106.

56   For the history of the Cramer family in Ireland, see: Julian Lyon, 'Coghills and Cramers', at *Wynch, Lyon, Coghill and Others*, http://gen.julianlyon.com, 2018; and 'Jane Cramer of Tipperary (1626)' at *The King's Candlesticks*, http://thekingscandlesticks.com/web/pedigrees/1626.html.

57   As above.

58   H.R. Thomas, 'Jocelyn Henry Connor Thomas', *Australian Dictionary of Biography*.

59   Tasmanian Pioneer Index (TPI): marriage, Torlesse-Hawthorn: 1362/1829/36, Hamilton.

60   'Shipping News: Yare' *CT*, 19 October 1831, p. 2.

61   Torlesse Family, 'Rathmore', at *The King's Candlesticks*, http://www.thekingscandlesticks.com/webs/pedigrees/1626.html.

62   Information sourced from the Tasmanian Aboriginal Centre, http://tacinc.com.au.

63   *Hawthorn v Steel* (1833) TASSC, *SG*, 11 June 1833, p. 4.

64   *Hawthorn v Steel* (1833) TASSC, *SG*, 11 June 1833, p. 4.

65   'Photograph – Supreme Court and Post Office 1838', NS1013/1/1670.

66   *Hawthorn v Steel* (1833) TASSC, *HTC*, 17 May 1833, p. 2.

67   *Hawthorn v Steel* (1833) TASSC, *HTC*, 14 May 1833, p. 2.

68   P.C. James, 'Joseph Tice Gellibrand', *Australian Dictionary of Biography*.

69   *Hawthorn v Steel* (1833) TASSC, *SG*, 11 June 1833, p. 4.

70   *Hawthorn v Steel* (1833) TASSC, *CT*, 14 May 1833, p. 3.

71   *Hawthorn v Steel* (1833) TASSC, *The Colonist*, 21 May 1833.

72   See: *SG*, 11 June 1833, p. 4; *Austral-Asiatic Review*, 14 May 1833, p. 3; *HTC*, 17 May 1833, p. 2; *The Colonist*, 21 May 1833, p. 3; *Launceston Advertiser*, 16 May 1833, p. 2; *CT*, 14 May 1833, pp. 2–3.

73   Addison, *Treatise on the Law of Contracts*, p. 579.

74   *Cork v Baker* 1 Str 33 as per Hold CJ. Cited in Addison, *Treatise on the Law of Contracts*, p. 578.

75  Addison, *Treatise on the Law of Contracts*, p. 579.
76  Kiera Lindsay, '"So Much Recklessness": Abduction in the Colony of New South Wales', *Australian Historical Studies* 44:3 (2013), pp. 438–56.
77  *Hawthorn v Steel* (1833) TASSC, *SG*, 11 June 1833, p. 4.
78  Poovey, *Uneven Developments: The Ideological Work of Gender in Mid-Victorian England* (University of Chicago Press, 1988), p. 32, cited in Russell, *A Wish of Distinction*, p. 92.
79  See Alecia Simmonds, 'Rebellious Bodies and Subversive Sniggers? Embodying Women's Humour and Laughter in Colonial Australia', *History Australia* 6:2 (2009).
80  *Hawthorn v Steel* (1833) TASSC, *SG*, 11 June 1833, p. 4.
81  *Hawthorn v Steel* (1833) TASSC, *SG*, Tuesday 11 June 1833, p. 4.
82  On the relationship between honour and feeling, see: Atkinson, 'Honour, Information and Religion', pp. 93–107.
83  Chitty, *A Practical Treatise on the Law of Contracts*, 1834, p. 426; See for example *Laurie v Beilby* SCNSW (1837), *SG*, 21 March 1837, p. 3.
84  *Cork v Baker* 1 Str 33 as per Hold CJ. Cited in Addison, *Treatise on the Law of Contracts*, p. 578.
85  *Hawthorn v Steel* (1833) TASSC, *HTC*, 14 May 1833, p. 2.
86  Steel Family Papers, 9 February 1833, Item: 1981.0134.00008.
87  Steel Family Papers, 30 January 1834, Item: 1981.0134.00008.
88  Dow, *Landfall in Van Diemen's Land*, p. 97.
89  Dow, *Landfall in Van Diemen's Land*, pp. 151–52.
90  Penny Russell, 'Honour, Morality and Sexuality in Nineteenth-Century Sydney', pp. 202–18.
91  Sarah Hawthorn and George F. Huston, *Registry of Births, Deaths and Marriages*: Reg No: 3003/1835/36, New Norfolk.
92  Carter and Bradmore, 'The Hawthorn Family in Van Diemen's Land', *Ancestry* 36:2 (2015), pp. 99–103.
93  James Boyce, *Van Diemen's Land*, p. 198.
94  James Boyce, *Van Diemen's Land*, p. 198.

## 5. Sexual Reputation and Global Mobility (*Stewart v Byrnes*, 1857)

1   *Stewart v Wise and Wife* (1857) NSWSC, *SMH*, 12 October 1857, p. 2.
2   *Stewart v Wise and Wife* (1857) NSWSC, *SMH*, 12 October 1857, p. 2.
3   *Stewart v Byrnes* (1857) NSWSC, *SMH*, 12 October 1857, p. 5.
4   *Stewart v Byrnes* (1858) NSWSC. This is noted in the archival documents for Byrnes' appeal decision. SRNSW, NRS 13472-1 [9/5759] 4/1858, 41-148, no.121.
5   *Stewart v Wise and Wife* (1857) NSWSC, *SMH*, 12 October 1857, p. 2.
6   *Stewart v Wise and Wife* (1857) NSWSC, *SMH*, 12 October 1857, p. 2; *Stewart v Byrnes* (1857) *SMH*, 12 October 1857, p. 5. Note that I have based my description of what parts were read aloud on the evidence given by Ellen, Henry and Ellen's mother in both cases.
7   *Stewart v Byrnes* (1857) NSWSC, *SMH*, 12 October 1857, p. 5.
8   *Stewart v Byrnes* (1857) NSWSC *SMH*, 12 October 1857, p. 5.
9   'Scandal', *BFP*, 7 October 1857, p. 2; 'Scandal', *Empire*, 13 October 1857, p. 2.
10  *Stewart v Byrnes* (1857) NSWSC, *SMH*, 12 October 1857, p. 5.
11  *Stewart v Wise and Wife* (1857) NSWSC, *SMH*, 12 October 1857, p. 2.

12   This distinction was made in Australia and Britain. For Australia see:
     Gwenda Jones, 'A Lady in Every Sense of the Word: A Study of the Governess
     in Australian Colonial Society', PhD Thesis, University of Melbourne, 1982,
     pp 37–43; Kate Matthew, 'Governesses', *Sydney Journal* 3:2 (2011), pp. 17–25; Kate
     Matthew, 'The Female Middle-class Emigration Society Governesses in Australia:
     A Failed Vision?', *Journal of Australian Colonial History* 14 (2012), pp. 107–130;
     Patricia Clarke, *The Governesses: Letters from the Colonies, 1862–82* (Vintage,
     1985). For Britain, see Mary Poovey, 'The Anathematized Race: The Governess
     and *Jane Eyre*', in *Uneven Developments*, pp. 126–63.

13   Charlotte Bronte, *Jane Eyre* (Oxford University Press, 2008); Thackeray,
     *Vanity Fair.*

14   Jones, 'A Lady in Every Sense of the Word', p. 31.

15   There is much on this theme. See: (British world) Kirsten McKenzie, *Imperial
     Underworld: An Escaped Convict and the Transformation of the British Colonial Order*
     (Cambridge University Press, 2016); Tony Ballantyne and Antoinette Burton (eds),
     *Moving Subjects: Gender, Mobility and Intimacy in an Age of Global Empire* (University
     of Illinois Press, 2009); Alan Lester, 'Imperial Circuits and Networks: Geographies
     of the British Empire, *History Compass* 4:1 (2006), pp. 124–41; Jennine Hurl-Eamon,
     'The Westminster Impostors: Impersonating Law Enforcement in Early Eighteenth-
     Century London', *Eighteenth-Century Studies* 38:3 (Spring 2005), pp. 461–83; Deacon
     et al., *Transnational Lives: Biographies of Global Modernity* (Palgrave Macmillan, 2010);
     (Indian Ocean) Clare Anderson, 'Multiple Border Crossings: "Convicts and Other
     Persons Escaped from Botany Bay and Residing in Calcutta"', *Journal of Australian
     Colonial History* 3:2 (2001); (Atlantic) Thomas Kidd, 'Passing as a Pastor: Clerical
     Imposture in the Colonial Atlantic World', *Religion and American Culture* 14:2 (Summer
     2004), pp. 149–74; Steven C. Bullock, 'A Mumper among the Gentle: Tom Bell, Colonial
     Confidence Man', *The William and Mary Quarterly* 55:2 (April 1998), p. 233.

16   See: Penny Russell, 'The Brash Colonial: Class and Comportment in Nineteenth-
     Century Australia', *Transactions of the Royal Historical Society* 12 (2002),
     pp. 431–53; Russell, *Savage or Civilised?*; Russell, *A Wish of Distinction*; McKenzie,
     *Scandal in the Colonies.*

17   Graeme Davison, 'The Dimensions of Mobility in Nineteenth-Century Australia',
     *Historical Studies* 2 (1979), pp. 10–12.

18   Dallas, Stewart and Steel Family Papers 1280–1963 MLMSS 1218/1.

19   Alexis de Tocqueville to the Chamber of Deputies in 1848. Cited in Eric
     Hobsbawm, *Age of Revolution: 1789–1848* (Hachette, 2010), pp. 7–27.

20   Dallas, Stewart and Steel Family Papers 1280–1963 MLMSS 1218/1.

21   Dallas, Stewart and Steel Family Papers 1280–1963 MLMSS 1218/1.

22   Dallas, Stewart and Steel Family Papers 1280–1963 MLMSS 1218/1.

23   Dallas, Stewart and Steel Family Papers 1280–1963 MLMSS 1218/1.

24   Dallas, Stewart and Steel Family Papers 1280–1963 MLMSS 1218/1 (author's
     translation).

25   Julia Gertrude Stewart, 'Lady's Treachery: The Sad Tale of Two Women's Destinies
     in the Colony of New South Wales', in Dallas, Stewart and Steel Family Papers
     1280–1963 MLMSS 1218/1.

26   Letter from Mrs Pinnock to Julia Gertrude Stewart 1849, Dallas, Stewart and Steel
     Family Papers 1280–1963 MLMSS 1218/1.

27  Poovey, 'The Anathematized Race', pp. 127–140.

28  Stewart, 'Lady's Treachery' in Dallas, Stewart and Steel Family Papers 1280–1963 MLMSS 1218/1.

29  'Shipping News', *The Argus*, 13 May 1850, p. 4.

30  Stewart, 'Lady's Treachery', in Dallas, Stewart and Steel Family Papers 1280–1963 MLMSS 1218/1.

31  See E. Windschuttle, *Ladies' Seminaries and Academies, Day and Boarding or Both* (1806–45), pp. 129-32.

32  Stewart, 'Lady's Treachery', in Dallas, Stewart and Steel Family Papers 1280–1963 MLMSS 1218/1.

33  Russell, *A Wish of Distinction*, pp. 7–11.

34  Stewart, 'Lady's Treachery', in Dallas, Stewart and Steel Family Papers 1280–1963 MLMSS 1218/1.

35  A.E. Bristow, Letter to her sister, Mrs Sarah Docker, 1 July 1856, Docker Papers, La Trobe Library.

36  Poovey, 'The Anathematized Race', pp. 127–35.

37  'Letters to my daughter, aged fifteen, on all the subjects calculated to influence the character and fate of a young women, from circumstances obliged early in life to quit the maternal guidance and protection and, in the "Halls of the Stranger" gain a scanty pittance as "The Governess!!" Dallas, Stewart and Steel Family Papers 1280–1963 MLMSS 1218/1.

38  Bronte, *Jane Eyre*, p. 5.

39  Poovey, 'The Anathematized Race', pp. 126–63.

40  Poovey, 'The Anathematized Race', p. 129.

41  Julia Gertrude Stewart, 'Passages in the Life of a Finishing Governess', Dallas, Stewart and Steel Family Papers 1280–1963 MLMSS 1218/1.

42  Stewart, 'Letters to my daughter', Dallas, Stewart and Steel Family Papers 1280–1963 MLMSS 1218/1.

43  *Stewart v Wise and Wife* (1857) NSWSC, *SMH*, 12 October 1857, p. 2.

44  'Law, Supreme Court Sitting in Banco', *SMH*, 8 September 1858, p. 2.

45  Jessica Lake, 'Whores Aboard and Laws Abroad: Reputation in Colonial New South Wales and the Global Slander of Women Movement', *Gender and History* (2022); for the New South Wales legislation, see *An Act to Amend the Law Respecting Defamatory Words and Libel* (1847), *New South Wales Government Gazette*, August 1847 (issue 74), p. 35.

46  *Stewart v Wise and Wife* (1857) NSWSC, *SMH*, 12 October 1857, p. 2.

47  *Stewart v Wise and Wife* (1857) NSWSC, *SMH*, 12 October 1857, p. 2.

48  *Stewart v Byrnes* (1857) NSWSC, *SMH*, October 1857, p. 5.

49  *Stewart v Wise and Wife* (1857) NSWSC, *SMH*. 12 October 1857, p. 2.

50  *Stewart v Byrnes* (1857) *SMH*, NSWSC, 12 October 1857, p. 5.

51  As cited in: Martha Rutledge, 'William Bede Dalley', *Australian Dictionary of Biography*.

52  Martha Rutledge, 'Sir Alfred Stephen', *Australian Dictionary of Biography*.

53  J.A. Ryan, 'Edward Wise', *Australian Dictionary of Biography*.

54  H.T.E. Holt, 'Arthur Todd Holroyd', *Australian Dictionary of Biography*. The *SMH* (12 October 1857) also lists Mr Stephen as an assisting barrister, although he never speaks or plays any role in the hearing. Mr Stephen was most likely his son, Matthew Henry.

55  *Stewart v Wise and Wife* (1857) NSWSC, *SMH*, 12 October 1857, p. 2; *Stewart v Byrnes* (1857) NSWSC, *SMH*, 12 October 1857, p. 5.

56  'Obituary', *Guardian Newspaper*, 21 June 1889, p. 5.

57  *Stewart v Wise and Wife* (1857) NSWSC, *SMH*, 12 October 1857, p. 2.

58  *Stewart v Wise and Wife* (1857) NSWSC, *SMH*, 12 October 1857, p. 2.

59  See: Jones, *A Lady in Every Sense of the Word*, pp 37–43; Matthew, 'Governesses'.

60  *Stewart v Wise and Wife* (1857) NSWSC, *SMH*, 12 October 1857, p. 2.

61  Poovey, 'The Anathematized Race', pp. 126–163.

62  Grimshaw et al., *Creating a Nation*, p. 116.

63  *Stewart v Wise and Wife* (1857) NSWSC, *SMH*, 12 October 1857, p. 2; *Stewart v Byrnes* (1857) NSWSC, *SMH*, 12 October 1857, p. 5.

64  Stewart, 'Lady's Treachery', Dallas, Stewart and Steel Family Papers 1280–1963 MLMSS 1218/1.

65  *Stewart v Byrnes* (1857) NSWSC, *SMH*, 12 October 1857, p. 5.

66  *Stewart v Byrnes* (1857) NSWSC, *SMH*, 12 October 1857, p. 5. Ellen and Henry's letters were read out in court and republished in the newspapers. The originals of Henry's (but not Ellen's) letters survive in the State Records Office of New South Wales: see SRNSW, NRS 13472-1 [9/5759] 4/1858, 41-148, no.121.

67  *Stewart v Byrnes* (1857) NSWSC, *SMH*, 12 October 1857, p. 5.

68  SRNSW, NRS 13472-1 [9/5759] 4/1858, 41-148, no. 121; *Stewart v Byrnes* (1857) NSWSC, *SMH*, 12 October 1857, p. 5.

69  *Stewart v Wise and Wife* (1857) NSWSC, *SMH*, 12 October 1857, p. 2.

70  *Stewart v Byrnes* (1857) *SMH*, NSWSC, 12 October 1857, p. 5.

71  *Stewart v Wise and Wife* (1857) NSWSC, *SMH*, 12 October 1857, p. 2.

72  *Stewart v Wise and Wife* (1857) NSWSC, *SMH*, 12 October 1857, p. 2.

73  *Stewart v Byrnes* (1857) NSWSC, *SMH*, 12 October 1857, p. 5.

74  For newspaper speculation, see: 'Sydney News', *MM*, 15 October 1857, p. 2; quote from Dalley, see: *Stewart v Byrnes* (1857), *SMH*, 12 October 1857, p. 5.

75  *Stewart v Wise and Wife* (1857) NSWSC, *SMH*, 12 October 1857, p. 2; *Stewart v Byrnes* (1857) *SMH*, 12 October 1857, p. 5.

76  Stewart, 'Lady's Treachery', Dallas, Stewart and Steel Family Papers 1280–1963 MLMSS 1218/1.

77  *Stewart v Wise and Wife* (1857) NSWSC, *SMH*, 12 October 185, p. 2.

78  Rutledge, 'Sir Alfred Stephen'.

79  On the disentanglement of manners from morals see Russell, *Savage or Civilised?* pp. 114–22.

80  Mary Elizabeth Braddon, *Lady Audley's Secret* (Oxford University Press, 1997); Louisa May Alcott, 'Behind a Mask; Or a Woman's Power', in *Behind a Mask: The Unknown Thrillers of Louisa May Alcott*, ed. Madeline Stern (Quill, 1984).

81  *Stewart v Byrnes* (1857) *SMH*, NSWSC, 12 October 1857, p. 5.

82  *Stewart v Byrnes* (1857) *SMH*, NSWSC, 12 October 1857, p. 5.

83  *Stewart v Byrnes* (1857) *SMH*, NSWSC, 12 October 1857, p. 5.

84  Giddens refers to women in this period as 'specialists of the heart'. See: Giddens, *The Transformation of Intimacy*, pp. 37–48. See also Francesca M. Cancian, *Love in America: Gender and Self-Development* (Cambridge University Press, 1990), p. 5.

85  See Anthony Giddens, *Transformation of Intimacy: Sexuality, Love and Eroticism* (Polity, 1992), pp. 37–48.

86    From the character Seth Pecksniff in Charles Dickens' *Martin Chuzzlewit*, whose meddlesome, insincere behaviour made the name Pecksniff associated with hypocrisy.

87    *Stewart v Wise and Wife* (1857) NSWSC, *SMH*, 12 October 1857, p. 2.

88    *Stewart v Byrnes* (1857) NSWSC, *SMH*, October 1857, p. 5; *Stewart v Byrnes*, SRNSW, NRS 13472-1 [9/5759] 4/1858, 41-148, no. 121.

89    Dallas, Stewart and Steel Family Papers 1280–1963 MLMSS 1218/1.

90    Michael W. Mosley, 'Stewart Castle Estate', *A Tour of Jamaica's Great Houses*, 2015, https://thelastgreatgreathouseblog.wordpress.com.

91    Patents, no. 26, p. 70, James Stewart, Entry 17 January 1754, Dallas, Stewart and Steel Family Papers 1280–1963 MLMSS 1218/1.

92    See: Christer Petley, *Slaveholders in Jamaica: Colonial Society and Culture During the Era of Abolition* (Routledge, 2015); Lesley Charles, *A New History of Jamaica* (Cambridge University Press, 2015).

93    Dallas, Stewart and Steel Family Papers 1280–1963 MLMSS 1218/1.

94    London, England, Church of England Baptisms, Marriages and Burials, 1538–1812, p. 330.

95    Deed of Mortgage of Stewart Castle, 23 September 1797, number 441, folio 213, Island Records Office.

96    Stewart, 'Lady's Treachery', in Dallas, Stewart and Steel Family Papers 1280–1963 MLMSS 1218/1.

97    Mosley, 'Stewart Castle Estate'.

98    *Royal Gazette*, August 2–9 1828; Dallas, Stewart and Steel Family Papers 1280–1963 MLMSS 1218/1.

99    'Pledge to WA Steel of Rockley', in Dallas, Stewart and Steel Family Papers 1280–1963 MLMSS 1218/1.

100   Anonymous, *Portrait von John Oliphant Murray*, cited at http://www.artnet.com; see also John Oliphant Murray, *The Peerage: A Genealogical Survey of the Peerage of Britain*, https://www.thepeerage.com/p3039.htm.

101   'Pledge to WA Steel of Rockley', in Dallas, Stewart and Steel Family Papers 1280–1963 MLMSS 1218/1.

102   Gertrude Marion Cardew in Dallas, Stewart and Steel Family Papers 1280–1963 MLMSS 1218/1.

103   'Passages in the Life', Dallas, Stewart and Steel Family Papers 1280–1963 MLMSS 1218/1.

104   Stewart, 'Lady's Treachery', Stewart and Steel Family Papers 1280–1963 MLMSS 1218/1.

105   'Legacies of British Slavery', University College London, http://www.ucl.ac.uk.

106   *Stewart v Byrnes* (1857) NSWSC, *SMH*, 12 October 1857.

107   Marsh, *Diaries*, Society for Australian Genealogists 02/000302.

108   Dallas, Stewart and Steel Family Papers 1280–1963 MLMSS 1218/1 and 2.

109   Dallas, Stewart and Steel Family Papers 1280–1963 MLMSS 1218/1 and 2.

110   Dallas, Stewart and Steel Family Papers 1280–1963 MLMSS 1218/1 and 2.

111   *Stewart v Byrnes* (1857) NSWSC, *SMH*, October 1857.

112   *Marriage Act 1855* (NSW). Note that Lord Hardwicke's *Marriage Act*, which demanded ceremony, did not apply in the colonies. See: *An Act for the Better Preventing of Clandestine Marriage 1753*, 26 Geo II, c. 33 ('Lord Hardwicke's Marriage Act').

113 *The Peerage: A Genealogical Survey of the Peerage of Britain*, https://www.the peerage.com/p3039.htm.

114 UK, Foreign and Overseas Registers of British Subjects, 1627–1965, Ellen Janet Mary, baptised 31 October 1837. p. 134.

115 Dallas, Stewart and Steel Family Papers 1280–1963 MLMSS 1218/1 and 2. Elizabeth Steele is described as a 'free quadroon' on *Ancestry*. 'Free quadroons', as James Stewart explained in his book *A View of the Past and Present State of the Island of Jamaica*, were the offspring of a 'white and a mulatto' (a mulatto was the 'offspring of a white and a black').

116 *Machon v Holt* cited in *Selden's Society Year Books*, p. 26.

117 'Rockley Historic Walking Tour' cited at https://www.bathurstregion.com.au/app/uploads/2020/07/UPDATE-Rockley-village.pdf.

118 'In Insolvency', *Government Gazette Private Notices – New South Wales Government Gazette* (Sydney: 1832–1900), 18 October 1859, p. 2290; *Empire*, 13 October 1859, p. 6. Note that Henry Byrnes also filed for insolvency earlier that year, to avoid paying for the breach of promise action. *SMH*, 7 May 1859, p. 5.

119 'Ellen Jane Marion Stewart', Insolvency Schedule, SRNSW, NRS 13654-1-(2/8981)-4636.

120 'Family Notices', *Empire*, 25 February 1860, p. 10.

121 Dallas, Stewart and Steel Family Papers *1280–1963* MLMSS 1218/2.

122 'Tapestry Samples by Julia Gertrude Stewart', Object Number A8825. See: https://collection.maas.museum/object/200167.

123 I would like to thank Kim Bagot at the Bathurst Archives for her expertise.

124 A variation on this argument has also been made by critics of the transnational turn. See: Matthew Pratt Guterl, 'Comment: The Futures of Transnational History,' *The American History Review* 118:1 (February 2013), pp. 130–39.

125 Thanks to Sarah Swift and Lee Steel for alerting me to this and for their knowledge of Chislehurst.

**Part 3 – Intimate Encounters: 1880–1914**

1 John Docker, *The Nervous Nineties: Australian Cultural Life in the 1890s* (Oxford University Press: 1991), pp. i–xx; Susan Magarey, Sue Rowley, Susan Sheridan (eds), *Debutante Nation: Feminism Contests the 1890s* (Allen and Unwin: 1993); Bruce Scates, *A New Australia: Citizenship, Radicalism and the First Republic* (Cambridge University Press: 1997); Grimshaw et al. (eds), *Creating a Nation*, pp. 151-209; Melissa Bellanta, 'Clearing Ground for the New Arcadia: Utopia, Labour and Environment in 1890s Australia', *Journal of Australian Studies* 26:72 (2002), pp. 13–20.

2 Virginia Woolf, *Mr Bennett and Mrs Brown* (Hogarth Press, 1924), pp. 4–5.

3 Bruce Scates, *A New Australia: Citizenship, Radicalism and the First Republic* (Cambridge University Press, 1997), p. 2; Clare Wright, 'Golden Opportunities: The Early Origins of Women's Suffrage in Victoria', *Victorian Historical Journal* (2008), p. 216; Docker, *The Nervous Nineties*, pp. i–xx; Marilyn Lake and Henry Reynolds, *Drawing the Global Colour Line: White Men's Countries and the Question of Racial Equality* (Melbourne University Press, 2008), p. 3.

4 *Immigration Restriction Act* (1901) Cth.

5 See Stephen Seidman, *Romantic Longings: Love in America, 1830–1980* (Routledge, 1991), p. 65ff; George Robb and Nancy Erber, 'Introduction', *Disorder in the Court: Trials and Sexual Conflict at the Turn of the Century* (Macmillan, 1999), pp. 1–5; Bongiorno, *The Sex Lives of Australians*, pp. 59–140; Bailey, *From Front Porch to Back Seat*.

6    Robb and Erber, 'Introduction', *Disorder in the Court,* p. 3.
7    Rebecca Tushnet, 'Rules of Engagement', *The Yale Law Journal* 107:8 (June 1998), p. 2586; Grossberg, *Governing the Hearth,* pp. 35–37; Lettmaier, *Broken Engagements,* p. 171; note that Ginger Frost states that the action continued to be used until the 1940s: Frost, *Promises Broken.*

## 6. Courtship, Coercion and Intimate Violence (*Vaughan v McRae,* 1891)

1    'Photograph of Myles McRae' in T.H. Higginson and G.W. Leighton (eds), *Jubilee Souvenir: Fifty Years of Progress* (Kogarah Municipal Council, 1935), p. 11. See also Betty Goodger, *Presentation to Oatley Heritage and Historical Society,* May 2017, https://oatleyhistory.org.au/wp-content/uploads/2017/07/MYLES-MCRAE-V2.pdf.
2    *McRae v McRae* (1891) NSW Divorce Court, *South Australian Chronicle,* 28 February 1891, p. 4.
3    *McRae v McRae* (1891) NSW Divorce Court, *National Advocate,* 24 February 1891, p. 3.
4    *McRae v McRae,* (1891) NSWSRO, Divorce Papers, Affidavit, 560/1890, shelf, 13/12395.
5    *McRae v McRae,* (1891) NSWSRO, Divorce Papers, Affidavit, 560/1890, shelf, 13/12395.
6    'The McRae Divorce Suit', *TACJ,* 28 February 1891, p. 14.
7    'Unclean Legislators', *TDT,* 26 February 1891, p. 4.
8    Marilyn Lake, 'Historical Reconsiderations IV: The Politics of Respectability: Identifying the Masculinist Context', *Australian Historical Studies* 22:86 (1986), p. 116.
9    Susan Magarey, 'Sexual Labour: Australia 1880–1910', in Magarey, Rowley and Sheridan (eds), *Debutante Nation,* p. 92.
10   On Mount Rennie, see: Kate Gleeson, 'White Natives and the Gang Rape at the Time of the Centenary', in Scott Poynting and George Morgan (eds), *Outrageous! Moral Panics in Australia* (ACYS Publishing, 2007), pp. 171–180; Juliette Peers, *What No Man Had Ever Done Before* (Dawn Revival Press, 1992); on castration: Bongiorno, *The Sex Lives of Australians,* p. 88.
11   Judith Allen, *Sex and Secrets: Crimes Involving Australian Women Since 1880* (Oxford University Press, 1990); Hilary Golder, *Divorce in Nineteenth-Century New South Wales* (UNSW Press, 1985); Alana Piper and Ana Stevenson, *Gender Violence in Australia: Historical Perspectives* (Monash University Publishing, 2019).
12   While scholars have recognised that the law sanctioned violence in marriage, there is no scholarship on how law sanctioned violence in courtship. See: Nancy Cott, *Public Vows: A History of Marriage and the Nation* (Harvard University Press, 2000); Norma Basch, 'Marriage and Domestic Relations', in Grossberg and Tomlins (eds), *The Cambridge History of Law in America* (Cambridge University Press, 2008), pp. 245–79; Regina Graycar and Jenny Morgan, *The Hidden Gender of Law* (Federation Press, 1990), p. 114; Heather Brook, *Conjugal Rights: Marriage and Marriage-Like Relationships Before the Law* (Palgrave, 2007), p. 7.
13   For courtship and women's agency see: Bailey, *From Front Porch to Back Seat;* Lystra, *Searching the Heart.*
14   I am indebted for this idea to Georges Vigarello, who argued it in relation to women in fin-de-siècle France: Vigarello, *A History of Rape: Sexual Violation in France from the Sixteenth to the Twentieth Century,* trans. Jean Birrell (Polity, 1998), p. 148.
15   Elizabeth Cady Stanton, 'The Solitude of Self', 18 January 1892.

16    Goodger, *Presentation to Oatley Heritage,* p. 3.

17    Goodger *Presentation to Oatley Heritage,* p. 2.

18    Goodger, *Presentation to Oatley Heritage,* p. 3.

19    'The Luck of Myles McRae', *NBN,* 30 April 1926, p. 2.

20    *McRae v McRae* (1891) NSWSRO, Divorce Papers, Affidavit, 560/1890, shelf, 13/12395

21    *McRae v McRae* (1891) NSWSRO, Divorce Papers, Affidavit, 560/1890, shelf, 13/12395.

22    This description is sourced from a range of materials, including G. Butler Earp, *The Gold Colonies of Australia* (Routledge and Co., 1852), p. 84; Beaufoy Merlin, 'Morpeth', in *At Work and Play* ML, 391842; 'Court House, Morpeth, Built in the Early Forties, Wings Added Later', ML, Graphic Collection, 836619.

23    Higginson and Leighton (eds), *Jubilee Souvenir.*

24    'The Nomination', *Maitland Mercury,* 15 February 1887, p. 4.

25    'The Nomination', *MM,* 15 February 1887, p. 4.

26    'Advertising', *MM,* 23 November 1889, p. 2.

27    'The Nomination', *MM,* 15 February 1887, p. 4.

28    *McRae v McRae,* (1891) NSWSRO, Divorce Papers, Affidavit, 560/1890, shelf, 13/12395.

29    'Protection Addresses', *MM,* 13 February 1890, p. 3.

30    'The Morpeth Election', *MM,* 24 February 1887, p. 8.

31    'Protection Addresses', *MM,* 13 February 1890, p. 3.

32    'The Morpeth Election', *MM,* 24 February 1887, p. 8.

33    'Original Correspondence', *MM,* 21 February 1885, p. 13.

34    'The Nomination', *MM,* 15 February, p. 2.

35    'Advertising', *MM,* 23 November 1889, p. 2.

36    *Macleay Argus,* 4 July 1890, p. 5.

37    *National Advocate,* 24 February 1891, p. 3.

38    Farge, *Le Gout d'Archives,* p. 26.

39    Farge, *Le Gout d'Archives,* p. 6.

40    *McRae v McRae,* (1891) NSWSRO, Divorce Papers, Affidavit, 560/1890, shelf, 13/12395.

41    Reported in the divorce hearing rather than the affidavit. See *National Advocate,* 24 February 1891, p. 3.

42    *McRae v McRae* (1891) NSWSRO, Divorce Papers, Affidavit, 560/1890, shelf, 13/12395.

43    *McRae v McRae* (1891) NSWSRO, Divorce Papers, Affidavit, 560/1890, shelf, 13/12395.

44    Erich Fromm, as cited in Jess Hill, *See What You Made Me Do: Power, Control and Domestic Abuse* (Black Inc., 2019), p. 119.

45    Goodger, *Presentation to Oatley Heritage,* p. 1.

46    William Blackstone, *Commentaries on the Laws of England, Vol. 1* (J.B. Lippincott, 1753), pp. 442–45. Blackstone was a popular text throughout the nineteenth century.

47    Golder, *Divorce in Nineteenth-Century New South Wales,* pp. 179–88.

48    *Married Women's Property Act* 1879 and 1882 (NSW); *Matrimonial Causes Act* 1873 (NSW); see: Golder, *Divorce in Nineteenth-Century New South Wales,* pp. 179–88.

49    *Vaughan v McRae,* 'Index to Judgment Books: Civil Jurisdiction: Civil Jurisdiction' (1891) SRNSW, 9/917; 'Judgment Papers', Container 20/11055; No. 3769 (1890). Innes J, Notebook NRS 6228 2/4565; 2/4537.

50    *Vaughan v McRae* (1891) NSWSC, *TDT,* 14 March 1891, p. 3.

51    *Vaughan v McRae* (1891) NSWSC, *The Australian Star,* 13 March 1891, p. 3.

52    Based on a description and a sketch of Ilma Vaughan in *The Bulletin,* 25 March 1891, p. 17.

53 *Vaughan v McRae* (1891) NSWSC, *Evening News,* 13 March 1891, p. 6.

54 *Vaughan v McRae* (1891) NSWSC, *Evening News,* 13 March 1891, p. 6.

55 K.G. Allars, 'Joseph George Long Innes', *Australian Dictionary of Biography.*

56 Vaughan versus McRae, *The Australian Star,* 13 March 1891, p. 3. See also: *SMH,* 17 March 1891, p. 7.

57 *Vaughan v McRae* (1891) NSWSC, *MM,* 17 March 1891, p. 7.

58 *Vaughan v McRae* (1891) NSWSC, *Evening News,* 13 March 1891, p. 6.

59 *McRae v McRae,* (1891) NSWSRO, Divorce Papers, Affidavit, 560/1890, shelf, 13/12395.

60 *Vaughan v McRae* (1891) NSWSC, *Evening News,* 13 March 1891, p 6.

61 As cited in Vigarello, *A History of Rape,* p. 44.

62 Joanna Bourke, *Rape: A History from 1860 to the Present* (Virago, 2007), p. 15.

63 *Bawden v Pascoe* SASC, *SAR,* 12 December 1882, p. 2.

64 *Bawden v Pascoe* SASC, *SAR,* 12 December 1882, p. 2.

65 *Yeo v Fox* (1903) NSWSC. *The Advertiser,* 5 September 1903, p. 10.

66 Hale, *The History of the Pleas of the Crown,* p. 629. On rape in marriage, see Wendy Larcombe and Mary Heath, 'Developing the Common Law and Rewriting the History of Rape in Marriage in Australia', *Sydney Law Review* 34:4 (2012), p. 785; Jill Elaine Hasday, 'Contest and Consent: A Legal History of Marital Rape', *California Law Review* 88:5 (2000), p. 1373.

67 Blackstone, *Commentaries on the Laws of England, Vol. 1,* p. 343.

68 *Bawden v Pascoe* (1882) SASC, *SAR,* 12 December 1882, p. 2.

69 Heather Lee Nelson, 'The Law and the Lady: Consent and Marriage in Nineteenth-Century British Literature', PhD thesis, Purdue University, 2015.

70 Frederick Pollock and Frederic William Maitland, *The History of English Law Before the Time of Edward I* (Cambridge University Press, 1895), p. 368.

71 Lettmaier, *Broken Engagements,* pp. 19-24.

72 Chitty, *A Practical Treatise on the Law of Contracts* (1872), pp. 490–91.

73 Simmonds, 'Gay Lotharios and Innocent Eves', p. 58.

74 *Vaughan v McRae* (1891) NSWSC, *SMH,* 17 March 1891, p. 7.

75 *Vaughan v McRae* (1891) NSWSC, *SMH,* 17 March 1891, p. 7.

76 'John Henry Want', *ML, Pictorial Collection,* GPO 1-11612.

77 *Vaughan v McRae* (1891) NSWSC, *SMH,* 14 March 1891, p. 3.

78 *Vaughan v McRae* (1891) NSWSC, *SMH,* 14 March 1891, p. 3.

79 *Vaughan v McRae* (1891) NSWSC, *SMH,* 14 March 1891, p. 3.

80 *Vaughan v McRae* (1891) NSWSC, *SMH,* 14 March 1891, p. 3.

81 *Vaughan v McRae* (1891) NSWSC, *SMH,* 14 March 1891, p. 3.

82 *Vaughan v McRae* (1891) NSWSC, *TDT,* 14 March 1891, p. 3.

83 *Vaughan v McRae* (1891) NSWSC, *TDT,* 14 March 1891, p. 3.

84 *Vaughan v McRae* (1891) NSWSC, *TDT,* 14 March 1891, p. 3.

85 *Vaughan v McRae* (1891) NSWSC, *MM,* 17 March 1891 at 7; *The Bulletin,* 25 March 1891; *TDT,* 14 March 1891, p. 3; *Evening News,* 13 March 1891, p 6.

86 *Vaughan v McRae* (1891) NSWSC, *TDT,* 14 March 1891, p. 3.

87 Roland Barthes, 'The Lady of the Camellias', in Susan Sontag (ed.), *A Barthes Reader* (Vintage, 2000), p. 89.

88 *Vaughan v McRae* (1891) NSWSC, *SMH,* 17 March 1891, p. 7.

89 *Vaughan v McRae* (1891) NSWSC, *SMH,* 17 March 1891, p. 7.

90 *Vaughan v McRae* (1891) NSWSC, *SMH,* 17 March 1891, p. 7.

91  For literature on this period, see: Allen, *Sex and Secrets*; Bongiorno, *The Sex Lives of Australians*; Liz Conor, *The Spectacular Modern Woman* (Indiana University Press, 2004); Gail Reekie, *Temptations: Sex, Selling and the Department Store* (Allen and Unwin, 1993); Seidman, *Romantic Longings*.

92  *Vaughan v McRae* (1891) NSWSC, *MM*, 17 March 1891, p. 7.

93  *Vaughan v McRae* (1891) NSWSC, *MM*, 17 March 1891, p. 7.

94  *Vaughan v McRae* (1891) NSWSC, *MM*, 17 March 1891, p. 7.

95  *Vaughan v McRae* (1891) NSWSC, *MM*, 17 March 1891, p. 7.

96  Vigarello, *A History of Rape*, p. 17.

97  *Vaughan v McRae* (1891) NSWSC, *MM*, 17 March 1891, p. 7.

98  Vigarello, *A History of Rape*, p. 17.

99  *Vaughan v McRae* (1891) NSWSC, *Sydney Truth* 13 March 1891, p. 4.

100  J.W. Smith, *A Manual of Common Law for Practitioners and Students* (Morrison, 1881), p. 194.

101  Graycar and Morgan, *The Hidden Gender of Law*, p. 114.

102  *Vaughan v McRae* (1891) NSWSC, *SMH*, 14 March 1891, p. 3.

103  Based on a description in *Evening News*, 20 March 1891, p. 5.

104  Bongiorno, *The Sex Lives of Australians*, p. 90.

105  Allen, *Sex and Secrets*, pp. 45-46; Barbara Caine and Moira Gatens (eds), *Australian Feminism: A Companion* (Oxford University Press, 1998), p. 256.

106  Allen, *Sex and Secrets*, p. 62.

107  Estelle Freedman, *Redefining Rape: Sexual Violence in the Era of Suffrage and Segregation* (Harvard University Press, 2013), p. 44.

108  My recreation of this day is taken from: *TDT*, 18 March 1891, p. 3; *Evening News*, 20 March 1891, p. 5; *MM*, 21 March 1891, p. 4; *GEPP*, 14 March 1891, p. 4; *TACJ*, 28 February 1891, p. 14; *Melbourne Punch*, 5 March 1891, p. 3; *SMH*, 26 February 1891, p. 4.

109  *Vaughan v McRae* (1891) NSWSC, *Evening News*, 20 March 1891, p. 5.

110  *Vaughan v McRae* (1891) NSWSC, *TDT*, 18 March 1891, p. 3; *Evening News*, 20 March 1891, p. 5; *MM*, 21 March 1891, p. 4; *GEPP*, 14 March 1891, p. 4; *TACJ*, 28 February 1891, p. 14; *Melbourne Punch*, 5 March 1891, p. 3; *SMH*, 26 February 1891, p. 4

111  *Vaughan v McRae* (1891) NSWSC, *Evening News*, 18 March 1891, p. 5.

112  Freedman, *Redefining Rape*, p. 44.

113  Simmonds, 'Gay Lotharios and Innocent Eves', p. 65.

114  *Vaughan v McRae* (1891) NSWSC, *Evening News*, 18 March 1891, p. 5.

115  *Vaughan v McRae* (1891) NSWSC, *Evening News*, 19 March 1891, p. 5.

116  *Vaughan v McRae* (1891) NSWSC, *Evening News*, 19 March 1891, p. 5.

117  *Vaughan v McRae* (1891) NSWSC, *SMH*, 20 March 1891, p. 3.

118  Pre-1901 Gosford Pioneeer Register, PNR 2250, Central Coast Family History Society (Ancestry.com).

119  Goodger, *Presentation to Oatley Heritage and Historical Society*.

120  'Mr Myles McRae', Parliament of New South Wales, https://www.parliament.nsw. gov.au/members/pages/member-details.aspx?pk=850.

## 7. Race, Religion and the Politics of Desire (*Lucas v Palmer*, 1892)

1  'Vehicle Collisions', *The Argus*, 28 June 1892, p. 6; 'Experiences at Ballarat, *Queensland Times*, 28 June 1892, p. 6; 'The Weather', *TDT*, 24 June 1892, p. 6.

2  Adele Chynoweth, 'Keeping Your Head Down at the Hyde Park Barracks Museum',

in Chynoweth (ed.), *Museums and the Working Class* (Routledge, 2022), pp. 145–160.

3   For descriptions of Colonna-Close and Clara Palmer, see: 'A Hong Kong
    Romance', *The Australian Star*, 29 June 1892, p. 2; 'Personal', *SMH*, 29 September,
    1905, p. 4; 'Mr Harold T Morgan', *Australian Star*, 24 February 1902, p. 5; 'Late
    Judge Gibson', *SMH*, 27 October 1914, p. 6.

4   *Lucas v Palmer* (1892) NSWDC, *Weekly Advance*, 1 July 1892, p. 3

5   'A Peculiar Action', *The Weekly Advance*, 1 July 1892, p. 3; 'A Hong Kong Romance',
    *The Australian Star*, 29 June 1892, p. 2.

6   A Peculiar Action', *The Weekly Advance*, 1 July 1892, p. 3; 'A Hong Kong Romance',
    *The Australian Star*, 29 June 1892, p. 2.

7   *Lucas v Palmer* (1892) NSWDC, *Weekly Advance*, 1 July 1892, p. 3; see also:
    'Peculiar Breach of Promise', *Evening News*, 29 June 1892, p. 4; 'Breach of Promise.
    A Peculiar Action', 'Breach of Promise', *Cumberland Mercury*, 2 July 1892, p. 2;
    'Metropolitan District Court', *SMH*, 29 June 1892, p. 4; 'A Hong Kong Romance',
    *Australian Star*, 29 June 1892, p. 2.

8   'A Hong Kong Romance', *Australian Star*, 29 June 1892, p. 2.

9   'Another Action: A Colored Lover and a White Girl', *TDT*, 29 June 1892, p. 6;
    'Blighted Affections' and 'A Man Sues for Breach of Promise', 29 June 1892 , p. 2,
    and 30 June 1892, p. 5.

10  'Another Action: A Colored Lover and a White Girl', *TDT*, 29 June 1892, p. 6;
    'Breach of Promise', *Cumberland Mercury*, 2 July 1892, p. 2; 'Breach of Promise
    Suit', *Leader*, 2 July 1892, p. 47.

11  'A Man Sues for Breach of Promise', *NMH*, 30 June 1892, p. 5; 'Peculiar Breach of
    Promise. FEMALE DEFENDANT', *Evening News*, 29 June 1892, p. 6.

12  See: David Roediger, *Working Towards Whiteness: How America's Immigrants
    Became White* (Basic Books, 2005), p. 5; and Matthew Frye Jacobson, *Whiteness
    of a Different Colour: European Immigration and the Alchemy of Race* (Harvard
    University Press, 1999).

13  *Coloured Races Restriction and Regulation Act 1896* (NSW).

14  *Immigration Restriction Act 1901* (Cth). See: Yarwood, *Asian Migration to
    Australia,* pp. 157–62.

15  Lake and Reynolds, *Drawing the Global Colour Line*, p. 3.

16  Lake and Reynolds, *Drawing the Global Colour Line*, p. 4.

17  Joseph Fraser, *Husbands: How to Select Them, How to Manage Them,
    How to Keep Them* (E.W. Cole, 1900), p. 32; Katherine Ellinghaus, *Taking
    Assimilation to Heart: Marriages of White Women and Indigenous Men in the
    United States and Australia, 1887–1937* (University of Nebraska Press, 2006),
    p. 149.

18  Henry Parkes, 'The Chinese Restriction Bill', *Kiama Independent and Shoalhaven
    Advertiser,* 22 May 1888, p. 4.

19  See: Ellinghaus, *Taking Assimilation to Heart*; McGrath, *Illicit Love*; Adams,
    'Immigration Law and the Regulation of Marriage', p. 1625ff; Peggy Pascoe,
    'Miscegenation Law, Court Cases and Ideologies of "Race" in Twentieth-Century
    America', The Journal of American History 83:1 (June 1996).

20  David Roediger, *The Wages of Whiteness* (Verso, 1992); N. Ignatiev, *How the
    Irish Became White* (Routledge, 1995); Lake and Reynolds, *Drawing the Global
    Colour Line*.

21  'Alleged Defamation', *The Telegraph*, 7 May 1915, p. 3; On British subjecthood and citizenship, see: Kartia Snoek, 'Empire, Race, Naturalisation: *The Naturalisation Act 1903*', *Melbourne Historical Journal* 40:1 (2012), pp. 103–27; Kate Bagnall, '*Potter v Minahan*: Chinese Australians, the Law and Belonging in White Australia', *History Australia* 15:3 (2018), pp. 458–74.

22  *Lucas v Palmer* (1892) NSWDC, *The Weekly Advance*, 1 July 1892, p. 3.

23  *Lucas v Palmer* (1892) NSWDC *The Weekly Advance*, 1 July 1892, p. 3; 'A Hong Kong Romance', *The Australian Star*, 29 June 1892, p. 2; 'Peculiar Breach of Promise', *Evening News*, 29 June 1892, p. 4; 'Breach of Promise', *The Cumberland Mercury*, 2 July 1892, p. 2.

24  Henri Bergson, *Laughter: An Essay on the Meaning of the Comic*, trans. C. Brereton and F. Rothwell (1900), p. 2.

25  *Another Action. A Colored Lover And A White Girl*', *TDT*, 29 June 1892, p. 6.

26  'Breach of Promise Suit', *Leader*, 2 July 1892, p. 47.

27  *Immigration Restriction Act 1901* (Cth). See: Alexander Yarwood, *Asian Migration to Australia: The Background to Exclusion, 1896–1923* (Melbourne University Press, 1964), pp. 157–62.

28  'The Loves of the "Nigers"', *The Australian*, 2 February 1826, p. 4.

29  Homi Bhabha, *The Location of Culture* (Routledge, 1994), p. 86.

30  'The Loves of the "Nigers"', *The Australian*, 2 February 1826, p. 4.

31  'A Hong Kong Romance', *Australian Star*, 29 June 1892, p. 2.

32  'A Hong Kong Romance', *Australian Star*, 29 June 1892, p. 2.

33  'A Hong Kong Romance', *Australian Star*, 29 June 1892, p. 2.

34  Katherine Ellinghaus, *Taking Assimilation to Heart*.

35  'A Hong Kong Romance', *The Australian Star*, 29 June 1892, p. 2.

36  Margaret Allen, '"A Fine Type of Hindoo" Meets the Australian "Type": British Indians in Australia and Diverse Masculinities', in Deacon et al. (eds), *Transnational Lives*, pp. 44–49.

37  Hsu-Ming Teo, *Desert Passions: Orientalism and Romance Novels* (University of Texas Press, 2012), pp. 1–20.

38  'A Hong Kong Romance', *The Australian Star*, 29 June 1892, p. 2.

39  'A Hong Kong Romance', *The Australian Star*, 29 June 1892, p. 2.

40  'The Loves of the "Nigers"', *The Australian*, 2 February 1826, p. 4.

41  *Lucas v Palmer* (1892) NSWDC, *The Weekly Advance*, 1 July 1892, p. 3; *The Australian Star*, 29 June 1892, p. 2. Also: *Evening News*, 29 June 1892, p. 4; *Cumberland Mercury*, 2 July 1892, p. 2; *SMH*, 29 June 1892, p. 4.

42  *Hong Kong Daily Press*, 2 July 1892.

43  'A Colored Lover and a White Girl', *TDT*, 29 June 1892, p. 6; , 'A Man Sues for Breach of Promise', *NMH*, 30 June 1892, p. 5; 'A Hong Kong Romance', *The Australian Star*, 29 June 1892, p. 2.

44  'Latest Colonial Intelligence', Perth Gazette, 28 November 1856, p. 3.

45  'Domestic Intelligence', *The Moreton Bay Courier*, 8 November 1856, p. 2.

46  Bagnall, 'Rewriting the History of Chinese Families in Nineteenth-Century Australia', *Australian Historical Studies* 42:1 (2011), p. 70.

47  Bagnall, 'Rewriting the History of Chinese Families', p. 70.

48  Yarwood, *Asian Migration to Australia*, p. 6; Lake and Reynolds, *Drawing the Global Colour Line*, pp. 3–4.

49 Yarwood, *Asian Migration to Australia,* p. 6.
50 Yarwood, *Asian Migration to Australia,* p. 163; for figures on Chinese during the gold rush, see 'Chinese Gold Miners', National Museum of Australia: https://www. nma.gov.au/explore/features/harvest-of-endurance/scroll/chinese-gold-miners
51 Yarwood, *Asian Migration to Australia,* p. 24.
52 See: *Bakar v Mighell* (1893), 'A Novel Breach of Promise Action', *West Australian,* 31 October 1893, p. 6.
53 *Gan Dah v Lenton* (1920), NSWSC, *SMH,* 9 June 1920, p. 9; *Rowan v Kooiso* (1923) DISCNSW, *National Advocate,* 22 September 1923, p. 2
54 *Gan Dah v Lenton* (1920) NSWDC, *SMH,* 9 June 1920, p .9
55 *Rowan v Kooiso* (1923) NSWDC, *National Advocate,* 22 September 1923, p. 2.
56 'Uncle's "Stranglehold", *The Bulletin,* 1 November 1923, p. 10.
57 Ariela Gross, *What Blood Won't Tell: A History of Race on Trial in America,* p. 75.
58 *Lucas v Palmer* (1892) NSWDC, *The Australian Star,* 29 June 1892, p. 2 .
59 *Cherrington v Malcolm* (1849) NSWSC, *SMH,* 6 August 1849, p. 2.
60 *Wiltshire v Hart* (1871) VICSC, 'Breach of Promise Case in Melbourne', *Empire,* 15 June 1871, p. 4.
61 *Noble v Crawford* (1880) NSWSC, *Evening News,* 16 September 1880, p. 3; *Leversha v Wrangham* (1889) VICSC, *Colac Herald,* 19 July 1889, p. 3.
62 'Women's Rights', *ATCJ,* October 1893, p. 34; Lettmaier has linked the increase in men suing to the suit's shift towards a more contractual emphasis. See *Broken Engagements,* p. 177).
63 'Bear It Like a Man', *Evening News,* 13 October 1903, p. 4.
64 *Lucas v Palmer* (1892) NSWDC *,The Australian Star,* p. 2.
65 Mitra Sharafi, *Law and Identity in Colonial South Asia: Parsi Legal Culture, 1772–1947,* pp. 1–18.
66 James Sorab Lucas, Certificate Exempting from Dictation Test No. 2829, 11 October 1921; Statutory Declaration, 5 September 1921, NAA ST84/1, 1921/315/51-60; SP42/1, C1923/6119; *Lucas v Roth* (1909) NSWSC, 'Judgment Papers', series NRS-13472, container 19/15892, file number 150, 1909, SRNSW; James Sorabjee Lucas, Carl Smith Collection, card number 143319 (1883); card number 120691 (1884–85; 1890–91), card number 120689 (1884, 1887, 1878, 1880, 1890, 1892; *Government Records Service of the Hong Kong Special Administrative Region.*
67 Renisa Mawani, *Across Oceans of Law: The Komagata Maru and Jurisdiction in the Time of Empire* (Duke University Press, 2018); Renisa Mawani and Iza Hussin, 'The Travels of Law: Indian Ocean Itineraries', *Law and History Review,* pp. 733–47; Lauren Benton, 'Oceans of Law: The Legal Geography of the Seventeenth-Century Seas', in *Seascapes, Littoral Cultures and Trans-Oceanic Exchanges* (Library of Congress, 2003), pp. 12–15.
68 James Sorab Lucas, Certificate Exempting from Dictation Test, no. 2829, 11 October 1921; Statutory Declaration, 5 September 1921; NAA: ST84/1, 1921/315/51-60; SP42/1, C1923/6119.
69 Campbell, *Gazetteer of the Bombay Presidency, Vol. II,* pp. 337–477; Tanya L. Luhrmann, *The Good Parsi: The Fate of a Colonial Elite in a Postcolonial Society* (Oxford University Press, 1996); Hans Raj Kumar, 'Colonialism and Agriculture in the First Half of the Nineteenth Century', *Proceedings of the Indian History Congress* 48, pp. 483–90.

70    Kumar, 'Colonialism and Agriculture'; Khojeste P. Mistree, 'Collision, Conflict
      and Accommodation: A Question of Survival and the Preservation of the
      Parsi Zoroastrian Identity', in Sarah Stewart et al. (eds), *The Zoroastrian Flame*
      (Bloomsbury, 2016), pp. 339, 345–51; Uma Das Gupta, *The World of the Indian
      Ocean Merchant, 1500–1800: Collected Essays of Ashin Das Gupta* (Oxford
      University Press, 2004), pp. 369–99; Meher P. Kelawala, 'The Parsis of Bharuch,
      1803–1947', *Journal of the K.R. Cama Oriental Institute*, p. 55.

71    I would like to thank Devleena Ghosh for pointing this out to me.

72    Kumar, 'Colonialism and Agriculture in the First Half of the Nineteenth Century'.

73    Luhrmann, *The Good Parsi*, pp. 333–34; J.M. Campbell, *Gazetteer of the Bombay
      Presidency, Vol. II* (Government Press, 1877), pp. 337ff.

74    Mistree, 'Collision, Conflict and Accommodation', pp. 345–51; Luhrmann, *The
      Good Parsi*, pp. 333–57; Sharafi, *Law and Identity*, pp. 7–18.

75    Sharafi, *Law and Identity*, pp. 7-18.

76    Sharafi, *Law and Identity*, p. 6.

77    Sharafi, *Law and Identity*, pp. 6–7.

78    Sharafi, *Law and Identity*, p. 6.

79    Kumar, 'Colonialism and Agriculture', pp. 483–90.

80    James said this in his slander action. See *Lucas v Roth* (1909) NSWSC, 'Judgment
      Papers', SRNSW, NRS-13472, container 19/15892, file number 150, 1909.

81    Sharafi, *Law and Identity*, p. 18.

82    James Sorabjee Lucas, Carl Smith Collection, card number 143319 (1883); card
      number 120691 (1884–85; 1890–91), card number 120689 (1884; 1887; 1878; 1880;
      1890; 1892); *Government Records Service of the Hong Kong Special Administrative
      Region*; Ho and Chu, *Policing Hong Kong*; Hamilton, *Watching Over Hong Kong*.

83    See the descriptions of Isabella Bird: Henrietta Amelia Bird, *Letters to Henrietta*,
      John Murray, 2002.

84    Lawrence K.K. Ho and You Kong Chu, *Policing Hong Kong, 1842–1969* (City
      University Hong Kong, 2012); *Sheila Hamilton, Watching Over Hong Kong: Private
      Policing 1841–1941* (Hong Kong University Press, 2012).

85    Ho and Chu, *Policing Hong Kong*.

86    James Sorabjee Lucas, Carl Smith Collection, card number 143319 (1883);
      card number 120691 (1884–5; 1890–91) Card Number 120689 (1884; 1887;
      1878; 1880; 1890; 1892), *Government Records Service of the Hong Kong Special
      Administrative Region*.

87    Achinto Roy and Reshmi Lahiri-Roy, 'World's Smallest Business Community:
      The Parsis of India', *International Journal of Interdisciplinary Social Science* 6:2
      (2011), p. 188.

88    James Sorabjee Lucas, Carl Smith Collection, card number 143319 (1883);
      card number 120691 (1884–85; 1890–91); card number 120689 (1884; 1887;
      1878; 1880; 1890; 1892); *Government Records Service of the Hong Kong Special
      Administrative Region*.

89    James Sorabjee Lucas, Carl Smith Collection, 1884.

90    James Sorabjee Lucas, Carl Smith Collection, 1887.

91    James Sorabjee Lucas, Carl Smith Collection, 1890.

92    This is seen in his immigration papers and in the Carl Smith Collection,
      *Government Records Service of HK*.

93 'A Peculiar Action', *The Weekly Advance*, 1 July 1892, p. 3; 'A Hong Kong Romance', *The Australian Star*, 29 June 1892, p. 2.

94 My description here is influenced by Philip Howell, 'Race, Space and the Regulation of Prostitution in Colonial Hong Kong', *Urban History* 31:2 (2004), pp. 229–48; and by Cecilia Chu, 'Combating Nuisance: Sanitation, Regulation and the Politics of Property in Colonial Hong Kong', in D.M. Pomfret and R. Peckham (eds), *Imperial Contagions: Medicine, Hygiene and Cultures of Planning in Asia* (Hong Kong University Press, 2013), pp. 17–36.

95 Yeu-Man Yeung, 'Cities That Work: Hong Kong and Singapore', in R.J. Fuchs et al. (eds), *Urbanisation and Urban Policies in Pacific Asia* (Routledge, 1989), pp. 257–74.

96 'A Peculiar Action', *The Weekly Advance*, 1 July 1892, p. 3; 'A Hong Kong Romance', *The Australian Star*, 29 June 1892, p. 2.

97 'A Peculiar Action', *The Weekly Advance*, 1 July 1892, p. 3; 'A Hong Kong Romance', *The Australian Star*, 29 June 1892, p. 2.

98 Sharifi, *Parsi Legal Culture*, p. 58.

99 'A Peculiar Action', *The Weekly Advance*, 1 July 1892, p. 3; 'A Hong Kong Romance', *The Australian Star*, 29 June 1892, p. 2.

100 'Shipping Intelligence', *The Age*, 21 January 1891, p. 4.

101 These descriptions were inspired by Graeme Davison, *The Rise and Fall of Marvellous Melbourne* (Melbourne University Press, 1978).

102 *Weekly Advance*, 1 July 1892, p. 3; *Australian Star*, 29 June 1892, p. 2.

103 *Lucas v Palmer* (1892) NSWDC, *The Australian Star*, 29 June 1892, p. 2.

104 Sharifi, *Parsi Legal Culture*, p. 41.

105 Patricia J. Williams, 'The Brass Ring and the Deep Blue Sea', in *The Alchemy of Race and Rights*, pp. 3-15.

106 James Sorab Lucas, Certificate Exempting From Dictation Test. No. 2829, 11 October 1921; Statutory Declaration, 5 September 1921, *NAA*, ST84/1, 1921/315/51–60; SP42/1, C1923/6119.

107 Nadia Rhook, 'Listen to Nodes of Empire: Speech and Whiteness in Victorian Hawker's License Courts', *Journal of Colonialism and Colonial History* 15:2 (2014), pp. 4–5.

108 See Yarwood, *Asian Migration to Australia*, pp. 157–62.

109 James Sorab Lucas, Certificate Exempting From Dictation Test No. 2829, 11 October 1921; Statutory Declaration, 5 September 1921, *NAA*: ST84/1, 1921/315/51–60; SP42/1, C1923/6119.

110 'Mudgee Police Court', *Mudgee Guardian*, 12 October 1903, p. 2.

111 *Lucas v Roth* (1909) NSWSC, SRNSW, NRS-13472, container 19/15892, file number 150, 1909.

112 Sharifi, *Parsi Legal Culture*, pp. 56ff.

113 James Sorab Lucas, Certificate Exempting From Dictation Test No. 2829, 11 October 1921; Statutory Declaration, 5 September 1921, *NAA*: ST84/1, 1921/315/51–60; SP42/1, C1923/6119.

## 8. Modernity, Migration and the Colour of Love (*Zathar v Hanna*, 1907)

1 Max Weber, *Economy and Society* (University of California Press, 1978), p. 225.

2 *Hanna Moses Joseph*, Bankruptcy Index 1888–1929, SRNSW, NRS 13655-1-[10/23531]-17464.

3   *Hanna Moses Joseph,* Bankruptcy Index 1888–1929, SRNSW, NRS 13655-1-
    [10/23531]-17464; see also Justice R.M. Sly, SRNSW, *Notebooks: Chambers,* NRS
    7682, 01.01.1907-31.12.1919; *Zathar v Hanna* (1907) SCNSW, *SMH,* 6 June, 1907,
    p. 4, 7 June, p. 4, 8 June, p. 10, 11 June, p. 5, 12 June, p. 6, 13 June, p. 4.

4   Weber, *Economy and Society,* p. 225.

5   'A Woman's Letter', *The Bulletin,* 13 June 1907, p. 22.

6   'A Woman's Letter', *The Bulletin,* 13 June 1907, p. 22.

7   'Syrians in the South: A Colony at Redfern', *Illustrated Sydney News,* p. 4.

8   Alys Weinbaum et al. (eds), *The Modern Girl Around the World: Consumption,
    Modernity and Globalization* (Duke University Press, 2008), p. 1.

9   There is surprisingly little on this in Australia. In America, see: Gross, *What
    Blood Won't Tell;* Kerry Arams, 'Immigration Law and the Regulation of Marriage',
    *Minnesota Law Review* 91 (2006), p. 1625ff; Peggy Pascoe, 'Miscegenation Law,
    Court Cases and Ideologies of Race in Twentieth-Century America', *The Journal of
    American History* 83:1 (June 1996).

10  On 'multiple modernities', see: Shmuel Eisenstadt, *Comparative Civilizations
    and Multiple Modernities: A Collection of Essays* (Brill, 2022); T.K. Oommen,
    'Recognising Multiple Modernities: A Prelude to Understanding Globalisation',
    Jawaharlal Nehru University, 1999; Robert Hefner, 'Multiple Modernities:
    Christianity, Islam and Hinduism in a Globalising Age', Annual Review of
    Anthropology 27 (1998), pp. 83–104. Exceptions to Anglocentric histories of love
    are Teo, *Desert Passions* and Samia Khatun, 'The Book of Marriage: Histories of
    Muslim Women in Twentieth-Century Australia', *Gender and History* 29:1 (April
    2017), pp. 8–30.

11  Alixa Naff, *A Social History of Zahle: The Principal Market Town in Nineteenth-
    Century Lebanon* (University of California Press, 1972), pp. 52ff.

12  Queenie Sada, *Biography of Cissie Zathar,* passed on to author by her descendants
    on 30 November 2021.

13  See Jim McKay, *Phoenician Farewell: Three Generations of Lebanese Christians
    in Australia* (Ashwood House Academic, 1989), pp. 27–29; Anne Monsour, *Not
    Quite White: Lebanese and the White Australia Policy, 1880–1947* (Post Pressed,
    2009), pp. 12–14; Karen Barky and George Gavrillis, 'The Ottoman Millet System:
    Non-Territorial Autonomy and Its Contemporary Legacy', *Ethnopolitics* 1:15
    (January 2016), pp. 24–42; Philip Mansel, *Levant: Splendour and Catastrophe
    on the Mediterranean* (Yale University Press, 2010), pp. 1–2; Eric C. Hooglund,
    'Introduction,' in Hooglund (ed.), *Crossing the Waters: Arabic-speaking
    Immigrants to the United States before 1940* (Smithsonian Institution Press, 1987),
    pp. 3–4.

14  Piperoglou, 'Migrant Acculturation via Naturalisation', p. 59.

15  Zathar v Hanna (1907) SCNSW, *SMH,* 6-8 June, 1907.

16  Andonis Piperoglou, 'Migrant Acculturation via Naturalisation: Comparing
    Syrian and Greek Applications for Naturalisation in White Australia', *Historical
    Studies in Ethnicity, Migration and Diaspora* 40:1 (2022), p. 59.

17  *Zathar v Hanna* (1907) SCNSW, *SMH,* 6 June, 1907, p. 4, 7 June, p. 4, 8 June, p. 10,
    11 June, p. 5, 12 June, p. 6, 13 June, p. 4.

18  Monsour, *Not Quite White,* p. 46ff; Yarwood, *Asian Migration to Australia,*
    pp. 157–162.

19    Paul Convy, *The Lebanese Quarter, Redfern: Time, Place and Extent* (Coogee Australian Lebanese Historical Society, 2009), pp. 6–18; Paul Convy and Anne Monsour, *Lebanese Settlement in NSW: A Thematic History* (Migration Heritage Centre, 2008), p. 18; Janis Wilton, *Hawking to Haberdashery: Immigrants in the Bush* (University of New England Printery, 1987), pp. 1–42.

20    Anne Monsour, 'Traders by Nature or Circumstance: The Occupational Pathways of Early Syrian/Lebanese Immigrants in Australia', *Labour and Management in Development* 15 (2014), p. 2; Convy and Monsour, 'Lebanese Settlement in NSW', p. 19.

21    See Monsour, 'Traders by Nature or Circumstance', who notes figures for 1898, 1899 and 1902, p. 2. For Redfern Local Court, see: Nadia Rhook, 'Turban-clad British Subjects: Tracking the Circuits of Mobility, Visibility and Sexuality in Settler Nation-making', *Transfers* 5:3 (December 2015), pp. 1–18.

22    Queenie Sada, *Biography of Cissie Zathar*.

23    Justice R.M. Sly, *Notebooks: Chambers*, SRNSW NRS 7682, 01.01.1907-31.12.1919; *Zathar v Hanna* (1907) SCNSW, *SMH*, 6 June, 1907, p. 4, 7 June, p. 4, 8 June, p. 10.

24    *Zathar v Hanna* (1907) SCNSW, *Evening News*, 5 June 1907, p. 5.

25    Lake and Reynolds, *Drawing the Global Colour Line*, p. 4.

26    For numbers, see Yarwood, *Asian Migration*, p. 141; Anne Monsour, 'Undesirable Alien to Good Citizen: Syrian/Lebanese in a "White" Australia', *Mahsriq and Mahjar: Journal of Middle East and North African Migration Studies* 3:1 (2015), p. 144.

27    Monsour, *Not Quite White*, p. 141ff.

28    Senator Thomas Playford, as cited in Monsour, *Not Quite White*, p. 52.

29    Abourik to Deakin (NAA: A1, 1910/3915), cited in Monsour, *Not Quite White*, p. 43.

30    Rhook, '"Turban-Clad " British Subjects', pp. 104–122.

31    'Syrian Hawkers', *ATCJ*, 11 January 1896, p. 18.

32    'The Syrian: A *Bulletin* Writer Dissects the Breed', *Wellington Times*, 25 January 1906, p. 6.

33    Monsour and Convy, 'Lebanese Settlement in NSW', p. 6.

34    J.K. McLaughlin, 'Richard Meares Sly', *Australian Dictionary of Biography*.

35    J.M. Bennett, 'Richard Windeyer', *Australian Dictionary of Biography*.

36    'A Leading Legal Light: The New Attorney General', *The St George Call*, 2 July 1904, p. 1.

37    Justice R.M.Sly, *Notebooks: Chambers*, SRNSW NRS 7682, 01.01.1907-31.12.1919; *Zathar v Hanna* (1907) SCNSW, *SMH*, 6 June, 1907, p. 4, 7 June, p. 4, 8 June, p. 10, 11 June, p. 5, 12 June, p. 6, 13 June, p. 4.

38    Justice R.M.Sly, *Notebooks: Chambers*, SRNSW NRS 7682, 01.01.1907-31.12.1919; *Zathar v Hanna* (1907) SCNSW, *SMH*, 6 June, 1907, p. 4, 7 June, p. 4, 8 June, p. 10, 11 June, p. 5, 12 June, p. 6, 13 June, p. 4.

39    'Society', *The Bulletin*, 20 June 1907, p. 10.

40    'Personal Items', *The Bulletin*, 13 June 1907, p. 18.

41    See for example: 'A Syrian Romance', *Wellington Times*, 6 June 1907, p. 4; 'Society', *The Bulletin*, 20 June 1907, p. 10.

42    See, for example: David Frisby, *Fragments of Modernity: Theories of Modernity in the Work of Simmel, Kracauer and Benjamin* (Routledge, 2013).

43   See: Sandra Lee Bartky, 'Foucault, Femininity and the Modernising of Patriarchal Power', in I. Diamond and L. Quinby (eds), *Feminism and Foucault: Reflections on Resistance* (Northeastern University Press, 1988), pp. 93–111; Liz Conor, *The Spectacular Modern Woman: Feminine Visibility in the 1920s* (Indiana University Press, 2004); Matthews, *Dance Hall and Picture Palace*; Gail Reekie, *Temptations: Sex, Selling and the Department Store* (Allen and Unwin, 1993).

44   Weinbaum et al. (eds), *The Modern Girl Around the World*.

45   Weinbaum et al. (eds), *The Modern Girl Around the World*; Eric Olund, 'Traffic in Souls: The "New Woman", Whiteness and Mobile Self-Possession', *Cultural Geographies* 16:4 (2009), pp. 485–504.

46   See Kate Bagnall and Julia Martinez (eds), *Locating Chinese Women: Historical Mobility Between China and Australia* (Hong Kong University Press, 2021), including Sophie Loy-Wilson, 'Daisy Kwok's Shanghai: Life in China Before and After 1949'; Samia Khatun, *Australianama: The South Asian Odyssey in Australia* (Oxford University Press, 2019); see also Liz Conor, *Skin Deep: Settler Impressions of Aboriginal Women* (UWA Press, 2016).

47   Conor, *The Spectacular Modern Woman*.

48   Monsour, *Not Quite White*, p. 90.

49   *Hanna Moses Joseph*, SRNSW, Bankruptcy Index 1888–1929, File Number 17464, 23.07/1907, NRS 13655-1- [10/23531]-17464.

50   'Syrians in the South: A Colony at Redfern', *Illustrated Sydney News*, 19 November 1892, p. 4. See also Convy, *The Lebanese Quarter, Redfern*, pp. 7–8.

51   Myra Morris, 'The Hawker', *The Bulletin*, 23 April 1925, p. 22.

52   Patrick White, *The Aunt's Story*, pp. 24–25.

53   'Syrians in the South: A Colony at Redfern', *Illustrated Sydney News*, 19 November 1892, p. 4.

54   *Ex parte McKay* (1907), Commonwealth Arbitration Reports Vol. 2, *Harvester*.

55   *Hanna Moses Joseph*, SRNSW, Bankruptcy Index 1888–1929, File Number 17464, 23.07/1907, NRS 13655-1-[10/23531]-17464.

56   See Monsour, *Not Quite White*, pp. 85ff.

57   'Personal Items', *The Bulletin* , 13 June 1907, p. 18.

58   'Lovers in Court', *Australian Star*, 7 June 1907, p. 6.

59   *Zathar v Hanna* (1907) SCNSW, *SMH*, 6 June, 1907, p. 4, 7 June, p. 4, 8 June, p. 10.

60   'Society', *The Bulletin,* 20 June 1907, p. 10.

61   'Society', *The Bulletin,* 20 June 1907, p. 10.

62   *Zathar v Hanna* (1907) SCNSW, *SMH*, 6 June, 1907, p. 4, 7 June, p. 4, 8 June, p. 10.

63   'Syrian Romance', *Evening News*, 7 June 1907, p. 6; 'Moses I Love You', *Australian Star*, 8 June 1907, p. 15.

64   *Zathar v Hanna* (1907) SCNSW, *SMH*, 6 June, 1907, p. 4, 7 June, p. 4, 8 June, p. 10.

65   Marilyn Lake, 'Female Desires: The Meaning of World War Two', *Australian Historical Studies* 24 (1990), pp. 267–84; Bartky, 'Foucault, Femininity', p. 74.

66   *Cherrington v Malcolm* (1849) NSWSC *SMH,* 6 August 1849, p. 2.

67   Aylette v Bolton (1879) TASSC, *The Cornwall Chronicle*, 14 November 1879, p. 2.

68   'Personal Items,' *The Bulletin*, 13 June 1907, p. 18.

69   *Zathar v Hanna* (1907) SCNSW, *SMH*, 6 June, 1907, p. 4, 7 June, p. 4, 8 June, p. 10.

70   'Peculiar Breach of Promise', *Evening News*, 29 June 1892, p. 4; 'A Hong Kong Romance', *Australian Star*, 29 June 1892, p. 2.

71 On the millet system, see: Barky and Gavrillis, 'The Ottoman Millet System';
J.T. Davidann and M.J. Gilbert, 'Empires of Difference: The Ottoman Model of
a Multicultural State' and 'The Millet System', in *Cross-cultural Encounters in
Modern World History, 1453 to the Present* (Routledge, 2019); Kamel S. Abu Jaber,
'The Millet System in the Nineteenth-Century Ottoman Empire', *The Muslim
World* 57:3 (1967), pp. 212–23; McKay, *Phoenician Farewell*, pp. 69ff.
72 Barky and Gavrillis, 'The Ottoman Millet System', pp. 24–42.
73 Monsour, 'Religion Matters', p. 96. Monsour's argument here is indebted to Philip
K. Hitti, *History of Syria, Including Lebanon and Palestine* (Macmillan, 1951).
74 *Zathar v Hanna* (1907) SCNSW, *SMH*, 6 June, 1907, p. 4, 7 June, p. 4, 8 June, p. 10.
75 There is a growing literature on law's movements across oceans, however it tends
to be mostly top-down. See: Iza Hussin, 'Circulations of Law: Cosmopolitan
Elites, Global Repertoires, Local Vernaculars', *Law and History Review* 32:4 (2014),
pp. 773–95; Resina Mawani and Iza Hussin, 'The Travels of Law: Indian Ocean
Itineraries', *Law and History Review* 32:4 (2014), pp. 733–47.
76 McKay, *Phoenician Farewell*, p. 41.
77 McKay, *Phoenician Farewell*, pp. 48–49, 68.
78 McKay, *Phoenician Farewell*, p. 49.
79 *Zathar v Hanna* (1907) SCNSW, *SMH*, 6 June, 1907, p. 4, 7 June, p. 4, 8 June, p. 10,
11 June, p. 5, 12 June, p. 6, 13 June, p. 4.
80 *Stores v Cottarn* (VICSC) 1901, *The Age*, 12 April, p. 6; see also *Parkinson v Wade*
(NSWDC) 1906, *National Advocate*, 24 July 1906, p. 3. For evidence of people
calling upon religion as a source of authority, see *Pattison v Dalley* (VICSC)
1877, *Riverine Herald*, 30 October 1877, p. 3; *McManus v Bennett* (VICSC) 1884,
*The Argus*, 14 August 1884, p. 10; *Schepper v Fuchs* (QLDSC) 1880, *Maryborough
Chronicle*, 13 July 1880, pp. 2–3; *Baker v Denman* (SASC) *SAR*, 20 October 1877,
p. 3.
81 *Zathar v Hanna* (1907) SCNSW, *SMH*, 6 June, 1907, p. 4, 7 June, p. 4, 8 June, p. 10,
11 June, p. 5, 12 June, p. 6, 13 June, p. 4.
82 'Breezy Bits from Sydney City', *Truth*, 1 September 1907, p. 3
83 Register of Firms Index, Item: 2/8545, File Number 25195, SRNSW.
84 *Hanna Moses Joseph*, SRNSW, Bankruptcy Index 1888-1929, File Number 17464,
23.07/1907, NRS 13655-1-[10/23531]-17464.
85 'In Bankruptcy. Re Moses Hanna, of Elizabeth Street, Redfern', *Government
Gazette of the State of New South Wales*, 14 July 1909, p. 3952.
86 'Moses Hanna Was New Australian Fifty Years This Month', *The Armidale Express*,
6 June 1951, p. 8 See also: 'Records of the Australian Lebanese Historical Society'
Box 4, MS 10162, *National Library of Australia*.
87 Private Papers of Cissie Zathar held in the author's possession.
88 Queenie Sada, *Biography of Cissie Zathar*.
89 Private Papers of Cissie Zathar held in the author's possession. See also: Khatun,
*Australianama*.
90 Queenie Sada, *Biography of Cissie Zathar*.
91 'A Woman's Letter', *The Bulletin*, 13 June 1907, p. 22

### 9. Courtship, Candour and Commodity Culture (*Rodriguez v O'Mara*, 1916)
1 Bailey, *From Front Porch to Back Seat*.
2 '"High Life" in Perth', *Sunday Times*, 17 December 1916, p. 6

3     '"High Life" in Perth', *Sunday Times*, 17 December 1916, p. 6.

4     *Rodriguez v O'Mara* (1916) WASC, *Daily News*, 11 December 1916, p. 8.

5     'Breach of Promise Action', *Western Argus,* Kalgoorlie, 19 December 1916, p. 23

6     *Rodriguez v O'Mara* (1916) WASC, *Western Argus*, 19 December 1916, p. 23; *Kalgoorlie Miner*, 12 December 1916, p. 5; *The West Australian*, 13 December 1916, p. 7; *The Register*, 13 December 1915, p. 9; *The Daily News*, 13 December 1916, p. 8; *Sunday Times*, 17 December 1916, p. 6

7     *Rodriguez v O'Mara* (1916) WASC, *Sunday Times*, 17 December 1916, p. 6

8     *Rodriguez v O'Mara* (1916) WASC, *Sunday Times*, 17 December 1916, p. 6

9     *Rodriguez v O'Mara* (1916) WASC, *Sunday Times*, 17 December 1916, p. 6.

10    *Rodriguez v O'Mara* (1916) WASC, *The Daily News*, 13 December 1916, p. 8

11    Tellingly, a search of Trove, the National Library of Australia's database of digitised Australian collections, returns the term 'keeper ring' 16,000 times between 1890 and 1899 and only 3000 times between 1870 and 1879. It then drops back to 2000 between 1920 and 1929.

12    For historical literature on early twentieth-century love and romance in Australia, see: Hsu-Ming Teo, 'The Americanisation of Romantic Love in Australia', in Curthoys and Lake (eds), *Connected Worlds: History in Transnational Perspective* (ANU Press, 2006), pp. 171–92; Teo, 'Love Writes: Gender and Romantic Love in Australian Love Letters, 1860–1960', *Australian Feminist Studies* 20:48 (2016), pp. 343–61; Reekie, *Temptations*; Bongiorno, *The Sex Lives of Australians*, p. 165. For Britain and America, see: Ilouz, *Consuming the Romantic Utopia*; Bailey, *From Front Porch to Back Seat*; Shumway, *Modern Love*; Seidman, *Romantic Longing*; Langhamer, *The English in Love*.

13    For literature on sexualised consumerism, see: Reekie, *Temptations*; Simmonds, 'Sex Smells', pp. 232–47; Weinbaum et al., *The Modern Girl Around the World*; Lake, 'Female Desires', pp. 267–84.

14    Langhamer, *The English in Love*, p. 160; See also: Lettmaier, *Broken Engagements*, p. 171.

15    Grossberg, *Governing the Hearth*, pp. 35–37; Tushnet, 'Rules of Engagement', p. 2586.

16    Obituary of Maria Caroline Verona Rodriguez, cited in 'Biographical Cuttings on Verona Rodriguez, socialite', NLA, BIB ID 495835.

17    *Daily News*, 16 November 1907, p. 13.

18    'Caroline Verona Rodriguez', *WA Pioneer Index*, 1896; Wendy Birman, 'Maria Caroline (Ronnie) Prevost', *Australian Dictionary of Biography*.

19    *Rodriguez v O'Mara* (1916) WASC, *The West Australian*, 13 December 1916, p. 7.

20    Michael Prevost, 'Filomeno Rodriguez, Master Pearler (1864–1943)', *Rodriguez Family History*, personal correspondence.

21    On Filomeno, see: J.F.J. de Lestang, *Reimagining Australia: Voices of Indigenous Australians of Filipino Descent* (Keeaira Press, 2016), pp. 29–34. On the pearling frontier, see: Filomeno Aguilar, 'Manilamen and Seafaring: Engaging the Maritime World Beyond the Spanish Realm', *Journal of Global History* 7:3 (2012), pp. 364–88; A. Shnukal, 'A Double Exile: Filipino Settlers in the Outer Torres Strait Islands, 1870–1940', *Aboriginal History* 35 (2011) pp. 161–78; Shnukal et al., *Navigating Boundaries: The Asian Diaspora in the Torres Strait* (Pandanus Books, 2017); Julia Martinez and Adrian Vickers, *The Pearl Frontier* (University of Hawaii

Press, 2015); Regina Ganter, *The Pearl-Shellers of Torres Strait: Resource Use, Development and Decline, 1860s–1960s* (Melbourne University Press, 1994); Adrian Cunningham, 'On Borrowed Time: The Australian Pearlshelling Industry, Asian Indentured Labour and the White Australia Policy, 1946–62', Masters of Letters thesis, Australian National University, 1992.

22  Prevost, 'Rodriguez Family History'.

23  Henry Reynolds, *Lectures on North Queensland History* (James Cook University, 1975), pp. 21–29.

24  Bamford, Final Report, 1916, cited in Ganter, *The Pearl-Shellers of Torres Strait*, p. 114; Pearling Conditions, A1/15 1914/12612, NAA.

25  Martinez and Vickers, *The Pearl Frontier*.

26  Prevost, 'Rodriguez Family History'; Lestang, *Reimagining Australia*.

27  See Julia Laite, *The Disappearance of Lydia Harvey: A True Story of Sex, Crime and the Meaning of Justice* (Profile Books, 2021), pp. 182–239.

28  'Prize Letter', *The Daily News*, 16 November 1907, p. 13; 'Prize Letter', *The Daily News*, 22 February 1908, p. 10; 'Prize Letter', *The Daily News*, 20 June 1908, p. 11; 'Prize Letter', *The Daily News*, 21 March 1908, p. 10; 'Events to Come', *The Daily News*, 13 February 1909, p. 10.

29  'School Prize Distributions', *The West Australian*, 15 December 1909, p. 9; 'Athletes in the Making', *The West Australian*, 7 November 1908, p. 12; 'School Prize Distributions', *West Australian*, 16 December 1910, p. 2.

30  '"High Life" in Perth', *Sunday Times*, 17 December 1916, p. 6.

31  '"High Life" in Perth', *Sunday Times*, 17 December 1916, p. 6.

32  *Rodriguez v O'Mara* (1916), consignment number 3548, item R26, SROWA.

33  'The Grave Divorce Case', *Western Mail*, 18 May 1917, p. 48.

34  '"High Life" in Perth', *The Sun,* 31 December 1916, p. 12.

35  Eric J. Edwards, 'Sir Robert Furse McMillan', *Australian Dictionary of Biography*; *Rodriguez v O'Mara* (1916) SROWA, consingment number 3548, item R26.

36  *Rodriguez v O'Mara* (1916) WASC, *Western Argus*, 19 December, 1916, p. 23; *Kalgoorlie Miner*, 12 December 1916, p. 5; *The West Australian*, 13 December 1916, p. 7; *The Register*, 13 December 1915, p. 9; *The Daily News*, 13 December 1916, p. 8; *Sunday Times*, 17 December 1916, p. 6.

37  Sir Robert Furse McMillan, *Bench Book*, 1916, p. 221.

38  *Rodriguez v O'Mara* (1916) WASC, *Western Argus*, 19 December 1916, p. 23; *Kalgoorlie Miner*, 12 December 1916, p. 5; *The West Australian*, 13 December 1916, p. 7; *The Register*, 13 December 1916, p. 9; *The Daily News*, 13 December 1916, p. 8; *Sunday Times*, 17 December 1916, p. 6.

39  'Claremont Colleen's Contretemps', *Truth*, 16 December 1916, p. 13.

40  'Alleged Breach of Promise', *The West Australian*, 12 December 1916, p. 8.

41  *Rodriguez v O'Mara* (1916) WASC, *Kalgoorlie Miner*, 12 December 1916, p. 5; *West Australian*, 13 December 1916, p. 7; *The Register*, 13 December 1916, p. 9; *Daily News*, 13 December 1916, p. 8; *Western Argus* , 19 December 1916, p. 23.

42  See Illouz, *Why Love Hurts*, pp. 42ff.

43  *Rodriguez v O'Mara* (1916) WASC, *Kalgoorlie Miner*, 12 December 1916, p. 5; *West Australian*, 13 December 1916, p. 7; *The Register*, 13 Dec 1916, p. 9; *Daily News*, 13 December 1916, p. 8; *Western Argus*, 19 December 1916, p. 23.

44  *Rodriguez v O'Mara* (1916) WASC, *Kalgoorlie Miner*, 12 December 1916, p. 5; *The West Australian*, 13 December 1916, p. 7; *The Register*, 13 December 1915, p. 9; 'Breach of Promise', *Daily News*, 13 December 1916, p. 8; *Western Argus*, 19 December 1916, p. 23.

45  Susman, 'Personality and the Making of Twentieth-Century Culture', pp. 271–85.

46  Conor, *The Spectacular Modern Woman*, p. 2. See also: Matthews, *Dance Hall and Picture Palace*; Bartky, 'Foucault, Femininity'; Reekie, *Temptations*; Kathy Peiss, *Hope in a Jar: The Making of America's Beauty Culture* (Henry Holt and Company, 1999).

47  Bailey, *From Front Porch to Back Seat*, p. 3.

48  Illouz, *Why Love Hurts*, p. 56.

49  Conor, *The Spectacular Modern Woman*.

50  *Rodriguez v O'Mara* (1916) WASC, *Kalgoorlie Miner*, 12 December 1916, p. 5; *The West Australian*, 13 December 1916, p. 7; *The Register*, 13 December, 1915, p. 9; 'Breach of Promise', *Daily News*, 13 December, 1916, p. 8; *Western Argus*, 19 December, 1916, p. 23.

51  *Rodriguez v O'Mara* (1916) WASC, *West Australian*, 12 December, 1916, p. 8.

52  See, for example, Eliza Leslie, *Miss Leslie's Behaviour Book: A guide and Manual for Ladies* (T.B. Peterson and Brothers, 1859), pp. 181–82; An Aristocrat, *Manners and Rules of Good Society* (F. Warne and Co., 1888), p. 231; *Chitty on Contract* (1912), p. 630; *Chitty on Contract* (1921), pp. 624ff.

53  *Horan v Earle* 53 (NY 267, 271), as cited in *Chitty on Contract* (1921), p. 624.

54  *Brown v Byham* (1909) VICSC, *Western Star*, 5 May 1909, p. 4.

55  *Bell v Pougoure* (1915) QLDSC, *Brisbane Courier*, 27 July 1915, p. 7.

56  *Manterfield v Bloomfield* (1927) TASSC, *The Mercury*, Friday 25 October 1929, p. 3.

57  *Rodriguez v O'Mara* (1916) WASC, *West Australian*, 12 December, 1916, p. 8.

58  Eleanor Aimes, *Book of Modern Etiquette* (New York, 1935), pp. 111ff.

59  *Wilcox v Robottom* (1920) QLDSC, *Darling Downs Gazette*, 10 September 1920, p. 3.

60  Aimes, *Book of Modern Etiquette*, pp. 111ff; *Robottom v Walker* (1914) WASC, *Kalgoorlie Miner*, 12 December 1914, p. 4; *Ezzy v Blondsmith* (1910) NSWSC, *Evening News*, 15 June 1910, p. 7.

61  *Horton v Keenan* (1904) VICSC, 'Breach of Promise', *The Argus*, 27 February 1904, p. 17.

62  *Wildie v Constable* (1900) NSWSC, 'Breach of Promise Case', *Evening News*, 30 November 1900, p. 3.

63  *Rodriguez v O'Mara* (1916) WASC, *The Daily News*, 13 December 1916, p. 8.

64  *Rodriguez v O'Mara* (1916) WASC, *The West Australian*, 13 December 1916, p. 7; *The Register*, 13 December 1915, p. 9; *The Daily News*, 13 December, 1916, p. 8.

65  *The West Australian*, 12 December 1916, p. 8.

66  *The Daily News*, 12 December 1916, p. 7.

67  Sir Robert Furse McMillan, *Bench Book 1916*, p. 220.

68  'Groperdom Gossip', *The Sun*, 17 December 1916, p. 5.

69  *Cost of Living of Adult Female Workers* (1918), NRS-670-1-[2/5768-2/5768], SRONSW.

70  'Abolition of Breach of Promise Actions', *SAR*, 10 July 1879, p. 4.

71  *Sykes v Huxley* (1901) QLDSC, *Evening Telegraph*, 4 December 1901, p. 2.

72  *Baldwin v Dickinson* (1907) Melb CC, *Sunday Times*, 26 May 1907, p. 12.

73  *Denver v Smith* (1910) NSW DC, *The Sun*, 20 September 1910, p. 5.

74 *Parker v Hallam* (1907) NSWSC, *Molong Argus,* 5 April 1907, p. 10; *Stanbrook v Carr* (1912) VICSC, *Ballarat Star,* 5 October 1912, p. 3.

75 *Anzelark v Smith* (NSWSC) 1912, *Bathurst Times,* 1 October 1912, p. 2; *Boyd v Chaplin,* Daylesford County Court, 1913, *The Argus,* 8 August 1913, p. 14.

76 *McQuilkin v Grogan* (VICSC) 1915, *The Argus,* 17 August 1915, p. 4.

77 *Flanagan v Cunningham-Armstrong* (1914) VICSC, *The Argus,* 31 March 1914, p. 7.

78 *Sharpies v Collier* (Wollongong District Court) 1921, *Illawarra Mercury,* 29 July 1921, p. 3.

79 See for example *Levett v Darcy* (1921) NSWDC, as cited in *Young Witness,* 2 December 1921, p. 1.

80 Liz Conor, *The Spectacular Modern Woman,* p. 24; Schaffer, 'Self-Evidence', 327–62.

81 Michael Prevost, personal correspondence.

82 'Breach of Promise Action', *Western Argus,* 19 December 1916, p. 23.

83 Breach of Promise Action', *Western Argus,* 19 December 1916, p. 23; 'Breach of Promise Action', *Kalgoorlie Miner,* 12 December 1916, p. 5; 'Evidence of the Plaintiff Concluded', *The West Australian,* 13 December 1916, p. 7; 'Breach of Promise Claim', *The Register,* 13 December 1915, p. 9; 'Breach of Promise', *The Daily News,* 13 December 1916, p. 8; *Sunday Times,* 17 December 1916, p. 6.

84 *Rodriguez v O'Mara* (1916) WASC, *Western Argus,* 19 December 1916, p. 23; *Kalgoorlie Miner,* 12 December 1916, p. 5; *The West Australian,* 13 December 1916, p. 7; *Western Argus,* 19 December 1916, p. 23; *The Register,* 13 December 1915, p. 9; *The Daily News,* 13 December 1916, p. 8.

85 Sir Robert Furse Mc Millan, Bench Book, 1916, p 220–22. *Rodriguez v O'Mara* (1916) WASC, *Western Argus,* 19 December 1916, p. 23; *Kalgoorlie Miner,* 12 December 1916, p. 5; *The West Australian,* 13 December 1916, p. 7; *The Register,* 13 December 1915, p. 9; *The Daily News,* 13 December 1916, p. 8; *Sunday Times,* 17 December 1916, p. 6.

86 *Rodriguez v O'Mara* (1916) WASC, *The Daily News,* 13 December 1916, p. 8.

87 *Rodriguez v O'Mara* (1916) WASC, *Western Argus,* 19 December 1916, p. 23; *Kalgoorlie Miner,* 12 December 1916, p. 5; *The West Australian,* 13 December 1916, p. 7; *The Register,* 13 December 1915, p. 9; *The Daily News,* 13 December 1916, p. 8; *Sunday Times,* 17 December 1916, p. 6.

88 *Grave v Grave* (1917) Divorce Court, *Western Argus,* 15 May 1917, p. 7; 'The Grave Divorce Case', *Western Mail,* 18 May 1917, p. 48; 'A Grave Situation', *Truth,* 19 May 1917, p. 5.

89 'The Grave Divorce Case', *Western Mail,* 18 May 1917, p. 48; 'A Grave Situation', *Truth,* 19 May 1917, p. 5.

90 *Grave v Grave* (1917) Divorce Court, *Western Argus,* 15 May 1917, p. 7.

91 *Grave v Grave* (1917) Divorce Court, *Western Argus,* 15 May 1917, p. 7.

92 Michael Prevost, personal correspondence.

93 Ian Mackersey, *The Life of Sir Charles Kingsford Smith* (Little Brown and Company, 1998), pp. 57–59

94 'Motors and Motoring', *Sunday Times,* 22 May 1927, p. 27.

95 Mary Gage et al., 'The Price of Pearls: A Two-hour, Two-act Play' (unpublished), 1977, Fyer Library, Queensland, H0605A.

96 'Family Notices', *The West Australian,* 12 August 1940, p. 11.

97 Gage, 'The Price of Pearls'.

98    Michael Prevost, personal correspondence.

99    Obituary of Maria Caroline Verona Rodriguez, cited in 'Biographical Cuttings on
      Verona Rodriguez, socialite', BIB ID 495835, NLA.

## 10. Proof, Performance and the Legal History of Heartbreak
## (*Daniels v Culverhouse*, 1920)

1     *Daniels v Culverhouse* (1920) VICSC, *The Argus*, 21 May 1920, p. 13.

2     *Daniels v Culverhouse* (1920) VICSC *Truth*, 30 May 1920, p. 9.

3     'Folies Marigny', *Le Radical*, 26 May 1914, p. 4. See also 'Ambassadeurs', *Le Frou
      Frou*, 5 July 1914, p. 18; 'Aux Ambassadeurs', *Le Figaro*, 29 May 1914, p. 5.

4     'Shocks and Thrills in Frock', *Table Talk*, 15 July 1915, p. 18.

5     'On and Off the Stage', *Table Talk*, 24 January 1918, p. 12.

6     'Stage Dancers in Court', *The Age*, 19 May 1920, p. 10.

7     'Simply Crazy with Love', *The Argus*, 20 May 1920, p. 8.

8     *Daniels v Culverhouse* (1920) VICSC, *The Argus*, 21 May 1920, p. 13.

9     *Daniels v Culverhouse* (1920) VICSC, *Truth*, 30 May 1920, p. 9.

10    For scholarly debate over awarding non-economic damages in tort law see,
      for example: Joseph H. King Jr, 'Pain and Suffering, Noneconomic Damages,
      and the Goals of Tort Law', *SMU Law Review* 57 (2004), pp. 1401–22; Rachel
      F. Moran, 'Law and Emotion, Love and Hate', *Journal of Contemporary Legal
      Issues* 11 (2001), pp. 747–84; Shuman, 'How We Should Address Mental and
      Emotional Harm Viewpoint', *Judicature* 90 (2006), pp. 789–920; John L. Ehrler,
      'Negligently Inflicted Emotional Harm: Let's Get Serious', *Colonial Lawyer* 18
      (1989), pp. 75–99.

11    Tushnet, 'Rules of Engagement', p. 2586; Grossberg, *Governing the Hearth*,
      pp. 35–37.

12    Lettmaier, *Broken Engagements*, p. 171. Frost argues that the action was used until
      the 1940s: Frost, *Promises Broken*.

13    *Evidence (Further Amendment) Act* (1869) 32 Vict., c. 68; assented to in all the
      Australian colonies except Victoria as *An Act for the Further Amendment of the
      Law of Evidence*, s. 2 (Western Australia in 1871; New South Wales in 1876; South
      Australia in 1870; Queensland in 1874; Tasmania in 1870). Victoria did pass an
      Act for the further amendment of the Law of Evidence (1876), however it did not
      require corroboration.

14    'A Charming Dancer's Progress', *Graphic of Australia*, 31 December 1918, p. 10.

15    'A Charming Dancer's Progress', *Graphic of Australia*, 31 December 1918, p. 10.

16    Robert Halliday, *Suffolk: Strange but True* (History Press, 2008); *The Ipswich
      Journal*, 22 March 1888; see also: *Bridport News*, 30 March 1888, p. 8; *Warrington
      Examiner*, 24 March 1999, p. 2.

17    1891 England Census, Suffolk, St Margaret, p. 30.

18    'Extraordinary Charge Against a Suffolk Rector', *The Ipswich Journal*,
      22 March 1888.

19    'An Act to remove Doubts as to the validity of Certain Marriages solemnized by a
      Person falsely pretending to be an ordained Clergyman of the Church of England',
      13 August 1888, in *Public General Statutes* (Great Britain), Volume 25, Chapter 28,
      p. 204.

20    'Extraordinary Charge Against A Suffolk Rector', *The Ipswich Journal*, 22 March
      1888; see also: 'Serious Charge Against a Clergyman', *Bridport News*, 30 March

1888, p. 8; 'The Reverend George Frederick Wilfrid Ellis', *Warrington Examiner*, 24 March 1999, p. 2; 'An Alleged Sham Clergyman', *The People*, 1 April 1888, p. 14.

21 Georg Simmel, 'The Metropolis and Mental Life', *The Sociology of Georg Simmel* (New York Free Press), pp. 409–24.

22 For literature on Vaudeville, see: Richard Waterhouse, *From Minstrel Show to Vaudeville: The Australian Popular Stage, 1788–1914*; Peter Jelavich, 'Modernity, Civic Identity and Metropolitan Entertainment: Vaudeville, Cabaret and Revue in Berlin, 1900–1933', in *Berlin: Culture and Metropolis* (University of Minnesota Press, 1987); Andrew Erdman, *Queen of Vaudeville: The Story of Eva Tanguay* (Cornell University Press, 2012).

23 Ernst von Wolzogen, as cited in Jelavich, 'Modernity, Civic Identity and Metropolitan Entertainment'.

24 'Divorce or Death', *The Register*, 21 September 1916, p. 5; 'Dancer and Dame', *Truth*, 23 September 1916, p. 6.

25 'Dick Whittington', *The Era*, 15 January 1910, p. 19; 'Daisy Yates: Always Blooming', Poster, 1910; 'Pavilion, Glasgow', *Music Hall and Theatre Review*, 1 December 1905; 'Daisy Yates', *Music Hall and Theatre Review*, 15 March 1907, p. 1; 'Hippodrome 7', *Port-Glasgow Express*, 17 February 1911, p. 2; 'Miss Daisy Yates', *Leicester Evening Mail*, 16 March 1912, p. 3.

26 'Revue', *Aurore*, 3 June 1914, p. 2; *Excelsior*, Paris, 4 June 1914, p. 10.

27 'Divorce or Death', *The Register*, 21 September 1916, p. 5; 'Dancer and Dame', *Truth*, 23 September 1916, p. 6.

28 'Musical Comedy Artists: Arrival of Mr and Miss Yates', *Daily Herald*, Adelaide, 17 May 1915, p. 3.

29 Alexis Witt, 'Networks of Performance and Patronage: Russian Artists in American Dance, Vaudeville and Opera, 1909–1947', PhD thesis, 2018; Robert Burnett, *The Global Jukebox: The International Music Industry, Vol. 18* (Psychology Press, 1996).

30 *Daniels v Culverhouse* (1920) VICSC, *The Age*, 19 May 1920, p. 10; *Daily Herald*, 17 May 1915, p. 3.

31 'Plays and People', *Sunday Times*, 12 March 1916, p. 961.

32 See 'Play, Players and Pictures', *The Mail*, 22 May 1915, p. 6; 'Tivoli Follies', *Daily Standard*, 23 July 1917, p. 2; 'Two Concerts', *TDT*, 22 March 1919, p. 18; 'Spectacular Dramatic Triumph', *The Advertiser*, 1 December 1916, p. 2.

33 'Dancer Issues Writ', *The Sun*, 26 November 1918, p. 5.

34 *Daniels v Culverhouse* (1920) VICSC, *The Age*, 19 May 1920, p. 10.

35 'Mother Hubbard', *Table Talk*, 24 December 1919, p. 10.

36 'Theatrical Tangle', *Truth*, 30 May 1920, p. 9.

37 *Daniels v Culverhouse* (1920) VICSC, *The Age*, 19 May 1920, p. 10.

38 *Daniels v Culverhouse* (1920) VICSC, *Geelong Advertiser*, 21 May 1920, p. 5.

39 *Daniels v Culverhouse* (1920) VICSC, *The Age*, 19 May 1920, p. 10.

40 *Daniels v Culverhouse* (1920) VICSC, *Daily Examiner*, 25 May 1920, p. 3.

41 *Daniels v Culverhouse* (1920) VICSC, *The Argus*, 21 May 1920, p. 13.

42 *Daniels v Culverhouse* (1920) VICSC, *The Age*, 19 May 1920, p. 10.

43 *Daniels v* Culverhouse (1920) VICSC *Truth* , 30 May 1920, p. 9.

44 *Daniels v Culverhouse* (1920) VICSC *The West Australian*, 19 May 1920. p. 6.

45 *Daniels v Culverhouse* (1920) VICSC, *Truth*, 30 May 1920, p. 9.

46   *Daniels v Culverhouse* (1920) VICSC, *Truth*, 30 May 1920, p. 9.
47   'Popular Dancers in a New Role', *The Herald*, 19 May 1920, p. 1.
48   *Daniels v Culverhouse* (1920) VICSC, *Truth*, 30 May 1920, p. 9.
49   'Popular Dancers in a New Role', *The Herald*, 19 May 1920, p. 1.
50   *Daniels v Culverhouse* (1920) VICSC, *The Age,* 22 May 1920, p. 40.
51   'Theatrical Dancer's Suit', *The Argus*, 21 May 1920, p. 13.
52   Chitty, *A Practical Treatise on the Law of Contracts*, 1872, pp. 585–87.
53   *Halley v Jackson* (1869) NSWSC, *Wagga Wagga Advertiser*, 13 October 1869, p. 2.
54   *Field v Nelson* (1850) NSWSC, *Bell's Life,* 6 July 1850, p. 1.
55   *Field v Christy* (1902) QLDSC, *Ipswich Herald and General Advertiser*, 8 November 1902, p. 3.
56   *Jaeger v Kuhl* (1916) SASC, *The Register*, 20 October 1916, p. 6.
57   *Cooper v Barnett* (1905) TASSC, *The Mercury*, 29 September 1905, p. 7.
58   *Newling v Smith* (1903) NSWSC, *SMH,* 19 December 1903, p. 11; *Garie v Mander* (1905) NSWSC, *The Advertiser*, 6 July 1905, p. 8; *Witt v Hay* (1905), *Daily News,* 6 May 1905, p. 8; *Swanston v Stick* (1908) VICSC, *The Argus,* 15 May 1908, p. 7.
59   *Broadhurst v Archer* (1918) VICSC, *Kalgoorlie Miner*, 16 April 1918, p. 3.
60   *Chadwick v Finch* (1919) TASSC, *The Mercury*, 6 March 1919, p. 7.
61   *Chadwick v Smith* (1951) QLDSC,*Truth*, 26 August 1951, p. 43; *Peel v Riley* (1912) VICSC, *BA,* 26 March 1912, p. 2; *Fox v Sims* (1918) NSWSC, *The Telegraph*, 18 June 1918, p. 7; *Ambler v Sheckleton* (1921) NSWSC, *The Argus*, 9 July 1921, p. 19.
62   *Lory v Lindsay* (1931) VICSC, PROV: VPRS 5328, P0000, Unit 90, No. 129, file no. 315.
63   Stephen Garton, *Medicine and Madness: A Social History of Insanity in New South Wales, 1880–1940* (UNSW Press, 1988), p. 40.
64   Garton, *Medicine and Madness,* p. 54.
65   Garton, *Medicine and Madness,* p. 64.
66   Garton, *Medicine and Madness,* p. 76.
67   Garton, *Medicine and Madness,* p. 76.
68   Josef Breuer et al., *Studies on Hysteria: The Pelican Freud Library, Vol. 3* (Penguin, 1974), p. 135.
69   Ernest Snowden, 'The Conversion Neurosis', *Postgraduate Medical Journal* 2:15 (1926), pp. 40–44.
70   See, for example: *Blunt v Olding* (1919) NSWSC, *Daily Examiner,* 6 September 1919; *Lodge v Boyce* (1919) WASC, *West Australian*, 27 June 1919.
71   *Broadhurst v Archer* (1918) VICSC.
72   *Chadwick v Finch* (TASSC) (1919), *The Mercury*, 6 March 1919, p. 7.
73   *White v Proude* (1908) SASC, *The Advertiser*, 19 September 1908, p. 7.
74   Yarrabend Asylum Patient Case Records, Public Records of Victoria (PROV) PVRS 07400, P0001, 000012.
75   *Medical Journal of Australia*, 1 August 1914, p. 117.
76   'Stage Dancers in Court', *The Age*, 19 May 1920, p. 10.
77   Illouz, *Why Love Hurts*, pp. 41–57.
78   Illouz, *Why Love Hurts*, pp. 41–58.
79   Illouz, *Why Love Hurts*, pp. 41–58.
80   John Tosh, 'Home and Away: The Flight from Domesticity in Late-Nineteenth-Century England Revisited' *Gender and History* 27:3 (2015), pp. 561–75; Martin Francis, 'The Domestication of the Male? Recent Research on Nineteenth- and Twentieth-Century British Masculinity', *The Historical Journal* 45:3 (2002), pp. 637–52.

81  *The Argus,* 22 May 1920, p. 22.

82  *The Argus,* 22 May 1920, p. 22.

83  See Matt Houlbrook, *Prince of Tricksters* (University of Chicago Press, 2016).

84  Houlbrook, *Prince of Tricksters.*

85  'Attractions', *Referee,* 5 September 1917, p. 14.

86  S.R. Henry, *By Heck: Fox Trot* (Albert's Music Stores, Sydney, 1914).

87  'Dancer Non Suited', *TDT,* 16 April 1924, p. 18.

88  'Dancer Non-Suited', *TDT,* 16 April 1924, p. 18.

89  'Dancer Non-Suited', *TDT,* 16 April 1924, p. 18.

90  Tivoli (vaudeville circuit), 3531752, National Library of Australia; 'Which Panto Are You?', *Kurt of Gerolstein* (blog), http://kurtofgerolstein.blogspot. com/2021/02/1913-which-panto-are-you.html.

91  'A Charming Dancer's Progress', *Graphic of Australia,* 31 December 1918, p. 10.

## 11. Love, Law and Feminist Consciousness (*Allan v Growden*, 1938)

1   *Allan v Growden* (1938) WASC, 3848, item 39, SROWA.

2   'Women's Gossip', *The Daily News,* 21 July 1934, p. 15.

3   'Supreme Healing Power', *The Wiluna Miner,* 11 December 1936, p. 4.

4   *Allan v Growden* (1938) WASC, 3848, item 39, SROWA; *West Australian* 21 October 1938, p. 14.

5   *Allan v Growden* (1938) WASC, 3848, item 39, SROWA.

6   'Growden Says He Was Merely a Friend', *The Daily News,* 20 October 1938, p. 1.

7   'Plaintiff's "Poetic" Leanings,' *The West Australian,* 21 October 1938, p. 14.

8   'Case Against Policeman,' *Townsville Daily Bulletin,* 4 December 1937, p. 9.

9   'The Police Sergeant and the Lady', *Mirror,* 4 December 1937, p. 19.

10  'CORRECTION. Sergeant Growden,' *The West Australian,* 4 December 1937, p. 20.

11  'The Police Sergeant and the Lady', *Mirror,* 4 December 1937, p. 19.

12  'Woman Sues Police Sergeant', *The Daily News,* 2 December 1937, p. 1.

13  'Plaintiff's "Poetic" Leanings,' *The West Australian,* 21 October 1938, p. 14.

14  Jeremy Birman, 'Sir John Patrick Dwyer', *Australian Dictionary of Biography.*

15  *Allan v Growden* (1938) WASC, *The West Australian,* 21 October 1938, p. 14.

16  *Allan v Growden* (1938) WASC, *Mirror,* 22 October 1938, p. 12.

17  *Allan v Growden* (1938) WASC, *Mirror,* 22 October 1938, p. 12.

18  *Allan v Growden* (1938) WASC, *The Daily News,* 20 October 1938, p. 7.

19  *Allan v Growden* (1938) WASC, *The West Australian,* 20 October 1938, p. 14.

20  *Allan v Growden* (1938) WASC, *The West Australian,* 20 October 1938, p. 14.

21  *Allan v Growden* (1938) WASC, *The West Australian,* 20 October 1938, p. 14.

22  Diane Kirkby, *Barmaids: A History of Women's Work in Pubs* (Cambridge University Press, 1997).

23  Alana Piper, 'Fortune-telling', in *A Companion to the History of Crime and Criminal Justice* (Policy Press, 2017) pp. 92–94.

24  Weinbaum et al., *The Modern Girl Around the World,* p. 8.

25  Victorian Registry of Births, Deaths and Marriages, Birth Index 1837–1917, Rubenia Marwick Allan, ref. 3106.

26  *Allan v Growden* (1938) WASC, 3848, item 39, SROWA; *The Daily News,* 21 July 1934, p. 15.

27  *Allan v Growden* (1938) WASC, 3848, item 39, SROWA.

28  *Allan v Growden* (1938) WASC, 3848, item 39, SROWA.

29  *Allan v Growden* (1938) WASC, 3848, item 39, SROWA.

30  *Allan v Growden* (1938) WASC, 3848, item 39, SROWA.

31  'Supreme Healing Power', *The Wiluna Miner*, 11 December 1936, p. 4.

32  Piper, 'Fortune-telling'.

33  *Allan v Growden* (1938) WASC, 3848, item 39, SROWA.

34  *Allan v Growden* (1938) WASC, 3848, item 39, SROWA.

35  *Allan v Growden* (1938) WASC, 3848, item 39, SROWA.

36  *Lory v Lindsay* (1931) VICSC, PROV. VPRS 5328, P0000, Unit 90, No. 129, File no. 315.

37  *Brown v Shearston* (1933) SCNSW, *Northern Star*, 31 August 1933, p. 7.

38  *Exton v Ambler* (1920) NSWSC, *Daily Observer*, 7 September 1920, p. 2.

39  See, for example, Sylvia Federici, *Revolution at Point Zero: Housework, Reproduction and Feminist Struggle* (PM Press, 2020); Ellen Malos (ed.), *The Politics of Housework* (New Clarion Press, 1995); James Keating, 'Woman as Wife, Mother, and Home-Maker: Equal Rights International and Australian Feminists' Interwar Advocacy for Mothers' Economic Rights', *Signs: Journal of Women in Culture and Society* 47:4 (2002), pp. 957–85.

40  *Hine v Schmidt* (1912) NSWSC, *Truth*, 22 December 1912, p. 5.

41  'Given £125 for Breach of Promise', *NMH*, 2 April 1946, p. 5.

42  *Allan v Growden* (1937) WASC, *The West Australian*, 4 December 1937, p. 20.

43  *Allan v Growden* (1938) WASC, *Mirror*, 22 October 1938, p. 12.

44  *Allan v Growden* (1938) WASC, *Mirror*, 22 October 1938, p. 12.

45  *Allan v Growden* (1938) WASC, *The Daily News*, 20 October 1938, p. 2.

46  *Allan v Growden* (1938) WASC, *The West Australian*, 21 October 1938, p. 14.

47  G.C. Bolton, 'Thomas John Hughes', *Australian Dictionary of Biography*.

48  *Allan v Growden* (1938) WASC, *The West Australian*, 21 October 1938, p. 14.

49  *Allan v Growden* (1938) WASC, *The West Australian*, 21 October 1938, p. 14.

50  *Allan v Growden* (1938) WASC, *Mirror*, 22 October 1938, p. 12; *West Australian*, 21 October 1938, p. 14.

51  *Allan v Growden* (1938) WASC, *The West Australian*, 21 October 1938, p. 14.

52  *Allan v Growden* (1938) WASC, *Mirror*, 22 October 1938, p. 12.

53  *Allan v Growden* (1938) WASC, *The West Australian*, 21 October 1938, p. 14.

54  *Allan v Growden* (1938) WASC, *The West Australian*, 21 October 1938, p. 14.

55  *Allan v Growden* (1937) WASC, *The Courier-Mail*, 3 December 1937, p. 18.

56  *Henry v Schwabe* (1912) NSWSC, *The Register*, 6 December 1912, p. 7.

57  *Bushby v Beardsall* (1913) NSWSC, *The Register*, 19 September 1913, p. 8.

58  *Caulfield v Edge* (1901) VICSC, *The Argus*, 29 August 1901, p. 7.

59  Frederick Octavius Arnold, *The Law of Damage and Compensation* (London, 1913), p. 440.

60  *Cooper v Barnett* (TASSC) (1905), *SMH*, 29 September 1905, p. 4.

61  *Bentley v Clews* (Rockhampton District Court QLD) (1913); *TWC*, 19 April 19, p. 11.

62  See Lake, 'Historical Reconsiderations IV: The Politics of Respectability'; Bongiorno, *The Sex Lives of Australians*, p. 63.

63  Teo, 'The Americanisation of Romantic Love in Australia', pp. 171–92.

64  *Ellis v Smith* (1931) QLDSC, *Arrow*, 11 September 1931, p. 6.

65  *Allan v Growden* (1938) WASC, 3848, item 39, SROWA; *Allan v Growden* (1938), per Dwyer J, *The Western Australian*, 22 October 1938, p. 9.

66  Linda Alcoff, *Rape and Resistance* (Wiley, 2018), p. 126.

67    Wendy Larcombe and Mary Heath, 'Developing the Common Law and Rewriting the History of Rape in Marriage in Australia', pp. 785–807.

68    Martin Pumphrey, 'The Flapper, the Housewife and the Making of Modernity', *Cultural Studies* 1:2 (1987), pp. 179–94; Bartky, 'Foucault, Femininity and the Modernising of Patriarchal Power', pp. 93–111.

69    *Allan v Growden*, (1938) WASC, *Mirror,* 22 October 1938, p. 12.

70    *Allan v Growden*, (1938) WASC, *Mirror,* 22 October 1938, p. 12.

71    *Allan v Growden*, (1938) WASC, *Mirror,* 22 October 1938, p. 12.

72    Tosh, 'Home and Away', pp. 561–75; Francis, 'The Domestication of the Male?', pp. 637–52; Lake, 'Historical Recollections IV: The Politics of Respectability'; Bongiorno, *The Sex Lives of Australians,* p. 63.

73    Illouz, *Why Love Hurts,* p. 56.

74    Illouz, *Why Love Hurts,* p. 56.

75    'Opinion', *The Daily News,* 9 February 1939, p. 4.

76    'Catty Criticism', *The Daily News,* 13 January 1948, p. 2; 'The War Spinster', *The Daily News,* 24 January 1941, p. 4.

77    'Women Move to Aid Evelyn Newman', *Mirror,* 26 April 1941, p. 4.

78    'Badly Treated Women', *The Daily News,* 3 May 1940, p. 4; 'Opinion', *The Daily News,* 30 July 1943, p. 2; 'Opinion', *The Daily News,* 26 December 1947, p. 4.

79    'Aboriginal MP, *The Daily News,* 26 June 1950, p. 4.

80    'Opinion', *The Daily News,* 12 June 1942, p. 2; 'Opinion', *The Daily News,* 12 January 1948, p. 2; 'Opinion', *The Daily News,* 19 October 1942, p. 2.

81    'Opinion Writer: She Gets Praise, Abuse and Marriage Offers', *The Daily News,* 20 April 1948, p. 2.

82    'Opinion Writer', *The Daily News,* 20 April 1948, p. 2.

83    'She Reunites Couples', *Mirror,* 29 September 1951, p. 8.

84    'She Reunites Couples', *Mirror,* 29 September 1951, p. 8.

85    See: (Australia) McKenzie, *Scandal in the Colonies,* pp 50ff; Simmonds, 'Promises and Pie-Crusts Were Made to Be Broke', pp. 99–120; Thornton, 'Historicising Citizenship', p. 1072; (Britain) Lettmaier, *Broken Engagements*; Frost, *Promises Broken*; (Canada) Coombe, 'The Most Disgusting, Disgraceful and Iniquitous Proceeding in Our Law', pp. 65–69; Patrick Brode, *Courted and Abandoned: Seduction in Canadian Law* (University of Toronto Press, 2002); (New Zealand) Megan Simpson, 'The Action for Breach of Promise of Marriage in Early Colonial New Zealand', p. 473.

86    Thornton, 'Historicising Citizenship', pp. 1072–86.

87    'Equality of Sexes and Breach of Promise', *The Advertiser,* 10 April 1940, p. 8.

88    *The Advertiser,* 10 April 1940, p. 8.

89    See Lettmaier, *Broken Engagements,* p. 173–78; Grossberg, *Governing the Hearth,* p. 34; Coombe, 'The Most Disgusting, Disgraceful, Iniquitous Proceeding in Our Law', pp. 64–108.

## 12. From Law to Therapy: Abolishing Breach of Promise of Marriage

1    *Canberra Times,* 3 June 1976, p. 3.

2    Ellicott, RJ, Second Reading, Marriage Amendment Bill 1976 (Cth), 3 June 1976, Hansard, p. 2492. See also: *Family Law Act 1975* (Cth) Part VI; Shurlee Swain and Diana Bryant, *Born in Hope: The Early Years of the Family Court in Australia* (UNSW Press, 2012), p. 3.

3   Ellicott, RJ, Second Reading, Marriage Amendment Bill (1976), 19 August 1976, Hansard, p. 425.

4   Birney, Second Reading, Marriage Amendment Bill (1976), 19 August 1976, Hansard, p. 412.

5   Ellicott, RJ, Second Reading, Marriage Amendment Bill (1976), 3 June 1976, Hansard, p. 2492.

6   Ellicott, RJ, Second Reading, Marriage Amendment Bill (1976), 3 June 1976, Hansard, p. 2492.

7   Britain: *Law Reform (Miscellaneous Provisions) Act* (1970); America: about half of the jurisdictions in America have abolished the action. See: Brinig, 'Rings and Promises', pp. 203–15; South Australia: *Action for Breach of Promise of Marriage (Abolition) Act* (1971); New Zealand: *Domestic Actions Act* (1975).

8   Lettmaier, *Broken Engagements*; Frost, *Promises Broken*. In Canada see: Coombe, 'The Most Disgusting, Disgraceful and Iniquitous Proceeding in Our Law', pp. 65–69. In New Zealand see: Simpson, 'The Action for Breach of Promise of Marriage in Early Colonial New Zealand', p. 473.

9   Illouz, *Why Love Hurts*, p. 4.

10  'Breach of Promise of Marriage', *The Goulburn Herald and Country of Argyle Advertiser*, 20 December 1856, p. 2.

11  'Miscellaneous', *Northern Argus*, 2 January 1885, p. 3.

12  Jane Austen, *Pride and Prejudice* (Penguin Classics, 2019), p. 16.

13  'General News', *The Daily Telegraph*, 7 May 1889, p. 4.

14  'Notes and Comments', *The Australian Star*, 18 May 1889, p. 4.

15  'Woman's Column', *The Newsletter*, 21 September 1907, p. 3.

16  'Matrimony on the Lay-By', *The Sun*, 9 February 1936, p. 45.

17  *Gabriel v Anthony* (1937) QLDSC, *Townsville Daily Bulletin*, 11 November 1937, p. 6.

18  Langhammer, *The English in Love*, pp. 126ff.

19  Marilyn Lake, 'The Desire for a Yank: Sexual Relations between Australian Women and American Servicemen During World War II', *Journal of the History of Sexuality* 2:4 (1992), pp. 621–33.

20  Illouz, *Why Love Hurts*; Illouz, *Cold Intimacies*.

21  'Matrimony on the Lay-By', *The Sun*, 9 February 1936, p. 45.

22  'Equality of Sexes and Breach of Promise of Marriage', *The Advertiser*, 10 April 1940, p. 8.

23  'Woman's Column', *The Newsletter*, 21 September 1907, p. 3.

24  See Regina Graycar and Jenny Morgan, *The Hidden Gender of Law* (Federation Press, 2002); Marilyn Lake, *Getting Equal: The History of Australian Feminism* (Allen and Unwin, 1999).

25  Langhamer, *The English in Love*.

26  'Breach of Promise – and the Law', *Pittsworth Sentinel*, 13 May 1949, p. 4; 'Your Marriage and the Law', *Australian Women's Weekly*, 11 November 1970, p. 143.

27  See: Tushnet, 'Rules of Engagement', p. 2586; Grossberg, *Governing the Hearth*, pp. 35–37; Lettmaier, *Broken Engagements*, p. 171; Langhamer, *The English in Love*, p. 160.

28  Weber, *Economy and Society*, p. 225.

29  Cohen, *Family Secrets*, pp. 224, 247.

30    Michel Foucault, *Discipline and Punish: The Birth of the Prison* (Pantheon Books, 1977).

31    Ellicott, Second Reading, Marriage Amendment Bill (1976), 3 June 1976, Hansard, p. 2492.

32    Ellicott, 'Explanatory Memorandum', Marriage (Amendment) Bill 1976, pp. 3019–32.

33    Susman, 'Personality', pp. 271–85; Illouz, *Why Love Hurts*.

34    Walter Beran Wolfe, *How to Be Happy Though Human* (Routledge, 1932), p. 296.

35    Kereen Reiger, 'The Coming of the Counsellors: The Development of Marriage Guidance in Australia', *Australian and New Zealand Journal of Sociology* 23:3 (1987); Illouz, *Saving the Modern Soul: Therapy, Emotions and the Culture of Self-Help* (University of California Press, 2008); Illouz, *Why Love Hurts*; Garton, *Madness and Medicine*; Ellen Herman, *The Romance of American Psychology: Political Culture in the Age of Experts* (University of California Press, 1995).

36    Hilda Holland, 'What Keeps You From the Altar', *Sunday Herald,* 25 February 1951, p. 7.

37    'What the Modern Girl Should Know: Freud, Love and Psychology', *Chronicle*, 1 October 1936, p. 48.

38    Deane, 'Psychological Advice: *The Sun*, 11 June 1939, p. 6.

39    *Choosing for Happiness* (1950)( https://www.youtube.com/watch?v=ocL1JXrBleA).

40    *Crowley v Dive* (1946) NSWSC, *The Sun*, 1 April 1946, p. 3.

41    *Lyons v Booth* (1935) NSWSC, *The Sun*, 5 September 1935, p. 21.

42    *Carr v Smith* (1937) NSWSC, *The Labor Daily,* 26 June 1937, p. 7.

43    *Carr v Smith* (1937) NSWSC, *The Labor Daily,* 26 June 1937, p. 7.

44    Illouz, *Why Love Hurts*; Herman, *The Romance of American Psychology*.

45    Swain, *Born in Hope.*

46    Illouz, *Saving the Modern Soul,* p. 114. Illouz is citing Herman, *The Romance of American Psychology*.

47    'Her Honour Takes a Look at Women's Rights', *Women's Weekly,* 24 January 1973, pp. 2–3.

48    Ellicott, RJ, Second Reading, Marriage Amendment Bill 1976 (Cth), 3 June 1976, Hansard, p. 2492.

### Epilogue

1    Renata Grossi and Miranda Kaye, 'Love, Law and Money', UTS Symposium, December 2022.

2    Stephanie Wood, *Fake* (Penguin, 2021).

3    Marilyn McMahon, 'The Lucrative Business of Romance Scams', *The Saturday Paper*, 15 October 2022; 'Findings', *Inquest into Renae Marsden,* State Coroner's Court of New South Wales, 20 February 2020.

4    McMahon, 'The Lucrative Business of Romance Scams'.

5    *Magill v Magill* [2006] 226 CLR 551.

6    Hasday, *Intimate Lies and the Law.*

7    *Tereze Burki v Seventy Thirty Ltd* (2018) EWHC 2151 (QB).

8    *A v B* CA 5258/98 [14 July 2004].

9    Justice Barak, *A v B* CA 5258/98 [14 July 2004], p. 336.

# Index

# Index

Fools' Paradise

"You could call your book 'Fools' Paradise'."

"Why's that?"

"Oh, because we were young and foolish," Julie answered. "Because we were living a dream. The dream of a golden afternoon."

She sighed, but she smiled. The last image faded as she slowly closed her photo album. That gleaming white yacht is gone now, like both the summer homes behind it.

"It was a lovely afternoon."

*Irene* Passing Wau Winet and Jewel Islands

# Fools' Paradise

ILLUMINATING.

## Remembering the Thousand Islands

Paul Malo

Copyright 2003 by the Laurentian Press

2 Harris Hill Road

Fulton, New York 13069-4723

(315) 598-4387   phmalo@syr.edu

00 01 02 03 04 05      6 5 4 3 2 1


Includes Notes, Appendices, Bibliography, and Index

ISBN 0-9669729-1-0

Library of Congress Control Number: 2003090589


PRINTED IN CANADA

The front cover shows Carleton Villa, Carleton Island, Cape Vincent, NY. Built in 1894, William Miller of Ithaca, NY, was its architect. The image was adapted from a postcard provided by Sam Williams of Cape Vincent. Marilyn and Phillip Wright contributed the photograph of the Opawaka Lodge gazebo that appears on the rear cover. The Afterword mentions sources of other illustrations.

For Julia Bingham McLean Hass,
my old friend, a fond memory from the past,

and

Amaliya and Mark Malo-Wellman,
my young children and bright hope for the future.

## The Way it Was

--and still is, in some places, as here at Blue Heron Point, out favorite summer retreat today. Here are spent many happy days—"golden afternoons"--with old friends, especially our generous hosts, Frank and Sandy Ellis. F. Courtney Ellis III was the model for "Courtney" in my Boldt Castle book.

# Contents

"It was indeed a fair scene, to . . . look afar off over the wharf with its gay crowd, over the boats gaily ridin' at anchor, and behold the fairy islands risin' from the blue waves crested with castles, and mansions and cottage ruffs, chimblyes and towers all set in the green of the surroundin' trees. And, off fur as the eye could see, way through, between and around, wuz other beautiful islands and trees covered with spires and ruffs peepin' out of the green. And way off, way off like white specks growing bigger every minute, wuz great ships floatin' in, and nearer along through the blue waves, sailin' on and goin' right by and mindin' their own bizness."

"Samantha" [Marietta Holley], 1911

"A Fair Scene"

"Thousand Island House Dock," A. C. McIntyre, Photographer, New York Public Library

PART I

# Conversations with Julie

"The dream of a golden afternoon, . . . a lovely afternoon."
Bluff Island, photograph by Underwood & Underwood, New York Public Library.

My swimming hole at Blue Heron Point with Prisoner's Island in the distance

Rowing over to an island, this curious youngster left his skiff to go exploring. Hidden in rampant growth a maze of old concrete walks emerged. Lichen-covered pavements wandered aimlessly through silvery waves of billowing grass, knee-high. The paths wound through overhanging brambles then disappeared into obscuring brush. One narrow vestige of a walk, hardly discernable, led towards a grove of enormous poplar trees. There, unseen from the water, long masked by acres of dense scrub, emerged a clearing. Amid shimmering leaves, rustling eternally in the island breeze stood a ruinous house.

Not so broad as some of the grand places on the water but tall, it rose into the overhanging trees, where swaying branches rubbed mossy wood shakes. Mottled shingles encrusted the walls like mussels on an ancient anchor. Windows shuttered, some slats hanging, the house seemed dead, every surface weather-beaten to a cadaver's gray. Rotted wooden steps warned against intrusion. But curious youngsters are adventurous.

The door was unlocked—ajar in fact. No one seemed to care. After the summer sun, internal darkness was cool, but forbidding. From brilliant shutter cracks streaked streams of dusty light across a cluttered floor. Inert forms began to emerge. The room was full of old stuff—but the place was mute. Rustling of leaves and drone of a distant motorboat seemed far away, filtered through shutters and broken glass. The muffled sound was a tenuous lifeline to a living world. Within, there was a dank torpor to the place, still occupied by human artifacts—rotting fabrics, musty books. Curious, I touched one. It felt clammy. What was that, over there?

On an oak tabletop, covered with crumbling plaster, a strange object appeared: like a giant fungus, a large horn seemed to be growing out of a wooden case. Strewn among the floor debris, revealed within decaying paper cases, were black cylinders: voices from the past, now still.

"Young man, what are you doing in here?"

I dropped the old phonograph record. Squatting on the floor, I had been reading titles of popular songs unheard for decades. When I turned, the tall figure was silhouetted against the light of the open door. The throaty voice, a skirt and a halo of white curls, luminously backlit, confirmed this to be a woman.

After assuring her that I meant no harm, but only had been curious, the lady—she seemed seven feet tall—escorted me back out. In the daylight I realized that she moved slowly and cautiously, probably because she wore one opaque lens in her glasses. I was surprised, because of her height, to realize that she was an *old* lady—as anyone past middle age is "old" to a youngster. She was not stooped, though; she was regal.

"Now tell me who you are," she commanded. "And what you are doing here." She studied me. "You don't look like a troublemaker."

I answered that I had rowed over in my skiff, as I often had done, from our place on the mainland. I told her that I had permission from the caretaker of one of the big houses to tie up there, whenever the family wasn't present. Recognizing the familiar name of the Edges, she smiled.

"Actually, I'm a visitor here myself," she confided. "I come to see friends here, but also live on the mainland, in Clayton." I noticed that she walked with a cane. "And as we're both visitors on Round Island," she continued, "we have something in common, don't we? And since you've told me who you are, I'll tell you who I am. I'm Julie."

\* \* \*

And so I met Julia Bingham McLean Hass. That was long ago, during the war years back in the 1940s. In high school, given an assignment to write the *Reader's Digest* sort of essay about "The Most Unforgettable Character I Have Known," I would attempt to characterize Julie. She became a friend of our family, spending much time at Steele's Point where my sister and I enjoyed long childhood summers. When Julie was not with us but stayed in town, I would regularly walk along the hot railroad tracks to visit her in the third-floor walk-up apartment on Riverside Drive, above Corbin's, where she lived in reduced circumstances. Julie had lost most of whatever she had—except her spirit—in the Great Depression, but she still cherished her friendship with more fortunate friends, who valued her as a remarkable person.

River Rats

Julia Bingham McLean Hass and the author at Steele's Point, Clayton, c. 1948.

Julie was of the generation that had known the Thousand Islands as young adults during the heyday of the resort at the beginning of the twentieth century. Not in the same league as May Irwin, one of the Thousand Islands' most famous summer residents who was a Broadway celebrity and superstar of the national vaudeville circuit, Julie nevertheless had an eventful theatrical career herself, as testified by many thick scrapbooks about which she reminisced often. Originally intending to become a professional singer, she became resigned to supporting roles after her vocal coach in Berlin "ruined my voice." Her stature and long legs probably were an asset on the stage. Julie never referred to herself as a "chorus girl," but in later years it occurred to me that was probably what she had been, at least much of the time.

Julie was connected to Round Island through her last husband, Kris, an ami-able Dane. His last name, although anglicized as "Hass," was pronounced to rhyme with "Oz." Kris was groundskeeper of Charles Emery's extensive prop-erties, including the grand Frontenac Hotel on Round Island. Julie's apartment had a marvelous view of Emery's Calumet Island, across the main channel from Clayton. I was enthralled with Calumet Castle, always boarded up in my youth — but irresistible and accessible to the trespassing youngsters in town.

"Oh, but you should have seen the island as it was," Julie would recall. "Such flowers! Kris had greenhouses over on Picton Island, you know, and set out thousands — hundreds of thousands, I suppose — of plants every spring on Calu-met and Round Island, as well as the Emery properties on Grindstone and Pic-ton. Flowers everywhere!" She had photographs of the huge floral displays that flanked the wide pavement leading from the pier to the huge hotel that once dominated Round Island and the region.

As an architect-to-be, I was even more interested in the vanished building than the gardens. Did she remember the hotel? Of course, and she recalled how it ended, with the fire that burned the huge structure to the ground — one of a series of fires that ended the halcyon days of the Thousand Islands. That old house on Round Island where we met, spared by the fire, had been the hotel manager's residence. Julie visited it occasionally, she said, to see if it was still there — since it was all that was left.

"I was a young woman then," she recalled. " It was so sad, the loss. It seemed that our youth was over, and I suppose it was, for then the First World War came along. So many young men never came back. All the great steam yachts, taken by the Navy for the war effort, they never came back, either. The age of steam had passed, you know. Then we had autos, so the train service from Manhattan declined. Tourist cabins replaced the grand hotels. It was never the same."

It seemed incredible that Julie had actually seen the big side-wheel steam-boats and the masted steam yachts, dozens of them more than a hundred feet long carrying crews of twelve or more — that she had seen the grand Frontenac Hotel rise to serve international celebrities and then watched it disappear in one night's spectacular fire, vanishing along with the yachts — and Julie had even seen astonishing Boldt Castle rise only to be abandoned. She had known so many of those rich and famous people, many of them now gone as well. And she remembered it all, wanting me to visualize how beautiful it had been. She was a voice from the past.

Depression Round Island

The Frontenac Yacht Club remained shuttered and overgrown during World War II,
photographed by the author. c. 1945.

My walks into Clayton usually were in the early afternoon, even if the railroad tracks were hot, smelling of creosote, because the fish didn't bite in the bright sunlight. I fished mostly before breakfast—providing breakfast, in fact. One afternoon, after Julie called, "Come in," when I didn't find her as usual, with her book at the table in her riverside kitchen, I was surprised to discover her in the living room on the street side, kneeling on the floor. She was peeking out over the windowsill, improbably peering intently through opera glasses. Encased in mother-of-pearl, they were the sort of elegant accessory favored by jeweled dowagers, held by a long handle. Noting my surprise, she laughed. "Oh, this is better than the opera. I police the 'Bucket of Blood'—that's what we call the saloon over there. It's amusing to keep tabs on who's meeting whom there, and which couples come out together."

My parents explained to me that Julie was living on welfare now—or had some sort of support because of her financial need and deteriorating eyesight. Actually, she may have told me that herself, since she was always candid and unpretentious. She saw the incongruity and laughed herself at viewing Clayton local life through opera glasses.

I suppose it was the incongruity that made Julie so fascinating to a youngster. As an actress, she spoke clearly and precisely in modulated tones—using the broad "A" appropriate to one of her previous lives in suburban Connecticut. That was while she was married to a wealthy businessman, prior to the stock market crash of 1929. Her sister had died. She had never had children, so as a widow was now was quite alone, except for many friends.

Julie came from a rather privileged family herself. She laughed to remember that she was one of the two "Bingham Sisters" — "rather notorious" — well known when they were striking debutantes in Watertown, New York. Their father was a physician in the small upstate city that both sisters left, gravitating to Europe and more cosmopolitan venues.

Rather than Riverside Drive, I was more interested in the view toward the river itself, where the great ships passed. This was before construction of the St. Lawrence Seaway, but there seemed to be more large vessels passing then, even if not the seagoing ships of today. And, of course, the river was alive with smaller boats, then as now — even with the Depression and then the war years, when gasoline rationing restricted travel on land and water. Some people — the more fortunate ones — didn't seem to be deterred by the economy or wars, however; they still came to the Thousand Islands. I suppose, in retrospect, that included us, but it never occurred to me at the time. That's the way my parents wanted it. My sister and I were told my mother's coat was "weasel," so we wouldn't know it was mink.

Julie and I often talked about Calumet Castle, that magnetic attraction to this budding architect, so visible from Julie's kitchen window. I had never seen the building opened — few people remembered it in use, since it had been boarded up for many years. The grounds were no longer tended and once-tidy landscaping had run rampant. The Emery family still retained a Clayton man as caretaker, however — but his function had dwindled to an occasional spin around the island to "check on things." Little care was spent on maintenance.

Despite its melancholy decline, Calumet Castle remained glorious. Surmounting a grassy mound on the island, its tiled roofs glistened in the sun. Many towers bristled in contrast to the languid, overgrown foliage engulfing the mansion. Walls of pink Potsdam sandstone clashed vibrantly with the orange roofs. Emery's own villa, even when closed, was sunnier and cheerier than the sad house of his hotel manager on Round Island.

Julie also had old photographs of Calumet Island, taken when her last husband, Kris, had been in charge of the grounds. From her kitchen window she could still make out vestiges of old flower beds he had planted, showing them to me in faded pictures. She remembered that Kris could identify eighty-one varieties of trees on the Emery properties. I asked Julie if she had visited Calumet, when the family was still there.

Calumet Island

The yacht *Nina* in the inner harbor, with the casino at left and main house in the distance. The boat became the Peacock's *Irene* when Emery acquired the much larger yacht, *Calumet*. Note how the skiff is pulled up on the ramp at the casino, and the houseboat in at the back of the harbor. The caretaker's house was out of the picture to the right.

"Oh, but the family is still around," she informed me. "Chuck Emery comes for a week or so of fishing now and then. He never opens the big house but stays in the caretaker's place. It's quite sizeable, you know. Have you seen it, on the other side of the island?" I reminded her that I rowed my skiff all over the river. "Of course," she continued. "Then you know about the other buildings on the island. I remember them well. The casino over the skiff house is the pleasantest place on the island. That's where we played bridge on summer afternoons. The big house was—well, too big."

"Was it dark and gloomy?" I was thinking of the decaying parlor where Julie had first appeared.

"Oh, not at all. There are huge—really enormous—windows behind those winter shutters. They have giant pieces of plate glass—curved in the tower windows—so the interior is really quite bright and sunny. But rooms are just very large, and there are so many of them. And the furnishings—well, they're 'Victorian,' you know. Not all overstuffed, but many summer things—fancy wicker and all that, but fussy. It's the sort of place where you should dress for tea, which would be carried in by a maid wearing a ruffled apron. I couldn't imagine Chuck Emery in there, in his old fishing garb, drinking beer with some current Hollywood girlfriend!"

"Did you go to parties over there?"

Ballroom Wing, Calumet Castle
Photograph by the author, c. 1945

"Oh, yes! The Emerys were very sociable. Irene Emery was very gracious. Her husband Charles was a jolly, round man, bald but with big, handlebar moustaches. We called him 'Judge' Emery — not because of any judicial qualification that I know of, but because he manufactured 'Old Judge' cigarettes.

"Emery was very cordial and built the big ballroom wing for parties. It was really a two-level party space. You see, a curved staircase in the ballroom connected it to another huge room the same size on the second floor. It was quite a sight, the guests in their fancy attire going up and down that staircase!

"And the new wing merely extended the main house, where there were . . . let me see, five large rooms that we saw, plus all that wide verandah and the terrace overlooking the river. It was all thrown open for those large events. Yes, it was really quite a party house, and Emery did throw parties in a big way.

"I remember the whole island illuminated with more than a thousand Japanese lanterns. There would be a couple hundred guests — and I'm not exaggerating. Most visitors had to dock at Clayton and be ferried across. The interiors of the house were banked with flowers and we would dance to music of Kapp's Orchestra and the Gananoque Band. The highlight of the evening would be a fireworks display reflected in the river. Oh, it was so gala!"

I wondered if the Emerys were so liberal in their views as to invite Kris, their gardener, to these parties. Julie laughed. "But I didn't even know Kris in those days. He was living over on Picton Island where the greenhouses were, behind the Emerys' big yacht house. We visitors didn't even see much of him — or know who he was — at the time. I knew the Emery children better, in fact — there were two daughters and a son, Frank. Nina was older, but I was about the same age as Francena, so was part of the 'younger set' on the river at the time. And what a time we had!

"I especially remember cruising in the evening on one or another of the yachts. Refreshments were served and we would sing popular songs of the day, accompanied by the mandolin or guitar. When passing close to Frontenac or another island, folks there might serenade us in return. So much laughter and gaiety, so much fun!"

*  *  *

You don't believe in psychic happenings? I don't either, normally, but let me tell you something odd. This happened about the time I'm recalling, when I was a young teenager, shortly after I had explored Round Island and met Julie in that strange place, the last, ruinous vestige of the vanished Frontenac Hotel.

I was studying piano at the time and after my weekly lessons in downtown Syracuse, I always visited the Public Library. There I devoured every book on architecture and poured through decades of back issues of architectural magazines. In the rear of one of these professional journals, where many small display ads pictured building products, one picture out of hundreds suddenly arrested my attention. At the time I couldn't imagine what it was about that particular image that struck me so vividly. The photograph showed only the portion of a large building, featuring a curved portico with tall classical columns. The columns were the product being sold, I think. The building was unidentified, so it meant nothing to me. The subject was hardly remarkable, and yet somehow it *did* mean something to me. What was it?

One day, at Julie's kitchen table, she was spreading out old photographs of Kris's gardens at the Frontenac Hotel. There it was. The image seen in the old magazine was so vividly imprinted on my mind that I recognized the place instantly. The grand Frontenac Hotel, burned long before I was born. I had never seen its imposing entrance before — or had I?

*  *  *

The Frontenac, J. W. Davidson, Architect

Charles Emery created the grand Frontenac, like his own villa, as a place to entertain and be entertained.  He was a great booster of the resort, even running ads in national magazines at his own expense to promote the region.  Like many other islanders, he wanted not merely a family country home, but a social community.  Emery supported the Thousand Islands Yacht Club and other regional organizations, but the grand hotels at Alexandria Bay–the Thousand Islands House and the Crossmon House–provided  exceptional dining and other social facilities.

Emery was oriented to Clayton rather than Alexandria Bay, however, and wanted Clayton to equal or surpass the Bay.  To accomplish this he acquired a large hotel on nearby Round Island which he greatly enlarged.  It became the Frontenac.  With more than four hundred rooms it was the biggest and (some would say) the best hotel "between the  Atlantic and the Great Lakes."

"Do you remember visiting the Frontenac?"

Julie seemed surprised. ìBut of course I do.  Not when Kris was thereóI mean, he may have been there, and probably I saw him, but I didnít know him.  The hotel burned in 1912, you know.  That was long before I knew Kris."

"What do you remember most about the Frontenac?"

"Why, the people. Such gorgeous people, and such clothes! They were really in a class by themselves—mostly New York City, of course, but international. I remember seeing the Gaekwar of Baroda—an Indian maharaja, said to be one of the wealthiest men in the world—stroll up the wide walk between the huge banks of flowers from the pier to that grand portico. It was a stately procession of dark men in London suits, dark women in Paris gowns, and liveried retinue in colorful silk Indian garb. Plumed turbans! Such a sight!"

"There were always many private yachts tied up at the long pier, but Round Island was a stop on all the big steamboat lines. That was one of the principle activities—watching the comings and goings from the pavilion overlooking the pier—or from the verandah of the Frontenac Yacht Club. It was closer to the water than the hotel or its big annex, both located in the middle of the island. You may have seen the yacht club building. It's one of the large houses now boarded up just below the pier.

"You'd never imagine today the glamour at the yacht clubs. I remember one of the Gold Cup Races—1905, I think, at Chippewa Bay—when there was a gala reception. What a stellar gathering! The Duke of Newcastle was there, and Mrs. Alfred Gwynn Vanderbilt, as well as Mrs. O.H.P. Belmont. She was Alva Vanderbilt, you know, mother of the Duchess of Marlborough. She usually was at Newport for the summer season but she came to the Frontenac for the races.

"I wasn't in that class, qualified to be invited to see the races from the Emery yacht, one of the largest on the river. I did watch from the club verandah, where the yacht party came afterwards for a party—but that was a different Gold Cup race, the one hosted by the Frontenac Yacht Club."

"What did people do at the hotel—all day, I mean, on that island? Fish?"

"Fish? Why, mostly they changed clothes. People came with huge trunks of clothes—several costumes for different times of day, never appearing twice in the same getup. It was madness," she laughed. "You'll see me wearing this same dress often enough, these days!"

"There must have been more to do, really."

"But of course. There were the usual things—tennis, croquet, even a small golf course around the hotel. And one could go out fishing with a guide. I don't think many serious fishermen chose to stay at the Frontenac, however. Serious drinkers, yes. And gambling. Surprised? These were high rollers, New Rich.

"A lot of money changed hands. We ladies played bridge in the hotel, but the serious wagering was done less conspicuously in a casino on the back side of the island. The building's a private cottage now."

"Was there much gambling other places?"

"Not nearly so much as at shore resorts and other fashionable watering holes. It was mostly an upper-class thing here."

"I suppose the food was good at the Frontenac."

"Oh, but eating is what you do at these places—and eating is almost as important as dressing.

"As you may imagine, the food was superb. The big dining room also was often cleared for balls. Then the diamonds came out. I'll bet you don't even know what a 'dancing master' or a 'cotillion' is. The dancing master was really an instructor—the big hotels hired them for work with young people. Harold Rielly at the Crossmon was wonderful.

"We used to get together during long summer days to practice steps—we danced in formation, with lots of moves, sort of like a marching band at midtime during a football game today, only far more elegant. We actually put on quite a performance—choreographed, you know. It was lovely, with the music, laughter—all the gowns and flowers. Never enough boys to go 'round, of course, but we shared. It was fun."

The Frontenac, Round Island

"It sounds quite different from that gloomy old house where we met."

"A different time. And things changed rapidly at that time. When I was a youngster, Round Island had been a staid Baptist resort—imagine that, so wholesome, so dull. The nineties were quite wicked in comparison, and by the turn of the century the new Frontenac had become sybaritic—a fleshpot on the St. Lawrence!" She laughed. "But we had a good time."

\* \* \*

From the cottage porches at Steele's Point we looked over at Round Island. Before I was allowed to row so far alone I used to gaze longingly at the big houses on the head of the island. I always wanted to be taken in the launch to see them once again. But even passing nearby wasn't enough. I wanted to stop, to go ashore. There was something mysteriously compelling about the dark, hulking structures lurking in the shadows of towering, wind-bent pine trees. What was it like, to actually be there?

Julie knew. One of her young friends had been Will Hays. His parents had built the great house on the point, at the time owned by the Edges from Delaware and now by the Withingtons of Watertown who spend as much of the year as possible on the island.

"Will was the life of the party," Julie recalled. "He took his banjo with him everywhere. We would sing as we cruised on his family yacht, *Columbia*, on our way to the Yacht Club. Many a song was sung sitting on the porch steps of that house—or inside, on rainy days. They had a grand staircase, freestanding in the middle of the main hall. It went up to a landing, where there was a large stained-glass window. Then the stairs broke into two flights going in different directions. The landing was like a stage, and Will would perform there. We used to sit on the two flights, serenading each other—sometimes the boys on one, the girls on another—or along the gallery railing of the two-story space. It was so romantic."

I wondered about the Hays family. Julie recalled that they came from New York City, like most of the prominent families on the river. Jacob Hays had one of the original seats on the New York Stock Exchange and his forebears had been prominent in the City, so the Hays were distinguished from many of the New Rich at the Frontenac and elsewhere on the river at the time.

Once I was free to row wherever my skiff would take me, I was allowed to tie up at the dock of the Hays house, then owned by the Edges — when they were not there, that is. Mr. Robbins, their kindly caretaker, lived behind us on Steele's Point. He never took me into the main house, though, but I could only walk around its high stone foundation, looking up at the shingled walls painted in dark red-and-green Victorian colors. I could, however, go in the wonderful casino, or playhouse, behind the boathouse. It was fitted out with elaborate cabinets for fishing gear and had been a rainy day venue for young people, provided with billiard and ping-pong tables. The main house had painted murals in some rooms, Julie said, but the dining room was its most distinctive feature. It occupied the large sort of round tower that projected on the front of the house. Inside the tower there was a continuous, curved window seat, upholstered in brilliant red velvet, particularly striking because the wood paneling was jet black, in contrast also to the blue-and-white Delft tiles of the fireplace at the opposite end of the room.

The Jacob Hays House, Round Island

"It's such an enchanted house," Julie observed, "so distinctive. It has decorative details on the porch devised of hemp rope — a sort of nautical touch. On the sun-dappled lawn they always put out one of those huge, glass gazing globes, hung from a sort of iron arch. Instead of concrete walks, they kept the original wooden boardwalks—such a nice touch. Lovely place, and so cool out on that point, catching the lake breezes in the afternoon."

After becoming an architect and historian, I realized that the Hays House, built in 1888, had been designed in the fashionable Shingle Style of that decade. I came to appreciate it as one of the architecturally finest buildings in the remarkable collection of Thousand Islands landmarks.

* * *

From the Steele's Point cottage porch I often tried to imagine how Round Island once appeared, with the grand hotel towering about the treetops, with huge steamboats puffing smoke and elegant masted yachts converging on the social center. The river was quieter during the lean years when I was a youngster—quieter than it had been at the beginning of the century and quieter, certainly, than today. I used to sleep out on that porch, where the lapping of water against the sea wall was the only sound, except for the regular ringing of the distant bell buoy off Round Island and the occasional puffing of a mysterious passing freighter. Occasionally I might be awakened by a blast of a foghorn. One blast meant intent to pass on the starboard; two blasts meant the port. Then I would wait for an echoing response from the other freighter, confirming the intent of huge ships to pass unseen in the night. Throughout the night a rotating beacon flashed off Round Island. There was a reassuring constancy to it all, timelessness.

The day begins early on the river, especially when sleeping outdoors. Fishermen rise before dawn, and I usually woke to the sound of distant motorboats. I was rarely the first to be out, but never the last. I might be on the water three hours before breakfast. The days were long and lazy. When not walking into town, I filled the hours with rowing my skiff many miles—and surreptitiously exploring abandoned houses and boathouses. The contents were amazing, for people simply walked away from many fine island villas during the Great Depression and war years. They left behind antique boats and furniture that would be highly prized today. I took nothing—nothing of great value, that is—except photos, which I prize highly today. One documented the dining room of the rambling stone house on Isle Imperial, across from Alexandria Bay, now gone.

The Isle Imperial dining room as I found it, abandoned, c. 1950

Carved, highback chairs were still around the table. Salt and pepper shakers remained where they had been placed for the last meal there. The people walked out, leaving the massive front door, with its leaded glass, open.

How I pleaded with my parents to acquire one of these white elephants! Many islands could be had then for back taxes. I recall the Thousand Islands Yacht Club, with its large building, tennis courts, and docks on Welcome Island, being advertised for $700. My parents only laughed when I suggested that we ought to own the Yacht Club. They laughed again when Calumet Castle, on its wonderful U-shaped island that enclosed a protected harbor, was offered for sale. With six buildings and a massive concrete pier, the island could have been acquired (as I recall) for thirteen or twenty-three thousand dollars. The exact figure is immaterial, for it was ridiculous. They laughed as well at the notion of owning one of the boarded-up houses on Round Island. Senator Richardson had brought twelve black servants with him from Delaware to operate his place. The woman who finally bought the big house complained that she spent her entire summer washing eighty-some windows.  Probably my parents were wise, but how grand to live in one of those glorious houses!

Many years later, friends on Round Island urged me to buy the fine Jacob Hays house at the head of Round Island.  Prices had risen by that time, and sixty-five thousand (as I remember it) seemed extravagant for a place to be used eight weeks or so a year.  Of course ever since I've regretted my failure to buy it, and I continue to envy the Withingtons—who fortunately appreciate what they have, now worth far more than ten times what I might have invested in the place.

If not a mansion, why not a boat?  My parents were equally wary.  I recall one day when a local fellow (we called him "Flukie," but I think his name was Flukiger or something like that) pulled up to our dock in a magnificent run-about—one of those long, gleaming wooden jobs with two cockpits and sumptuous tufted leather upholstery. Due to hard times, Flukie wanted to get rid of the boat.  My parents could have had it for $400.  But that was a lot of money during the Depression, and few people (my parents included) needed a big, high-maintenance powerboat.  I don't know what happened to Flukie's boat.  Maybe it's in the Antique Boat Museum at Clayton, or possibly on the market—not for ten times, but more likely a hundred times the price asked back about 1940.

Mothballed

Senator Richardson's Round Island summer home was shuttered and engulfed in scrub brush when I took this photograph during World War II.

If grand country houses were bargains to acquire, filling the showplaces was something else. The single woman who bought Senator Richardson's place—she who complained about window washing—was faced with the prospect of furnishing it. The lady and a friend regularly went to flea markets and garage sales to sweep up enough stuff to fill at least some of the many rooms.

The Frontenac Yacht Club next door was also boarded up when I was a youngster, but fortunately an appreciative owner eventually bought that property. The Colonial Revival house, evidencing much architectural distinction, was originally built as Die Lorelie, for Mrs. Frank A. Peck of Syracuse.

Many of the dozens of cottages on Round Island were maintained during those difficult years; some are still today in families that have been on the island for generations, such as the Potters, who have Brunarche, another of the big houses at the head of the island, next to the Jacob Hays house. It's similarly a Shingle-Style villa of the same period. There was a third imposing residence in this row, but it burned in later years. Only the interesting boathouse remains there. Called Onondaga, the third large villa was the summer home of colorful Sim Dunfee, the pugnacious Irishman who annoyed Charles Emery by driving up the cost of Round Island by bidding against him. Emery had arranged to acquire the entire property at an attractive price at a foreclosure auction. The association apparently was in arrears to repaying improvement loans from Emery, but the common impression was that the transaction was not made under duress but amicably. Emery was supposed to be the only bidder, before Dunfee surprised everyone by disrupting the plan. Emery wanted to enlarge and improve the hotel in the center of the island, which had been developed by a Baptist association, but wanted title to the property before making such a substantial investment. Private summer homes built on leased land were transferred from the association to Emery in the deal. Dunfee didn't like living on Emery's property.

Sim Dunfee was a rough-and-tumble, self-made millionaire from Syracuse whose fortune derived mostly from building trolley lines. Sim was one of many islander fishing cronies in an age of common political graft and corruption. Dunfee acquired Onondaga from James Belden, a Syracuse canal builder who had been prosecuted on corruption charges. Governor Thomas "Old Salt" Alvord, whose island (now called "Governors") was just above Emery's, was identified with the Canal Ring. Construction of the Erie Canal, a colossal New York State public project, offered many opportunities to the enterprising. Mayor Kirk of Syracuse was another politician residing on Round Island. His big house was called, appropriately, "Tammany Hall."

Tammany Hall
One of the lost houses of Round Island was built by Mayor Kirk of Syracuse.

There were, and still are, other large summer homes on Round Island. Many of the smaller cottages on the island are also distinctive. Most of the open land in the center of the island, once a golf course, has grown up to be wooded. An association maintains communal tennis courts and a public dock, retaining a post office building that was in use until service was discontinued in more recent years. Much of the island is still owned in common, purchased collectively from the Emery estate at a time when cottagers acquired title from the estate to the many private properties around the edge of the island.

\* \* \*

Charles Emery was in the big leagues, compared to these Upstate yokels, particularly when it came to being prosecuted by the government. Emery was a major shareholder and treasurer of the American Tobacco Company, charged with anti-trust violation. The trial was one of the government's "trust-busting" precedents. Because of the historical importance of three notable islanders, Emery as well as George Pullman and Frederick Bourne warrant special articles, which follow.

\* \* \*

"You didn't climb that tower!" Julie was aghast, or perhaps feigned appreciation of my daring. "Didn't you see the signs warning visitors that it's dangerous?" I confessed that I ignored them, but failed to admit that I took one of the signs as a souvenir. Looking across the main channel from her kitchen window, I asked Julie if she had ever climbed to the top of the tall, freestanding tower on the far side of the island. Yes, she told me. That was part of the usual tour, back when the stairs were safer—if one was young enough to want to climb all the flights to the top. The tower provided a good view, she recalled, especially of the rest of the island with its many buildings.

The island was called "Calumet," a Native American name supposedly for the peace pipe, since it was shaped something like Sherlock Holmes' pipe, with a mound at the bowl of the pipe, where the Castle rose, while the stem wound around a lovely internal harbor. Actually, it had been practically two islands, which were connected by a narrow causeway to enclose and shelter the harbor from the prevailing winds off the lake. Ringed around the harbor were the skiff house, with a recreation room above, then a massive stone icehouse built into the hill under the Castle, and nearby a powerhouse that generated electricity. Then, across the harbor was the laundry building, with the great tower behind it, and finally the big caretaker's house.

What was in the tower originally, I wondered? The lower several stories were built of stone; the upper part was clad in wood shingles.

"Mostly the inside was just a hollow space containing stairways, winding up and up," Julie recalled. I suppose there were some rooms in the larger square part at the bottom. There was a big water tank high up, and that was the real purpose of the thing, I suppose, but there was an observation gallery at the very top, with a balcony running all around the outside. It was delightful —exciting, and even a little scary. Mr. Emery became concerned about someone falling, though, so put up a sign prohibiting us young people from going up there any more. You can image that at parties, after partaking a bit too much of the liquid refreshment, you wouldn't want your guests climbing to the top."

"You mentioned the skiff house. Wasn't there a bigger boathouse? What's the difference?"

"Well, there are three different kinds of buildings for boats: a skiff house, a boathouse, and a yacht house. The skiff house doesn't have water inside, with slips so that boats can enter while in the water. Instead it has a ramp on the outside going down into the water, so the skiffs and canoes can be pulled out of the water and into the building. Larger launches require a boathouse, which as you know, is where you can drive the boat in, keeping it in the water but out of the weather—and the sun, so bad for varnished wood, you know.

Calumet Tower

Beyond the terrace roof of the stone icehouse rises the powerhouse,
viewed from the castle, photographed by the author about 1945.

"The yacht house is really just a huge boathouse, but it had special requirements, since there was a crew to be housed—maybe twelve or more men—and the boiler for the steam engine would have to be fired up while in the building, so the smoke would have to be removed. There had to be lots of coal storage, and a way of receiving the coal from a barge and getting it up into the coal bin. A yacht house also had to have special jacks so that the vessel could be raised out of the water, which froze in the winter, of course."

"You know a lot about these things."

"I've been around a lot of boats and boathouses."

"But you only mentioned a skiff house on the island."

"There once was a boathouse, but when the Emerys got the big yacht, the island was too small, so they built a huge yacht house over on Picton Island and took down the smaller one. Picton is where Kris lived, you know."

*Irene* at Peacock Yacht House, Boldt Yacht House at right.

"But it's a long way from Calumet."

"Oh, the Emerys had so much help, that didn't worry them. They had men constantly ferrying boats back and forth over the couple of miles. They'd just call for a boat, like you or I might call for a cab. Of course the big yacht was too slow to be much use on a day-to-day basis, so they had a fleet of smaller, faster boats, naturally.

"There was so much coming and going, back in those days. In addition to Picton Island, where the greenhouses were—and orchards—the Emerys had a farm over on Grindstone. The family thought of the Frontenac as their annex, and did a lot of entertaining there. They wanted to show off the new hotel, and to show how elegant it could be. Actually, the hotel Annex, built shortly after the Frontenac became a great success, was even more *soigné*. The Annex was where the most elite guests stayed—the maharaja and Mrs. Belmont—in luxurious suites. The Annex had its own verandah, which was where one was invited to tea, if one was anybody. That left me out. I was just a young doctor's daughter from Watertown, always on the fringes of *le haut monde*.

"The Annex survived the fire, and operated for a few years, as I recall, but then it also burned. Fire has always been a menace on these islands. That's why the Boldts took down their big frame showplace, then rebuilt it in masonry and steel. The Boldts imitated the Emerys, you know."

"No, I didn't know. How?"

"Well the Emerys did everything first, and the Boldts simply mimicked them. You see, Emery was fifteen years older than Boldt. The Emerys came from the City, like the Boldts, and were wealthy patrons of Boldt's Waldorf-Astoria. They had just built the stone Castle when the Boldts first came. They had a ballroom, a farm, a big yacht house on another island—the Boldts imitated them in everything. But the Boldts went to the Bay, and intended to confirm that town as the social center. That probably had something to do with Charles Emery's attempts to make Clayton rival the Bay."

"Did you see the fire?"

"Everybody saw it, for miles around. What a huge firetrap that big wooden hotel was. It was a disaster waiting to happen. We all knew about fires. Hotels had burned here before, and would burn again."

"The fire was spectacular, I suppose."

"Oh, it lit up the River. The building was so tall, and it went up in flames so quickly."

"It was full of people?"

"Yes, it was height of the season. But everyone got out. The minute it started, everyone knew it was a goner. There was no real fire protection. So everyone simply went out on the lawns and watched it burn. Of course, it was inconvenient for guests, who had to be taken off the island—and this in the evening—to be put up in all sorts of emergency quarters around town. And lots of people lost things. In the rush to get out, much was left behind. That was the reason for the only casualty."

"How was that?"

"Well, one fellow—not a guest of the hotel, or even an employee, I think—who came over when the fire started, realized that wealthy guests had left things behind. He was greedy. He never got out."

"Emery didn't want to rebuild it?"

"Oh, he had an architect draw plans for a fireproof hotel. I remember seeing a drawing of it, over at Calumet Island. It was going to be lower, more sprawling, but built of stone. It never happened. I suppose that we all knew that the glory days were over. You see, the Boldts' stables burned the same night as the Frontenac, and the Columbian Hotel burned the next year, taking much of Thousand Island Park with it. It was the second big hotel there to go up in flames."

"They could have built fireproof structures."

"Yes, but the season is so short here—only eight weeks or so out of the year. Then the First World War came, and the big yachts went. That was the end. But it was also just the changing of generations. After Mrs. Emery died, Charles didn't have the heart to keep up the social life of the Castle—just as George Boldt didn't when Louise died. Even in that he imitated Charles Emery, who closed up the Castle when his wife died. The kids didn't want any part of their parents' follies—neither Frank Emery nor Clover Boldt. Times changed, and they preferred a more casual lifestyle."

Off to Tea

A Benson party departs from Mississauga

I supposed that Julie's family had one of the big summer places when she was young. "Oh, no," she laughed, "my father was a physician in Watertown. He couldn't spend much time on the river, because he always was on call in town. He wanted us to have the advantages this place offered, however. Many of his patients spend summers here, and we knew lots of them socially. Watertown is only twenty miles or so from the river, you know.

"We knew the Flower family in Watertown and I was close in age to Emma Flower. She was the daughter of Roswell Pettibone Flower, who was New York State Governor and congressman who made a multi-million-dollar fortune in railroads and on Wall Street. He was clever, as you can imagine — sometimes called 'the sly Flower.' Governor Flower was prominent on the river, always recognized by his inevitable broad-brimmed straw hat. He was a great story-teller, with lots of funny fish tales. Flower had been a farmer who became a grain trader and then had the largest brokerage firm in the country at the time — I'm talking about the 1890s now. Flower was nationally known as a 'famous plunger' who was the 'biggest bull' in the Great Bull Market at the turn of the century.

"The Flower family was the key that opened doors for me. Everyone knew Governor Flower. His daughter Emma was not much of a socialite, but had credentials. Once you knew one family here, you quickly became acquainted with others, since the Islands were so very sociable.

Off to Tea in Grand Style

In contrast to the Bensons in the previous picture, the Peacocks did things with
bravura. Here they are headed for Boldt's Wellesley House, not in their yacht
(which is moored outside the center yacht house in the distance) but in one of
their smaller boats. Note the uniformed captain and engineer in the forward
cockpit. The Rafferty yacht house appears at the left and the Boldt yacht
house, with the great houseboat, *La Duchesse*, moored along side, is on the right.

The Thousand Islands Yacht Club, near Alexandria Bay, was a place were you
could meet almost everyone, and on the Boldt's golf course — or at the grand hotels. There were the cotillions, the tennis tournaments, the polo matches on
Wellesley Island, horse races at Edgewood — 'the Driving Park,' we called it then.
For young folks, it was a constant round of events — and parties."

"Emma married John Taylor, and they had a big cottage at St. Lawrence Park
where the governor and other family stayed, but sometimes they favored hotels.
Emma and John had a daughter, Rosemary, and a son, Fred. Their father had
Taylor Instrument Company in Rochester and was interested in Watertown
utilities, as I recall. John and Emma divorced soon, however. Divorces were uncommon then, and not widely condoned socially.

"John Taylor continued to come to the river, buying Point Marguerite on the
mainland below Alexandria Bay — that's called Pine Tree Point now — about the
time of World War I. He built a fine stone house there. What a lovely terrace on
the point there, overlooking the main channel and their pretty little cove. His
son, Fred, has Mink Island on the Canadian side.

"There were other Taylors on the river, which was always confusing. Margaret Taylor was a great tennis player, I remember. She was from Club Island,
daughter of those Taylors. Another tennis champion was Mary Packer, said to
be the wealthiest heiress in America. Her family was at Sport Island and after

marriage to Charles Cummings. They had Little Lehigh, across that great iron bridge from Sport Island. Mary was older than I, so I suppose young Dick Macsherry would be her great-grandson. He's about your age. That family, running from the Packers to the Macsherrys, is one of the river dynasties. They married with the Hammonds of the Ledges, who were connected to the Hollands of Bonnie Castle. Jean Hammond is a bit younger than I. Her family was at Sylvan Island. The genealogical network gets complicated."

"Did you know George Boldt?"

"I can't say I knew him, since he was an older man and mostly I was familiar with younger people. I remember seeing him on many occasions. Although short, he stood out because of his trimmed beard and pince-nez spectacles—and his elegant attire. He wore a dramatic cape when on the river, along with his captain's hat. He was the soul of courtesy—which was his business, you know, as a hotel man. He overdid it a bit—kissing ladies' hands in the European manner—but with his money he was above reproach. Yes, he could have taught some of his neighbors manners. What a courtly gentleman—suave—with the barest trace of a German accent. Affable and likable, if a bit remote. He was not in the same class of hale-fellow-well-met as the likes of Gilbert Rafferty. Boldt was a gentleman.

"I was of the same generation as his daughter, Clover Boldt—but I didn't see so much of her either, since she was in a set that moved from resort to resort, visiting other country houses, and when here she was always involved in competitive sporting events—out of my league athletically as well as socially. I saw more of Ed Noble, whose family came from Gouverneur, here in the North Country. His father, Harvey, had a cottage on Murray Isle. Ed was on the river more regularly throughout the summer, and he was on the fringes here, as I was—back in those days, that is. How differently our lives have gone!"

"Noble is the Life Savers man, who bought the Boldt estate and built the Thousand Islands Club?"

"Yes, Life Savers to start with, then Beechnut Foods, then the American Broadcasting Company, and Paramount Pictures, and many other things, I've heard. But he lives in a log cabin over on the Lake of the Isles. How times have changed!"

\* \* \*

As usual, I was gazing across the kitchen table at Calumet Castle, seeming so near yet so far. I wondered how visitors would arrive, since the front of the house didn't face the harbor in the center of the island.

Calumet Vista

Entrance steps appear at left and Round Island is in the right distance.

"Well, you'd arrive differently than today. The inner harbor really provided more the service functions of the island. At one time there was a big deep-water pier for yachts on this side. It was over by that little island, which Emery more or less created by building a seawall on a shoal. It was one big flowerpot, really, which Kris filled with hundreds of annuals each spring. Approach and arrival at Calumet was a thrill, since the castle was so dramatically situated.

"As one approached it appeared splendid, crowning its little hill. There used to be a long boardwalk, gradually ascending the grassy slope. Concrete later replaced the wood and then a semicircular stone terrace extended out in front of the entrance steps. You can see the curved retaining wall from here. There's a low wall running around the edge and steps down to the lawn below.

"I remember being impressed by the big windows—all that plate glass glistening. They must have washed windows every day! The house was rather formal. The main front is symmetrical, with a center entrance and matched corner towers. There was a very broad porch across the front, curving around the

towers—even this was recalled at Boldt Castle. As you may imagine, the verandah was furnished with the usual rocking chairs and such, but it had many oriental rugs and potted palms, so it seemed more of an extended outdoor living area.

"Going through the wide front door, you found a large, square hall—very
wide, a room rather than a corridor. There was a granite fireplace on the wall
opposite the entry, and the broad oak stairs went up to the left of the fireplace.
The room, although large, was only one story high, unlike the Wyckoffs' hall at
Carleton Villa. That's one instance where Boldt imitated someone other than
Emery. Carleton Villa rivaled Calumet Castle as the finest house on the river,
before Boldt Castle beat them all."

"I don't know about that place. Where is it?"

"It's beyond your rowing range, up on the head of Carleton Island, near
Cape Vincent. You've probably never seen Dark Island Castle either, have you?
That's way down-river, near Chippewa Bay. You'll have to get your parents to
let you use a motorboat, if you're going to visit all of the great houses."

"I've been to Castle Rest."

"Oh, yes. That's the other 'castle,' the Pullman place. It's boarded up, like
Calumet, isn't it? I've not been there in years."

"Yes. I didn't get inside, but it's wonderful on the outside. But tell me more
about the inside of Calumet Castle."

"Where was I? Oh, yes. Well, four rooms opened off the big, square hall. It
was very spacious, with wide archways linking the rooms. On the front there
were two matched sitting rooms, one on each side—especially pleasant because
they had the round spaces with big, curved windows in the towers. Behind the
sitting room on the left there was another room. It was more closed in, and
darker I suppose, after they added the ballroom wing. I remember it had a small
stained-glass window built into the chimney over the fireplace. This became
mostly a link between the main hall and the big ballroom—larger than the
Boldts', in fact. On the right side of the ballroom the curved stair went up to the
second story billiard room. On the left side was a big semicircular bay window
that had steps down to the lawns and a marvelous view upriver. At the far end
of the ballroom wing were two more circular towers, with round alcoves in
them. What was wonderful place this was for large parties!

"Then on the right-hand side of the hall, behind the front sitting room, was
the big dining room. Because of the slope, it extended out to be quite high above
the ground at the far end, where there was a delightful breakfast area in another
very glassy sort of bay window. It overlooked the harbor and skiff house below.

Behind the hall fireplace there were smaller rooms in the service wing. I don't recall getting back there much. I suppose the kitchen was in a lower level, since the sloping site gave the basement exterior exposure on the harbor side. Many houses of the time had kitchens at lower levels, using a dumbwaiter. They didn't want the kitchen to be close to the dining room because of the heat from the big, coal-burning cook stoves and the cooking odors as well as noise. I can't imagine how they got the coal up to the Castle—or the ice from the lower icehouse. There was a very steep and very long flight of stairs that led up to the Castle from the harbor on this back side. But manpower—and woman-power—was very plentiful back in those days."

"What a shame that the place hasn't been used in all these years."

"You can imagine why Frank and Chuck Emery haven't opened it—all those rooms—to use as a fishing camp? The big, frame caretaker's house probably is more livable. It's very attractive, you know. But there's a sad story that goes with the place. The caretaker's family used to stay on the island year-round, crossing over the ice in the winter. This can be treacherous. One day the husband was taking the children over the ice to school on Grindstone Island. It was a bright warm day, and his wife stood on the porch after waving them off. You can imagine what happened. They suddenly disappeared from view. All were drowned, as I recall."

Caretaker's House, Calumet Island

It was inevitable—irresistible. I had to see the inside of Calumet Castle myself. I was warned about the caretaker, who circled the island regularly to "keep an eye on it" and, presumably, to ward off trespassers. No one was using any of the buildings for any purpose at the time. The island was absolutely still and lifeless, except for encroaching wildlife. Supposing that the caretaker would merely encircle the outside of the island, rather than coming into the harbor, it was not very difficult to find a fairly inconspicuous spot to tie up my skiff. I suppose I left it on the less visible side of the skiff house.

It was not too difficult to find a way into the Castle, either. I was not the first, or last, Clayton youngster to go exploring there. That was apparent from the debris scattered about—some drawers pulled out, contents spilled on the floors.

Like the abandoned house on Round Island, the lifeless interior, with windows boarded up so that it was dark inside, was eerie. Large pieces of furniture, some shrouded with sheets, were ghostly. There was not enough light to get much of a sense of the place, and I hadn't thought to bring a flashlight. Light poured down the main staircase, however, and on ascending I found more windows uncovered on the second story. It was apparent that others before me had been prowling, judging from the mess.

The budding architect was also a budding historian, so all of this refuse, especially paper, intrigued me. In a bathroom, on a sink, where apparently someone had carried it to find better light, was a large sort of book, missing most of its pages. It had handwriting inside on the margin of pages left attached to the binding. I quickly recognized that this was a checkbook—Charles G. Emery's own checkbook, in which he had entered expenditures for the operation of Calumet Island and the rest of his estate. It was fascinating. On one page was an entry for a contribution to the Clayton chapter of the W.C.T.U. (Women's Christian Temperance Union). The ladies' mission was to eliminate the scourge of alcohol. Two stubs below was a check for two barrels of rum.

I was so engrossed, standing in that white-tiled bathroom reading this account of life in the past, that I recognized with a start the sound of a motorboat, becoming louder. It was approaching the island. That would be the caretaker. I looked out the small, unshuttered bathroom window. Yes, the boat was circling the island. But it turned, and came into the harbor. There was no escape, since my skiff was tied up there.

If it was the caretaker, he must have been going through the motions with his mind elsewhere, or perhaps the visitor was merely another sightseer, unconcerned to notice my skiff. I was relieved by the sound of the outboard motor receding on departure. Counting myself lucky, I headed back. I confess I took the checkbook with me, rationalizing that it would be of no value to anyone else except other another historian crazy enough to care about such things.

* * *

Calumet Harbor

Photographed by the author from his skiff (oar handle shown) on landing,
about 1945. The powerhouse appears at right, in front of the stone icehouse.
A steep flight of stairs led up to the shuttered castle.

Calumet Castle is gone now. I was not alone in grieving. Vincent J. Dee, with whom I worked in later years when he was Chairman of the Thousand Islands Bridge Authority, was outraged. It was Vince who saved Boldt Castle when it was threatened with demolition, and it was Vince who initiated a campaign of restoration there. As I write, Dark Island, the last "castle" of the region to be privately owned and inhabited, has been sold in a multi-million dollar transaction. The loss of Calumet Castle might have been averted if the building could have survived until interest in these properties revived.

Calumet Castle, like some other important island buildings, might have been demolished even earlier to avoid payment of property taxes, but apparently the builder, Charles G. Emery, averted this by foresight, stipulating in his will that disposition of the property would await decision of his grandson, when he reached his majority. Emery's own son didn't seem to care much for the place and probably would have been rid of it earlier, except for this provision. When the grandson came of age, the building was doomed. The contents were auctioned off, out on the lawn. It was so sad—and a fiasco. A huge Oriental rug, said to be 74 by 35 feet and supposedly worth $30,000, sold for $220. Then, as I recall, the purchasers didn't come in a boat big enough to carry the huge thing back to the mainland, so they left it, intending to return the next day with a larger boat. When they came, the rug had disappeared.

Although a group of Clayton people then opened the Castle to the public, after only one season (as I recall) this course was abandoned. New owners of the island were more interested in use of the harbor as a marina than in preserving a historic monument. There was a fire one night and the Castle was gutted. The stone walls then were deemed a hazard, and were pulled down. What a loss for Clayton and the region! Today Calumet Castle would be an important resource for tourism. When the stone walls came down, a document appeared in the cornerstone. Placed there by Charles G. Emery, it conveyed his vision for the future of the Thousand Islands and his confidence that generations of Emerys would return to Calumet Island, regarding it as their family seat, a place of reunion built for the centuries. It didn't last one century.

* * *

I asked Julie if she had ever been on the Emerys' big yacht. "Which one?" She laughed. "They had several. Emery was always trying to keep out in front of the Joneses down at the Bay, so moved up to bigger and bigger boats. He sold one lovely yacht to the Peacocks down there, replacing it with the gorgeous *Calumet*, one of the breathtaking sights on the river. But Emery was outclassed by the Laughlins, Pittsburgh steel people, down at the Bay. Nobody was going to beat them at the game, after their *Corona* arrived. It was so colossal that they couldn't go many places among the islands, only up and down the main channel."

"Did you go on any of these big boats?"

"Oh, that's what they were for—not merely for display, which was part of it, surely, but to entertain. Attractive young people always seemed to enhance a party, and with all those yachts, there was no end to entertaining on board. There were some silly parties. I remember Clover Boldt's hayride. The decks of the elegant *Louise* were strewn with hay from their farm, in which we lolled as we steamed up the river to the Frontenac, where Clover had arranged a dinner party. We must have been a sight, coming up those broad steps into the grand portico, covered with straw!"

"Really? I imagined people were much more formal—very Victorian, you know—looking at the pictures. Everyone was so overdressed, in the middle of the summer."

"That's true. We suffered with layers of clothes, always wearing hats. Seems insane now, but that's what we thought proper. But appearances are deceiving. Behavior wasn't stiff. You'd be surprised at some of our antics.

The Boldt Yacht, *Louise*

Aboard, from the right, the steward, two sailors, captain, male passenger, chef, and engineer.

"Remember that most of the people here came from simple backgrounds. George Boldt had been a kitchen helper, you know. There were all sorts of im-migrant accents heard at the Yacht Club—Boldt's Prussian, Rafferty's Irish. Gilbert Rafferty! Now there was a diamond in the rough! He and Sim Dunfee were quite a pair of Irish brawlers. Alex Peacock was Welsh. May Irwin was Canadian. We had quite a mix—and there was a Jewish contingent as well. That was one of the amusing aspects of the place, the improbable mix of people. They were really more interesting—people who had done something, accomplished something themselves—more so than at exclusive resorts, where what you got were second or third generations of wealth. Most of those folks had learned to do nothing except to spend inherited money."

"May Irwin was an actress, like you?"

"Let's say, charitably, that we were entertainers. But May hit the big time, becoming a Broadway superstar and touring the nation for decades on the vaudeville circuit. I was lucky to get on stage at all.

May Irwin

Photograph in an early role is the frontispiece of her cookbook,
which contains her recipe for Thousand Islands Fish Chowder

"May was a case in point about these islanders. She was a very funny, earthy woman. She couldn't abide the dressy tea set at the Yacht Club, preferring to tromp around her mainland farm in muddy boots. She had that Canadian sort of quick wit—eh? She poked fun at the pretensions of some New Money—like the Boldts' preposterous Castle."

"But May Irwin had an island near here, didn't she? I've rowed around it."

"Oh, she built a fine house off the head of Grindstone, but never really cared for it, preferring farm life. In later years she used the island building as an inn, while she stayed mostly on the farm.

"May was a national celebrity, so her arrival at the Clayton depot always attracted a crowd. Here's a photo. She had just come off that private railroad car, to be welcomed by admirers (mostly male, it seems). Some of them may have been members of her own troop. May sometimes rehearsed her company for Broadway openings at the Clayton Opera House. She was a producer, even a composer, and quite a businesswoman herself, investing in real estate and becoming very wealthy—although she was assisted by a business manager, Kurt Eisfeldt, whom she married in later years.

May Irwin

Disembarking from a private car, May and company are welcomed at the
Clayton railroad dock.  May wears the man's fedora hat and veil.

"After divorcing her first husband, for much of her life May was a single mother,
raising two sons alone.  She lost interest in her splendid island home.  May
turned the place into an inn, which was popular because of her celebrity.  I suppose the mainland farm was partly for the boys—better than hanging out with
the fast set at the Yacht Club.  We were not always the most wholesome or admi-
rable youngsters."

"How do you mean?  Drinking?"

"May was not averse to a nip now and then.  When she left her farm one fall,
she tacked a note to the door.  She scrawled, 'Don't break the door down, boys.
It's open and the liquor's on the kitchen table.'

"Everybody drank prodigiously back then.  There were those two Donohue
brothers—'always drunk,' as Fred Beach says (but he knew them better than I),"
she added, with a wink.

St. John's Island, Summer Home of the Donohue Family.

Previously called "Plantagenet," when owned by A. E. Hume of Charleston, S.C., the island now known as "Steamboat" is summer home to author John Keats. The old house, built in 1881, represented the Stick Style of the 1870s but unfortunately is gone.

"The Donohues were an interesting family—Irish, like the Raffertys. Although they gave the land for the Catholic church at the Bay and were generous benefactors, they had a chapel in their big house at St. John's Island where a priest came to say Mass. The judge's sister-in-law dropped a check for a thousand dollars in the collection basket one Sunday at St. Cyril's."

"Who were the Donohues?"

"He was a New York State Supreme Court judge, well known in New York City for not being a team player with Irish cronies on the police force. Donohue tried to shut down 'disorderly houses' in the City. He was also the nemesis of railroad men Jay Gould and Russell Sage. Fred Beach was talking about the sons, who were such drinkers. Frank was also a great tennis player and marksman and was a novelist as well. The big house at St. John's was so awful it was wonderful!

"We had our share of alcoholics—wives especially. It's odd that people characterize those times as decorous. But I was thinking of more sinister things." Julie paused, apparently wondering if she should go on. "Personal things."

I waited expectantly, so she continued. "There was this rather dirty affair, quite a scandal, at the Bay. One of the young men in the Yacht Club set was attracted to a local girl who lived in Alexandria Bay. The boy's mother, who was socially ambitious, disapproved of the relationship. You see, one of the basic functions of the Yacht Club was the matching and mating of 'suitable' young people—those whose parents belonged to the Club, of course. This local girl was *outré.*

"The girl disappeared. Kidnapped—not for long, but long enough to ruin her reputation. She came back as 'spoiled goods,' you see (if you follow me)—then she was supposed to be even less appropriate as a mate for a gilded youth. Naturally, the young woman was outraged, bringing charges against her kidnapper, who turned out to be another rich hoodlum, supposedly a 'friend' of the girl's islander boyfriend. In the ensuing investigation, the kidnapper revealed that he had transported the young lady for a sojourn at the behest of his 'friend's' mother, the social climber. You see, we were not all very nice people."

"Did the boy and his girlfriend get together again after that?"

"I wish I could say so, as that might make a happier ending. Perhaps the mother's scheme worked by making the girl seem less attractive to her son. I expect, however, that the young lady was totally disgusted with these people. Would you want to marry into that kind of family?"

"Clayton attracted more theater people than the Bay or other river communities," Julie recalled. "Here at Clayton we had not only May Irwin but the Opera House. May opened some of her shows there, bound for Broadway. I think the first performance in the house was the premier of her New York hit, *Mrs. Black is Back.*

"We also had another famous actor as a summer resident, James K. Hackett. Oh, he was more thrilling to us young ladies than any of our millionaires. Hackett was a matinee idol of the nineties—he was literally tall, dark, and handsome. Jim married Mary Mannering, another stage star of the time. They enjoyed a fine summer home below Clayton on Bartlett Point where Jim, like May Irwin, had a mainland farm. He called his estate "Zenda," after one of his most famous roles, the *Prisoner of Zenda*. He was a spectacular, swashbuckling type—I remember some snide critic saying one of his shows was notable mostly for his legs in tights.

"Hackett had been born on nearby Wolfe Island so, like May, he was from 'the Queen's domain,' as we used to say. But don't think Jim was a farm boy. His father had been a famous American actor and his mother was an actress as well. They had summered on Wolfe Island. Jim Hackett was a friend of Frederic Remington, the famous painter down at Chippewa Bay." [Much of the Zenda Farm property has been acquired by the Thousand Islands Land Trust, which maintains the remarkable barns as well as protecting the open space.]

"Other famous performers frequented Clayton," Julie continued. "The co-median Joe Weber, half of the Weber & Fields vaudeville team, was an avid fish-erman and regular visitor to river hotels. The Hubbard House at Clayton was popular with theater people. Joe talked of buying a place—possibly Florence Island, but that that never happened. May Irwin bought her island from another actor, Hugo Toland. Naturally these theatrical folks brought show-business col-leagues with them to the river. I was more in awe of Charles Frohman than the performers, since he was a great Broadway producer of my day. Albert Bial was another important producer who came here. One of the most famous visitors was composer Irving Berlin, who stayed with friends at Pt. Vivian. Fay Temple-ton, another Broadway star, vacationed here—staying at the Frontenac and renting one of the grand villas on Cherry Island, just above Alexandria Bay. Geraldine Farrar, a famous opera diva, rented George Boldt's Chalet. She was a close friend of May Irwin, and these celebrities naturally knew one another."

Some of the major cultural events took place not in any of the mainland vil-lages, but on Wellesley Island—then accessible only by boat. Thousand Island Park had grown to be a village itself, a cottage community with a grand hotel and the Tabernacle—the place had been founded as a Methodist camp meeting ground. The State of New York built a facility there to serve continuing educa-tion of teachers, which contributed to a Chautauqua-like sort of cultural pro-gram. Music was a feature, with ambitious choral and orchestral performances at the big Tabernacle—they did big things like Rossini's "Stabat Mater." The music director was Welsh, Tali Esen Morgan, and some world-renowned soloists per-formed, such as Madam Schumann-Heinck. They performed Shakespear there as well.

The Tabernacle
The huge auditorium at Thousand Island Park collapsed in 1936

Clayton during the Depression and war years was less upscale than it has become today, now that it is enhanced by many galleries and boutiques. Clayton nevertheless had a charm, and some features unfortunately were lost to "progress," like the median that ran down the center of Riverside Drive, filled with flowers. The Ellis block was at the foot of James Street, with a drug store (and soda fountain) adjoining a gourmet grocery store, which provisioned many island homes. The Riverside Drive facility had a dock at the rear.

"That's where we saw many of the nearby islanders most often," Julie recalled, " — there and at the post office in town. Islanders didn't have to come in often for provisions, however, since many farmers went from island to island, selling produce from boats. Some of the Canadian islands were even served by a marine mailman, who would sound his horn and the cottagers would run down to the dock to fetch their mail. On the big islands where there was a hotel, it provided ice, milk, water and such to nearby cottagers. But elsewhere one of the chores of children often was a daily row to some nearby island with a farm to get milk."

Some of the islanders who patronized Clayton provisioners lived in relative seclusion above the village, around the head of Grindstone Island, where tour boats didn't pass. Many of these families have been there for generations and are closely linked by intermarriage, following river romances of young people.

"It's complicated," Julie observed, "trying to keep track. The Remingtons, the arms and typewriter people at Thousand Island Park, were related to the Dodges off the head of Grindstone. They were New York City merchants who made their money mostly from munitions and copper mining. Then the Dodges were related by marriage to the Morgans, some of whom married Leavitts, a Pruyn, Thacher, White and David Goodrich, chairman of the rubber company—and so it goes, on and on." Laurie Rush, an anthropologist, in an article about water recreation on the river, characterized these head-of-Grindstone families as Old Money, in contrast with many islanders down-river.

"I've known some of the Grindstone set," Julie commented, "but mostly I associated with those people merely by running into them here in town. Those families seem to keep pretty much to themselves out on their islands. Of course, we went over that way to fish, because that's where the bass were, so we passed the big houses regularly.

"The Bohlens' Mid-River Farm had a special aura. Chip Bohlen is prominent in Washington, you know, and ambassador to France. The house was designed by the architects of Grand Central Station in New York. The Bacons bought the place and entertained international diplomats and statesmen. Robert Low Bacon was a congressman from New York whose father was Secretary of State and also ambassador to France.

"Hickory Island is another wonderful place. I've been there often—a big house on vast lawns, but likewise comfortable. All the rooms are finished in natural wood, with big stone fireplaces. There's a delightful terrace where we'd have cocktails with the Woods, looking out through the Oak Trees to the distant islands. J. Walter Wood was a New York stockbroker. One of his two sons became an architect and designed the strange but wonderful reinforced concrete villa for the Pratts, on nearby Niagara Island. The Woods were such nice people, compared to some of the arrogant types down at the Bay. Ethel Roosevelt visited the Morgans at Papoose. I saw her here in town, but I wasn't in that set."

"They're very exclusive over there?"

"Not snobs, if that's what you mean. My friend, Sis Morgan Pruyn, is as natural and unaffected as you can imagine—very down-to-earth. Those people simply enjoy themselves and don't need the sort of showy socializing that many people have wanted here. When you see the Grindstone folks buying groceries at the Ellis store, or on the Clayton golf course, you don't think 'money,' but 'classy.'

Rum Point, 1908

A few friends at the complex owned by Boston surgeon James White. Rum Point served as a recreation center for related families and friends at the head of Grindstone Island. Pictured, from left, are Mary White, Lawrence Butler, Beatrice Morgan ("Sis") Pruyn, and E. Boelker—as well as the dog, Turnips and another in the background.

"They play here, at our rather ragged facility, rather than at the more prestigious Thousand Islands Club, which is characteristic of their tastes."

"I know Mr. Morgan," I volunteered.

"Really? William Fellowes Morgan? How?"

"I caddied for him at the Clayton Golf Club. Not for long, though. I proved to be a terrible caddy. I couldn't follow the ball, because of my astigmatism."

\* \* \*

Since Julie's family had never owned a summer home here, I wondered how she came to know so much about the river. "Like you," she laughed. "I impose on the hospitality of my friends."

"You didn't even have your own boat, then?"

"There were so many boats. You didn't have to own one. People were so sociable, wanting to take you everywhere! But of course there were also the big steamboats. They made regular rounds, stopping at all the major resort communities on the islands. They'd go from Clayton to Round Island, then over to Grenell, then stop at Murray, and on to T.I. Park. Then they went down to St.

Lawrence Park and stopped again at Pt. Vivian before arriving at the Bay and Westminster Park. What a loss the steamboats are to the river! There's nothing to compare with them today. They had large, elegant interiors, serving refreshments, and had live music on board. I can still hear the sound of the band, with people singing, coming across the water. That and the sound of paddle wheels—and the sight of white clouds of smoke rising behind distant islands, or at night, with the glittering lights reflected in the water. It was so lovely."

The *St. Lawrence* on her searchlight tour

There were, and still are, many resort communities on islands and the mainland. Thousand Island Park is the largest. Historically and architecturally it is the most important—a veritable museum of cottage architecture. T.I. Park is interesting moreover for its mode of community organization. It's not a village municipality but rather a corporation, which holds title to the common facilities. Residents own variable quantities of shares of stock in the corporation. Thousand Island Park has proved to be a workable model for a community, but it has taken great effort as a participatory exercise. Controversy and dispute seems to have been endemic, but the place seems to thrive on it.

Thousand Island Park is a case study in what we call "gentrification," or in less critical terms, the continuing improvement of properties as they increase in value. I first knew the place as a youngster, rowing there in my skiff. During the Depression and war years it had become seedy, since many families could not, or did not care to maintain, summer cottages. Many charming Victorian houses were vacant or in disrepair. One could buy one of them for a few thousand dollars. Recently one sold for more than six hundred thousand dollars.

While increasing property values generally please people, some families sigh when they feel they no longer can refuse offers to sell at such attractive prices. Furthermore, upgrading of the community has entailed communal improvements, which have burdened some older residents with increased annual bills from the corporation.

Affluent new owners can well afford to restore and maintain properties. That's the upside. On the downside, investors in costly properties often want to improve the places, so as to bring them into line with their price. "Improvement" often means additions or alterations that affect the historic character of the buildings—although the historic character contributed to the quality that brought new residents to Thousand Island Park in the first place.

Will Thousand Island Park be spoiled by success? Not if the strong local preservation organization can prevent it. Spearheaded by the indomitable Trude Fitelson, Park preservationists have prevailed upon the corporation to create preservation regulations and a review board, required to approve proposed alterations. The remarkable character—and economic boom—at Thousand Island Park is evidence that this process has worked.

\* \* \*

Thousand Island Park is listed on the National Register of Historic Places and rightly so, for it is a remarkable survival of a nineteenth-century village, largely intact and unchanged. Its survival is all the more remarkable because two disastrous fires have swept a portion of the park, taking two hotels built on the same site, together with many cottages and other buildings. Julie remembered the last conflagration, in the summer of 1912.

"Was the Thousand Island Park fire as exciting as the Frontenac fire?"

"Don't be so ghoulish," she replied. "It was doubly disheartening because the Park fire came the very next summer after the Frontenac burned. The Park's Columbian Hotel wasn't so colossal as the Frontenac, but it was large and very popular. The cross-shaped building was located where the big village green is now, much of which then served as its front lawn. The fire started in the hotel kitchen—always the Achilles' heel of these island buildings, especially then, due the big coal or wood-burning stoves.

Thousand Island Park
East Coast Avenue, destroyed in the 1912 fire.

"Like the Frontenac, the smaller hotel went up in flames quickly, but the total disaster was worse, since the fire consumed much of the village. Next to the hotel was the State Education facility, another large frame building, quickly destroyed. The fire, spread by the breeze from the west, burned most of the eastern part of the Park. The Iron Cottage, which still stands at the corner of the green by the water, was spared because the owners had the foresight to clad it in metal."

"That part of the Park is rebuilt now, isn't it?"

"Pretty much, but there are still more vacant lots there, and you can tell by their style that the buildings are not so old. The really quaint part now is to the west of the green."

"They didn't rebuild the hotel."

"It was the second big hotel on that site to burn. Even more pointedly, the grand Frontenac at Round Island had burned the previous summer. We had been living in a fools' paradise."

"Those fires ended the heyday of the Islands?"

"Well, certainly they contributed to the change, but I suppose it was more generally a change of the times. Even more basically, there was a change of generations. Louise Boldt died in 1904, when her incredible project was abandoned.

That was dismaying. Then four years later Irene Emery died. In 1908 the lights went off at Calumet—three years before Emery's Frontenac Hotel burned. Neither Boldt nor Emery, probably the two major boosters of the resort whose rivalry did so much to glamorize it—neither of them had the heart to continue. And their children didn't want the same things from life. The coming generation didn't want castles and steam yachts and farms, operations with hundreds of people on the payrolls. They wanted to fish and play golf."

"What happened to the Thousand Islands Yacht Club?"

"The new Thousand Islands Country Club—a golf club really—competed with the nearby, older facility. The new facility seemed more stylish, I suppose—but in the twenties people were playing more golf than yachting. The old club kept going, largely from loyalty of a smaller and smaller group of old river families, but when World War II came, following the long, lean years of the Great Depression, many people who couldn't get to the Islands, or couldn't open the big houses because of labor shortage, gave up paying the hefty dues required to keep the facility operating. It closed shortly after the war broke out, as I recall. After being vacant for years, the island finally went for back taxes, more or less, about 1950, I suppose."

*  *  *

I supposed Julie had seen Boldt Castle being built. This budding architect wondered if that was exciting.

"Oh, their crazy projects were always the talk of the river. What would they do next? The Alster Tower was odd enough, but then came that massive triumphal arch—totally without redeeming purpose. You can imagine the reaction when we heard that their huge house was to be demolished, so that they could build another there of stone! Construction of the castle went on for years. Boldt's tug, the *Queen*, towed barge after barge of granite from the Oak Island quarry. Every bit of stone in that colossal structure was pushed up the hill in wheelbarrows. There were hundreds of men working on the project.

"Boldt's stone chateau was intended to outdo Emery's towered house on Calumet. Boldt even followed Emery's precedent by relocating the original structure on another island. Emery's first summer home was a large, wooden structure, built in 1883. When Emery built the stone castle ten years later, the old frame house was dismantled and moved over to Picton Island. You must know the place, since you've rowed around these islands," Julie added.

Boldt Castle, Hewitt & Hewitt, Architects

"There's only one house on the whole island."

"Yes, now that Kris's house is gone. Emery provided Kris with a regular, year-round house, up on the hill above the big yacht house. There were coal bins there for the steam yacht and for boilers to heat the greenhouses so there was plenty of heat during the winter—but the place was very isolated. The bigger summer home, moved from Calumet, was some distance from these buildings, so it was more private. The gossip was that Charles, Senior, fitted up his big, old house as a pied-a-terre for his mistress, who stayed on Picton and never set foot on Calumet. I never met the woman, so I can't testify to that relationship personally. My friends the Hinemans bought the island. The old house from Calumet is now their summer home. I'm fortunate, since they have me over there often.

"And rowing around the island, you must have noticed the old granite quarry on the far side of the island. That was just one of Emery's enterprises here. The red stone used for the Museum of Natural History in New York City came from Picton Island. Emery also constructed a big, four-story building in Clayton for the company he formed with Dr. Bain to build boats. Their skiffs were famous. Emery also was a major benefactor of the Catholic church here, which is one reason its stone building is so fine. He also donated an Italian painting of the Madonna when the building was completed. Charles Emery was not merely a promoter of the summer resort, but Mr. and Mrs. Emery contributed substantially to the village in many ways."

\* \* \*

I had known Kris Hass before he died, but as a youngster I didn't know him well. I remember him as a jovial Dane, rugged and weather-beaten even as an old (or so he seemed to me) man. Although I didn't like pulling in eels any more than most fishermen, Kris prevailed upon me never to cut the line, but always to bring the slithering creature to him. As a Dane, he relished eels as a rich delicacy, pickling them himself. Pickled eels weren't Julie's favorite fare.

Julie met Kris on the river. This was in the thirties, during the Great Depression. Julie always conveyed an optimistic confidence, however, managing to seem regal even when surviving on welfare. When they wed, they supposed that their combined resources would assure some semblance of financial security. The moment of truth came in Havana, when the check came for lunch. "I hope you can take care of this," Kris said. "I'm broke."

"Me too," Julie replied. They didn't cry, but laughed. That's the way they were. Blithe spirits.

\* \* \*

Recollections of exploring the islands by skiff are as much about the sound as the sights. The rhythmic creaking of the wooden oars, metal pins rubbing against leather oarlocks, was so constant, so pervasive, as to be indelibly imprinted in my memory. Yes, there were drones of motors even then, but they were mostly distant sounds. The immediate reality was the wooden oar in the callused palm.

The sound of gulls and terns also speak of the river. Their shrill cries were so common as to become unnoticed background to daily life. And of course there was the lapping of the water, against the hull, against the sea wall. And the wind—that was the more fearsome sound. Breeze might be friendly on land, but on the water, wind was less welcome. The thermals, the wind from the west originating over Lake Ontario and the other Great Lakes, might please the sailboat skipper, but was not welcome when rowing upstream in late afternoon. Although the river might be glassy in the morning, the wind predictably came up later on warm days. I learned to plot my courses with current and wind in mind.

It seems odd that my parents thought me safer in a skiff than a powerboat. Perhaps I was, since I never had any misfortune on the water. It could be scary, however, when both wind and current slowed homeward progress through the whitecaps. I remember telling my little sister to lie down in the skiff, not because there was any danger of her going overboard, or even to reduce wind resistance, but because I didn't want her to be as terrified as I was.

Around the point from our cottages was a deep bay — now a marina filled with white, plastic boats. Then it was filled with water lilies, with winding channels among them. I would row the skiff and my sister picked the big white and smaller yellow blossoms to fill a bowl on our porch dining table.

I found my perfect island, Hogsback, on the main channel off Little Round Island. Actually there were two small islands extending the larger one in a chain. As the name suggested, the granite island was long and narrow, rising to a ridge, with a rocky head where the waves crashed, contrasting with the more protected slips between the islets at its foot. Nothing had ever been built there; it was pristine, with some tall, windswept white pines and other trees scattered around the shores and grassy intervals between the exposed granite of the crest. The outlook in each direction was different: looking down on the picturesque islets at the foot, while off the head were open waters with Clayton and Calumet Island, castle roofs glistening in the sun, or silhouetted in the western sunset.

View from Smoke Island

McIntyre left his case and black hood in the left corner of this famous photograph.

On one side, Little Round Island (then undeveloped) was close by, while on the other was the broad main channel, where huge ships passed—astoundingly close to Hogsback. Some might object to their noise at night, but I found the puffing sound, as well as the sight of the lights, five or six stories of them, passing in the darkness, thrilling. Of course, the foghorn would shake the house, if one were trying to sleep there, but that did not dissuade me, nor the crashing waves, as swells from the giant freighters broke against the rocky shore. The flashing navigation light and constantly ringing bell buoy were nearer here than to our mainland quarters—but for me these were attractions, not liabilities.

The budding architect had a house designed for Hogsback—I remember drawing sketches of it when I should have been taking notes in college. It would have been the iconic Thousand Islands house, in my view—with tall, steep roofs dotted with many dormers, the whole building covered with weathered shingle to merge into the natural character of the island. It was pure fantasy, of course. The Edges (who owned the Jacob Hays House and Sim Dunfee's Onondaga at the head of Round Island) owned Hogsback and had no intention of selling it. Fortunately the subsequent owner acquired it to keep it wild, which probably is better for all concerned, although for an architect it still presents a stimulating prospect as a building site.

I would tie up my skiff and visit most of the islands within my range. Pine Island, not far from Hogsback, was somewhat larger but still a small island, similar in character, rising even higher as a granite knoll. There was a house here, built fairly recently at the time (in the early thirties) but of the character I envisioned for Hogsback. It already appeared old and weather-beaten by the forties — which was my style. Because of the Great Depression and then the war, many of these properties had been abandoned or unmaintained for a decade or so. The ramshackle look was the Thousand Islands look that I loved, growing up with it.

Grindstone was — and still is — another world. What impressed me most as a youngster was the way that youngsters my age — maybe ten or twelve years old — wheeled around the large island in automobiles! This was "west of the Pecos" for law enforcement. There was no bridge to the island, but the cars came over the ice in the winter. They couldn't get back to the mainland readily and had limited use on the island, so they usually were decrepit vehicles when they came. They didn't last long and few islanders made the effort to tow them back across the ice to the mainland once they stopped running. The first sight to greet a visitor, tying up at Aunt Jane's Bay, was a pile of junked cars — part of the charm of Grindstone.

Once past the rusting relics, Grindstone became the nineteenth century. Roads were all dirt, with no telephone poles or power lines. There were still a few farms inland, for the cheese factory still operated then. Rocky outcroppings, dotted with pines, erupted into broad hay fields, like islands in green water. It was so quiet, so remote, so otherworldly. But I can't evoke this special place so poignantly as Stanley Norcom has done in his beautiful Grindstone Island memoir, fondly recalling other boyhood summers spent on this island.

* * *

I never fell in love with motorboats. Of course I enjoy looking at antique wooden runabouts and covet them, in fact, but outboard motors — never my thing. Oars don't give out on you.

Rum Point Confrontation

Introducing my wife-to-be to the hidden charms of the Islands, we were on the north side of Grindstone, exploring a bay, when the propeller became fouled in weeds. The motor stalled, became flooded, and wouldn't be cajoled into restarting. I took to the oars, but it was a long way back to Clayton. Fortunately, out in Eel Bay a passing boat noticed me rowing the cumbersome boat, outboard raised, and stopped to tow us over to Thousand Island Park where someone who had more rapport with motors got us started. Since then neither of us has volunteered another nautical outing, unless someone else provides a well-maintained boat with a mechanic on board.

Our attitude towards cottages is the same as our attitude towards boats—better to be a guest, and let someone else take care of the place. Having enough properties already to maintain, we have resisted many tempting island real estate investments. Instead, we have imposed on friends for decades—mainly Frank Ellis ("Courtney" of mythical "Heron Island," who appeared in my Boldt Castle book) and his generous wife, Sandy.

Of course, I've operated many motor boats over the years. When younger and wilder, I would sometimes skipper a boat full of friends around the river. Our final destination was often some abandoned island, such as Belle, across from Alexandria Bay, which had a dandy harbor and a grassy site ready-made for spreading a blanket. We would indulge in that University of Virginia classic, the picnic Mint Julep: a handful of mint and as much cracked ice as could be packed in one of those old Mason glass canning jars. Then the jar was filled with bourbon, which would last the afternoon—if we could last that long. It was a quart jar. As the song went, "I'm glad I'm not young any more".

The itinerary for such an outing might include Boldt Castle out of season or after hours. It was far more mysterious and romantic when forbidden. The reward for sneaking in and prowling up flights of dark stairways was the view of moonlight on the river from the top floor observation terrace.

* * *

My life would have been different had I not known the Thousand Islands or discovered Boldt Castle. My epiphany occurred when quite young. Like all visitors, at some point I took the usual boat tour—and I took those tours many times, as my parents found putting me on board a good way of getting rid of me for the afternoon. Actually, I think I was alone on my first visit to Heart Island, as I remember bringing back to the cottage the little booklet, *Heart Island: Its Castle and Towers*. I was so entranced that I read the text aloud to the adults gathered on the porch—not once, but so often thereafter that they began to mock me by reciting some of the purple prose verbatim. It was inevitable that more than a half century later I would write a book about Boldt Castle.

As a youngster I was overwhelmed with the mysterious ruin—it was far more romantic then than now. It was more tragic, abandoned, the island overgrown. Within, workmen's tools still lay where they had been dropped when the famous telegram came. I didn't quite understand the place or the people then, of course, so well as I do sixty years later. What was clear was that I wanted to build something like that. I became an architect—but never had clients like the Boldts.

* * *

As I grew older my parents gravitated to the Thousand Islands Club, then in its heyday when owned and subsidized by Ed Noble. Julie had known the multimillionaire when young, but the two River Rats had gone different ways.

"I missed my main chance," she laughed.

"You mean you might have been . . ."

"Who knows? We were friends, and Ed was an attractive, likable fellow. But it was not to be."

Thousand Islands Club

Noble was now a multimillionaire, Julie was on welfare. "He had the magic touch," she observed. "Luckiest fellow I ever knew. Of course, he didn't start a poor boy exactly, but his parents weren't in the ranks of the real swells on the river. Ed went to Yale and there he and a friend, pretty much as a lark, bought a small, local shop that sold hard candy made out in the back room. They put their heads together and thought of ways to promote the candy as distinctive. They came up with the idea of putting a hole in the center of each piece, called the product 'Life Savers.' That little hole made their ordinary hard candy distinctive. What really made the difference was Ed's novel marketing idea. He had metal stands made with racks to hold the tubes of wrapped candy, and gave the stands to merchants to place on the counter next to the cash register. That's what did it."

"It was as simple as that—and he became a millionaire?"

"Well, as Ed said, it all happened so fast, so easily, he could hardly believe it himself. What a lucky fellow!"

The food at the T.I. Club was the attraction for my father. Cuisine was basic to his French heritage. Lewis Beers, then the manager, told how Noble had engaged an "efficiency expert" to try to find the leaks in the cash flow. He reported a major problem: it was the French chef. "Every time he turns around," the consultant related, "in goes a pound of butter." The food was superb.

We used to stay not in the main building, but in the Chalet, where the rooms were larger and cooler. Built by Boldt, that large villa has since been divided into condominiums. Nearby was Wellesley House, which Noble also acquired when he purchased the Boldt property. It was another of the ghostly relics that affected me deeply. I knew that Wellesley House had been George Boldt's summer home for the final thirteen years of his life, after his wife's death. From there he had gazed across the water to the Castle, which he never revisited. There was a sense of tragedy about this place as well, heightened by its appearance.

Noble had no use for Wellesley House. It was a gloomy derelict, its once cream-colored shingles now weathered gray like the nearby Boldt Yacht House. It was not shuttered or boarded up, however, and not a pane of glass was broken, miraculously, since the property was untended and wide open to intruders like me.

Wellesley House was big, naturally—since it was a Boldt property. Fifty-six rooms. Like other Boldt buildings, it had steep roofs with many dormers (the motif I envisioned for my dream house on Hogsback). It had the inevitable Boldt tower. On stone pedestals iron lanterns of the same sort that Boldt used elsewhere flanked a pair of curving flights of steps leading up to the entry.

It was not a cheery place. The rooms, darkened by the tall trees around the house, had no furniture and were not particularly interesting. What was interesting, however, was what had been left behind when the furnishings were removed. Among the paper debris that apparently meant nothing to anyone else I discovered original blueprints for Boldt Castle and photographs of Louise Boldt.

A bridge across a canal connected Wellesley House to other buildings—the Tennis House and the Play Pavilion, originally situated in extensive gardens, now overgrown. The canal, lined with concrete walls, had been the entry to an elaborate system of waterways dug throughout the island. Other bridges still crossed the waterways, connecting concrete walks once lined with flowers. I had visions of all this from old postcards that I had been collecting for years.

Noble soon demolished Wellesley House. Like so many huge summer homes on the river at the time, it was considered a white elephant. Noble also owned and demolished the Peacock's regal villa on Belle Isle. Grant Peacock took that hard—said that Noble was always a "wrecker." But with the Depression, of course, there was little demand for grand summer homes.

The Boldt's great houseboat, *La Duchesse*, sank in the Boldt Yacht House, which Noble also owned. That remarkable building became increasingly shabby during these lean years, as did Boldt Castle, which Noble owned and operated as a public attraction. Noble did, however, maintain the Thousand Islands Club with its golf course in tip-top condition. That was his baby. The gardens were spectacular during those years. At the time the place was reputed to be "one of the richest and most exclusive" establishments in the country. That's questionable, since they let *us* in — even when I arrived with a company of college friends in tow. I was surprised (but too cool to show it) when the headwaiter seated us at Ed Noble's own table for the duration of our stay. Enthroned in the best corner, we received smiles and familiar nods from total strangers (young men have always been in short supply at summer resorts).

The Thousand Islands Club is still a fine restaurant, although no longer an inn. A wing was demolished, but otherwise the place looks much the same. Although I still enjoy the place, it no longer has the aura of privilege that it once had, back in the days when we college students dined at Noble's own table.

\* \* \*

Julie was appreciative of outings to venues that no longer were readily accessible to her, due to her vision and financial problems. In Clayton, Harold Bertrand's restaurant in his historic hotel, the old Hubbard House, was tops, but Harold had few customers in his dining room during those hard times. His wife did the cooking. As a youngster I preferred Tessie Grimaldi's on James Street, busier because her Italian food was lower priced. Tessie was everyone's stereotype of a big, jolly Mama Mia—and could she make "Stuffa-da-Pep"! Bertrand's brick hotel is gone now, replaced by a frame motel. Grimaldi's restaurant also is long gone, but the large brick house is still there, now a private residence.

Before the Thousand Islands International Bridge (which I remember being built) there used to be a ferry that connected Clayton and Gananoque, Ontario, on the far side of Grindstone Island. "Gan," as we called it, was a sleepy, rural town at the time. There were few tourist facilities then, but the attraction to us was the Golden Apple TeaRoom, which still functions (now as a full restaurant) in a historic stone house. It was just tea and scones at the time, however.

Some American friends of ours bought a Canadian island near Gananoque—improbably, since both were scared of the water and dreaded getting to their island, where they spent most of the visit worrying about getting off. They kept their boat at Mercier's in Clayton, and relied on one of the fellows there to pilot the boat around Grindstone. Since he would have to return to Clayton, they were left stranded on their island, hoping to see him return to rescue them. Of course, bad weather would come, terrifying these stranded, improbable island-ers. Eventually they came to their senses and decided island living wasn't for them.

* * *

Cape Vincent was beyond my rowing orbit, so I knew about one of the great houses, Carleton Villa, only from old photos and descriptions. Julie recalled that it had been far better known when built in 1894. "The mansion at the head of Carleton Island was the most ambitious house on the river at the time," Julie recalled. "We all went to see it, of course. It was a marvel. The lower part of the building was built of marble; the upper stories were half-timbered, in the English Tudor style. Like many grand houses here, it had steep roofs and a tower."

"Did you know the people who built it?"

"Not well, since it was quite a trip in the boats of those days up to Cape Vincent. The Wyckoffs were Ithaca people, but their money came from Remington Arms, which had a big plant in Ilion, New York. They made the Remington typewriter and rifles. I think the army was their biggest customer. William O. Wyckoff took over sales of the Remington typewriter, which made his personal fortune."

"Did you go in the house?"

"They were proud of it, naturally, and glad to show it off. The house certainly was astonishing—especially before Calumet, or Boldt, or Dark Island Castles appeared. There was a tall, open space in the center, ringed with a gallery on the second floor. Boldt may have got the idea for his great hall there. Waronoco Island had a similar arrangement, but that came later.

"There were lots of big rooms, but I don't remember much more after all these years. We didn't get back there much because William Wyckoff died and then there was the depression of the nineties. He didn't get much use out of the extravagant villa."

"What happened to it?"

"I think it's still there, but I don't get up that way much anymore. I've heard it is falling into ruin and there's a fence around it so no one will be injured trying to go in to it."

"Was Carleton Villa the big house farthest from here?"

"Maybe, but the Nichols' place over on the Bateau Channel seemed pretty far from here. That was Nokomis Lodge, on Howe Island, above Gananoque—that's a Canadian island, of course.

"The Nichols, like so many folks here, were from New York City. William H. Nichols was head of the Nichols Copper Co and chairman of the Allied Chemical

Nokomis Lodge, Howe Island, with yacht *Nokomis* at dock.

and Dye Co. The first house, built in 1898, was even more splendid than the present one. It burned in 1914. I remember seeing the great yacht, *Nokomis*, drifting down the river when the sky was lit from the fire. They cut the beautiful boat loose to save her, which was fortunate, since the yacht house burned as well.

Yacht *Nokomis*

We saw more of the Nichols than the Wyckoffs, since the Nichols hung onto their money and stayed on the river for a long time. They were sociable, attending events at the Frontenac, despite the distance."

\* \* \*

The Thousand Islands extend for some fifty miles of the St. Lawrence's run from Lake Ontario to the sea. The season is short, and most summer residents know only the environs of their insular retreats. Bound by the limits of my rowing, my summer world was small. Occasional afternoon tour boat excursions expanded the horizons of the Thousand Islands, but even those long cruises covered only the river between Clayton and the Bay. Julie took me back in time, as well as afar in place.

If Carleton Villa and Nokomis Lodge were so far from Clayton—both about ten miles—how far off were the other great houses? I learned about another pair of fantastic places farther down the river, about eighteen and thirty miles way, one American and the other Canadian. Dark Island Castle—the name alone was romantic—and Fulford Place. The first was near Chippewa Bay and the other at Brockville, Ontario. They were little known and rarely seen by visitors.

Fulford Place

The Fulford's great steam yacht, *Magadoma* is at the boathouse. To the left is the extensive rock garden. Greenhouses are at the lower right. Above is the fine Ladies' Home Fulford built as a contribution to the Brockville community.

Dark Island, like other remote villas, existed for me merely as images on old photographs for many years, until when much older I undertook a thorough study of these places, finally inspecting and documenting them. I began by collecting five-cent postcards on my afternoon walks into Clayton, then discovered that I could buy old books and paper ephemera from dealers. Over the years I built quite a collection, which I gave to the Antique Boat Museum at Clayton. It became the nucleus of the library there.

Did Julie know the Bournes — she pronounced it 'Born' — at Dark Island Castle? "Oh, they were far out of my league," she explained. "They hardly mixed even with the Chippewa Bay crowd. Frederick Bourne was probably the richest man here. He made Boldt look like a prosperous social climber. His wife was Emma Keeler, of an old New York family, so the Bournes were more than New Money. Bourne was Commodore of the New York Yacht Club — we always called him 'Commodore.' He bought the King of Belgium's ocean-going yacht and owned the largest estate on Long Island.

"People in that class didn't always come to the river for the summer, but only visited occasionally. Much of the time they were at other fashionable spas or guests at country houses elsewhere. They kept their island establishments running at the ready, however, in case they should drop in."

"Who was this Bourne fellow?"

"Frederick Bourne was president of the Singer Manufacturing Company, which he developed into a world-wide organization—really one of first global corporations — with plants in places like Scotland, Australia, and Russia. He built the tallest building in Manhattan, the Singer Tower, and had the same architect, Ernest Flagg, design his Long Island country house and Dark Island, too. Flagg was one of America's leading architects. He designed the Naval Academy at West Point."

"Did you ever even meet the Bournes?"

"The daughter, Marjorie, was my age. We called her 'Margie'. She had six sisters and brothers, mostly older than we were. She and Clover Boldt and Jean Chapman and a number of us at the Club played golf often, and tennis, too, so we knew one another socially. We played bridge on rainy days—that sort of thing.

"Marjorie married Alec Thayer. Margie loved the river and Dark Island, so in later years used it more than others in the family. It was her favorite, lifelong summer home after her parents' death. She got it only after a bitter quarrel with one of her brothers, who also wanted it. There was a legal battle. Margie was a pal of Clover Boldt—both were marvelous sportswomen. That's where I saw them, on the Boldts' golf course and the tennis courts, at the Thousand Islands Club and on Dark Island, and other places. It was such a treat to play at Dark Island! Like Clover, Margie owned and raced fast boats—handling them herself. She had the *Moike*, which would do twenty-six miles per hour—very fast back them—and many others. There was later the even speedier *Running Wild*, for instance—supposed to be the fastest boat on the river. The *Messenger* went the eighteen miles from Dark Island to Frontenac in forty minutes, and that included a stop in the Bay. The *Messenger* would have competed in the Gold Cup Races and might have won over the *Dixie*, but the Bournes' boat was fifty feet long, ten feet longer than the maximum allowed. They also had the *Stranger*, which also competed and won races—so many boats—-even an electrified Venetian gondola—would you believe it?"

"Dark Island was truly a fantasy castle. It was a folly from the start. The Commodore originally came to the river alone—not to fish so much as to hunt in the fall. The duck hunting was especially good down there at Chippewa Bay. There was the Fish and Gunning Club of nine New York men that had a clubhouse on Oak Island. Boldt belonged, and that's how Bourne came to the river, I suppose, but he belonged to some of the same clubs as Emery and others in the city, so was already acquainted with islanders.

Dark Island Castle

Commodore Bourne called his "shooting box" "The Towers."

"Boldt was building his colossal castle at the time, and Bourne got the bug. His stone walls were going up when Louise Boldt died. Borne finished his place, though—and what a place! He called it "The Towers" but didn't tell the family about it for years, while he came alone to the river to watch it rise. Joseph Reid was the contractor. He built many of the landmarks on the river. When finished, the Commodore finally suggested that the family visit the river for the first time. He told them only that he had built a 'shooting box' for fall hunting on one of the islands. Imagine the astonishment when, rounding an island, they saw far out in the water the great stone pile rising on the summit of Dark Island! Quite a 'shooting box'!"

"Was the place used only in the fall?"

"Oh, no. There were many Bourne children who liked summer fun here better than on the big Long Island estate. Their father fished as well as hunted. The kids called him 'The Old Fisherman.' He was a real outdoorsman—loved the river and often stayed late in the fall, after most of the summer people had left."

I wondered about the clock tower in front of the Castle, connected by the arched, stone bridge. "What was that for, do you suppose?"

"I can't imagine why they needed the big clock faces, showing the time in three directions, but the tower served a purpose. It provided a way of getting from the big boathouse and the main dock up to the castle if the weather was disagreeable. There were all sorts of winding stairs in that place. It was mostly up-and-down — more fanciful than Boldt Castle, more like their Alster Tower. "

"You say the Boldts knew the Bournes?"

"Of course. Frederick Bourne was a pallbearer at George Boldt's funeral. And Clover was a friend of Margie, but I don't think their parents were really very close — although the Boldts would have liked to be more intimate, of course. They were ambitious that way. But everyone saw everyone at the Yacht Club or at the Boldts' lavish recreational facilities nearby. Boldt built the big covered pier at the Thousand Islands Club, a stone's throw from the Yacht Club on Welcome Island. He had moved part of the old frame house from Heart Island over to Wellesley Island, where it became the Golf House. There were more and better tennis courts there than at the Yacht Club itself, and there was the polo field, where we gathered with parasols to watch the dashing young men play. Boldt had a stable full of marvelous polo ponies. Actually, it was his son-in-law, Clover's husband, who was the playboy polo player."

"I'm confused about the Yacht Club and the Thousand Islands Club — and you mentioned the Golf House. They were all different?"

"Yes, it was a strange mix. The Yacht Club came first, with the big clubhouse built on Welcome Island. Then the Boldts developed the golf course and other facilities on nearby Wellesley Island, making them available to members of the Yacht Club. Boldt built that huge pier for our boats. The Golf House was there first, before the Thousand Islands Club was built. That larger building was constructed by Ed Noble and Boldt's son-in-law in the early twenties, after George Boldt had died. That's why it's sort of Florida Mediterranean in style. That was the vogue then."

"A lot of these places had tile roofs. Dark Island too."

"That was because of the concern for fire. Wood shingles were a hazard, when fires were going in cook stoves and fireplaces. The Bradley's big house — about forty rooms — over on the north side of Wellesley had people inside, not even aware that the roof had been ignited by a spark from the chimney, until a passer-by in a boat called up from the water. There was no saving it. They never rebuilt, although they had a big estate, with farm and all, on the island. They went to Newport instead. I understand they built the biggest house there, larger even than the Vanderbilts' mansion."

SCENES ON THE POLO FIELD

Polo on Wellesley Island

A page from the nearby Hotel Westminster's booklet

"Who were the Bradleys?"

"Whisky—'Old Crow,'" as I recall. Edson Bradley had one of the splendid steam yachts. There were so many of the beautiful big boats at the peak of the resort, at the beginning of the twentieth century."

"The Bournes' yacht must have been something, if it belonged to the King of Belgium."

"Oh, they didn't bring that boat here from Long Island. They used it for trips abroad. They had smaller, faster yachts for the river, the *Artemis* was one, I remember—Dark Island was some distance from the Bay, or from anywhere else, you know, isolated several miles from either mainland shore. It was a mysterious, moody place, especially on gray days, and we get our share of them here, certainly."

"It was supposed to be that way, as a castle, I imagine."

"Yes, that seemed to be the idea. The New York Times ran a big, illustrated article—I have the clipping here: 'Castle of Mysteries.' There were secret passages and hidden doors—that sort of thing. The kids had a lot of fun, running around them, rapping on walls. The Commodore had read those novels by Sir Walter Scott, and this was supposed to be one of those romantic piles. They lit the place by candles at first. It certainly was extraordinary."

"It doesn't sound pleasant as a place to live: 'Dark Island' — gloomy."

"Well, in reality not so much so as you might think. On a sunny day, there were lots of flowers; it could be inviting. There's a huge, curved ramp leading up from the main dock that was lined with flowers. There weren't many big trees on the island, so it was really quite sunny, on a good day. It's the wooded islands than can be really damp and chilly in bad weather. Dark Island was really bright and breezy.

"Inside the massive entry doors, the main hall was a bit more forbidding. It was all stone, floors, walls, with stone vaulting overhead — rather dark and cave-like. Lifelike suits of armor — men carrying weapons — didn't appeal to the ladies, either. I suppose it was intended to be a man's place, but it wasn't full of the usual hunting trophies or mounted fish. None of that. Too tacky for the Bournes. They had medieval things, as I recall, and more sumptuous furnishings.

"There was a big, comfortable library off the lower hall — a retreat for bad weather. We played bridge in front of the fireplace there. With the thick stone walls and small windows covered with velvet draperies, one would never know that the wind was howling outside. The main part of the house was upstairs, however. One went up a grand staircase of several flights with landings. It was very broad, I remember, and turned a couple of times, since it was inside the main tower. There was a huge tapestry on one of the stone walls, with some sort of coat-of-arms on it.

"At the top, one went into what was really the main hall — the one below had been really more of a foyer, one realized. The big room on the second story was very high, running through two stories. It was brighter, since there were huge windows on two sides. The most interesting features were the alcoves. They said the Commodore got the idea from railroad cars, divided into small compartments. Each window opened into a sort of small room, which in turn opened into the main hall. The deep alcoves were designed to serve smaller groups or individual use, being set up for various activities like games, letter writing, or tea. Since these compartments were only one story high, there was a hidden space above them running around the central hall. This contained one of the secret passages, where one might spy on goings-on below. You could open a hinged painting and look down on the party in the main hall."

Dark Island Castle (The Towers), Lower Hall

"You went through some of these passages?"

"Oh, they were not really so secret—the point of having them was to show them to visitors. Margie loved taking us through the place.

"Off the great hall was the big dining room. I never had dinner there, since my visits were informal, mostly to play tennis. Margie expanded the house by adding the big room at the end of the dining room, a music room for perform-ances, but also a sort of 'morning room,' as we would have called it—a more casual place to dine, lingering over many cups of coffee in the morning, or over several glasses of wine at midday. It was brighter, with tall, Gothic sort of openings on three sides, and incredible views, as it was very high. On the main channel side, French doors opened out onto a broad terrace, where dining moved in good weather."

"That sounds more pleasant than the gloomy stone parts of the castle."

"Yes, and there were still other options: off the main hall was a large sitting room above the library which had windows on both sides and, beyond that, the sun room, all windows on three sides. It was furnished in rattan, very casual, and was the breeziest spot on the island during a hot afternoon. The high sun-room looked far up the river in one direction, and down on the tennis courts on the opposite side. A huge, level terrace had been built for the courts on the summit of the island, with stone retaining walls on all sides. A tunnel underneath allowed supplies to come from the service dock on the back of the island, where the stone yacht house was, together with the remarkable powerhouse. Such a collection of dials and switches, mounted on white marble slabs!"

"Marjorie Bourne didn't mind being isolated on that island, so far from everyone, even in bad weather?"

"Oh, I suppose when you have that kind of money, even weather can be ignored. Margie wasn't isolated. Like many wealthy islanders, she zipped around the region, chauffeured in what we call a 'sedan,' — sort of a water limousine with comfortable upholstered chairs in an enclosed, rear cabin — or raced in one of her runabouts. Those powerful boats were unfazed by rough water. In bad weather, one could use the sedan; the velvet curtains could be drawn if one didn't want to see the white caps. These water taxis had to be powerful and fast. Dark Island was more then ten miles down river from the Yacht Club.

Off to Dinner in the Sedan

"But there were plenty of things to do on the island, even if the weather was inclement. They had a squash court in another stone building, so athletic Margie could get her exercise, regardless. That was on one side of the tennis-court terrace. At the end opposite the sunroom wing of the castle there was a lovely garden pergola, where we might have tea.

"And Margie was always pressing visitors to engage in activities, some not quite to my taste. Down by the water, on the back side, was a terrace with stone seats, as I recall, where one went to shoot clay pigeons. Some sort of mechanism shot them up into the air, over the water. I didn't care for guns, but Margie was regarded as the best shot around here and around their Long Island place — next to her father and better than her brothers. Dark Island had been a hunting lodge and Margie carried on the family tradition. We often forget that fall duck hunting was once an important activity here.

"Margie was a superb horsewoman, like Clover Bolt. It's interesting that both girls seemed to have more dash than their brothers. Margie was a real speed demon, crazy about fast cars as well as boats. Her Long Island garage held sixty cars and had an electric revolving floor. We all thought that Margie was really a daring driver. She once raced her auto against the Long Island Express train — and she won."

"It's hard to relate that to tea parties — you mentioned having tea there. That sounds rather formal."

"Oh, it wasn't formal at all — at least it didn't seem so at the time. We were accustomed to eating dinner later in the evening, so some sort of snack about five was welcome. And the liquid refreshment wasn't always tea, to be sure. During Prohibition in the 1920s, they say that the Bournes kept their ample collection of fine wines — and cache of Scotch whisky — on a nearby Canadian island that they owned. The butler had to navigate to get to his wine cellar!"

* * *

Fulford Place, the other more distant great house Julie had mentioned, was closer to thirty miles below Alexandria Bay. It was at Brockville where the Thousand Islands began with the Three Sisters. Fulford Place was built overlooking them, on the mainland. Because of the distance, it was more a destination for yachting parties than for frequent social calls. George Fulford was a yachtsman. His *Magadoma* remains the last of the river's great steam yachts, although gone from the region today. Being Canadian, it didn't go to the US Navy like many of the big boats for the First World War. It was turned over to the Canadian Navy during World War II.

"Fulford Place hasn't changed a bit," Julie observed. "It's stayed in the family, and the family has stayed wealthy. The money came from — would you believe it? — 'Pink Pills for Pale People'."

"Fulford must have sold a lot of little pills."

"All over the world. It was pure marketing. There wasn't much medicinal value in the pills. Like Emery, Fulford was one of the first to use modern advertising. Like Bourne, he was one of the first to develop truly global marketing.

Fulford Place, Brockville, Fuller and Pitcher, Architects

"Fulford was a Brockville druggist originally but he became a Canadian senator. He entertained the Prince of Wales and all sorts of prominent people at his splendid stone mansion. Brockville is not far from Ottawa, you know. Sir Clifford and Lady Sifton had Assiniboine Lodge, a fine summer home on the mainland above Brockville, closer to Chippewa Bay. Sifton was prominent as a cabinet member in several Canadian governments. The family is still there, down by Brown's Bay and Jones Creek.

"If you want to see how this set lived back when the century began, you should visit Fulford Place. In some ways it's more representative than Dark Island, which was more a romantic folly. Fulford Place is sort of mainstream rich, with all the conventions of the period—a French style drawing room, full of elegant but not very comfortable furniture. Lots of gilt and curlicues, you know. It has the huge dining room, with one of those mahogany tables to seat twenty-four, as I recall, plus a smaller table at the far end, like the Emery's arrangement. There's the wood-panelled library, with a rich coffered ceiling, opening off a wide center hall that runs through the house. Broad verandahs run around two sides, offering a splendid outlook from the high vantage point, down over expansive lawns, to the river with the alluring masted yacht waiting there.

"On the side of the house was its special glory, the garden. The grounds were designed by Olmsted, the famous American landscape architect.

"George and Mary Fulford belonged to the Yacht Club and came to the Bay to socialize. I remember their sensational arrival one night. They had just acquired the huge *Magadoma*, which few of us had seen. They steamed up at twilight and approached the grand hotels when it was dark. We were having dinner at the Crossmon (where the food was wonderful) when I heard the gasp from the many people on the verandah outside the open windows. We all went to see the sight. The Fulfords had waited until in full view of the three hotels before throwing the switch that turned on hundreds of electric lights, strung on the rigging of the tall masts. Reflected in the rippling water, the effect was dazzling."

"Were there other big places that far down the river?"

"Yes, there's Thornton Cliff — a romantic, Gothic sort of house. Then there's quite a cottage colony around Fernbank, just above Brockville. The group of islands there is lovely, but few visitors to this part of the river even know about that area, since it's too far for tour boats to go from here. There are boat tours out of Brockville, however. And Sir Clifford and Lady Sifton built Assinaboine Lodge this side of Brockville. That's still the family summer home.

Cottage at Fernbank, Brockville

Thornton Cliff
Brockville, Ontario

Were the hotels at Alexandria Bay so grand as the Frontenac?  Julie admitted she had been partial to the Round Island establishment, which was the largest and probably most elite, when built.  The grand hotels at the Bay were older, after thirty years already somewhat dated in the early years of the twentieth century, when the enlarged Frontenac was new.

"But the older hotels still provided fine restaurants," Julie recalled, "and were patronized by many loyal guests who returned year after year.  The Crossmon had the best food, in my estimation, and was a bit less Nouveau Riche than the larger Thousand Islands House.  That big building was impressive, however—especially from the water, with its two-story colonnade running the length of the building.  It was the Saratoga style, if you know those enormous summer hotels built earlier in the nineteenth century.  The original hotel on Round Island had been similar, but the mode seemed dated by the turn of the century.  That was one reason why Emery changed the character of the place, painting it light colors instead of the somber old Victorian hues.

"The Crossmon was the oldest hotel at the bay, which may have accounted for more Old Families in its clientele.  Charles Crossmon took over his father-in-law□s tavern in 1848.  The family, now the Thomsons, is still in the hotel business here.  Crossmon had been one of the American invaders of Canada captured at the Battle of the Windmill down at Prescott, Ontario.  He was fortunate in being spared the fate of many, who were executed or exiled to the British penal colony at Tasmania, on the other side of the globe.  Charles was just a teenager at the time, so he was allowed to go home.

"The first visitors had been fishermen, coming without families.  When the railroads arrived, it was less arduous and time-consuming for families to come.  The resort really developed with a boom in the 1870s.  It was triggered by publicity about a visit of President Grant, together with the Civil War heros, Generals Sherman and Sheridan.  Pullman entertained the presidential party for several days on his island.  Perhaps it was no accident that the presidential visit occurred simultaneously with a convention of three hundred newspaper editors here, or that Pullman entertained them on his island as well.  They spread an account of Pullman's entertainment of the presidential party in papers through the eastern United States.  It was quite a bash.  They said that President Grant did 'not take kindly to water at that time in any form.'  You may interpret that as you wish—but Capt. Visger reported that due to his aversion to water the President fell in the river.  They also reported that General Grant, even wet, was so entranced with the region that at one point 'he had his purse raised to buy an island'.

*Wednesday, August, 11th, 1886.*

### SOUPS.

Consommé Vermicelli.                    Purèe of tomatoes.

### FISH.

Baked filet of bass.                    Potatoes Quèlin,
Raw Tomatoes.                           Cucumbers.

### RELEVE.

Boiled leg of mutton caper sauce. Boiled beef piquant sauce.

### ENTREES.

Chicken livers sautes
Salmi of tame duck with olives.
Stewed lamb, parisienne.
Baked macaroni with cheese

### ROASTS.

Ribs of beef.    Roast Turkay.    Lamb mint sauce.
Ham, champagne sauce.

LOBSTER salad.                          CHICKEN Salad.

### VEGETABLES.

Mashed *and* new boiled Potatoes,      Stewed tomatoes,
Boiled onions cream sauce         New peas.
Green corn on the Ear.        Beets.

### PASTRY.

Vanilla Ice cream.

Rice pudding.
Blackberry Pie                    Custard Pie.
Assorted cake.

### DESSERT.

Almonds.    Nuts.    Pecan nuts.        Filberts.
Fruit,                Raisins.         Coffee.

*Hours for Meals*  *Breakfast from 6:00 to 10:00  Dinner 1:00 to 2:30  Tea 6:30 to 9:00*
**SUNDAY DINNER AT 2:00.**
*For Children and Servants.*  *Breakfast at 7:00  Dinner at 1:00  Tea at 6:00*

1000 **ISLAND HOUSE.**
*Alexandria Bay, N. Y.*

Thousand Island House

The Crossmon House appears in the distance, beyond Cornwall & Walton's
stone store and the steamboat landing on the Alexandria Bay waterfront.

"The publicity resulted in the 'Rush of '72,' as they liked to call it, when Alexandria Bay was inundated with visitors. Big hotels followed immediately, as did development of many summer communities like Thousand Island Park. It was quite a boom."

"Did Grant ever buy an island?"

"Well, that summer Pullman tried to purchase Friendly Island for President Grant—too bad he didn't succeed. The Pullmans lived quite simply on their island originally. It was just a 'camp,' as we would say. George Pullman was one of the first generation of fishermen who came for the sport, not for socializing—at least not the sort of dressy socializing that developed after the wives arrived. But even then the Pullmans were regarded as something special, because they came all the way from Chicago in their private railroad cars."

"How did they find the Thousand Islands?"

"The whole resort might not be here, but for St. Lawrence University at Canton. One of the Pullman boys went there, so that's probably how the family discovered the charms of the St. Lawrence River. It was George Pullman's mother who was the real River Rat. She adored the place and summered on several islands. Her son acquired Pullman Island, near the Yacht Club, and built Castle Rest for her.

"Castle Rest was a great showplace, but George's wife hated it—maybe because it was really her mother-in-law's. Hattie preferred their other summer home on the Jersey shore, at fashionable Long Branch. President Grant also had a cottage there. George insisted the family convene at Castle Rest for his mother's birthday, however. Mrs. Crossmon, wife of Charles Crossmon, proprietor of the Crossmon House at Alexandria Bay, always make birthday cake. Mrs. Pullman tolerated the ordeal, assisted by liquid medications." Julie winked.

"Mrs. Pullman was one of the women who drank heavily?"

"I can't attest to that personally, since the Pullmans were really even more out of my orbit than the Bournes, but I heard stories from their chief housekeeper. It was what we would call a 'dysfunctional family.' That wasn't unusual, since these very successful men often were obsessed with their work, leaving wives amply provided with means to escape, one way or another. It wasn't just alcohol either. But what was a woman supposed to do, when waited on hand-and-foot by servants? She wasn't supposed to have any ideas. Thinking wasn't ladylike. Nannies cared for the children. Even if she was close to them, what did she do once the children were raised—and especially after the daughters were married off?

"George Pullman was famously devoted to his mother but otherwise was known as 'a tough customer.' They said that he was as 'equally ruthless' as Jay Gould, the notorious financier (with whom Pullman was associated in New York City transit development).

"Pullman had become even more nationally notorious because of his stubborn resistance to the workers' strike at his Chicago works and company town. I remember that summer, when he was holed up in his castle, while the US Army moved into Chicago and reporters hovered around his island. After the strike he became more wary of the public and newspaper men. We were in awe of Pullman. He personified power—symbolized by the great Corliss steam engine, largest in the world, which had been the centerpiece of the Philadelphia World's Fair. Pullman was the only bidder for the colossus, carrying it to his Chicago works on a train of thirty-five cars.

"The family didn't socialize much with other islanders but did come over to the club often. All chatter would stop on the verandah when they came up the steps. The great man was not imposing physically—he was rather short and chubby. But he was a little Napoleon. He assumed command. Andrew Carnegie said, 'Pullman monopolized everything.'

CastleRest, S. S. Beman, Architect

"But once clearly in charge, he had a sense of humor. I remember some of his rejoinders that we passed around merrily. A reporter innocently asked if, when he was a youngster, Pullman had ever dreamed of being so successful. He shot back, 'No, I did not. If I had dreamed then, I'd be dreaming still.' Then when S. S. Beman, his architect—of both Castle Rest and of Pullman, Illinois—suggested that the town might be called 'Beman' to recognize the architect's contribution, Pullman cheerily replied, 'I'll tell you what we'll do. We'll take the first half of your name and the last half of mine.' Pullman seemed affable in the billiard room at the club and was courteous to the ladies, if a bit remote. He was a busy man and seemed to be thinking of something else most of the time."

Castle Rest

The Shingle Style character is even more apparent on the side of the building where we see the five stories of the main block, with two more in the stone tower partially concealed behind the roof dormer. The towering landmark probably influenced design of Boldt Castle, which likewise would have seven stories. The kitchen wing extends to the left at the lowest level.

I wondered what people did at the club. Julie laughed. "Why, we showed off our clothes and gossiped, of course. That's what you do—the girls and their mothers, anyway. Many families, like the Pullmans, came for lunch, sometimes bringing guests for a change of scene. A small island can seem confining. Mr. Pullman often came alone, I recall, and we would see him reading, smoking, or playing billiards with other men—some of whom probably wanted to get away from their wives.

"Life at Castle Rest was odd—as I suppose the life of the very rich often is, especially when the father is such a dynamo. Boldt was a workaholic, too, you know—that's not unusual for self-made men. Moreover, Hattie was overwhelmed by George's mother and her family at the Thousand Islands. George even stipulated in his will that Castle Rest had to be opened for his mother's birthday for a family reunion. Hattie couldn't escape, even when her mother-in-law was in the grave. Castle Rest was a Pullman family institution. Hattie much preferred her own summer home on the Jersey shore—a sunnier sort of place. There she had her own friends, socializing with the Grants and other notables.

"George and his siblings were a strange mix of oil and water—intense George, called by the press a 'ruthless' tycoon, and his amiable minister brothers. As they said, their 'worlds were poles apart.' And then the Pullmans had some stressful differences, not merely between the adults, but between parents and children.

"The Pullman boys, Walter and George, Jr.—they were twins—had their father's wit, but not his ambition. The boys were a disappointment, eventually regarded by their father as being incorrigible. The twins were cut-ups, given to practical jokes that didn't amuse everyone—like riding horses into the house to break up a formal dinner party. They were wild playboys, eventually marrying the glamorous West sisters who were both divorcées, said to be 'blue-eyed and statuesque, with beautifully rounded forms.' The spontaneous elopement of Walter Pullman and Louise West was a great sensation. The other twin, George, Jr., married Louise's sister shortly afterward. Pullman didn't quite disinherit his sons, but left each of them only a modest annual income of $3000 a year, while the bulk of his great fortune went to his wife Hattie and their two daughters."

"You said one of the girls was adopted?"

"Yes, the younger was a little child when adopted. She became Mrs. Francis Carolan, who had a grand estate near San Fransisco. I saw more of the elder daughter, who was more my age and came to the nightly hops at the club. Florence Pullman was more responsible than her brothers. She married Frank Lowden, who became Governor of Illinois. We also called him 'Col. Lowden.' He was also a major figure in Nabisco, as I recall. Their main estate was Sinnissippi Farm at Oregon, Illinois. Here on the river they had the yacht *Venice* and built a golf course of their own on Wellesley Island. I remember one son and three daughters; one of them is Florence Lowden Miller now. The Lowdens continued to come to Castle Rest for many years, but that place like others became a white elephant—not that the family couldn't well afford to maintain it. Rather, the distance from Chicago, San Fransisco, Baltimore, and other cities, with the decline of railway service, made visits difficult. Andy McNally, also from Chicago, solved that problem by buying an airplane and landing on Wellesley Island, but the Lowdens didn't care that much for the place. The house was really rather dark—very Victorian, you know. The rooms really aren't so large as you might suppose, although there are a lot of them. That's the way they liked it, back then."

Hall, Castle Rest

Julie noticed my disappointment so continued, " — but it's quite intriguing on the outside, isn't it? It's been a high point of the boat tours for a half-century."

"And it's in good shape, even if they never open it any more."

"Yes, the family retains a caretaker. They think of the place as a memorial to George Pullman—and to his mother, which George himself wanted. The family knows the landmark is a public feature of the island tours. Pullman intended, like Charles Emery, to have the house remain for the future a place of family reunions, as his mother had done. But conditions change, don't they?" She laughed. "Look at me."

\* \* \*

Castle Rest subsequently was demolished by the distant family, which found it impractical to use. The property would have been maintained as a memorial to George M. Pullman and his mother, as he wished, had the Village of Alexandria Bay cooperated with tax abatement. Loss of this prime landmark and boat-tour attraction for the entire region has been greater than the loss of taxes to the Village of Alexandria Bay.

In later years I recognized more fully the architectural importance of Castle Rest. It was not merely of local interest as the first of the Thousand Islands "castles," built in 1888. It was one of the most distinctive designs of any building here, the work of Solon Spencer Beman, the Chicago architect who designed Pullman's famous company town, Pullman, Illinois, at the huge railroad-car works there, with buildings likewise designed by Beman. Castle Rest was unusual here for being somewhat "rustic," at a time when taste favored showy evidence of expenditure. Beman designed a building integrated into its natural setting. There were no lawns or elaborate beds of floral displays. The house, with its great tower of rough stone and mass of dark shingles, was artfully inserted into the existing landscape. When completed, all evidence of disruption was masked by planting disturbed earth with ground cover of ivy and ferns. The intent was to create a home in harmony with nature, characterized by a natural ease. That was very different from the prevailing taste of the time, which required a display of labor-intensive grounds, with "bedding out" of hundreds of greenhouse-grown annuals each spring and manicuring of luxurious lawns.

The designer's vision may not have been consistent with the life of the place, however, given the strained dynamics of the Pullman family. Probably George's mother appreciated its serene design quality, at least when others were not quarreling there. Perhaps they behaved themselves on occasions celebrating her family role—but the twin boys apparently were not up to behaving. At any event, the birthday of George's mother was an event known to everyone around, since he featured a spectacular display of fireworks, with filial sentiments conveyed in letters of dazzling light. Pullman used locomotive headlights— "powerful calcium lights"—to make his stone tower a beacon at night, a "tower of light."

The natural serenity conveyed by the artful design and the festive nightly illuminations seemed especially incongruous in July of 1894, when reporters hovered around Pullman Island. It was during the severe depression of the nineties, when Pullman had to cut back production of his railroad cars. He had retreated to his island while the President of the United States ordered the Army to put down the strike of Pullman workers, supported by other railroad unions, that was crippling railroad transportation in the United States. Pullman, who considered himself a philanthropic benefactor because of the model company town he had built, felt betrayed by his employees and was adamant about yielding. The issue became a national concern. Pullman did not come out the winner, even though the strike was suppressed.

Castle Rest, 1888

George M. Pullman, right, chats with with a visitor to his new
summer home. One of his daughters is on the second story deck.

The 1894 strike was a public relations disaster. Pullman was portrayed by much of the press—and has continued to be regarded by many historians—as a villain, a symbol of industrial greed and callousness towards labor. He did not see himself that way, of course. Although dismayed, he "looked five years younger," they said, the summer following the agony of the strike. He died three years later, in his view a misunderstood man.

\* \* \*

"I suppose the Pullmans also had one of the big yachts."

"No, they didn't even own a big boat." Julie responded. "They merely rented one while here. They were probably the best known people on the river at the time, so they didn't need to prove anything to anyone. Of course, they came in luxurious private railroad cars, which said enough.

"The Clayton railroad dock was quite a sight in those days. Some days sixteen trains arrived. Several families had luxurious private cars that awaited them on sidings there—I remember the Packer-Wilburs of Sport Island, the Hays of Round Island, the Haydens of Fairyland, and of course the Pullmans, were among them. The trains stopped right at the water's edge, where yachts and runabouts, as well as big commercial steamboats, picked up passengers and baggage, bound for the island communites or private summer homes.

"Private railroad cars were not unusual. The Packer-Wilbur family of Sport Island came in two cars, one carrying the family, the other the servants. Far more affluent islanders came on the regular trains, however. Since most wealthy summer people came from New York City and belonged to the Thousand Islands Yacht Club, there was a special Club train that left Grand Central Station late Friday afternoon. After a leisurely dinner overlooking the Hudson River, club members would retire to private compartments, waking on Saturday morning to the sound of water lapping on the dock. They would disembark to be greeted by the captain of their yachts or launches, to be carried to their islands for breakfast. The big steamboats jockeyed for position at the dock to take on passengers and baggage bound for the island resorts. It was so easy and comfortable then, compared to the interminable automobile trip today from New York City to the Thousand Islands. It's no wonder that there were far more New Yorkers, and far more wealth, on the River then than now."

\* \* \*

I wondered if the family that had two private cars came from New York City. No, Julie said, the Packers, and the Wilburs after them, came from Pennsylvania. This was unusual, but the North Country connection was their Lehigh Valley Railroad, which extended up through New York State, connecting to Oswego, on Lake Ontario. The family had the only side-wheel steam yacht on the river, the *Sport*, which carried them to Sport Island.

"They were two families, the Packers and the Wilburs?"

"Yes, but practically one, since Wilbur inherited the family enterprise — leadership of the railroad, that is. He was sort of an adopted son. Asa Packer was a heroic pioneer of railroading. His early line served the anthracite coal fields originally but was expanded to become a major link in the national railroad network. The elder Packer gave away much of a huge fortune, founding Lehigh University. He had two sons, but they didn't survive long to carry on. That's when young Elisha Packer Wilbur emerged as the successor. He had been groomed for leadership by the senior Packer. The Packers and Wilburs have been on the river since the beginning, practically, since they bought one of the first islands sold by Cornwall and Walton, who owned most of them at the time, which was just after the Civil War.

"Azariah Walton was an old-timer, of the generation of early fishermen who patronized Charles Crossmon's rustic inn at Alexandria Bay. In advancing years, Walton took as a younger partner Andrew Cornwall, an astute Alexandria Bay businessman who had the vision of developing a resort here. The Cornwall & Walton firm had acquired most of the American islands, most which were of little value for agriculture. They did have timber, however, which the firm cut and sold as fuel for passing steamboats. Once shorn of large trees, the smaller, rocky islands were fairly worthless. Andrew Cornwall saw the fishermen who patronized Charles Crossmon's inn. He sensed a market and offered islands for sale at very reasonable prices, stipulating that a cottage had to be built within a certain number of years. The Packers were one of his earliest customers, selecting Sport Island, a couple of miles below Alexandria Bay. The Packers bought Sport Island for twenty-five dollars in 1872."

"They built the big house there?"

"Yes, but Wilbur remodeled it in a more fashionable style at the turn of the century, when he acquired the island. The Packers built the big iron bridge over to Little Lehigh Island with its charming cottage, which also was remodeled in the same style as the big house.

The Iron Bridge between Sport and Little Lehigh Islands

"Little Lehigh was the home of Mary Packer, reputedly the wealthiest heiress in America when her father died. She married Charles Cummings and their family is still on the river."

" Did you visit Sport Island?"

"Occasionally. They had many youngsters. I remember that on Sunday the Wilburs gave all the help the day off. The big side-wheel yacht carried them over to church at the Bay. If you visited on Sunday evening, you could be sure of getting nothing but sandwiches made by the butler — he was the only staff person who stayed on the island. Like most owners of these big places, the Packers and Wilburs had a huge staff — far more people than we might imagine required to run even a large house. After all, these were supposed to be summer places. Butlers? It finally occurred to me why the Wilburs brought a whole railroad car full of servants to the river — not because they needed them here, but because they didn't want to leave them back at the big house in town all summer. A couple of months on the river was something of a treat to most of the help as well as the family. The staff had their own swimming spot on Sport Island. You may think that the idle rich took for granted the service of staff. Nothing could be farther from the truth. As someone said, life in one of these big houses 'revolved around keeping the help happy.'

Eight Maids at Sport Island

"In some ways island life was more casual than formality required in town, but it was difficult to maintain the illusion of informality with butlers and maids hovering around. Everything was expected to be so labor intensive, back in those days. There were big lawns on Sport Island, but they never used any efficient mechanical mowers. You would see three gardeners, on their knees, clipping grass with scissors. It took the three of them a week to get from one end of the island to the other. The next Monday they started all over again, back at the other end of the island.

"And the laundry! Every meal required a fresh linen tablecloth and napkins, all not only newly washed but ironed. Then there were all the family, guest, and staff bed linens. Big island establishments had laundry buildings and a full-time laundry staff. It's hard for us to imagine the labor required to keep these places going—at least in the manner to which the families were accustomed."

"It sounds feudal. Could you be comfortable with all those servants on a little island? It doesn't sound very relaxing—or even decent, somehow."

"Yes, even then there were critics who complained about the extravagant ways of the rich. But think about the jobs they gave all of these people. Most of the Wilburs' maids were single Irish girls, recent immigrants, who had few opportunities otherwise to support themselves. Islander families were not so selfish as you might imagine. Many really thought it their duty to use their wealth to provide jobs."

"I never thought of it that way."

"Local people here did, you can be sure of that. There was a sort of love-hate relationship between the natives and the summer people. That was usual for resorts anywhere, I suppose."

"It must have been wonderful, living in one of these great houses — if you were a member of the family, or a guest, that is. Didn't you envy these people?"

"Well, to be honest, yes and no. So much was so alluring about it. But I was close enough to that way of life to know how unhappy some of those people were. One of the Wilbur boys was always depressed. He used to hide in the big boathouse and drink alone in there, we supposed. Poor fellow, we always tried to avoid him because of his unpredictable behavior. He was hardly joyous about his privilege.

"And Mrs. Wilbur, she was a great lady, really patrician in her manner — but what a job, running that sort of establishment, with all those employees! It wasn't all fun, to be sure, when your summer home was a veritable hotel of which you were the manager. It was a great responsibility, and their businessmen husbands weren't much help, being gone most of the time and wanting to relax, being spared problems when on the island."

"Did other members of the family drink much?"

"Liquor? It flowed like water. Everyone drank, it seemed. I remember seeing on Little Lehigh, in the front hall, a jug on a stand with a spigot. You might suppose it was water. I don't think it was. Maids served ice water there. Gents sipped their whisky neat, gulped in one swallow from a little shot glass. A faucet in the hall was convenient, you see."

\* \* \*

Julie didn't smoke, but one day I spotted a silver object on her kitchen table. It was the size of a cigarette case, but I had never seen anything like it. There was a raised image on the cover, showing a sleigh being pulled through the snow by three horses. I rubbed my finger over it to feel the high relief.

Mississauga Laundry

"That's called *repoussè*—the silver is pounded out from the back to form the image. Do you recognize the picture? It's a Russian *Troika*."

"It's a cigarette case, isn't it?"

"Yes, turn it over." The other side was even stranger, with all sorts of words in an odd script, running every which way on the cover. They were raised in gold, applied somehow to the silver case. There was also a small oval piece of thick glass, framed in gold, covering a faded picture of a young woman. "It's Russian," Julie explained. "It was made for a young officer in the Czar's service. On the eve of his departure for the front, his friends gave him a farewell party. Afterward, to commemorate the event, they all signed a piece of paper, which they sent to the silversmith, who replicated their signatures in gold, as you see them there. As you might guess, the young woman in the photograph was the officer's girlfriend. They sent the cigarette case to him at the front. I've often wondered were she might be now, and what became of the officer. So many of them were killed. If he were still alive, he'd probably have the case now."

"How did you get this?"

"I was at a party—not here on the river, but back in Connecticut. Igor Sikorski was there—he's the inventor of the helicopter, you know, and he produces them. While we were chatting, he pulled out this cigarette case and offered me one. I admired the unusual case and asked questions. I was astonished when, out of the blue, he smiled and said, 'I want you to have it'."

When I told the story to my mother, who was something of a cynic, she laughed and commented, "Well, I believe most of it, except for that 'out of the blue' bit."

\* \* \*

I missed seeing May Irwin perform, although she was still on the river when I was young. Julie was more familiar with the star and admired her achievement as a fellow actress. "May was really out in front. She skyrocketed to stardom by singing a ribald man's song that came from a brothel in St. Louis—imagine, a woman, and this back in the nineties. It really shocked even sophisticated Manhattan audiences. This was the age of sentimental operetta, when sopranos twittered about sweet mysteries of life or, at the worst, about being birds in gilded cages. And along comes May, belting out a song about a cut-throat gangster with a knife.

"May was a born comedienne, moreover. She and her sister had been on the stage since they were children, and May was a seasoned professional by the time she was a young woman. Although her reputation was established on Broadway, she was known to millions of Americans from her decades of travel on the vaudeville circuit, where she kept audiences rolling in the aisles. President Wilson called her 'America's Ambassador of Laughter.' Unlike some performers, May wasn't funny merely on the stage, but all the time. She was so popular she could get away with anything. She dressed as she chose, lived as she chose—and was so different in this way from most of the wealthy grand dames here, who slavishly did whatever was supposed to be proper. Propriety didn't mean a thing to May, for its own sake, although in truth she was a very wonderful person. She just loved to shock people. I remember that she wrote a famous article that appeared covering most of the front page of the sections of a New York City newspaper. I think the headline read, "How I Told My Sons About Sex." Sex! That three-letter word was hardly whispered at the time. And here was May, an unconventional single mother who was raising teen-age boys, telling other American mothers how to tell their sons the facts of life. That was May for you!

"One of May's real contributions was her support for Negro music and musicians. Today some of her material would be offensive, to be sure—but at the time every minority was the subject of jokes, and many of May's songs were composed humorously by Negroes about Negroes. But naturally, when a white person says the same thing, it can be disagreeable. But May really appreciated the Negro culture. She spent many of her free evenings at clubs in the Tenderloin District, absorbing Negro music. Again, she was way ahead of the time in this. Her singing began to take on the Negro style, which gave her distinction, particularly as a woman entertainer.

"May's great gift was in working an audience. She didn't go through the motions of performing. She got out there and made eye contact, trying to engage every person in the house. This is not easy to do, particularly in those huge vaudeville houses that were packed with thousands. One of her tricks, I discovered, was the 'we' tactic. She had wonderful timing and was a master of the pause, so effective with innuendo.

"Building to an implied punch line, she'd stop, look around the hall, and slyly wink, as if to confide to each person, 'We get it, don't we?' Of course, they did, and they loved it. Half the time she never even gave them a punch line. They got it, and broke up before she needed to deliver it."

"Was May Irwin ever in the movies?"

"That was one of her most sensational innovations — the first motion picture kiss. Movies were still a novelty, and May boldly gave the public, not passive acceptance of her partner's kiss, nor merely did she give her partner a discrete little affectionate peck on the cheek, but they merged in long, long lips-to-lips, honest-to-goodness kiss. Blown up as a closeup on the big theater screen, the impact was sensational."

"I'd like to see that."

"I'm sure you can, since it's a part of motion picture history now, reproduced in many film anthologies. But May never enjoyed making pictures the way she enjoyed the stage. They were silent films, originally, and certainly May needed live delivery of her lines and songs. She really required a live audience, and she knew it. She had to work the audience. That was her gift.

"She was always performing, in the sense that she was always entertaining whomever was around. You'd see her engaging a group of strangers on Riverside Drive, delivering wise cracks. She was generous with her talent and wealth, contributing much to the Clayton Boys' Club, for instance, a favorite cause."

* * *

Benson Boys

George Frothingham Benson and William Davenport Benson

It occurred to me that Julie seemed to be talking mostly about people on the US side. What was happening over on the Candian side? "Well, I did mention Nokomis Lodge—but the Nichols were New Yorkers, of course. So were the Woods on Hickory—I think we talked about that place, which is just over the boundary lime. But the Fulfords and Siftons were Canadian, down Brockville way. There's a lot of river in between, though—and more Canadian than US islands, you know. But there was a title problem with the Native Americans, who retained a claim of some sort, so the government didn't put many Canadian islands on the market until the US islands were already more developed. When they did so, they only auctioned off a small number each year, so we didn't see so many summer homes being built over there.

"The most prominent place that comes to mind in the mid-island stretch is Mississauga, the Bensons' beautiful summer home in one of the most beautiful groups of islands. The Canadian span of the International Bridge crosses just below Rabbit Island, as they call it now. The house is not so large as most of those we've talked about, and life there was less burdened by excessive staff and labor-intensive display. The building always attracts admiration from passing tour boats, however. It was designed by the Montreal architect, Robert Findley, in a sort of English Tudor style, I suppose. Do you know the place?"

"I've passed it on the tours. The boats go through Benson's Rift, that narrow passage alongside the island, with the big house on one side and 'Grandmother's Garden,' as they call it, on the other. It's a big flower garden on a slope."

"Yes, that's on Hill Island. They used to have a sheep pasture over there. The Bensons were a lovely family. They had the cutest little boys!

"They were from Montreal. The family fortune came from making starch. Actually, they lived on this side of Montreal, in suburban Cardinal, where they had a big, stone house. They kept their islands (there were several linked together with foot bridges) natural—no lawns—which was refreshing compared to many showplaces in 'Millionaire's Row' over at the Bay. The Bensons also lived fairly simply, as these things went—which means only a few servants, not dozens. The house is not really as big as it appears. I don't suppose you've been inside."

Mississauga, Robert Findley, Architect

"No. It's always been occupied. I only break into abandoned houses."

Julie laughed. "The interior is all wood, fairly dark as I recall—which is not unusual for these places. They often avoided plaster in summer homes that were not heated through the winter. Repetitive varnishing darkens the wood, just as layers of varnish darken an oil painting. The Benson place isn't self-consciously rustic, however. No rough stone fireplaces—they're brick, as I recall. It's just a commodious, attractive house.

"The Bensons were not so intently social as many over on the American side—which is one reason the house is less grand. It was just a family summer home, not a virtual hotel. But the Bensons did belong to the Thousand Islands Yacht Club. They would come over through the International Rift and Lake of the Isles, taking the shortcut through the Mary Island canal.

"The Bensons didn't have many immediate neighbors, but they seemed to enjoy the relative isolation—and there were always all the tour boats going by. It's rather amusing at first to sit on the verandah and hear the tour guide's amplified comments about you and your house—but a dozen times a day—after the hundredth time—it wears a bit thin.

"There were several other grand houses in that vicinity, among the Canadian islands on the north side of Wellesley Island. One the tour boat guides called 'The House of the Seven Gables.' The imposing place was said to have been the largest residence on a Canadian Island when built in 1900. It was acquired by Ohio Congressman Himes, whose fortune came from Pittsburgh steel. Actually the building doesn't have seven gables, but has many dormers—two stories of them—in the huge roof. The white house with its very long porch stretches along the top of a rocky cliff. It's not at all rustic, but is large, not overly ostentatious, and especially attractive.

"Nearby, the Devine Cottage was another roofy place with many dormers. It likewise picturesquely crowned a small, rocky island (Madawaska) in a densely packed group of Canadian islands near the International Bridge. Although their cottage seems less grand than many, the Devines surprisingly were one of eighteen or more island families to maintain farms, and even more surprisingly, the Devines kept polo ponies on theirs. New Yorker Andrew Devine, said to be a founder of Columbia Records, was a member of the Thousand Islands Yacht Club.

"But don't judge the wealth of an islander by the size of the island and house." Julie laughed. "The Redpaths of Montreal—a sugar fortune— have a tiny place they call 'Just Room Enough,' off Hill Island."

Opawaka Lodge was the summer home of Pittsburgh steel man, Washington D.C. resident, and Ohio Congressman Joseph Hendrix Himes (1885-1960). Tour guides often called the Canadian landmark "The House of Seven Gables."

One of the most photographed places on the river has been Zavikon Island, also Canadian and likewise featuring one of these houses with big, steep roofs and long porches. Not so large as "Seven Gables," Zavikon is notably picturesque because the cottage crowns a small island, completing a triangular compostition, It's connected to an even smaller island with a graceful bridge. Since the islet is on the US side of the boundary line, the span is pointed out by tour boat guides as "the smallest international bridge in the world."

These were some especially memorable landmark homes in the central Canadian islands. The big Bradley house that burned, mentioned previously, also was in this vicinity, although it was located on Wellesley Island in the United States. The Pratt's unique, modernistic villa on Niagara Island came somewhat later — in the thirties. The Pratts are American — Standard Oil fortune, like the Rockefellers. There were, of course, many other cottages here and in other groups of Canadian islands, but not nearly so many notable landmark structures as on the US side of the river.

* * *

The Rippeteaus' summer home on Wellesley Island below Alexandria Bay recalls the big-roofed houses on the Canadian islands, except that it has a gambrel roof rather than a simple gable. Similarly, the roof comes down over the second story to the long porch across the front, and the roof is broken by many dormers. This device appears again at Long Rock Island, a smaller but architecturally distinctive summer home, originally of the Vandergrifts, a family prominently identified with Pittsburgh steel. Long Rock is closer to Clayton, the island located directly above Grenell Island. At Long Rock a gambrel roof similarly was brought down to the main floor level, providing second story bedrooms with dormers. The intent was to make the form less boxy, appearing to rise more gradually from the ground.

As the Victorian became the Edwardian period, following the highly influential Chicago World's Fair — the "Great White City" — taste changed. White paint reappeared with renewed appreciation for more classical (or purportedly "Colonial") forms and some measure of classical restraint. The Vandergrifts were as wealthy as most owners of island show places, but blatant ostentation no longer seemed tasteful. Probably Long Rock was thought to be "Dutch Colonial" when built.

"The interior seemed very modern, when we first knew it," Julie recalled. "There weren't a lot of little parlors filled with fussy furniture, but a big living hall with the simple Stickley or Mission style furniture. The plainer look came as a reaction — you know, those big, squarish pieces made out of flat oak boards and slats, with brown leather cushions.

"The Vandergrifts had taste. They were more akin to the folks at the head of Grindstone — which may be why they preferred the Clayton area to the Bay. The Vandergrifts moved from Pittsburgh to Washington, D.C. — which is indicative, since they didn't care for New York City. They were not New Rich but were second generation — Standard Oil money originally, plus steel and banking. I knew Alice, the daughter, better than her parents, Harry and Alice. We first became acquainted at the Frontenac, where they stayed and where they kept their earlier, smaller boat, before they built the Long Rock house. The Vandergrifts also had a farm on Grindstone, like Emery. Their big yacht house was over there, for the larger *Cherokee*. It was one of those alluring vessels, over a hundred feet long."

I wondered what the inside of the house was like. "Of course there was a big fireplace in the hall," Julie explained, "and another smaller one in a little library off the hall. Most living was done on a big, screened porch, however—it was really a room, furnished like one. The smaller buildings on the island were especially charming—a fancy water tower, a skiff house, an icehouse and others that I can't remember. But you've rowed around that island, I'm sure."

"Yes, I've taken pictures from the water. It's one of my favorites. It's a lot like Hogsback, with the waves breaking that long, rocky point at the upper end of the island, and the tall, wind-swept pines towering over the house. I could live there."

\* \* \*

"The Thousand Islands Yacht Club was the center of life on the river in those days—at least for those who could afford the high life. The big, shingled building was a barn of a place," Julie remembered. "There was a long verandah across the front, which was where most people congregated. You'd walk along it, chatting with acquaintances as you went. There were regulars of course, who you'd come to know after awhile. The stalwarts tended to be mostly the people who lived nearby, naturally, like Emma Hagan from Ina Island. She had a regular post on the verandah at the head of the steps, where you couldn't miss her. You couldn't forget her either. She was enormous and had one wild eye that was always looking somewhere else. We'd see less of folks like the Fulfords, who had to cruise thirty miles for special events.

The Thousand Islands Yacht Club

Tea Time at the Thousand Islands Yacht Club

"The interior of the building was not very cozy—just big. It reminded me of the interior of one of those shingled yacht houses, dark and echoing. In fact, some of the interior walls were covered with the same shingles used on the outside. Odd. No one ever sat in the cavernous hall, which only came alive for dances in the evening. There was a huge fireplace, seven feet wide. Charles Emery gave a couple of enormous Chinese vases. I think they were about as tall as I was. There were smaller rooms that were more congenial, however— billiard and smoking rooms for the men, and a pleasant reading room. But mostly we sat on the verandah—170 feet long.

"The café at the end of the long building was livelier, naturally, for that's where one went for refreshment. Of course, drinks could be ordered on the verandah, but that was more the genteel venue—mostly ladies ordered tea out there. The gents and the younger set favored the café. It adjoined the tennis courts, which was convenient. Of course, we had to shuttle across the bay to the Boldt facilities for larger tennis matches, since there was room only for four courts on little Welcome Island. Over on Wellesley there was a big loggia overlooking the courts. We'd also go over there for golf and polo. Nobody did much swimming back in those days. Well, there was an exception, and a girl at that. Mary Donohue at St. John's Island (they call it "Steamboat" now) used to swim from her island to the mainland. That's about three-quarters of a mile and took her about an hour and a half.

"A few adventurous folks had toboggans—slides that landed in the water—but no one stayed in very long. There was one at Thousand Island Park and another at Ina Island. The Boldts had indoor as well as outdoor 'plunges,' as they called swimming pools, but they were hardly more than big bathtubs. One just jumped in to get wet, then jumped out."

"Why did you do it?"

"Why, it was an opportunity to change costume once again—and to appear in a bathing suit!" She winked. "But those heavy woolen things don't seem very fetching today. How times change!" She laughed. "But we did get to see the men's legs (or 'limbs,' as they might be more genteely called)—more of theirs than they saw of ours, in our black leggings.

"Bathing, as we called it in those days, was more for young men, and then only in the hottest weather, when needless to say we girls regarded the boys' activity as a very interesting curiosity. We adventurous ladies had to calculate the risk in appearing in closely fitting tights, a low-necked bodice, and a shirt just covering our hips—with arms bared to the shoulders and, even daringly exposing our 'limbs' to the knees—for the effect would be a calcuated sensation, welcomed by the boys but deplored by our feminine rivals. We notorious Bingham Sisters were always cautiously and nervously on the edge between admiring notice and disparaging disapproval. We were 'modern girls,' however, fancying ourselves to be two of the 'New Women.'

"A major concern of the ladies was their complexion, especially if we were the least bit athletic. My sister and I played golf and tennis, fished, and were on the water as much as possible. We even enjoyed collecting wild blueberries on some unpopulated island. But tans were not admired in those days, and proper ladies stayed indoors, carried parasols, or wore big hats to preserve their pallid appearance. I suppose those of us who were active had to reconcile ourselves to looking like farm girls. We had the consolation of good company, however, since Clover Boldt and Margie Bourne also had the ruddy complexions of sports women."

\* \* \*

Bathing, Fulford Place

The small bay outside the Yacht Club was activated by boats and enhanced with architectural splendor. Within stone's throw of one another were the clubhouse, the big Boldt Pier, with its casino on the second floor, Pullman's Castle Rest, its tall stone tower rivaled by that of Hopewell Hall nearby. Hopewell Hall was then the summer home of George and Louise Boldt's daughter, Clover Boldt Miles—later Johaneson.

"The tower was once much taller," Julie commented, showing me an old postcard. "These towers had to be high, so as to provide adequate water pressure, since their real purpose was to contain tanks that would serve bathrooms on the third floors of most houses—that's where the servants usually slept. The tanks had to be higher, to provide gravity pressure. And at Hopewell Hall there originally were more dormers in the roof, to light the servants' rooms. But after we acquired electric pumps, water tanks weren't necessary, nor these tall towers. And with fewer servants, third floor bedrooms (usually hot) were not required either, so dormers were removed. Hopewell Hall is not nearly so imposing to-day as it once was, since practical Clover simplified the house. Even the big yacht house is gone now."

"Hopewell Hall was built by William Browning, who made his fortune making uniforms for Civil War soldiers. After the war Browning was one of the active boosters of the resort who envisioned it becoming more of a social colony, centered on a yacht club. He was one of the men that induced the Boldts to buy Hart Island.

"Boldt bought Hopewell Hall, adding it to his collection of summer homes here, and Clover chose it as the place she preferred. It has lovely gardens and a good outlook, being high and dry, which was more than Wellesley House was, down in the reclaimed swamps—those canals were mosquito heaven— with no breeze."

"What was her house like inside?"

"Well, Clover was not one for display, as her pruning down the exterior showed. The rooms were rather small—typical of these big houses back in the nineties. Lots of little parlors cluttered with lots of furniture. Clover didn't spend much time indoors, however, preferring to be active outdoors. I got the sense that she didn't pay much attention to décor. I think she hired decorators now and then to make the place more spiffy.

"Clover loved flowers, however, like her father. The Brownings had devel-oped all those elaborate stepped gardens around the cliffs of the site, contained in granite retaining walls. They built a real folly, a huge set of symmetrical stone flights of steps that didn't go anywhere or serve any purpose. There were all these stone masons here—the same ones built stone ornaments on many of the islands, which is why the style seems so similar and characteristic of the Islands now."

"Like those crazy gargoyles on the shore, over at Cherry Island?"

"Exactly. They never served any purpose either. Or the pretty stone bridge out to that little island at the head of Nobby—a rather costly way to get across a few yards of water. It was all for fun.

"Nobby was one of the islands around the Yacht Club bay, like Pullman's island which had its rustic stone work as well. On Wellesley there was the Cha-let. Many celebrities rented that big house from Boldt. Next door, fronting on the bay, was 'The Junior's' summer home, The Birches. That was George Boldt, Jr. His wife, Estelle, was widely regarded as one of the most striking women on the river, seeming exotic, since she was Mexican. After they divorced, Estelle continued to come with her daughters, whom George, Senior, adored. Estelle and the girls didn't stay at the Birches any longer, however, but preferred the smaller Tennis House, part of the Wellesley House complex. The Birches was once much larger, but it was cut down to be merely a one-story cottage when big summer homes became a burden.

"You should have seen that bay, when the Yacht Club was in its prime, attracting so many of the alluring boats. They had to use the big Boldt pier on Wellesley Island, or moor out in the bay, since Welcome Island couldn't provide sufficient dockage. A club tender would shuttle people around the bay. It was a lively place."

\* \* \*

My collection of postcards and old souvenir books was growing. I would take new acquisitions purchased in Clayton directly up to her apartment. Julie was an appreciative viewer. Like a jeweler inspecting a diamond, she'd hold each item close to the thick glass over her one good eye. Julie provided many informative comments. It was like taking one of the old steamboat tours with a good guide. There were so many of these island showplaces, many of them gone now. Naturally, Julie told me more about the places she had known personally.

"Casa Blanca—the place with the big stone gargoyles, a river landmark—was built by a Cuban sugar planter. How did he ever get way up here? Well, the Marx family was wealthy, so they spent time in New York City—which I expect was really more their home base, rather than Cuba. They were Jewish, as were the Abraham and Straus families who lived next door on Cherry Island, in the famous Twin Cottages. Luis Marx married Nathan Straus's sister.

"The Marx family came in the nineties. You don't remember the Spanish-American War, of course, but that's when Teddy Roosevelt and his Rough Riders stole Cuba from Spain—a jolly little war—and American interests were served, especially for investors in sugar production there. The great Sugar Trust was put together in those days, following the model of Emery's Tobacco Trust. A lot of money was made, selling stock in these new giant corporations. I suppose that Marx had a windfall from selling his plantations and production facilities in Cuba to the new trust. There was so much money being made over the turn of the century. This place was awash in money.

"Luis Marx bought Melrose Lodge, as they called it then, on Cherry Island. It was one of the Pullman family places. The original cottage is now the back part of the big house. Marx outbid everyone at an auction in 1897 and then improved the property."

Casa Blanca, Cherry Island, Alexandria Bay

"The Marxs' daughter was about my age, so we naturally became acquainted — but not at the Yacht Club. I don't remember any of the Jewish families going over there. They favored the big hotels at the Bay, which really had better food and a more diverse clientele. We met different people for a change at the hotel dances, people other than the familiar set at the Club. But parents were often concerned about youngsters socializing at the hotels for this reason. There always were some questionable types there. One wondered where they got their money — or if they really had money, or were merely out to get it. Some girls were not allowed to socialize in the Bay, but I was less constrained, being given pretty much free run of the river. My sister cut quite a figure on the grounds of the Thousand Islands House, I remember—she use to have a pair of Italian grey-hounds on a leash. You should have seen the heads turn to watch us from the verandah. We were 'Those Bingham Sisters'."

"She was tall like you?"

"Yes, we were a pair, just like her dogs! We also had a certain advantage, being from Watertown, not so far off, since we could bring our 'turnout,' which was what our horse, carriage, and coachman was called. Most people who came farther by train were stranded as pedestrians on land, while we could pull up to the mainland hotels and country houses in great style in our elegant victoria with its prancing team of bays and colored coachman. Needless to say, all the city folks appreciated a carriage ride—even though the roads were awful." Julie sighed and began to drift off in reverie.

"You were telling me about Casa Blanca."

"Yes, that was a lovely place. Just a large frame house, really—not much more than you might find on Coast Avenue at Thousand Island Park—but the Cherry Island location was so splendid, right across the from Castle Rest, not far from the Bay or the Yacht Club. The Marx family bought it just in time for their daughter to be married there, which was a big event. They installed a big foun-tain in front of the house, which they lighted with electricity every night. They got the idea from the Chicago World's Fair, a few years earlier. The 'electric fountain' was a sensation, when electricity itself was still a novelty here. All the big steamboats would pass close by Casa Blanca on the 'illumination tours,' after dark."

"What were they?"

"Oh, romantic outings, with big searchlights picking out the towers on the islands, which were all aglow with outdoor lighting—paper lanterns with can-dles, or kerosene lanterns with colored glass globes. People vied for the most spectacular displays. Islands were identified by different symbols outlined in lights, their porches and often whole seawalls ringed with lights. They Boldts were supposed to have had one man whose only job was to take care of their kerosene lanterns, washing all the hundreds of globes every day, filling them, lighting and extinguishing them at night. The 'illuminations,' as they were known, brought whole trainloads of excursionists from cities in the region. The lighted steamboats moving among the dark islands, over the sparkling water, added motion to the scene, as well as sound, not only from the steam engines and paddle wheels, but from the bands playing aboard.

"The illuminations became one of the popular attractions of the resort. Thousands of people came every week to see the spectacle. Imagine the scene around Alexandria Bay, where the verandahs of the big hotel were outlined with strings of lights, and the great tower of the Thousand Islands House—a huge lantern of colored stained glass—was a beacon seen for miles. Then imagine all this accompanied by strains of music from many steamboats, some growing louder, some diminishing as they mixed with the orchestras playing in the big hotels How enchanting!"

*   *   *

The "Twin Cottages" were another major feature pointed out on every steamboat tour. At the head of Cherry Island, they were visible from the upper dock at the Bay—the more so because they were large and rose high above the river. Either one would have been imposing, but what was so unusual was that one was the mirror image of the other, and they were built very close to each other.

Abraham & Straus was a major department store in Brooklyn, and the partners were very close friends as well as business associates. Their identical cottages were testimony to their filial bond. Nathan Straus, owner of Belora, the most visible house at the head of the island, was the more prominent of the two. He was perhaps the most distinguished summer resident on the river, at least judged by his civic contributions—even if he was not so rich as some islanders, such as Commodore Bourne or the Haydens of Fairyland. Straus was not nearly so well known as May Irwin, either. But he was wealthy enough—the fortune coming mostly from his family business, Macy's in Manhattan, the largest department store in the world.

102

Hopewell Hall and Castle Rest

Nathan Straus was respected as "one of the outstanding philanthropists of his time." He probably was best known for distributing free pasturized milk to poor children of New York City. Straus was admired, not only in the city, but internationally, for he was a major contributor to the Zionist movement. Cleveland Amory, in his book about the American Jewish aristocracy, *Our Crowd*, observed that the Straus family became "foremost among the inner circle of the "Jewish Grand Dukes."

"But don't think of Nathan Straus as a stuffed shirt," Julie cautioned. "He was addicted to fast horses. Straus and George Boldt were both keen fanciers and excellent drivers. In the City, they drove together in Central Park. Up here Straus kept his stable over on the mainland, at Edgewood, where there was a race track.

"When his summer home was finally completed, Straus had a big party over at the Thousand Island House for all the workmen. Straus was that sort of person—which I couldn't say for everyone here. We were all distressed by an accident, which might have been comical if it had not been serious. Yachts used to have little cannons on board—we called then 'sunset guns,' because they would be fired at twilight, when the US flag was lowered. They were also used to salute distinguished guests coming on board, or even the family on arrival at the Clayton railroad pier. As Nathan Straus approached his lovely boat, the *Siscilina*, the skipper give the command to fire the cannon. The shot hit Nathan in the face. The injury wasn't life-threatening, but painful and embarrassing to all concerned."

Belora, Summer Home of Nathan Straus, Williams & Johnson, Architects

"How about the Abrahams who lived in the other Twin Cottage?"

"That place was called 'Olympia.' The Abrahams weren't so visible on the River as the Straus family, nor as prominent in the City. Nathan's brother, Oscar, was a cabinet member in Washington and was also well known nationally. We saw him on the river often."

"Are any of the families still here?"

"No. The Abraham house was demolished recently. Having two identical houses side by side did seem rather redundant, and Abrahams' Olympia was situated very close to Belora, which was plenty large itself. When his friend Abraham died, Nathan Straus didn't have the heart to continue coming. But other famous people have summered on the foot of Cherry Island. One was Fay Templeton, a Broadway star who was a contemporary of May Irwin. John D. Archibold was guest of Royal Vilas when he rented the place. Another national celebrity who summered regularly there was Arthur Brisbane, the syndicated New York columnist. His 'Today' column reached thirty million readers every day. The Brisbanes cut quite a figure—they were on the 'best dressed' lists of the time and were very elegant.

104

Belora Dining Room  The late Harry Marley awaits luncheon guests.

"It's curious that the foot of Cherry Island once again is identified with Jewish families, even though they may not have had any real connection to earlier residents. Straus sold Belora to James Dawes, said to be an 'oil magnate' of Philadelphia, but the property was vacant during the late Depression and war years. Abe Cooper of Syracuse came to the Bay to salvage metal for war effort — Boldt Castle's radiators and plumbing were scrapped at this time. The Thousand Islands House was then being demolished and Cooper was collecting its materials when he learned that the big houses at the foot of Cherry Island might also be acquired, likewise to be demolished for salvage. Cooper went over to inspect the places and was astonished to find that Belora was completely furnished, even to the china, silver, and linens. He bought the property but fortunately for history he did not demolish Belora. Instead he kept it as a family summer home. The Abraham house next door was removed, to be replaced by a swimming pool, but Belora, like nearby Casa Blanca on Cherry Island, is a veritable museum. The Coopers added modern electric table lamps but otherwise the interiors are as they were when the twentieth century opened.

"Were there other prominent Jewish families here at the time?"

"Yes—Julius Breitenbach was quite a character. He was generous, giving Alexandria Bay its first fire boat, sponsoring the local hockey team, supporting the Boy Scouts—but he was eccentric and occasionally cantankerous. He had an island deer park and an aviary full of tropical birds (like Boldt)."

"Where did he live?"

"Oh, several places, as I recall. He was at The Ledges for a while, until the Hammonds bought it. Sigmund Stern, a diamond broker, built the fine house called "Deva Loka" at Brown Bay Point on Wellesley Island. Sam Brown of Cleveland bought Sunnyside Island and renamed it 'Hadassah.' That was the name of a women's Zionist organization. Nathan Straus was a big financial contributor to that group."

The cottage of Cleveland steel-maker Samuel E. Brown on Hadassah Island was designed by famed New York City architect H. J. Hardenbergh, who designed Boldt's Waldorf-Astoria and the Plaza hotels, among many urban landmarks. The island, in the Summerland Group, also has been called "Sunnyside"

"Was there much anti-Semitism here?"

"Oh, we were aware of who was Jewish and who wasn't—and who came to the Thousand Islands Yacht Club and who didn't, but beyond that I certainly didn't worry much about it. There was a boy's camp on Grindstone Island, called "Camp Frontenac" It attracted many Jewish youngsters, but I don't think it was exclusively Jewish, just as I don't recall the big hotels discriminating. Money was what talked here.

"There was another yacht club at Alexandria Bay that the Jewish families favored, but it was not exclusively Jewish.  Col. Staples, proprietor of the Thousand Islands House, had a fine boat and was active in that club—may have even formed it in part to serve his regular guests, who didn't belong to the T.I. Yacht Club.  I mentioned that the Jewish families gravitated to the large hotels.

"There were other yacht clubs here at the time.  The major competitor to the T.I Yacht Club was another group down at Chippewa Bay.  Although they didn't have such a grand clubhouse, they were serious about racing and competed in the International Gold Cup Races, which they hosted one summer, after winning the trophy the previous season.

"There were even more yacht clubs  at the time, one at Clayton and another at Thousand Island Park, for instance.  This was such a clubby place."

\* \* \*

"The Fifth Avenue of the St. Lawrence," they called the American channel between Alexandria Bay and Clayton.  The Thousand Islands in their heyday, as the twentieth century opened, were predominantly a New York City resort—or certainly most of the wealthy families who built large summer homes, as well as most of the clientele of the grand hotels, came from the metropolitan New York area.  Excellent rail service made this possible.

"You'd be amazed," Julie recalled, "to see all the New York City newspapers on the stands here.  The dailies arrived by train about four in the afternoon.  The *Tribune* was the most popular, I think.  The sidewheel steamboat *St. Lawrence* would carry the several  New York newspapers to all the resorts down the river.  People would be waiting on the dock to get them."

In the fast lane of their day, the New Yorkers were "always out for a good time," according to a contemporary Syracuse newspaper.  There were so many of them on the river that the *New York Times* had a special correspondent here, as did other papers.

Second in social importance to  New Yorkers was probably the contingent from Chicago, followed by the group from Pittsburgh.  Nearer cities of Upstate New  York such as Syracuse, Rochester, and Watertown were well represented, as proximity might suggest, but more typically by middle-class cottagers.  The makeup of the resort community was far different then than now, when a much larger proportion finds access to the river convenient by automobile.  In contrast, New  York City is now very remote, without service by overnight trains.  Many people in "The City" today have never even heard of the Thousand Islands.

The Thousand Islands were a more important national resort a century ago than now—but of course they have always been international, since more than half of them are in Canada. But there have been fewer wealthy Canadian families for the same reason that fewer came from Upstate cities. New York, Chicago, Pittsburgh—that's where the great fortunes were concentrated when the twentieth century began.

Why was there so little representation of Boston? Much of the reason was the proximity to that city of Atlantic shore resorts as well as New England mountain resorts. Part of the reason may be affinity of the Boston elite to New England, which to the New Rich of other American cities may have seemed less congenial. Furthermore rail connections between Boston and northern New York did not facilite access so readily as from Manhattan.

* * *

The Chicgo contingent was led by the Pullmans, who were among the most prominent citizens of that city and certainly of this resort. Several other families originally from Chicago have been coming to the Islands for generations: the Clarks of Comfort Island and the McNallys of Wellesley Island, as well as kin such as the Vilas family.

"Jack Vilas was one of our early aviators," Julie remembered. "He caused a sensation on the river when he raced his airplane against a fast boat. Jack won easily, of course. That was at the time of the First World War. Automobiles had been the sensation a few decades earlier. Times were changing fast. Thousand Islands Yacht Club members formed the Aero Club, buying specially designed planes. They landed on the Boldts' golf course, or on a field outside of Alexandria Bay.

"Where did Vilas live?"

"The family had a big house at Oswegatchie Point, near Isle Royal, the McNally's place on Wellesley Island, across from Pt. Vivian . That's where Andy McNally keeps the big Boldt houseboat, you know. The Vilas' daughter became Mrs. McNally."

"That's the Rand-McNally map company family from Chicago?"

"Yes. The Vilas business was making special brakes for railroad cars. Their grand summer home is gone. Only a stone pump house remains on Wellesley Island."

Alexandria Bay

The Thousand Islands House dominated the village, but the Crossmon House, beyond the picture to the right, rivaled it in size and elegance. The smaller hotel in front of Boldt Castle was the Marsden House. All of these hotels, plus many of the other buildings seen here, have vanished.

Talking about vanished houses like Oswagatchie Point, in addition to the countless remaining places seen on the boat tours, began to impress on me how elusive was the past reality of the place. "How many of these big summer homes were there at one time?" I asked. "I'm having trouble keeping them all straight."

" I couldn't begin to guess," Julie replied, "without sitting down with a map to try to count all the places. Just in the Manhattan Group and what they now call 'Millionaires' Row' there were dozens, certainly. On a single island like Round Island were several truly grand houses. It would be quite a task to compile a complete list."

In later years I worked on a compilation, discovering to my astonishment that about 150 prominent New York City families were regular Islanders — and they merely represented that one city. Fifty of those families were listed in the *Social Register*, but the number did not include many of the most distinguished Islanders, such as Nathan Straus or George Boldt. Wealth was not the criterion for that distinction, but rather "family." Jews and immigrants apparently didn't have "family." At the beginning of the twentieth century, island residents came from sixteen states and two provinces. Although Islanders were predominantly Manhattanites, New York City itself was a polyglot cultural mixing pot at the time, so the Thousand Islands became quite a cosmopolitan place.

Disembarking from the Cornwall Dock, Alexandria Bay

Julie stressed how mixed the islanders were at the time, but she had said there were no Jewish families at the Thousand Islands Yacht Club. I wondered about this. "Weren't they accepted as member?"

"But that wasn't even a question," she responded. "At least I never heard of any Jews applying for membership."

"Did they know they would be refused?"

"How could they know, if they never asked? You see, one of the primary functions of the Yacht Club was finding suitable mates for offspring—daughters especially. If you were Jewish, and wanted your children to meet and mate with other Jewish young people, you wouldn't send them to a place where they might be attracted to others, would you? The Jewish families just naturally associated mostly with one another. The rest of us knew them very casually—sort of nodding acquaintances. The adults might be closer. I think George Boldt knew Nathan Straus quite well, for instance. But the children weren't supposed to become too close, you see.

"Naturally there were smaller circles of friends, usually neighbors. This is a big region, remember. Probably few residents of Chippewa Bay knew Islanders at the head of Grindstone either. In both areas some prominent families resided in relative isolation, which was what they wanted. Julie remembered one exception—Mrs. Post of Scow Island

"She hated being out on that rock", Julie recalled. "I suppose she would have preferred being in the thick of things, near the yacht club—if she *had* to be here at all. She really would have relished Newport far more than a remote island in Chippewa Bay. The Bradleys migrated to Newport after their house burned, you recall. But we had one Islander family, the Lorillard Spencers, who divided their time between Newport, Chippewa Bay, and Lucerne, Switzerland, while the Bostwicks of Bella Vista Lodge came to the river from Newport.

"I liked young Fanny Post. We played tennis on her courts at Scow Island. But her mother—well, she was no fun. So pretentious. She came from Ogdensburg, but you'd think she was a duchess, with her regal airs. They had a fast yacht, the *Karma*, and William Post built a great house for his wife, but still she was unhappy at Chippewa Bay. She shouldn't have been lonely, since there were many Ogdensburg people there—that nearby city was very affluent at the time. The Ogdensburg architectural firm of Williams and Johnson designed the Posts' place and another beautiful house not far way, on Rob Roy Island. They look something alike. That firm also designed the Twin Cottages on Cherry Island, and probably they were responsible for many other fine buildings here."

"Did you go aboard some of the big yachts like the Posts'?"

"Theirs wasn't among the largest, only half as long as the monster yachts, but was very fast for its size. I think it would go twenty-one miles per hour, which was speedy for a boat sixty-five feet long. They wanted speed because Scow Island was about ten miles from the Thousand Islands Yacht Club. They could do the run in about a half hour. Fanny carried us over there to play tennis many a day."

"How many big summer homes were there in that area, so far from the Bay?"

"Well, we here in Clayton may think of it as far away, since it's in the opposite direction from the Bay, meaning that Chippewa Bay is about twenty miles from here. But Scow Island was no father from the Bay than Round Island. We're about ten miles distant, you know. But how many summer homes were down there? Probably at least ten or more outstanding places, like Wyanoke Island, the grand establishment of the Orcutts. We had tennis tournaments there. But of course the real celebrity of Chippewa Bay didn't live in a mansion, but in a small cottage on Ingleneuk Island."

Frederic Remington at his studio, Ingleneuk Island, Chippewa Bay

"Who was that?"

"Frederic Remington, the famous artist. You've probably seen his paintings of the American West—or those bronzes of cowboys on bucking broncos. Remington had a studio there, but I never met him. He was always so busy with his work when he wasn't out on the river. Eve Remington sometimes brought their guests to the club. He was a great outdoors enthusiast—really the antithesis of his neighbor, the white-gloved Mrs. Post."

When not painting, Frederic Remington preferred Teddy Roosevelt's "strenuous life" of the outdoorsman to socializing. The exercise never helped his figure, however.

I wondered if a painter could be rich enough to have an island among the millionaires. "Rich?" Julie laughed. "Rich is just what people are if they have more money than you. That's what everyone is today, to me."

* * *

Chippewa Bay otherwise might have remained little known except to residents (who liked it that way), but suddenly the place became internationally prominent. The little Chippewa Bay Yacht Club, which held meetings in the playroom above a member's boathouse, won the Gold Cup Race of the American Power Boat Association, held on the Hudson River. It would have been less surprising had the Thousand Islands Yacht Club entered a world-class speedboat. It was astonishing that the Chippewa Bay club not only entered the 1904 race, but won. Without a proper clubhouse, the little Chippewa Bay Yacht Club became host for the races the following year on the St. Lawrence, and for three more years after that, since their boats kept winning the Gold Cup. The leading edge of Chippewa Bay may be explained by the business of some summer residents there: national shipbuilding enterprises.

The Gold Cup Races stayed on the St. Lawrence for the next five years, when the trophy was won four times by Thousand Islands Yacht Club and once by Frontenac Yacht Club. Appendix D summarizes nine years of Gold Cup racing at the Thousand Islands.

Design of boats and engines changed rapidly during those few years; the Gold Cup Races showcased the most innovative developments. The racing craft were costly and not designed for general recreational use, so syndicates of yacht club men often provided financing. Although entered in competition in the name of the club, they were privately owned. Frederick Burnham, an insurance executive who rented Boldt's Chalet, was a principle backer one of the famous *Dixie* racers. He personally offered $50,000 (more like $800,000 today) for any boat that would attain the speed of fifty miles per hour.

The Peacocks' *Dusquesne II*

In addition to the celebrities, I asked Julie if some families didn't stand out among so many at the resort because of their involvement in local affairs.

"Well, of course there were the Boldts. They certainly were in the forefront, since Boldt made the Thousand Islands Yacht Club almost an annex to the Waldorf-Astoria, provisioning major events and even sending up floral décor from the City. He also offered all the recreational facilities nearby on Wellesley Island, including the Golf House. Clover continued to be a real leader socially, but more in terms of athletic and informal events—not so much balls and other dressy occasions. There were some families that were far more sociable than others, like the Hagans of Ina Isle. They had that huge ballroom over their boathouse, which was popular for dancing. Then there were the Wheelers of Wau Winet—they had that lovely big sunroom or glassed-in porch. And the Johnstons of Whippoorwill Island—they call that Wintergreen nowadays.

"Naturally, I was mostly aware of people my age, and therefore of certain families like the Raffertys. They had a slew of children (they were Irish, of course) including some dashing boys with those Irish good looks. Their dad—that was Gilbert Rafferty, 'the Coke King' from Pittsburgh—built a lot of fast boats for them and they really cut a swath on the river. Rafferty sold his big coke operation—the coal product is used to make steel, you know—to US Steel when that huge corporation was being put together. Like Emery, Rafferty had a sudden cash windfall, as did his neighbor, Alex Peacock, who had a stake in Carnegie's company.

"Gilbert Rafferty became Commodore of the Thousand Islands Yacht Club somehow, but he was such a difficult person they ousted him. He was quarrelsome, suing Alex Peacock over some trivial property dispute involving their yacht houses. Like Boldt, their yachts were too big to be housed on their own islands, so the three of them had giant buildings on Wellesley Island."

"Where did the Raffertys live?"

"Isle Imperial, just above the Boldts—or rather next above the little island that tour guides like to call Boldt's 'Mother-In-Law's.'"

"Oh, I've been to Imperial. The big stone house is abandoned, still with stuff in it. I took a picture of the dining room. Sad."

"Yes, and to think they were so much fun—when the dad wasn't in a belligerent mood, that is. He also sued Alexandria Bay because he didn't like the village sewage being dumped into the river."

"Can't blame him for that."

"He was ahead of his time, maybe, but the village had been doing it forever. Rafferty bought Bonnie Castle when he should have realized it was just below the town. Bonnie Castle was the mainland summer home of J.G. Holland, a famous author and publisher, even before my time."

"Rafferty had two places then?"

"Yes, I suppose he followed Boldt's lead, renting extra homes. He got $3,000 a season from Bonnie Castle, which we thought was a lot of money back in those days—I still think it's a lot. The original house there was quite different—more the style of the charming gazebo that remains—before they turned the mansion into a Georgian sort of house.

"The Raffertys were very sociable, throwing huge parties. We girls adored the Rafferty boys. Charles was captain of the Yale football team, and he always brought a bunch of Yalies to the river. I remember some the Yale crew also. And the boys were in the Aero Club here. They were 'fast,' you might say." Julie winked. "One of their boats, the *Stroller* was among the fastest on the river. The Raffertys had tennis courts, where we often played. Like the Boldts, they also had a houseboat, in addition to the yacht. Such good times. Such attractive boys!

"But attractions can be fatal. I told you about the local girl in Alexandria Bay who fell for one of the Rafferty boys, and he fell for her. She was the lovely daughter of McIntyre, the photographer whose work was well known here. Mrs. Rafferty didn't think the young lady was 'suitable.' I think I mentioned that unsavory episode. It was bizarre. It appeared in the papers that John Hayden, whose family was perhaps the richest on the river—they were over on Fairyland—was arrested in 1902 for kidnapping the young woman. How unreal life was in this strata of the very rich! John (who was known as J. Harold Hayden) married Elsie Vilas of Oswagatchie Point. She was a noted tennis player and he a star boat racer—won one of the Gold Cup Races with his *Mitt II*.

* * *

"As you might expect of a large Irish family, the Raffertys    were Catholic. I r emember going to a daughter's confirmation at St. Cyril's in the Bay—a church they helped build. It was interesting that here, unlike many elite communities, the Episcopal Church wasn't preeminent. Oddly, the big stone Dutch Reformed Church was established early in Alexandria Bay, not because there were many Dutch up here, but because one of the cronies in the early fishing fraternity was a minister of that denomination. He left his flock down on the Hudson River for a summer sojourn at Charles Crossmon's little inn at Alexandria Bay. Rev. George Bethune became chaplain for the group of regulars—mostly politicians—and he and passed the hat to build a church. As I mentioned, we had a number of prominent Jewish families, and we also had different colonies of church-oriented folks—the Methodists at Thousand Island Park, the Baptists at Round Island, and Presbyterians at Westminster Park. They had a fine church there, on 'Mt. Beulah,' as they called it, which was quite a landmark while it lasted. A charming Episcopal church in the Bay served some island as well as mainland families. The Boldts had been 'born again fashionable,' becoming Episcopalians. Many prominent families were generous to local churches but weren't to be seen regularly by Sunday congregations. They had house parties to entertain, of course."

Steamboat Leaving Alexandria Bay

The view from the Crossmon House shows the Thousand
Island House in the distance, behind Cornwall's stone store.

I remember Sunday mornings on the River, hearing the tolling of distant church
bells across the water. We attended St. Mary's Catholic Church in Clayton,
where we would listen to a litany of French-Canadian names in announcements
of current committees and projects. I felt quite at home, given my own French-
Canadian name.

There is a delightful chapel on Grenell Island, serving that community, and
another historic church of the period at Dinsmore Bay, on Wellesley Island,
serving some of the families down that way. Today some seventy weddings take
place every summer on Heart Island because of its romantic associations rather
than any religious reason. Of course larger mainland communities have many
churches of various denominations.

* * *

The contrast of the sacred and the profane was striking at the Thousand Islands.
The Methodists at Thousand Island Park were so strict in enforcing proper behavior—no dancing, let alone drinking—that police prohibited any boat arriving
or departing from the community on Sunday. The policy contributed to the
prosperity of neighboring Fine View, where boats could work on the Sab-
bath—and to a tavern there, which had no compunctions on serving thirsty gents

from T.I. Park. Alternately, they might row the short distance over to the Hub House, a hotel that totally covered a small island just above T.I. Park.

"Thousand Island Park wasn't one of my favored venues," Julie commented. "As you can imagine, we livewires thought it rather dull. We pitied the young folks there. But they did have marvelous performances at the Tabernacle —really a huge, open-air shed. We went to hear the music and sometimes the famous soloists. You could take one of the big steamboats over, and dine and have your drinks on board, if you required fortification for the temperance ordeal.

"From the steamboat landing at T.I. Park you could look over and see the huge hotel rising above the trees on Round Island. What a contrast between those places! I felt sorry for the young people trapped at the Park, imagining them looking longingly over at the grand Frontenac, wonder what the high life was like. It was more my style, to be sure."

"You spent a lot of time there?"

"As much as possible."

Frontenac Pier

"It was such a thrill, to disembark on that long pier lined with alluring yachts, all those masts bristling and uniformed crews standing by. And then to stroll with all the gorgeously-dressed people up the broad walk towards the towering hotel with its imposing portico. One wondered who all the people were on the verandah, supposing that they were the rich and famous of the day. This was where you went to see and be seen—far more than the Yacht Club, where we always recognized the same familiar faces. At the Frontenac you'd see the visitors, many of whom came on the big luxury steamboats that regularly sailed up and down the St. Lawrence, connecting major cities of Canada and other Great Lakes ports.

"The Frontenac Hotel was so much more cosmopolitan, more worldly, than the other resort establishments—although the grand hotels at the Bay had a regular clientele, mostly of New Yorkers, and many folks were loyal to the smaller inns of Clayton, which attracted serious fishermen—and women. Mrs. Mann and Mrs. Skinner were Clayton's champion fisherwomen. Some families that really loved the river, like the Raffertys, would spend the shoulder seasons at the hotels, before and after their island establishments were open. Even after the Club was closed for the season, we'd find friends at the hotels."

"But you said," I recalled, "that some parents didn't want youngsters hanging around the big hotels."

"I was lucky." Julie laughed. "My father trusted our judgment, allowing 'those Bingham Sisters' to have free reign on the river. And we never got into any serious trouble. Even life in the 'fast set' was pretty tame, by today's standards."

Julie spoke only of her father, so I supposed that something had happened that she didn't care to recall about her mother. "As I probably told you, my father was so busy with his medical practice that he couldn't chaperone us himself, so we pretty much had to rely on our common sense.

"I should have had more sense about money, however. We never had to be concerned about where it came from, so I supposed it always would be coming. Then it stopped. And here I am."

Julie was not one to feel sorry for herself; she would laugh and shake her white curls. "But I'm still here, so that's something. So many others are gone. The place has gone, too—at least this place that I knew when I was young."

Peacocks and friends aboard the *Irene* at Belle Isle

Peacock Luncheon at Belle Isle

What other families stood out in the Island community, I wondered. "The Pea-cocks, of course," Julie shot back. "They had the island next to the Raffertys. No doubt about it, those families were in the very center of things — geographically as well as socially. Belle Isle was directly across from the grand hotels at the Bay, and the big white house, with its tall columns, was a central landmark. Boldt built it, you know. His family used it one summer or so while the castle was rising, then he rented it, as he did the Chalet, to prominent New York people who became acquainted with him at the Waldorf. The Peacocks' name facilitated many jokes, but they were no more ostentatious than most families of means.

"Alex Peacock was another Islander who became suddenly very rich through the formation of the huge trusts, giant companies like U.S. Steel, called 'the first billion-dollar corporation.' Alex was Carnegie's chief marketing man. He and other sold their interests to J.P. Morgan for fantastic sums when he put together the steel combine. Alex enjoyed his money, like a boy with a new toy — many new toys, to be sure. Since another Pittsburgh millionaire had two gilded grand pianos in his mansion, Peacock ordered four. No one in the family played the instrument.

"Alex became a regular at Boldt's Waldorf-Astoria while building one of the great show houses of Pittsburgh. After renting Boldt's Belle Isle for a couple of years, he bought it. He also acquired Charles Emery's beautiful yacht, the *Nina*, which he renamed the *Irene*. That was his daughter's name. Emery replaced that boat with an even larger yacht, the *Calumet*. Not everyone cared for Alex Peacock. Jean Hammond remembers him as insolent. Well, a lot of the New Rich were overbearing. Alex and his neighbor Gilbert Rafferty were a match for each other. I mentioned that silly lawsuit that dragged on in the courts for ten years, over a bit of property.

"Mrs. Peacock loved to serve afternoon tea to guests while cruising among the islands — and we loved the ritual as well. Irene, Jean, Clarence, Rolland and Grant Peacock were in my age group. Grant was a champion golfer. I remember him breaking the club record, doing eighteen holes in seventy — and the Boldt course was considered the longest in America at the time. Irene was also a far better golfer than I. She won a ladies' tournament when only thirteen years old.

Peacock boys in one of their sixteen fast boats

"The Peacocks vied with the neighboring Raffertys by acquiring fast boats. They had sixteen — yes, sixteen — of them. I remember their *Pirate* as a trophy winner. But they had so many! Alex offered a handsome sum, $100,000 (twice as much as Frederick Burnham) to anyone building a boat to go fifty miles per hour. The Peacocks also had that marvelous yacht house over on Wellesley Island. It was like a cathedral inside, with soaring arches tall enough to allow the big yacht to enter with her masts standing. Incredible!

A Regal Entry

The *Irene* at the Peacock Yacht House

"Like the Raffertys on the next island, the Peacock boys were livewires—into everything. They brought college chums with them to the river—but from Princeton rather than Yale. Princeton had a champion baseball team at the time, so the rival collegians challenged the Princetonians to a game at Frontenac—but the Yalies were no match for the nationally renowned visitors. Clarence Peacock was captain of the Alexandria Bay baseball team. Those boys were so athletic, so . . . dashing!

The Peacocks in their electric boat

"The young Peacocks and Raffertys were really the core of the younger set—if not the leaders such as Clover Boldt or Marjorie Bourne. There were so many events to fill our summers. I mentioned the balls and cotillions. We also put on shows. The fellows liked minstrel routines. I wish I had pictures of them in blackface! We even made a film once, in 1911—'The Island Comedy,' we called it. Six reels of film—I wonder whatever happened to them. They'd be priceless today."

"What else did you do?"

"Well, some of the families were very horsy. We rode, mostly on Wellesley Island where the Boldts had fine stables and miles of horse paths. Automobiles were quite a novelty when they came in, and there were miles of roads over there as well—a few paved. I wasn't an enthusiast. The first automobiles were always breaking down, leaving us stranded out in the country somewhere. Even if they just stalled (which they did regularly) someone had to get out and crank to get the machine going. The fellows thought it challenging, but not me. We had to wear veils and goggles—or thought we did—because the early models were wide open and the roads dusty in the summer.

"Then there were those rickety, early airplanes—I mentioned the Aero Club. And of course there were always the old-fashioned picnics, walks, and romantic canoe rides to secluded coves. We even went berry picking, if you can imagine Gilded Youths doing such a thing. Many wealthy families had farms at the time—but not such large operations as Boldt's. The Peacocks had a smaller farm on Wellesley Island—mostly for growing fresh produce for the table.

"Like Boldt, who took his estate superintendent to court, Peacock learned that he couldn't trust those to whom he delegated responsibility. An apparently virtuous aid stole $150,000 (a far larger sum then than now). Alex commented bitterly, 'I'm tired of these psalm singers 'round the office. You don't expect them to rob you, but they do. I think I'll hire real burglars after what I've lived through.'

"Alex Peacock had been an immigrant clerk. His wife was considered an 'obscure woman' without what we used to call 'good breeding,' while her husband 'never did get polish,' as they said. The Peacocks, like the Raffertys next door, really characterized the New Rich. But they surely did enjoy life and spent their money with gay abandon. But if not suave, the Peacocks were decent. Alex Peacock, when he suddenly came into his huge fortune, looked up all his old friends and paid off all their debts. The Peacocks were good people.

Peacocks and Friends Aboard the *Irene*

Julie hadn't mentioned fishing among the favored activities of the younger set. "Fishing? Well, it goes without saying that people fish here. That was a more sedate occupation of more mature folks, I suppose. Youngsters don't have much patience for sitting in a boat, holding a pole and waiting for something to happen—which rarely does. Some of the older men were very serious anglers, and a few women as well. The Anglers' Association was one of the major all-river organizations. All the prominent Islanders supported its conservation mission, which required lobbying the state to control commercial fishing and to re-stock the waters. Netting of fish was a big issue, especially up Cape Vincent way.

"The Anglers' Association was really a men's club, with hundreds of members—more than four hundred at one time. It was well known, said to have 'almost a national reputation.' Boldt, Pullman, Emery and most other prominent islanders belonged. The men enjoyed steamboat excursions accompanied by a band to elaborately catered picnics at Mary Island or some other destination. The high point of the evening would be a big bonfire when the confiscated nets were soaked in kerosene and burned. The clubmen raised funds for restocking black bass ingerlings as well as for legal actions and a patrol boat. Arresting local men was not popular with everyone, as you may imagine. Commercial fishing was the livelihood of some breadwinners here.

"The real star of the fishing world here was Seth Green from Rochester, who summered on Manhattan Island in one of the earliest island cottages. Seth was our great fish expert, a scientific pisciculturalist, the State Commissioner of Fisheries, and widely known as a proficient fisherman. He held the record distance for fly-casting—eighty-four feet. He was a proponent of fly-casting for bass.

"Probably the most lasting effect of the St. Lawrence River Angler's Association are our parks. The association selected sites from Cedar to Kring Points, prevailing upon to New York State to acquire them for public use. The association was involved as well in creating the Canadian National Park system here. The organization also selected many of these islands, originally proposing them together with New York State sites for a single International Park.

"Shore dinners were the reward for hours of inactivity on the river. They were not mere picnics, but full dinners cooked on wild islands by our guides. The menu was simple—fish, of course (we could rely on that, much as I deride the inactivity)—but the ritual was a refreshing contrast to the white linens of the grand hotels or the lavish silver services of the great houses.

"Her First Muskallonge"

Frederic Remington depicted Thousand Islands subjects in many paintings and drawings, occasionally appearing as magazine illustrations.

"It seemed that visitors did more fishing than residents, maybe because the novelty wore off for those who were here regularly. Many people came just to fish,
however. It was quite a sight, if you rose early enough, to see the chains of skiffs
being towed out from Clayton and the Bay. A steam yacht or motorboat would

haul many of them linked end-to-end, like a great necklace, to the fishing grounds, where they would disperse. Fishing parties would return to the yacht for lunch and liquid refreshments, if they didn't dine on some island.

"While more young people were thrilled by fast motorboats than by sailing, there were groups devoted to working the wind. Sailing is quieter, to be sure—I never cared for the noise of those powerful engines—but sailing is akin to fishing, in that it requires patience to work with nature. Particularly arcane is the art of sailing skiffs without a rudder and only a small centerboard, while carrying a huge amount of canvas. That wasn't for me. Too scary, and too wet. But it still has its devotees who have mastered the art. They do that over at the head of Grindstone, you know.

"They even sailed canoes here. The American Canoe Association held international meets on the river. They were big events, attracting a thousand or more campers. They moved their tent city from place to place in different years, as they alternated US and Canadian sites. Eventually the ACA acquired property over on Sugar Island. Some island families first discovered the region when attending one of these gatherings.

"The encampments were jolly events, with lots of high jinks. They welcomed us visitors to their big bonfires at night and staged minstrel shows as well as a famous 'burlesque circus' and impromptu parades in crazy costumes at all hours of the day or night. How different from the high-toned Gold Cup Races! The canoe folks pitched tents, whereas the Gold Cup set demanded the luxury of grand hotels and country house parties."

* * *

I wondered about class distinctions here, back at the beginning of the twentieth century. "Well, it's fair to say," Julie observed, "that few poor people vacationed here—except the servants brought by wealthy families. It took time and money to get here, let alone to stay here. But there were many excursions of less affluent people who came by rail from nearby cities. They would disembark from a train at Clayton and board one of the big steamboats, spending much of the day on the river, returning to the train in the late afternoon. Excursions were organized by fraternal groups and the like, the whole organization's membership coming together, often accompanied by a band. Singing was popular, as was drinking, you can be sure. At least no one had to drive.

"People who owned summer homes obviously had to be able to afford them and also needed time away from work to use them. It's surprising that so many

cottage communities sprang up towards the end of the nineteenth century, because they generally were made up of middle-class folks — shopkeepers' and professional men's families, typically. It was a sign of the growing prosperity of
America that my father's generation could afford second homes."

"Was there a distinct division between the upper and lower classes here?'

"Hardly. Emma Hagan, for instance, had been a laundress but became a
fixture at the Thousand Islands Yacht Club. There were a lot of diamonds-in-the-
rough here. You couldn't tell much by how a person spoke or even behaved.
You could tell something by the size of their yacht, however. That's the way it
was.

Beatrice Morgan Pruyn Thibault ("Sis")"

"The Thousand Islands were very different from the Adirondacks, which are not
far from us, up here in northern New York. Sis Morgan (that's "Beatrice," actually) married Frederick Pruyn, whose family had one of the Great Camps of the
Adirondacks. How different over there! People retreated into huge tracts of
wilderness, never to be seen by anyone. The Pruyns had twelve thousand acres
of forest surrounding their great log villa. They were five miles by private road
from a tiny hamlet, which was a day's drive from any real social life. There were
no yacht clubs, no golf courses, no dances.

"The Pruyns, you see, were not New Rich. They didn't care to be seen playing a social role, at least not during the summer. They had a huge place in town
where they were required to be sociable during the winter. In the woods they
preferred a self-sufficient country house where they entertained house parties.
Beyond their invited guests, they didn't care to participate in the larger social
community of a resort.

"Sis is such a real person—no put-on airs. She's like her mother, Emma, that way. Emma Leavitt Morgan was a great outdoorswoman. She and Virginia Murray Bacon (of Mid-River Farm) were dedicated fisherwomen, and Emma was quite a softball player. But Emma, who didn't aspire to be a socialite, entertained the Whitneys and Ethel Roosevelt, daughter of the President, at Papoose Island—and Emma once left two diamond pins, worth $10,000, under her mattress on the sleeping car coming up to the river once.

"Sis always remarks on what a change it is, to come from the Pruyn place in the Adirondacks back to her own family summer home on the River. Here we're so social, always coming and going to cocktails at different islands or setting off to dine in restaurants, or running over to play golf or tennis somewhere. That doesn't happen in the woods.

"At the Thousand Islands people built huge houses to be admired by passing tourists, adorned with splendid yachts as ornaments. But the Great Camps of the Adirondacks were deliberately hidden away in the wilderness. What's the difference? The Pruyns were Old Money, not New Rich. Virtually every builder of a Great Camp in the Adirondacks was of the second or third generation of wealth. Patricians, they were brought up with privilege, were educated differently, acquiring different tastes and culture.

"Sis loves her husband's family retreat in the woods, of course, and looks forward to return visits. But Sis was born a River Rat. I think she'll spend the rest of her life here."

* * *

"There were, of course, some social distinctions, even among wealthy Islanders," Julie recalled. The Bournes lived near Chippewa Bay—from where you can see Dark Island Castle rising a mile or so across the main channel—but the Bournes were more like the Pruyns, keeping to themselves rather than engaging in the the social life of the neighborhood. Mrs. Bourne, like Mrs. Pruyn, was of an old family, so had acquired more patrician customs. Of course the Commodore was in a totally different league in the business world than anyone in Chippewa Bay—or at the Thousand Islands, probably. Dark Island was only one of the Bourne's several country places. They didn't come here to be part of a community for an entire season. Similarly, Pink-Pills Fulford (even as Senator Fulford) probably was not in the same social strata as his neighbors, Sir Clifford and Lady Sifton. Senator Fulford might entertain cabinet members. Sir Clifford was one.

"On a less exalted social level, however, the Boldts and Emerys wanted to be engaged in the social life of the place. Both men were major boosters of the resort and avid joiners of community organizations.  They were more typical of Islanders than was Commodore Bourne or Sir Clifford Sifton.  Even so, the cas-tle-dwellers' extravagant way of life caused others to regard them with some awe, creating a certain distance.  This was certainly true of George Pullman as well, since he was a nationally prominent figure who entertained Presidents and celebrities, as was May Irwin, a national celebrity herself.  But clear distinctions blurred when it came to the hundreds of other wealthy families here.  In its own way, the Thousand Islands Yacht Club was democratic.  All it required was money — lots of it."

Thousand Island Yacht Club Verandah

Certainly one of the fundamental purposes of the Yacht Club was getting young people together. At the club parents might monitor daughters' social life, intro-ducing young ladies to appropriate suitors.  No question about it — that was pretty basic.  River romances abounded, which is natural when you put young people together at a certain age, giving them the leisure to become acquainted and little else to do but socialize.  Many Islanders are related though intermarriage over several generations. Of course, some marriages worked; others didn't. Despite concern of wealthy parents for fortune hunters, even scions of peers could turn out to be duds.

"Clover and Gus were as predictable as you might imagine," Julie observed. "If you were going to write a novel about a very rich family, you'd probably invent these characters and their relationship. After Louise died, George Boldt had pressed Clover into service as his hostess—and George Boldt entertained lavishly and constantly. Having grown up with this, Clover was socially adroit. But she'd rather be on the golf course. I think she became increasingly resentful of her obligations—or rather of her father's social duties which, in truth, were much related to his business.

"There was a period of mourning after Louise's death. This came at a time in Clover's life when she was just 'coming out,' being introduced to society and developing a life of her own. George Boldt could be very insistent, in his Prussian way. Clover's personal life was put on hold.

"Then along came Gus. He was a character—a local character, that is. He was not some fortune hunter at one of the grand hotels but was the son of Islander parents of means. They were at Lotus Land. His father ran the oldest ale brewery in New York City. 'Gus' was A. Graham Miles. He was one of our dashing young men, a sportsman—and Clover was a sportswoman. But Gus turned out to be a 'sport' in another sense of the word. He was your stereotypical playboy. Gus never finished college, where he played football and had a good time, but was not sufficiently self-disciplined to succeed.

"Gus was a barrel of fun, always ready to party, and probably was just what Clover needed at that moment. George Boldt must have been dismayed, but he put Clover's wishes ahead of his own. After they wed, there were several years of gaiety. Gus decided to go into polo, and to accommodate his son-in-law, Boldt acquired a costly stable of polo ponies, built a polo field, and entertained visiting polo teams. During winters he tried to put Gus to work in the City at one of the Boldt enterprises—to find that he was about as effectual as his own son, 'The Junior.' Clover had the brains—maybe more than the two young men together—and eventually she came to her senses and divorced Gus. It was a messy business, however, for he had become increasingly a problem, causing public disturbances. It was sad, because he had been such a likable fellow. But he was, as Grant Peacock said, 'a crazy loon'."

"Did they have children before the divorce?"

"Yes, Clover had only one child, Clover Boldt Morrisset. She's married to a physician. I don't know if she sees much of her father. He dropped out of sight, both here and in the City after the divorce. I hear he remarried and is up in Connecticut some place.

"George Boldt's daughter did much better on her second marriage, we all thought. She found 'Sunny Jim,' we called him, Nils Johaneson. But eventually that marriage didn't work either. I suppose wealthy wives, when they have more means than their husbands, experience particular difficulty in a marital relationship. I had my difficulties, to be sure—but it wasn't because I had too much money!"

Griffin and Gazebo, Melrose Lodge, Cherry Island

When I think of idyllic places I have known, not merely the Thousand Islands as a whole but several spots on the River come immediately to mind. One of these was Wau Winet Lodge. It had been the summer home of the Thomas Wheelers in "Millionaire's Row," above Alexandria Bay. Wheeler was an associate of John D. Rockefeller in Standard Oil. By the time I knew the house it no longer served as a private residence but had become a public restaurant. Wau Winet was not a very commercial operation, however. It was still more like a summer home. Because access was by boat, it was off the usual tourist circuit.

The island was long and narrow, so that the big house was built virtually out to the waters' edge on front and back. When inside, one had the sense of being in a boat. I remember that the drawing room had a ceiling entirely covered with gold leaf, dazzling as the sun reflected from the moving water up onto it through big plate glass windows in shimmering patterns.

This much gold leaf probably sounds pretentious, but in truth the house was fairly simple, as these places went—comfortable, but not grandiose. The biggest and best feature was a huge sort of sunroom at the lower end of the building—large enough for dances, which made the house suitable as a restaurant. There were wonderful outlooks to the water on three sides. We spent many a happy hour there—until Wau Winet suffered the fate of so many island building: it burned. The large boathouse subsequently has become a residence, but only the granite foundation walls and steps of Wau Winet Lodge remain as a reminder.

Nearby was Jewel Island, where there was another fine house, sufficiently grand to be said to "eclipse anything on the river" when built in 1883. It became even more so when rebuilt as a "delightful granite castle" five years later, at the same time that Pullman's Castle Rest was rising nearby. Most cottages had been built entirely of wood, but the villa on Stony Crest (later Jewel) Island, like Castle Rest, introduced massive masonry. H. H. Warner was said to have paid $50 for his island but $40,000 for his grand mansion (in dollars of the time). Warner's new villa was built at the same time as Pullman's Castle Rest (1888). Both houses featured novel electric lighting. Warner was said to have used a water wheel to generate electricity from the river current.

"Safe Cure" Warner, like "Pink-Pills" Fulford, was a patent medicine producer. Like Fulford—and like Emery—the Rochester millionaire's achievement was not so much providing a new product of real value as it was marketing. In the manner of Fulford, Warner sold his "Safe Cure" around the world, combining high volume production with mass marketing. His real genius was for advertising. In 1906 the Pure Food and Drug Act curtailed unregulated prosperity of patent medicines in the United States, but the severe depression that struck in 1893 had already ruined Warner. It was rumored that summer that he had fled to Europe to avoid his creditors. The island was in his wife's name, but his ninety-seven foot Herreshoff yacht, *Siesta*, reportedly built at a cost of $50,000 (more than the house), was bought at auction for $4000 by Capt. Davis of Alexandria Bay. After bankruptcy proceedings, Mrs. Warner sold the island and the family disappeared from the river. While he was here, however, H.H. War-

ner, a colorful character who wore large diamond studs as president of the Anglers' Association, was very active as a fishing enthusiast and conservationist,
volunteering his personal funds for restocking the fish population when it was
being depleted by commercial fishing.

Jewel Island was dynamited to widen the main channel for the St. Lawrence
Seaway.

A Herreshoff Yacht

The Peacocks replaced their *Irene* with the larger *Irene II* in 1910. They sold the *Irene*, originally Emery's
*Nina*, to the Burkes of Jewel Island. M. Crouse Klock of Bartlett's Point acquired the *Nina* in 1921.
The *Irene II* was was photographed at the Peacock Yacht House.

The name Herreshoff became to yachts what Rolls Royce has been to automobiles. The Herreshoffs of Bristol, Rhode Island began to dominate American
yachting in the 1880s. The first Herreshoff boat on the river was built in the late
seventies for the famous author, J. G. Holland of Bonnie-Castle. His *Camilla* was
a steam yacht, considered very fast for its time, doing fourteen miles per hour.
More than twenty Herreshoff yachts built prior to the end of World War I,
graced the river.

Many of the largest private vessels were not Herreshoff boats, however. The
colossal *Corona*, 172 feet long, weighing 304 tons, was built at Clyde, Scotland in

1905, designed by Alfred H. Brown. Because of her excessive length and twelve-foot draft she was not well adapted to cruising among the islands. The owner, Henry Laughlin, had to build a new pier at Alexandria Bay to accommodate the ship. That long public dock in upper bay used to be known as the Carona Dock. Although Pittsburgh's Laughlin, of Jones & Laughlin Steel, summered in a relatively modest cottage (Craigside, now the Coast Guard Station on Wellesley Island) his *Corona* was the nautical response to Boldt Castle—the trophy yacht vying with the trophy house. The *Corona* carried a crew of twenty-two men.

It's a stretch of the imagination today to envision the Thousand Islands at the beginning of the twentieth century, when there were fourteen or more splendid steam yachts longer than a hundred feet. They plied the "Fifth Avenue of the St. Lawrence," along with scores of boats more than fifty feet long. Capt. Visger recalled "thirty or forty steam yachts of millionaires."

"His and Hers" Yachts

Fulfords' *Dora* at left and the larger *Magadoma* at Fulford Place Dock

Author J. G. Holland is hardly remembered today. When he is mentioned, likely it is as friend and mentor to poetess Emily Dickenson—although even she may may known mostly by poetry readers. Few read Josiah Gilbert Holland's novels and long poems any more, except scholars of American literature. Holland is often recalled for his influence on the literary scene, however. He was a founder and editor of *Scribner's Monthly* magazine, which became the *Century*. In his editorial role Holland encouraged many American writers of his time such as Walt Whitman. In fact, Holland envisioned creating a writers' colony at Bonnie Castle, on the other side of the lower harbor below Alexandria Bay.

Dr. Holland stood out here, bringing urban style to the Bay, where he astonished folks by appearing in a white flannel suit. When he became an Islander, Holland was a far more important figure in America than he is remembered today. He was said to be "the most successful man of letters in the United States" and its "most popular lay moralist of the mid-nineteenth century." His books sold widely and his magazine also served as a pulpit. It was said that "he could think the thoughts and speak the speech of the common people." Holland's preaching instinct, however, together with changing notions of propriety, contributed to twentieth-century decline of his popularity.

Holland had an artist's "astonishingly good taste", of which his summer home, built in 1878, was considered evidence. He also had an artist's appreciation for the Thousand Islands, of which he became passionately fond. J. G. Holland was one of the great boosters of the resort, which he promoted through his journalistic connections in New York City. He appreciated the natural qualities of the Thousand Islands, advising readers that here "real play may be unrestricted by any of the conventionalities of society." He did not foresee the increasing social convention of High Life that would follow him at Alexandria Bay. He did not live to see Boldt Castle rise across from his frame house.

Holland was one of an earlier generation of Islanders. He bought his river property with proceeds from his novel, *Arthur Bonniecastle*. Its title accounts for the name of his summer place (originally hyphenated as "Bonnie-Castle"). The fine cottage was thought to be "one of the river's first five summer houses." Holland discovered one of the intangible costs of living in a showplace. "He would sometimes at Bonnie-Castle hide his face in his hands, with sort of terror, when he saw strangers approaching, but he would never refuse to see and show them about the place." He died in 1881, long before Julie could have known him, although his family remained on the river after his death. J. G. Holland was remembered by the Holland Memorial Library at Alexandria Bay and by a plaque in the Reformed Church, opposite that of his contemporary, also a key figure of the early resort, Rev. George Bethune. Few today visiting the large Bonnie Castle hotel and restaurant facility realize that it was the home of a famous public figure of the nineteenth century. Little there is left from Holland's time except Bonnie Castle's extraordinary gazebo, still charming amid the tall pines on the rocky point. His final thoughts and memorable last words were about this place: "It is to me the sweetest spot on earth."

Bonnie Castle Gazebo, 1878

"Holland was before my time," Julie said, "but I remember another author, Marietta Holley. You probably don't know about her, but she was a very funny lady. She wrote a whole series of popular books about her character, 'Samantha.' She was something of a feminist for her time, an outspoken, independent woman—always poking fun at her old-fashioned, conservative husband. One story was set here in the islands. Holley made some good cracks about Boldt's folly and other things. She liked to stay at Thousand Island Park, where she had friends. She was more the down-homey type.

"Will Carleton was another author who had a large following. He was a poet—and wildly popular, believe it or not. Back in the nineteenth century people read those long poems—really stories in verse. Holland wrote some of those book-length poems too. Carleton did some readings at the Tabernacle, but I recall him staying on Round Island." Julie went to a bookcase. "Let me see if I can put my hand on *Samantha*—here, let me read you a bit. She's describing her landing from a big steamboat at the Thousand Islands House in Alexandria Bay:

It was indeed a fair scene, to turn round when you wuz about half way up the flower strewn declivity and look afar off over the wharf with its gay crowd, over the boats gaily ridin' at anchor, and behold the fairy islands risin' from the blue waves crested with castles, and mansions and cottage ruffs, chimbleys and towers all set in the green of the surroundin' trees.

And when she came to Heart Island, she had this to say:

Heart Island . . . is almost covered with buildin's of different sizes and ruined castles (the ruins all new, you know; ruined a-purpose), the buildin's made of the gray stun the island is compose of. And there are gorgeous flower beds and lawns green as emerald, and windin' walks lined with statuary, and rare vases runnin' over with blossoms and foliage, and a long, cool harbor, fenced in with posies where white swans sail, archin' up their proud necks as if lookin' down on common ducks and geese. They wuz ancient stun architecture, and modern wood rustic work, and I sez to Josiah, "They believe in not slightin' any of the centuries; they've got some of most every kine of architecture from Queen Mary down to Taft."

"Heart Island wasn't always abandoned, you know. It's such a dreary place now." Julie sighed.

"Mysterious, I'd say—kind of exciting."

"Well, it *was* exciting in a livelier way, when the Boldts lived there. They were in the big frame house, before they took it down for the Castle. The Alster Tower was brand new, when I first came—and was the talk of the river, you may be sure. Those crazy Boldts!

"Clover was more my age—a teenager—and 'Cricket' (that was 'The Junior's' other nickname) was a bit older. He was starting college—Cornell. Sometimes he came with a few chums, 'Older Men,' to us pre-debs. They'd stay at the new Alster Tower. There are several floors of bedrooms, you know, stacked one atop another in the upper floors. Nearby, close to the shore, there was the 'Roman Plunge', as they called the swimming pool—hardly more than a big bathtub. It was ringed with a terra cotta balustrade, and the fellows would sit atop it, waving to the passing girls, giggling in their launches. The young men were in bathing suits, of course, with their 'limbs' (legs, that is) hanging over. As you can imagine, the place was irresistible to us."

"Did you go ashore to visit?"

Alster Tower, Heart Island, photographed c. 1900

"Oh, yes. I saw Clover mostly at the club, or more likely at the Golf House or tennis courts, which were public—sort of, if you belonged. We didn't get invited much to Heart Island because that's where her parents entertained prominent visitors. Since I didn't have parents here on the river, I was somewhat out of that adult set. Young people were supposed to be 'seen but not heard" in those days. Women in general were not supposed to speak up, especially young women. Of course with people our own age we girls spoke out and had plenty to say.

"And I will say that the boys were interested, so we did get included in the fun of the younger set—and I did get to visit the Alster Tower."

"What was it like?"

"Indescribable. Pure fantasy. You've seen it, haven't you?"

"Yes, but it's a ruin now. When I was there some other kids were pulling apart a stained glass window, to take home pieces as souvenirs."

"What a shame. It was so unique—no square rooms or hardly any straight lines, as I recall—and the spaces at different levels, with balconies looking down from one room into another."

"They were furnished then?"

"Of course, chock full of stuff. This is the era of the 'Oriental Nook,' with piles of cushions and lots of glass-beaded lanterns—that sort of thing. It was supposed to be sumptuously decadent. We in the nineties thought ourselves rather daring if we affected an exotic pose."

"What did you do in there?"

Julie laughed. "Such an indelicate question! But we really were so innocent, back in those days. For a young woman simply to be in that bizarre place without a chaperone was considered daring, and it could be dangerous to one's reputation. We girls were supposed to be attended by an older woman, to avert trouble. But in those days there were always servants about, so in truth there was little chance to get away with anything. But there was no butler down at the Alster Tower and one had to ring the main house for service, so we were fairly unsupervised.

"The miniature kitchen was one of the remarkable features of the playhouse—which is what it was. Normally we never even saw kitchens, since servants prepared and served all our meals in dining rooms that were remote from the mysterious source of the food. An elegant kitchenette was a novelty to us at the Alster Tower, where we were allowed to prepare our own snacks! None of us even knew how to make toast or coffee, but we had a lot of fun messing around there. Our disastrous experiments caused much merriment.

"The Alster Tower's little kitchen was very different from the institutional operations in big houses. Instead of being hidden away as a utilitarian function, the kitchen was a finished room, open to the others, with carved wood cabinets and decorative tile. People have a way of congregating in kitchens, you know, but this social custom was unknown in our set, so hanging around the stove and sink was quite a novelty for the young folks.

"I was introduced to bowling at the Alster Tower. The alleys there were probably the first on the river and must have been very early for any in the country. The game was new to all of us, so our clumsiness was riotously funny. I remember the noise of heavy balls dropped, pins falling, and laughter, echoing in that subterranean tunnel. I was impressed to learn that pin boys had their own stairway down to the far end of the alleys, magically appearing to reset the pins—the few pins that we actually managed to knock down.

"The bowling alley was not segregated as a separate facility but was wide open to the main space, up a half flight of steps. The steps went under a balcony that served as a performance stage, or for musicians when we danced. The big room was called the 'Shell Room' because the ceiling was like a seashell—sort of a scalloped dome.  Other smaller rooms—a library, billiard room — surrounded the main space on different levels, having balconies overlooking the Shell Room. As you can imagine, it was a great party place!"

* * *

"You mentioned going with Clover  on the Boldt's yacht for a hayride.  What was the boat like?"

"Well, as yachts went here, it was lovely, of course, but nothing exceptional. The Boldts bought it from the Haydens.  They're the family over at Fairyland, you know.  There were many larger boats on the river, but the *Louise* was elegant.  I remember most the sailors in their spotless whites."  She smiled.  "But the houseboat—that was something else!  *La Duchesse* was—still is—a floating mansion, complete with fireplaces in the main rooms.   Talk about luxury! Imagine a party aboard, with music on the huge dancing deck at the upper level, behind the main saloon.  The deck was roofed, with lights sparkling around the edges of the canopy, above long boxes of flowers.  The orchestra would play in a bay window that projected onto the deck, where there was a green piano painted with Chinese scenes, as I recall.  The musicians were highlighted by illuminated stained glass overhead—Tiffany, I believe.

"The craft might be moored on the Boldt Canal, next to Wellesley House, full of partying people, or the floating palace might be towed across the moonlit river by the Boldts' tug, the *Queen*.  Now *that* was living!"

* * *

"Oh, the Yacht Club was special, and the hotels were grand, the private ballrooms impressive, but really some of the most enjoyable events happened at less pretentious island communities.  Frank Taylor, the artist over on Round Island, was a marvelous organizer of social events there.  He was the island's unofficial master of ceremonies, officiating at a regular series of big bonfire parties on the island.  He promoted all sorts of amateur presentations and outdoor parlor games.  As usual, we sang popular songs of the day.  There was much more group singing back in those days, before we had radio and records.  Frank's neighbor was a New York City fireworks manufacturer, so these evenings wound up spectacularly.

*La Duchesse* at Wellesley House

The Tennis House appears at the right. A barge loaded with forms for canal concrete walls
is under the bridge. The canal banks in the distance have not yet been completed.

"Then there were the dances under the stars—so much more romantic than any
ballroom. They used to have them at Summerland. The way from the dock
would be lit by torch flares, leading to a dance platform illuminated by big kerosene lamps with reflectors. We danced from sunset to midnight, then cruised
home by moonlight. How entrancing it was!"

\* \* \*

I wondered where Julie and her sister stayed on the river, if they didn't have a
family summer home here. "Well, it was complicated," she recalled. "My father
could only come on occasions, and then we could properly stay at a hotel. From
Watertown to the River was quite a trip back then, before we had reliable automobiles and good highways. The roads were dreadful in the early part of the
century. Occasionally, once we were registered at a hotel, my father might slip
away and return to his practice briefly, but it wouldn't do for single ladies to be
living there alone. Gossips might suggest they were up to no good." She gave
me another of her knowing smiles. "George Boldt first admitted single women to
the Waldorf-Astoria about this time, but he and New York City were a step ahead
of the hinterlands.

"Friends took pity on us, so we worked the house-party circuit for all it was worth. I still do," she laughed. "There were the Taylors at St. Lawrence Park and Pine Tree Point—they were the Watertown people who helped to introduce us around, and gave us entrée to the Yacht Club. But we couldn't impose on them or any other family for an entire season, so it took some initiative to get ourselves invited to other summer homes. It helped that we were rather attractive, played golf and tennis well, and we did fit in smoothly with the young people at the Club and elsewhere. On the other hand there was always a shortage of young men here. You should have seen the crowds on the docks at the big hotels, all the girls anxiously watching arriving guests, hoping to see some boys. We young ladies had to shine, since a hostess didn't covet extra young ladies so much as college men. It took some doing. Did you ever read *The House of Mirth?*" She explained that the novel by Edith Wharton conveyed the world of lavish house parties and the plight of an ambitious young woman caught up in this strange life of the very rich.

"I'll tell you candidly that some people suspected that we were on the make—gold diggers, you know. We should have been so lucky!"

"Your first marriage was to a successful businessman, wasn't it?"

"Yes, but that wasn't a river romance. I was on stage in the City when we met, and he never cared to travel so far for weekends—by that time the railroad service to the river had been reduced—and he couldn't leave his business for the summer. So during that previous life as Mrs. McLean I spent many seasons away from the river.

" I did make some river connections in the city, however. There were so many Thousand Islands folks there during the winter, and they tended to see one another at social events. That's how I met Charles Hudson—what a charmer. He should have been an actor—but why? He did so much better on Wall Street. Charisma was his special gift, his magic ticket. Charlie was a high-school dropout, a messenger boy making a delivery to Jay Gould, when the multimillionaire financier took a shine to him. Out of the blue, Gould not merely gave the youngster a stock market tip, but actually gave the boy the stock—900 shares of Union Pacific. Young Charlie made a killing. Within twenty days he sold the stock making a profit of $19,000—which would be hundreds of thousands today. Quite a tip, eh? A 'tip' in both senses of the word. No longer a messenger boy, the windfall set him up as a stockbroker. With Jay Gould as a mentor, Charlie's charm won him a large following of wealthy clients.

Sportswear

"Winning personality and attractive appearance contributed to the success of many men here. Boldt is a good example, like Hudson—and Commodore Bourne. You know how Bourne got his start? The young man sang in a choir. His voice appealed to Edward Clark, millionaire president of the Singer Manufacturing Company. Clark took a shine to young Frederick and made him his personal secretary. When Clark died, Frederick became manager of the Clark estate and soon became president himself of the Singer company. If you've actually read any of the Horatio Alger novels (few people have) you'd recognize the formula. Young men didn't succeed so much by true grit as by the lucky break. They won the patronage of some angel."

"Hudson had a place here on the river?"

"Yes, The Ledges—a big barn of a house, one of those shingle-style places from the 1880s. It's gone now but was between Bonnie Castle and Pine Tree Point, the Taylors' place where we often visited. The Taylors were mutual friends who introduced me to the Hudson family in the City. Mrs. Taylor's father, who was Governor Flower of New York State, was also a big Wall Street operator, you know. I was as much on the margins of that New York scene as I was up here on the river—really more so in the City. We lived up in Connecticut, so I wasn't part of the social scene down there

"Charlie married well—as you would expect of a charmer. Sara Kierrstede gave him elite family connections and polish. Until she died recently she had one of the finest estates on Long Island, filled with European antiques, and she wintered at the Everglades Club in Palm Beach. There are four Hudson children, who are more my age. Of course I've lost touch with all those people now. Clayton in the winter is a long way from Palm Beach."

\* \* \*

Thousand Islands families often were linked in many ways—by common family and social ties, as well as by business interests in Manhattan and other places. There were at least seven prominent stockbrokers from New York City here, while many of those who were not professional brokers were heavily interested in the stock market. Much of the conversation on the Club train coming up to the river was devoted to common business interests.

"One of the most shocking news stories on the river," Julie recalled, "was the murder of James Oliphant. He was a New York stockbroker who was shot by a client who despaired about his losses in the 1907 panic. The Oliphants had the lovely house, Neh Mahbin, at the head of Comfort Island—and one of the prettiest boathouses. But there may be a jinx to the place. The Charles Lipes from Syracuse—he was heir to an industrial fortune—bought Neh Mahbin. The young couple was on their way to the Club when hit by a tour boat and killed."

Neh Mahbin, photograph c. 1900

This house, built in 1893 to replace a burned cottage, evidenced advanced taste. Across the main channel the cottage at Emerald Park (Louisiana Point) represents an earlier style.

Across from the sunny golf course where I had attempted to caddy, near a thriving marina and two roadside restaurants just east of Clayton, an inconspicuous road leads through a sort of scattered suburb of houses—all built since my youth, when these were open fields full of Queen Anne's Lace and, later in the season, goldenrod. Approaching the River, the cottages are more familiar—mostly unchanged after a half century. These are not the grand houses built a half-century earlier. They are "camps," as we called them. These one-and-a-half story frame cottages appeared between the two world wars of the twentieth century. They were little like those grand summer homes that had been occupied by wealthy families, coming by train from afar for the entire season with trunks full of belongings. These were more typically weekend cottages for middle-class commuters who drove from nearby cities—or, as in my family's case, where wives and children might spend the weeks, but working husbands would come for weekends.

The undistinguished lane, lined with small garages, would hardly affect others as it did me. Every detail had been imprinted. I remembered the many-hued sweet peas that used to grow on that fence in June, when we would first arrive at Steele's Point. How many times I walked this road, headed for Clayton and my regular visits with Julie! It was uncanny that it remained almost as it had been, so long ago. Several generations of youngsters have shared my own experiences here since then.

I drove to the very end of the road, where it dipped down and disappeared in the water. Here we were, at the cottages where I spent so many happy summers—several of them acquired during the Depression years when banks foreclosed on mortgages. I had no idea who these strange people were now, mowing our grass and hanging their beach towels on our line to dry. They no doubt wondered who I was, driving to this dead end at the water and stopping to stare.

A neighboring summer cottage had been supplanted by a year-round residence. Someone improbably had built a good-sized house on little Board Island, only a hundred yards or so offshore. But, my ideal island, Hogsback, farther off, was still out there, just as I had left it, still wild and natural. My own fantasy house for that special place was still there, in my mind's eye. Farther distant, Pine, Bluff and other islands receded, still beckoning as they had to the boy in his skiff. The place, so changed in some ways, was still so little changed in others. It was still magically alluring. It still called.

Across the water was the head of Round Island, with its imposing houses and the Edge's (now the Withingtons') dark red boathouse where I had tied up my skiff so often. I imagined how the grand Frontenac Hotel had once towered so much higher than the trees.  And those huge poplar trees were still there, leaves rustling in the breeze.  It struck me as odd how trees outlast us, and how buildings outlast their builders.  The shimmering poplars marked the place where that decaying house had been—I supposed it must be gone now, like so much else—the place where a curious boy, investigating old cylinder records, was startled to first hear Julie's voice.

The Author at Boldt Castle, c. 1968

Early impressions of Thousand Islands buildings led to my career as an architect, educator, and author of books and articles about historic buildings of New York State, including Boldt Castle.

# PART II

# Castles and Cottages
## Three Castles and Their Builders

Castle Rest

The Pullman summer home as photographed from the tower of Hopewell Hall shows the new Thousand Islands Yacht Club behind it, at the left. The building's cedar shingle roof is still bright, not yet weathered. The Castle Rest powerhouse, seen in the foreground, survived demolition of the main house.

The Towers

# Frederick   Bourne

## The Singer Sewing Machine and Dark Island

Frederick Gilbert Bourne (1851-1919) attended New York City public schools. Young Frederick didn't seem destined to be a giant of American industry. He was inclined towards music. Bourne had a fine baritone voice and sang as a soloist in many fashionable New York City churches and with the Mendelssohn Glee Club. It was at a New York City concert of that group that Edward Clark discovered him.

Edward Clark was President and said to be "the business brains" of the Singer Manufacturing Company, producers of the Singer sewing machine. Forty years older than Bourne, Clark asked Frederick to become his personal secretary. Their relationship developed. Clark had an estate, Fernleigh, at Cooperstown, New York. Bourne was thirty-one years old in 1882 when Clark died at age seventy-one. Bourne then became manager of the Clark estate. Edward's only son and sole surviving heir, Alfred Corning Clark, who also was older than Frederick, thereupon continued to be Bourne's patron. Alfred, like his father, was fond of music. The year following Edward Clark's death Bourne became a Singer director and two years later, when thirty-four years old, he became secretary of the company. Then in four more years, when only thirty-eight years old, Frederick Bourne became President of the Singer Manufacturing Company.

Although the Bourne's summer home is sometimes called "Singer Castle," Isaac Singer, founder of I. M. Singer & Co., moved to Europe when Bourne was twenty-four years old. Probably the two never met. Bourne built Dark Island Castle more than a quarter century after Singer's 1875 death in Europe; visitors should not be misled by suggestion that Singer built, or even visited, the Dark Island landmark.


At age twenty-four Frederick Bourne married Emma Keeler of New York. They had three sons, Arthur, Alfred, and George, and four daughters, May, Marion, Florence, and Marjorie. For many years the family lived in New York City in a fourteen-room apartment in the famous Dakota on Central Park West. Built by Edward Clark, this was one of the first prestigious apartment buildings in New York City, now a well-known historic landmark occupied by celebrities.

George Boldt was building his castle when Frederick Bourne became a new member of the Thousand Islands Yacht Club. Bourne had purchased Dark Island and in the summer of 1903 he was said to be "getting ready to build." He commissioned from prominent architect Ernest Flagg a "castellated residence and other buildings." That same year he was elected Commodore of the New York Yacht Club.

During the next two summers architect Flagg often accompanied Bourne aboard his yacht, *Artemis*, inspecting construction of the massive buildings on Dark Island. Joseph A. Reid was the contractor.

The main structure was five stories high and it crowned the island so as to be a landmark seen for miles. The house was not nearly so large as Boldt Castle, however, or as many other summer homes here, in fact. There were only twenty-eight rooms in the original portion, which was subsequently expanded. "The Towers," as Bourne called the place, was monumental, however, and romantically picturesque. At Bourne's request, Flagg evoked the Scottish castles described in Sir Walter Scott's historical novels, particularly the Old Royal Lodge described *Woodstock*.

To the Library from the Entry Hall

One of the curiosities of Dark Island Castle is the hinged portrait of Charles I of England that may be opened from a concealed passage on the mezzanine level of the seventeen-foot-high main hall, affording a view of activity on the floor below. This feature apparently was inspired by Scott's novel, *Woodstock*, according to Mardges Bacon, author of *Ernest Flagg*, who also mentions that "there were other such passages running both horizontally and vertically, via two spiral stone staircases. Passages in nearly every room of the house were entered from doors disguised either as wainscoting, as part of a chimney piece, or a bedroom closet wall. These doors were activated by a variety of curious devices including push buttons concealed behind lighting fixtures, thermostats, or even closet hooks. Subterranean passages led from the kitchen to the powerhouse and boathouse. Heralded as a 'Castle of Mysteries' by the *New York Times*, upon its completion in the fall of 1905, 'The Towers' was surrounded by a veil of secrecy which Bourne, Flagg, and the building superintendent, Arthur Sutcliffe, all encouraged. During the summer of 1905 as the house was nearing completion, Sutcliffe privately reflected on the reaction of the Italian workmen to their first experience within 'the mysterious passage.' 'They were quite frightened,' wrote Sutcliffe, and said they would never come into the house again'" (166-7).

Bourne, who was Commodore of the New York Yacht Club (1903-5) and a member of other yacht clubs here and elsewhere, had many vessels and boats. The *Artemis*, which was housed in the stone quarters on Dark Island, was 131 feet long with a beam of 12.6 feet, powered by a twin-screw steam engine. His first yacht, acquired in 1902, was the colossal 253-long *Maria*, which he renamed the *Delaware*. This was followed by the *Diana* (1905) and the *Little Sovereign* (1909), which became the *Sioux*. The great *Calonia* was similarly powered but was 189 feet long with a 22.6—foot beam. This was probably had been the *Alberta*, the vessel bought in 1899 from Albert, King of Belgium, and later kept at the Long Island estate. The *Scat* was a seventy-foot powerboat with internal combustion engine and was seventy feet long with beam of 9.7 feet. Bourne also had a sail-boat on the river, the *Reverie*. It was 48 feet long with 14-foot beam, and on the ocean had the sloops *Constitution* and *Meridian*. His numerous smaller craft in-cluded the *Squaw, Pilot, Express, Sparks, Ginty, Meriah*, and the very fast boats, *Wanderer, Messenger, Dark Island*, which would do twenty miles per hour, *Moike*, which would do twenty-six m.p.h. and *Stranger*, which took the Frontenac Cup in 1907. The *Running Wild* was a later fast boat. There was even an electrified Venetian gondola at Dark Island. As new Commodore of the New York Yacht Club Bourne, who sailed internationally with Sir Thomas Lipton, commissioned from Herreshoff the famous 1903 international racing sailboat, *Reliance*.

A Dark Island tragedy occurred in 1916, a year before Bourne's death. Peter Larivière, a French-Canadian who had been the Dark Island steward for eleven years, had gone fishing on Sunday, his day off. When Peter didn☐t reappear, no one wanted to guess what happened but everyone feared the worst. They found Peter's body by grappling. He had drowned on Sunday night, when he was within ten feet of the dock.

Marjorie Bourne married Alexander Dallas Thayer of Philadelphia. The Thayers added two wings were to the main house   A breakfast room off the dining room was removed and replaced by the music room that extended the dining room wing the full length of the existing terrace and service rooms below. This extension provided an additional room on the floors above as well. On the north side of the house, a portion of the "piazza" or porch off the main hall was enclosed, creating the "loggia" with large stone fireplace, and the sunroom be-yond.

In 1905, the year that Dark Island Castle was completed, Frederick Bourne announced that he was not a candidate for continued presidency of the Singer Manufacturing Company. After sixteen years as president, he retired when only fifty-four years old. He died fourteen years later, in 1919.

Indian Neck Hall, the vast Bourne estate at Oakdale, N.Y. was mentioned and illustrated in Appendix B, "Some Great American Country Houses of the Gilded Age," in this author's book, *Boldt Castle*. The huge Long Island house was also designed by Ernest Flagg. Bourne spent some six million dollars on the estate, which would be at least ten times that today. Both the Long Island and Dark Island properties were bequeathed to La Salle Academy. Indian Neck Hall is now known as La Salle Center.

Dark Island was purchased in 1965 by the Harold Martin Evangelistic Association. Martin and his wife resided here for decades, enjoying tax-exempt status because of the religious nature of their operation. This amounted mainly to offering Sunday services in the music room. The Martin operation was not favored by nearby Chippewa Bay residents, who duly paid their property taxes.

Dark Island was offered for sale for many years. In 2002 a German investment syndicate, American Castles Holding, Ltd., acquired the property for the purpose of restoring the buildings and opening them to the public.

Dark Island, Ernest Flagg, Architect

Led by Frederick Bourne, the Singer Manufacturing Company initiated global marketing, so important a century later. Bourne is remembered for his "genius for marketing" of what has been called the "first domestic appliance."

As then practiced, distribution was unsatisfactory. Middle men did not develop markets but merely marked up the price. Singer created demand by demontstratinghe sewing machine directly to potential users. Singer was the first mass producer to form its own sales organization.

The Singer Company was innovator of direct sales to customers. The company became the "world-wide pioneer of installment selling," with Bourne as its "world-traveling, forceful executive." He made it "America's pioneer in foreign fields," the "United States' first international company" and "perhaps the first modern multinational industrial enterprise of any nationality." Bourne said proudly, "The American sewing-machine is the sewing-machine of the world."

By 1900 the company had 1700 branch offices with "sixty-thousand sales persons in almost every inhabitable portion of the world." Singer held "a near monopoly of world markets." Bourne visited Russia in 1892 but was "not impressed with its potential." Nevertheless, Singer built a plant there, becoming one of the two largest industrial firms in Imperial Russia. Singer lost a hundred million dollars in the Russian Revolution.

The Singer company was "among the most important innovators in building vertically integrated firms." Bourne was responsible for "Singer's power [which] lay in its organization," which was "a world-wide sales and marketing organization." With its own retail network, Singer provided a full range of customer services, including demonstration, installation, after-sales service and repair, as well as offering consumer credit. Prior to Singer's example, producers were little concerned with consumer service, being twice removed from users. Producers generally distributed their products to wholesalers who then supplied retailers. Singer established the direct link between producer and consumer.

The architect Ernest Flagg designed the New York City headquarters for Singer, built in several stages. Addition of the Bourne Building in 1906 included a forty-seven-story tower that made it the tallest building in the world at the time. The landmark unfortunately was demolished.

Bourne's global view was not totally commercial. He believed that "poverty could be removed from society by self-help" and that the domestic sewing machine, made obtainable worldwide through rental and installment sales plans, contributed to self-help of poorer people around the globe.

# Charles    Emery

## The American Tobacco Corporation and Calumet Island

The career of Charles Goodwin Emery (1836-1915) is the story of the rapid transformation of American business from the small family firm into the giant corporation. Emery's New York City business, Goodwin & Co., was the fifth largest
American producer of tobacco products when absorbed into the American Tobacco Company, the "Tobacco Trust" assembled by James B. Duke.

To produce "Old Judge" pipe tobacco, cigars, and cigarettes, Emery employed mainly Russian immigrants who came via London, where they had become experienced in cigarette factories. Goodwin & Co. also produced the
"Canvas Back" and "Welcome" brands of tobacco products.

Competition among the five major American tobacco firms had been vigorous. Because there was little real difference between tobacco products, advertising became critical to gain brand recognition. Emery was effective marketing

his products and, moreover, he had the Emery Cigarette Machine that produced cigarettes efficiently, bringing the cost down more than ninety per cent. He also had competition from the Bonsack cigarette machine, but so long as Emery had his own patent, the proposed tobacco trust couldn't monopolize efficient mechanical production. Emery was able to negotiate a very profitable deal with Duke in 1890. He sold his cigarette machine patent to Bonsack and became treasurer of the new corporation—which was "outrageously overcapitalized," yielding a bonanza to Emery. Goodwin & Co. got 2.5 million dollars in stock. The tangible assets of the new corporation were merely 3.9 million, exclusive of 1.8 million contributed in notes by the organizers. The extraordinary success of the American Tobacco Company was due to its control of the cigarette machine, so Emery's participation had been critical.

Like other earlier manufacturers of tobacco products, Emery disposed of most of his interest in American Tobacco by 1898 when large investors without tobacco experience such as Thomas Fortune Ryan became directors of the corporation. There was talk of "certain shady stock manipulations" that had raised the value of stock previously bought by company insiders. In time, Emery's original New York City production facility was transferred to Durham, N.C.

President Roosevelt and the U.S. government sought to break up the "Tobacco Trust" as an illegal monopoly in 1907. Emery testified in the famous court proceedings that lasted four years before the trust was disassembled.

The foresight of the American Tobacco Company was recognition that the cigarette machine, using a virtually labor-free continuous process, could produce such a volume of the product that a global organization would be required to provide adequate marketing and distribution. Although American Tobacco was broken up, this international vision was the wave of the future. It was recognized by Commodore Bourne of Singer as well, for this was the beginning of truly global enterprises.

Charles Goodwin Emery married Irene Smith Boyton. They had three children. Their two daughters were Mable ("Nina") and Francena. Their son was Frank Whitney Emery. The family resided in Brooklyn and subsequently on the Upper East Side of Manhattan. They came to the Thousand Islands in the early 1880s, staying at various hotels such as the Thousand Islands House in 1881 and the Crossmon House in 1885, both in Alexandria Bay, and at Clayton's Hubbard House in 1886. They became Clayton converts.

Charles Emery and Guide

Note that the guide holds a bat, part of his equipment when
bringing in such a large muskellunge.

Emery purchased Powderhorn Island opposite Clayton from the Lawrence estate in 1882 for $1000 and renamed it "Calumet." The name referred to the Native American peace pipe, since the island, as defined by Emery's fill behind sea walls, was pipe-shaped. A fine new frame cottage, "one of the finest among the islands," was being built in June of 1883 and was ready for occupancy late in that season.

Emery did not acquire a yacht initially but, like Pullman, he chartered boats. In 1881 he rented the new *R. P. Flower*, provided with captain and crew of two. In 1883 and 1884 he leased the *Juanita* and continued to charter yachts, such as the *Valetta* in 1892. In 1894 he employed the *Serius* to inspect work on his construction projects and in 1897 he chartered the yacht *Columbia* for use until his own, new yacht, *Calumet*, arrived.

Calumet Castle

The author photographed the shuttered building from the water tower, c. 1945

Ten years after building the frame cottage, Emery decided a finer summer home was in order and he commissioned architect John W. Griffen of Watertown to design it. Although built in 1893, the year a grave depression set in, Emery's windfall from the formation of American Tobacco allowed him to build a splendid trophy house—one that would cost as much (it was noted pointedly) as Wyckoff's new Carleton Villa, reputedly $50,000. The other model no doubt was Castle Rest, summer home of George Pullman, built five years earlier. Emery would continue the Thousand Islands "castle" motif. Griffen designed a towered villa built of Potsdam red sandstone and Grindstone Island granite. Other buildings and improvements to the island brought the total cost to more than $100,000. A two-story ballroom wing was added in 1901. It measured twenty feet wide by fifty feet long, adding two more towers and extending the mass of the Castle.

To make way for the new mansion, Emery removed the frame cottage from Calumet Island, rebuilding it on Robbins Island which he had acquired and re-named "Picton" Island. As seen in the contemporary photograph on page 255, Picton Island eventually had two large greenhouses and a poultry farm. Five mammoth incubators hatched 7-8000 chickens and ducks seasonally. A well 500 feet deep provided water that "sparkles as if charged," but Emery eventually acquired Frontenac Crystal Springs on the mainland to supply drinking water to his facilities and to other users.

In 1893 Emery purchased nearby Governor's Island for $5000. Emery continued to acquire properties, including several farms on the foot of Grindstone Island, which became his Frontenac Farm.  In 1899 he built a creamery where milk was "aerated, sterilized, and bottled."  Emery was proud of his "fine, blooded Jersey stock" at Frontenac Farm.  In 1901 he purchased the Delaney and McCrary farms on Grindstone, about 600 acres total, for about $30,000, expanding the Frontenac Farm.

Although Emery chartered yachts for many years, by 1897 he had acquired the Herreshoff-built yacht, *Nina*.  He supplemented this with "a houseboat, two naphtha launches and numerous trim skiffs."  In 1902 Emery sold the *Nina* for $30,000 to Alexander Peacock of Belle Isle, who renamed it the *Irene*.  Emery then visited Herreshoff and ordered a new yacht, to cost $100,000.  Reportedly she he would be 147 feet long with a twenty-foot beam, and do eighteen knots per hour (twenty miles per hour, twenty-four maximum)—speed unexcelled on the river.  By another account she was actually 144 feet long with 17.6-foot beam, said to have cost $75,000.  In 1904 the grand new *Calumet* came from the Bristol yards in Rhode Island via the ocean and down the St. Lawrence.  She required a crew of seventeen.

Charles Emery was not merely an idle vacationer on the river.  He was actively a promoter and developer of local many projects.  His many plans and five offers over the years to rebuild the retail district of Clayton came to naught, but in 1887, with I. D. Little, Emery founded the St. Lawrence River Skiff, Canoe & Steamboat Co., a major Clayton business that eventually relocated in Ogdensburg.

In 1903 Emery purchased Grandview Park, a community of summer residents on Wellesley Island that included a hotel.  This was really an interest of Mrs. Irene Emery, who intended to use the hotel building as a summer facility for less privileged New York City children.

Charles Emery acquired Round Island, with all its summer homes as well as the large hotel and related facilities.  That large island had been developed by a Baptist association, which had leased lots in a manner similar to Thousand Island Park.  That association was supplanted by another that was secular but still retained much of the island for common use and built a large hotel, pier, and made other improvements.  Emery gained Round Island when the association went through foreclosure proceedings.  Excluded from the auctioned property were only the Hays and Whedon lots (indicated on a contemporary map as 'The Reservation").

Foreclosure followed the depression of the mid-nineties, but observers commented that Round Island Hotel seemed to be prospering, observing that the sale was made "in order to make a more perfect title in certain interested persons than from any lack of means to carry on the business." Apparently the proceedings were really intended to liquidate the extant association and allow Emery to develop the Frontenac Hotel as his own property. Emery did not bid himself. Probably, if his interest had been known, the price would have been forced up much higher. Jacob Hays of New York, who had the fine house at the head of the island, initiated the bidding. He was said to represent a syndicate of six Round Islanders, with no reference to Emery.

"At 11 o'clock this morning a little group of men gathered under the clump of trees on the Frontenac lawn and [the] Sheriff . . . of Jefferson County sold [virtually] the entire Round Island property at auction. The sale was short but exciting. It had been thought that the holders of the second mortgage headed by Jacob Hays of New York and including James J. Belden of Syracuse [and others] might bid in the property. . . . But John Dunfee of Syracuse happened to be standing in the ring and when Mr. Hays started the bidding at $30,000, he spoke up. . . . It was generally believed that the bidding would not go above [the total indebtedness of $33,283.56 to an off-island lender represented by a banker] but Mr. Dunfee forced it up $1000 a clip until Mr. Hays reached $37,000. Then [the banker] called Mr. Dunfee aside and off, and the property was knocked down to Mr. Hays at $37,000."

No mention of Emery was made at the time, but "Mr. Hays said that the association would be reorganized at once and that many improvements would be made. The present season has been a prosperous one and the future looks very bright for Round Island." The following spring title passed from Jacob Hays to the Round Island Company, a corporation with six stockholders including Jacob and Will Hays, as well as their next-door neighbor, Hubert Van Wagenen, and three others, but not yet including Emery. In the fall of that year, however, Emery and Van Wagenen bought out the other stockholders and then, late in 1898, work began on Emery's grand Frontenac Hotel.

Many improvements followed, funded by Emery, "principle stockholder of the Round Island Company," such as construction of a large annex structure and establishment of the Frontenac Yacht Club, of which Emery was commodore, with a fine clubhouse, now a private residence. Emery reportedly purchased nearby Little Round Island for $15,000 in 1900.

Although Emery had his own yachts, in 1900 he leased the *Gryphon*, which he placed at the disposal of Frontenac Hotel guests, also using the yacht as a private shuttle for guests arriving from the Clayton railroad terminus.

This construction photograph of the Frontenac shows the
dining room and kitchen wing on the back of the building.

Charles Emery was a member of the New York Yacht Club, of which Frederick
Bourne was Commodore. In addition to the magnificent steam yacht, *Calumet*,
he had acquired the smaller yachts *Juanita* and the *Molly C* and a work tug *Alice
R*. With properties on many islands, much transport was required.

Irene Boynton Emery fell ill 1905—the year after Louise Boldt died, leaving
Boldt Castle unfinished. Mrs. Emery only enjoyed the great yacht *Calumet* during one short summer.

The following season Charles Emery did not open Calumet Castle, but instead during the summer of 1906 he stayed at the Frontenac. His wife died the
following year, 1907, after two years of illness. Emery Castle was never re-
opened. Like George Boldt, Charles Emery left his splendid house unoccupied.

Calumet Island was not illuminated in 1908, disappointing many in the
Clayton region. The darkness was not mere mourning for Irene Emery however;
high water had damaged the powerhouse. Charles Emery returned to his island,
but subsequently he occupied the large frame caretaker's house. Again, like George
Boldt, he merely contemplated the great castle, which remained boarded up
during his last years.

Emery gave up the great yacht, *Calumet*, as well—not disposing of it but, like
the castle, leaving it unused. The yacht was hauled up by marine railroad onto
Washington Island, near Clayton, where he could see the huge vessel dry-docked
summer after summer. Emery used the smaller *Mollie C* in later seasons.

In 1910 the Town of Clayton "went dry," prohibiting the sale of alcohol. The
effect on the hospitality business was devastating. Considering his huge hotel in
the town, one can only imagine Emery's reaction—remembering as well that
Clayton had spurned his repeated offers to assist in rebuilding its waterfront.

Ironically, his wife Irene had supported the local Women's Christian Temperance Union, and Charles Emery had contributed to the ladies' crusade. He was hoisted on their petard. The grand Frontenac Hotel burned to the ground in 1911. The disastrous fire sounded a death knell for the glamorous resort. The First World War would finally end an era a few years later. The great yachts disappeared; the fools' paradise vanished.

Foolish or not, Emery continued to be an optimistic booster of the resort. Like Boldt, he continued to be involved in projects here. Emery was involved in a 1912 meeting about rebuilding the two grand hotels and had architects prepare plans for a new, fireproof Frontenac. But, again like Boldt's fireproof hotel begun about the same time on Wellesley Island, the project was never built.

Charles Goodwin Emery died in 1915, a year before the death of George Boldt. Frederick Bourne died three years after. It was the passing of a generation of castle builders, as the First World War approached.

The great yacht, *Calumet*, in dry dock for several years, was sold the year after Emery's death to James Farrell, President of the United States Steel Corporation.

Emery was known as an art collector, and his paintings were shown for sale in New York City galleries in 1924. His estate included thirty-three islands and stipulated that Calumet Island could not be sold until his grandson, Charles Gordon Emery, reached age thirty. Emery had set aside an $800,000 fund to maintain the property that he loved. His son, Frank, was sole trustee of the multi-million-dollar estate.

Frank, who built a fine home in Pasadena, California, was not much interested in the Thousand Islands, but his son, "Chuck," came to the river occasionally to fish. He would use the commodious caretaker's house on back side of Calumet Island, never reopening his grandfather's castle. These were the Depression and war years. In 1935 the grandson traded in the antique "Mollie C" for new Christ Craft. Chuck waited until age thirty, when the property could be sold.

For many seasons it was understood locally that Calumet Island could be had for back taxes or for some modest amount less than $25,000. It was finally sold in 1950. Sadly, the period contents were auctioned. The shutters were taken off the windows for the first time in almost a half-century and briefly the Castle was opened to the public. This apparently did not prove promising, however. One night in 1957 a fire gutted the Castle, which then was demolished as a hazard to public safety. The Clayton owner at the time was interested in developing a marina facility on the island.

When the masonry walls of Calumet Castle were knocked down, the hollow cornerstone revealed a poignant message from the past. Charles Emery's note conveyed a confident vision for the future of the Thousand Islands and for his proud house, built to serve untold generations of Emerys as their true family seat, a place of happy reunions for centuries to come. The next two generations never even opened the place.

In addition to providing a maintenance fund for the property, Emery set aside a trust fund for his grandson, Charles Gordon Emery. The bequest was provisional on the condition that he abstain from intoxicants and—you guessed it—tobacco.

Calumet Castle, Jown W. Griffen, Architect.

Pullmans and Lowdens at Castle Rest, 1897

This was the last summer in the life of George M. Pullman, seated at right. His wife, Harriet Pullman sits on the left. Between them is the Reverend Royal H. Pullman of Baltimore and Camp Royal, Wellesley Island. Standing behind him is the Reverend James M. Pullman of New York City and Summerland Island. One of the Pullman twin sons stands at the right and daughter Florence Pullman Lowden stands at left, next to her husband, Frank O. Lowden, who holds their infant son, Pullman Lowden. The Lowdens inherited Castle Rest, which they enjoyed for many summers. Frank Lowden became Governor of Illinois. George's recently deceased mother, Emily Minton Pullman, appears in the painting behind the group.

# George Pullman

## The Pullman Palace Car Company and Castle Rest

George Mortimer Pullman (1831- 1897) is a key figure in American business history, remembered not merely for building a major industrial concern but also for the model company town of Pullman, Illinois, which survives today as a historic community. Most significantly, however, Pullman is recalled for the famous Pullman Strike of 1894, which triggered a national crisis for railroad transportation. The President's use of federal troops to break the strike has continued to be controversial. Admiration for Pullman's achievement has been tempered by frequent condemnation for his labor practices. Pullman regarded himself, however, as beneficent when he could be and reasonable otherwise.

The Pullmans were among the earliest summer residents on the islands. George Pullman's mother, Emily Minton Pullman, was the real the key to the family's presence on the river. She came first not with her son George but with his brother, Royal. Emily returned to the river almost every year of her life and was the nucleus for reunions here of her large family.

Emily had married James Lewis Pullman (called "Lewis") who moved from Onondaga County in Central New York to nearby Auburn where they were wed. The Pullmans were a large family — ten children. George was their third son, born near Buffalo after his parents had moved there. The Thousand Islands might seem remote from western New York today, when few summer people commute so far by automobile. We may forget, however, that steamboat service on Lake Ontario and the St. Lawrence River made the region accessible in the mid-nineteenth century, long before roads were much used for long-distance travel to the Thousand Islands.

Two of George Pullman's brothers attended St. Lawrence University, at Canton in New York's North Country. James Minton Pullman graduated in 1861, Frank William Pullman in 1872. George did not attend college but went to work for a country merchant at age fourteen. He became acquainted with James E. Lyon of nearby Ogdensburg. They formed an early venture, Lyon, Pullman & Co., doing business in Colorado. On his return from that state, George visited the Thousand Islands with a brother and sister, Henry and Helen, in the summer of 1863 or 1864. He bought Sweet Island from the large landowners, Cornwall & Walton, in 1864, when it became known as Pullman Island. That was the year that Pullman built his famous Pioneer, a luxurious railroad car that revolutionized passenger travel. It carried President Lincoln's body across a mourning nation after his assassination. President Grant subsequently occupied the Pioneer when he traveled through the West. Because of the car's unusual width, many tracks required widening while station platforms had to be altered. National use of the Pioneer promoted standardization of railroad lines, facilitating through passage with less transferring of passengers between cars of different widths.

George Pullman married Harriet A. Sanger and they had four children, a daughter, Florence Pullman Lowden and an adopted daughter, Harriet Pullman Carolans Schermerhorn, as well as twin sons, George M. Pullman, Jr. and Walter Sanger Pullman.

In 1871, seven years after buying his island, Pullman began to entertain prominent guests. His accommodations were simple initially, since the Thousand Islands at the time were largely favored by sportsmen. Tenting was common, and the Pullmans retained tents on their island even after Castle Rest was built. Prior to that project, they placed a Pullman Palace Car on the shore, doors and windows removed, to serve as a summerhouse. It "attract[ed] much attention from the river."

George Pullman's mother, Emily Caroline, enjoyed other places here. According to one story, it was she who urged purchase of island property when visiting with one of her sons, Royal Henry. She reportedly induced another son, George, to acquire two islands, Sweet (Pullman Island, site of Castle Rest) and Nobby, paying $40 for each. James Minton Pullman and Joseph H. Clowes purchased Nobby four years later, but according to the deed they acquired it from Walton, not from Pullman. Subsequently they sold Nobby to Henry R. Heath.

Another son, George's brother James Minton Pullman of Lynn, Mass. and Chicago, built a cottage on Cherry Island in 1881. It's still there, having become the rear wing of Casa Blanca. This was the second cottage on the island, which the firm of Cornwall & Walton had given to Rev. George Rockwell. He built the original island cottage, Sunnyside, at the head of the island, later supplanted by the fine villa of Frederick Frazer. It was said that Pullman purchased the entire island for $40 in the early 1870s; if so, probably it was from Rev. Rockwell.

James Pullman's Cherry Island cottage passed to another brother, Albert Benton Pullman, general superintendent of the Pullman car operations. He called the place Melrose Lodge. In later years, his wife shared the property with her friend, Mrs. G. B. Marsh, both of Chicago. Mrs. Marsh erected the landmark gargoyles on the Cherry Island shore. Luis Marx acquired the property from the estate of A. B. Pullman, enlarging the building to become Casa Blanca.  Confusion about Cherry Island properties is caused by Mrs. Marsh also owning the adjacent property, Ingleside, which was acquired by Abraham and Straus.  There they built their twin cottages, Olympia and Belora.

Griffins Guard Melrose Lodge, Cherry Island, Alexandria Bay

So  two of George Pullman's brothers successively owned the Cherry Island property where their mother often stayed.  Another brother, Rev. Royal Henry Pullman of Baltimore, owned Camp Royal on Wellesley Island, a short distance from Pullman Island.  These two brothers were partners in a business near Buffalo.  Royal Henry Pullman, like brother James, became a Universalist minister.  Royal also served as secretary to Clara Barton, founder of the American Red Cross and a frequent guest at Camp Royal, where the Red Cross flag often flew.  In contrast to George, who built a magnificent island home, Royal Henry preferred to tent at his "camp" on the nearby shore.  Like his mother, Royal Henry was a devoted and loyal River Rat.  He returned every summer but two to the river, thirty-four seasons, finally coming against physicians' advice after he had been paralyzed by a stroke.  He died at his beloved Camp Royal in 1900 at age seventy four.

Castle Rest, back side. The powerhouse is at right, with the tall chimney.

Brother George, the industrialist, was, of course, in a class by himself in this clan. His family traveled in a chain of private railroad cars, carrying twelve servants and baggage in one car, while a stable car with six stalls usually carried five horses, and three vehicles. That car had berths and sitting room for grooms. The family's private car, the Monitor, was staffed by a conductor, cook, and two waiters. It had a parlor organ and even a bathtub. The monitor was famous because it was used by every President of the United States during the many years when it was in service.

Despite their regal mode of transportation, George Pullman and his family enjoyed a fairly simple life on their island for several seasons when fishing was thought to be the main reason for being there. For years he did not acquire a yacht but chartered one as required — for many years the *Valetta* from Oswego, which Emery also chartered occasionally.  The Pullmans did not always require a private boat to take them from the Clayton railroad terminus to their island, but often took the regular steamboat to Alexandria Bay, where a boatman from their island met them.  Regularly "a little naphtha launch that plied back and forth from the Bay to his island satisfied Mr. Pullman's modest wants."  Pullman eventually did own a small yacht, *Little Billee,* and then the *Monitor,* named after his famous railroad car.  The larger boat was similar to Capt. Visger's familiar touring yacht.

The Pullmans became more sociable in 1871, however.  In that year they visited President Grant and his wife at Long Branch on the Jersey shore before coming to the river.  The next summer President Grant visited them at their island, accompanied by a retinue that included the Civil War heroes, Generals Philip Henry Sheridan and William Tecumseh Sherman.  That event put the Thousand Islands on the map.

A contemporary novelist told a  charming story of the presidential visit in *Under the Tamaracks, or a Summer with General Grant.*  A boy whose family was on a nearby island was curious about all the commotion on Pullman's island.  He rowed over there with his skiff.  When he approached, a bearded man, standing alone while smoking a cigar on the shore, beckoned him.  The man called out, asking if he could have a ride in the skiff.  The youngster rowed over to the nearby dock and grabbed a cleat to steady the craft as the well-dressed gentleman, appearing not too confident about small boats, carefully stepped in.  The fellow was very talkative, curious about everything as they rowed around nearby islands.  Then the man sighed and said he supposed it was time to get back.  He told the lad that he was happy to get away for a little while from all the socializing on that island.  Only after the boy left the man back on Pullman's Island and went home to relate his story, describing his passenger, did he learn that he had given the tour to the President of the United States.

The Pullmans continued to entertain prominent visitors on occasion, such as Presidential candidate James G. Blaine, and General Schofield, highest-ranking officer of the U.S. Army, as well as prominent jurists and other politicians.  As George and Harriet Pullman divided the summer between Castle Rest and Fairlawn, their other summer home at Elberon, near Long Branch on the Jersey shore, and as much of the month on the river was filled with family reunion events, they were less noted here as hosts than were the Boldts.  Pullman was a member of Georgia's Jekyll Island Club.  Commodore Frederick Bourne was club president.

Prior to construction of Castle Rest, two large frame cottage—Packers' (1879) on Sport Island and Deweys' on Friendly Island (1887)—were most admired. When built in 1888, Castle Rest surpassed them as a marvel, odd for its intentional rusticity, but admired for its boldness and picturesque composition. The first of the Thousand Islands "castles," the design was thought to be "after the German fortress style." The main tower, six stories high on the summit of the island, rose 127 feet above the water as a prominent landmark. Local contractor Seth G. Pope employed 122 men for the project. The most conspicuous features were built of rough stone, introducing substantial masonry to the regional cottage style. While other stone features on the island conveyed a substantial character, the several buildings were mostly of wood frame construction, clad with shingles in the manner favored during the 1880s. A detached building for a steam engine to power an electric generator and other mechanical equipment was a notable feature introduced here. Provision of five hundred electric lights on the island was notable in 1888, for this was the first island home to be electrified. Emery, Boldt, and Bourne subsequently also built powerhouses on their "castle" islands.

Castle Rest contained fifty-eight rooms in the main house, which was supplemented by several ancillary structures. A feature of Castle Rest was "the historic room occupied by President Grant preserved as a relic." It was salvaged from the old cottage and relocated in the new structure. Prior to construction, Castle Rest was estimated to cost $100,000—perhaps 1.5 million in today's dollars—but when completed its cost was said to be about $150,000, exclusive of furnishings, or closer to 2.5 million dollars. When completed, Castle Rest "so enraptured a wealthy gentleman residing in Europe that he sent a noted artist here to paint an elaborate picture of it." The artist was W. A. Hilliard of Paris, who stayed with his wife at the Crossmon House, Alexandria Bay. The painting was to be shown at the Royal Academy, London, but whether it was is not known. If existing, it would be a true collector's item, but its location today is also unknown.

The rustic character of Castle Rest may have seemed odd, but a year after construction the "curious Norman structure begins to appear at home on the rocky heights of the celebrated island." The large freestanding chimney of the powerhouse, seventy-five feet tall, was reportedly "built to gratify a whim of Mr. Pullman, who said that he had become so used to seeing chimneys in his manufacturing city of Pullman, Illinois that he would get lonesome in a place where he could see none." Of course this was Pullman's wit. In fact the chimney was tall because the nearby house was so tall. Beman, the architect, adroitly made use of the striking feature in composing the massing of the complex. The remaining powerhouse and nearby boathouse evidence the picturesque character of Beman's design.

Exterior lighting of the landmark tower by means of locomotive headlights made it a feature on the evening boat tours. Not only did lights shine up on the stone tower of Castle Rest, but "from the tower a brilliant electric light throws a beam to the opposite shore." A special treat was Pullman's annual display of fireworks on his mother's birthday.

Castle Rest Powerhouse Interior

The View from the Top

Castle Rest's tower observation room looked down on the Thousand Islands Yacht Club, at left, and Knobby Island, right. Boldt Castle rises in the center distance.

Not only members of George Pullman's immediate household were regular visitors to the Pullman Island. The family of his elder daughter, Florence Pullman Lowden, made Castle Rest their summer home for many decades, observing the required custom of celebrating the birthday of George's mother with a family reunion. Apparently wary of spoiling their children like Florence's wayward brothers may have seemed, the Lowdens demanded good behavior. George[?] Dobbins, a regular fishing guide for the Lowdens, when taking the sister and brother fishing, disciplined the boy, who angrily replied that he would tell his father. The next day Gov. Lowden, without further comment, thanked Dobbins for the special care he gave his son.

George Pullman's sisters were frequent visitors—Mrs. L. Flurher, whose husband was a New York City doctor, and Mrs. George West whose husband was a doctor of Providence, Rhode Island.

George's brother, Rev. James Minton Pullman, often used Castle Rest when otherwise unoccupied, but James had his own cottage, Cliff, at Summerland, where he was known as "J.M." Said to be the first cottage on the island, it was visited by President Grant and later acquired by Dr. Asa Saxe. It was James who said "he would never ask a woman if she loved him but 'did she love the Thousand Islands'?" Perhaps James had his brother's wife, Hattie Pullman, in mind.

James became pastor of the Sixth Universalist Church in New York City but on the river was a member of the Reformed Church at Alexandria Bay. An alumnus of St. Lawrence University, James Minton Pullman became a trustee of the university, which continued to attract Pullmans. Tracy Minton Pullman graduated from St. Lawrence University in 1925.

George M. Pullman, who was a player in national railroad manipulations as well as New York City transit, was benefactor of technical colleges and the University of Chicago.

Castle Rest, like the other Thousand Islands castles, was a trophy house. Pullman's company became the seventh largest industry in the United States. The company was "the leading symbol of big business in the years after 1893." The Thousand Islands monument celebrated not merely Pullman's personal achievement, however, but building of the castle in 1888 marked the high point of railroad road development in the United States. Construction of new lines set a historic record during the previous year. Decline in railroad transportation has dimmed recollection of the Pullman car and its innovative service, so that George M. Pullman is less well known today. Nevertheless a historian has recently observed that "his name entered several languages as a near synonym for luxury and comfort, and both here and abroad it became a byword for American business genius."

Although prominent elsewhere, the Pullmans, Lowdens, Carolans, and others of the large family are gone from the river now. Castle Rest is gone as well. Only the powerhouse and some smaller structures were spared demolition. The region might never have developed as it did, however, without the Pullmans, who really initiated the Thousand Islands as an international resort.

Pullman Boathouse

The Iron Bridge to Little Lehigh from Sport Island

This stereopticon view was made prior to remodeling
the cottages in more fashionable Shingle Style.

# Two Grand Country Houses

Important houses extended over some forty-five miles of the St. Lawrence River, from Carleton Villa, near Cape Vincent, New York to Fulford Place, at Brockville, Ontario—and from Nokomis Lodge, on the Bateau Channel to Dark Island, near Chippewa Bay. Between were hundreds of notable properties. Only a sampling can be mentioned here.

There were four major "castles," so-called because of substantial masonry construction and towered forms: Castle Rest (1888), Calumet Castle (1893), Boldt Castle (1900), and Dark Island Castle (1903). Three of these landmarks and their owners have been discussed here; the most famous is the subject of a companion volume by the author, *Boldt Castle: In Search of the Lost Story*. A few more prominent villas may be mentioned more briefly.

## Carleton Villa and the Wyckoffs

Prior to construction of Boldt Castle, the Wyckoff mansion on Carleton Island vied for importance with Castle Rest and Calumet Castle; some thought it to be the most ambitious house on the river. Designed by architect William Miller of Ithaca, it was built in 1894. That was the year following construction of Emery's Calumet Castle, but Haddock in his new book noted, ". . . In point of elegance of design and completeness of finish, [Carleton Villa] is easily first among all the summer palaces on the river. All others, including the celebrated 'Castle Rest' and 'Greystone Villa' must take second place." (The latter was the fine house of H. H. Warner.) A few years later, shortly before Boldt Castle was begun, Carleton Villa was still "one of the most costly and perfectly appointed [houses] on the river, and architecturally is not surpassed even by the wonderful summer palaces at Alexandria Bay." The site of Carleton Villa on Government Point at the head of the island, below the ruins of Fort Haldimand, was enhanced by Revolutionary War history while being favored with prevailing breezes from Lake Ontario and fine black bass fishing in the environs.

While not so much a "castle" in character, Carleton Villa (illustrated on the front cover) did feature an enormous campanile (now gone) and small towers on the corners of the front façade. It had the steep, hipped roofs characteristic of the island castle style. Indeed, the influence on Boldt Castle is evident. In addition to the lofty hall within, previously mentioned, there is a matched pair of huge hipped roofs, steeply pitched, very much like those in the center of Boldt Castle on the main channel side. Boldt Castle also has a turret above its main entrance similar to the small corner towers of Carleton Villa. Construction employed substantial masonry — the lower walls are of masonry faced with Gouverneur marble. The upper walls, in a half-beam Tudor style, are clad in scalloped and diamond-shaped wood shingles. In 1893 Wyckoff acquired about 450 acres, a large portion of Carleton Island. The estate included a "great farm" behind the villa.

It was an amusing but telling paradox that Philo Remington, who was president of the Remington Arms Company, summered modestly in a frame cottage at Thousand Island Park, while his super-salesman, William O. Wyckoff, built this staggering showplace on Carleton Island.

Firearms producers such as Remington were leaders in mass production which spread to other industries after the Civil War. The Remington was the first successful typewriter, having the market to itself for ten years before competitors began production. William O. Wyckoff "believed in the machine from the time he saw the first crude model, and was among the very first to use and sell it. . . . [He] had not only the faith to invest his money in the enterprise at the dawn of its history, in spite of the protests and the ridicule of his friends, but had also that prescience which told him that sooner or later the whole civilized world would want typewriters."

William Osmun Wyckoff (1845-1895) was known familiarly as "Capt. Wyckoff" since he was "a gallant soldier of the late rebellion." He and his two partners in Wyckoff, Seamans & Benedict Co. were sales agents who developed national markets for the Remington Typewriter. Their company acquired the entire enterprise in 1886. Like some other outstanding business achievers of the time such as Bourne and Emery — or of a succeeding generation, like Noble — it was not inventors of new product who built great fortunes so much as imaginative and aggressive marketers of existing products. This was the historical moment when improved transportation and expanding media made national and global markets accessible. Like Frederick Bourne for the Singer sewing machine, William Wyckoff was a leader in building a network of franchised dealers for the Remington typewriter.

William O. Wyckoff enjoyed his grand villa only one season, for he died there in 1895, the year after completion. He had two sons. The elder, Clarence F. Wyckoff, acquired Carleton Villa. His brother, Edward G. Wyckoff, a Syracuse merchant, had another summer home, Edgemore Lodge, nearby on Government Point .

Carleton Villa still stood in 2003, as seen below.  The property had been secured by fences for many decades, to avert vandalism and to protect curious visitors from the the building's hazardous condition.  Rapidly advancing deterioration suggested that Carleton Villa might soon be gone, but to this hopeful architect the basic structure appeared remarkably sound, plumb and square, with little sagging or leaning.  The walls were solidly built.  There might be hope for the place yet.

Carleton Villa

William Miller was architect of the Wyckoff mansion on Carleton Island.  The substantial building survived many decades of neglect.  As shown on the front cover, the upper exterior walls originally were covered with wood shingles applied between the wood "half-timber" members.

Harry Packer built the original cottage on Sport Island in 1879.

## Sport, Little Lehigh, Idlewild Islands
## The Packer-Wilbur-Cummings-Eggleston Families

The story of Sport Island and nearby family islands spans the golden age of the resort. This saga of intertwined clans also conveys the emergence of American industry from primitive beginnings through the age of corporate consolidation. Asa Packer had almost single-handedly built a pioneer railroad, but towards the end of the story, the financier J. P. Morgan wrested control from the family as part of his national consolidation of railroads.

Asa and Sarah Packer's three children, Harry, Bob and Mary Hannah, none of them yet married, first came to the River and Sport Island with their young friends. Harry Packer bought Sport Island in a milestone year. The "Rush of '72" had been triggered by the visit of President Grant's party to Pullman's island. Because the Packers' wealth derived largely from railroads, the family may have become acquainted with the Thousand Islands through George Pullman. Sport Island was close to Summerland, where George□s brother, Rev. James Minton Pullman, built the first cottage.

Harry Packer was a twenty-two year old bachelor when he acquired the island. He had graduated two years earlier from Lehigh University, an institution created by his father, Asa Packer, with a fortune derived from Pennsylvania's Lehigh Valley Railroad. Asa was sixty-six years old when Harry bought Sport Island. The father apparently was grooming younger son Harry for leadership, probably because he seemed more promising than his elder brother, Robert Packer.

After their marriage, Harry brought his bride, Mary Augusta Lockhart ("Gussie") and brother Bob his new wife, Emily Victorine Poillet, to the island. Sister Mary Hannah married one of the island sojourner friends, Charles Cummings. When Sport Island was made comfortable, the siblings brought their mother, Sarah Packer, on their summer visits. Their father, Asa Packer, died just as the new cottage was nearing completion in the spring of 1879.

Sport Island (as the name suggests) originally may have been envisioned as a bachelor's simple fishing camp. Soon it became a large summer home, nucleus of a constellation of family island cottages. Although the Packers traveled from

Sport Island's Main House Before Alteration

Pennsylvania, their railroad extended northwards to Oswego on Lake Ontario. From that port the family could travel by water or could continue in their private railroad cars by connecting rail lines directly to Clayton. There they transferred to their commodious side-wheel steam yacht, the *Sport*, to be conveyed to their island.

If initially intended as a casual holiday retreat, Sport Island never was rustic. Even the first house was elegant. The life style at Sport Island likewise was not simple, since the families brought many servants with them. The crew of the yacht alone numbered seven men.

Young Harry Packer died within a few years, but his family continued to enjoy the island. Brother Bob became the virtual proprietor of the place, planning many improvements. For his own family Bob bought a nearby island which he and Emily renamed "Idlewild." After Bob Packer's death, his widow Emily married banker Richard Henry Eggleston of New York City. Their family enjoyed the very large house on Idlewild. Sister Mary and her husband, Charles H. Cummings, built a charming cottage on Little Lehigh Island, which became part of the complex when connected by an ambitious iron footbridge.

Harry's older brother Bob never succeeded his father and brother as head of the family enterprises. Neither Harry, Bob, nor Mary Packer had children. Their father, Asa Packer, had a trusted young protégé, Elisha Packer Wilbur, his sister's son. E. Packer Wilbur assumed management of the business. In 1889 he took over Sport Island as well.

E. P. Wilbur expanded and remodeled the main house at Sport Island. He and his wife, Stella, in contrast to the Packer siblings, had a very large family — eight sons and one daughter. They came to the river with thirty-eight servants on one occasion, but more regularly the transient staff numbered eighteen, plus a crew of seven for the yacht, bringing the number to twenty-five. The Wilburs employed four more local men to tend the grounds. Furthermore they retained two local fishing guides. The family of eleven and many guests — making about twenty normally at the table — were served by more than thirty people. In 1888 E. P. Wilbur launched a campaign of Sport Island improvements to facilitate operation of what was much like a private hotel and restaurant.

Sport Island and Little Lehigh, remodeled twelve years later in the same style, now represent the taste of the late 1880s and 'nineties — the Shingle Style that is so characteristic of the Thousand Islands.

Little Lehigh Island and the Iron Bridge

One of the loveliest views recorded by A.J. McIntyre, the famous Thousand Islands photographer, was taken from the cupola of the main house on Sport Island, viewing the original cottage of Packer heiress, Mary Packer Cummings. The cottage, a fine example of the Stick Style of the 1870s, subsequently was remodeled in a more fashionable Shingle Style.

This work was done at the same time Castle Rest was being built. 1888 was a very good year for island architecture, as the Jacob Hays house at the head of Round Island and H.H. Warner's fine villa, Stony Crest on Jewel Island, were built at the same time. Although an architect for the Sport Island work is not known, James Ellis of Alexandria Bay was architect and contractor for the Little Lehigh remodeling.

As a childless widow Mary Packer Cummings, the sole Packer heiress, devoted herself to philanthropy until her death in 1912. Little Lehigh Island passed to Col. Rollin H. Wilbur, second son of E. P. Wilbur. "Rollie" and his wife "Nannie" had one daughter, Dorothy. Her son, Richard R. Macsherry married Mary Hammond, daughter of J. Sidney and Jean Chapman Hammond of the Ledges. Jean Chapman's family had Sylvan Island. The Macsherrys, who live on a mainland point at Goose Bay, are benefactors of the Macsherry Library at Alexandria Bay.

The main house at Sport Island as remodeled by E. P. Wilbur

Idlewild

Idlewild was known for tennis. Matches on its court attracted prominent ob-servers and became social events. Richard H. Eggleston, Jr. ("Dick") was profi-cient, as was his half-sister, Sarah Packer, who had been adopted by Emily and Robert Packer before his death and Emily's subsequent remarriage to Richard Eggleston. Young Dick Eggleston married Helen Rafferty of Isle Imperial. They lived at Bonnie Castle, which her father, Gilbert Rafferty, had acquired from the Holland family and remodeled in newly fashionable Georgian style.

Robert Wilbur, one of E. P. Wilbur's sons, acquired Sylvan Island, Jean Chapman Hammond's family summer home. Another son, Col. Harry Packer Wilbur, bought Canadian Reveille Island in 1926. His son, E. Packer Wilbur III ("Packer") and his wife Elisabeth enjoyed Reveille until Packer's death in 1991.

Sport Island and the families associated with it have been well documented over the years with many photographs as well as guest books, ledgers, and other records. The Packers commissioned the local photographer McIntyre on many occasions. Especially remarkable is an album of one of the maids which records life of the staff. Since Wilburs remained on the river until recent years, and since others of the family are with us still, the information conveyed by personal ac-counts is considerable, supplementing newspaper accounts of this prominent family's comings and goings. The amount of material suggests a separate vol-ume devoted to these islands, their related families, houses, boats, and lifestyle.

# Thousand Islands Summer Homes

Belle Isle
The view from the verandah of the grand Peacock House encompassed
Boldt Castle, in the farthest distance, and Isle Imperial. The square
stone tower of the Rafferty house appears at the right.

The "castles" and other grand country houses of the Thousand Islands may be
the most prominent individual landmarks. Collectively, however, colonies of
smaller cottages are equally characteristic and distinctive. The prosperity that
created great wealth for some islanders also enabled the middle class to acquire
second homes, facilitated by new railroad access to the river and steamboat
service to island communities.

There is something of a Thousand Islands style, due in part to the relation of
buildings to the water and to rocky, wooded sites. Because the resort developed
during the half century between 1870 and 1920, styles of this period seem characteristic.

Cottage styles varied not merely because tastes changed but also because "the plans are designed by architects wherever the visitor happens to reside" during the rest of the year. Prominent architects of New York City, Philadelphia, Chicago and Montreal were represented, as well as many from other cities of the United States and Canada. There were capable local architects, while native builders did some interesting work, sometimes adapting stock plans but often inventing new forms. Seth Pope and Joseph Reid were prominent contractors.

The typical early cottage at Thousand Island Park was T-shape in plan, with "piazzas" running around three sides of a parlor that projected towards the street. On three sides French doors provided cross ventilation. The piazzas were not porches, as many have become, after being enclosed by railings and screens. Originally the piazzas were more like low terraces (or modern decks).

The hundreds of cottages at Thousand Island Park evidence remarkable variation, particularly of the elaborate "gingerbread" details, no two cottages being identical. Much of the complicated wood detail for these fanciful buildings was milled by Strough's lumberyard at Clayton, which by 1883 had "built up a nice trade" for these products. The firm became Strough and Brooks, with John W. Williams as "architect and supervising foreman on all their job work outside."

Early buildings generally reflected the Eastlake or Stick Style, as we know the mode today, but an 1882 article referred a "Newport cottage," presumably because similar houses were popular at that fashionable resort. Holland's original Bonnie-Castle was a model of Stick Style or Eastlake design.

Early Thousand Island Park Cottages

Thousand Island Park is a veritable museum of "gingerbread" cottages of the period. In 1883 "the growing taste for harmonious combinations of colors gives the park residences an air of neatness and comfort, besides which the white dwellings look cold and uninviting."

Bonnie-Castle

Towards the end of the 1880s taste turned from flatter surfaces with linear banding, hallmarks of the Stick Style as seen at Bonnie Castle or the Iron Cottage at Thousand Island Park. Builders adopted more sculptural masses of the Shingle Style. This mode also favored natural materials intended to become more integrated into the surroundings. "There is a new fashion in cottages," a river commentator observed. "Instead of painting them in bright colors, the latest and most elegant are left unpainted to take on the soft grays of age, and so blending more perfectly with the landscape. It is a marked contrast with the fashion of the past [which was] to make the cottage as conspicuous as possible. In some cases the painted roofs have been torn off to be replaced by unpainted shingles which are encouraged to take tints and moss and look old and respectable." Bonnie-Castle and Castle Rest both retained natural setting, restoring original landscaping.

The taste of the late 1880s produced some of the region's finest buildings such as the Hays and Van Wagenen Houses, both at the head of Round Island, as well as Pullman's landmark Castle Rest. That fashion was short lived, however, for soon the 1894 Chicago World's Fair, "the Great White City," popularized Classical motifs and sold countless gallons of white paint. Peacock's Belle Isle villa (1902), with its monumental portico (like that of the grand Frontenac Hotel) represented the newer style, as did, at a smaller scale, the Holden Library at Thousand Island Park.

Colonial Revivalism began in New England about the time of the national centennial of 1876, but was a minor stream of style that gradually became more widely popular, merging with Classical Revivalism and love of white paint. The gambrel roof, a familiar barn shape identified with Dutch colonial models, became fashionable at the turn of the century. The gambrel roof appeared on islands such as Long Rock, Sylvan, and Hadassah, as well as most prominently on the grand Frontenac Hotel.

Towards the end of the Golden Age, prior to World War I, some cottages were built in a free style, often influenced by the Craftsman or Bungalow mode. The fine Frazer summer home at the head of Cherry Island was one of the last of the important houses to be built during this period. Several local architects contributed many buildings to the region's remarkable collection, among them G. Cook, John Griffen, and Frank Lent. Williams & Johnson of Ogdensburg, designed some fine villas in Chippewa Bay and Belora on Cherry Island. John D. Williams of Clayton's Strough & Brooks Lumber Yard planned many cottages.

Hadassah (Sunnyside) Island. H. J. Hardenbergh Architect

Nelfred, summer home of Frederick and Nellie Frazer, head of Cherry Island

Several new island villas have appeared recently that reflect models built a hundred years earlier. Sculptural forms, steep roofs, towers, and shingle siding are features often employed. This modern Shingle Style idiom seems congenial, resonating with the regional tradition.

Boathouses contribute to the distinctive Thousand Islands landscape, as do gazebos and other follies. The tower became a striking motif, whether engaged to the building or detached. The feature derived less from the romantic notion of the castle than from utility. Before the days of electricity, water would be periodically pumped by a coal-fired steam engine to the high tank, where it could be drawn by gravity without operating the pump. On some islands with smaller cottages, pumping was done by hand. Once a day someone would have the tiresome task of pumping at length to refill the high tank.

Electricity did not become available until the end of the nineteenth century. Grand establishments like Castle Rest, Calumet and Boldt Castles, and Dark Island had their own powerhouses, generating electricity by coal-fired steam engines before the mainland villages had electric power. Cottages usually relied on kerosene lanterns and stoves, but some produced acetylene gas, or a gasoline generator made electricity. Some of these systems have been used on more remote islands until recent times. Underwater cables now provide most islands with electricity. Electric water pumps have obviated the need for tall water towers, although they remain a romantic feature of some new homes.

The pump house became a feature of many islands, often as a whimsical small structure at the water's edge. Pumps were noisy, so the building might be fairly remote from the main house — sometimes, as at Basswood Island, it was even situated off shore, reached by a causeway or bridge. Icehouses were common before the advent of electric refrigeration. Delivery of ice to remote islands was a nuisance, so ice cut from the river often was kept through the summer in small, well-insulated buildings or buried in sawdust.

Sewage? Don't ask. Obstreperous Gilbert Rafferty sued the village of Alexandria Bay after purchasing Bonnie Castle when he discovered the place was downstream from the village sewage outlet. Only in more modern times has the local organization, Save the River, prevailed upon most islanders to cease dumping into the river.

Residence of Jim and Peggy Pontious, a new house at Zenda Farms, Grater Architects, Clayton

For their recently-built summer home on Arcadia Island, Mike and Julie Chavoustie began with a stock traditional plan, adapting it with their local builder, Gary Piche.

The verandah has always been a basic component of the summer cottage — even castles had them, except for Dark Island's, where the architect apparently prevailed, probably arguing that medieval castles didn't have porches. Verandahs were veritable open-air living rooms, frequently much broader than we think typical for a "porch." Usually owners furnished them with carpets (often oriental), and potted palms, as well as wicker tables and chairs. Roll-down awnings might shelter one direction or another from rain or sun. Cottagers didn't dine outdoors, however. Eating was taken seriously, invariably done in the formal dining room, attended by servants.

Even middle-class families often had one or several servants. It was common to engage a cook in the days of wood stoves, when summer food preparation could be unpleasant, with heat adding to the work of carrying fuel in and ashes out, as well as bringing in large chunks of ice from the icehouse.

Islanders feared fire on their remote islands, with concern especially for sparks from the stacks of passing steamboats igniting dry, wooden shingle roofs. With prosperity towards the turn of the century, some islanders built summer homes of fire-resistant construction, but cost deterred most island residents, who lived constantly with the threat to their fool's paradise.

Playrooms were often located over boathouses, but large villas frequently had billiard rooms in the main house. The loft of a large boathouse might become a ballroom, as at Ina Island, or it could be used to house yacht crew or male servants, since female servants might have bedrooms on the third floor of the main house, and separation was considered proper.

A complete island establishment might have as many as nine or more buildings: main house, boathouses, icehouse, powerhouse, pump house, water tower, laundry and perhaps some guest cottages or detached servant quarters—to say nothing of gazebos, docks, and bridges to maintain. These ambitious properties provided much employment locally. It was common to retain from twenty to forty people to run a major country house. Because boats are such high-maintenance follies, the payroll for a Thousand Islands operation was probably greater than for most country places.

### Some Sport Island Staff

Eight housemaids are joined by the captain, engineer, and three sailors from the yacht *Sport* and two other men, one perhaps the butler. One sailor holds another by the hair while a maid offers him a flower.

Fishing attracted sportsmen before
the Civil War. Even in the nineteenth
century they complained that fishing
"isn't what it used to be." We still hear
this, but guides continue to take parties
out to favored fishing grounds. Fish
are still caught--even big Muskies, as
we see here.

Illustration byHoward Pyle
*Scribner's Monthly*, April 1878

PART III

# Thousand Islands Life
## A Summer Colony Develops

Back in the 1840s, when the overland stage trip from Utica was difficult, access to the Thousand Islands was most comfortable by steamboat. The water trip was lengthy, however. One might travel the Erie Canal to Oswego, then take a larger steamboat such as the *Cataract* from that port to Alexandria Bay. The railroad extended as far as Oswego by 1848. Legislators who enjoyed a lengthy summer recess had time for leisurely fishing outings on the distant St. Lawrence River, and the earliest summer visitors were largely politicians.

New York State Governor Silas Wright, who lived in nearby Canton, became an influential U. S. Senator and major figure in Washington. He was the magnetic nucleus of the fishing cohort. Wright attracted President Martin Van Buren and New York State Governor William Seward of Auburn, together with a group of regulars whose names were more familiar a century and a half ago than now. It was said, ". . . If a list had been kept of the names of visitors, it would have embraced nearly all the prominent statesmen during the administrations of Jackson, Van Buren, Polk and Buchanan."

The unofficial chaplain for the politicos was the Rev. George W. Bethune, who first came in 1846 all the way from the Hudson Valley, and in 1851 was instrumental in establishing the Church of the Thousand Islands at Alexandria Bay.

Azariah Walton, the great island landowner and Alexandria Bay merchant, served as an unofficial host, conducting a rustic salon in his general store where fishermen gathered to hear his stories and exchange tall tales. Charles Crossmon was the more literal host for many. He took over his father-in-law's Alexandria Bay tavern in 1848. Crossmon offered ten rooms for visitors, gradually expanding his facilities through the latter half of the century until his Crossmon House became one of the grand hotels of the river.

Walton and a partner, Parsons, had acquired title to most of the islands in 1846. The smaller were poorly suited for agriculture, so they were valued mostly for timber cut during the winter. Hauled over the ice, it served the following season as fuel for passing steamboats as well as for barrel staves. In 1852, as Walton was elderly, he took on young Andrew Cornwall as a partner. Timber on many of the islands had been cut, but fishermen found the region attractive, so the partners began offering islands for sale as summer cottage sites. Walton died in 1855, and Cornwall acquired title to the islands. He carried on the business, becoming one of the major figures in development of the resort.

The railroad arrived in 1852, providing much faster access to the Thousand Islands. Its first terminus on the river was at Cape Vincent, from whence steamboats carried vacationers to Alexandria Bay. Clayton at the time was largely a commercial port, prosperous from ship building and timber trade. Timber rafts made here were sent down to Montreal. Stephen Decatur Johnson began hotel keeping at Clayton in 1849, the year after Crossmon began at Alexandria Bay. There had been earlier inns in this commercial town, however. Moffatt's Inn became the Hubbard House in 1850. Although Clayton was never so exclusively a resort town as Alexandria Bay, fishermen began to stay here after the railroad arrived. Clayton had the advantage of being closer to the Cape Vincent terminus than the Bay. By 1868 fishing guides ("oarsmen") were serving visitors at the Hubbard House.

There was not much of a market for real estate during the Civil War, however — particularly for recreational use. Many tourists avoided the St. Lawrence during the war years for fear of Confederate agents crossing from Canada. Local author John Haddock related the "Mystery of Maple Island," possibly an 1865 refuge a member of the ring of Lincoln's assassins. Some Civil War deserters fled to Canada. Canadian sympathy for the South antagonized many on the US side. Nevertheless "crowds of sportsmen and pleasure seekers" were coming even during the war years.

"In the early days tents were to be seen on every suitable island or point of the mainland on both sides of the American channel from Clayton to Alexandria Bay," according to a late nineteenth-century account. "Then little by little the tents were replaced by wooden cottages and later still, in many cases, by stone palaces."

The oldest island summer cottage, according to some accounts, was built about 1850 by Seth Green of Rochester, the famed fish expert mentioned elsewhere. Green bought Manhattan Island below Alexandria Bay and built a cottage on it, which still stands. Green sold the property to Judge Spencer in 1868. Cornwall and Walton were selling small islands like Occident and Orient, near Fisher's Landing, for $5 each in 1862. By 1864, when Pullman acquired his island, the price was $25, but in 1864 Capt. James A. Taylor bought large Hemlock Island for "$100 cash and trade." Harry Packer purchased Sport Island for $100 in 1872 but other islands (perhaps to less affluent customers) were sold for forty and fifty dollars apiece. According to one report, "in 1871 there was not a cottage . . . that could be call habitable," but clearly as we see Seth Green's cottage today it had been more than merely habitable, so this comment is suspect (although the original building was "restored" by Judge Spencer in 1868). By another account there were in 1872 "perhaps a half-dozen" island cottages, probably including Rev. Rockwell's on Cherry Island (where there was "a small, rough cottage, irregularly occupied by camping parties as early as 1860"). Also early were the cottages of Henry Spicer, Fernbank, on Hemlock Island, of Dr. Whedon on Round Island, and Henry Heath's first cottage on Nobby Island, built in 1872. That was the same year that Pullman built a better house on his island, in addition to the "comfortable old building at the water's edge." But Eugene Robinson's house on Pine Island, built in 1874, was said to be the fourth island cottage, which seems dubious. Regardless of the number, or which were the earliest, there were few summer homes on the river prior to the boom, beginning with the much-publicized events and consequent "Rush" of 1872.

Early cottages on the green at Thousand Island Park

There had been farmhouses on larger islands, however, and visitors' early notice of summer cottages generally overlooked these residents. The first house on Round Island, for instance, was not Dr. Whedon's summer home, but a cabin built by the local owner of the island, now incorporated into the cottage of Volker Wiess.

Early buildings were frequently moved, "like checkers" usually during winter when they could be skidded over ice. The earlier Hart House was relocated from Heart Island to Wellesley Island, and another portion of the Boldt's frame house sent to another site to become Wellesley House.

Andrew Cornwall was not merely an astute businessman but was visionary, foreseeing the potential for the Thousand Islands to become a great resort. He offered the islands for sale at attractive prices but stipulated that a building be built within a short time — in the case of Sport Island one costing at least $400, or four times the price of the island. Cornwall gave the prime property on the Alexandria Bay waterfront for construction of the Thousand Islands House, recognizing that the grand hotel would enhance the appeal of the region.

The "Rush of '72" was followed the next season by connection of rail service to Clayton. This contributed to the influx of visitors and the sudden appearance of grand hotels to accommodate them. The Crossmon House at Alexandria Bay was enlarged for the second time and the magnificent Thousand Islands House appeared, becoming a dominant landmark on the shoreline of Alexandria Bay. New steamboats soon were built expressly for the tourist excursion trade and to serve rapidly developing island communities, many of which sprouted large hotels. Thousand Island Park was planned in 1875. By 1887 at the height of the season some sixty coaches and two to three thousand people arrived by train daily at Clayton.

Cornwall's vision was fulfilled. After the Civil War, due to "wealth accumulated at home while soldiers were fighting . . . there was a decided movement toward beautifying the Thousand Islands Archipelago." By the late 1880s there were some ten thousand summer residents on the river.

A landmark hotel, said to be "Byzantine" in style, opened 1883 at Thousand Island Park. Ominously, the Hub House on a nearby island burned that year. Seven years later the much larger Thousand Island Park House and other buildings burned to the ground with loss of one life. A Rochester newspaper observed that the disaster was no surprise, since the huge wooden hotel building was "admirably adapted to make a magnificent bonfire." The report noted that it was a "little less than miraculous that a score or more of people were not killed. . . . The conditions seemed perfect for a terrible holocaust." The article reported that some men, staying up late playing cards, first became aware of the fire and spread the alarm. The article concluded that other hotel guests "should present the three young men at least with a new pack of cards."

The First Thousand Island Park Hotel

But the fools rebuilt their paradise. The following year fifty-three cottages rose at Thousand Island Park. The grand new Columbian Hotel opened in 1894. That one lasted eight years. When it burned, it took much of Thousand Island Park—the New York State Institute, three large boarding houses and another fifty or so cottages—with it. But fools will be fools. Immediately an architect was commissioned to prepare drawings for a third hotel, this one to be built of concrete so as to be fireproof. That never happened. Storm clouds were brewing in Europe and soon the First World War ended the fools' paradise.

## Recollections of a Golden Afternoon

Julie stressed that this was once a New York City resort. "Yes, there were people from Chicago, Pittsburgh, and other places," she recalled, "but the New York crowd was the main show. I was a provincial girl, from Watertown, far Upstate.

Belle Isle with Yacht *Irene*

"None of the New Yorkers had ever heard of Watertown. Nowadays they've never heard of the Thousand Islands. Back then, you'd recognize lots of faces from the river at the Waldorf, or driving in Central Park, or at the New York Yacht Club. That's hard to believe now. Everything has changed so much."

I ventured that there must have been fine restaurants, elegant shops . . . just like New York. "Oh, don't think we were terribly sophisticated. That set went to the Adirondacks or Bar Harbor, or such places, I suppose. We were merely rich—not me, of course. The folks I knew here were largely a rough-and-tumble crowd. Sig Stern—he was a New York wholesale diamond dealer, someone you might expect to be sophisticated—well, he went after Herb Hutchinson, the boat builder at the Bay—I mean, really attacked him. Herb had Sig arrested for assault. It wasn't a matter of merely throwing a punch; Sig did that, but then took after Herb with a knife."

"What was that all about?"

"I don't recall, exactly. Something about a boat, no doubt. Hutchinson was the big boat builder at the Bay. People tend to be emotional about boats, you know. But Herb won in court and got a big settlement."

"Where was the Stern place?"

"That was Devaloka Lodge, one of the big Wellesley Island houses on the Main Channel. Hutchinson had another run-in more recently, I've heard, over that crazy boat, the *Pardon Me*. It's for sale now, if you want to buy it."

"What kind of boat?"

"One of a kind—that's the problem. Like the Purple Cow—one's too many. As I hear the story, Charlie Lyons had the thing built to his specifications, making it the world's largest and fastest runabout. Actually, until you get close to it you'd think it merely a runabout. But it's huge, propelled by two engines, one of them designed for a PT boat—1800 horse power. He wanted a big, fast boat."

"What was the problem? Wasn't it fast enough?"

"I expect Charlie could zip over from Oak Island—that's in Chippewa Bay— to Kingston for lunch in a half hour, it was so fast. The problem was the fuel. He'd have to keep refueling the damn thing—with 100-octane aviation fuel—to keep it going any distance. It burns 150 gallons an hour. Totally impractical. And he paid $50,000 it. That would take care of me the rest of my days."

"So he was unhappy with the boat?

"Never really used it. Blamed Hutchinson, the builder, but actually it was designed by Hacker. I can't imagine what Charlie's complaint was. Folks down his way regard him as a playboy, saying he never worked a day in his life. He had a string of fast boats. There was *Vamoose I* that burned and then its successor, *Vamoose II*, both also Hacker designs, built at the Bay—but the latter had merely a 250 horsepower engine that would go forty-five miles per hour—not 1800 horse power!

"And speaking of characters and Chippewa Bay, there was the time that Sid Quarrier was coming home to Scow Island—from a party, I suppose, bringing his mother. Approaching that big boathouse, intending to slow down, rather than going into reverse he carelessly increased speed forward. His famous cry, much quoted for years afterwards, was, "Hang on, Mother. We're going through!"

"He went all the way through, breaking out the other end?"

"That's the story—mostly remembered for that great line."

"I thought the Posts were at Scow Island."

"They were, but sold it to the Quarriers—who were not newcomers either. They had been at Chippewa Bay since the 1880s. Sid, the careless skipper, was an All-American football hero." She laughed. "He didn't go to parties *before* games, apparently.

"People were here to have a good time, you know. There were some, like Mrs. Post, who put on airs and never relaxed, but you found that mostly among the New Rich. They were often insecure, you see—uncertain about how to behave with their money. The old families generally were more casual—more genuine. There was a lot of silliness at Rum Point, where the families around the head of Grindstone got together regularly. Men playing baseball in drag—that sort of thing. Mrs. Post would not approve!

Baseball at Rum Point
William Fellowes Morgan, Jr. and John Walter Wood

Rum Point Tennis

"Those folks didn't require big yachts, like Mrs. Post with her *Karma*. The Grindstoners cared more for their sailing skiffs—that was their style."

"But they had as much money?"

"How would I know? Chris Wolfe, who was one of that gang, was said to be one of the wealthiest men on the river—a multi-millionaire. But he was just an architect, I think—probably inherited family money. He built a house on Coral, which he renamed Whisky Island. That tells you something.

"The Kips over on the Canadian side of Grindstone were another wealthy New York family that was old—not merely Old Money, but Old Family—Dutch New York. They had a big mansion at West Orange, New Jersey and a splendid place at the head of Leak Island. It was unusual for the river, being built of logs. No fancy castles for the Kips. They were very different from the Boldts. Ira Kip was a stockbroker. He gave his island for use as a hospital and service camp during the First World War. It burned shortly thereafter. Leak Island is called "Thwartway" now. There was another Kip—Charles Hayden Kip, who had Kip Island, down by the Bay.

"I've mentioned the Hays, at the head of Round Island. Although not Dutch, they were also an old New York family. An earlier Jacob Hays was High Constable of New York City, at the beginning of the nineteenth century. The

Hasbroucks, on Manhattan and Huguenot Islands, were old New York families, I believe, and some wives, such as Emma Keeler Bourne and Sara Kierstede Hudson, as I mentioned, brought some family gentility to New Rich husbands. In the main, however, we were not patrician — just rich (excluding me, of course)."

Stylish Anglers

The Bensons evidence fashionable taste in fishing attire.
Their guide however is without hat, coat, or tie.

# Heyday

The Golden Age — the "first" Golden Age, we hope — of the Thousand Islands lasted for about a half century, roughly the period between the Civil War and the First World War. The flowering of this resort, like most others, was possible because of larger conditions. An emerging middle class, social mobility, economic prosperity, and the Great Bull Market at the turn of the twentieth century were factors. As the saying goes, the "rising tide raises all boats." Many Americans moved from the expanding middle class upwards, becoming the New Rich.

Improved transportation — first by steamboats on the Great Lakes and St. Lawrence, and then railroads — was another factor. The next major transportation changes, with advent of the automobile and air travel, were in turn factors in the decline of the resort, which became paradoxically less accessible to urban populations.

Benefits from resort development were not merely economic but also social. Boosters of the summer colony foresaw the quality of a more communal life here. Landowner Andrew Cornwall had the most to gain financially and was astute in encouraging improvements. But publicity provided by cottager George Pullman triggered major development. Probably concurrence of his entertainment of the presidential party in 1872 with entertainment of newspaper editors was not mere coincidence, nor the "Rush" of that year a total surprise. Cornwall sprung into action, immediately offering land for construction of the grand Thousand Islands House.

Some twenty years later, a group of cottagers at Alexandria Bay rallied interest in establishing a yacht club as a social center for the summer colony. They recruited George and Louise Boldt to become members of the community, inducing them to acquire Hart Island and take a stake in the new Thousand Islands Yacht Club. Boldt became of one the greatest promoters of the resort. Probably the neighbors who first recruited him were aware of his extensive social connections through his elite Waldorf-Astoria Hotel in New York City. Boldt had a rival up at Clayton, Charles Emery, who was motivated to have that sector of the river vie with Alexandria Bay. Emery invested heavily in development here, such as the grand Frontenac Hotel, and promoted the region in national publications. There were many other boosters of the place, some having business interests here, such as tour boat operators like Capt. Visger, others like George Rockwell or Frank Taylor merely being personal enthusiasts who wanted to share the good news with others.

The ascendancy of the resort peaked at the turn of the century, when Boldt Castle was rising. It had crested by 1904, when Louise Boldt died and construction ceased at Heart Island. Conditions were changing. The Great Bull Market was over; optimism was less boundless. Bourne began his "castle" before Louise Boldt died. But Charles Emery closed Calumet Castle after the death of his wife. No more colossal trophy houses would be built, and no more grand hotels. In 1910 the Towns of Clayton and Orleans enacted local prohibition laws. Without income from bars, hotels found the short season marginally profitable. There was grave concern that the large Murray Hill Hotel and even the great Frontenac would close. But the opulent way of life continued for about another decade. The end was announced in 1911.

"That's the end of it." Midnight, August 23, 1911

At the time sixteen trains a day continued to arrive at the Clayton terminus. In June one of the Yacht Club trains came with eleven cars, all filled. But following local prohibition, the Manatauk and Murray Hill Hotels near Clayton were closed. That summer at least ten cottages burned and, at the height of the season, while George Boldt's stables were on fire, the grand Frontenac Hotel burned to the ground. The flames from the spectacular fire were seen even on the north side of Grindstone Island where Dick McRae commented, "That's the end of it. The Bay is finished and so is Clayton." As if to confirm his premonition, the next summer the big Columbian Hotel at Thousand Island Park burned, taking much of the Park along with it. It had been, as Julie, observed, "a fools' paradise."

Capt. Visger noted that after these events "all large excursion steamers were withdrawn" and water traffic decreased about fifty per cent. Towards the end of the next summer, when the 1913 social season culminated with the usual gala events, there was a mock "funeral" at the Thousand Islands Yacht Club. The *PDQ IV* rested like a coffin in banks of flowers within the club hall. The boat had failed to win the Gold Cup that summer, and so after nine years the trophy and the annual Gold Cup races left the St. Lawrence River.

Then came World War I. The great steam yachts vanished, many going to serve the Navy during the war when all private boats were "subject to call of the national government for war purposes." Lightning struck and fire demolished the Frontenac annex in 1917, but its contents had been sold previously. Even by

1916 islanders already were looking back to "the days when the Islands were at their height as a summer resort." The years 1915-1920 were severely depressed here, not merely because of the war but because of loss of prestigious facilities and because of local ineptness, depressing business by enacting town prohibition laws—by some of the same people who had rejected Emery's five offers to improve the Clayton waterfront and business district.

The world had changed after the First World War. With better roads automobile use increased while railroad transportation declined. Tourist cabins supplanted grand hotels. Still, many families continued to return to island summer homes during the twenties, when E. J. Noble and A. G. Miles, Boldt's son-in-law, built the new Thousand Islands Club on Wellesley Island to supplement the Yacht Club. Smaller motor yachts replaced the big steam yachts. But the stock market crash in 1929 was another dire event. The next two decades were the low point of the resort during the Great Depression followed by World War II when gas rationing and shortage of help made big summer homes impractical or obsolete. These were the decades when I first knew the Thousand Islands, the years of my conversations with Julia Bingham Hass.

Thousand Islands Yacht Club, Mock Funeral, *PDQ IV*, 1913

The Peacocks Party Aboard the *Irene*

# Pastimes of a Gilded Age

## A Half-Century of Thousand Islands Life, 1870-1920

Fishing was the first occupation of early visitors, but boating became a mania during the five decades that were the halcyon days of the resort. There were not merely the three major yacht clubs, the Thousand Islands, Chippewa Bay, and Frontenac organizations, but there were ten other yacht clubs plus eleven boat clubs. Boats were everywhere, then as now.

During these four decades boating changed dramatically. Conventions of the American Canoe Association had attracted thousands at the end of the nineteenth century. "Where are the canoes?" asked an article in 1911, which continued, "A few years ago the river was dotted with canoes. Now scarcely one is seen between Clayton and Alexandria Bay." Another item that same year urged enacting a law to muffle noisy motor boats, noting that "as early as 5 A.M. one is wakened by the burst of explosions." In 1915 it was reported that "formerly sailboats were a familiar sight on the St. Lawrence, but the motorboat has completely ousted the sloop of bygone days. One man still stands by the sailing craft, Dr. J. H. Dower of Syracuse and Thousand Island Park." Houseboats became a craze in the 1890s. Introduced to the river by the Clarks of Comfort Island, soon the Deweys, Emerys, Nichols and Oliphants also acquired them. Houseboats were especially popular with the ladies, six women acquiring them as well as many other men. Some were for charter. Probably about thirty houseboats, several more than a hundred feet long, floated on the river at the turn of the century. Although Boldt's *La Duchesse* is often thought to have been the largest, in fact Samuel Maxwell's *Pamela* was larger, as noted in the appendix about houseboats.

During the 1890s, when Victorian propriety began to relax, athletic activities became more popular, for women as well as men. Archery and croquet were popular, the latter often played late into the night, illuminated by lanterns. One of the attractions of croquet was its requirement of shorter skirts of the young ladies. At the Thousand Islands, as elsewhere in America at the time, baseball was the most popular team sport. Teams representing most island resort communities competed fiercely in an Inter-River League. The games were reported regularly for a decade or so in newspapers of distant cities such as Syracuse. James K. Hackett of Zenda Farm, a famous actor of the time, was an ardent amateur baseball player.

Golf was introduced in the 1890s and tennis, appearing in the previous decade, became widely popular. Thousand Island Park provided an early tennis court in 1883. At first "Lawn tennis, . . .that popular society game," was played on grass courts at Idlewild Island and elsewhere, but enthusiasts such as Clover Boldt and Marjorie Bourne soon had faster clay courts on their properties. Given leisurely summers, some islanders became proficient athletes. Harold Hayden of Fairyland was considered a tennis expert, but he had serious competition from other young men on the river.

Central (St. Lawrence) Park had an early golf course in 1899. Edgewood and Westminster Park had courses by 1913, when Thousand Island Park was planning a new course. Few islands were suited to that rage of the nineties, the bicycle, while mainland roads were abominable, but readers were advised by an article, "Where to Wheel on the St. Lawrence"—quite a trick. By 1896 "a person who does not ride is a curiosity." The Boldts built many miles of good roads on

Wellesley Island, but more for their carriages and pony carts, and especially for the subsequent rage, motorcars. As noted at the time, "This was the heyday of the automobile, socially speaking."

A few Islanders took to air, experimenting with novel airplanes. The Aero Club, comprised of aviator members of the Thousand Islands Yacht Club, in 1910 had its own innovative Brigham Biplane, designed by Dr. Miles Gibbons of St. Lawrence Park and made by Brigham in Syracuse, and another built at Lloyd Boat Works, Morristown. The first weighed only 180 pounds (with an aluminum motor). The Aero Club used the farm field of Benjamin Petrie outside Alexandria Bay and the Boldts' Wellesley Island golf links as landing fields for trial flights. Jack Vilas, that "fearless aviator" who "created a sensation" in 1917 by easily winning the race between his "aeroplane"and a fast motorboat, was also "a daring motorboat enthusiast."

Many islanders were horse people. Nathan Straus leased the Edgewood track for his racehorses. The Boldts introduced polo to the river in 1913 and had a large stable, including many fine polo ponies. The Devines also kept polo horses on their Canadian mainland farm. Grant Peacock recalled that his family brought their stableman from Pittsburgh to tend their riding horses on Wellesley Island.

Hunting, especially duck shooting in the fall, was popular with many, being "almost as favored as fishing" in 1898. One hunting club at Chippewa Bay has been mentioned; another, the Ice Island Shooting Company, owned Canadian Chimney Island, the familiar landmark between Mallorytown Landing and Brown's Bay. The Wilburs of Sport Island were also avid hunters. Duck hunting was both a late fall an early spring activity. This explains why many "summer homes" here had heating systems, as did the Fish and Gunning clubhouse on Oak Island. Boldt also had a shooting blind on an island in the Lake of the Isles. It was connected to the mainland and New York City by a telephone cable.

Many men, including artist Frederic Remington of Ingleneuk Island, were keen on trap shooting, and some women too, not merely as spectators but as participants—Marjorie Bourne was a crack shot and Elsie Vilas competed in meets. The Thousand Islands and Chippewa Bay Yacht Clubs were rivals in trap shoots attended by hundreds of members. S. H. Vandergrift of Long Rock Island awarded a splendid trophy, a silver cup with gold lining the "finest ever offered for any event at the Thousand Islands Yacht Club." Gilbert Rafferty sponsored shoots on his Wellesley Island property, offering prizes to both men and women. If a woman made the highest score, she was awarded both prizes.

The Stylish Hunter
The dog seems bemused by the top hat as a sportsman takes
aim on Crossmon Point, across the bay from Holland's Bonnie Castle.

The Thousand Islands Yacht Club conducted annual golf and tennis tournaments. Charles Hudson of The Ledges gave one trophy cup for golf and Gilbert
Rafferty of Isle Imperial donated the Commodore's Cup, given to the winner of
two golf tournaments, played on the Wellesley Island links, "said to be the longest in the world." A gallery of two hundred or so followed the tournament
games. Royal Vilas of Oswagatchie Point gave the R. C. V. Tennis Challenge
Cup. The Schultz Cup went to the woman who won three times. Dr. Carl
Schultz of Oak Lodge produced "Lithia Water." His daughter, Elsie, was an
avid tennis player. S. H. Vandergrift of Long Rock Island donated the Cherokee
Cup, awarded to the winner of the annual club tennis tournament. The solid
silver trophy stood about twenty inches high and had three handles. The cup
was "one of the handsomest and costliest in the United States." Tennis herea-
bouts was taken seriously.

The club held an annual bench show, a popular event. "Several ribbons were awarded to the dogs from George C. Boldt's kennels." Even the dog show was an excuse for subsequent celebratory and consolation dinner parties. In addition the Aero Club, formed in 1909, the Yacht Club even had a baseball team—not a very good one in competition with other river teams, such as arch rival Thousand Island Park which usually defeated their upscale Wellesley Island neighbors.

Contrary to frequent snide comments by others, club members did actually do some boating—even if mostly the work of captains and crews. The club held an annual regatta. Whereas the initial marine impulse probably was display of costly yachts, shortly after the turn of the century when internal combustion engines were being improved, motorboat speed became an obsession.

By 1904 "some of the fastest powerboats in the world are entered in the races on the St. Lawrence." Five years later it became evident that winning powerboat races was a matter of spending money—more than one's competitors— on state-of-the-art engines. Owners of the fast boats generally didn't even operate them personally. Like owners of racehorses who hire jockeys, proud owners of powerful race boats usually engaged a pilot and engineer to run the tricky and dangerous machines. Some members of the Thousand Islands Yacht Club who appreciated handling skill countered this development by acquired identical racing boats from Joe Leyare of Ogdensburg. He built nineteen of these one-design craft, called "number boats" because they were identified by number. They were V-transomed runabouts, twenty-eight feet long. Each had a thirty-horsepower Jencick three-cylinder, two-cycle engine. Unlike the more competitive race boats, these craft could be used for other purposes. Because their speed was merely moderate, at times mechanics adjusted the engines for more speed, eventually undermining the initial one-design concept.

The number boats were for amateurs, however. The glory days of powerboat racing at the Thousand Island began in 1904, when the *Vingt-Et-Un II*, owned by Willis Sharpe Kilmer of Binghamton, New York won the second race of the American Power Boat Association. Her record speed exceeded twenty-five

*Vingt-et-Un II*

Winning the Gold Cup

The *Dixie II* passes the finish line at Chippewa Bay, 1908

miles an hour in the Gold Cup Race on the Hudson River. The owner, "of turf fame," was well known for his "Kilmer's Swamp Root" medication. When visiting here Kilmer sometimes stayed at the Frontenac Hotel. Because his boat had been sponsored by the Chippewa Bay Yacht Club, the splendid gold trophy came to the Thousand Islands. Consequently the Chippewa Bay club held the Gold Cup Race during the following summer. In 1905 the host club sponsored the *Chip*, owned by J. M. Wainwright of Philadelphia and Ojibway, Chippewa Bay. His boat won three heats decisively at Chippewa Bay, so the trophy stayed on the river. In the following two summers the races were again held at Chippewa Bay and were won by another Wainwright boat, the *Chip II*.

Then in 1908 E. J. Schroeder's *Dixie II* won at Chippewa Bay, passing the Gold Cup to the Thousand Islands Yacht Club, sponsor of the boat. Schroeder, from Bayonne, N. J., stayed at the Thousand Islands House. Schroeder's boat won again the following year at the races held near Alexandria Bay. In 1910 the *Dixie III* won — not owned by Schroeder but by Frederick K. Burnham, a New York City insurance executive who stayed at Boldt's Chalet. The Duke of Westminster entered a boat in that race but instead of taking the cup he gave a cup, to the Thousand Islands Yacht Club, as "a token appreciation for courtesies of many members." To be awarded to the winner of a [one]-design-class race, the gesture was said to be "a slap in the face of [other] fashionable New York City yachtsmen."

Burnham's *Dixie III* was sponsored by the Frontenac Yacht Club, so that club hosted the event the following summer. At the course off Round Island the *MIT II* won. That boat, owned by J. H. Hayden of Fairyland, returned the trophy to the Thousand Islands Yacht Club. The *P.D.Q. II*, owned by George

The *Dixie III* passing the Frontenac Hotel in the Gold Cup Race of 1911

Boldt's son-in-law, Alfred G. Miles, won the 1912 race, so the 1913 Gold Cup races were again hosted by the club. That summer the trophy passed from the river, the races going to Lake George, but the Gold Cup had remained at the Thousand Islands for nine years.

According to an 1897 report, "One form of amusement that has never been popular at this resort has suddenly sprung into marked favor. . . during the past week. . . . Bathing parties have become quite the thing." At the Thousand Island Yacht Club a swimming club was organized in 1904 to conduct races and perform "aquatic feats as a novel part of club entertainment."

Even for sporting events dress was improbably formal. The jacket was "always worn" on the river, exception being made only for the most strenuous warm-weather activities such as baseball. In the privacy of one's own boat "knickerbockers and blue flannel shirt" might be allowed. Either the summers were cooler then, or people suffered for their appearance. Men even wore vests in the summer and after dark the better-dressed man might carry a "light summer overcoat, even on sweltering evenings." Relaxation of formality as the century waned was expressed by more casual attire. "The knit skull caps with the gaudy teasel, which are worn by many of the [Thousand Islands] park people, give them a decidedly youthful appearance, except when some of them forget to put in their false teeth." On the other hand, at the turn of the century men members of the Thousand Islands Yacht Club wore matching navy blue blazers identified with the club burgee, regardless of the temperature. Ladies even golfed in splendor. Mrs. Burton Proctor Smith of New York lost on the golf links her pearl necklace, which had a clasp of diamonds and emeralds.

214

Yachting Party Aboard the Fulford's *Magadoma*

Bowling was a "pastime which is constantly growing in favor at all the River resorts, especially at Frontenac" during the nineties, although the Thousand Islands House had alleys earlier, in the seventies. In later years the Thousand Island House Casino on Staples Island at Alexandria Bay had bowling alleys, but the Frontenac alleys were "the best of any along the river." Ladies as well as gentlemen enjoyed bowling—"no pastime is more enjoyed by the athletic maiden than bowling." Young women didn't participate in greased-pole climbing or tub races, however—popular frolics of the day. Croquet, archery and bicycling were more appropriate for athletic ladies.

Many island establishments had "casinos" or recreation buildings for rainy day amusements. Billiards and ping-pong were commonly played. The Bournes built an indoor squash court. Most common during inclement weather were "little games of euchre and whist" when "mamas get together to discuss the prospective dances of their respective daughters." Card parties were probably the most common entertainment at the Thousand Islands Yacht Club and elsewhere.

Festivals were popular, such as the annual Water Carnivals at Alexandria Bay and the Venetian Carnival at St. Lawrence Park, where participants wore domino costumes and engaged in a "grand confetti battle" under hundreds of electric lights strung among the trees. On one Fourth of July twenty thousand visitors listened to seven brass bands at Alexandria Bay.

American Canoe Association Carnival

Activities of "the smart set" peaked in August, as the season approached its close. The last week of the month was "the week of all weeks on the River," attracting "some of the wealthiest society folk from Newport, Saratoga, and New York." The grand hotels had gala affairs. The final ball of the season at the Thousand Islands Yacht Club, that "Mecca for those that worship at society's shrine," was the climactic event for members. Festively illuminated islands surrounded yachts as they assembled in the bay. "The centerpiece was Senator Fulford's magnificent yacht [*Magadoma*], ablaze in red and white electric lights from waterline to top of masts." Welcome Island and its big clubhouse glittered with lights. An orchestra played on the verandah as members came up the broad steps from the dock, regaled in evening wear. A large reception committee of clubwomen greeted guests in the main hall, the long list of prominent names beginning with Mrs. G. C. Boldt.

The interiors were spectacularly decorated with greenery and floral displays, arrangements supervised personally by George Boldt—"palms, cut flowers, festoons of cedar and evergreen, arranged in various designs." On one wall a tree in bloom was simulated by "limbs covered with dark leaves of oak . . . mingled with white asters." Another wall featured a sixty-foot United States flag. Ceilings "formed a perfect lattice work of cedar, from which were suspended red and white ribbons, the colors of the club." On each table red carnations and asparagus fern formed different emblems, while columns were entwined with smilax, flowers hung from chandeliers overhead, and between them were strung flags of some two hundred yacht clubs. The club orchestra alternated with the Gananoque Band, the latter providing music for "two-steps" while the orchestra played more sedate waltzes. At midnight supper was served in the dining room, concluding what was "always the swellest event of the season on the river."

So what did Julie think of all that, I asked. "Oh, we hardly *thought*," she replied. "We just *felt*, you know—we were too excited, too thrilled to really think about it. Just carried away on a glorious wave of euphoria. It made you feel like a queen—even if you were in borrowed regalia that had to be returned when the clock struck twelve."

"What do you mean?"

"Well, some of us really were mere visitors in this fantasy land. We knew we really weren't part of it—or suspected it couldn't last. It didn't, of course, but in the meantime, for a few good years, as they use to say in the society columns, 'A good time was had by all'."

Shipshape and Yare

The Peacock's Yacht, *Irene*, with the Thousand Islands House in the background

What happened to all those people? They're all gone, of course, remembered merely by fading photographs and some hundred-year-old buildings, and a few boats—and by a few families still on the river.

Their way of life vanished, for the most part. During the mid-1920s, after E. P. Wilbur died, his family gave up Sport Island. Some members moved to less burdensome island properties. One of the last of his generation on the river, Alex Peacock, so aptly named, died in 1927, and his family gave up their grand villa. They reportedly paid $100,000 for the island and 25-room main house, spent $27,000 on the great yacht house, and improved the estate with other buildings and their fifteen-acre Wellesley Island farm. The property was on the market for $150,000. Ed Noble got it for $100, even before the stock market crashed the following year. Noble tore the place down. Grant Peacock provided the family scrapbook with many of the photographs seen here. Fred Beach recorded a delightful interview with Grant, who recalled life here at the turn of the twentieth century. The paper is in the files of the Antique Boat Museum.

A few of the big places, here as elsewhere, were given to institutions. Marjorie Bourne gave Dark Island as well as the huge estate on Long Island to La Salle Academy. The Raffertys gave their properties to the local Catholic church. Very few of the landmark houses remained in original families for long. Hopewell Hall, owned by George Boldt's daughter and then her daughter in turn, was a rare exception. Even that property now has passed from the family.

218

# ADIEU, JULIE

I wondered what Julie remembered most vividly. She had seen Boldt Castle rise. She had partied at the Alster Tower. What was best? She laughed.

"Oh, none of those things. Yes, they were interesting. But what comes back—has never gone, really, and stays with me now when I really can't see out that window the way you do—was the river itself, those entrancing evenings when we would drift by the illuminated islands, Will Hays playing his banjo, and all of us singing. That was pure heaven. The balls, the diamonds, the gorgeous gowns—nothing could compare with just being on the river. You know it's true what they say—about the best things in life being free. . . . I'm lucky to feel that way, don't you think—seeing as how what is left now is what is free, or at least cheap.

Julie

"I can still smell the river, even when the big freighters passing my window are just fuzzy blobs. That aroma, and the sound of distant boats, and the fog horns at night. . . . I still savor those things that I still have.

"I don't miss Boldt Castle or the fancy dress parties. I do miss some of the people, of course. Even that ornery Gilbert Rafferty, but more his dashing sons! And the equally dashing gals—Margie Bourne and Clover Boldt. There was zest to life, when powerboats kept getting faster and faster and the seasons ended with the roar of the Gold Cup Races. Those were the days!

Dark Island

"If it seems like fantasy now, it did even then. I suppose none of us were really surprised that the mirage vanished. There was no way to go on like that, to keep living with such abandon. Such excess. But it was so beautiful while it lasted—so lovely. I hope the memory can be kept alive, to share with others." The way Julie smiled, I imagined her vision was still good enough to see the rapt expression on my face. "You're such a good audience, my young friend."

I told her that I was collecting old books and pictures. Someday, when I was older, I would put them together into a new book, to bring it all back.

She seemed to sniff, as if to be sure the river was still out there, then laughed.

"Do you think they'll believe any of this really happened? I sometimes wonder myself."

*　*　*

*"Looking foolish does the spirit good."*
John Updike

# An Album of Images of Thousand Islands Life

"The Gents"

More Rum Point nonsense from the album of "Sis" Morgan Pruyn Thibault

Belle Isle Verandah

Peacock Girls

Mississauga Hall

Benson Boys

Victorian Bedroom, Castle Rest, c. 1890

Guide and Skiff

The Bensons' guide returns from netting minnows, placed in the barrel at left, carried with his net in a St. Lawrence skiff. The indigenous boat, similar to the Adirondack Guide Boat, is still being made and used in the region.

Edwardian Bedroom, Belle Isle, c. 1910

More Sport Island Staff Nonsense

The Yacht Steward watches as a maid is about to cool off a chicken plucker.

Back Side of Belle Isle, with Peacock and Boldt Yacht houses at left.

Some of the Wilbur staff aboard the *Sport*

226

Front side of Belle Isle, with Peacock Yacht House at right. Boldt's Wellesley House is at left.

Boldt Yacht House Crew

Peacocks' *Damphino*, another of their sixteen fast boats

Library, Fulford Place

Peacocks' *Irene*

Drawing Room, Fulford Place

The Columbian Hotel, Thousand Island Park, burned 1912

Luncheon aboard the Fulfords' *Magadoma*

Pullman House, off Grenell Island

Senator George Fulford (in yachting cap) and friends at Fulford Place

231

Early Thousand Island Park corner, site of future Wellesley Hotel

"Pink Pills" Fulford (with cigar) and friends

Early dock scene, Thousand Island Park, with paddle-wheel ferry, Round Island in distance.

At the Boldt Country Club, Wellesley Island

Interiors of Peacocks' *Irene*

Young Salt
George Frothingham Benson tries to fill his dad's boots.

Frontenac Yacht Club, Round Island

Grand Dame
Mrs. William Thomas Benson, George's grandmother, with her dog

The Swimming Lesson
Sis and Fritzi Pruyn, watched by a concerned Bunny Carter

Afternoon Gathering, Rum Point
The "Kids' Team" includes Carey and Camilla Morgan, third from left and from right.

"Moms Keeps Score"
Emma Leavitt Morgan and friends at Rum Point

Morning Gathering, Rum Point
Hostess Emma Morgan (with racket) and houseguest Ethel Roosevelt (looking down)

Vegetable garden on Peacock Farm, Wellesley Island

Skiffing
Bensons' oarsman takes dad and son for a spin

Garden, Fulford Place

"Intimate" at Rum Point
Tom Blumer, Camilla Morgan, M. S. Barger

Frederic Remington and his canoe

Benson Picnic

Visitors Arrive at Mississauga

Mississauga Bridge

241

A Festive Event

Balloon ascension at the Thousand Island House, Alexandria Bay
A Mathew Brady photograph.

President Arthur at the Crossmon House, 1882
A Mathew Brady photograph.

### Socializing

An elegant afternoon assemblage at the Hollands' Bonnie-Castle.
The Crossmon House at Alexandria Bay appears across water in the distance.
From a stereoscopic view by A. C. McIntyre, Photographer.

Sport Island Maids

### Westminster Park Chapel

Westminster Park was originally a Presbyterian community. This landmark on Mt. Beulah, built in 1891-2, was considered to be "more ornamental than useful—but then, people at Westminster are good enough anyway." The ambitious non-denominational church replaced the earlier Bethune Chapel that blew down in 1885. Although recalled by a whimsically-named "Cathedral Avenue," the second building is now gone as well, as are the original pier and freight house, located on the site of the Boldt Yacht House. A canal that created Mary Island gave ferry access to the new dock at the hotel site on Poplar Bay. New York State acquired Mary Island, originally part of Westminster Park, for use as a public facility.

## A Landmark Villa at Westminster Park

Andrew Cornwall of Alexandria Bay, one of the key promoters of the resort, was the driving force in developing this cottage colony at the foot of Wellesley Island. Following the lead of Thousand Island Park, the community originally was denominational but soon lost its religious tone. With regular ferry service to the Bay, the Westminster Park Hotel became one of the liveliest social centers or the region, where an orchestra played for dancing regularly. Proximity to golf and tennis facilities, as well as to the polo grounds, attracted a steady clientele. Like the hotel, this large summer home has vanished. Westminster Park today is a different sort of place—a small, quiet neighborhood where some residents live year-round.

Dining Room, Thousand Islands Yacht Club

Thousand Islands Yacht Club, Welcome Island

Estelle Savin Boldt

Probably the event that marked the social high point in the history of the Thousand Islands Yacht Club was George Boldt's 1906 reception to introduce his new daughter-in-law to the community. Estelle Savin Boldt was considered a glamorous beauty, rather exotic because she was Mexican.

Hall, Thousand Islands Yacht Club

Canvas stretched over a metal frame formed the skiff shelter at Belle Isle. The billiard room shown on the facing page was in the wing on this side, reached by the walk and steps behind the shelter.

Spring cleaning is an annual chore of "opening." The dress here suggests that these are cottage owners, not servants, probably the Bensons at their earlier cottage on Hill Island

Parlor

The Belle Isle house was Colonial Revival in style, but innovative electrical lighting fixtures were prominently displayed, as were the Peacocks' many silver trophies. In addition to five on the mantel and one on the center table, the cabinet in the right corner is full of trophies, while another appears on the cabinet at far left.

Billiard Room

The mate to the parlor on the other side of large center hall at Belle Isle was the Billiard Room with two tables, surrounded by verandah on three sides.

Skull & Bones

George Douglass Miller of Albany and New York City designed several inventive buildings at his summer home, Deer Island. He willed the property to Yale's Skull and Bones Society. Many distinguished members and guests have enjoyed this secluded retreat, which still retains interesting structures. Two of the larger were destroyed in fires at the mid-twentieth century, however, with great loss of valuable contents. The cottage shown is one that remains.

"Overboard" at Rum Point

Back of the House: the Cook at Mississauga

Front of the House: the Bensons at Mississauga

Boldt staff arrive from Alexandria Bay for work at Wellesley House.  The butler stands on the dock.

A Boldt employee at Wellesley House

Isle Imperial and Heart Island, seen from the tower of the Thousand Island House, before construction of Boldt Castle. The Alster Tower had been completed; the Arch of Triumph and Boldt Yacht House were being built. The Rafferty boathouse appears behind their island, but the Peacock Yacht House has not yet been built. The Boldt Play House on Wellesley Island however appears at the extreme left.

The Boldt Castle Rotunda, as seen from the ballroom about 1950, before renovations by the Thousand Islands Bridge Authority.

The President's "Gone Fishin"

Chester Arthur's sojourn at the Thousand Islands was documented by the famous photographer, Mathew Brady, who accompanied the President. The additional skiffs pulled ashore in the distance indicate the presence of others in the presidential party. Collection of the Library of Congress.

The Emery yacht house, boat house, and farm buildings on Robbins' Island [Piction], seen from Bluff Island. Residence of Kris Hass, Julie's husband, appears next to the greenhouses above the large yacht house, and a large vegetable garden is on the slope below the orchard to the left of the barns.

Spectacular flower borders flanked the approach to the Frontenac Hotel, the work of Kris Hass.

The Frontenac, Round Island

The *Islander* approaches Frontenac dock

The Frontenac dining room served as the resort's largest ballroom. Note the musicians' balcony.

Frontenac Verandah

Young George at the earlier Benson cottage on Hill Island

George Campbell, Guide, by Howard Pyle, 1878

258

Frontenac Girls

The tall girls might be "Those Bingham Sisters" posing with friends at the new Frontenac. Even more probably, the man in the distance may be Kris Hass, Julie's future husband, who was in charge of the grounds on the Emery properties. The huge American flag atop the building was not destroyed by the fire, but is at the Thousand Islands Museum, Clayton. Judging from the costumes, this stereopticon photograph, published by Strohmeyer & Weyman, New York, probably was taken in 1899 when the enlarged hotel opened. The wooden walk was replaced with concrete in 1908. Julie would have been about the age of these tall girls in 1899.                    Collection of the Library of Congress.

## Ghosts

Dubious about including this illustration, I first tried to lighten and straighten it. Something was lost. The bleakness of this late autumn view of Wellesley House, its grim darkness together with the amateur quality of the photograph, seemed of a piece with the poignant subject. Someone on the staff probably took this snapshot about the time of George Boldt's death. The elderly woman seen here may have been the housekeeper, photographed with her visiting granddaughter. Like the building and its builder, both of these people probably are gone now. I discovered Wellesley House some twenty-five years later—a half-century ago now—as another grand, but sad, vacant house, soon to be demolished.

The illustration, like several included earlier in the book, was contributed by Bud and Eleanor Forrest, present owners of the property, who received the pictures from Roger Lucas, compiler of several works about the Boldts.

# AFTERWORD

Some people (often the young) are disinterested in history. Others find accounts of the past entertaining. Some moreover value history not merely as amusement. For them, history provides a "shock of recognition," a revelation of who we are — a discovery of our identity. Some of us have a special relationship with a region. Its distinctive past intensifies the present reality of the place that we love.

The special magic of the Thousand Islands derives in large part from the sense of an island's disengagement from the world. Dislocated fragments of reality seem adrift, positions indeterminate when we move among them. Larger chunks of land break apart, becoming still more smaller islands. Islands appear and disappear, receding through layered veils of haze. There is a sense of unreal illusion in a world of islands, a sense of the unknown that has appealed to builders of fantastic castles and generations of romantic escapists.

Words and pictures cannot fully convey a sense of place. Missing are the sounds and smells — the fishy smell of the water, blended with the aroma of varnish on the sun-warmed wooden boat, and the whiff of gasoline that evokes the iridescent shimmer of oil on water, rolling about a dock, or the warm fragrance of an old cottage bedroom, all natural wood — sloping floor, unfinished walls, and underside of roof now dark with age.

Water lapping under a dock, waves echoing in a boathouse; the creak of old leather, binding against the metal pins of the skiff; the nudging of boats, bumpers and lines squeaking, or a the sail luffing, halyard flapping against the mast: these are the simple sounds of life on the river that poignantly evoke fond memories of summers past, as alluring but elusive as the whine of a distant motorboat, receding into the wind.

Words and pictures can neither capture the shriek of gulls, the aroma of pine needles baking on warm rock, nor does this book present the history of the Thousand Islands. That would require a much larger volume — or the many books that have been written about our past. This account has been more a personal memoir, or an evocation of the place as it was, recalling its unique lifestyle. The fuller history of the Thousand Islands has been documented in many fine works, as suggested by the bibliography. I have avoided duplicating most of their content, seeking images that are fresh as well as factual information that is not readily available elsewhere.

From a stereoscopic photograph by James Esson

Why are the Thousand Islands worth remembering? Because they are *ours*, first of all. We're partial. The place, moreover, was and is beautiful, and beauty requires no rationale. Natural scenery has been enriched lovingly by many generations of inhabitants, creating a world of fragmented land and endless water layered with a historic culture that retains alluring boats and splendid buildings, virtually irreplaceable. The Thousand Islands are not merely a veritable museum of historical artifacts; the place as a whole is a collective work of art.

This was a "fools' paradise" in the sense that art is foolish, considered in practical terms. Living on an island is foolhardy—a romantic folly. Restoring and maintaining antique wooden boats is foolish. Uselessness is a characteristic of art. George Boldt was a fool, we may suppose, because he spent millions of dollars on a place he visited only a few weeks of the year. If the investment seems absurd economically, we should realize that for Boldt the place had value beyond utility. We who come to the river for only ten weeks or so *know* that the place awaits us the other forty-two weeks. Our knowing has value, sustaining us throughout the year. As John Updike observed, "Looking foolish does the spirit good." Foolishness is good for us, when it's the art of fools.

Of course, many islanders were foolish in their extravagance, like the Boldts, the Peacocks, or many others. Aging William O. Wyckoff, who built the grand villa on our cover, enjoyed it only one summer. As the saying goes, "A fool and his money are soon parted." But the fools would probably answer, "That's what money's for."

The Thousand Islands are not especially memorable because many wealthy people have come here. Although some boosters bravely asserted that the islands once "threatened to rival" Newport as the favored summer resort of the Americanrich, that was never much of a threat but mere bravado. We have generally had, as Ron Hollander observed in *Town and Country* magazine, "third class millionaires." At the turn of the twentieth century the wealthy patronized dozens of American resorts. At many enclaves of the rich, astounding wealth accumulated during the Great Bull Market created what Henry James (referring to Boldt's Waldorf-Astoria) characterized as "a great golden blur."

The Antique Boat Museum at Clayton celebrates the remarkable marine culture of the Thousand Islands and other water-oriented recreational communities. Herreshoff and other leading boat designers and builders of the time were were represented on the river. Gilbart Mercier documented many of the great steam yachts in his fine book, *Pleasure Yachts of the Thousand Islands circa 1900*. The bibliography mentions works of Tony Mollica, Bonnie Wilkinson Mark and others.

Viewed collectively, it seems that relatively few of these islanders were industrial entrepreneurs like George Pullman. Most amassed fortunes not from inventing new products, nor even from manufacturing them, but more from mass marketing of consumer commodities—some of dubious value, like the patent medicines purveyed by Fulford, Warner, Breitenbach, Comstock and Kilmer—to say nothing of Emery's cigarettes or Bradley's whisky. Philo Remington summered in his modest cottage at Thousand Island Park while William Wyckoff built Carleton Villa with the fortune made from marketing Remington's products.

The success of these marketers, as Alfred Chandler observed more generally about the business trend of the time, resulted less from responding to existing demand than from creating demand by promotion, making products more readily accessible by improved distribution. The phenomenon of the Thousand Islands at the turn of the twentieth century was in large part a consequence of a new consumer culture.

Change in business organization contributed to these fortunes. The turn of the twentieth century saw the consolidation of smaller enterprises into giant corporations. The big three of the controversial new "trusts" were represented here: American Tobacco by Charles Emery, Standard Oil by Wheeler, Pratt, and Vandergrift, U.S. Steel by Peacock. In addition to these largest American corporations of the time, the Pullman Company was seventh in size, Singer was twelfth.

The interdependence of modern business was evident: Wilbur's railroad required Pullman's cars, which required Peacock's or Laughlin's steel, which required Rafferty's coke, which in turn required coal mined by Wilbur—all to distribute Remington's typewriters, Browning's clothing, or Fulford's Pink Pills to Straus's department store—or to take the New Rich to George Boldt's prestigious hotel.

While the disastrous fires of 1911 and 1912 signaled the end of an era, they were not the cause. Even in England, as Clive Aslet observed, 1910 was about the end of the "social country house" period and a way of life that required large staffs to maintain grand establishments. Labor, particularly with twentieth century wars depleting the supply, became less readily obtainable. Furthemore, as Alfred Thimm noted, "the American economy slowly approached economic stagnation between 1905 and 1913." Just as the death of Louise Boldt was not the sole reason for abandoning Boldt Castle before its completion, the fires in the next decade were not the sole cause for ending the heyday of the Thousand Islands.

Although fishing and hunting provided impetus for development of the resort, few islanders acquired the wilderness mystique that characterized the nearby Adirondack Mountains. They continued to fish—some six hundred men served as oarsmen-guides in 1894. But people went into the Adirondacks to escape from the city while people coming to the islands brought urbanity with them. An 1883 local newspaper reported the arrival of the "first living dude, . . . a full-fledged dude, with banged hair and toothpick shoes." Few islanders huddled around campfires, playing noble savage. They preferred socializing on the verandahs of grand hotels or making matches for daughters at the yacht club, showing off their big yachts and fine clothes. They wore white gloves to prove they need not get them soiled.

Although islanders often were delighted to show off costly new toys, they were fairly inclusive. Many had been immigrants themselves. George Boldt, Frank Ritter, Carl Schultz, and Nathan Straus were German-born, for instance. The grand hotels evidenced no anti-Semitism. Nathan Straus stayed at the elite Frontenac before building his summer home and he patronized the Thousand Island House occasionally. It may be surprising today to learn how many African Americans were on the river at the turn of the twentieth century—far more than today, since they served on the staff of many grand hotels and on the crew of steamboats. Some islanders brought black servants; the Wilburs at Sport Island had a black butler.

A. C. McIntyre photographed this unidentified group, probably from the staff of a hotel.
From an undated stereoscopic print, c. 1885.

Some African Americans had been here for generations, coming via the Underground Railroad to settle on islands such as Atlantis and Wyanoke in Chippewa Bay and Isle of Pines, near Fishers Landing. By the turn of the century African Americans were organizing social events here. Cakewalks were popularly noted in the press. May Irwin, the first major white performer to introduce black music to mainstream audiences in New York City, had a farm on the mainland a short row from Round Island, where the huge hotel had many African-American employees. May became a patron of black composers and performers and a fan of African-American music performed at New York clubs.

The second generation of island families was not always so inclusive. After the First World War children educated at elite finishing schools may have acquired more polished in manners, but when they closed their doors to others they sealed the fate of their society. Within a few decades the supposedly exclusive but now anti-Semitic Thousand Islands Yacht Club stood vacant. Overt racism at Alexandria Bay, clearly intended to drive the black community from the river, is a blot on our history. One person was killed in a race riot at the Bay. As Julie observed, "We were not always nice people."

Whereas Great Camps of the Adirondacks, isolated amid thousands of acres of forest, were generally retreats of Old Money, the social life of the Thousand Islands provided a group identity to New Money. The dancing masters of the grand hotels educated the young in urbane manners while clubs provided common social experiences for their elders. What these diverse people had in common was not just money. They were generally unfamiliar with wealth, and had children who needed to learn how to behave with money. The parents were linked by friendships of offspring—not merely as summer pals on the river, but as classmates in the sort of elite private schools that their parents never attended. If our islanders were in the main less genteel than well-educated second and third generations of wealth, our islanders were in the main more accomplished. They earned their yachts and great trophy houses, built with huge fortunes not merely acquired from prior generations but made with their own hands. In parlance of the times, our islanders were not "nobs" who inherited their silver spoons, but were mostly "swells," who had to earn them. Our islanders were the more interesting people. They were funnier. How could you take seriously airs put on by someone like Mayor W. H. Comstock of Brockville and Morristown, who sailed around the islands in the splendor of his fine yacht, *Albani*, but who peddled Dr. Morse's Indian Root Pills, Dead Shot Worm Pellets, and McKenzie's Dead Shot Worm Candy?

\* \* \* \* \*

The story of the more recent fifty years might fill another book. Like many people of my generation, I regret that I didn't buy a cottage at Thousand Island Park back in the Depression and War decades when they went begging for a few thousand—or in some cases hundred—dollars. Recently one sold for more than six-hundred thousand dollars. Some hotels on both sides of the river now operate year-round. After expenditure of more than fourteen million dollars, Boldt Castle draws hundreds of thousands of visitors each summer. Gananoque now has a new casino as well as the thriving Gananoque Playhouse. We see new million-dollar villas being built. It's sad that revival didn't begin fifty years earlier, when many grand houses might have been saved. We might still be gathering at the Thousand Islands Yacht Club on Welcome Island, or dancing in the ballroom of Calumet Castle—which would be a multi-million dollar property today.

Lost Keewaydin

Demolition of Keewaydin was an outrage. The State of New York acquired the lovely estate on the mainland above Alexandria Bay. At the same time that the State's Division for Historic Preservation worked to recognize landmarks such as this, its parent Department of Parks and Recreation demolished the major buildings at Keewayden. To make matters worse, instead of reusing the fine house, they replaced the historic structure with a modern building to serve as regional park headquarters.

The Peacock Yacht House was another sad loss. Other than the nearby Boldt Yacht House, the landmark building was the last of the tall Thousand Islands yacht houses, designed to house masted steam yachts. It was particularly distinctive for its unusual structure, employing parabolic wood arches fabricated by bolting together wood planks. Architect Rick Tague devoted his master's thesis to the building and tried to rally support for its preservation, to no avail.

As a student, for my own 1955 architectural thesis I developed an imaginary Thousand Islands project—a new yacht club facility on the site of Boldt's Wellesley House. We were required to have a purported "client" and so I approached Grant Mitchell, then executive director of the Thousand Islands Bridge Authority and owner of the Monticello Hotel at the Bay. We did not hit it off well. He thought, "this place will be a lot better off as soon as we get rid of all those old wrecks." No doubt he was pleased when the State demolished the Keewaydin villa.

I dedicated my recent book about Boldt Castle to the late Vincent J. Dee, chairman of the Thousand Islands Bridge Authority. I recall Vince again here as valiantly stemming the tide of destruction. He saved Boldt Castle. That will be his enduring monument. Vince was heartsick, however, to see Calumet Castle go, within view of his Clayton restaurant, McCormick's. Vince nevertheless would be pleased to see how the Clayton mentality has changed, albeit belatedly. The Antique Boat Museum (which Vince was instrumental in founding) continues to build and expand, leading a village renaissance. Andy McNally has given the great Boldt houseboat, *La Duchesse*, to the museum. As mentioned earlier, Clayton has become less a tourist depot than an upscale destination, offering fine shops and dining. As I write, Bill Danforth, previous director of the Antique Boat Museum, is leading a campaign to restore and improve the Clayton Opera House as a performing arts facility.

From Brockville to Cape Vincent, facilities are being improved and culture being enriched. My sense of what the Thousand Islands are, my grasp of the entire region as an identity, has expanded over the years. As a youngster, the place was defined by how far I could row in my skiff. That view changed as I took the afternoon motorboat tours offered tourists, so that the circuit around Wellesley Island came to define the place. Then I became more independent, able to travel farther with my own motorboat. As a young adult I became acquainted with others who summered farther from my old haunts. Chippewa Bay was a revelation. I realized that others had different perspectives of the region.

My friend and colleague, Ian Coristine, when visiting Clayton, commented that the center of my boyhood summer world seemed like a remote extremity from his Canadian island down by Jones Creek. His familiar world was bracketed by Alexandria Bay and Brockville. Down that far, Kingston, which is fifty miles west of Brockville, hardly seemed part of the neighborhood.

Yet as I grow older, Kingston has become a magnet. It's an urbane city, not a rustic retreat. Kingston is a marvelously civil and cultured small city, a university town. It's a special place. Perhaps because I'm both an architect and historian, the distinctive character of this old Canadian city, enriched with many historic landmarks, resonates—particularly when so many American cities have become so much alike. Kingston was a city for generations bypassed by progress and modernization—a blessing in disguise. Kingston now realizes what it has. Encouraging visitors, it rightly proclaims, "You'll be amazed!"

Kingston

Domes and towers from Fort Henry, with Royal Military College in foreground. Heather Hall print.

Ah, Kingston! By the time of my late lunch on a sunny afternoon, following an errand to my bank across the square, most of the chatting crowd has left the sidewalk café. I gaze across tables of the Café Max, strewn with cups and glasses. Framed in the iron curlicues of the awning supports is the colorful abundance of the Saturday farmer's market. Beyond rises the monumental stone mass and copper dome of the City Hall. Built to serve as the capitol of Upper Canada, the robust sculptured limestone is a beloved icon—as is domed St. George's Cathedral, another massive limestone structure nearby, and the tall tower of the Catholic Cathedral, crowning the highest point of the downtown. This is a walking city, full of historic buildings, intriguing boutiques, sidewalk cafés, hidden patios, and fine restaurants. This is an urbanist's town.

My favorite approach to Kingston is across the water. The great citadel, Ft. Henry, atop its hill, together with the old and new buildings of the Military College on the point nearby, and the domes and towers of the skyline of the historic city, become an expanding panorama as the ship approaches the shore, festive with parks, marinas, and hotels.

Kingston

Kingston is not merely another river village; it's a Great Lakes city. Here one senses the larger presence of vast Lake Ontario. There's expansiveness to the horizon, looking westward as the Great Lakes open, and even a different smell to the westerly breeze, coming hundreds of miles across the water that stretches from horizon to horizon. Kingston is neither central to the Thousand Islands nor is typical of a river community. It seems more a European than American city—a leisurely paced city of cafés and students, a retirement destination of choice for many. It's a city of history, a city built of stone, a city of education and culture. Kingston is not characteristic of the Thousand Islands but this charming city provides another dimension to the regional experience.

What will be the future of the Thousand Islands region? Should we wish for a return of its prominence as a resort, with bigger and better hotels, marinas, residential complexes—more development? Should we stop development, to retain what is left of the natural quality of the region? Or should we opt for "Smart Growth," weighing benefits against costs?

Development is always a mixed blessing. Several decades ago, when Robert Charron and I were doing a survey of historic buildings here, an owner of an island in Chippewa Bay, Sidney Manes, being told that we might use the material to attract interest to the region, responded, "Get outta here. That's the last thing we want!" Many people deplore the congestion of too many boats and other recreational watercraft, often operated inconsiderately if not irresponsibly. Many islanders deplore the proliferation of buildings and trailer parks, the dearth of parking in town, the blatant commercialization of the "strip" development along the highways. While understandable, this view may be interpreted as merely, "We got here first. Let's keep everybody else away."

Planners and architects (like me) may respond that development may be better or worse depending on how it's done. The intensive use of the region during its first Golden Age might be a model. Grand hotels offered attractive resources for dining and recreation while having small footprint on the landscape. Dense communities like Thousand Island Park were compact. They continue to demonstrate a "New Urbanism" principle that alternatives to "Suburban Sprawl" can have charm and appeal. It's a joy to see folks at the Park happily running around the place in their electric golf carts, leaving the big automobiles parked. How we use the inheritance from the past may be different, but there is much to be learned and valued in our past.

The Thousand Islands Land Trust has secured much of our natural scenic resource for the future. This fine organization continues, with help of many members and donors, to acquire land and otherwise save it from development. Save the River works to improve and maintain the environmental quality of the region. The Canadian Thousand Islands Heritage Conservancy and the Thousand Islands Association play similar roles on their side of the border.

As a historian, my first wish for the Thousand Islands is that the Fulford's *Magadoma*, currently awaiting completion of its restoration, might return to the river. The steam yacht could become a companion attraction to the Boldt houseboat. The tall-masted ship, rigged with flags and electric lights, with her alluring clipper bow and fantail stern, would be a distinctive and elegant icon for the Thousand Islands, a symbol to recall our special marine tradition and colorful social history.

I also hope that Carleton Villa, shown on the front cover, can be saved from total ruin before it is lost forever. Because the bearing walls apparently were constructed of solid masonry on bedrock, they seem generally sound. No doubt this is why the building for many decades has survived neglect and partial dismantling. Prior to World War II the General Electric Company acquired the property and contracted demolition of the villa. This explains removal of all the windows. Ownership of salvaged materials was controversial, however, and then the war intervened before the structure was fully razed. Many Carleton Island and Cape Vincent residents continued to remove materials with permission of the owner at the time. The top three stories of the great tower fell shortly before 1946. Now the roof is going and the building will soon be a mere shell. Can it be saved? As we see million-dollar villas being constructed elsewhere in the region, and as Boldt Castle has been largely restored with more than fourteen million dollars from paid admissions, Carleton Villa ought not to be written off as beyond salvation.

As I write, new owners of Dark Island plan restoration of its buildings, opening them to the public. A landmark attraction at Cape Vincent would anchor this end of the region on the U.S. side, as Kingston does across the river, and as Dark Island and Fulford Place do at the lower end. We might look to other regions that have developed collections of historic buildings, such as Natchez, Mississippi. A week of "open houses" celebrates the resources of Charleston, South Carolina, offering events such as afternoon teas and candlelight receptions. Similarly, the Thousand Islands region, especially when historic Kingston is viewed as integral, might be better presented as a remarkable historic resource, comparable to destinations such as Newport, Rhode Island.

Kingston

Kingston Ambiance
Water, history, and culture contribute to the city's sense of place, identity, and lifestyle.

Not only is the city of Kingston urbane in contrast to the natural quality of much of the surrounding river and lake country; its built fabric also recalls a history older and more varied than that of the region elsewhere. Count Frontenac established a French fort here in 1693. Kingston became capital of the Province of Canada in 1841. The grand City Hall, designed by George Brown, was built to serve as the capitol building. Distinctive Martello towers dot the waterfront (as seen above), extending the monumental fortification of Fort Henry. Prominently situated on a bluff overlooking the city, the citadel protected the juncture of lake, river, and the historic Rideau Canal. This picturesque waterway, built between 1826 and 1832, connects many lakes of the Laurentian Shield, linking the Thousand Islands and Ottawa, providing a popular boating resource.

Fort Henry, built in the 1830s, attracts more than 150,000 visitors annually. The national historic site offers regular tours and spectacular military and musical performances. Billed as "a cultural capital of Canada," with Queens University, the Royal Military College, and other institutions, Kingston provides rich theater, music, and entertainment fare, as well as many diverse ethnic restaurants and lively bistros. Many fine shops make the city a shopper's delight. An Olympic Harbor and other marinas relate the city to Lake Ontario, the Rideau Canal, and the Thousand Islands.

Kingston's historic charm, waterfront ambiance, educational institutions, theater, music, fine shops and dining, combine to make the major city of the Thousand Islands region culturally lively.

Kingston Market. A Heather Hall Print

Kingston is a festive city, offering an extensive program of street fairs and community events.

"Spirit of Sir John A.," Kingston. A Heather Hall Print

The Author and Friend

When frequently asked, "How long did it take you to write the book?" I reply, "a lifetime" or perhaps "sixty years." I've been doing research that long. Although I gave much material to the Antique Boat Museum several decades ago, I still have huge files of notes. What appears here is but a sampling.

To mention all the historic buildings of the region might provide an inventory—a catalogue perhaps useful for reference but about as readable as a telephone directory. There has been no attempt to select these few examples according to any ranked merit, although obviously I have featured the principle landmark "castles." Boldt Castle has been covered in my previous book devoted to it alone.

Similarly, much more might have been presented about some other islanders, such as May Irwin, Arthur Brisbane, J. G. Holland or Nathan Straus—people who were more internationally important in their time. Families less noted in larger history, like the Peacocks, appear more conspicuously here. The reason, of course, is simply that they have left albums of photographs that convey a sense of Thousand Islands life. The Peacocks and Bensons, like the families that gath-

276

ered at Rum Point, represent hundreds of others whose photographic records were not so readily accessible. As other family albums become available, subsequent publications may follow (a hint that I would welcome material).

Needless to say, my conversations with Julie don't literally record our actual exchanges of some sixty years past. Most of the content in the dialogue, other than related to Julie's personal life, derives from my research, largely in period newspapers, and from information provided by many people. I've enjoyed conversations not only with Julie but also with many others, such as Vincent Dee, Pierre Du Prey, Jean Hammond, Hal McCarney, Virginia Minnick, Hazel Simpson McMane, and Bonnie Wilkinson Mark. I hesitate to mention these few because there have been more whom I probably neglect.

So many people have helped over the years, contributing to this book by sharing their views, experiences, and materials, that adequate thanks here would overburden this book. I must acknowledge substantial contributions by a few people, however, such as Fred Beach, Jack Brown Verda Corbin, Bud and Eleanor Forrest, Bob and Patty Mondore, Gene Kleinhans, E. Packer Wilbur III and other Wilburs, Grant Peacock (via Fred Beach and Rick Tague), Beatrice Morgan Pruyn Thibault ("Sis"), all of whom provided many of the photographs, as did Kingston's Maritime Museum, the Chicago Historical Society, which holds Pullman materials; the Ontario Heritage Foundation, which holds Fulford materials; and the Queens University Archives, which holds Benson materials. The New York State Historical Association and the Remington Museum at Ogdensburg have provided Remington material, and many images come from the Library of Congress, the New York Public Library, and the New York State Archives. The photograph of the interior of Dark Island Castle is reproduced with permission from Mardges Bacon's excellent book about the architect, *Ernest Flagg*. Heather Greg (KEDCO), Heather Hall, Bob Johnson , Bonnie Wilkinson Mark, John Schuck, Sam Williams, and Marilyn and Phillip Wright shared photographs. Phoebe Tritton, librarian, and Rebecca Hopfinger, curator of the Antique Boat Museum, often confirmed facts, as did Nan Dixon, Trude Fitelson, Charles and William Millar, Tony Mollica, Jeanne Snow — and so many others over so many decades that recalling them all here seems impossible. I'm especially grateful to Robert Charron, who assisted me for many years in doing field research in the region and who has contributed several photographs, as has Ian Coristine, who has also shared his publishing and marketing experience and has been a constant encouragement in these ventures.

"It is to me the sweetest spot on earth."

Last words of Josiah Gilbert Holland, 1881

A new generation enjoys the Pullmans' island, living with momentos of the past. The dock, gazebo, and retaining wall along the approach walk are more than 115 years old. The boys are young men now, as Robert Charron took this photograph about fifteen years ago. Soon one more generation of youngsters will be fishing from this stone dock, where steam yachts once tied up to the iron ring, where ladies in bustles once strolled with parasols up the walk to Castle Rest, and where the Pullman twins, when about the same ages these boys, once fished from this same spot.

# Appendix A

# Some Notable Boats of the Thousand Islands

Islanders had yachts designed by many of the leading marine architects of the day such as Hacker, but most notably by Herreshoff. "Of all the men who have worked in the field of yacht design, Nathanael Greene Herreshoff has had the widest and most lasting influence."[1] There were more than twenty Herreshoff-designed boats on the River, built between the 1870s and 1917.[2] They did not

---

[1] Bill Robinson continues, "Whole books have been written about his remarkable career. . . . The 'Wizard of Bristol' belongs at the head of the list" of American marine architects (Bill Robinson, 11). John and Nathanael Herreshoff began to dominate the American yacht scene in the 1880s (John Allen Krout, 74-75).

[2] The first Herreshoff yacht, and the first steam yacht, on the river was the fast (14 mph) *Camilla*, built in the late seventies at Bristol, RI for Joshiah C. Holland of Bonnie-Castle (*Syracuse Standard*, 16 July 1897.) Other Herreshoff yachts were: *Aida*, 1882; *Neried*, 1882; *Now Then*, 1887; *Say When*, 1888; *Lotus Seeker*, 1892; *Louise*, 1893; *Jean*, 1897; *Nina*, 1897; *Empress*, 1900; *Clover*, 1901; *Stroller*, 1901; *Wana*, 1903; *Sioux*, 1904; *Ellen*, 1917. Gilbart Mercier identified all of these but two, the *Louise* and *Neried*. The *Louise* was attributed to Herreshoff in an description of the yacht in the *Watertown Daily Times* (10 July 1893.) She was owned by Charles H. Hayden of Fairyland at least until 1897 (Edwin Wildman). Roger Lucas maintains that this *Louise* was acquired by George Boldt, but provides neither date nor source (*Boldt's Boats*, and *Thousand Islands Sun Vacationer*, 14 July 1993, 17). The *Nereid* was described as new by the *Watertown Daily Times*, (21 April 1882, 3). Other Herreshoff boats, not identified by Mercier, dates of construction unknown, were Gilbert Rafferty's *Consuelo* (*Syracuse Standard*, 19 July 1896), M.B. Bush's *Idle Hour* (*Watertown Daily Times*, 7 September 1883), the *Lucille* (11 September 1885), S.A. Jacob's *Say Now* (*Syracuse Herald*, 25 August 1907), H.H. Warner's *Siesta* (16 August 1893) George Boldt's *Dawn*, acquired from John S. Newberry of Detroit in 1909 (Syracuse *Post-Standard*, 21 July 1909), and S.B. Van Dusen's *Vacuna* (*Syracuse Standard*, 19 July 1896, called the *Vacretia* by the same paper on 16 July 1897). Changes of boat names when owners changed have created some confusion, as has similarity of names. In addition to the *Now Then* and *Say When*, there was a *Say Now* and a *Where Now*. The *Now Then* may have been called the *Cresceus* briefly, for a boat of her distinctive torpedo shape was so identified in a photograph, said to be owned by Commodore Luchenbach (*Syracuse Herald*, 30 August 1903).

include the largest (that dubious honor belonged the Laughlin's colossal *Corona*).[3] The Herreshoff boats were among the most beautiful and innovative, however.

Islanders vied to possess not only the largest, but fastest boats on the River. During the first decade of the resort's golden period, boats were powered either by oar (the famous St. Lawrence Skiff), by steam, or by wind. With advent of the naphtha engine, introduced in the mid-eighties, came rapid development of launches, generally larger than rowed skiffs, but smaller than steam yachts. Electric boats appeared remarkably early here: Rushton offered one for sale in 1883.[3] By 1887 naphtha launches were "much used among the Thousand Islands."[5] By 1904, when more than a hundred new naphtha launches were built at Alexandria Bay alone, skiffs were regarded as "a thing of the past."[6] "Put-put" gasoline motors appeared shortly after the turn of the century; these quickly were developed to power a new class of speedboats.[7] By 1904 "the whole River has been seized with the craze for boat racing."[8] Naturally, the coveted title as fastest craft on the River was passed from boat to boat over the years, as technology allowed greater speed. Islanders' racing craft, representing the cutting edge of development, dominated the national scene during the first two decades of the twentieth century. Three local yacht clubs took the Gold Cup of the American

---

[3] The *Corona* was described on pp. 135-136 (Mercier, 20). The *Corona* was even longer than Harkeness' *Peerless*, which at 170 feet had been the most magnificent private yacht ever to visit the Thousand Islands when she called in 1892. Although but two feet longer, the *Corona* carried five more crew, numbering twenty two.

[4] The famous boat builder of Canton, N. Y. soon dropped the electric boat from his catalogue, as it was difficult to start and to recharge (Durant, 16). By the turn of the century, technology had improved and several electric boats were operating on the river. Charles Emery had one in 1900, and the Laughlins carried one aboard their great *Corona* as a tender.

[5] *Forest and Stream*, 1887, quoted by Durrant, 13. Patented in 1883, the naphtha engine was not yet an internal combustion engine. Basically, it was still similar to a steam engine, but it employed vaporized naphtha, a petroleum product like gasoline, instead of vaporized water. Production of naphtha engines began in 1885. Because they did not require a license to operate, as did a steam engine, they quickly became popular. Even children operated naphtha launches. They were dangerous, however, and "blaze ups" were not infrequent (Durant, 10-20).

[6] *Syracuse Herald*, 19 June 1904.

[7] John Allen Krout, 76.

[8] *Syracuse Herald*, 14 August 1904.

Power Boat Association, consequently bringing its international Gold Cup race and much publicity to the Thousand Islands.[9]

Frederick Gilbert Bourne was uncontested as the preeminent yachtsman on the river. As Commodore of the New York Yacht Club in 1903 he commissioned the America Cup defender, "Reliance," from Herreshoff. Bourne had a large fleet of yachts, including an ocean-going vessel that he bought from the King of Belgium.[10] Many of his boats were mentioned previously (p. 156).[11] In addition to the New York and other Thousand Islands yacht clubs, Bourne belonged to the Seawanhaka, Corinthian, and Larchmont clubs.

Marjorie Bourne's 1904 *Moike* today at the Antique Boat Museum, Clayton.
The runabout is 36'-9" long with a 150-hp engine.

[9] As mentioned in the narrative, boats representing the Chippewa, Thousand Islands, and Frontenac Yacht Clubs won the Gold Cup, retaining it on the river during the first nine years of its history.

[10] Bourne bought King Leopold's [*sic*] yacht in 1899 (Syracuse *Post-Standard*, 18 May 1899.) Mrs. Van Rensselaer recalled that the "magnificent yacht" was the *Alberta*, kept at the Bourne's Indian Neck estate on Long Island (*Social Ladder*, p. 296.)

[11] H. D. B., 39-40; New York *Social Register*, Summer 1906; Syracuse *Post-Standard*, 8 July 1903.

Old Tradition, New Building

Architect Bill Grater (rowing the skiff) designed a new boathouse for St. Margarettes Island in a style recalling the old house, at right below. The larger view appeared on the front page of the *New York Times'* "Home" section, September 5, 1996, photograph by Suzanne DeChillo.

# Appendix B
# Houseboats of the Thousand Islands

The houseboat was a phenomenon of the nineties.[1] Introduced to the river by the Clarks of Comfort Island, they were followed by the Deweys, Emerys, Nichols and Oliphants, who immediately acquired houseboats.[2] Orchestras on board were a novel feature, enjoyed by many, as their music carried far across the water.[3] The houseboats were more mobile than we might imagine, travelling up the Rideau Canal to Ottawa and to the Bay of Quinte.[4] Many more houseboats appeared during the decade, some quite grand.[5] The *Rowena* was a 69-ton vessel,

---

[1] The houseboat craze was more general: "the most popular book in America" for a short time was John K. Bang's *A House-Boat on the Styx* (1896), an account of a trip on an English houseboat (Francis Hyde Bangs, 166-7). Articles about houseboats appeared in the following two years, in the press (Syracuse *Standard*, 8 August 1897 and 31 July 1898) and national journals (*Outlook*, v; 56, 316). The houseboat was introduced on the river six years earlier, in 1890 (*Watertown Daily Times*, 22 June 1891). Social cachet was assured by Pierre Lorillard's acquisition of a houseboat the following year (*Watertown Daily Times*, 22 July 1891). The houseboat was "a new feature of the River" in 1893 (*Watertown Daily Times*, 15 July 1893). "The new feature is borrowed from the English," according to the *Watertown Daily Times* (1 August 1893). In 1899, houseboating was "becoming more popular each year on the St. Lawrence" (Syracuse *Herald* 8 June 1899). A photograph, "A House-Boat on the St. Lawrence River," appeared in *Country Life*, 3 May 1903 (Vol. IV, 11).

[2] *Watertown Daily Times*, 10 July 1893. The Deweys' houseboat was then the largest, having cost $20,000 (more like $300,000 today.) Capt. Visger also mentioned the Emery houseboat. Somewhat later, the Burkes, of Jewel Island, planned "a floating palace" of a houseboat, 55 feet long, to be "the gem of the present age" (*Thousand Islands Sun*, 24 August 1911.) Was the gem ever built?

[3] *Watertown Daily Times*, 17 July 1893.

[4] Syracuse *Herald*, 1 September 1901 and 27 July 1902; Syracuse *Post-Standard*, 1 July 1900 and 30 July 1912.

[5] Houseboats were apparently popular with the ladies on the River, for after 1893 Mrs. J. Brown, Mrs. Emily M. Cox, Mrs. Walter Gibb, Mrs. Robert Osborne, and Mrs. W. J. Townsend acquired them and somewhat later Mrs. Julia Burke had one designed. Other owners were M. J. Lawrence, S. A. Maxwell, and E. W. Wheeler. The houseboats *Clover* and *Virginia* were available for charter, and Capt. D. H. Hass was pilot of the *Dora*. Other houseboats were the *Halcyon*, Mrs. Walter Gibb's *Idler*, and Chauncey Wheeler's *Skips* (Syracuse *Standard*, 11 July 1895, *Post-Standard*, July 1900 and 30 August 1912, and Syracuse *Herald*, 6 August 1899, 21 July 1907).

ninety-six feet long, that was "much admired."[6]  The houseboat, *Lysander*, the "finest of its kind on the River," belonged to Gen. Andrew C. Fields.[7]  The *Winona*, "one of the most beautiful houseboats on the River," belonged to Charles E. Johnson of New York and Wintergreen Island.  She had a seventeen-foot beam and was ninety-eight feet long, accommodating six staterooms.[8]   In the same class, at a hundred feet long, was the *Amaryllis* of Mrs. M. T. Cox, which provided double, single and twin staterooms, each with a full bathroom.[9]  A houseboat *Amaryllis* remains a familiar sight, moored among the Canadian islands.  Another large houseboat was identified with the head of Cherry Island, probably used by the Straus, Abraham or Marx families.  The hundred-foot length and seventeen-foot beam of Edson Bradley's *Arcadia* provided seven staterooms and three baths, with hot and cold water in every room, as well as hot-water heating.[10]  Commodore Lawrence's was even broader, with an 18-foot beam.[11]  George Boldt's *La Duchesse* exceeded these, of course.[12]  With a beam of

---

[6]  The *Rowena* was built in Detroit for D. P. McQueen of Schenectady at a cost of $35,000, equivalent today to more than a half-million dollars.  Date uncertain, she was sold in 1909 to Joseph Witmann (Syracuse *Post-Standard*, 7 August 1909).

[7]  The Fields' houseboat was towed by their yacht, when not anchored off Hub Island (*Syracuse Herald*, 20 July 1902).  The houseboat *Lysander* previously may have belonged to the Roses, as she was photographed at Rose Island.  The *Lysander* was purchased in 1902 by Andrew C. Fields of Hub Island (*Syracuse Herald*, 20 July 1902).

[8]  Tender for the *Winona* was the *Juanita* (Syracuse *Post-Standard*, 24 June 1909).  The *Winona* apparently was acquired by General John A. Johns[t]on of Wintergreen Island (Syracuse *Herald*, 26 July 1903, *Post-Standard*, 1 July 1904).  Gen. Johns[t]on sold the *Wynona* (*sic*) to Joseph H. Brown (*Thousand Islands Sun*, 21 September 1916).  This article provides a more detailed description of the houseboat.  The *Winona* apparently was renamed the *Zilpha C.* on which Mrs. Brown entertained (Syracuse *Herald* 19 July 1914).

[9]  The *Amaryllis* serves as a bed-and-breakfast inn near Rockport, Ontario, operated by fifth-generation Islanders, Pieter Bergen and Janet Rodier.  The *Amaryllis* is said to have been built at Cape Vincent in 1911, probably by Peo.  Mrs. Cox was owner in 1911 (*Thousand Islands Sun*, 1 June 1911).  The Gillespies of Basswood Island owned the houseboat at one time.

[10]  *Thousand Islands Sun*, 14 September 1911.  Bradley sold the *Arcadia* to Robert Osborne (Syracuse *Post-Standard*, 12 July 1916).  Edson Bradley also owned the fine, 117-foot yacht, *Klotawah* (Mercier, 46-47).  The Bradley estate, Arcadia, on the north shore of Wellesley Island, is now Wellesley Island State Park.

[11]  The Lawrence houseboat was 94 feet long, with a beam of 18 feet, nine inches (*Thousand Islands Sun*, December 11, 1913).

[12]  The Boldts' 104-foot *La Duchesse* was preceded by an earlier houseboat of the same name:  Mr. C. D. Perry of Englewood, "owner of the famous Chermont ranch of 40,000 acres" was cruising on that houseboat in 1900 (Syracuse *Post-Standard*, 9 August 1900).

twenty-one feet, she provided ten staterooms and five baths, and fireplaces in parlor and dining room. The late Andrew McNally III restored *La Duchesse*, replacing the wood hull with one of steel, a bit longer, wider and deeper than the original. Mr. McNally arranged for *La Duchesse* to go to the Antique Boat Museum, Clayton. Roger Lucas provides further information about the houseboat in *Boldt's Boats*.

Even the great Boldt houseboat, although said to be "the largest in the world," may not have been the largest on the River.[13] Samuel Maxwell's *Pamela*, although a foot shorter, had a twenty-four foot beam. The *Pamela* (originally the *Wannegan*) had an area on the water of 2472 square feet, compared to 2184 of *La Duchesse*. The Maxwell houseboat moreover had two full levels of enclosed quarters (one below deck), with a third, full "promenade deck," covered but open-air, on top. *La Duchesse* has but one full and one half-level of enclosed quarters, both levels above the main deck, with her "promenade deck" located at the stern of the upper level. *La Duchesse* is more of a barge or flatboat, with a building constructed atop, whereas the *Pamela* had a conventional boat hull. She was built by Leon L. Peo of Cape Vincent, as he proudly related in his catalogue, and was probably designed by him. Some of the rooms may have been larger aboard the *Pamela*, for she had nine staterooms, compared to ten aboard *La Duchesse*, and three, rather than five, bathrooms, but only one fireplace, rather than two.[14] The "splendid" Maxwell houseboat, "one of the finest . . . on the River and a well-known fixture of the Thousand Islands region," was called the *Wannegan* in 1899.[15] The *Waunegan* or *Wanegan* (sic) subsequently was identified with F. Schmidt of New York.[16] The Maxwell houseboat was a familiar landmark of the Canadian islands, near the present Thousand Islands Bridge.

---

A houseboat, *Duchess* was owned by E. W. Wheeler of New York City (Syracuse *Herald*, 1 September 1901).

[13] Lydia S. Dubin, 468.

[14] Data from Bonnie Wilkinson, 30.

[15] Syracuse *Standard*, 28 June 1899.

[16] *Thousand Islands Sun*, 22 September 1910, 18 May 1911, and 27 April 1911.

The modern kayak may be supplanting the old canoe, but
its form recalls the early Canadian decked canoe.

Surveying the nautical scene, 1908

# Appendix C
# Smaller Craft

The St. Lawrence Skiff is widely recognized as the generic boat of the region. This rowboat evolved during the nineteenth century, although Xavier Colon was said to have built the first skiff at Clayton in 1868.[1] By the 1880s skiffs rigged with bat-wing sails were being raced here. A reporter commented, "The race of the little skiffs, with their immense sails and the boats rudderless and oarless, was a remarkable sight as they were turned and turned with as much ease and rapidity as though they were toys working on pivots. To see the natives handle oar and sail is a liberal education."[2] To facilitate sailing, by 1880 "most all the skiff owners are having Atwood's patent centre-board put in their skiffs."[3] In 1891 a London member of the Royal Yacht Club ordered a Clayton boat.[4] The St. Lawrence River Skiff became known nationally and internationally, particularly through exposure at the Chicago World's Fair of 1893, where the boats "won the highest possible awards."[5] During the 1890s the St. Lawrence Skiff and Sailing Association conducted a series of championship races, with skiffs entered from as far as Kingston and Ogdensburg.

Other types of recreational craft have been common on the river at different times. Sculling was very popular in the 1880s, when competitive races for substantial purses were widely attended. Sailing, of larger boats as well as skiffs, was far more popular in the nineteenth than during most of the twentieth century. In the earlier period the alternative to rowing small boats was use of a steam engine, using kerosene as fuel. Operation of a steam engine required a professional captain and engineer, however. New naphtha engines (patented in 1883) averted this necessity.[6] Because anyone could operate them without a license, naphtha launches were widely used on the river over the turn of the century, even when frequent "blaze-up" accidents proved them dangerous.[7]

---

[1] Ann Hutchinson. *Along the Trail and Into the Past.* Seaway Trail, 1986.

[2] *Watertown Daily Times,* 10 July 1882.

[3] *Watertown Daily Times, 27 July 1880.*

[4] *Watertown Daily Times* 29 August 1891.

[5] An excellent article appeared in the *Watertown Daily Times,* 17 October 1893.

[6] Kenneth Durant. *The Naphtha Launch.* Adirondack Museum, 1976; Estelle Hawley, *The History of Summerland,* 1961.

[7] Durant. *The Naphtha Launch.*

Gasoline engines for boats appeared here early as 1891, but technical problems made them slow to be practical.[8] The first boats with internal combustion engines were often taken to be electric boats (already available) because they showed no visible evidence of how they were propelled. Outboard motors with an internal combustion or "explosive engine" came on the market in 1900.[9] They were slow to be improved and accepted, however, and rarely were seen here until about 1915. Shortly after the turn of the century many skiffs were converted to "skiff-putts," which might employ a single-cycle, 2-cylindar engine, with no neutral or reverse gears, using rope steering [10] About 1905 the mania for fast boats powered by internal combustion engines took hold. Not merely the national Gold Cup Races but other matches on the river after 1900, particularly at Chippewa Bay and Frontenac, created a fiercely competitive game. By 1907 boat shops were working overtime trying to satisfy demand for motorboats.[11] The powerboats were dangerous. Two persons were killed in 1908 when the racer *Delawanna II* struck another boat, cutting it in two.[12]

Ralph and Russell Britton in their naphtha launch at Mudlunta Island

[8] E. Bertrand of Clayton built the 35' gasoline launch, *Hazel*, during the winter 1890-91 (*Watertown Daily Times*, 9 July 1891), also *Syracuse Standard*, 10 August 1895.

[9] Kenneth Durant, *The Naphtha Launch*, Adirondack Museum, 1976.

[10] D. W. Fostle, "The Boat Builders of Alexandria Bay," *Wooden Boat*, Sep/Oct 1982.

[11] *Syracuse Herald*, 4 August 1907.

[12] Syracuse *Post-Standard*, 21 August 1908.

Boat building in the region is too large a subject to summarize here. D. W. Fostle, Bonnie Wilkinson, and others have written extensively about local boats and their builders. Firms and individuals on both sides of the river generally built several types of boats rather than specializing in one sort of craft. Prominent for St. Lawrence River skiffs was Dr. Bain of Clayton, who consolidated the operations of many individual builders into one firm, A. Bain & Co. of Clayton. This company was absorbed by the St. Lawrence River Skiff, Canoe & Steam Launch Co., a stock corporation subsequently absorbed by the national sporting goods firm, A. G. Spaulding,

During the 1880s there were various popular makes of canoes and skiffs, but J. H. Rushton of Alexandria Bay and Canton emerged the region's premier canoe builder.[13] Frederic Remington owned Rushton canoes, perhaps one or both of the two types of canoes that appear in photographs reproduced here. By the late 1890s canoeing was one of the most popular sports at the Thousand Islands. We may think of romantic couples idling among the water lilies of secluded bays, but at the turn of the twentieth century sportsmen used canoes more competitively. Canadian canoes often were decked over, more like modern kayaks.[14]

The American Canoe Association often met at the Thousand Islands, beginning in 1880 with an encampment at Canadian Stave Island. In 1884 the canoeists convened at Delaney's (Canoe) Point at the foot of Grindstone Island and again the following summer, when about a hundred tents were pitched there, including one occupied by Rushton, who brought a full assortment of his canoes and replacement parts in case of accidents. Races were the focus of the meets, Rushton contributing paddles as prizes. The ACA continued to meet at Canoe Point for several seasons, attracting hundreds of canoeists from places as remote as San Francisco, Jacksonville, St. Paul, and England. After an 1888 meet on Lake George, the ACA returned to the river in 1889, attracting about a thousand people to the meet, again at Stave Island in Canada. The organization established a policy of alternating Canadian and U.S. sites for annual meets. In 1893 some 2000 canoeists came to the meet, the fifth held on the river, this time at Brophy's Point on Canadian Long (Wolfe) Island, about six miles below Kingston. In 1896 the meet again was held at Canoe Point (with the ladies' tents at nearby Squaw Point). Preference for this venue led to return the next season (despite the alternating policy), but in 1898 the meet was again at the head of Stave Island in

---

[13] *Watertown Daily Times,* 10 July 1884.

[14] D. W. Fostle, "The Boat Builders of Alexandria Bay." *Wooden Boat, Sept/Oct 1982.*

Canada. New York State had acquired Canoe and Squaw Points for a public park. The ACA in 1899 met at Canadian Hay Island, which was less exposed than Stave Island. In 1901 the Canadian government leased Sugar Island to the ACA for ninety-nine years. After a year's absence, the ACA returned in that year to the river to meet at Canadian Mudlunta Island, but attendance was diminished, as it continued to be at subsequent meets held at Sugar Island. "Where are the canoes?" they asked in 1911, while complaining that a law should quiet noisy motor boats.[15] The golden age of canoeing, and of skiff sailing, had passed. The wilderness mystique, the frontier game-playing of the early fishermen's gatherings, was gone.

Thousand Islands fishing camp, drawn by Howard Pyle, 1878

---

[15] "A few years ago the river was dotted with canoes. Now scarcely one is seen between Clayton and Alexandria Bay" (Syracuse *Post-Standard*, 31 July 1911). "As early as 5 A. M. one is wakened by the burst of explosions" (*Thousand Islands Sun*, 6 June 1911).

# Appendix D

# Gold Cup Races of the American Power Boat Association

| Year | Host Club | Winning Boat | Owner | Length | Speed |
|------|-----------|--------------|-------|--------|-------|
| 1904[1] | | Standard | Carl Riotte | 60 | 23.160 |
| 1904 | | Vingt-Et-Un II | W. Sharpe Kilmer | 38' 9" | 24.900 |
| 1905 | CBYC | Chip I | J.M. Wainwright | 27 | 15.000 |
| 1906 | CBYC | Chip II | J.M. Wainwright | 30 | 25.000 |
| 1907 | CBYC | Chip II | J.M. Wainwright | 30 | 23.903 |
| 1908 | CBYC | Dixie II | E.J. Schroeder | 39 | 29.938 |
| 1909 | TIYC | Dixie II | E.J. Schroeder | 39 | 29.590 |
| 1910 | TIYC | Dixie III | F.K. Burnham | 39 | 32.473 |
| 1911 | FYC | MIT II | J.H. Hayden | | 37.000 |
| 1912 | TIYC | P.D.Q. II | A.G. Miles | 20 | 39.462 |
| 1913 | TIYC | Ankle Deep | C.S. Mankowski | 32 | 42.779 |

*Chip I*, a fledgling powerboat

Clinton Crane designed five of the winning boats; H.L Leighton designed the two *Chips*. In 1904 the *Standard* was sixty feet long; in 1912 the *P.D.Q. II* at twenty feet was a third of that length. Power of the *Chip I* was a mere 10.25 HP compared to 220 HP for the *Dixie II*. Generally the trend was for shorter, more powerful boats.

---

[1]  New York City's Columbia Yacht Club won the first race of the Association in May of 1904 on the Hudson River, but retained the trophy for only four months before yielding it in September to the Chippewa Yacht Club (*Thousand Islands Sun*, 17 August 1911).

# Appendix E
# Online References

Supplemental material about the following topics may be found on the web site:

## 1000islandsbooks.com.

New York City Islanders

Ohio Islanders

Chicago Islanders

Syracuse Islanders

Pennsylvania Islanders

Canadian Islanders

These lists identify many regular visitors to the Thousand Islands, mentioning their island properties or boats, with amplifying notes. Another extensive list is:

Thousand Islands Organizations

This list surveys clubs and organizations during the period covered in the book.

Other Thousand Islands material may be placed on the web site from time to time.

The Shore Dinner prepared by the fishing guide is a tradition of the Thousand Islands extending back about 150 years. The ritual is still cherished today. Note the bottles on the table. 1878. drawing by Howard Pyle.

# Bibliography

A basic but incomplete survey of works published prior to 1975 pertaining to the Thousand Islands region within New York State is:

*Northern New York Historical Materials*, Second Edition, Canton, N.Y., North
    Country Reference and Research Resources Council, 1976.

The Onondaga County Public Library at Syracuse has holdings related to the Thousand Islands not included in this New York State North Country library survey. A comprehensive bibliography of Canadian material published prior to 1977 is provided by Adrian G. Ten Cate and Mary Beacock Fryer, *Pictorial History of the Thousand Islands of the St. Lawrence River*, cited below. Susan Smith also provides a full bibliography in *The First Summer People*, also cited below. Queens University, Kingston, holds a large collection of Thousand Islands material, as does the Antique Boat Museum, Clayton.

Some older works devoted to the Thousand Islands:

Albro, John. *The Thousand Islands, and the Thousand Island House, Season of '87.*
    New York: Liberty Printing, c. 1887.
> Well written, this volume contains two poems by the author, "Down the
> St. Lawrence," and "Isles of Beauty."

*Alexandria Bay and the Thousand Islands.* Watertown, N.Y.: Post job printing
    establishment, 1874.

*American Architect and Building News*, October 13, 1900.
> This journal published plans and River front elevation of Fulford Place.

*Benson Album*, unpublished volume of original photographs with
    handwritten notes, at Queens University Archives, Kingston, Ontario.

Brooks, Eldridge S. *Under the Tamaracks or A Summer with General Grant at the
    Thousand Islands.* Philadelphia: The Penn Publishing Company, 1896.

Browne, George Waldo. *The St. Lawrence River.* New York, Putnams, 1905.
    reprinted: New York, Weathervane, n.d.

[Chapin, Jennie.] *Boyd's Handbook and Picturesque Guide Among the Thousand
    Islands and River St. Lawrence* (etc.), by Andrew Boyd, Syracuse: Central City
    Publishing House, 1879 (also appearing as *Summering Among the Thousand
    Islands, River St. Lawrence,* etc.)
> This early publication is valuable for recording island owners and their
> improvements during the first half-dozen years of the resort's major period of
> development. Jenny Chapin was identified as the author by a handwritten notation
> in the copy now in the collection of the Onondaga County Public Library.

Crémazie, Joseph Octave. *Ouevres Completes de Ocatave Cremazie.* Montréal, C. O.
    Beauchemin & fils, 1882.
> The complete works contain a long poem in French about the Thousand Islands.

Darling, J.D.W. *Sketch of the Early History of the Front Concessions of Lansdowne and
    Thousand Islands Group.* c1925 [at Queens University].

*Earth's Grandest River, The St. Lawrence and the Thousand Islands, an Unrivaled Summer Resort* (cover: *The Thousand Islands, St. Lawrence River and the Crossmon.*) Watertown, N. Y.: H. H. Coates, 1890,1897. Also: Watertown, N.Y.: Hungerford & Coates, 1895, in CIHM/ICMH Microfiche series (Internet: www.nlc-bnc.ca/cihm).

Fulford Papers, with many photographs, at Fulford Place, Brockville, Ont.

Gould, Horace Graeme. *'Round the Islands with Capt. "Dud" Gould.* [Syracuse, N.Y.], c. 1928.

*Guide Book to the Thousand Island House for 1875* [cover title], or *Alexandria Bay and the Thousand Islands: A Summer Resort for Pleasure Seekers* [title page]. Watertown, N. Y.: Post Job Printing Establishment, 1874, 1884.[1]

H. D. B., *Dark Island*, private printing, n.p., n.d. (c. 1925.)

Haddock, John A. *A Souvenir of the Thousand Islands of the St. Lawrence River, from Kingston and Cape Vincent to Morristown and Brockville, with Their Recorded History, from the Earliest Times, Their Legends, Their Romances, Their Fortifications, and Their Contests, Including Both the American and Canadian Channels.* Alexandria Bay, J. A. Haddock (Under the Patronage of the Thousand Islands Club of Alexandria Bay,) 1895.

A second edition, abridged from 256 to 146 pages, was published in 1896. Although some articles were omitted, some amplification was included.

Holley, Marietta. *Samantha at Coney Island and a Thousand Other Islands.* New York: Christian Herald, 1911.

Hough, Franklin Benjamin. *Thousand Islands of the River St. Lawrence, with Descriptions of Their Scenery as Given by Travellers from Different Countries at Various Periods.* Syracuse: Davis, Bardeen, 1880.

Johnston, Capt. Henry S. *A Tour of the 1000 Islands, the American Venice of the St. Lawrence River.* Clayton, N.Y.: Aldrich, 1936.

——. *The Thousand Islands of the St. Lawrence River with Descriptions of the Scenery and Reminiscences With Which They are Associated.* Boston: Christopher, 1937.

Lantier, Margaret McCormick. *The Thousand Islands, Vacation Paradise.* Ogdensburg, N. Y.: North Country Life, rev. 1956

Lawrence, H.J., ed. *The Thousand Islands of the St. Lawrence River. A Weekly Journal, Devoted to Hours of Recreation Among the Thousand Islands of River St. Lawrence.* Alexandria, N.Y., 1872 (one issue at Queens University).

Machar, Agnes Maule. *The Thousand Islands.* Toronto: Ryerson Press, c. 1935.

McIntrye, A. C. *Sunlight Picture of the Thousand Islands: Half-tones from Photographs by McIntyre.* New York: The Artotype Publishing Co., 1895.

---

[1]   The Thousand Island House, like the Crossmon House, Capt. Visger's boat lines, and other enterprises, published booklets, revised occasionally, even annually. Souvenir booklets likewise appeared in many editions, often with slight variations. This particular publication, for example, reappeared in 1876, with 44 rather than 32 pages.

*Picturesque Thousand Islands of the St. Lawrence.* New York, The Albertype co. [1891].

Pyle, Howard. "Among the Thousand Islands." *Scribner's Monthly* 15, no.6 (April 1878).

> J. G. Holland was editor of *Scribners'* and probably commissioned this article. It is valuable for recollections of early summer visitors and many fine illustrations by Howard Pyle, some of which are reproduced here. The full article is available online: athttp://cdl.library.cornell.edu/cgi-bin/moa/moa-cgi?notisid=ABP7664-0015-135.

Rockwell, Rev. George N. [One Who Has Been There, pseud.]. *Hints for Pleasure Seekers: The Thousand Islands and the Crossmon House, the Summer Paradise of the St. Lawrence River.* Watertown, New York, Times and Reformer Printing and Publishing House, 1882, 1883.

—. *Hints for Pleasure Seekers: The Thousand Islands, the Archipelago of the St. Lawrence River.* Watertown, New York, Times and Reformer Printing and Publishing House, 1886, 1890.

—. *Map of Part of the Thousand Islands of the St. Lawrence River, near Alexandria Bay, New York, Based Upon the English Charts from Surveys of Capt. W. F. W. Owen, R. N., 1818, Corrected from U. S. Government Charts of 1876,* Fulton, New York [?]: George Rockwell, 1883.[2]

—. *Meanderings Among a Thousand Islands, or, An Account of Capt. Visger's Daily Trip on the River St. Lawrence,* Watertown, Times and Reformer Printing and Publishing House, 1881, 1882.

—. [The Wanderer, pseud.] *Meanderings Among a Thousand Islands: An Illustrated and Descriptive Handbook of the Picturesque Daily Excursion on the St. Lawrence,* Watertown, Watertown Post Book and Job Printing Establishment, 1884, 1888, 1890.

Simcoe, Elizabeth. *A Simcoe Relic : Among the Thousand Isles in 1796 : Fragment of a MS. Journal of Mrs. Simcoe.* H. Scadding, ed. Toronto: 1896. CIHM/ICMH Microfiche Series, no. 13621.

Taylor, Frank H. [?]. *Souvenir of the Thousand Islands and River St. Lawrence : Comprising a Short History of the Survey and Division of the Islands between Canada and the United States; the Transfer of the Islands from the Government to Individual Owners; Their Popularity as a National Resort; the Protection and Propagation of Game Fish, Fishing, Hunting, etc.* Grand Rapids, Mich. : J. Bayne. [c1900]. Microfiche series: CIHM/ICMH; no. 13864.

*1000 Island House Season of '88.* Alexandria Bay: Thousand Island Hotel Co., [1888].

*The Thousand Islands Red Book,* Alexandria Bay, James, 1895.

> Queen's University Archives, Kingston, and Redpath Library, McGill University, Montréal, hold microform copies of this rare directory. The original is in the Library of Congress, Washington, D. C.

*Views and Vistas of the Thousand Islands.* New York: The Artotype publishing Co. [1895].

---

[2]  Rockwell also published a map, copyrighted 1873 (Corbin Collection, River Heritage Gallery, Clayton.)

Visger, Walter. *Capt. Visger's Standard Guide to the Thousand Islands.* Alexandria Bay, c. 1898, 1900, 1934, 1936. (There were many other editions.)

Walsh , George J., and David C. Bennett. *A Tour Among the Thousand Islands: The Finest Souvenir View Book Ever Published on the American Continent.* Syracuse: Walsh & Bennett, n.d.

White, James. *Place Names in the Thousand Islands, St. Lawrence River.* Ottawa: Government Printing Office, 1910.

Wildman, Edwin "Cottage Life on the St. Lawrence." *Munsey's Magazine* 19 (May 1898): 194.

Several county histories and gazetteers provide historical articles about the Thousand Islands:

Child, Hamilton. *Geographical Gazetteer of Jefferson County, N. Y., 1684-1890.* Syracuse, N. Y.: The Syracuse Journal Co., 1890.

[Durant, Samuel W.] *History of Jefferson County, New York.* Philadelphia: L. H. Everts and Company, 1878.

Haddock, John A. *The Growth of a Century, as Illustrated in the History of Jefferson County.* Philadelphia: Sherman, 1894.

Hough, Franklin Benjamin. *A History of Jefferson County in the State of New York, from the Earliest Period to the Present Time.* Albany: J. Munsell; Watertown: Stirling and Riddell, 1854.

——. *History of St. Lawrence and Franklin Counties, New York, from the Earliest Period to the Present Time.* Albany: Little & Co., 1853.

McKenzie, Ruth. *A History of Leeds and Grenville County.* Toronto: University of Toronto Press, 1967.

Histories of many regional localities have been published. Devoted to mainland communities are:

*Brockville: a Social History, 1890-1930.* Brockville: Waterway Press, 1975.

Casler, Nellie Horton. *Cape Vincent and Its History.* Watertown: Hungerford-Holbrook, 1906.

Corbin, Verda S. and Shane A. Hutchinson. *Images of America: Clayton.* Charleston, S.C.: Arcadia, 1998.

Disotell, Russ. *Brockville: the River City.* Toronto: Natural Heritage, 1997.

Fryer, Mary Beacock and Arthur Ten Cate. *Brockville: A Pictorial History.* Brockville: Besancourt, 1986. (See also listing by Ten Cate, Adrian, below).

Gordon, Fred. C. and Thos. Southworth. *Brockville : the City of the Thousand Islands.* [Brockville, Ont.: T. Southworth and F. C. Gordon, 1888?]

Hawke, H. William. *Historic Gananoque.* Belleville, Ont.: Mika, 1974.

Lewis, Roy D., ed., and others. *Our Living History: an Historical Guide to the United Counties of Leeds and Grenville.* Mallorytown, Ont.: Thousand Islands River Heritage Society, 2000.

Minnick, Virginia. *Clayton on the St. Lawrence, 1872-1972.* Clayton: Clayton Travelers Club, 1972.

Moore, Arthur W. *The Thousand Island Park at Wellesley Island : Its Origin & Progress as an International Centre of Moral, Religious & Scientific Thought and a Health Giving Summer Resort.* Montreal: J. Dougall. [c1877 –1881].

Ten Cate, Adrian G., and H. C. L. McNaughton. *Brockville, A Pictorial History.* Brockville, Ont.: Besancourt, 1972.

So many works have been devoted to the historic City of Kingston as to require a special bibliography. A recent, comprehensive volume that may serve as an introduction is:

Osborne, Brian S., and Donald Swainson. *Kingston: Building on the Past.* Westport, Ontario: Butternut Press 1988.

Others books about Kingston:

Angus, Margaret. *The Old Stones of Kingston: Its Buildings before 1867.* Toronto: University of Toronto Press, 1966.

Mika, Nick and Helma, with Derek F. Crawley, Kathy Harding, Capt. J. R. McKenzie, and Frances K. Smith. *Kingston, Historic City.* Belleville, Ontario: Mika Publishing Company, 1987.

Tulchinsky, Gerald, Editor. *To Preserve & Defend: Essays on Kingston in the Nineteenth Century.* Montréal: McGill-Queen's University Press, 1975

A history of the largest of the islands is provided by:

Spankie, R. M. "Wolfe Island, Past and Present." *Proceedings of the New York State Historical Association: The Fifteenth Annual Meeting* [etc.] XIII, New York State Historical Association, 1914.

Histories of island summer communites are:

Allan, Jane R. *The Story of Grenadier Island: Metamorphosis of an Island, Its People, and Its Purpose.* Kingston: St. Lawrence College, 1971.

Hawley, Estelle. *The History of Summerland, or More "Rambles at Random."* Rochester: Burnett, 1961.

Jacox, Helen P., and Eugene B. Kleinhans. *Thousand Island Park: One Hundred Years, and Then Some; A Centennial History.* Thousand Island Park: Centennial Book Project, 1975.

Malo, Paul. "Architecture of Thousand Island Park." *Thousand Island Park: One Hundred Years, and Then Some; A Centennial History.* Thousand Island Park: Centennial Book Project, 1975.

Manes, Susan, Editor. *Whose Up?* 1980.

In this delightful collection of essays, residents of Chippewa Bay recall histories of their islands.

Nulty, Margaret, and Doris Mosher. *Murray Isle*, 1972.

Pratt, Alice Olivia. *The Story of Grenell.* Watertown, 1946.

Stamp, Elizabeth P. *Glimpses of Grand View.* Spokane, Wash., 1988.

Westminster Park Association. *The Westminster Park Association of the Thousand Islands.* Syracuse : Truair, Smith & Bruce , 1878.


Some more recent general works about the Thousand Islands:


Corbett, Marjorie R., Editor. *Greenline Parks: Land Conservation for the Eighties and Beyond.* Washington, D. C.: National Parks and Conservation Association, 1983.

Coristine, Ian. *The 1000 Islands.* Hudson Heights, Q.C.: 1000 Islands Photo Art, 2002.

de Visser, John, and Patricia Flemming. *1,000 Islands.* Erin, Ontario: Boston Mills Press, 1990.

Gill, Brendan, and Dudley Witney. *Summer Places.* New York: Methuen, 1978.

Hirvonen, R. P. and R.A. Woods. *Integrated Resource Survey of St. Lawrence Islands National Park and Surrounding Areas.* [Ottawa]: Canadian Forestry Service, Environment Canada, 1978.

Hollander, Ron. "The Thousand Islands." *Town and Country*, August 1978.

Nulton, Laurie Ann. *The Golden Age of the Thousand Islands: Its People and Its Castles; The Thousand Islands of the Saint Lawrence River: A Social History of Its Resort Development, 1890-1904.* Hop Bottom, Pa.: Thomas Nulton, 1981.
The late Miss Nulton's Master's Thesis at Georgetown University provides a good general history of the resort. Unfortunately, it is out of print, and will not be reprinted, according to the expressed intentions of the publisher, the author's father, who views the limited edition as a memorial to his daughter.

Osborne, Brian S. *The Thousand Islands Region, 1650-1850: a Study of Exploration, Settlement and Development.* [Ottawa]: Parks Canada, c. 1976.

Rayburn, Alan "The Thousand Islands: There Really are 1,149." *Canadian Geographic* 105 (October-November 1985) 88-89.

Ross, Don. *Discovering the Thousand Islands.* Kingston: Quarry Press, 2001.

——. *St. Lawrence Islands National Park.* Vancouver: Douglas & McIntyre, in association with Parks Canada, 1983.

Rush, Laurie W. *Fishing and Folk Art of the St. Lawrence River.* Typescript and illustrations at the Antique Boat Museum, Clayton, New York.

Rush, Laurie W., with technical assistance and research contributions from Philip Gillesse. "Water Sports and Social Class in the Late Nineteenth Century: A Look at the St. Lawrence Skiff in the Thousands Islands of the St. Lawrence River." *The Sports Historian: The Journal of the British Society of Sports History* 13 (May 1993). Available on line: www2.umist.ac.uk/sport/rush.html.

Smith, Susan. *The First Summer People: The Thousand Islands 1650-1991.* Erin, Ont.: Boston Mills Press, 1993.

An initial "Historical Review" provides a familiar survey, enriched with some original research. The major portion, "Island Descriptions," derives from extensive study of primary sources related to surveying, naming and selling of the islands. Some remarkable, previously unpublished photographs are among the many well-reproduced illustrations.

Stanley, George F. G. *Conflicts and Social Notes : the War of 1812-1814, the Patriot War, 1837-8.* [Ottawa]: Parks Canada, c. 1976.

Sykes, Pamela, & Michael Sykes. *Food & Folklore of the 1,000 Island : Savor the Flavor of the Islands.* Gananoque, Ont.: Dove Cottage Press, 1995.

Tague, Rick Wagoner. *The Peacock Yacht House.* Unpublished Master's Thesis, Columbia University, 1982.

Ten Cate, Adrian G., and Mary Beacock Fryer. *Pictorial History of the Thousand Islands of the St. Lawrence River.* Brockville, Ont.: Besancourt, 1977, reprinted 2002.

As the title suggests, this large volume was intended primarily to be an archive of historic illustrations. The brief text is readable and reliable, particularly devoted to early history, especially of the Canadian shore.

Thompson, Shawn. *River Rats: The People of the Thousand Islands.* Burnstown, Ont.: General Store, 1989.

——. *River's Edge: Reprobates, Rum-runners and Other Folk of the Thousand Islands.* Burnstown, Ont.: General Store, 1991.

——. *A River Rat's Guide to the Thousand Islands.* Erin, Ont.: Boston Mills, 1998.

——. *Soul of the River: Life in the Thousand Islands.* Burnstown, Ont.: General Store, 1997.

Shawn Thompson has invented a new genre of regional literature. His river books are comprised mostly of interviews with islanders today, reported with Thompson's journalistic flair.

All Wet at Rum Point

## Memoirs of Island Life

Beach, Frederick G. *The Burtch-Beach Interview*. Unpublished transcript of an interview with Elisha Burtch, Alexandria Bay, New York, 1947, typescript at the Antique Boat Museum, Clayton, New York.

——. *The Peacock-Beach Interview*. Unpublished transcript of an interview with Grant Peacock, Alexandria Bay, New York, 1976, typescript at the Antique Boat Museum, Clayton, New York.

Clayton Guides' Association. "Traditional Guides' Shore Dinner Friday." *Thousand Islands Sun Vacationer*, 14 July 1993, 21.

Daw, Polly Flynn. "Epilogue: When We Were Rather Young." In Margaret Nulty and Doris Mosher. *Murray Isle*, 1972.

Gustke, Nancy L. *The Special Artist in American Culture: a Biography of Frank Hamilton Taylor (1846-1927)*. New York: P. Lang, c.1995.

Keats, John. *Of Time and an Island: The Writer Reflects on his Life in the Thousand Islands--and on Life in America*. New York: Charterhouse, 1974. Reprinted by Syracuse University Press, 1987.

This beautifully written memoir has become a classic.

Lashomb, Audrey . *Going Home: Grindstone Island*. Clayton, N.Y.: Grindstone Press, 1998.

Lucas, Roger. Reference to his and other works about Boldt Castle are in the author's companion volume, *Boldt Castle: In Search of the Lost Story* (below).

Malo, Paul. *Boldt Castle: In Search of the Lost Story*. Fulton, N.Y.: Laurentian, 2001.

Mondore, Robert and Patricia, *Dark Island's Castle of Mysteries*, (video). Jamesville, N.Y.: Gold-Mountain, 2003 (http://gold-mountain.com).

A substantial presentation has derived from extensive research as well as personal association with the place and its previous owners.

Newberry, Jessie Matthews. *The Longest Winter*. [Clayton. N.Y.?]: 1989.

This moving, personal account of the hard life of native Islanders on Grindstone Island surely will become a classic.

——. *The Summer After*. [Clayton, N.Y.?]: 1989.

Following *The Longest Winter*, this compelling memoir in effect comprises the concluding volume of a Grindstone trilogy, with Stanley Norcom's larger book serving as a more comprehensive, introductory first volume. The three books may well be read in this order.

Norcom, Stanley. *Grindstone: An Island World Remembered*. New Cumberland, Pa.: Robert Edwards, 1993.

A beautiful memoir, edited, introduced and appended by Norvin Hein, recalls eighty-some summers on Grindstone Island. Chapter 12, "The Coterie at the Head of the Island," appended by the editor, presents the complex network of related families there.

Russell, Robert. *The Island*. New York: Vanguard, 1973. Another classic memoir.

Stearns, Charles. "Memories of the Thousand Islands." *Thousand Islands Sun Vacationer*, 4 August 1993. Still another valuable recollection of island life.

## Boats, Boat Builders, and Boat Captains

"Afloat on the St. Lawrence." *Pittsburgh's Illustrated Weekly.* 18 May 1907.

Brown, Jack. *Simon Johnston and the Ships of Clayton.* Mallorytown, Ont.: River Heritage, 1988.
> This work of meticulous scholarship by the noted Canadian scholar set a high standard for historical studies of the region.

Corbin, Les and Verda. *The Visgers' World.* Clayton, N.Y.: Corbin, 1987.
> The colorful era of steamboat excursions and elegant yacht tours has been portrayed by this thorough study of a prominent family of river captains.

Durant, Kenneth. *The Naphtha Launch.* Blue Mountain Lake, N.Y.: Adirondack Museum, 1976.

Editors of Time-Life Books. *The Classic Boat,* Alexandria, Virginia: Time-Life Library of Boating, 1977.

Fostle, D. W. "The Boat Builders of Alexandria Bay", Part I. *Wooden Boat,* Number 48, September-October, 1982.

Keats, John. *The Skiff and The River.* Nantucket, Mass.: Herrick Collection, 1988.
> Reproductions of paintings by the noted river artist, Michael Ringer, enhance this beautiful book. It is less a historical study than an extended essay about the romance of the St. Lawrence skiff.

Krout, John Allen. *Annals of American Sport.* New Haven, Conn.: Oxford, 1929.

Mercier, Gilbart B. *Pleasure Yachts of the Thousand Islands, Circa 1900.* Clayton, N.Y.: The Shipyard Press, 1981.
> This marvelous work represents the long research of a dedicated scholar, the late Gilbart Mercier of Clayton. Now out of print, it warrants a new addition.

Mollica, Tony. *American Wooden Runabouts.* St. Paul, Minn: Motorbooks, 2002.

Peo, Leon L. *Boats of All Kinds.* Cape Vincent, N. Y.: n.d.

Robinson, Bill. *The Great American Yacht Designers.* New York: Knopf, 1974.

Wilkinson [Mark], Bonnie J. *Boat Building in the Thousand Islands.* Typescript, Antique Boat Museum, Clayton, New York.
> This work in progress incorporates much original research, promising to become an excellent book.

Watching for Otter

This is a scene among the thousand islands of the St. Lawrence where the Canadian Frenchmen have a habit of shooting the otter instead of trapping him.  It would seem that at certain localities these curious creatures are very abundant, and the hunters, by remaining perfectly quiet on the margin of an island or the main shore, discover the animals as they pop their heads above the water, and then shoot them.  The birchen canoe, though somewhat too small, is a fair specimen of that kind of craft.

*Illustrated London News,* March 27, 1858

# Index

Thousand Islands Life, c. 1900

The steamer *Islander*, one of many making the rounds of the
river resorts, brings Frontenac Hotel guests to Round Island.
The team of horses hitched to the wagon awaits their baggage.

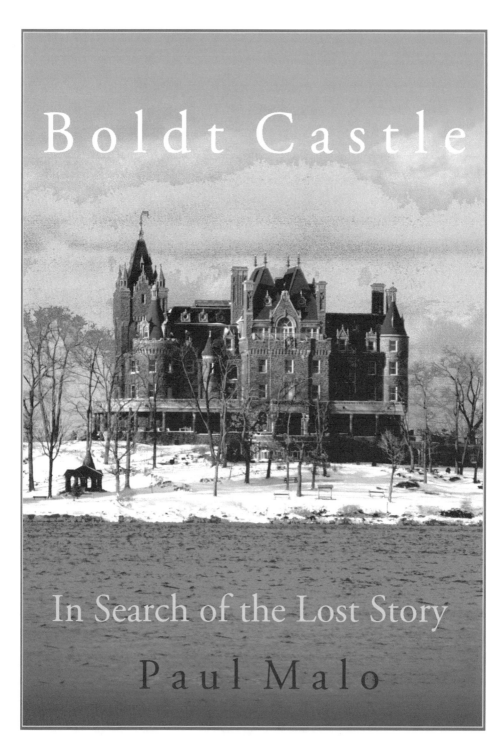

# Boldt Castle

## In Search of the Lost Story

### Paul Malo

This book complements a previously published volume, a
companion in format, about the Boldts and their castle.

314